Image and value

An invitation to literature

Image
and value

An invitation to literature

By Martha Heasley Cox / *San Jose State College*

Harcourt, Brace & World, Inc.

New York / Chicago / Burlingame

PN 6014 C648

Library of Congress Catalog Card Number: 66–16059

Printed in the United States of America

COPYRIGHTS AND ACKNOWLEDGMENTS

The author thanks the following publishers and copyright holders for their permission to use the selections reprinted in this book.

Agnes Rogers Allen.   For "Lines to a Daughter—Any Daughter," *Harper's Magazine,* February, 1947.

Ashley Famous Agency, Inc.   For *The Apollo of Bellac* by Jean Giraudoux.
Adapted by Maurice Valency. Copyright 1954 by Maurice Valency. Reprinted by
permission of Maurice Valency and his representative, Audrey Wood, Ashley Fa-
mous Agency, Inc.   For *The Ghost of an Apprehension* by Walter van Tilburg
Clark. © 1949, Pacific Spectator. Reprinted by permission of Ashley Famous
Agency, Inc.

Bantam Books, Inc.   For "Appearance of Wisdom," "Inscription for a Monument," and "On Magical Whiskers." Reprinted from *Greek Lyric Poetry* translated
by Willis Barnstone; copyright © 1962, by Bantam Books, Inc., by permission of
the publisher.

Chatto and Windus, Ltd.   For "Strange Meeting," "Dulce et Decorum Est," and
"The Parable of the Old Men and the Young" from *Collected Poems* by Wilfred
Owen, Chatto and Windus, Ltd., 1963. By permission of the publishers and Mr.
Harold Owen.   For "The Lady with the Dog" from *The Lady with the Dog and
Other Stories* by Anton Chekhov, translated by Constance Garnett.

Curtis Brown, Ltd.   For "Polonius, Yes, Polonius, No" from *The Private Dining
Room* by Ogden Nash. Reprinted by permission of the author. The poem was
originally published in *The New Yorker* magazine © 1952, by Ogden Nash.

iv

Preface

The stories, plays, and poems in this anthology are arranged so that they may be read as a representative introduction to the literary genres; every selection has been chosen as well, however, for its relevancy and contribution to the thematic topics listed in the alternate table of contents. A course based upon these concepts will provide a closely inter-woven study of varying aspects of subject matter, theme, method, and tone. It should also invite lively discussion and writing.

The many selections long popular with both students and teachers are supplemented by a number of fresh and uncommonly interesting works: Eugene O'Neill's last full-length drama, *A Touch of the Poet*; a recent one-act play from the theater of the absurd by a young Spanish playwright; a modern Japanese short story which is a counterpart of the Book of Ruth; a new story by the contemporary Spanish author, Ana María Matute, especially translated for this anthology; traditional ballads and native American folk songs, accompanied by scores keyed to the guitar and prepared specifically for this collection; selections from the Greeks, including advice on the worth of a beard; and Howard Nemerov's comments on contemporary education.

This, then, is an invitation to the student to read and consider the image authors here and abroad have created of objects, people, and events, and the value implicit in each such presentation.

M. H. C.

San Jose State College
San Jose, California
December, 1965

Table of Contents

DRAMA

POETRY

Thematic Table of Contents

IMAGE

LOVE

CONFLICT

VALUE

Fiction

Note

The first story, "The Portable Phonograph" by Walter Van Tilburg Clark, is accompanied by an essay, "The Ghost of an Apprehension," the author's detailed account of the birth and development of his ideas for the story and the principles that guided him as he wrote it. This pairing is intended to serve as an introduction to the study of the stories that follow.

The Portable Phonograph

Walter Van Tilburg Clark

The red sunset, with narrow black cloud strips like threats across it, lay on the curved horizon of the prairie. The air was still and cold, and in it settled the mute darkness and greater cold of night. High in the air there was wind, for through the veil of the dusk the clouds could be seen gliding rapidly south and changing shapes. A queer sensation of torment, of two-sided, unpredictable nature, arose from the stillness of the earth air beneath the violence of the upper air. Out of the sunset, through the dead, matted grass and isolated weed stalks of the prairie, crept the narrow and deeply rutted remains of a road. In the road, in places, there were crusts of shallow, brittle ice. There were little islands of an old oiled pavement in the road too, but most of it was mud, now frozen rigid. The frozen mud still bore the toothed impress of great tanks, and a wanderer on the neighboring undulations might have stumbled, in this light, into large, partially filled-in and weed-grown cavities, their banks channeled and beginning to spread into badlands. These pits were such as might have been made by falling meteors, but they were not. They were the scars of gigantic bombs, their rawness already made a little natural by rain, seed, and time. Along the road there were rakish remnants of fence. There was also, just visible, one portion of tangled and multiple barbed wire still erect, behind which was a shelving ditch with small caves, now very quiet and empty, at intervals in its back wall. Otherwise there was no structure or remnant of a structure visible over the dome of the darkling earth, but only, in sheltered hollows, the darker shadows of young trees trying again.

Under the wuthering arch of the high wind a V of wild geese fled south. The rush of their pinions sounded briefly, and the faint, plaintive notes of their expeditionary talk. Then they left a still greater vacancy. There was the smell and expectation of snow, as there is likely to be when the wild geese fly south. From the remote distance, towards the red sky, came faintly the protracted howl and quick yap-yap of a prairie wolf.

North of the road, perhaps a hundred yards, lay the parallel and deeply intrenched course of a small creek, lined with leafless alders and willows. The creek was already silent under ice. Into the bank above it was dug a sort of cell, with a single opening, like the mouth of a mine tunnel. Within the cell there was a little red of fire, which showed dully through the opening, like a reflection or a deception of the imagination. The light came from the chary burning of four blocks of poorly aged peat, which gave off a petty warmth and much acrid smoke. But the precious remnants of wood, old fenceposts and timbers from the long-deserted dugouts, had to be saved for the real cold, for the time when a man's breath blew white, the moisture in his nostrils stiffened at once when he stepped out, and the expansive blizzards paraded for days over the vast open, swirling and settling and thickening, till the dawn of the cleared day when the sky was thin blue-green and the terrible cold, in which a man could not live for three hours unwarmed, lay over the uniformly drifted swell of the plain.

Around the smoldering peat four men were seated cross-legged. Behind them, traversed by their shadows, was the earth bench, with two old and dirty army blankets, where the owner of the cell slept. In a niche in the opposite wall were a few tin utensils which caught the glint of the coals. The host was rewrapping in a piece of daubed burlap four fine, leather-bound books. He worked slowly and very carefully and at last tied the bundle securely with a piece of grass-woven cord. The other three looked intently upon the process, as if a great significance lay in it. As the host tied the cord he spoke. He was an old man, his long, matted beard and hair gray to nearly white. The shadows made his brows and cheekbones appear gnarled, his eyes and cheeks deeply sunken. His big hands, rough with frost and swollen by rheumatism, were awkward but gentle at their task. He was like a prehistoric priest performing a fateful ceremonial rite. Also his voice had in it a suitable quality of deep, reverent despair, yet perhaps at the moment a sharpness of selfish satisfaction.

"When I perceived what was happening," he said, "I told myself, 'It is the end. I cannot take much; I will take these.' "

"Perhaps I was impractical," he continued. "But for myself, I do not regret, and what do we know of those who will come after us? We are the doddering remnant of a race of mechanical fools. I have saved what I love; the soul of what was good in us is here; perhaps the new ones will make a strong enough beginning not to fall behind when they become clever."

He rose with slow pain and placed the wrapped volumes in the niche with his utensils. The others watched him with the same ritualistic gaze.

"Shakespeare, the Bible, *Moby Dick, The Divine Comedy,*" one of them said softly. "You might have done worse, much worse."

"You will have a little soul left until you die," said another harshly. "That is more than is true of us. My brain becomes thick, like my hands." He held the big, battered hands, with their black nails, in the glow to be seen.

"I want paper to write on," he said. "And there is none."

The fourth man said nothing. He sat in the shadow farthest from the fire, and sometimes his body jerked in its rags from the cold. Although he was still young, he was sick and coughed often. Writing implied a greater future than he now felt able to consider.

The old man seated himself laboriously and reached out, groaning at the movement, to put another block of peat on the fire. With bowed heads and averted eyes his three guests acknowledged his magnanimity.

"We thank you, Dr. Jenkins, for the reading," said the man who had named the books.

They seemed then to be waiting for something. Dr. Jenkins understood but was loath to comply. In an ordinary moment he would have said nothing. But the words of *The Tempest,* which he had been reading, and the religious attention of the three made this an unusual occasion.

"You wish to hear the phonograph," he said grudgingly.

The two middle-aged men stared into the fire, unable to formulate and expose the enormity of their desire.

The young man, however, said anxiously, between suppressed coughs, "Oh, please," like an excited child.

The old man rose again in his difficult way and went to the back of the cell. He returned and placed tenderly upon the packed floor, where the firelight might fall upon it, an old portable phonograph in a black case. He smoothed the top with his hand and then opened it. The lovely green-felt-covered disk became visible.

"I have been using thorns as needles," he said. "But tonight, because we have a musician among us"—he bent his head to the young man, almost invisible in the shadow—"I will use a steel needle. There are only three left."

The two middle-aged men stared at him in speechless adoration. The one with the big hands, who wanted to write, moved his lips, but the whisper was not audible.

"Oh, don't!" cried the young man, as if he were hurt. "The thorns will do beautifully."

"No," the old man said. "I have become accustomed to the thorns, but they are not really good. For you, my young friend, we will have good music tonight."

"After all," he added generously, and beginning to wind the phonograph, which creaked, "they can't last forever."

"No, nor we," the man who needed to write said harshly. "The needle, by all means."

"Oh, thanks," said the young man. "Thanks," he said again in a low, excited voice, and then stifled his coughing with a bowed head.

"The records, though," said the old man when he had finished winding, "are a different matter. Already they are very worn. I do not play them more than once a week. One, once a week, that is what I allow myself.

"More than a week I cannot stand it; not to hear them," he apologized.

"No, how could you?" cried the young man. "And with them here like this."

"A man can stand anything," said the man who wanted to write, in his harsh, antagonistic voice.

"Please, the music," said the young man.

"Only the one," said the old man. "In the long run, we will remember more that way."

He had a dozen records with luxuriant gold and red seals. Even in that light the others could see that the threads of the records were becoming worn. Slowly he read out the titles and the tremendous, dead names of the composers and the artists and the orchestras. The three worked upon the names in their minds, carefully. It was difficult to select from such a wealth what they would at once most like to remember. Finally the man who wanted to write named Gershwin's "New York."

"Oh, no!" cried the sick young man, and then could say nothing more because he had to cough. The others understood him, and the harsh man withdrew his selection and waited for the musician to choose.

The musician begged Dr. Jenkins to read the titles again, very slowly, so that he could remember the sounds. While they were read he lay back against the wall, his eyes closed, his thin, horny hand pulling at his light beard, and listened to the voices and the orchestras and the single instruments in his mind.

When the reading was done he spoke despairingly. "I have forgotten," he complained. "I cannot hear them clearly."

"There are things missing," he explained.

"I know," said Dr. Jenkins. "I thought that I knew all of Shelley by heart. I should have brought Shelley."

"That's more soul that we can use," said the harsh man. "*Moby Dick* is better.

"By God, we can understand that," he emphasized.

The Doctor nodded.

"Still," said the man who had admired the books, "we need the absolute if we are to keep a grasp on anything.

"Anything but these sticks and peat clods and rabbit snares," he said bitterly.

"Shelley desired an ultimate absolute," said the harsh man. "It's too much," he said. "It's no good; no earthly good."

The musician selected a Debussy nocturne. The others considered and approved. They rose to their knees to watch the Doctor prepare for the playing, so that they appeared to be actually in an attitude of worship. The peat glow showed the thinness of their bearded faces, and the deep lines in them, and revealed the condition of their garments. The other two continued to kneel as the old man carefully lowered the needle onto the spinning disk, but the musician suddenly drew back against the wall again, with his knees up, and buried his face in his hands.

At the first notes of the piano the listeners were startled. They stared at each other. Even the musician lifted his head in amazement but then quickly bowed it again, strainingly, as if he were suffering from a pain he might not be able to endure. They were all listening deeply, without movement. The wet, blue-green notes tinkled forth from the old machine and were individual, delectable presences in the cell. The individual, delectable presences swept into a sudden tide of unbearably beautiful dissonance and then continued fully the swelling and ebbing of that tide, the dissonant inpourings, and the resolutions, and the diminishments, and the little, quiet wavelets of interlude lapping between. Every sound was piercing and singularly sweet. In all the men except the musician there occurred rapid sequences of tragically heightened recollection. He heard nothing but what was there. At the final, whispering disappearance, but moving quietly so that the others would not hear him and look at him, he let his head fall back in agony, as if it were drawn there by the hair, and clenched the fingers of one hand over his teeth. He sat that way while the others were silent and until they began to breathe again normally. His drawn-up legs were trembling violently.

Quickly Dr. Jenkins lifted the needle off, to save it and not to spoil the recollection with scraping. When he had stopped the whirling of the sacred disk he courteously left the phonograph open and by the fire, in sight.

The others, however, understood. The musician rose last, but then abruptly, and went quickly out at the door without saying anything. The others stopped at the door and gave their thanks in low voices. The Doctor nodded magnificently.

"Come again," he invited, "in a week. We will have the 'New York.' "

When the two had gone together, out towards the rimed road, he stood in the entrance, peering and listening. At first there was only the resonant boom of the wind overhead, and then far over the dome of the dead, dark plain the wolf cry lamenting. In the rifts of clouds the Doctor saw four stars flying. It impressed the Doctor that one of them had just been obscured by the beginning of a flying cloud at the very moment he heard what he had been listening for, a sound of suppressed coughing. It was not near by, however. He believed that down against the pale alders he could see the moving shadow.

With nervous hands he lowered the piece of canvas which served as his door and pegged it at the bottom. Then quickly and quietly, looking at the piece of canvas frequently, he slipped the records into the case, snapped the lid shut, and carried the phonograph to his couch. There, pausing often to stare at the canvas and listen, he dug earth from the wall and disclosed a piece of board. Behind this there was a deep hole in the wall, into which he put the phonograph. After a moment's consideration he went over and reached down his bundle of books and inserted it also. Then, guardedly, he once more sealed up the hole with the board and the earth. He also changed his blankets and the grass-stuffed sack which served as a pillow, so that he could lie facing the entrance. After carefully placing two more blocks of peat upon the fire he stood for a long time watching the stretched canvas, but it seemed to billow naturally with the first gust of a lowering wind. At last he prayed, and got in under his blankets, and closed his smoke-smarting eyes. On the inside of the bed, next the wall, he could feel with his hand the comfortable piece of lead pipe.

The Ghost of an Apprehension

Walter Van Tilburg Clark

Since the story took place in my mind somewhat as a play might, the intention producing the scene, the scene and the intention selecting the cast, and all three, by means of certain guiding principles which developed with them, dictating the action, and since its approach has occurred often with me, in novels as well as in stories, it will help both to shape the discussion to follow and in a measure to widen its application, if we put the synopsis itself into something like dramatic form. To brief the brief, then (the story is only eight pages long):

THE SCENE   Interior of a dugout above a creek thinly lined with alders. A small, smoky, peat fire in the center. In one wall a niche containing a few battered cooking utensils. In the opposite wall an earth bunk with two old army blankets on it. Above the entrance, a rolled canvas, which is the door. Outside (the back-drop, so to speak) a desolate prairie, pitted by craters and grooved by the frozen ruts of huge wheels and caterpillar treads. Here and there a remnant of highway pavement, a spidery entanglement of barbed wire, and, in the depressions, a few small, shadowy trees. On the far horizon, a red sunset with bars of black cloud across it. Overhead, changing clouds gliding rapidly south before a high, booming wind. A single wedge of wild geese passes over, going southward more swiftly than the clouds and conversing faintly among themselves. A prairie wolf yaps in the distance. There is no other sound or motion. The air near the ground is still and full of the cold promise of winter.

THE CAST   Four men, all dirty, ragged, and bearded: Dr. Jenkins, a former professor and the host, and three visitors: a powerful, sardonic man, once a writer; a polite, conciliatory soul, whose past is not revealed; and a very thin, nervous young man with a bad cough, who has been a musician. The writer and the conciliatory soul have evidently been here before, though not often, but the musician is making his first call.

9

THE ACTION   Dr. Jenkins has just finished reading *The Tempest* aloud, and while he wraps up his library, Shakespeare, the Bible, *The Divine Comedy,* and *Moby Dick,* is discussing with the writer and the anonymous one, the present, and possibly future, worth of the books. When he has put the books into the niche with the pots, there is a brief, coercive silence, after which he reluctantly produces an old portable phonograph and twelve records. They may hear one record; one record, once a week, is his rule. He reads the titles. A Gershwin named by the writer is rejected as too sharp a reminder. The musician is given the choice, and after hearing the titles again, and complaining that there are parts he can't remember, he selects a Debussy nocturne. Dr. Jenkins, in a sudden, penitent gesture, takes out one of his three remaining steel needles, though he has been using thorns himself. The visitors rise to their knees in a reverent semicircle to watch him insert the needle and set the record on. At the first note of the piano, however, the musician shrinks back against the wall, where he struggles silently against his cough and the agony of hearing music again.

When the record is finished, the visitors rise. The musician is the last to rise, but then he goes out at once, without a word. The other two leave more slowly and formally. Dr. Jenkins lingers in the doorway, peering down into the dusk and listening. At last, just as a cloud erases one of four visible stars, he hears a faint cough from down among the alders. He lowers the canvas and pegs it down, and puts the phonograph and records, and then the books too, into a hole above the bunk and seals them in. After changing his blankets around so that he will lie facing the door, and putting more fuel on the fire, he stands watching the canvas again. Still only the wind, which has at last come down to earth, moves it. He prays and gets under his blankets, where, "On the inside of the bed, next the wall, he could feel with his hand the comfortable piece of lead pipe."

Even so brief a retelling, when we remember that the story first appeared in the fall of 1941, suggests fully enough all we need to know about the apprehension which was the source of the idea. It also brings us at once to the crux of the writing problem, for it was just the very universality of that apprehension which placed the severest strictures upon the design of the story, and so compelled me, in the first stage, to formulate the guiding principles already mentioned.

Clearly I could justify the use of such a theme only by bringing that universal apprehension into sharp focus, by so heightening the reader's reaction to what he already knew and feared as to make the vaguely possible into the concretely probable. Gradually it became evident that the means to such a concentration and heightening must be three. First, if I were to avoid the flavor of Wellsian[1] prophecy, the great apprehension itself must be touched upon lightly and indirectly, must be little more than a taken-for-granted backdrop. Secondly, the incident played against that backdrop, and the characters engaged in it, had to be highly credible, not in terms of their situation, but in terms of an everyday American life. In short, it didn't seem to me that the desired tone could be achieved in the key of either the incident or the scene alone, but that it must arise out of the dissonant juxtaposition of the two. And finally, the manner of the story had to convey the same contrast, had to be fiddle light on the surface and bass viol deep beneath, which is to say, it had to be satirical. One cannot afford to speak seriously of the end of the world. All of these necessities, the minor and credible activity, presented against a background of doom, in a manner calculated to sustain the dissonance, added up, of course, to a very short story. One does not strain a joke about the end of the world, either.

I didn't, naturally, start with a notion of saying something about the finality of modern war, and out of that melancholy fog evolve a set of rules, and out of them a story. The process was not that orderly. First, I just began to write. I can't remember exactly what set me off. Probably it was some intensifying item of the day's news, stirring me when I had time to sit and brood on it until I had to get rid of the emotion it built up, and the first, suggestive images began to appear. Almost always, whatever may have been working up to it in my mind, recognized and unrecognized, it is some image suddenly coming alive and suggesting more to follow, or to precede, that makes me reach for a pencil. In this case it was the prairie, the vast, desolated backdrop of the dugout, which first appeared, accompanied by a feeling that such a scene implied in itself all that one could afford to say directly about a final war. In short, the critical process began with the creative, and by the time I had completed the introductory description (a slow procedure, involving much cutting, rewriting, and rearranging) the controlling principles, more or less as I have stated them, were already in full operation, the cast had appeared and been approved, and the incident had arisen out of their gathering. The story was finished, ex-

[1] H. G. Wells (1866–1946), English novelist and journalist, is known for his popular fantasies on pseudoscientific themes.

cept for putting it down, which meant little more than keeping an ear open for that desirable dissonance.

The prairie first appeared blackened by old fires, full of shell craters, deeply scored everywhere by the tracks of enormous tank battles and the vestiges of hopeless entrenchment, and devoid of all present signs of human life. There were no houses, or even shells of houses, no barns, no windmills, no fences, no recognizable fields or even stubs of groves or orchards. It was bare as the moon. It suggested a warfare of almost cosmic proportions (since Hiroshima, we can delete the "almost") which was what I wanted, and it suggested also, that a good deal of time had passed since the battle. That hint of time softening the edges of all detail, but unable to restore anything, made the destruction even more final, and sufficiently indicated, it seemed to me, that the survivors necessary to the story must be so few, and so far set back, as to be without hope or use. But then I saw that the mooniness was too complete, and could just as well mean a region that had always been desert as it could the ruin of a productive region. Yet it seemed wrong to name the place, and I still didn't want any skeletons of building against the sky. I preferred that tundralike emptiness stretching away to the western horizon. (I was looking west, perhaps because Americans have that habit, perhaps because the war we most dreaded was raging in Europe, and so, in the story, would have gone across America westward, but probably just because the scene had first appeared in an end-of-day light, and one would naturally be looking toward the sunset.) So there appeared the broken remnants of a highway as unobtrusive tokens of the past. Clearer signs of time elapsed since the fighting were also needed, yet signs which would not too much relieve the sterility of the earth, so there grew up the sparse lines of willows and alders in the trenches and creek beds, and the stunted, new trees in the craters.

Sometime during its first viewing, though I avoided the narrowing effect of a name (the nature of the land, and the fact that the four men were unquestionably American, seemed enough in the way of location) the region became definitely the American Middle West, because it spread the devastation over the whole world to show the heart of the most isolated major power swept over, and the grain lands gone in a warfare which concentrated on cities. It made the place not only a field of the final war, but the final field as well.

Late autumn became the necessary time of year, the last season before the complete death and the somehow healing secrecy of winter, just as sunset, the last hour of vision before the secrecy of night, was the proper time of day. To begin with, the sky had been cloudless, the sunset one of those infinitely penetrable, green-gold fadings that come with cold, but now such a horizon seemed too peaceful, and even suggestive of hope. There had to be some motion in that inert landscape, some threat in the sky. So that clouds formed, moving in a wintry wind, and the sunset turned red, and then, although that came as an afterthought, in part because the professor had to hear that last faint cough down in the alders, the unmoving lower air settled in. The chief intent was that the dissonance of the two regions of air should furnish a physical lead into the moral dissonance of the action, and also that it should reinforce the threat of the black clouds across the sunset, suggest apprehension by ear and skin as well as by eye. Finally, for by now the story was fully in view, some touch of conscious life was needed, by which to move from the backdrop into the play. Hence, as also maintaining the mood, the far-off yapping of the wolf, unheard in those parts for generations, and the brief, almost invisible passage of the geese, unconcerned with the land except as a distance to get over.

The action of the story, prepared all during the arranging and rearranging of this backdrop, moved forward so swiftly, almost automatically, in its details, as to be now largely beyond recall. I do remember the vital factors of the preparation, however. I remember that the cast first appeared to me as three in number, the three who became the professor, the writer, and the musician; that they were all men because even one woman might imply a future; and that they became men of highly mental pasts because that rendered them more nearly helpless, increased their recession, and made it more likely that they would retain the necessary surface of polite conduct. I remember also that the three men first came together in the open, around a wood fire down by the creek, but that somehow nothing would happen among them there. The size and finality of the setting shrank them and paralyzed them with futility. I could not even seem to discover any reason for their bothering to get together, save an animal loneliness which had no dramatic potential except through a much longer development than I could afford. When at last it became clear that it was the scene which rendered them so unusable, the dugout, as in keeping with the tank tracks and the barbed wire, appeared in the bank behind me, and we moved into it. That was all it took. The men not only came alive, but swelled to more than life-size, filling the little cave enormously, assuming the importance for me that they had for each other, and setting the lifeless prairie away into its proper backdrop perspective. The vestigial touches of homemaking effort became possible: the few and battered utensils, kept in a niche, like a saint; the peat fire and the earthen bunk, hinting of a nearly woodless world; the army blankets and the canvas. Also, the home made necessary the host, and the professor, as likely to be the most provident and the most chairmanly, at once assumed that role, and with it his manner and his more numerous years. Indeed it was only then that he certainly became a professor, a kind of epitome of civilized man in his most familiar form, suggesting thereby a great deal through his mere presence in a cave.

When the fragments of possible conversation among the three men, the professor, the writer, and a third who was for a time alternately a painter and a musician, began to occur in the midst of the backdrop details, I shortly felt the need of a fourth man, not only because I sensed that the musician-painter was going to be nearly inarticulate, and, for the sake of variety and interplay, three speakers were preferable to two, but also because the trio was a bit too patly symbolic, and so likely to resist the individualization without which they couldn't convince. (The writer was first seen as a sculptor—which has something to do with the physical characteristics he retained—but changed his profession, partly for the same reason, to break up the rigid one-two-three alignment by drawing nearer to the professor's interests, making a one-two grouping, and partly because it better suited the intent of the tale that he should be thwarted by an absence of that so-common commodity, paper. Of clay there would still be aplenty.) So the fourth man joined the group, the man with the unknown past, the representative of the great, departed audience whose need had produced the specialists. He was a real help, for not only did he relieve the stiffness of the allegory, but he also furnished a contrasting attitude, a second psychological level, being a trifle deferential in the presence of the more specific abilities of the others, but also more resigned because his individual needs were less acute. He was, in short, different in kind, whereas the other three, all upon one level of bolder individuality, were different only in particulars: the harsh cynicism of the frustrated writer; the advanced tuberculosis which makes time so important to the musician; the grave, reluctant, orderly air of the professor. Furthermore, I believe that I had found in him another sufficiently concealed means to irony, for his deference was, of course, wholly pointless in that place and time, a mere hang-over from an irrecoverable social pattern, and yet it was just that trace of deference, that touch of the conciliatory, that held together, by its remnant of drawing-room conduct, a group that otherwise would almost certainly have broken into an undesirable violence.

Once we were in the dugout, and the anonymous fourth had entered, there seemed to be only one thing lacking, that precipitating agent which would settle the whole narrative out in visible form, the reason for the gathering. I cannot remember how many reasons I fleetingly considered off the top of my mind while I completed the backdrop and caught unusable but suggestive glimpses of the civilized pasts of the men. (The professor, for instance, had taught English in a Midwestern college, specializing in Victorian Literature, but had a wide range of interests beyond that. He had lived in a small, white, frame house, with vines on the front porch, and a dark, somewhat stuffy study in it, with heavy rugs, too much furniture, and the walls lined with books, mostly old and worn, but here and there in bright, new bindings or dust jackets. He had two children, but both were grown and away from home, and he was rather lonely, because he had retired just a couple of years before the war, and his wife, a plump, bespectacled woman, although a fine mother and housekeeper, did not share any of his intellectual interests.) I remember very clearly, however, that the happiest moment of the whole preliminary came with the discovery of the portable phonograph. Beyond question it was the very object, the key symbol, for which I'd been hunting ever since my first dusky glimpse of the prairie. It was portable, which was important. It would seem valuable enough to such a man as the professor, to be worth carrying off in a crisis. It was a universally familiar object, and so would derive its dramatic virtue entirely from its present rarity. In its combined material inconsequence—for certainly it was one of the lesser gadgets of our abundantly gadgeted civilization—and spiritual consequence, as the only remaining vehicle of perhaps the highest achievement of mind and emotion of that same civilization, it became the very centerpiece of the desired dissonance, the touchstone for action and language. The title arrived with it, of course. In its presence, the relationships of the cast were rapidly established. It became evident that the small, suppressed element of conflict that was needed must spring from it and form the music it produced. As a result, the musician at once assumed the brief future that would make him desperate, and became certainly a musician rather than a painter, and also the newcomer, the stranger in the group, the man in whom the restraint of association would play the smallest part and the hunger for music the greatest. At once, also, the professor, as the owner of the treasure, became the antagonist. To all intents the story was complete.

There remained only to discover a valid and contributory means of prolonging, though backwards, into the hours before the tale opens, a meeting which would otherwise be incredibly brief, and which could not, obviously, be extended by eating and drinking. Books were beyond question the means, and certainly, in this context, the reasons for selecting the four the professor had brought with him are equally clear, at least by the time the writer has spoken of *Moby Dick* as something they can all understand now (he might usefully have dropped a word about Ishmael's coffin-boat) and added that Shelley had too much soul, and was "no earthly good." Nor is there any mystery about his selecting *The Tempest* for the reading, once we realize that Caliban and Ariel are at it again over the portable phonograph. The act of reading and the reverence accorded the books serve also as a kind of induction to the high sacrament of the music, in which the professor becomes the priest of a doomed faith and the visitors literally assume kneeling positions around the phonograph.

It is intended that the conclusion should leave with the reader a sense of unity, of the opening dissonance resolved, though not into peace, but rather by means, gently, gently, of almost entirely reducing the professor to the cave man, blending him, as it were, into the terrible landscape. As he stands suspiciously in the doorway, after the guests have departed, he sees, at the very instant he hears the coughing down in the alders, one of four bright stars suddenly hidden by a cloud. It is a sufficient sign to the primitive credulity revived in him, and indirectly, we hope, in the reader. Then also, as he stands watching the canvas he has pegged down, it is moved by "the first gusts of a lowering wind." The opening dissonance between the wuthering upper air and the still ground air is also resolved, and again, as in the case of the human dissonance, by suggesting an end, by bringing winter to the door. Yet, in the last line, as the professor lies on the earth bench, facing the billowing canvas, "On the inside of the bed, next the wall, he could feel with his hand the comfortable piece of lead pipe." His weapon still comes from that lost world of gadgets. He cannot bring even violence to the level of the new—the very old—world in which he now lives. And of course futility, in any but the meanest and most temporary sense, attends the defense for which he is prepared.

It seemed to me that sentence plucked the proper closing note, one that might linger for a time with a tenuous but moving reminder of the whole intention. If so, it was so, happily, by means of the very last phrase, and particularly by means of the one word "comfortable." Nothing in the phrase was considered, not "comfortable" any more than the rest, but even as it came, that "comfortable" tickled me, not so much because of its immediate implication, in which the paradox was clear enough, as for some more remote, redoubling connotation which I could not, at the moment, catch hold of. Then, a few seconds after I had poked home the final period, it came to me. I had done a bit of lucky thieving from Bill of Avon. (Perhaps the professor's volume of Shakespeare had put it out handy for the borrowing.) Remember how Juliet, waking in the tomb, and not yet aware that Romeo is dead, murmurs drowsily to the gentle Friar Lawrence, "Oh, comfortable Friar—"? [2] Oh, poor professor, with only his lead pipe. And I was sure that at least the ghost of that old, warm, trusting "comfortable" would lurk to trouble the reader as it had troubled me. Nor could I feel, considering the grim little twist I had given it, that Bill would begrudge me his word. After all, he was no mean shakes of a borrower himself.

Many Moons   *James Thurber*

Once upon a time, in a kingdom by the sea, there lived a little princess named Lenore. She was ten years old, going on eleven. One day Lenore fell ill of a surfeit of raspberry tarts and took to her bed.

The royal physician came to see her and took her temperature and felt her pulse and made her stick out her tongue. The royal physician was worried. He sent for the king, Lenore's father, and the king came to see her.

"I will get you anything your heart desires," the king said. "Is there anything your heart desires?"

"Yes," said the princess. "I want the moon. If I can have the moon, I will be well again."

Now the king had a great many wise men who always got for him anything he wanted, so he told his daughter that she could have the moon. Then he went to the throne room and pulled a bell cord, three

[2] See *Romeo and Juliet*, V. iii. 148.

long pulls and a short pull, and presently the lord high chamberlain came into the room.

The lord high chamberlain was a large, fat man who wore thick glasses which made his eyes seem twice as big as they really were. This made the lord high chamberlain seem twice as wise as he really was.

"I want you to get the moon," said the king. "The Princess Lenore wants the moon. If she can have the moon, she will get well again."

"The moon?" exclaimed the lord high chamberlain, his eyes widening. This made him look four times as wise as he really was.

"Yes, the moon," said the king. "M-o-o-n, moon. Get it tonight, tomorrow at the latest."

The lord high chamberlain wiped his forehead with a handkerchief and then blew his nose loudly. "I have got a great many things for you in my time, Your Majesty," he said. "It just happens that I have with me a list of the things I have got for you in my time." He pulled a long scroll of parchment out of his pocket. "Let me see, now." He glanced at the list, frowning. "I have got ivory, apes, and peacocks, rubies, opals, and emeralds, black orchids, pink elephants, and blue poodles, gold bugs, scarabs, and flies in amber, humming-birds' tongues, angels' feathers, and unicorns' horns, giants, midgets, and mermaids, frankincense, ambergris, and myrrh, troubadours, minstrels, and dancing women, a pound of butter, two dozen eggs, and a sack of sugar— sorry, my wife wrote that in there."

"I don't remember any blue poodles," said the king.

"It says blue poodles right here on the list, and they are checked off with a little check mark," said the lord high chamberlain. "So there must have been blue poodles. You just forget."

"Never mind the blue poodles," said the king. "What I want now is the moon."

"I have sent as far as Samarkand and Araby and Zanzibar to get things for you, Your Majesty," said the lord high chamberlain. "But the moon is out of the question. It is thirty-five thousand miles away and it is bigger than the room the princess lies in. Furthermore, it is made of molten copper. I cannot get the moon for you. Blue poodles, yes; the moon, no."

The king flew into a rage and told the lord high chamberlain to leave the room and to send the royal wizard to the throne room.

The royal wizard was a little, thin man with a long face. He wore a high red peaked hat covered with silver stars, and a long blue robe covered with golden owls. His face grew very pale when the king told him that he wanted the moon for his little daughter, and that he expected the royal wizard to get it.

"I have worked a great deal of magic for you in my time, Your Majesty," said the royal wizard. "As a matter of fact, I just happen to have in my pocket a list of the wizardries I have performed for you." He drew a paper from a deep pocket of his robe. "It begins: 'Dear Royal Wizard: I am returning herewith the so-called philosopher's stone which you claimed'—no, that isn't it." The royal wizard brought a long scroll of parchment from another pocket of his robe. "Here it is," he said. "Now, let's see. I have squeezed blood out of turnips for you, and turnips out of blood. I have produced rabbits out of silk hats, and silk hats out of rabbits. I have conjured up flowers, tambourines, and doves out of nowhere, and nowhere out of flowers, tambourines, and doves. I have brought you divining rods, magic wands, and crystal spheres in which to behold the future. I have compounded philters, unguents, and potions, to cure heartbreak, surfeit, and ringing in the ears. I have made you my own special mixture of wolfbane, nightshade, and eagles' tears, to ward off witches, demons and things that go bump in the night. I have given you seven-league boots, the golden touch, and a cloak of invisibility—"

"It didn't work," said the king. "The cloak of invisibility didn't work."

"Yes, it did," said the royal wizard.

"No, it didn't," said the king. "I kept bumping into things, the same as ever."

"The cloak is supposed to make you invisible," said the royal wizard. "It is not supposed to keep you from bumping into things."

"All I know is, I kept bumping into things," said the king.

The royal wizard looked at his list again. "I got you," he said, "horns from Elfland, sand from the Sandman, and gold from the rainbow. Also a spool of thread, a paper of needles, and a lump of beeswax— sorry, those are things my wife wrote down for me to get her."

"What I want you to do now," said the king, "is to get me the moon. The Princess Lenore wants the moon, and when she gets it, she will be well again."

"Nobody can get the moon," said the royal wizard. "It is a hundred and fifty thousand miles away, and it is made of green cheese, and it is twice as big as this palace."

The king flew into another rage and sent the royal wizard back to his cave. Then he rang a gong and summoned the royal mathematician.

The royal mathematician was a bald-headed, near-sighted man, with a skullcap on his head and a pencil behind each ear. He wore a black suit with white numbers on it.

"I don't want to hear a long list of all the things you have figured out for me since 1907," the king said to him. "I want you to figure out right now how to get the moon for the Princess Lenore. When she gets the moon, she will be well again."

"I am glad you mentioned all the things I have figured out for you since 1907," said the royal mathematician. "It so happens that I have a list of them with me."

He pulled a long scroll of parchment out of a pocket and looked at it. "Now let me see. I have figured out for you the distance between the horns of a dilemma, night and day, and A and Z. I have computed how far is Up, how long it takes to get to Away, and what becomes of Gone. I have discovered the length of the sea serpent, the price of the priceless and the square of the hippopotamus. I know where you are when you are at Sixes and Sevens, how much Is you have to have to make an Are, and how many birds you can catch with the salt in the ocean—187,796,132, if it would interest you to know."

"There aren't that many birds," said the king.

"I didn't say there were," said the royal mathematician. "I said if there were."

"I don't want to hear about seven hundred million imaginary birds," said the king. "I want you to get the moon for the Princess Lenore."

"The moon is three hundred thousand miles away," said the royal mathematician. "It is round and flat like a coin, only it is made of asbestos, and it is half the size of this kingdom. Furthermore, it is pasted on the sky. Nobody can get the moon."

The king flew into still another rage and sent the royal mathematician away. Then he rang for the court jester. The jester came bounding into the throne room in his motley and his cap and bells, and sat at the foot of the throne.

"What can I do for you, Your Majesty?" asked the court jester.

"Nobody can do anything for me," said the king mournfully. "The Princess Lenore wants the moon, and she cannot be well till she gets it, but nobody can get it for her. Every time I ask anybody for the moon, it gets larger and farther away. There is nothing you can do for me except play on your lute. Something sad."

"How big do they say the moon is," asked the court jester, "and how far away?"

"The lord high chamberlain says it is thirty-five thousand miles away, and bigger than the Princess Lenore's room," said the king. "The royal wizard says it is a hundred and fifty thousand miles away, and twice as big as this palace. The royal mathematician says it is three hundred thousand miles away, and half the size of this kingdom."

The court jester strummed on his lute for a little while. "They are all wise men," he said, "and so they must all be right. If they are all right, then the moon must be just as large and as far away as each person thinks it is. The thing to do is find out how big the Princess Lenore thinks it is, and how far away."

"I never thought of that," said the king.

"I will go and ask her, Your Majesty," said the court jester. And he crept softly into the little girl's room.

The Princess Lenore was awake, and she was glad to see the court jester, but her face was very pale and her voice very weak.

"Have you brought the moon to me?" she asked.

"Not yet," said the court jester, "but I will get it for you right away. How big do you think it is?"

"It is just a little smaller than my thumbnail," she said, "for when I hold my thumbnail up at the moon, it just covers it."

"And how far away is it?" asked the court jester.

"It is not at high as the big tree outside my window," said the princess, "for sometimes it gets caught in the top branches."

"It will be very easy to get the moon for you," said the court jester. "I will climb the tree tonight when it gets caught in the top branches and bring it to you."

Then he thought of something else. "What is the moon made of, princess?" he asked.

"Oh," she said, "it's made of gold, of course, silly."

The court jester left the Princess Lenore's room and went to see the royal goldsmith. He had the royal goldsmith make a tiny round golden moon just a little smaller than the thumbnail of the Princess Lenore. Then he had him string it on a golden chain so the princess could wear it around her neck.

"What is this thing I have made?" asked the royal goldsmith when he had finished it.

"You have made the moon," said the court jester. "That is the moon."

"But the moon," said the royal goldsmith, "is five hundred thousand miles away and is made of bronze and is round like a marble."

"That's what you think," said the court jester as he went away with the moon.

The court jester took the moon to the Princess Lenore, and she was overjoyed. The next day she was well again and could get up and go out in the gardens to play.

But the king's worries were not yet over. He knew that the moon would shine in the sky again that night, and he did not want the Princess Lenore to see it. If she did, she would know that the moon she wore on a chain around her neck was not the real moon.

So the king sent for the lord high chamberlain and said: "We must keep the Princess Lenore from seeing the moon when it shines in the sky tonight. Think of something."

The lord high chamberlain tapped his forehead with his fingers thoughtfully and said: "I know just the thing. We can make some dark glasses for the Princess Lenore. We can make them so dark that she will not be able to see anything at all through them. Then she will not be able to see the moon when it shines in the sky."

This made the king very angry, and he shook his head from side to side. "If she wore dark glasses, she would bump into things," he said, "and then she would be ill again." So he sent the lord high chamberlain away and called the royal wizard.

"We must hide the moon," said the king, "so that the Princess Lenore will not see it when it shines in the sky tonight. How are we going to do that?"

The royal wizard stood on his hands and then he stood on his head and then he stood on his feet again. "I know what we can do," he said. "We can stretch some black velvet curtains on poles. The curtains will cover all the palace gardens like a circus tent, and the Princess Lenore will not be able to see through them, so she will not see the moon in the sky."

The king was so angry at this that he waved his arms around. "Black velvet curtains would keep out the air," he said. "The Princess Lenore would not be able to breathe, and she would be ill again." So he sent the royal wizard away and summoned the royal mathematician.

"We must do something," said the king, "so that the Princess Lenore will not see the moon when it shines in the sky tonight. If you know so much, figure out a way to do that."

The royal mathematician walked around in a circle, and then he walked around in a square, and then he stood still. "I have it!" he said. "We can set off fireworks in the gardens every night. We will make a lot of silver fountains and golden cascades, and when they go off, they will fill the sky with so many sparks that it will be as light as day and the Princess Lenore will not be able to see the moon."

The king flew into such a rage that he began jumping up and down. "Fireworks would keep the Princess Lenore awake," he said. "She would not get any sleep at all and she would be ill again." So the king sent the royal mathematician away.

When he looked up again, it was dark outside and he saw the bright rim of the moon just peeping over the horizon. He jumped up in a great fright and rang for the court jester. The court jester came bounding into the room and sat down at the foot of the throne.

"What can I do for you, Your Majesty?" he asked.

"Nobody can do anything for me," said the king, mournfully. "The moon is coming up again. It will shine into the Princess Lenore's bedroom, and she will know it is still in the sky and that she does not wear it on a golden chain around her neck. Play me something on your lute, something very sad, for when the princess sees the moon, she will be ill again."

The court jester strummed on his lute. "What do your wise men say?" he asked.

"They can think of no way to hide the moon that will not make the Princess Lenore ill," said the king.

The court jester played another song, very softly. "Your wise men know everything," he said, "and if they cannot hide the moon, then it cannot be hidden."

The king put his head in his hands again and sighed. Suddenly he jumped up from his throne and pointed to the windows. "Look!" he cried. "The moon is already shining into the Princess Lenore's bedroom. Who can explain how the moon can be shining in the sky when it is hanging on a golden chain around her neck?"

The court jester stopped playing on his lute. "Who could explain how to get the moon when your wise men said it was too large and too far away? It was the Princess Lenore. Therefore, the Princess Lenore is wiser than your wise men and knows more about the moon than they do. So I will ask *her*." And before the king could stop him, the court jester slipped quietly out of the throne room and up the wide marble staircase to the Princess Lenore's bedroom.

The princess was lying in bed but she was wide awake and she was looking out the window at the moon shining in the sky. Shining in her hand was the moon the court jester had got for her. He looked very sad, and there seemed to be tears in his eyes.

"Tell me, Princess Lenore," he said mournfully, "how can the moon be shining in the sky when it is hanging on a golden chain around your neck?"

The princess looked at him and laughed. "That is easy, silly," she said. "When I lose a tooth, a new one grows in its place, doesn't it?"

"Of course," said the court jester. "And when the unicorn loses his horn in the forest, a new one grows in the middle of his forehead."

"That is right," said the princess. "And when the royal gardener cuts the flowers in the garden, other flowers come to take their place."

"I should have thought of that," said the court jester, "for it is the same way with the daylight."

"And it is the same way with the moon," said the Princess Lenore. "I guess it is the same way with everything." Her voice became very low and faded away, and the court jester saw that she was asleep. Gently he tucked the covers in around the sleeping princess.

But before he left the room, he went over to the window and winked at the moon, for it seemed to the court jester that the moon had winked at him.

A Day's Wait   *Ernest Hemingway*

He came into the room to shut the windows while we were still in bed and I saw he looked ill. He was shivering, his face was white, and he walked slowly as though it ached to move.

"What's the matter, Schatz?"

"I've got a headache."

"You better go back to bed."

"No. I'm all right."

"You go to bed. I'll see you when I'm dressed."

But when I came downstairs he was dressed, sitting by the fire, looking a very sick and miserable boy of nine years. When I put my hand on his forehead I knew he had a fever.

"You go up to bed," I said, "you're sick."

"I'm all right," he said.

When the doctor came he took the boy's temperature.

"What is it?" I asked him.

"One hundred and two."

Downstairs, the doctor left three different medicines in different colored capsules with instructions for giving them. One was to bring down the fever, another a purgative, the third to overcome an acid condition. The germs of influenza can only exist in an acid condition, he explained. He seemed to know all about influenza and said there was nothing to worry about if the fever did not go above one hundred and four degrees. This was a light epidemic of flu and there was no danger if you avoided pneumonia.

Back in the room I wrote the boy's temperature down and made a note of the time to give the various capsules.

"Do you want me to read to you?"

"All right. If you want to," said the boy. His face was very white and there were dark areas under his eyes. He lay still in the bed and seemed very detached from what was going on.

I read aloud from Howard Pyle's *Book of Pirates;* but I could see he was not following what I was reading.

"How do you feel, Schatz?" I asked him.

"Just the same, so far," he said.

I sat at the foot of the bed and read to myself while I waited for it to be time to give another capsule. It would have been natural for him to go to sleep, but when I looked up he was looking at the foot of the bed, looking very strangely.

"Why don't you try to go to sleep? I'll wake you up for the medicine."

"I'd rather stay awake."

After a while he said to me, "You don't have to stay in here with me, Papa, if it bothers you."

"It doesn't bother me."

"No, I mean you don't have to stay if it's going to bother you."

I thought perhaps he was a little lightheaded and after giving him the prescribed capsules at eleven o'clock I went out for a while.

It was a bright, cold day, the ground covered with a sleet that had frozen so that it seemed as if all the bare trees, the bushes, the cut brush and all the grass and the bare ground had been varnished with ice. I took the young Irish setter for a little walk up the road and along a frozen creek, but it was difficult to stand or walk on the glassy surface and the red dog slipped and slithered and I fell twice, hard, once dropping my gun and having it slide away over the ice.

We flushed a covey of quail under a high clay bank with overhanging brush and I killed two as they went out of sight over the top of the bank. Some of the covey lit in trees, but most of them scattered into brush piles and it was necessary to jump on the ice-coated mounds of brush several times before they would flush. Coming out while you were poised unsteadily on the icy, springy brush they made difficult shooting and I killed two, missed five, and started back pleased to have found a covey close to the house and happy there were so many left to find on another day.

At the house they said the boy had refused to let any one come into the room.

"You can't come in," he said. "You mustn't get what I have."

I went up to him and found him in exactly the position I had left him, white-faced, but with the tops of his cheeks flushed by the fever, staring still, as he had stared, at the foot of the bed.

I took his temperature.

"What is it?"

"Something like a hundred," I said. It was one hundred and two and four tenths.

"It was a hundred and two," he said.

"Who said so?"

"The doctor."

"Your temperature is all right," I said. "It's nothing to worry about."

"I don't worry," he said, "but I can't keep from thinking."

"Don't think," I said. "Just take it easy."

"I'm taking it easy," he said and looked straight ahead. He was evidently holding tight onto himself about something.

"Take this with water."

"Do you think it will do any good?"

"Of course it will."

I sat down and opened the *Pirate* book and commenced to read, but I could see he was not following, so I stopped.

"About what time do you think I'm going to die?" he asked.

"What?"

"About how long will it be before I die?"

"You aren't going to die. What's the matter with you?"

"Oh, yes, I am. I heard him say a hundred and two."

"People don't die with a fever of one hundred and two. That's a silly way to talk."

"I know they do. At school in France the boys told me you can't live with forty-four degrees. I've got a hundred and two."

He had been waiting to die all day, ever since nine o'clock in the morning.

"You poor Schatz," I said. "Poor old Schatz. It's like miles and kilometers. You aren't going to die. That's a different thermometer. On that thermometer thirty-seven is normal. On this kind its ninety-eight."

"Are you sure?"

"Absolutely," I said. "It's like miles and kilometers. You know, like how many kilometers we make when we do seventy miles in the car?"

"Oh," he said.

But his gaze at the foot of the bed relaxed slowly. The hold over himself relaxed too, finally, and the next day it was very slack and he cried very easily at little things that were of no importance.

Why I Live at the P.O.   *Eudora Welty*

I was getting along fine with Mama, Papa-Daddy and Uncle Rondo until my sister Stella-Rondo just separated from her husband and came back home again. Mr. Whitaker! Of course I went with Mr. Whitaker first, when he first appeared here in China Grove, taking "Pose Yourself" photos, and Stella-Rondo broke us up. Told him I was one-sided. Bigger on one side than the other, which is a deliberate, calculated falsehood: I'm the same. Stella-Rondo is exactly twelve months to the day younger than I am and for that reason she's spoiled.

She's always had anything in the world she wanted and then she'd throw it away. Papa-Daddy gave her this gorgeous Add-a-Pearl necklace when she was eight years old and she threw it away playing baseball when she was nine, with only two pearls.

So as soon as she got married and moved away from home the first thing she did was separate! From Mr. Whitaker! This photographer with the popeyes she said she trusted. Came home from one of those towns up in Illinois and to our complete surprise brought this child of two.

Mama said she like to made her drop dead for a second. "Here you had this marvelous blonde child and never so much as wrote your mother a word about it," says Mama. "I'm thoroughly ashamed of you." But of course she wasn't.

Stella-Rondo just calmly takes off this *hat,* I wish you could see it. She says, "Why, Mama, Shirley-T.'s adopted, I can prove it."

"How?" says Mama, but all I says was, "H'm!" There I was over the hot stove, trying to stretch two chickens over five people and a completely unexpected child into the bargain, without one moment's notice.

"What do you mean—'H'm'?" says Stella-Rondo, and Mama says, "I heard that, Sister."

I said that oh, I didn't mean a thing, only that whoever Shirley-T. was, she was the spit-image of Papa-Daddy if he'd cut off his beard, which of course he'd never do in the world. Papa-Daddy's Mama's papa and sulks.

Stella-Rondo got furious! She said, "Sister, I don't need to tell you you got a lot of nerve and always did have and I'll thank you to make no future reference to my adopted child whatsoever."

"Very well," I said. "Very well, very well. Of course I noticed at once she looks like Mr. Whitaker's side too. That frown. She looks like a cross between Mr. Whitaker and Papa-Daddy."

"Well, all I can say is she isn't."

"She looks exactly like Shirley Temple to me," says Mama, but Shirley-T. just ran away from her.

So the first thing Stella-Rondo did at the table was turn Papa-Daddy against me.

"Papa-Daddy," she said. He was trying to cut up his meat. "Papa-Daddy!" I was taken completely by surprise. Papa-Daddy is about a million years old and's got this long-long beard. "Papa-Daddy, Sister says she fails to understand why you don't cut off your beard."

So Papa-Daddy l-a-y-s down his knife and fork! He's real rich. Mama says he is, he says he isn't. So he says, "Have I heard correctly? You don't understand why I don't cut off my beard?"

"Why," I says, "Papa-Daddy, of course I understand, I did not say any such of a thing, the idea!"

He says, "Hussy!"

I says, "Pappa-Daddy, you know I wouldn't any more want you to cut off your beard than the man in the moon. It was the farthest thing from my mind! Stella-Rondo sat there and made that up while she was eating breast of chicken."

But he says, "So the postmistress fails to understand why I don't cut off my beard. Which job I got you through my influence with the government. 'Bird's nest'—is that what you call it?"

Not that it isn't the next to smallest P.O. in the entire state of Mississippi.

I says, "Oh, Papa-Daddy," I says, "I didn't say any such of a thing, I never dreamed it was a bird's nest, I have always been grateful though this is the next to smallest P.O. in the state of Mississippi, and I do not enjoy being referred to as a hussy by my own grandfather."

But Stella-Rondo says, "Yes, you did say it too. Anybody in the world could of heard you, that had ears."

"Stop right there," says Mama, looking at *me.*

So I pulled my napkin straight back through the napkin ring and left the table.

As soon as I was out of the room Mama says, "Call her back, or she'll starve to death," but Papa-Daddy says, "This is the beard I started growing on the Coast when I was fifteen years old." He would of gone on till nightfall if Shirley-T. hadn't lost the Milky Way she ate in Cairo.

So Papa-Daddy says, "I am going out and lie in the hammock, and you can all sit here and remember my words: I'll never cut off my beard as long as I live, even one inch, and I don't appreciate it in you at all." Passed right by me in the hall and went straight out and got in the hammock.

It would be a holiday. It wasn't five minutes before Uncle Rondo suddenly appeared in the hall in one of Stella-Rondo's flesh-colored kimonos, all cut on the bias, like something Mr. Whitaker probably thought was gorgeous.

"Uncle Rondo!" I says. "I didn't know who that was! Where are you going?"

"Sister," he says, "get out of my way, I'm poisoned."

"If you're poisoned stay away from Papa-Daddy," I says. "Keep out of the hammock. Papa-Daddy will certainly beat you on the head if you come within forty miles of him. He thinks I deliberately said he ought to cut off his beard after he got me the P.O., and I've told him and told him and told him, and he acts like he just don't hear me. Papa-Daddy must of gone stone deaf."

"He picked a fine day to do it then," says Uncle Rondo, and before you could say "Jack Robinson" flew out in the yard.

What he'd really done, he'd drunk another bottle of that prescription. He does it every single Fourth of July as sure as shooting, and it's horribly expensive. Then he falls over in the hammock and snores. So he insisted on zigzagging right on out to the hammock, looking like a half-wit.

Papa-Daddy woke up with this horrible yell and right there without moving an inch he tried to turn Uncle Rondo against me. I heard every word he said. Oh, he told Uncle Rondo I didn't learn to read till I was eight years old and he didn't see how in the world I ever got the mail put up at the P.O., much less read it all, and he said if Uncle Rondo could only fathom the lengths he had gone to to get me that job! And he said on the other hand he thought Stella-Rondo had a brilliant mind and deserved credit for getting out of town. All the time he was just lying there swinging as pretty as you please and looping out his beard, and poor Uncle Rondo was *pleading* with him to slow down the hammock, it was making him as dizzy as a witch to watch it. But that's what Papa-Daddy likes about a hammock. So Uncle Rondo was too dizzy to get turned against me for the time being. He's Mama's only brother and is a good case of a one-track mind. Ask anybody. A certified pharmacist.

Just then I heard Stella-Rondo raising the upstairs window. While she was married she got this peculiar idea that it's cooler with the windows shut and locked. So she has to raise the window before she can make a soul hear her outdoors.

So she raises the window and says, *"Oh!"* You would have thought she was mortally wounded.

Uncle Rondo and Papa-Daddy didn't even look up, but kept right on with what they were doing. I had to laugh.

I flew up the stairs and threw the door open! I says, "What in the wide world's the matter, Stella-Rondo? You mortally wounded?"

"No," she says, "I am not mortally wounded but I wish you would do me the favor of looking out that window there and telling me what you see."

So I shade my eyes and look out the window.

"I see the front yard," I says.

"Don't you see any human beings?" she says.

"I see Uncle Rondo trying to run Papa-Daddy out of the hammock," I says. "Nothing more. Naturally, it's so suffocating-hot in the house, with all the windows shut and locked, everybody who cares to stay in their right mind will have to go out and get in the hammock before the Fourth of July is over."

"Don't you notice anything different about Uncle Rondo?" asks Stella-Rondo.

"Why, no, except he's got on some terrible-looking flesh-colored contraption I wouldn't be found dead in, is all I can see," I says.

"Never mind, you won't be found dead in it, because it happens to be part of my trousseau, and Mr. Whitaker took several dozen photographs of me in it," says Stella-Rondo. "What on earth could Uncle Rondo *mean* by wearing part of my trousseau out in the broad open daylight without saying so much as 'Kiss my foot,' *knowing* I only got home this morning after my separation and hung my negligee up on the bathroom door, just as nervous as I could be?"

"I'm sure I don't know, and what do you expect me to do about it?" I says. "Jump out the window?"

"No, I expect nothing of the kind. I simply declare that Uncle Rondo looks like a fool in it, that's all," she says. "It makes me sick to my stomach."

"Well, he looks as good as he can," I says. "As good as anybody in reason could." I stood up for Uncle Rondo, please remember. And I said to Stella-Rondo, "I think I would do well not to criticize so freely if I were you and came home with a two-year-old child I had never said a word about, and no explanation whatever about my separation."

"I asked you the instant I entered this house not to refer one more time to my adopted child, and you gave me your word of honor you would not," was all Stella-Rondo would say, and started pulling out every one of her eyebrows with some cheap Kress tweezers.

So I merely slammed the door behind me and went down and made some green-tomato pickle. Somebody had to do it. Of course Mama had turned both the niggers loose; she always said no earthly power could hold one anyway on the Fourth of July, so she wouldn't even try. It turned out that Jaypan fell in the lake and came within a very narrow limit of drowning.

So Mama trots in. Lifts up the lid and says, "H'm! Not very good for your Uncle Rondo in his precarious condition, I must say. Or poor little adopted Shirley-T. Shame on you!"

That made me tired. I says, "Well, Stella-Rondo had better thank her lucky stars it was her instead of me came trotting in with that very peculiar-looking child. Now if it had been me that trotted in from Illinois and brought a peculiar-looking child of two, I shudder to think of the reception I'd of got, much less controlled the diet of an entire family.

"But you must remember, Sister, that you were never married to Mr. Whitaker in the first place and didn't go up to Illinois to live," says Mama, shaking a spoon in my face. "If you had I would of been just as overjoyed to see you and your little adopted girl as I was to see Stella-Rondo, when you wound up with your separation and came on back home."

"You would not," I says.

"Don't contradict me, I would," says Mama.

But I said she couldn't convince me though she talked till she was blue in the face. Then I said, "Besides, you know as well as I do that that child is not adopted."

"She most certainly is adopted," says Mama, stiff as a poker.

I says, "Why, Mama, Stella-Rondo had her just as sure as anything in this world, and just too stuck up to admit it."

"Why, Sister," said Mama. "Here I thought we were going to have a pleasant Fourth of July, and you start right out not believing a word your own baby sister tells you!"

"Just like Cousin Annie Flo. Went to her grave denying the facts of life," I reminded Mama.

"I told you if you ever mentioned Annie Flo's name I'd slap your face," says Mama, and slaps my face.

"All right, you wait and see," I says.

"I," says Mama, "*I* prefer to take my children's word for anything when it's humanly possible." You ought to see Mama, she weighs two hundred pounds and has real tiny feet.

Just then something perfectly horrible occurred to me.

"Mama," I says, "can that child talk?" I simply had to whisper! "Mama, I wonder if that child can be—you know—in any way? Do you realize," I says, "that she hasn't spoken one single, solitary word to a human being up to the minute? This is the way she looks," I says, and I looked like this.

Well, Mama and I just stood there and stared at each other. It was horrible!

"I remember well that Joe Whitaker frequently drank like a fish," says Mama. "I believed to my soul he drank *chemicals.*" And without another word she marches to the foot of the stairs and calls Stella-Rondo.

"Stella-Rondo? O-o-o-o-o! Stella-Rondo!"

"What?" says Stella-Rondo from upstairs. Not even the grace to get up off the bed.

"Can that child of yours talk?" asks Mama.

Stella-Rondo says, "Can she what?"

"Talk! Talk!" says Mama. "Burdyburdyburdyburdy!"

So Stella-Rondo yells back, "Who says she can't talk?"

"Sister says so," says Mama.

"You didn't have to tell me, I know whose word of honor don't mean a thing in this house," says Stella-Rondo.

And in a minute the loudest Yankee voice I ever heard in my life yells out, "OE'm Pop-OE the Sailor-r-r Ma-a-an!" and then somebody jumps up and down in the upstairs hall. In another second the house would of fallen down.

"Not only talks, she can tap-dance!" calls Stella-Rondo. "Which is more than some people I won't name can do."

"Why, the little precious darling thing!" Mama says, so surprised. "Just as smart as she can be!" Starts talking baby talk right there. Then she turns on me. "Sister, you ought to be thoroughly ashamed! Run upstairs this instant and apologize to Stella-Rondo and Shirley-T."

"Apologize for what?" I says. "I merely wondered if the child was normal, that's all. Now that she's proved she is, why, I have nothing further to say."

But Mama just turned on her heel and flew out, furious. She ran right upstairs and hugged the baby. She believed it was adopted. Stella-Rondo hadn't done a thing but turn her against me from upstairs while I stood there helpless over the hot stove. So that made Mama, Papa-Daddy and the baby all on Stella-Rondo's side.

Next, Uncle Rondo.

I must say that Uncle Rondo has been marvelous to me at various times in the past and I was completely unprepared to be made to jump out of my skin, the way it turned out. Once Stella-Rondo did something perfectly horrible to him—broke a chain letter from Flanders Field—and he took the radio back he had given her and gave it to me. Stella-Rondo was furious! For six months we all had to call her Stella instead of Stella-Rondo, or she wouldn't answer. I always thought Uncle Rondo had all the brains of the entire family.

Another time he sent me to Mammoth Cave, with all expenses paid.

But this would be the day he was drinking that prescription, the Fourth of July.

So at supper Stella-Rondo speaks up and says she thinks Uncle Rondo ought to try to eat a little something. So finally Uncle Rondo said he would try a little cold biscuits and ketchup, but that was all. So *she* brought it to him.

"Do you think it wise to disport with ketchup in Stella-Rondo's flesh-colored kimono?" I says. Trying to be considerate! If Stella-Rondo couldn't watch out for her trousseau, somebody had to.

"Any objections?" asks Uncle Rondo, just about to pour out all the ketchup.

"Don't mind what she says, Uncle Rondo," says Stella-Rondo. "Sister has been devoting this solid afternoon to sneering out my bedroom window at the way you look."

"What's that?" says Uncle Rondo. Uncle Rondo has got the most terrible temper in the world. Anything is liable to make him tear the house down if it comes at the wrong time.

So Stella-Rondo says, "Sister says, 'Uncle Rondo certainly does look like a fool in that pink kimono!' "

Do you remember who it was really said that?

Uncle Rondo spills out all the ketchup and jumps out of his chair and tears off the kimono and throws it down on the dirty floor and puts his foot on it. It had to be sent all the way to Jackson to the cleaners and re-pleated.

"So that's your opinion of your Uncle Rondo, is it?" he says. "I look like a fool, do I? Well, that's the last straw. A whole day in this house with nothing to do, and then to hear you come out with a remark like that behind my back!"

"I didn't say any such of a thing, Uncle Rondo," I says, "and I'm not saying who did, either. Why, I think you look all right. Just try to take care of yourself and not talk and eat at the same time," I says. "I think you better go lie down."

"Lie down my foot," says Uncle Rondo. I ought to of known by that he was fixing to do something perfectly horrible.

So he didn't do anything that night in the precarious state he was in—just played Casino with Mama and Stella-Rondo and Shirley-T. and gave Shirley-T. a nickel with a head on both sides. It tickled her nearly to death, and she called him "Papa." But at 6:30 A.M. the next morning, he threw a whole five-cent package of some unsold one-inch firecrackers from the store as hard as he could into my bedroom and they every one went off. Not one bad one in the string. Anybody else, there'd be one that wouldn't go off.

Well, I'm just terribly susceptible to noise of any kind, the doctor has always told me I was the most sensitive person he had ever seen in his whole life, and I was simply prostrated. I couldn't eat! People tell me they heard it as far as the cemetery, and old Aunt Jep Patterson, that had been holding her own so good, thought it was Judgment Day and she was going to meet her whole family. It's usually so quiet here.

And I'll tell you it didn't take me any longer than a minute to make up my mind what to do. There I was with the whole entire house on Stella-Rondo's side and turned against me. If I have anything at all I have pride.

So I just decided I'd go straight down to the P.O. There's plenty of room there in the back, I says to myself.

Well! I made no bones about letting the family catch on to what I was up to. I didn't try to conceal it.

The first thing they knew, I marched in where they were all playing Old Maid and pulled the electric oscillating fan out by the plug, and everything got real hot. Next I snatched the pillow I'd done the needlepoint on right off the davenport from behind Papa-Daddy. He went "Ugh!" I beat Stella-Rondo up the stairs and finally found my charm bracelet in her bureau drawer under a picture of Nelson Eddy.

"So that's the way the land lies," says Uncle Rondo. There he was, piecing on the ham. "Well, Sister, I'll be glad to donate my army cot if you got any place to set it up, providing you'll leave right this minute and let me get some peace." Uncle Rondo was in France.

"Thank you kindly for the cot and 'peace' is hardly the word I would select if I had to resort to firecrackers at 6:30 A.M. in a young girl's bedroom," I says back to him. "And as to where I intend to go, you seem to forget my position as postmistress of China Grove, Mississippi," I says. "I've always got the P.O."

Well, that made them all sit up and take notice.

I went out front and started digging up some four-o'clocks to plant around the P.O.

"Ah-ah-ah!" says Mama, raising the window. "Those happen to be my four-o'clocks. Everything planted in that star is mine. I've never known you to make anything grow in your life."

"Very well," I says. "But I take the fern. Even you, Mama, can't stand there and deny that I'm the one watered that fern. And I happen to know where I can send in a box top and get a packet of one thousand mixed seeds, no two the same kind, free."

"Oh, where?" Mama wants to know.

But I says, "Too late. You 'tend to your house, and I'll 'tend to mine. You hear things like that all the time if you know how to listen to the radio. Perfectly marvelous offers. Get anything you want free."

So I hope to tell you I marched in and got that radio, and they could of all bit a nail in two, especially Stella-Rondo, that it used to belong to, and she well knew she couldn't get it back, I'd sue for it like a shot. And I very politely took the sewing-machine motor I helped pay the most on to give Mama for Christmas back in 1929, and a good big calendar, with the first-aid remedies on it. The thermometer and the Hawaiian ukulele certainly were rightfully mine, and I stood on the step-ladder and got all my watermelon-rind preserves and every fruit and vegetable I'd put up, every jar. Then I began to pull the tacks out of the bluebird wall vases on the archway to the dining room.

"Who told you you could have those, Miss Priss?" says Mama, fanning as hard as she could.

"I bought 'em and I'll keep track of 'em," I says. "I'll tack 'em up one on each side of the post-office window, and you can see 'em when you come to ask me for your mail, if you're so dead to see 'em."

"Not I! I'll never darken the door to that post office again if I live to be a hundred," Mama says. "Ungrateful child! After all the money we spent on you at the Normal."

"Me either," says Stella-Rondo. "You can just let my mail lie there and *rot,* for all I care. I'll never come and relieve you of a single, solitary piece."

"I should worry," I says. "And who you think's going to sit down and write you all those big fat letters and postcards, by the way? Mr. Whitaker? Just because he was the only man ever dropped down in China Grove and you got him—unfairly—is he going to sit down and write you a lengthy correspondence after you come home giving no rhyme nor reason whatsoever for your separation and no explanation for the presence of that child? I may not have your brilliant mind, but I fail to see it."

So Mama says, "Sister, I've told you a thousand times that Stella-Rondo simply got homesick, and this child is far too big to be hers," and she says, "Now, why don't you all just sit down and play Casino?"

Then Shirley-T. sticks out her tongue at me in this perfectly horrible way. She has no more manners than the man in the moon. I told her she was going to cross her eyes like that some day and they'd stick.

"It's too late to stop me now," I says. "You should have tried that yesterday. I'm going to the P.O. and the only way you can possibly see me is to visit me there."

So Papa-Daddy says, "You'll never catch me setting foot in that post office, even if I should take a notion into my head to write a letter some place." He says, "I won't have you reachin' out of that little old window with a pair of shears and cuttin' off any beard of mine. I'm too smart for you!"

"We all are," says Stella-Rondo.

But I said, "If you're so smart, where's Mr. Whitaker?"

So then Uncle Rondo says, "I'll thank you from now on to stop reading all the orders I get on postcards and telling everybody in China Grove what you think is the matter with them," but I says, "I draw my own conclusions and will continue in the future to draw them." I says, "If people want to write their inmost secrets on penny postcards, there's nothing in the wide world you can do about it, Uncle Rondo."

"And if you think we'll ever *write* another postcard you're sadly mistaken," says Mama.

"Cutting off your nose to spite your face then," I says. "But if you're all determined to have no more to do with the U.S. mail, think of this: What will Stella-Rondo do now, if she wants to tell Mr. Whitaker to come after her?"

"Wah!" says Stella-Rondo. I knew she'd cry. She had a conniption fit right there in the kitchen.

"It will be interesting to see how long she holds out," I says. "And now—I am leaving."

"Good-bye," says Uncle Rondo.

"Oh, I declare," says Mama, "to think that a family of mine should quarrel on the Fourth of July, or the day after, over Stella-Rondo leaving old Mr. Whitaker and having the sweetest little adopted child! It looks like we'd all be glad!"

"Wah!" says Stella-Rondo, and has a fresh conniption fit.

"*He* left *her*—you mark my words," I says. "That's Mr. Whitaker. I know Mr. Whitaker. After all, I knew him first. I said from the beginning he'd up and leave her. I foretold every single thing that's happened."

"Where did he go?" asks Mama.

"Probably to the North Pole, if he knows what's good for him," I says.

But Stella-Rondo just bawled and wouldn't say another word. She flew to her room and slammed the door.

"Now look what you've gone and done, Sister," says Mama. "You go apologize."

"I haven't got time, I'm leaving," I says.

"Well, what are you waiting around for?" asks Uncle Rondo.

So I just picked up the kitchen clock and marched off, without saying "Kiss my foot" or anything, and never did tell Stella-Rondo good-bye.

There was a nigger girl going along on a little wagon right in front.

"Nigger girl," I says, "come help me haul these things down the hill, I'm going to live in the post office."

Took her nine trips in her express wagon. Uncle Rondo came out on the porch and threw her a nickel.

And that's the last I've laid eyes on any of my family or my family laid eyes on me for five solid days and nights. Stella-Rondo may be telling the most horrible tales in the world about Mr. Whitaker, but I haven't heard them. As I tell everybody, I draw my own conclusions.

But oh, I like it here. It's ideal, as I've been saying. You see, I've got everything cater-cornered, the way I like it. Hear the radio? All the war news. Radio, sewing machine, book ends, ironing board and that great big piano lamp—peace, that's what I like. Butter-bean vines planted all along the front where the strings are.

Of course, there's not much mail. My family are naturally the main people in China Grove, and if they prefer to vanish from the face of the earth, for all the mail they get or the mail they write, why, I'm not going to open my mouth. Some of the folks here in town are taking up for me and some turned against me. I know which is which. There are always people who will quit buying stamps just to get on the right side of Papa-Daddy.

But here I am, and here I'll stay. I want the world to know I'm happy.

And if Stella-Rondo should come to me this minute, on bended knees, and *attempt* to explain the incidents of her life with Mr. Whitaker, I'd simply put my fingers in both my ears and refuse to listen.

Miss Brill   *Katherine Mansfield*

Although it was so brilliantly fine—the blue sky powdered with gold and great spots of light like white wine splashed over the Jardins Publiques—Miss Brill was glad that she had decided on her fur. The air was motionless, but when you opened your mouth there was just a faint chill, like a chill from a glass of iced water before you sip, and now and again a leaf came drifting—from nowhere, from the sky. Miss Brill put up her hand and touched her fur. Dear little thing! It was nice to feel it again. She had taken it out of its box that afternoon, shaken out the moth-powder, given it a good brush, and rubbed the life back into the dim little eyes. "What has been happening to me?" said the sad little eyes. Oh, how sweet it was to see them snap at her again from the red eiderdown! . . . . But the nose, which was of some black composition, wasn't at all firm. It must have had a knock, somehow. Never mind— a little dab of black sealing-wax when the time came—when it was absolutely necessary. . . . Little rogue! Yes, she really felt like that about it. Little rogue biting its tail just by her left ear. She could have taken it off and laid it on her lap and stroked it. She felt a tingling in her hands and arms, but that came from walking, she supposed. And when she breathed, something light and sad—no, not sad, exactly —something gentle seemed to move in her bosom.

There were a number of people out this afternoon, far more than last Sunday. And the band sounded louder and gayer. That was be-cause the Season had begun. For although the band played all the year round on Sundays, out of season it was never the same. It was like some one playing with only the family to listen; it didn't care how it played if there weren't any strangers present. Wasn't the conductor wearing a new coat, too? She was sure it was new. He scraped with his foot and flapped his arms like a rooster about to crow, and the bandsmen sitting in the green rotunda blew out their cheeks and glared at the music. Now there came a little "flutey" bit—very pretty!—a little chain of bright drops. She was sure it would be repeated. It was; she lifted her head and smiled.

Only two people shared her "special" seat: a fine old man in a velvet coat, his hands clasped over a huge carved walking-stick, and a big old woman, sitting upright, with a roll of knitting on her embroidered apron. They did not speak. This was disappointing, for Miss Brill always looked forward to the conversation. She had become really quite expert, she thought, at listening as though she didn't listen, at sitting in other people's lives just for a minute while they talked round her.

She glanced, sideways, at the old couple. Perhaps they would go soon. Last Sunday, too, hadn't been as interesting as usual. An Englishman and his wife, he wearing a dreadful Panama hat and she button boots. And she'd gone on the whole time about how she ought to wear spectacles; she knew she needed them; but that it was no good getting any; they'd be sure to break and they'd never keep on. And he'd been so patient. He'd suggested everything—gold rims, the kind that curved round your ears, little pads inside the bridge. No, nothing would please her. "They'll always be sliding down my nose!" Miss Brill had wanted to shake her.

The old people sat on the bench, still as statues. Never mind, there was always the crowd to watch. To and fro, in front of the flower-beds and the band rotunda, the couples and groups paraded, stopped to talk, to greet, to buy a handful of flowers from the old beggar who had his tray fixed to the railings. Little children ran among them, swooping and laughing; little boys with big white silk bows under their chins, little girls, little French dolls, dressed up in velvet and lace. And sometimes a tiny staggerer came suddenly rocking into the open from under the trees, stopped, stared, as suddenly sat down "flop," until its small high-stepping mother, like a young hen, rushed scolding to its rescue. Other people sat on the benches and green chairs, but they were nearly always the same, Sunday after Sunday, and—Miss Brill had often noticed—there was something funny about nearly all of them. They were odd, silent, nearly all old, and from the way they stared they looked as though they'd just come from dark little rooms or even—even cupboards!

Behind the rotunda the slender trees with yellow leaves down drooping, and through them just a line of sea, and beyond the blue sky with gold-veined clouds.

Tum-tum-tum tiddle-um! tiddle-um! tum tiddley-um tum ta! blew the band.

Two young girls in red came by and two young soldiers in blue met them, and they laughed and paired and went off arm-in-arm. Two peasant women with funny straw hats passed, gravely, leading beautiful smoke-colored donkeys. A cold, pale nun hurried by. A beautiful woman came along and dropped her bunch of violets, and a little boy ran after to hand them to her, and she took them and threw them away as if they'd been poisoned. Dear me! Miss Brill didn't know whether to admire that or not! And now an ermine toque and a gentleman in gray met just in front of her. He was tall, stiff, dignified, and she was wearing the ermine toque she'd bought when her hair was yellow. Now everything, her hair, her face, even her eyes, was the same color as the shabby ermine, and her hand, in its cleaned glove, lifted to dab her lips, was a tiny yellowish paw. Oh, she was so pleased to see him—delighted! She rather thought they were going to meet that afternoon. She described where she'd been—everywhere, here, there, along by the sea. The day was so charming—didn't he agree? And wouldn't he, perhaps? . . . But he shook his head, lighted a cigarette, slowly breathed a great deep puff into her face, and, even while she was still talking and laughing, flicked the match away and walked on. The ermine toque was alone; she smiled more brightly than ever. But even the band seemed to know what she was feeling and played more softly, played tenderly, and the drum beat, "The Brute! The Brute!" over and over. What would she do? What was going to happen now? But as Miss Brill wondered, the ermine toque turned, raised her hand as though she'd seen some one else, much nicer, just over there, and pattered away. And the band changed again and played more quickly, more gayly than ever, and the old couple on Miss Brill's seat got up and marched away, and such a funny old man with long whiskers hobbled along in time to the music and was nearly knocked over by four girls walking abreast.

Oh, how fascinating it was! How she enjoyed it! How she loved sitting here, watching it all! It was like a play. It was exactly like a play. Who could believe the sky at the back wasn't painted? But it wasn't till a little brown dog trotted on solemn and then slowly trotted off, like a little "theater" dog, a little dog that had been drugged, that Miss Brill discovered what it was that made it so exciting. They were all on the stage. They weren't only the audience, not only looking on; they were acting. Even she had a part and came every Sunday. No doubt somebody would have noticed if she hadn't been there; she was part of the performance after all. How strange she'd never thought of it like that before! And yet it explained why she made such a point of starting from home at just the same time each week—so as not to be late for the performance—and it also explained why she had quite a queer, shy feeling at telling her English pupils how she spent her Sunday afternoons. No wonder! Miss Brill nearly laughed out loud. She was on the stage. She thought of the old invalid gentleman to whom she read the newspaper four afternoons a week while he slept in the garden. She had got quite used to the frail head on the cotton pillow, the hollowed eyes, the open mouth and the high pinched nose. If he'd been dead she mightn't have noticed for weeks; she wouldn't have minded. But suddenly he knew he was having the paper read to him by an actress! "An actress!" The old head lifted; two points of light quivered in the old eyes. "An actress—are ye?" And Miss Brill smoothed the newspaper as thought it were the manuscript of her part and said gently: "Yes, I have been an actress for a long time."

The band had been having a rest. Now they started again. And what they played was warm, sunny, yet there was just a faint chill—a something, what was it?—not sadness—no, not sadness—a something that made you want to sing. The tune lifted, lifted, the light shone; and it seemed to Miss Brill that in another moment all of them, all the whole company, would begin singing. The young ones, the laughing ones who were moving together, they would begin, and the men's voices, very resolute and brave, would join them. And then she too, she too, and the others on the benches—they would come in with a kind of accompaniment—something low, that scarcely rose or fell, something so beautiful—moving. . . . And Miss Brill's eyes filled with tears and she looked smiling at all the other members of the company. Yes, we understand, we understand, she thought—though what they understood she didn't know.

Just at that moment a boy and a girl came and sat down where the old couple had been. They were beautifully dressed; they were in love. The hero and heroine, of course, just arrived from his father's yacht. And still soundlessly singing, still with that trembling smile, Miss Brill prepared to listen.

"No, not now," said the girl. "Not here, I can't."

"But why? Because of that stupid old thing at the end there?" asked the boy. "Why does she come here at all—who wants her? Why doesn't she keep her silly old mug at home?"

"It's her fu-fur which is so funny," giggled the girl. "It's exactly like a fried whiting."

"Ah, be off with you!" said the boy in an angry whisper. Then: "Tell me, ma petite chère—"

"No, not here," said the girl. "Not *yet*."

*   *   *

On her way home she usually bought a slice of honeycake at the baker's. It was her Sunday treat. Sometimes there was an almond in her slice, sometimes not. It made a great difference. If there was an almond it was like carrying home a tiny present—a surprise—something that might very well not have been there. She hurried on the almond Sundays and struck the match for the kettle in quite a dashing way.

But to-day she passed the baker's by, climbed the stairs, went into the little dark room—her room like a cupboard—and sat down on the red eiderdown. She sat there for a long time. The box that the fur came out of was on the bed. She unclasped the necklet quickly, without looking, laid it inside. But when she put the lid on she thought she heard something crying.

The Downward Path to Wisdom   *Katherine Anne Porter*

In the square bedroom with the big window Mama and Papa were lolling back on their pillows handing each other things from the wide black tray on the small table with crossed legs. They were smiling and they smiled even more when the little boy, with the feeling of sleep still in his skin and hair, came in and walked up to the bed. Leaning against it, his bare toes wriggling in the white fur rug, he went on eating peanuts which he took from his pajama pocket. He was four years old.

"Here's my baby," said Mama. "Lift him up, will you?"

He went limp as a rag for Papa to take him under the arms and swing him up over a broad, tough chest. He sank between his parents like a bear cub in a warm litter, and lay there comfortably. He took another peanut between his teeth, cracked the shell, picked out the nut whole and ate it.

"Running around without his slippers again," said Mama. "His feet are like icicles."

"He crunches like a horse," said Papa. "Eating peanuts before breakfast will ruin his stomach. Where did he get them?"

"You brought them yesterday," said Mama with exact memory, "in a grisly little cellophane sack. I have asked you dozens of times not to bring him things to eat. Put him out, will you? He's spilling shells all over me."

Almost at once the little boy found himself on the floor again. He moved around to Mama's side of the bed and leaned confidingly near her and began another peanut. As he chewed he gazed solemnly in her eyes.

"Bright-looking specimen, isn't he?" asked Papa, stretching his long legs and reaching for his bathrobe. "I suppose you'll say it's my fault he's dumb as an ox."

"He's my little baby, my only baby," said Mama richly, hugging him, "and he's a dear lamb." His neck and shoulders were quite boneless in her firm embrace. He stopped chewing long enough to receive a kiss on his crumby chin. "He's sweet as clover," said Mama. The baby went on chewing.

"Look at him staring like an owl," said Papa.

Mama said, "He's an angel and I'll never get used to having him."

"We'd be better off if we never *had* had him," said Papa. He was walking about the room and his back was turned when he said that. There was silence for a moment. The little boy stopped eating, and stared deeply at his Mama. She was looking at the back of Papa's head, and her eyes were almost black. "You're going to say that just once too often," she told him in a low voice. "I hate you when you say that."

Papa said, "You spoil him to death. You never correct him for anything. And you don't take care of him. You let him run around eating peanuts before breakfast."

"You gave him the peanuts, remember that," said Mama. She sat up and hugged her only baby once more. He nuzzled softly in the pit of her arm. "Run along, my darling," she told him in her gentlest voice, smiling at him straight in the eyes. "Run along," she said, her arms falling away from him. "Get your breakfast."

The little boy had to pass his father on the way to the door. He shrank into himself when he saw the big hand raised above him. "Yes, get out of here and stay out," said Papa, giving him a little shove toward the door. It was not a hard shove, but it hurt the little boy. He slunk out, and trotted down the hall trying not to look back. He was afraid something was coming after him, he could not imagine what. Something hurt him all over, he did not know why.

He did not want his breakfast; he would not have it. He sat and stirred it round in the yellow bowl, letting it stream off the spoon and spill on the table, on his front, on the chair. He liked seeing it spill. It was hateful stuff, but looked funny running in white rivulets down his pajamas.

"Now look what you're doing, dirty boy," said Marjory. "You dirty little old boy."

The little boy opened his mouth to speak for the first time. "You're dirty yourself," he told her.

"That's right," said Marjory, leaning over him and speaking so her voice would not carry. "That's right, just like your papa. Mean," she whispered, "mean."

The little boy took up his yellow bowl full of cream and oatmeal and sugar with both hands and brought it down with a crash on the table. It burst and some of the wreck lay in chunks and some of it ran all over everything. He felt better.

"You see?" said Marjory, dragging him out of the chair and scrubbing him with a napkin. She scrubbed him as roughly as she dared until he cried out. "That's just what I said. That's exactly it." Through his tears he saw her face terribly near, red and frowning under a stiff white band, looking like the face of somebody who came at night and stood over him and scolded him when he could not move or get away. "Just like your papa, *mean*."

The little boy went out into the garden and sat on a green bench dangling his legs. He was clean. His hair was wet and his blue woolly pull-over made his nose itch. His face felt stiff from the soap. He saw Marjory going past a window with the black tray. The curtains were still closed at the window he knew opened into Mama's room. Papa's room. Mommanpoppasroom, the word was pleasant, it made a mumbling snapping noise between his lips; it ran in his mind while his eyes wandered about looking for something to do, something to play with.

Mommanpoppas' voices kept attracting his attention. Mama was being cross with Papa again. He could tell by the sound. That was what Marjory always said when their voices rose and fell and shot up to a point and crashed and rolled like the two tomcats who fought at night. Papa was being cross, too, much crosser than Mama this time. He grew cold and disturbed and sat very still, wanting to go to the bathroom, but it was just next to Mommanpoppasroom; he didn't dare think of it. As the voices grew louder he could hardly hear them any more, he wanted so badly to go to the bathroom. The kitchen door opened suddenly and Marjory ran out, making the motion with her hand that meant he was to come to her. He didn't move. She came to him, her face still red and frowning, but she was not angry; she was scared just as he was. She said, "Come on, honey, we've got to go to your gran'ma's again." She took his hand and pulled him. "Come on quick, your gran'ma is waiting for you." He slid off the bench. His mother's voice rose in a terrible scream, screaming something he could not understand, but she was furious; he had seen her clenching her fists and stamping in one spot, screaming with her eyes shut; he knew how she looked. She was screaming in a tantrum, just as he remembered having heard himself. He stood still, doubled over, and all his body seemed to dissolve, sickly, from the pit of his stomach.

"Oh, my God," said Marjory. "Oh, my God. Now look at you. Oh, my God. I can't stop to clean you up."

He did not know how he got to his grandma's house, but he was there at last, wet and soiled, being handled with disgust in the big bathtub. His grandma was there in long black skirts saying, "Maybe he's sick; maybe we should send for the doctor."

"I don't think so, m'am," said Marjory. "He hasn't et anything; he's just scared."

The little boy couldn't raise his eyes, he was so heavy with shame. "Take this note to his mother," said Grandma.

She sat in a wide chair and ran her hands over his head, combing his hair with her fingers; she lifted his chin and kissed him. "Poor little fellow," she said. "Never you mind. You always have a good time at your grandma's, don't you? You're going to have a nice little visit, just like the last time."

The little boy leaned against the stiff, dry-smelling clothes and felt horribly grieved about something. He began to whimper and said, "I'm hungry. I want something to eat." This reminded him. He began to bellow at the top of his voice; he threw himself upon the carpet and rubbed his nose in a dusty woolly bouquet of roses. "I want my peanuts," he howled. "Somebody took my peanuts."

His grandma knelt beside him and gathered him up so tightly he could hardly move. She called in a calm voice above his howls to Old Janet in the doorway, "Bring me some bread and butter with strawberry jam."

"I want peanuts," yelled the little boy desperately.

"No, you don't, darling," said his grandma. "You don't want horrid old peanuts to make you sick. You're going to have some of grandma's nice fresh bread with good strawberries on it. That's what you're going to have." He sat afterward very quietly and ate and ate. His grandma sat near him and Old Janet stood by, near a tray with a loaf and a glass bowl of jam upon the table at the window. Outside there was a trellis with tube-shaped red flowers clinging all over it, and brown bees singing.

"I hardly know what to do," said Grandma, "it's very . . ."

"Yes, ma'am," said Old Janet, "it certainly is . . ."

Grandma said, "I can't possibly see the end of it. It's a terrible . . ."

"It certainly is bad," said Old Janet, "all this upset all the time and him such a baby."

Their voices ran on soothingly. The little boy ate and forgot to listen. He did not know these women, except by name. He could not understand what they were talking about; their hands and their clothes and their voices were dry and far away; they examined him with crinkled eyes without any expression that he could see. He sat there waiting for whatever they would do next with him. He hoped they would let him go out and play in the yard. The room was full of flowers and dark red curtains and big soft chairs, and the windows were open, but it was still dark in there somehow; dark, and a place he did not know, or trust.

"Now drink your milk," said Old Janet, holding out a silver cup.

"I don't want any milk," he said, turning his head away.

"Very well, Janet, he doesn't have to drink it," said Grandma quickly. "Now run out in the garden and play, darling. Janet, get his hoop."

A big strange man came home in the evenings who treated the little boy very confusingly. "Say 'please,' and 'thank you,' young man," he would roar, terrifyingly, when he gave any smallest object to the little boy. "Well, fellow, are you ready for a fight?" he would say, again, doubling up huge, hairy fists and making passes at him. "Come on now, you must learn to box." After the first few times this was fun.

"Don't teach him to be rough," said Grandma. "Time enough for all that."

"Now, Mother, we don't want him to be a sissy," said the big man. "He's got to toughen up early. Come on now, fellow, put up your mitts." The little boy liked this new word for hands. He learned to throw himself upon the strange big man, whose name was Uncle David, and hit him on the chest as hard as he could; the big man would laugh and hit him back with his huge, loose fists. Sometimes, but not often, Uncle David came home in the middle of the day. The little boy missed him on the other days, and would hang on the gate looking down the street for him. One evening he brought a large square package under his arm.

"Come over here, fellow, and see what I've got," he said, pulling off quantities of green paper and string from the box which was full of flat, folded colors. He put something in the little boy's hand. It was limp and silky and bright green with a tube on the end. "Thank you," said the little boy nicely, but not knowing what to do with it.

"Balloons," said Uncle David in triumph. "Now just put your mouth here and blow hard." The little boy blew hard and the green thing began to grow round and thin and silvery.

"Good for your chest," said Uncle David. "Blow some more." The little boy went on blowing and the balloon swelled steadily.

"Stop," said Uncle David, "that's enough." He twisted the tube to keep the air in. "That's the way," he said. "Now I'll blow one, and you blow one, and let's see who can blow up a big balloon the fastest."

They blew and blew, especially Uncle David. He puffed and panted and blew with all his might, but the little boy won. His balloon was perfectly round before Uncle David could even get started. The little boy was so proud he began to dance and shout, "I beat, I beat," and blew in his balloon again. It burst in his face and frightened him so he felt sick. "Ha ha, ho ho ho," whooped Uncle David. "That's the boy. I bet I can't do that. Now let's see." He blew until the beautiful bubble grew and wavered and burst into thin air, and there was only a small colored rag in his hand. This was a fine game. They went on with it until Grandma came in and said, "Time for supper now. No, you can't blow balloons at the table. Tomorrow maybe." And it was all over.

The next day, instead of being given balloons, he was hustled out of bed early, bathed in warm soapy water and given a big breakfast of soft-boiled eggs with toast and jam and milk. His grandma came in to kiss him good morning. "And I hope you'll be a good boy and obey your teacher," she told him.

"What's teacher?" asked the little boy.

"Teacher is at school," said Grandma. "She'll tell you all sorts of things and you must do as she says."

Mama and Papa had talked a great deal about School, and how they must send him there. They had told him it was a fine place with all kinds of toys and other children to play with. He felt he knew about School. "I didn't know it was time, Grandma," he said. "Is it today?"

"It's this very minute," said Grandma. "I told you a week ago."

Old Janet came in with her bonnet on. It was a prickly looking bundle held with a black rubber band under her black hair. "Come on," she said. "This is my busy day." She wore a dead cat slung around her neck, its sharp ears bent over under her baggy chin.

The little boy was excited and wanted to run ahead. "Hold to my hand like I told you," said Old Janet. "Don't go running off like that and get yourself killed."

"I'm going to get killed, I'm going to get killed," sang the little boy, making a tune of his own.

"Don't say that, you give me the creeps," said Old Janet. "Hold to my hand now." She bent over and looked at him, not at his face but at something on his clothes. His eyes followed hers.

"I declare," said Old Janet, "I did forget. I was going to sew it up. I might have known. I *told* your grandma it would be that way from now on."

"What?" asked the little boy.

"Just look at yourself," said Old Janet crossly. He looked at himself. There was a little end of him showing through the slit in his short blue flannel trousers. The trousers came halfway to his knees above, and his socks came halfway to his knees below, and all winter long his knees were cold. He remembered now how cold his knees were in cold weather. And how sometimes he would have to put the part of him that came through the slit back again, because he was cold there too. He saw at once what was wrong, and tried to arrange himself, but his mittens got in the way. Janet said, "Stop that, you bad boy," and with a firm thumb she set him in order, at the same time reaching under his belt to pull down and fold his knit undershirt over his front.

"There now," she said, "try not to disgrace yourself today." He felt guilty and red all over, because he had something that showed when he was dressed that was not supposed to show then. The different women who bathed him always wrapped him quickly in towels and hurried him into his clothes, because they saw something about him he could not see for himself. They hurried him so he never had a chance to see whatever it was they saw, and though he looked at himself when his clothes were off, he could not find out what was wrong with him. Outside, in his clothes, he knew he looked like everybody else, but inside his clothes there was something bad the matter with him. It worried him and confused him and he wondered about it. The only people who never seemed to notice there was something wrong with him were Mommanpoppa. They never called him a bad boy, and all summer long they had taken all his clothes off and let him run in the sand beside a big ocean.

"Look at him, isn't he a love?" Mama would say and Papa would look, and say, "He's got a back like a prize fighter." Uncle David was a prize fighter when he doubled up his mitts and said, "Come on, fellow."

Old Janet held him firmly and took long steps under her big rustling skirts. He did not like Old Janet's smell. It made him a little quivery in the stomach; it was just like wet chicken feathers.

School was easy. Teacher was a square-shaped woman with square short hair and short skirts. She got in the way sometimes, but not often. The people around him were his size; he didn't have always to be stretching his neck up to faces bent over him, and he could sit on the chairs without having to climb. All the children had names, like Frances and Evelyn and Agatha and Edward and Martin, and his own name was Stephen. He was not Mama's "Baby," nor Papa's "Old Man"; he was not Uncle David's "Fellow" or Grandma's "Darling," or even Old Janet's "Bad Boy." He was Stephen. He was learning to read, and to sing a tune to some strange-looking letters or marks written in chalk on a blackboard. You talked one kind of lettering, and you sang another. All the children talked and sang in turn, and then all together. Stephen thought it a fine game. He felt awake and happy. They had soft clay and paper and wires and squares of colors in tin boxes to play with, colored blocks to build houses with. Afterward they all danced in a big ring, and then they danced in pairs, boys with girls. Stephen danced with Frances, and Frances kept saying, "Now you just follow me." She was a little taller than he was, and her hair stood up in short, shiny curls, the color of an ash tray on Papa's desk. She would say, "You can't dance." "I can dance too," said Stephen, jumping around holding her hands, "I can, too, dance." He was certain of it. "*You* can't dance," he told Frances, "you can't dance at all."

Then they had to change partners, and when they came round again, Frances said, "I don't *like* the way you dance." This was different. He felt uneasy about it. He didn't jump quite so high when the phonograph record started going dumdiddy dumdiddy again. "Go ahead, Stephen, you're doing fine," said Teacher, waving her hands together very fast. The dance ended, and they all played "relaxing" for five minutes. They relaxed by swinging their arms back and forth, then rolling their heads round and round. When Old Janet came for him he didn't want to go home. At lunch his grandma told him twice to keep his face out of his plate. "Is that what they teach you at school?" she asked. Uncle David was at home. "Here you are, fellow," he said and gave Stephen two balloons. "Thank you," said Stephen. He put the balloons in his pocket and forgot about them. "I told you that boy could learn something," said Uncle David to Grandma. "Hear him say 'thank you'?"

In the afternoon at school Teacher handed out big wads of clay and told the children to make something out of it. Anything they liked. Stephen decided to make a cat, like Mama's Meeow at home. He did not like Meeow, but he thought it would be easy to make a cat. He could not get the clay to work at all. It simply fell into one lump after another. So he stopped, wiped his hands on his pull-over, remembered his balloons and began blowing one.

"Look at Stephen's horse," said Frances. "Just look at it."

"It's not a horse, it's a cat," said Stephen. The other children gathered around. "It looks like a horse, a little," said Martin.

"It is a cat," said Stephen, stamping his foot, feeling his face turning hot. The other children all laughed and exclaimed over Stephen's cat that looked like a horse. Teacher came down among them. She sat usually at the top of the room before a big table covered with papers and playthings. She picked up Stephen's lump of clay and turned it round and examined it with her kind eyes. "Now, children," she said, "everybody has the right to make anything the way he pleases. If Stephen says this is a cat, it *is* a cat. Maybe you were thinking about a horse, Stephen?"

"It's a *cat*," said Stephen. He was aching all over. He knew then he should have said at first, "Yes, it's a horse." Then they would have let him alone. They would never have known he was trying to make a cat. "It's Meeow," he said in a trembling voice, "but I forgot how she looks."

His balloon was perfectly flat. He started blowing it up again, trying not to cry. Then it was time to go home, and Old Janet came looking for him. While Teacher was talking to other grown-up people who came to take other children home, Frances said, "Give me your balloon; I haven't got a balloon." Stephen handed it to her. He was happy to give it. He reached in his pocket and took out the other.

Happily, he gave her that one too. Frances took it, then handed it back. "Now you blow up one and I'll blow up the other, and let's have a race," she said. When their balloons were only half filled Old Janet took Stephen by the arm and said, "Come on here, this is my busy day."

Frances ran after them, calling, "Stephen, you give me back my balloon," and snatched it away. Stephen did not know whether he was surprised to find himself going away with Frances' balloon, or whether he was surprised to see her snatching it as if it really belonged to her. He was badly mixed up in his mind, and Old Janet was hauling him along. One thing he knew, he liked Frances, he was going to see her again tomorrow, and he was going to bring her more balloons.

That evening Stephen boxed awhile with his uncle David, and Uncle David gave him a beautiful orange. "Eat that," he said, "it's good for your health."

"Uncle David, may I have some more balloons?" asked Stephen.

"Well, what do you say first?" asked Uncle David, reaching for the box on the top bookshelf.

"Please," said Stephen.

"That's the word," said Uncle David. He brought out two balloons, a red and a yellow one. Stephen noticed for the first time they had letters on them, very small letters that grew taller and wider as the balloon grew rounder. "Now that's all, fellow," said Uncle David. "Don't ask for any more because that's all." He put the box back on the bookshelf, but not before Stephen had seen that the box was almost full of balloons. He didn't say a word, but went on blowing, and Uncle David blew also. Stephen thought it was the nicest game he had ever known.

He had only one left, the next day, but he took it to school and gave it to Frances. "There are a lot," he said, feeling very proud and warm; "I'll bring you a lot of them."

Frances blew it up until it made a beautiful bubble, and said, "Look, I want to show you something." She took a sharp-pointed stick they used in working the clay; she poked the balloon, and it exploded. "Look at that," she said.

"That's nothing," said Stephen, "I'll bring you some more."

After school, before Uncle David came home, while Grandma was resting, when Old Janet had given him his milk and told him to run away and not bother her, Stephen dragged a chair to the bookshelf, stood upon it and reached into the box. He did not take three or four as he believed he intended; once his hands were upon them he seized what they could hold and jumped off the chair, hugging them to him. He stuffed them into his reefer pocket where they folded down and hardly made a lump.

He gave them all to Frances. There were so many, Frances gave most of them away to the other children. Stephen, flushed with his new joy, the lavish pleasure of giving presents, found almost at once still another happiness. Suddenly he was popular among the children; they invited him specially to join whatever games were up; they fell in at once with his own notions for play, and asked him what he would like to do next. They had festivals of blowing up the beautiful globes, fuller and rounder and thinner, changing as they went from deep color to lighter, paler tones, growing glassy thin, bubbly thin, then bursting with a thrilling loud noise like a toy pistol.

For the first time in his life Stephen had almost too much of something he wanted, and his head was so turned he forgot how this full-ness came about, and no longer thought of it as a secret. The next day was Saturday, and Frances came to visit him with her nurse. The nurse and Old Janet sat in Old Janet's room drinking coffee and gossiping, and the children sat on the side porch blowing balloons. Stephen chose an apple-colored one and Frances a pale green one. Between them on the bench lay a tumbled heap of delights still to come.

"I once had a silver balloon," said Frances, "a beyootiful silver one, not round like these; it was a long one. But these are even nicer, I think," she added quickly, for she did want to be polite.

"When you get through with that one," said Stephen, gazing at her with the pure bliss of giving added to loving, "you can blow up a blue one and then a pink one and a yellow one and a purple one." He pushed the heap of limp objects toward her. Her clear-looking eyes, with fine little rays of brown in them like the spokes of a wheel, were full of approval for Stephen. "I wouldn't want to be greedy, though, and blow up all your balloons."

"There'll be plenty more left," said Stephen, and his heart rose under his thin ribs. He felt his ribs with his fingers and discovered with some surprise that they stopped somewhere in front, while Frances sat blow-ing balloons rather halfheartedly. The truth was, she was tired of balloons. After you blow six or seven your chest gets hollow and your lips feel puckery. She had been blowing balloons steadily for three days now. She had begun to hope they were giving out. "There's boxes and boxes more of them, Frances," said Stephen happily. "Millions more. I guess they'd last and last if we didn't blow too many every day."

Frances said somewhat timidly, "I tell you what. Let's rest awhile and fix some liquish water. Do you like liquish?"

"Yes, I do," said Stephen, "but I haven't got any."

"Couldn't we buy some?" asked Frances. "It's only a cent a stick, the nice rubbery, twisty kind. We can put it in a bottle with some water, and shake it and shake it, and it makes foam on top like soda pop and we can drink it. I'm kind of thirsty," she said in a small, weak voice. "Blowing balloons all the time makes you thirsty, I think."

Stephen, in silence, realized a dreadful truth and a numb feeling crept over him. He did not have a cent to buy licorice for Frances and she was tired of his balloons. This was the first real dismay of his whole life, and he aged at least a year in the next minute, huddled, with his deep, serious blue eyes focused down his nose in intense speculation. What could he do to please Frances that would not cost money? Only yesterday· Uncle David had given him a nickel, and he had thrown it away on gumdrops. He regretted that nickel so bitterly his neck and forehead were damp. He was thirsty too.

"I tell you what," he said, brightening with a splendid idea, lamely trailing off on second thought, "I know something we can do, I'll—I . . ."

"I *am* thirsty," said Frances with gentle persistence. "I think I'm so thirsty maybe I'll have to go home." She did not leave the bench, though, but sat, turning her grieved mouth toward Stephen.

Stephen quivered with the terrors of the adventure before him, but he said boldly, "I'll make some lemonade. I'll get sugar and lemon and some ice and we'll have lemonade."

"Oh, I love lemonade," cried Frances. "I'd rather have lemonade than liquish."

"You stay right here," said Stephen, "and I'll get everything."

He ran around the house, and under Old Janet's window he heard the dry, chattering voices of the two old women whom he must outwit. He sneaked on tiptoe to the pantry, took a lemon lying there by itself, a handful of lump sugar and a china teapot, smooth, round, with flowers and leaves all over it. These he left on the kitchen table while he broke a piece of ice with a sharp metal pick he had been forbidden to touch. He put the ice in the pot, cut the lemon and squeezed it as well as he could—a lemon was tougher and more slippery than he had thought—and mixed sugar and water. He decided there was not enough sugar so he sneaked back and took another handful. He was back on the porch in an astonishingly short time, his face tight, his knees trembling, carrying iced lemonade to thirsty Frances with both his devoted hands.

A pace distant from her he stopped, literally stabbed through with a thought. Here he stood in broad daylight carrying a teapot with lemonade in it, and his grandma or Old Janet might walk through the door at any moment.

"Come on, Frances," he whispered loudly. "Let's go round to the back behind the rose bushes where it's shady." Frances leaped up and ran like a deer beside him, her face wise with knowledge of why they ran; Stephen ran stiffly, cherishing his teapot with clenched hands.

It was shady behind the rose bushes, and much safer. They sat side by side on the dampish ground, legs doubled under, drinking in turn from the slender spout. Stephen took his just share in large, cool, delicious swallows. When Frances drank she set her round pink mouth daintily to the spout and her throat beat steadily as a heart. Stephen was thinking he had really done something pretty nice for Frances. He did not know where his own happiness was; it was mixed with the sweet-sour taste in his mouth and a cool feeling in his bosom because Frances was there drinking his lemonade which he had got for her with great danger.

Frances said, "My, what big swallows you take," when his turn came next.

"No bigger than yours," he told her downrightly. "You take awfully big swallows."

"Well," said Frances, turning this criticism into an argument for her rightness about things, "that's the way to drink lemonade anyway." She peered into the teapot. There was quite a lot of lemonade left and she was beginning to feel she had enough. "Let's make up a game and see who can take the biggest swallows."

This was such a wonderful notion they grew reckless, tipping the spout into their opened mouths above their heads until lemonade welled up and ran over their chins in rills down their fronts. When they tired of this there was still lemonade left in the pot. They played first at giving the rosebush a drink and ended by baptizing it. "Name father son holygoat," shouted Stephen, pouring. At this sound Old Janet's face appeared over the low hedge, with the tan, disgusted-looking face of Frances' nurse hanging over her shoulder.

"Well, just as I thought," said Old Janet. "Just as I expected." The bag under her chin waggled.

"We were thirsty," he said; "we were awfully thirsty." Frances said nothing, but she gazed steadily at the toes of her shoes.

"Give me that teapot," said Old Janet, taking it with a rude snatch. "Just because you're thirsty is no reason," said Old Janet. "You can ask for things. You don't have to steal."

"We didn't steal," cried Frances suddenly. "We didn't. We didn't!"

"That's enough from you, missy," said her nurse. "Come straight out of there. You have nothing to do with this."

"Oh, I don't know," said Old Janet with a hard stare at Frances' nurse. "*He* never did such a thing before, by himself."

"Come on," said the nurse to Frances, "this is no place for you." She held Frances by the wrist and started walking away so fast Frances had to run to keep up. "Nobody can call *us* thieves and get away with it."

"You don't have to steal, even if others do," said Old Janet to Stephen, in a high carrying voice. "If you so much as pick up a lemon in somebody else's house you're a little thief." She lowered her voice then and said, "Now I'm going to tell your grandma and you'll see what you get."

"He went in the icebox and left it open," Janet told Grandma, "and he got into the lump sugar and spilt it all over the floor. Lumps everywhere underfoot. He dribbled water all over the clean kitchen floor, and he baptized the rose bush, blaspheming. And he took your Spode teapot."

"I didn't either," said Stephen loudly, trying to free his hand from Old Janet's big hard fist.

"Don't tell fibs," said Old Janet; "that's the last straw."

"Oh, dear," said Grandma. "He's not a baby any more." She shut the book she was reading and pulled the wet front of his pull-over toward her. "What's this sticky stuff on him?" she asked and straightened her glasses.

"Lemonade," said Old Janet. "He took the last lemon."

They were in the big dark room with the red curtains. Uncle David walked in from the room with the bookcases, holding a box in his uplifted hand. "Look here," he said to Stephen. "What's become of all my balloons?"

Stephen knew well that Uncle David was not really asking a question.

Stephen, sitting on a footstool at his grandma's knee, felt sleepy. He leaned heavily and wished he could put his head on her lap, but he might go to sleep, and it would be wrong to go to sleep while Uncle David was still talking. Uncle David walked about the room with his hands in his pockets, talking to Grandma. Now and then he would walk over to a lamp and, leaning, peer into the top of the shade, winking in the light, as if he expected to find something there.

"It's simply in the blood, I told her," said Uncle David. "I told her she would simply have to come and get him, and keep him. She asked me if I meant to call him a thief and I said if she could think of a more exact word I'd be glad to hear it."

"You shouldn't have said that," commented Grandma calmly.

"Why not? She might as well know the facts. . . . I suppose he can't help it," said Uncle David, stopping now in front of Stephen and dropping his chin into his collar, "I shouldn't expect too much of him, but you can't begin too early—"

"The trouble is," said Grandma, and while she spoke she took Stephen by the chin and held it up so that he had to meet her eye; she talked steadily in a mournful tone, but Stephen could not understand. She ended, "It's not just about the balloons, of course."

"It *is* about the balloons," said Uncle David angrily, "because balloons now mean something worse later. But what can you expect? His father—well, it's in the blood. He—"

"That's your sister's husband you're talking about," said Grandma, "and there is no use making things worse. Besides, you don't really *know*."

"I *do* know," said Uncle David. And he talked again very fast, walking up and down. Stephen tried to understand, but the sounds were strange and floating just over his head. They were talking about his father, and they did not like him. Uncle David came over and stood above Stephen and Grandma. He hunched over them with a frowning face, a long, crooked shadow from him falling across them to the wall. To Stephen he looked like his father, and he shrank against his grandma's skirts.

"The question is, what to do with him now?" asked Uncle David. "If we keep him here, he'd just be a—I won't be bothered with him. Why can't they take care of their own child? That house is crazy. Too far gone already, I'm afraid. No training. No example."

"You're right, they must take him and keep him," said Grandma. She ran her hands over Stephen's head; tenderly she pinched the nape of his neck between thumb and forefinger. "You're your Grandma's darling," she told him, "and you've had a nice long visit, and now you're going home. Mama is coming for you in a few minutes. Won't that be nice?"

"I want my mama," said Stephen, whimpering, for his grandma's face frightened him. There was something wrong with her smile.   .

Uncle David sat down. "Come over here, fellow," he said, wagging a forefinger at Stephen. Stephen went over slowly, and Uncle David drew him between his wide knees in their loose, rough clothes. "You ought to be ashamed of yourself," he said, "stealing Uncle David's balloons when he had already given you so many."

"It wasn't that," said Grandma quickly. "Don't say that. It will make an impression—"

"I hope it does," said Uncle David in a louder voice; "I hope he remembers it all his life. If he belonged to me I'd give him a good thrashing."

Stephen felt his mouth, his chin, his whole face jerking. He opened his mouth to take a breath, and tears and noise burst from him. "Stop that, fellow, stop that," said Uncle David, shaking him gently by the shoulders, but Stephen could not stop. He drew his breath again and it came back in a howl. Old Janet came to the door.

"Bring me some cold water," called Grandma. There was a flurry, a commotion, a breath of cool air from the hall, the door slammed, and Stephen heard his mother's voice. His howl died away, his breath sobbed and fluttered, he turned his dimmed eyes and saw her standing there. His heart turned over within him and he bleated like a lamb, "Maaaaama," running toward her. Uncle David stood back as Mama swooped in and fell on her knees beside Stephen. She gathered him to her and stood up with him in her arms.

"What are you doing to my baby?" she asked Uncle David in a thickened voice. "I should never have let him come here. I should have known better—"

"You always should know better," said Uncle David, "and you never do. And you never will. You haven't got it here," he told her, tapping his forehead.

"David," said Grandma, "that's your—"

"Yes, I know, she's my sister," said Uncle David. "I know it. But if she must run away and marry a—"

"Shut up," said Mama.

"And bring more like him into the world, let her keep them at home. I say let her keep—"

Mama set Stephen on the floor and, holding him by the hand, she said to Grandma all in a rush as if she were reading something, "Good-by, Mother. This is the last time, really the last. I can't bear it any longer. Say good-by to Stephen; you'll never see him again. You let this happen. It's your fault. You know David was a coward and a bully and a self-righteous little beast all his life and you never crossed him in anything. You let him bully me all my life and you let him slander my husband and call my baby a thief, and now this is the end. . . . He calls my baby a thief over a few horrible little balloons because he doesn't like my husband. . . ."

She was panting and staring about from one to the other. They were all standing. Now Grandma said, "Go home, daughter. Go away, David. I'm sick of your quarreling. I've never had a day's peace or comfort from either of you. I'm sick of you both. Now let me alone and stop this noise. Go away," said Grandma in a wavering voice. She took out her handkerchief and wiped first one eye and then the other and said, "All this hate, hate—what is it for? . . . So this is the way it turns out. Well, let me alone."

"You and your little advertising balloons," said Mama to Uncle David. "The big honest businessman advertises with balloons and if he loses one he'll be ruined. And your beastly little moral notions . . ."

Grandma went to the door to meet Old Janet, who handed her a glass of water. Grandma drank it all, standing there.

"Is your husband coming for you, or are you going home by yourself?" she asked Mama.

"I'm driving myself," said Mama in a far-away voice as if her mind had wandered. "You know he wouldn't set foot in this house."

"I should think not," said Uncle David.

"Come on, Stephen darling," said Mama. "It's far past his bedtime," she said, to no one in particular. "Imagine keeping a baby up to torture him about a few miserable little bits of colored rubber." She smiled at Uncle David with both rows of teeth as she passed him on the way to the door, keeping between him and Stephen. "Ah, where would we be without high moral standards," she said, and then to Grandma, "Good night, Mother," in quite her usual voice. "I'll see you in a day or so."

"Yes, indeed," said Grandma cheerfully, coming out into the hall with Stephen and Mama. "Let me hear from you. Ring me up tomorrow. I hope you'll be feeling better."

"I feel very well now," said Mama brightly, laughing. She bent down and kissed Stephen. "Sleepy, darling? Papa's waiting to see you. Don't go to sleep until you've kissed your papa good night."

Stephen woke with a sharp jerk. He raised his head and put out his chin a little. "I don't want to go home," he said; "I want to go to school. I don't want to see Papa, I don't like him."

Mama laid her palm over his mouth softly. "Darling, don't."

Uncle David put his head out with a kind of snort. "There you are," he said. "There you've got a statement from headquarters."

Mama opened the door and ran, almost carrying Stephen. She ran across the sidewalk, jerking open the car door and dragging Stephen in after her. She spun the car around and dashed forward so sharply Stephen was almost flung out of the seat. He sat braced then with all his might, hands digging into the cushions. The car speeded up and the trees and houses whizzed by all flattened out. Stephen began suddenly to sing to himself, a quiet, inside song so Mama would not hear. He sang his new secret; it was a comfortable, sleepy song: "I hate Papa, I hate Mama, I hate Grandma, I hate Uncle David, I hate Old Janet, I hate Marjory, I hate Papa, I hate Mama . . ."

His head bobbed, leaned, came to rest on Mama's knee, eyes closed. Mama drew him closer and slowed down, driving with one hand.

Tomorrow and Tomorrow and So Forth   *John Updike*

Whirling, talking, 11D began to enter Room 109. From the quality of their excitement Mark Prosser guessed it would rain. He had been teaching high school for three years, yet his students still impressed him; they were such sensitive animals. They reacted so infallibly to merely barometric pressure.

In the doorway, Brute Young paused while little Barry Snyder giggled at his elbow. Barry's stagy laugh rose and fell, dipping down toward some vile secret that had to be tasted and retasted, then soaring artificially to proclaim that he, little Barry, shared such a secret with the school's fullback. Being Brute's stooge was precious to Barry. The fullback paid no attention to him; he twisted his neck to stare at something not yet coming through the door. He yielded heavily to the procession pressing him forward.

Right under Prosser's eyes, like a murder suddenly appearing in an annalistic frieze of kings and queens, someone stabbed a girl in the back with a pencil. She ignored the assault saucily. Another hand yanked out Geoffrey Langer's shirt-tail. Geoffrey, a bright student, was uncertain whether to laugh it off or defend himself with anger, and made a weak, half-turning gesture of compromise, wearing an expression of distant arrogance that Prosser instantly coördinated with feelings of fear he used to have. All along the line, in the glitter of key chains and the acute angles of turned-back shirt cuffs, an electricity was expressed which simple weather couldn't generate.

Mark wondered if today Gloria Angstrom wore that sweater, an ember-pink angora, with very brief sleeves. The virtual sleevelessness was the disturbing factor: the exposure of those two serene arms to the air, white as thighs against the delicate wool.

His guess was correct. A vivid pink patch flashed through the jiggle of arms and shoulders as the final knot of youngsters entered the room.

"Take your seats," Mr. Prosser said. "Come on. Let's go."

Most obeyed, but Peter Forrester, who had been at the center of the group around Gloria, still lingered in the doorway with her, finishing some story, apparently determined to make her laugh or gasp. When she did gasp, he tossed his head with satisfaction. His orange hair bobbed. Redheads are all alike, Mark thought, with their white eyelashes and pale puffy faces and thyroid eyes, their mouths always twisted with preposterous self-confidence. Bluffers, the whole bunch.

When Gloria, moving in a considered, stately way, had taken her seat, and Peter had swerved into his, Mr. Prosser said, "Peter Forrester."

"Yes?" Peter rose, scrabbling through his book for the right place.

"Kindly tell the class the exact meaning of the words 'Tomorrow, and tomorrow, and tomorrow/Creeps in this petty pace from day to day.' "

Peter glanced down at the high-school edition of *Macbeth* lying open on his desk. One of the duller girls tittered expectantly from the back of the room. Peter was popular with the girls; girls that age had minds like moths.

"Peter. With your book shut. We have all memorized this passage for today. Remember?" The girl in the back of the room squealed in delight. Gloria laid her own book face-open on her desk, where Peter could see it.

Peter shut his book with a bang and stared into Gloria's. "Why," he said at last, "I think it means pretty much what it says."

"Which is?"

"Why, that tomorrow is something we often think about. It creeps into our conversation all the time. We couldn't make any plans without thinking about tomorrow."

"I see. Then you would say that Macbeth is here referring to the, the date-book aspect of life?"

Geoffrey Langer laughed, no doubt to please Mr. Prosser. For a moment, he *was* pleased. Then he realized he had been playing for laughs at a student's expense.

His paraphrase had made Peter's reading of the lines seem more ridiculous than it was. He began to retract. "I admit—"

But Peter was going on; redheads never know when to quit. "Macbeth means that if we quit worrying about tomorrow, and just lived for today, we could appreciate all the wonderful things that are going on under our noses."

Mark considered this a moment before he spoke. He would not be sarcastic. "Uh, without denying that there is truth in what you say, Peter, do you think it likely that Macbeth, in his situation, would be expressing such"—he couldn't help himself—"such sunny sentiments?"

Geoffrey laughed again. Peter's neck reddened; he studied the floor. Gloria glared at Mr. Prosser, the anger in her face clearly meant for him to see.

Mark hurried to undo his mistake. "Don't misunderstand me, please," he told Peter. "I don't have all the answers myself. But it seems to me the whole speech, down to 'Signifying nothing,' is saying that life is—well, a *fraud*. Nothing wonderful about it."

"Did Shakespeare really think that?" Geoffrey Langer asked, a nervous quickness pitching his voice high.

Mark read into Geoffrey's question his own adolescent premonitions of the terrible truth. The attempt he must make was plain. He told Peter he could sit down and looked through the window toward the steadying sky. The clouds were gaining intensity. "There is," Mr. Prosser slowly began, "much darkness in Shakespeare's work, and no play is darker than 'Macbeth.' The atmosphere is poisonous, oppressive. One critic has said that in this play, humanity suffocates." This was too fancy.

"In the middle of his career, Shakespeare wrote plays about men like Hamlet and Othello and Macbeth—men who aren't allowed by their society, or bad luck, or some minor flaw in themselves, to become the great men they might have been. Even Shakespeare's comedies of this period deal with a world gone sour. It is as if he had seen through the bright, bold surface of his earlier comedies and histories and had looked upon something terrible. It frightened him, just as some day it may frighten some of you." In his determination to find the right words, he had been staring at Gloria, without meaning to. Embarrassed, she nodded, and, realizing what had happened, he smiled at her.

He tried to make his remarks gentler, even diffident. "But then I think Shakespeare sensed a redeeming truth. His last plays are serene and symbolical, as if he had pierced through the ugly facts and reached a realm where the facts are again beautiful. In this way, Shakespeare's total work is a more complete image of life than that of any other writer, except perhaps for Dante, an Italian poet who wrote several centuries earlier." He had been taken far from the Macbeth soliloquy. Other teachers had been happy to tell him how the kids made a game of getting him talking. He looked toward Geoffrey. The boy was doodling on his tablet, indifferent. Mr. Prosser concluded, "The last play Shakespeare wrote is an extraordinary poem called 'The Tempest.' Some of you may want to read it for your next book reports—the ones due May 10th. It's a short play."

The class had been taking a holiday. Barry Snyder was snicking BBs off the blackboard and glancing over at Brute Young to see if he noticed. "Once more, Barry," Mr. Prosser said, "and out you go." Barry blushed, and grinned to cover the blush, his eyeballs sliding toward Brute. The dull girl in the rear of the room was putting on lipstick. "Put that away, Alice," Mr. Prosser commanded. She giggled and obeyed. Sejak, the Polish boy who worked nights, was asleep at his desk, his cheek white with pressure against the varnished wood, his mouth sagging sidewise. Mr. Prosser had an impulse to let him sleep. But the impulse might not be true kindness, but just the self-congratulatory, kindly pose in which he sometimes discovered himself. Besides, one breach of discipline encouraged others. He strode down the aisle and shook Sejak awake. Then he turned his attention to the mumble growing at the front of the room.

Peter Forrester was whispering to Gloria, trying to make her laugh. The girl's face, though, was cool and solemn, as if a thought had been provoked in her head. Perhaps at least *she* had been listening to what Mr. Prosser had been saying. With a bracing sense of chivalrous intercession, Mark said, "Peter, I gather from this noise that you have something to add to your theories."

Peter responded courteously. "No, sir. I honestly don't understand the speech. Please, sir, what *does* it mean?"

This candid admission and odd request stunned the class. Every white, round face, eager, for once, to learn, turned toward Mark. He said, "I don't know. I was hoping *you* would tell *me*."

In college, when a professor made such a remark, it was with grand effect. The professor's humility, the necessity for creative interplay between teacher and student were dramatically impressed upon the group. But to 11D, ignorance in an instructor was as wrong as a hole in a roof. It was as if he had held forty strings pulling forty faces taut toward him and then had slashed the strings. Heads waggled, eyes dropped, voices buzzed. Some of the discipline problems, like Peter Forrester, smirked signals to one another.

"Quiet!" Mr. Prosser shouted. "All of you. Poetry isn't arithmetic. There's no single right answer. I don't want to force my own impression on you, even if I *have* had much more experience with literature." He made this last clause very loud and distinct, and some of the weaker students seemed reassured. "I know none of *you* want that," he told them.

Whether or not they believed him, they subsided, somewhat. Mark judged he could safely reassume his human-among-humans attitude again. He perched on the edge of the desk and leaned forward beseechingly. "Now, honestly. Don't any of you have some personal feeling about the lines that you would like to share with the class and me?"

One hand, with a flowered handkerchief balled in it, unsteadily rose. "Go ahead, Teresa," Mr. Prosser said encouragingly. She was a timid, clumsy girl whose mother was a Jehovah's Witness.

"It makes me think of cloud shadows," Teresa said.

Geoffrey Langer laughed. "Don't be rude, Geoff," Mr. Prosser said sideways, softly, before throwing his voice forward: "Thank you, Teresa. I think that's an interesting and valid impression. Cloud movement has something in it of the slow, monotonous rhythm one feels in the line 'Tomorrow, and tomorrow, and tomorrow.' It's a very gray line, isn't it, class?" No one agreed or disagreed.

Beyond the windows actual clouds were bunching rapidly, and erratic sections of sunlight slid around the room. Gloria's arm, crooked gracefully above her head, turned gold. "Gloria?" Mr. Prosser asked.

She looked up from something on her desk with a face of sullen radiance. "I think what Teresa said was very good," she said, glaring in the direction of Geoffrey Langer. Geoffrey chuckled defiantly. "And I have a question. What does 'petty pace' mean?"

"It means the trivial day-to-day sort of life that, say, a bookkeeper or a bank clerk leads. Or a schoolteacher," he added, smiling.

She did not smile back. Thought wrinkles irritated her perfect brow. "But Macbeth has been fighting wars, and killing kings, and being a king himself, and all," she pointed out.

"Yes, but it's just these acts Macbeth is condemning as 'nothing.' Can you see that?"

Gloria shook her head. "Another thing I worry about—isn't it silly for Macbeth to be talking to himself right in the middle of this war, with his wife just dead, and all?"

"I don't think so, Gloria. No matter how fast events happen, thought is faster."

His answer was weak; everyone knew it, even if Gloria hadn't mused, supposedly to herself, but in a voice the entire class could hear, "It seems so *stupid*."

Mark winced, pierced by the awful clarity with which his students saw him. Through their eyes, how queer he looked, with his long hands, and his horn-rimmed glasses, and his hair never slicked down, all wrapped up in "literature," where, when things get rough, the king mumbles a poem nobody understands. The delight Mr. Prosser took in such crazy junk made not only his good sense but his masculinity a matter of doubt. It was gentle of them not to laugh him out of the room. He looked down and rubbed his fingertips together, trying to erase the chalk dust. The class noise sifted into unnatural quiet. "It's getting late," he said finally. "Let's start the recitations of the memorized passage. Bernard Amilson, you begin."

Bernard had trouble enunciating, and his rendition began " 'T'mau 'n' t'mau 'n' t'mau.' " It was reassuring, the extent to which the class tried to repress its laughter. Mr. Prosser wrote "A" in his marking book opposite Bernard's name. He always gave Bernard A on recitations, despite the school nurse, who claimed there was nothing organically wrong with the boy's mouth.

It was the custom, cruel but traditional, to deliver recitations from the front of the room. Alice, when her turn came, was reduced to a helpless state by the first funny face Peter Forrester made at her. Mark let her hang up there a good minute while her face ripened to cherry redness, and at last forgave her. She may try it later. Many of the youngsters knew the passage gratifyingly well, though there was a tendency to leave out the line "To the last syllable of recorded time" and to turn "struts and frets" into "frets and struts" or simply "struts and struts." Even Sejak, who couldn't have looked at the passage before he came to class, got through it as far as "And then is heard no more."

Geoffrey Langer showed off, as he always did, by interrupting his own recitation with bright questions. " 'Tomorrow, and tomorrow, and tomorrow,' " he said, " 'creeps in'—shouldn't that be *'creep* in,' Mr. Prosser?"

"It is 'creeps.' The trio is in effect singular. Go on." Mr. Prosser was tired of coddling Langer. If you let them, these smart students will run away with the class. "Without the footnotes."

" 'Creep*sss* in this petty pace from day to day, to the last syllable of recorded time, and all our yesterdays have lighted fools the way to dusty death. Out, out—' "

"No, no!" Mr. Prosser jumped out of his chair. "This is poetry. Don't mushmouth it! Pause a little after 'fools.' " Geoffrey looked genuinely startled this time, and Mark himself did not quite understand his annoyance and, mentally turning to see what was behind him, seemed to glimpse in the humid undergrowth the two stern eyes of the indignant look Gloria had thrown Geoffrey. He glimpsed himself in the absurd position of acting as Gloria's champion in her private war with this intelligent boy. He sighed apologetically. "Poetry is made up of lines," he began, turning to the class. Gloria was passing a note to Peter Forrester.

The rudeness of it! To pass notes during a scolding that she herself had caused! Mark caged in his hand the girl's frail wrist and ripped the note from her fingers. He read it to himself, letting the class see he was reading it, though he despised such methods of discipline. The note went:

Pete—I think you're *wrong* about Mr. Prosser. I think he's wonderful and I get a lot out of his class. He's heavenly with poetry. I think I love him. I really do *love* him. So there.

Mr. Prosser folded the note once and slipped it into his side coat pocket. "See me after class, Gloria," he said. Then, to Geoffrey, "Let's try it again. Begin at the beginning."

While the boy was reciting the passage, the buzzer sounded the end of the period. It was the last class of the day. The room quickly emptied, except for Gloria. The noise of lockers slamming open and books being thrown against metal and shouts drifted in.

"Who has a car?"

"Lend me a cig, pig."

"We can't have practice in this slop."

Mark hadn't noticed exactly when the rain started, but it was coming down fast now. He moved around the room with the window pole, closing windows and pulling down shades. Spray bounced in on his hands. He began to talk to Gloria in a crisp voice that, like his device of shutting the windows, was intended to protect them both from embarrassment.

"About note passing." She sat motionless at her desk in the front of the room, her short, brushed-up hair like a cool torch. From the way she sat, her naked arms folded at her breasts and her shoulders hunched, he felt she was chilly. "It is not only rude to scribble when a teacher is talking, it is stupid to put one's words down on paper, where they look much more foolish than they might have sounded if spoken." He leaned the window pole in its corner and walked toward his desk.

"And about love. 'Love' is one of those words that illustrate what happens to an old, overworked language. These days, with movie stars and crooners and preachers and psychiatrists all pronouncing the word, it's come to mean nothing but a vague fondness for something. In this sense, I love the rain, this blackboard, these desks, you. It means nothing, you see, whereas once the word signified a quite explicit thing—a desire to share all you own and are with someone else. It is time we coined a new word to mean that, and when you think up the word *you* want to use, I suggest that you be economical with it. Treat it as something you can spend only once—if not for your own sake, for the good of the language." He walked over to his own desk and dropped two pencils on it, as if to say, "That's all."

"I'm sorry," Gloria said.

Rather surprised, Mr. Prosser said, "Don't be."

"But you don't understand."

"Of course I don't. I probably never did. At your age, I was like Geoffrey Langer."

"I bet you weren't." The girl was almost crying; he was sure of that.

"Come on, Gloria. Run along. Forget it." She slowly cradled her books between her bare arm and her sweater, and left the room with that melancholy shuffling teen-age gait, so that her body above her thighs seemed to float over the desks.

What was it, Mark asked himself, these kids were after? What did they want? Glide, he decided, the quality of glide. To slip along, always in rhythm, always cool, the little wheels humming under you, going nowhere special. If Heaven existed, that's the way it would be there. "He's heavenly with poetry." They loved the word. Heaven was in half their songs.

"Christ, he's humming." Strunk, the physical ed teacher, had come into the room without Mark's noticing. Gloria had left the door ajar.

"Ah," Mark said, "a fallen angel, full of grit."

"What the hell makes you so happy?"

"I'm not happy, I'm just serene. I don't know why you don't appreciate me."

"Say." Strunk came up an aisle with a disagreeably effeminate waddle, pregnant with gossip. "Did you hear about Murchison?"

"No." Mark mimicked Strunk's whisper.

"He got the pants kidded off him today."

"Oh dear."

Strunk started to laugh, as he always did before beginning a story. "You know what a goddam lady's man he thinks he is?"

"You bet," Mark said, although Strunk said that about every male member of the faculty.

"You have Gloria Angstrom, don't you?"

"You bet."

"Well, this morning Murky intercepts a note she was writing, and the note says what a damn neat guy she thinks Murchison is and how she *loves* him!" Strunk waited for Mark to say something, and then, when he didn't, continued, "You could see he was tickled pink. But— get this—it turns out at lunch that the same damn thing happened to Fryeburg in history yesterday!" Strunk laughed and cracked his knuckles viciously. "The girl's too dumb to have thought it up herself. We all think it was Peter Forrester's idea."

"Probably was," Mark agreed. Strunk followed him out to his locker, describing Murchison's expression when Fryeburg (in all innocence, mind you) told what had happened to him.

Mark turned the combination of his locker, 18–24–3. "Would you excuse me, Dave?" he said. "My wife's in town waiting."

Strunk was too thick to catch Mark's anger. "I got to get over to the gym. Can't take the little darlings outside in the rain; their mommies'll write notes to teacher." He clattered down the hall and wheeled at the far end, shouting, "Now don't tell You-know-who!"

Mr. Prosser took his coat from the locker and shrugged it on. He placed his hat upon his head. He fitted his rubbers over his shoes, pinching his fingers painfully, and lifted his umbrella off the hook. He thought of opening it right there in the vacant hall, as a kind of joke, and decided not to. The girl had been almost crying; he was sure of that.

Boy in the Summer Sun   *Mark Schorer*

Unalloyed, summer had lingered miraculously into late September without a suggestion that autumn was at hand. Leaves and grass were green still, smoke had not yet come into the air, and the lake was calm, almost sapphire blue. Mid-mornings were hot, like mornings in July. So they walked where the woods were thickest, where the air was always slightly damp and the cool of night never quite gone. They did not speak much but went silently along the path, almost shoulder to shoulder, their hands touching, or their arms, as they moved. Now and then the girl spoke, quietly, briefly pointed out a bird, a flower, once a green snake gliding through the grass, and the boy answered with a nod or a monosyllable, his face touched with abstraction and a slight worry. After they came to a place in the wood where they stretched out now with their arms about each other lightly as if the place and this gesture were habitual, they did not speak at all until at last the girl, Rachel, asked suddenly, "Why are you so quiet? Is it Max? Are you angry because he's coming, Will?"

The boy started and looked into her face. "Angry? No, I'm not angry . . . I was just thinking about that lousy job. When I'm out here it's hard to believe that a job like that can be waiting for me when I get back."

The girl looked away into the depth of the wood. "Is it, Will?" she asked. "Or is it just that in college we never learn that for most people life finally comes down to work?"

"Maybe that's it."

"Or is it foul, Will? Is it worse then most jobs in the city, in summer?"

"Maybe not. But it's still foul."

They were quiet again, and it seemed a long time later, to him, when Rachel said, "Anyway, I'm glad it isn't Max."

His arms tightened around her shoulders. Then he sat up, his eyes narrowed in the shade, and he asked, "Why should it be?"

She said, "It shouldn't."

He lay down beside her again. He stared up into the lace-work of green leaves arched above them, and at the rare patches of blue sky that the leaves did not cover. Why should it be Max? Or why should she think it might be?

He had been awakened that morning by the ringing telephone, and lay sleepily in bed listening to Rachel's voice talking to someone in a way that did disturb him vaguely then, although now it seemed only mildly irritating that this week-end should be intruded upon. "But darling!" her voice had cried over the telephone. "What are you doing here? Come over at once! Mind? Of course not! We'll love it! In two hours? Good!"

When he came to breakfast, she smiled brightly and cried,

"Guess who's coming, Will! Max Garey! He got bored and started out early this morning, and just now called from the village. Isn't it grand? Mother's so fond of him—she'll take care of him."

"Does your mother know him? I didn't know she did."

"Oh, yes! I must have told you."

"No, you didn't," he said. And now he wondered why she had not told him.

Then Mrs. Harley came out on the porch. "Good morning, Will," she said brightly as she patted her white hair. "Isn't it *nice* that Mr. Garey can come! I'm so fond of Mr. Garey!"

"Yes, isn't it?" Will said into his coffee, and looked across the table into Rachel's eyes, which, shining with pleasure, were heedless of the question in his.

"Did you have any work with Mr. Garey, Will? Rachel thought him such a splendid teacher."

"No, I didn't," Will said. "His classes were always filled with girls."

Rachel looked at him quickly. "Now you're being unfair, Will. Everybody thinks he's a good teacher."

"I'm sorry," he said, and felt suddenly lonely in the bright morning with Rachel only across the table from him.

He was feeling that loneliness again now. "Maybe it's more than the job," he said. "Everything's different since June. I don't know why."

"What do you mean, Will?"

"Just a feeling that everything's breaking up."

They were quiet then until Rachel said, "I know. I'm different, too. Something's changed in me. There's something sad, some ache . . ."

Will knew that something had changed in her. She was older than she had been in June. There was something about her now that bewildered him, the feeling that she had lived without him, an aloofness and self-sufficiency which was new. She was like a woman, sometimes, putting up with a boy. He had felt it almost every week-end, and this and the more general sadness of the summer had darkened otherwise bright hours. Yet her kisses, her sweet arms around him, her yielding body, all denied his feeling. With him, there still came from her throat a little moan of pain and passion which he knew no one else had ever heard. And yet, now in the deep cool wood as she lay in his arms, he felt that she had forgotten him beside her.

She spoke at last as with an effort, as if recalling herself from a dream. "You know, Will, after you left college, in that week I stayed on, I saw Max rather often. Then mother met him. She invited him to come up. He was here earlier in the summer. Didn't I tell you?"

"No," he said, his throat contracting. "You must have forgotten."

His sadness knotted in his throat intensely, and he remembered then very clearly, almost as if she were saying it again now, something she had said before he left her in June. "Sometimes I wonder if this can last. We know each other as I think people almost never do. Now it begins to seem a little unreal, perhaps because it's been too lovely, part of this unreal life we're leaving. I wonder if that sometimes happens, Will."

Then he had laughed; but now, as he remembered, his arms tightened around her suddenly, as if from fright, and he leaned down and kissed her. Her lips were quiet, without response. He saw that her eyes were fixed on some remote object in the arch of trees or beyond, some dream, something far from him. He stood up and moved away. "Let's go back," he said, and without waiting for her started quickly up the path, toward the house.

All the afternoon they lay on the raft, Rachel between them. Max talked, his voice reflective and lazy, mixing with the sun of that afternoon and the endless laziness in the sounds that insects made in the woods and in the long grass along the shore, his voice spinning itself out, pausing now and then to listen to itself, and going on again, with Rachel lying quiet between them, her eyes closed and the oil gleaming on her brown skin. Will's head was turned toward her, his eyes wandering back and forth from her parted lips and her gleaming lashes to the swell of her breasts under her white swimming suit, to her long browned legs and her crossed feet at the end of the raft.

All the time Max's voice went on, the lazy, professor's voice. Will could tell as he heard it that it was a voice that always talked and that always had listeners, and yet, now, it did not irritate him. He was almost content to lie in the sun with the sensation of burning on his skin, the soft warm glow of skin absorbing bright sun enough in the afternoon to allay for the moment the morning's inarticulate fears, even though it was Max who was lying stretched out beyond Rachel, who was talking, pausing, talking, sometimes falling silent and no word coming from Rachel or himself, and then starting up again, the voice spinning itself out softly in the afternoon sun, with all the laziness of the afternoon in his slow words.

". . . and so in Donne the central factor is death . . . death, of course . . . he, more than any of the poets, built what he wrote upon what may be called a metaphysic of death . . . death as the great leveler on the one hand, the great destroyer of everything, beauty, love . . . and death as the figure at the gate of Heaven . . . these two, this one . . . the central factor, always present . . ."

His voice was slow, modulated, a little affected, quite soft, and in it, Will knew as he looked at Rachel's face, there was some magic of wisdom and experience that enthralled her.

Rachel's voice began, slow and soft as if infected by Max's voice, as warm as the sun, and speaking lines that Max first spoke to her, perhaps—only perhaps—in the classroom:

> "When I died last, and, Dear, I die
>   As often as from thee I go,
>   Though it be but an hour ago,
> And Lovers hours be full eternity,
> I can remember yet, that I
>   Something did say, and something did bestow. . . ."

Max laughed. "But darling," he said, "that's still another kind of death, not so serious."

Rachel said nothing. And the sun wove around them its bright and golden web, and the whole world then as they lay there had slipped away and left the three of them stranded together in an unreality of sunlight on burning skin and closed eyelids, and nothing more. And Will, too, felt out of the world of fact, was empty of feeling, as if pure sensation had replaced it. And only slowly did a faint jangling come into his mind, the jangle of Max's word *darling,* like something shaken in a metal box, some harsh sound, or a feeling perhaps, shaking him abruptly from the web. He stirred. He turned. And in turning the web was broken, and he was free of it again, his hand plunged in the cold blue water of the lake and left to dangle there, his eyes turned from Rachel and Max for the moment but seeing nothing in the indeterminable depths of the blue water that gently lapped his hand.

"Not nearly so serious," Max said. "Only a metaphor, a way of speaking . . ."

Will turned toward them again and he saw in Rachel's face how serious it was, for she looked suddenly ill for all the glow of her skin, her face turned away from him and her lips fallen apart, and every line in her face and body taut suddenly, yearning, aching suddenly with sharp longing, sharp pain, she quite sick for love. Will's hands closed at his sides and opened again, turned empty to the sun.

"Poetry is full of such conventions, formalized short cuts to express familiar sentiments," Max was saying. "In Donne, of course, there's enough fire, usually, to vitalize them, but in others . . . mere metaphors . . ."

Something in Will's mind snapped, then seemed to shout, *Who cares? For God's sake, who cares?* He was enraged beyond endurance by the man's pompous classroom manner, his easy presence, his way of excluding Will, as if he were alone with Rachel and no one else existed. He hated him, and the very presence of Rachel there made his throat ache with something like the pressure of tears coming. The sun had lost its spell. The buzz of insects on the shore seemed for a moment unbearably loud, and the sun no longer warm, but hot, searing, parching his throat and mouth, blinding him. For now he hated Max, and he knew as he remembered Rachel's voice speaking those lines, that she was lost to him, that he had nothing more for her, that Max had all. And there Max lay, as if he belonged there, had every right to be there, talking and priding himself in his talk, delighting to hear his own words, lecturing as though he were in the classroom and Rachel in the front row looking up at him with wide eyes, lecturing as though Rachel and he were alone in the room and Will did not exist.

Will's eyes clouded in anger as he stared down into the water disturbed by his hand. He tried not to hear what their low voices said, and only when they were silent did he turn again suddenly on the raft to see how their bodies had moved together, so that their legs touched, and Max's hand lay quite near Rachel's hair. He stood abruptly, stirring the raft in the water, and then dived deep, swam quickly out and away from them, his arms beating the water in his anger, in a frantic effort to forget the hurt which came from Rachel's willing reception of the man's intolerable arrogance.

He struck out into the lake. The water was cold on his skin, and as he swam his anger cooled. But when his anger was gone, he felt sad and futile again, swam more slowly, felt helpless and wounded, felt almost weak in the water, so that he grew angry with himself instead and wished that he could hold that other anger. When he turned back and swam slowly toward the shore, only the hurt remained, and he did not go to the raft. There Max's words would still be spinning themselves out in the sunlight, catching Rachel's mind in their spell, catching her heart firmly and her whole mind and life, and holding them there, as if the words were really magic.

He walked up the beach and stretched out on the sand. He lay on his back and looked up into the blue sky, and as he lay there he felt suddenly that this was the last time in his life that he would be doing quite this. All summer he had been coming from the sweltering, grimy city, and in seeing Rachel in the country, in living in her mother's friendly house, in swimming and dancing and drinking and finding cool spots in the woods where the moss was thick and only the trees and birds made sound—in all of this it had seemed that nothing had changed or was ending. And this in spite of the fact that when they parted in June, when they walked for the last time along familiar walks between familiar buildings, they had vaguely felt that an end had come to a period, that a new life was waiting for both of them, and that (Rachel felt) somehow they were therefore ending for one another. But then Max was nothing to him, only a professor whom she liked; so for him nothing really ended.

Now the golden day was unbearable. He turned over on his stomach and put his face in his arms. Almost at once he could feel the sun burning his neck, his back. But it alleviated nothing. There was the dull ache in his chest and throat, the constant feeling that at any moment he would cry out like a child in sobs. It was a pressure in his body that he could not put into thoughts, only the feeling that something was ending, inevitably ending. He thought of his past and it was all gold, all brightness and gold, all magic landscape, all an idyl, all a bright day, and all ending.

He thought he must cry. All his youth was gathered into a knot of pain that choked him, that, dull and heavy, pressed against his heart. He thought of going back to the city, to the hot office, to stupid work sweating over accounts, of the years he had ahead of him in which to slave there. And he knew as he lay in the sand, really *knew* for the first time, that all of that was no mere interlude.

He felt a touch on his shoulder, turned, and looked up. It was Rachel, brown in the sun, saying, "Darling, don't be rude."

He sat up. "Am I being rude?"

"Does he bore you?"

"Yes. I don't like him much."

"Well, I'm sorry he came, Will, but I couldn't help it. Come back and try to bear him. He's not bad, you know."

"No?" Will asked as he got up.

She looked at him swiftly, then smiled. "Don't be silly, darling."

"No, *darling*."

"Good."

Then they went up the shore, back to the raft where Max still lay in the lessening glare of the sun.

Then finally he could put up with him no longer. The whole thing, suddenly, was impossible, too much for him. He sat at the table for a minute more and fought against the impulse to leave. But Mrs. Harley, cooing in a voice that almost made him ill ("But how *interesting*, Mr. Garey. *Do* go on! Do you *really* believe that?") and Max, toying with his fork and smiling with what Will supposed was great "charm" before continuing his monologue, decided him. He looked quickly at Rachel. She sat at the end of the table, opposite her mother. She looked very cool in a white dress, brown throat and arms cool and lovely, her lips slightly parted, her eyes fixed—lost to him.

Then he rose quickly to his feet. "Excuse me, please," he said, and went to the porch, and then outside, down the steps, stumbled down toward the shore under the pines. He sat down in the grass. His fingers fumbled for a cigarette and a match in his pocket. Then he stared out at the water and the new moon hanging close over the opposite shore. In the reeds the frogs sang. From above came the ring of silver on china. He bit hard into his lower lip when he knew suddenly that the salt he tasted was of tears.

Then everything broke, collapsed in him like a sail when the wind dies. He wept as he had not wept since he was a small boy; and there, for a time in the night, he felt that he was a small boy still, alone in the dark and empty night. He lay on the grass and sobbed, and there was a violence in his weeping as of a body tortured. He smothered the sound in the grass.

But he could not smother the pain in his chest. It was like a live thing in his heart, heavy and pressing, torturing, not relieved by sobs. It came over him in waves of torment, and now it was no longer anything of the mind, but of the body alone, a physical pressure, wracking and violent, eruptive and convulsive, as if his very life, well-loved, were ending in the torment.

He did not feel Rachel's hand on his shoulder. It was her voice that recalled him: "Will—darling—please!"

Even then he could not prevent his sobs from coming. It was as if they were something separate from him, separate from his will, as if they had their own life, must come to their own slow end. He felt no shame before her, had no feelings at all, no thoughts, was given over entirely to what seemed wholly a physical act. Then slowly, at last, his shoulders grew quieter. Slowly his breathing quieted. Slowly his eyes dried. And it was over at last. He felt empty, weak, desolate as he turned slowly over on his back to look at her.

The moon was almost in the water. He could see it, touching the opposite shore. The sky was dark, sprinkled with cold stars. These too he saw, blurred and faint, unsteady in the darkness. Beside him knelt Rachel, her white dress a vague lightness, her face above him a blur. She spoke again: "Darling, what is it, what's *wrong?*"

He swallowed hard but could not speak. He lay on his back and looked at the blur of her face. His hand reached out and seized hers, held it tightly. Then she lay down beside him suddenly, put her arms around him, and her cheek to his mouth. He smelled the familiar perfume of her hair and moved away from her a little. Now he could see the stars more clearly; their light was brighter, harder, they were steadier in the sky, fixed and remote. Then, although Rachel's arms

were around him and her face so close that he could feel her warm
breath sweet on his face, he was alone, desolate, empty, alone on the
shore under the stars. He did not say this then, nor did he even quite
feel it, but he knew it, his body, empty and quiet, knew it—the cold
loneliness of the stars even on a summer night. He lay still and looked
up. Something momentous had happened.

"I felt sick," he said at last, though Rachel had not spoken again.

She said nothing for a while, then whispered, "I'm sorry."

"It's all right now."

As if startled by the deadly quiet of his voice, she sat up and looked
closely into his face. "*Are* you all right now, Will?"

"Yes, it's all right now." He said it clearly.

"What was it, though?" she asked.

"You know."

"No."

"Yes, you do."

"Not *Max*, Will?"

"What else?"

"Oh, but *darling*—"

"It doesn't matter, Rachel."

"What do you mean—doesn't matter? Do you think—"

"I know, Rachel. I knew it this morning. But only tonight, suddenly,
at the table, when I saw your face while he was talking—it took that
long until I really could believe it. But it doesn't matter now."

"You think I love him?"

"You do love him."

Then she did not answer.

"Yesterday I wouldn't have believed that things like this happen. For
over a year . . ." He paused. Then, "Nothing will ever be the same
again—love, or anything."

"Please, Will. Nothing's happened."

"Everything's happened. Now it's over."

She looked at him closely. Then she said, "I've never heard you talk
like that. You're different. Your voice—it's . . ."

"What?"

"You're different. Your voice frightens me. It's so quiet and cold and
far away, so different—" She spoke jerkily. "So dead!"

He sat up, leaned back on his elbows. The moon was gone, sunk
under the water. The sky was darker, and the stars seemed brighter

still, separate, and farther away. Then he lay down again and she beside him. They were both very quiet. Finally she said, "Do you hate me?"

He turned to her. "No," he answered. He watched her face. He saw her eyes sparkling with tears. He said, "What are you crying for?"

"I can't tell you why, I can't say, I don't know. I'm afraid. I do love you, Will. Only now I'm afraid, because I do love someone else—more. I don't want to. But I do. It frightens me!"

Now she was no longer older than he. She was a girl again, her woman's poise, given her briefly by this new love, taken from her again by that same love because, in the face of it, she was afraid. She was afraid of its swiftness, of what it might hold, of her own heart, turning. Now he felt older than she, felt that he could tell her something. He said, "I know what it is. It isn't just that we've been in love. We've had such a fine time. I don't know if I can say this, but it's something like this anyway—you weren't just yourself for me, and I wasn't just myself for you. We were both in love with much more than each other. You were all of that life for me, and maybe I was that for you, too. We were that whole life for each other, and we didn't want to lose it, but we couldn't help ourselves, we couldn't keep it any longer."

She was crying. She put her face on his shoulder and he felt her tears on his neck. Then he put his arms around her and held her close. But he felt no less alone. And he thought then that this aloneness would never entirely leave him again, but that when he got back to the city next day, after he had been there a while, working in the office, after a week or two or perhaps a whole year, finally anyway, it would have left him somewhat less empty, less deadly calm. Then this day and this summer and all the golden days would have become the dream; and the other life would be real.

"How did your poem go, Rachel? 'When I last died, and, dear, I die whenever you go from me . . .' ?"

"Please—don't," she said.

He began to stroke her hair. She was quiet now, no longer crying, held close in his arms. He said. "Maybe it's always like this. Maybe the end of every love is a kind of little death, when you have to put behind more than just the love itself, but all the life, too, in which the love was wrapped. Maybe living is really a lot of little dyings."

For a moment more they sat together and then she said, "We must go back. They'll wonder . . ."

"All right," he said.

Then, clinging together like children still under the stars, helping each other up the slope, they went back to the house, where the lights were and the sounds of voices.

Things   *D. H. Lawrence*

They were true idealists, from New England. But that is some time ago: before the war. Several years before the war, they met and married; he a tall, keen-eyed young man from Connecticut, she a smallish, demure, Puritan-looking young woman from Massachusetts. They both had a little money. Not much, however. Even added together, it didn't make three thousand dollars a year. Still—they were free. Free!

Ah! Freedom! To be free to live one's own life! To be twenty-five and twenty-seven, a pair of true idealists with a mutual love of beauty, and an inclination towards "Indian thought"—meaning alas, Mrs. Besant—and an income a little under three thousand dollars a year! But what is money? All one wishes to do is to live a full and beautiful life. In Europe, of course, right at the fountainhead of tradition. It might possibly be done in America: in New England, for example. But at a forfeiture of a certain amount of "beauty." True beauty takes a long time to mature. The baroque is only half-beautiful, half-matured. No, the real silver bloom, the real golden-sweet bouquet of beauty had its roots in the Renaissance, not in any later or shallower period.

Therefore the two idealists, who were married in New Haven, sailed at once to Paris: Paris of the old days. They had a studio apartment on the Boulevard Montparnasse, and they became real Parisians, in the old, delightful sense, not in the modern, vulgar. It was the shimmer of the pure impressionists, Monet[1] and his followers, the world seen in terms of pure light, light broken and unbroken. How lovely! How lovely the nights, the river, the mornings in the old streets and by the flower-stalls and the book-stalls, the afternoons up on Montmartre or in the Tuileries, the evenings on the boulevards!

They both painted, but not desperately. Art had not taken them by

---

[1] Claude Monet (1840–1926), a French landscape painter, was one of the leading figures of impressionism.

the throat, and they did not take Art by the throat. They painted: that's all. They knew people—nice people, if possible, though one had to take them mixed. And they were happy.

Yet it seems as if human beings must set their claws in *something*. To be "free," to be "living a full and beautiful life," you must, alas, be attached to something. A "full and beautiful life" means a tight attachment to *something*—at least, it is so for all idealists—or else a certain boredom supervenes; there is a certain waving of loose ends upon the air, like the waving, yearning tendrils of the vine that spread and rotate, seeking something to clutch, something up which to climb towards the necessary sun. Finding nothing, the vine can only trail, half-fulfilled, upon the ground. Such is freedom!—a clutching of the right pole. And human beings are all vines. But especially the idealist. He is a vine, and he needs to clutch and climb. And he despises the man who is a mere *potato,* or turnip, or lump of wood.

Our idealists were frightfully happy, but they were all the time reaching out for something to cotton on to. At first, Paris was enough. They explored Paris *thoroughly.* And they learned French till they almost felt like French people, they could speak it so glibly.

Still, you know, you never talk French with your *soul.* It can't be done. And though it's very thrilling, at first, talking in French to clever Frenchmen—they seem *so* much cleverer than oneself—still, in the long run, it is not satisfying. The endlessly clever *materialism* of the French leaves you cold, in the end, gives a sense of barrenness and incompatibility with true New England depth. So our two idealists felt.

They turned away from France—but ever so gently. France had disappointed them. "We've loved it, and we've got a great deal out of it. But after a while, after a considerable while, several years, in fact, Paris leaves one feeling disappointed. It hasn't quite got what one wants."

"But Paris isn't France."

"No, perhaps not. France is quite different from Paris. And France is lovely—quite lovely. But *to us,* though we love it, it doesn't say a great deal."

So, when the war came, the idealists moved to Italy. And they loved Italy. They found it beautiful, and more poignant than France. It seemed much nearer to the New England conception of beauty: something pure, and full of sympathy, without the *materialism* and the *cynicism* of the French. The two idealists seemed to breathe their own true air in Italy.

And in Italy, much more than in Paris, they felt they could thrill
to the teachings of the Buddha. They entered the swelling stream of
modern Buddhistic emotion, and they read the books, and they prac-
tised meditation, and they deliberately set themselves to eliminate
from their own souls greed, pain, and sorrow. They did not realize—
yet—that Buddha's very eagerness to free himself from pain and sorrow
is in itself a sort of greed. No, they dreamed of a perfect world, from
which all greed, and nearly all pain, and a great deal of sorrow, were
eliminated.

But America entered the war, so the two idealists had to help. They
did hospital work. And though their experience made them realize more
than ever that greed, pain, and sorrow *should* be eliminated from the
world, nevertheless the Buddhism, or the theosophy, didn't emerge very
triumphant from the long crisis. Somehow, somewhere, in some part
of themselves, they felt that greed, pain, and sorrow would never be
eliminated, because most people don't care about eliminating them,
and never will care. Our idealists were far too western to think of
abandoning all the world to damnation, while they saved their two
selves. They were far too unselfish to sit tight under a bho-tree and
reach Nirvana in a mere couple.

It was more than that, though. They simply hadn't enough *Sitzfleisch*
to squat under a bho-tree and get to Nirvana by contemplating anything, least of all their own navel. If the whole wide world was not
going to be saved, they, personally, were not so very keen on being
saved just by themselves. No, it would be so lonesome. They were
New Englanders, so it must be all or nothing. Greed, pain, and sorrow
must either be eliminated from *all the world,* or else, what was the use
of eliminating them from oneself? No use at all! One was just a victim.

And so, although they still *loved* "Indian thought," and felt very
tender about it: well, to go back to our metaphor, the pole up which
the green and anxious vines had clambered so far now proved dry-
rotten. It snapped, and the vines came slowly subsiding to earth again.
There was no crack and crash. The vines held themselves up by their
own foliage, for a while. But they subsided. The beanstalk of "Indian
thought" had given way before Jack and Jill had climbed off the tip of
it to a further world.

They subsided with a slow rustle back to earth again. But they made
no outcry. They were again "disappointed." But they never admitted
it. "Indian thought" had let them down. But they never complained.
Even to one another, they never said a word. They were disappointed,

faintly but deeply disillusioned, and they both knew it. But the knowledge was tacit.

And they still had so much in their lives. They still had Italy—dear Italy. And they still had freedom, the priceless treasure. And they still had so much "beauty." About the fulness of their lives they were not quite so sure. They had one little boy, whom they loved as parents should love their children, but whom they wisely refrained from fastening upon, to build their lives on him. No, no, they must live their own lives! They still had strength of mind to know that.

But they were now no longer so very young. Twenty-five and twenty-seven had become thirty-five and thirty-seven. And though they had had a very wonderful time in Europe, and though they still loved Italy—dear Italy!—yet: they were disappointed. They had got a lot out of it: oh, a very great deal indeed! Still, it hadn't given them quite, not *quite,* what they had expected. Europe was lovely, but it was dead. Living in Europe, you were living on the past. And Europeans, with all their superficial charm, were not *really* charming. They were materialistic, they had no *real* soul. They just did not understand the inner urge of the spirit, because the inner urge was dead in them, they were all survivals. There, that was the truth about Europeans: they were survivals, with no more getting ahead in them.

It was another bean-pole, another vine-support crumbled under the green life of the vine. And very bitter it was, this time. For up the old tree trunk of Europe the green vine had been clambering silently for more than ten years, ten hugely important years, the years of real living. The two idealists had *lived* in Europe, lived on Europe and on European life and European things as vines in an everlasting vineyard.

They had made their home here: a home such as you could never make in America. Their watchword had been "beauty." They had rented, the last four years, the second floor of an old Palazzo on the Arno, and here they had all their "things." And they derived a profound, profound satisfaction from their apartment: the lofty, silent, ancient rooms with windows on the river, with glistening dark-red floors, and the beautiful furniture that the idealists had "picked up."

Yes, unknown to themselves, the lives of the idealists had been running with a fierce swiftness horizontally, all the time. They had become tense, fierce hunters of "things" for their home. While their souls were climbing up to the sun of old European culture or old Indian thought, their passions were running horizontally, clutching at "things." Of course they did not buy the things for the things' sakes, but for the sake of "beauty." They looked upon their home as a place entirely furnished by loveliness, not by "things" at all. Valerie had some very lovely curtains at the windows of the long *salotto*,[2] looking on the river: curtains of queer ancient material that looked like finely-knitted silk, most beautifully faded down from vermilion and orange, and gold, and black, down to a sheer soft glow. Valerie hardly ever came into the *salotto* without mentally falling on her knees before the curtains. "Chartres!"[3] she said. "To me they are Chartres!" And Melville never turned and looked at his sixteenth-century Venetian bookcase, with its two or three dozen of choice books, without feeling his marrow stir in his bones. The holy of holies!

The child silently, almost sinisterly, avoided any rude contact with these ancient monuments of furniture, as if they had been nests of sleeping cobras, or that "thing" most perilous to the touch, the Ark of the Covenant. His childish awe was silent and cold, but final.

Still, a couple of New England idealists cannot live merely on the bygone glory of their furniture. At least, one couple could not. They got used to the marvellous Bologna cupboard, they got used to the wonderful Venetian bookcase, and the books, and the Siena curtains and bronzes, and the lovely sofas and side-tables and chairs they had "picked up" in Paris. Oh, they had been picking things up since the first day they landed in Europe. And they were still at it. It is the last interest Europe can offer to an outsider: or to an insider either.

When people came, and were thrilled by the Melville interior, then Valerie and Erasmus felt they had not lived in vain: that they still were living. But in the long mornings, when Erasmus was desultorily working at Renaissance Florentine literature, and Valerie was attending to the apartment: and in the long hours after lunch; and in the long, usually very cold and oppressive evenings in the ancient palazzo: then the halo died from around the furniture, and the things became things, lumps of matter that just stood there or hung there, *ad infinitum*,[4] and said nothing; and Valerie and Erasmus almost hated them. The glow of beauty, like every other glow, dies down unless it is fed. The idealists still dearly loved their things. But they had got them. And the sad fact is, things that glow vividly while you're getting them, go almost quite cold after a year or two. Unless, of course, people

[2] Parlor.
[3] Chartres is a city in north central France which is known for its Gothic cathedral.
[4] Endlessly.

envy them very much, and the museums are pining for them. And the Melvilles' "things," though very good, were not quite so good as that.

So, the glow gradually went out of everything, out of Europe, out of Italy—"the Italians are *dears*"—even out of that marvellous apartment on the Arno. "Why, if I had this apartment, I'd never, never even want to go out of doors! It's too lovely and perfect." That was something, of course—to hear that.

And yet Valerie and Erasmus went out of doors: they even went out to get away from its ancient, cold-floored, stone-heavy silence and dead dignity. "We're living on the past, you know, Dick," said Valerie to her husband. She called him Dick.

They were grimly hanging on. They did not like to give in. They did not like to own up that they were through. For twelve years now, they had been "free" people living a "full and beautiful life." And America for twelve years had been their anathema, the Sodom and Gomorrah[5] of industrial materialism.

It wasn't easy to own that you were "through." They hated to admit that they wanted to go back. But at last, reluctantly, they decided to go, "for the boy's sake."—"We can't *bear* to leave Europe. But Peter is an American, so he had better look at America while he's young." The Melvilles had an entirely English accent and manner; almost; a little Italian and French here and there.

They left Europe behind, but they took as much of it along with them as possible. Several van-loads, as a matter of fact. All those adorable and irreplaceable "things." And all arrived in New York, idealists, child, and the huge bulk of Europe they had lugged along.

Valerie had dreamed of a pleasant apartment, perhaps on Riverside Drive, where it was not so expensive as east of Fifth Avenue, and where all their wonderful things would look marvellous. She and Erasmus house-hunted. But alas! their income was quite under three thousand dollars a year. They found—well, everybody knows what they found. Two small rooms and a kitchenette, and don't let us unpack a *thing!*

The chunk of Europe which they had bitten off went into a warehouse, at fifty dollars a month. And they sat in two small rooms and a kitchenette, and wondered why they'd done it.

Erasmus, of course, ought to get a job. This was what was written on the wall, and what they both pretended not to see. But it had been

---

[5] Two cities, described in the Old Testament, that were destroyed with fire and brimstone from heaven because of their wickedness.

the strange, vague threat that the Statue of Liberty had always held over them: "Thou shalt get a job!" Erasmus had the tickets, as they say. A scholastic career was still possible for him. He had taken his exams brilliantly at Yale, and had kept up his "researches," all the time he had been in Europe.

But both he and Valerie shuddered. A scholastic career! The scholastic world! The *American* scholastic world! Shudder upon shudder! Give up their freedom, their full and beautiful life? Never! Never! Erasmus would be forty next birthday.

The "things" remained in the warehouse. Valerie went to look at them. It cost her a dollar an hour, and horrid pangs. The "things," poor things, looked a bit shabby and wretched, in that warehouse.

However, New York was not all America. There was the great clean West. So the Melvilles went West, with Peter, but without the things. They tried living the simple life, in the mountains. But doing their own chores became almost a nightmare. "Things" are all very well to look at, but it's awful handling them, even when they're beautiful. To be the slave of hideous things, to keep a stove going, cook meals, wash dishes, carry water and clean floors: pure horror of sordid anti-life!

In the cabin on the mountains, Valerie dreamed of Florence, the lost apartment; and her Bologna cupboard and Louis-Quinze chairs, above all, her "Chartres" curtains, stood in New York and costing fifty dollars a month.

A millionaire friend came to the rescue, offering them a cottage on the California Coast—California! Where the new soul is to be born in man. With joy the idealists moved a little farther west, catching at new vine-props of hope.

And finding them straws! The millionaire cottage was perfectly equipped. It was perhaps as labour-savingly perfect as is possible: electric heating and cooking, a white-and-pearl enameled kitchen, nothing to make dirt except the human being himself. In an hour or so the idealists had got through their chores. They were "free"—free to hear the great Pacific pounding the coast, and to feel a new soul filling their bodies.

Alas! the Pacific pounded the coast with hideous brutality, brute force itself! And the new soul, instead of sweetly stealing into their bodies, seemed only meanly to gnaw the old soul out of their bodies. To feel you are under the fist of the most blind and crunching brute force: to feel that your cherished idealist's soul is being gnawed out of you, and only irritation left in place of it: well, it isn't good enough.

After about nine months, the idealists departed from the California West. It had been a great experience, they were glad to have had it. But, in the long run, the West was not the place for them, and they knew it. No, the people who wanted new souls had better get them. They, Valerie and Erasmus Melville, would like to develop the old soul a little further. Anyway, they had not felt any influx of new soul, on the California coast. On the contrary.

So, with a slight hole in their material capital, they returned to Massachusetts and paid a visit to Valerie's parents, taking the boy along. The grandparents welcomed the child—poor expatriated boy— and were rather cold to Valerie, but really cold to Erasmus. Valerie's mother definitely said to Valerie, one day, that Erasmus ought to take a job, so that Valerie could live decently. Valerie haughtily reminded her mother of the beautiful apartment on the Arno, and the "wonderful" things in store in New York, and of the "marvellous and satisfying life" she and Erasmus had led. Valerie's mother said that she didn't think her daughter's life looked so very marvellous at present: homeless, with a husband idle at the age of forty, a child to educate, and a dwindling capital: looked the reverse of marvellous to *her*. Let Erasmus take some post in one of the universities.

"What post? What university?" interrupted Valerie.

"That could be found, considering your father's connections and Erasmus's qualifications," replied Valerie's mother. "And you could get all your valuable things out of store, and have a really lovely home, which everybody in America would be proud to visit. As it is, your furniture is eating up your income, and you are living like rats in a hole, with nowhere to go to."

This was very true. Valerie was beginning to pine for a home, with her "things." Of course she could have sold her furniture for a substantial sum. But nothing would have induced her to. Whatever else passed away, religions, cultures, continents, and hopes, Valerie would *never* part from the "things" which she and Erasmus had collected with such passion. To these she was nailed.

But she and Erasmus still would not give up that freedom, that full and beautiful life they had so believed in. Erasmus cursed America. He did not *want* to earn a living. He panted for Europe.

Leaving the boy in charge of Valerie's parents, the two idealists once more set off for Europe. In New York they paid two dollars and looked for a brief, bitter hour at their "things." They sailed "student class"—that is, third. Their income now was less than two thousand dollars, instead of three. And they made straight for Paris—cheap Paris.

They found Europe, this time, a complete failure. "We have returned like dogs to our vomit," said Erasmus; "but the vomit has staled in the meantime." He found he couldn't stand Europe. It irritated every nerve in his body. He hated America too. But America at least was a darn sight better than this miserable, dirt-eating continent; which was by no means cheap any more, either.

Valerie, with her heart on her things—she had really burned to get them out of that warehouse, where they had stood now for three years, eating up two thousand dollars—wrote to her mother she thought Erasmus would come back if he could get some suitable work in America. Erasmus, in a state of frustration bordering on rage and insanity, just went round Italy in a poverty-stricken fashion, his coat-cuffs frayed, hating everything with intensity. And when a post was found for him in Cleveland University, to teach French, Italian, and Spanish literature, his eyes grew more beady, and his long, queer face grew sharper and more rat-like, with utter baffled fury. He was forty, and the job was upon him.

"I think you'd better accept, dear. You don't care for Europe any longer. As you say, it's dead and finished. They offer us a house on the college lot, and mother says there's room in it for all our things. I think we'd better cable 'Accept.'"

He glowered at her like a cornered rat. One almost expected to see rat's whiskers twitching at the sides of the sharp nose.

"Shall I send the cablegram?" she asked.

"Send it!" he blurted.

And she went out and sent it.

He was a changed man, quieter, much less irritable. A load was off him. He was inside the cage.

But when he looked at the furnaces of Cleveland, vast and like the greatest of black forests, with red and white-hot cascades of gushing metal, and tiny gnomes of men, and terrific noises, gigantic, he said to Valerie:

"Say what you like, Valerie, this is the biggest thing the modern world has to show."

And when they were in their up-to-date little house on the college lot of Cleveland University, and that woebegone débris of Europe,

Bologna cupboard, Venice book-shelves, Ravenna bishop's chair, Louis-Quinze side-tables, "Chartres" curtains, Siena bronze lamps, all were arrayed, and all looked perfectly out of keeping, and therefore very impressive; and when the idealists had had a bunch of gaping people in, and Erasmus had showed off in his best European manner, but still quite cordial and American; and Valerie had been most ladylike, but for all that, "we prefer America"; then Erasmus said, looking at her with the queer sharp eyes of a rat:

"Europe's the mayonnaise all right, but America supplies the good old lobster—what?"

"Every time!" she said, with satisfaction.

And he peered at her. He was in the cage: but it was safe inside. And she, evidently, was her real self at last. She had got the goods. Yet round his nose was a queer, evil, scholastic look, of pure scepticism. But he liked lobster.

The Machine Stops   *E. M. Forster*

1. THE AIR-SHIP

Imagine, if you can, a small room, hexagonal in shape, like the cell of a bee. It is lighted neither by window nor by lamp, yet it is filled with a soft radiance. There are no apertures for ventilation, yet the air is fresh. There are no musical instruments, and yet, at the moment that my meditation opens, this room is throbbing with melodious sounds. An arm-chair is in the center, by its side a reading-desk— that is all the furniture. And in the armchair there sits a swaddled lump of flesh—a woman, about five feet high, with a face as white as a fungus. It is to her that the little room belongs.

An electric bell rang.

The woman touched a switch and the music was silent.

"I suppose I must see who it is," she thought, and set her chair in motion. The chair, like the music, was worked by machinery, and it rolled her to the other side of the room, where the bell still rang importunately.

"Who is it?" she called. Her voice was irritable, for she had been interrupted often since the music began. She knew several thousand people; in certain directions human intercourse had advanced enormously.

But when she listened into the receiver, her white face wrinkled into smiles, and she said:

"Very well. Let us talk, I will isolate myself. I do not expect anything important will happen for the next five minutes—for I can give you fully five minutes, Kuno. Then I must deliver my lecture on 'Music during the Australian Period.' "

She touched the isolation knob, so that no one else could speak to her. Then she touched the lighting apparatus, and the little room was plunged into darkness.

"Be quick!" she called, her irritation returning. "Be quick, Kuno; here I am in the dark wasting my time."

But it was fully fifteen seconds before the round plate that she held in her hands began to glow. A faint blue light shot across it, darkening to purple, and presently she could see the image of her son, who lived on the other side of the earth, and he could see her.

"Kuno, how slow you are."

He smiled gravely.

"I really believe you enjoy dawdling."

"I have called you before, mother, but you were always busy or isolated. I have something particular to say."

"What is it, dearest boy? Be quick. Why could you not send it by pneumatic post?"

"Because I prefer saying such a thing. I want—"

"Well?"

"I want you to come and see me."

Vashti watched his face in the blue plate.

"But I can see you!" she exclaimed. "What more do you want?"

"I want to see you not through the Machine," said Kuno. "I want to speak to you not through the wearisome Machine."

"Oh, hush!" said his mother, vaguely shocked. "You mustn't say anything against the Machine."

"Why not?"

"One mustn't."

"You talk as if a god had made the Machine," cried the other. "I believe that you pray to it when you are unhappy. Men made it, do not forget that. Great men, but men. The Machine is much, but it is not everything. I see something like you in this plate, but I do not see you. I hear something like you through this telephone, but I do not hear you. That is why I want you to come. Come and stop with me. Pay me a visit, so that we can meet face to face, and talk about the hopes that are in my mind."

She replied that she could scarcely spare the time for a visit.

"The air-ship barely takes two days to fly between me and you."

"I dislike air-ships."

"Why?"

"I dislike seeing the horrible brown earth, and the sea, and the stars when it is dark. I get no ideas in an air-ship."

"I do not get them anywhere else."

"What kind of ideas can the air give you?"

He paused for an instant.

"Do you not know four big stars that form an oblong, and three stars close together in the middle of the oblong, and hanging from these stars, three other stars?"

"No, I do not. I dislike the stars. But did they give you an idea? How interesting; tell me."

"I had an idea that they were like a man."

"I do not understand."

"The four big stars are the man's shoulders and his knees. The three stars in the middle are like the belts that men wore once, and the three stars hanging are like a sword."

"A sword?"

"Men carried swords about with them, to kill animals and other men."

"It does not strike me as a very good idea, but it is certainly original. When did it come to you first?"

"In the air-ship—" He broke off, and she fancied that he looked sad. She could not be sure, for the Machine did not transmit *nuances*[1] of expression. It only gave a general idea of people—an idea that was good enough for all practical purposes, Vashti thought. The imponderable bloom, declared by a discredited philosophy to be the actual essence of intercourse, was rightly ignored by the Machine, just as the imponderable bloom of the grape was ignored by the manufacturers of artificial fruit. Something "good enough" had long since been accepted by our race.

"The truth is," he continued, "that I want to see these stars again. They are curious stars. I want to see them not from the air-ship,

[1] Subtle variations.

but from the surface of the earth, as our ancestors did, thousands of years ago. I want to visit the surface of the earth."

She was shocked again.

"Mother, you must come, if only to explain to me what is the harm of visiting the surface of the earth."

"No harm," she replied, controlling herself. "But no advantage. The surface of the earth is only dust and mud, no life remains on it, and you would need a respirator, or the cold of the outer air would kill you. One dies immediately in the outer air."

"I know; of course I shall take all precautions."

"And besides—"

"Well?"

She considered, and chose her words with care. Her son had a queer temper, and she wished to dissuade him from the expedition.

"It is contrary to the spirit of the age," she asserted.

"Do you mean by that, contrary to the Machine?"

"In a sense, but—"

His image in the blue plate faded.

"Kuno!"

He had isolated himself.

For a moment Vashti felt lonely.

Then she generated the light, and the sight of her room, flooded with radiance and studded with electric buttons, revived her. There were buttons and switches everywhere—buttons to call for food, for music, for clothing. There was the hot-bath button, by pressure of which a basin of (imitation) marble rose out of the floor, filled to the brim with a warm deodorized liquid. There was the cold-bath button. There was the button that produced literature. And there were of course the buttons by which she communicated with her friends. The room, though it contained nothing, was in touch with all that she cared for in the world.

Vashti's next move was to turn off the isolation-switch, and all the accumulations of the last three minutes burst upon her. The room was filled with the noise of bells, and speaking-tubes. What was the new food like? Could she recommend it? Had she had any ideas lately? Might one tell her one's own ideas? Would she make an engagement to visit the public nurseries at an early date?—say this day month.

To most of these questions she replied with irritation—a growing quality in that accelerated age. She said that the new food was horrible. That she could not visit the public nurseries through press of engagements. That she had no ideas of her own but had just been told one—that four stars and three in the middle were like a man: she doubted there was much in it. Then she switched off her correspondents, for it was time to deliver her lecture on Australian music.

The clumsy system of public gatherings had been long since abandoned; neither Vashti nor her audience stirred from their rooms. Seated in her arm-chair she spoke, while they in their arm-chairs heard her, fairly well, and saw her, fairly well. She opened with a humorous account of music in the pre-Mongolian epoch, and went on to describe the great outburst of song that followed the Chinese conquest. Remote and primeval as were the methods of I-San-So and the Brisbane school, she yet felt (she said) that study of them might repay the musician of today: they had freshness; they had, above all, ideas.

Her lecture, which lasted ten minutes, was well received, and at its conclusion she and many of her audience listened to a lecture on the sea; there were ideas to be got from the sea; the speaker had donned a respirator and visited it lately. Then she fed, talked to many friends, had a bath, talked again, and summoned her bed.

The bed was not to her liking. It was too large, and she had a feeling for a small bed. Complaint was useless, for beds were of the same dimension all over the world, and to have had an alternative size would have involved vast alterations in the Machine. Vashti isolated herself—it was necessary, for neither day nor night existed under the ground—and reviewed all that had happened since she had summoned the bed last. Ideas? Scarcely any. Events—was Kuno's invitation an event?

By her side, on the little reading-desk, was a survival from the ages of litter—one book. This was the Book of the Machine. In it were instructions against every possible contingency. If she was hot or cold or dyspeptic or at loss for a word, she went to the book, and it told her which button to press. The Central Committee published it. In accordance with a growing habit, it was richly bound.

Sitting up in the bed, she took it reverently in her hands. She glanced round the glowing room as if someone might be watching her. Then, half ashamed, half joyful, she murmured "O Machine! O Machine!" and raised the volume to her lips. Thrice she kissed it, thrice inclined her head, thrice she felt the delirium of acquiescence. Her ritual performed, she turned to page 1367, which gave the times of the departure of the air-ships from the island in the southern hemisphere, under whose soil she lived, to the island in the northern hemisphere, where-under lived her son.

She thought, "I have not the time."

She made the room dark and slept; she awoke and made the room light; she ate and exchanged ideas with her friends, and listened to music and attended lectures; she made the room dark and slept. Above her, beneath her, and around her, the Machine hummed eternally; she did not notice the noise, for she had been born with it in her ears. The earth, carrying her, hummed as it sped through silence, turning her now to the invisible sun, now to the invisible stars. She awoke and made the room light.

"Kuno!"

"I will not talk to you," he answered, "until you come."

"Have you been on the surface of the earth since we spoke last?"

His image faded.

Again she consulted the book. She became very nervous and lay back in her chair palpitating. Think of her as without teeth or hair. Presently she directed the chair to the wall, and pressed an unfamiliar button. The wall swung apart slowly. Through the opening she saw a tunnel that curved slightly, so that its goal was not visible. Should she go to see her son, here was the beginning of the journey.

Of course she knew all about the communication-system. There was nothing mysterious in it. She would summon a car and it would fly with her down the tunnel until it reached the lift that communicated with the air-ship station: the system had been in use for many, many years, long before the universal establishment of the Machine. And of course she had studied the civilization that had immediately preceded her own—the civilization that had mistaken the functions of the system, and had used it for bringing people to things, instead of for bringing things to people. Those funny old days, when men went for change of air instead of changing the air in their rooms! And yet—she was frightened of the tunnel: she had not seen it since her last child was born. It curved—but not quite as she remembered; it was brilliant—but not quite as brilliant as a lecturer had suggested. Vashti was seized with the terrors of direct experience. She shrank back into the room, and the wall closed up again.

"Kuno," she said, "I cannot come to see you. I am not well."

Immediately an enormous apparatus fell on to her out of the ceiling, a thermometer was automatically inserted between her lips, a stethoscope was automatically laid upon her heart. She lay powerless. Cool pads soothed her forehead. Kuno had telegraphed in her doctor.

So the human passions still blundered up and down in the Machine. Vashti drank the medicine that the doctor projected into her mouth, and the machinery retired into the ceiling. The voice of Kuno was heard asking how she felt.

"Better." Then with irritation: "But why do you not come to me instead?"

"Because I cannot leave this place."

"Why?"

"Because, any moment, something tremendous may happen."

"Have you been on the surface of the earth yet?"

"Not yet."

"Then what is it?"

"I will not tell you through the Machine."

She resumed her life.

But she thought of Kuno as a baby, his birth, his removal to the public nurseries, her one visit to him there, his visits to her—visits which stopped when the Machine had assigned him a room on the other side of the earth. "Parents, duties of," said the book of the Machine, "cease at the moment of birth. P. 422327483." True, but there was something special about Kuno—indeed there had been something special about all her children—and, after all, she must brave the journey if he desired it. And "something tremendous might happen." What did that mean? The nonsense of a youthful man, no doubt, but she must go. Again she pressed the unfamiliar button, again the wall swung back, and she saw the tunnel that curved out of sight. Clasping the Book, she rose, tottered on to the platform, and summoned the car. Her room closed behind her: the journey to the northern hemisphere had begun.

Of course it was perfectly easy. The car approached and in it she found armchairs exactly like her own. When she signaled, it stopped, and she tottered into the lift. One other passenger was in the lift, the first fellow creature she had seen face to face for months. Few traveled in these days, for, thanks to the advance of science, the earth was exactly alike all over. Rapid intercourse, from which the previous civilization had hoped so much, had ended by defeating itself. What was the good of going to Pekin when it was just like Shrewsbury? Why return to Shrewsbury when it would be just like Pekin? Men seldom moved their bodies; all unrest was concentrated in the soul.

The air-ship service was a relic from the former age. It was kept up, because it was easier to keep it up than to stop it or to diminish it, but it now far exceeded the wants of the population. Vessel after vessel would rise from the vomitories of Rye or of Christchurch (I use the antique names), would sail into the crowded sky, and would draw up at the wharves of the south—empty. So nicely adjusted was the system, so independent of meteorology, that the sky, whether calm or cloudy, resembled a vast kaleidoscope whereon the same patterns periodically recurred. The ship on which Vashti sailed started now at sunset, now at dawn. But always, as it passed above Rheims, it would neighbor the ship that served between Helsingfors and the Brazils, and, every third time it surmounted the Alps, the fleet of Palermo would cross its track behind. Night and day, wind and storm, tide and earthquake, impeded man no longer. He had harnessed Leviathan. All the old literature, with its praise of Nature, and its fear of Nature, rang false as the prattle of a child.

Yet as Vashti saw the vast flank of the ship, stained with exposure to the outer air, her horror of direct experience returned. It was not quite like the air-ship in the cinematophote. For one thing it smelt—not strongly or unpleasantly, but it did smell, and with her eyes shut she should have known that a new thing was close to her. Then she had to walk to it from the lift, had to submit to glances from the other passengers. The man in front dropped his Book—no great matter but it disquieted them all. In the rooms, if the Book was dropped, the floor raised it mechanically, but the gangway to the air-ship was not so prepared, and the sacred volume lay motionless. They stopped—the thing was unforeseen—and the man, instead of picking up his property, felt the muscles of his arm to see how they had failed him. Then someone actually said with direct utterance: "We shall be late" —and they trooped on board, Vashti treading on the pages as she did so.

Inside, her anxiety increased. The arrangements were old-fashioned and rough. There was even a female attendant, to whom she would have to announce her wants during the voyage. Of course a revolving platform ran the length of the boat, but she was expected to walk from it to her cabin. Some cabins were better than others, and she did not get the best. She thought the attendant had been unfair, and spasms of rage shook her. The glass valves had closed, she could not go back. She saw, at the end of the vestibule, the lift in which she had ascended going quietly up and down, empty. Beneath those corridors of shining tiles were rooms, tier below tier, reaching far into the earth, and in each room there sat a human being, eating, or sleeping, or producing ideas. And buried deep in the hive was her own room. Vashti was afraid.

"O Machine! O Machine!" she murmured, and caressed her Book, and was comforted.

Then the sides of the vestibule seemed to melt together, as do the passages that we see in dreams, the lift vanished, the Book that had been dropped slid to the left and vanished, polished tiles rushed by like a stream of water, there was a slight jar, and the air-ship, issuing from its tunnel, soared above the waters of a tropical ocean.

It was night. For a moment she saw the coast of Sumatra edged by the phosphorescence of waves, and crowned by lighthouses, still sending forth their disregarded beams. They also vanished, and only the stars distracted her. They were not motionless, but swayed to and fro above her head, thronging out of one skylight into another, as if the universe and not the air-ship was careening. And, as often happens on clear nights, they seemed now to be in perspective, now on a plane; now piled tier beyond tier into the infinite heavens, now concealing infinity, a roof limiting for ever the visions of men. In either case they seemed intolerable. "Are we to travel in the dark?" called the passengers angrily, and the attendant, who had been careless, generated the light, and pulled down the blinds of pliable metal. When the air-ships had been built, the desire to look direct at things still lingered in the world. Hence the extraordinary number of skylights and windows, and the proportionate discomfort to those who were civilized and refined. Even in Vashti's cabin one star peeped through a flaw in the blind, and after a few hours' uneasy slumber, she was disturbed by an unfamiliar glow, which was the dawn.

Quick as the ship had sped westwards, the earth had rolled eastwards quicker still, and had dragged back Vashti and her companions towards the sun. Science could prolong the night, but only for a little, and those high hopes of neutralizing the earth's diurnal revolution had passed, together with hopes that were possibly higher. To "keep pace with the sun," or even to outstrip it, had been the aim of the civilization preceding this. Racing aeroplanes had been built for the purpose, capable of enormous speed, and steered by the greatest intellects of the epoch. Round the globe they went, round and round, westward, westward, round and round, amidst humanity's applause. In vain. The globe went eastward quicker still, horrible accidents occurred, and the Committee of the Machine, at the time rising into prominence, declared the pursuit illegal, unmechanical, and punishable by Homelessness.

Of Homelessness more will be said later.

Doubtless the Committee was right. Yet the attempt to "defeat the sun" aroused the last common interest that our race experienced about the heavenly bodies, or indeed about anything. It was the last time that men were compacted by thinking of a power outside the world. The sun had conquered, yet it was the end of his spiritual dominion. Dawn, midday, twilight, the zodiacal path, touched neither men's lives nor their hearts, and science retreated into the ground, to concentrate herself upon problems that she was certain of solving.

So when Vashti found her cabin invaded by a rosy finger of light, she was annoyed, and tried to adjust the blind. But the blind flew up altogether, and she saw through the skylight small pink clouds, swaying against a background of blue, and as the sun crept higher, its radiance entered direct, brimming down the wall, like a golden sea. It rose and fell with the air-ship's motion, just as waves rise and fall, but it advanced steadily, as a tide advances. Unless she was careful, it would strike her face. A spasm of horror shook her and she rang for the attendant. The attendant too was horrified, but she could do nothing; it was not her place to mend the blind. She could only suggest that the lady should change her cabin, which she accordingly prepared to do.

People were almost exactly alike all over the world, but the attendant of the air-ship, perhaps owing to her exceptional duties, had grown a little out of the common. She had often to address passengers with direct speech, and this had given her a certain roughness and originality of manner. When Vashti swerved away from the sunbeams with a cry, she behaved barbarically—she put out her hand to steady her.

"How dare you!" exclaimed the passenger. "You forget yourself!"

The woman was confused, and apologized for not having let her fall. People never touched one another. The custom had become obsolete, owing to the Machine.

"Where are we now?" asked Vashti haughtily.

"We are over Asia," said the attendant, anxious to be polite.

"Asia?"

"You must excuse my common way of speaking. I have got into the habit of calling places over which I pass by their unmechanical names."

"Oh, I remember Asia. The Mongols came from it."

"Beneath us, in the open air, stood a city that was once called Simla."

"Have you ever heard of the Mongols and of the Brisbane school?"

"No."

"Brisbane also stood in the open air."

"Those mountains to the right—let me show you them." She pushed back a metal blind. The main chain of the Himalayas was revealed. "They were once called the Roof of the World, those mountains."

"What a foolish name!"

"You must remember that, before the dawn of civilization, they seemed to be an impenetrable wall that touched the stars. It was supposed that no one but the gods could exist above their summits. How we have advanced, thanks to the Machine!"

"How we have advanced, thanks to the Machine!" said Vashti.

"How we have advanced, thanks to the Machine!" echoed the passenger who had dropped his Book the night before, and who was standing in the passage.

"And that white stuff in the cracks?—what is it?"

"I have forgotten its name."

"Cover the window, please. These mountains give me no ideas."

The northern aspect of the Himalayas was in deep shadow: on the Indian slope the sun had just prevailed. The forests had been destroyed during the literature epoch for the purpose of making newspaper-pulp, but the snows were awakening to their morning glory, and clouds still hung on the breasts of Kinchinjunga. In the plain were seen the ruins of cities, with diminished rivers creeping by their walls, and by the sides of these were sometimes the signs of vomitories, marking the cities of today. Over the whole prospect air-ships rushed, crossing and intercrossing with incredible aplomb, and rising nonchalantly when they desired to escape the perturbations of the lower atmosphere and to traverse the Roof of the World.

"We have indeed advanced, thanks to the Machine," repeated the attendant, and hid the Himalayas behind a metal blind.

The day dragged wearily forward. The passengers sat each in his cabin, avoiding one another with an almost physical repulsion and longing to be once more under the surface of the earth. There were eight or ten of them, mostly young males, sent out from the public nurseries to inhabit the rooms of those who had died in various parts of the earth. The man who had dropped his Book was on the homeward journey. He had been sent to Sumatra for the purpose of propagating the race. Vashti alone was traveling by her private will.

At midday she took a second glance at the earth. The air-ship was crossing another range of mountains, but she could see little, owing to clouds. Masses of black rock hovered below her, and merged indistinctly into gray. Their shapes were fantastic; one of them resembled a prostrate man.

"No ideas here," murmured Vashti, and hid the Caucasus behind a metal blind.

In the evening she looked again. They were crossing a golden sea, in which lay many small islands and one peninsula.

She repeated, "No ideas here," and hid Greece behind a metal blind.

2. THE MENDING APPARATUS

By a vestibule, by a lift, by a tubular railway, by a platform, by a sliding door—by reversing all the steps of her departure did Vashti arrive at her son's room, which exactly resembled her own. She might well declare that the visit was superfluous. The buttons, the knobs, the reading-desk with the Book, the temperature, the atmosphere, the illumination—all were exactly the same. And if Kuno himself, flesh of her flesh, stood close beside her at last, what profit was there in that? She was too well-bred to shake him by the hand.

Averting her eyes, she spoke as follows:

"Here I am. I have had the most terrible journey and greatly retarded the development of my soul. It is not worth it, Kuno, it is not worth it. My time is too precious. The sunlight almost touched me, and I have met with the rudest people. I can only stop a few minutes. Say what you want to say, and then I must return."

"I have been threatened with Homelessness," said Kuno.

She looked at him now.

"I have been threatened with Homelessness, and I could not tell you such a thing through the Machine."

Homelessness means death. The victim is exposed to the air, which kills him.

"I have been outside since I spoke to you last. The tremendous thing has happened, and they have discovered me."

"But why shouldn't you go outside!" she exclaimed. "It is perfectly legal, perfectly mechanical, to visit the surface of the earth. I have lately been to a lecture on the sea; there is no objection to that; one simply summons a respirator and gets an Egression-permit. It is not the kind of thing that spiritually-minded people do, and I begged you not to do it, but there is no legal objection to it."

"I did not get an Egression-permit."

"Then how did you get out?"

"I found out a way of my own."

The phrase conveyed no meaning to her, and he had to repeat it.

"A way of your own?" she whispered. "But that would be wrong."

"Why?"

The question shocked her beyond measure.

"You are beginning to worship the Machine," he said coldly. "You think it irreligious of me to have found out a way of my own. It was just what the Committee thought, when they threatened me with Homelessness."

At this she grew angry. "I worship nothing!" she cried. "I am most advanced. I don't think you irreligious, for there is no such thing as religion left. All the fear and the superstition that existed once have been destroyed by the Machine. I only meant that to find out a way of your own was— Besides, there is no new way out."

"So it is always supposed."

"Except through the vomitories, for which one must have an Egression-permit, it is impossible to get out. The Book says so."

"Well, the Book's wrong, for I have been out on my feet."

For Kuno was possessed of a certain physical strength.

By these days it was a demerit to be muscular. Each infant was examined at birth, and all who promised undue strength were destroyed. Humanitarians may protest, but it would have been no true kindness to let an athlete live; he would never have been happy in that state of life to which the Machine had called him; he would have yearned for trees to climb, rivers to bathe in, meadows and hills against which he might measure his body. Man must be adapted to his surroundings, must he not? In the dawn of the world our weakly must be exposed on Mount Taygetus, in its twilight our strong will suffer euthanasia, that the Machine may progress, that the Machine may progress, that the Machine may progress eternally.

"You know that we have lost the sense of space. We say 'space is annihilated,' but we have annihilated not space, but the sense thereof. We have lost a part of ourselves. I determined to recover it, and I began by walking up and down the platform of the railway outside my room. Up and down, until I was tired, and so did recapture the meaning of 'Near' and 'Far.' 'Near' is a place to which I can get quickly *on my feet,* not a place to which the train or the air-ship will take me quickly. 'Far' is a place to which I cannot get quickly on my feet; the vomitory is 'far,' though I could be there in thirty-eight seconds by summoning the train. Man is the measure. That was my first lesson. Man's feet are the measure for distance, his hands are the measure for ownership, his body is the measure for all that is lovable and desirable and strong. Then I went further: it was then that I called to you for the first time, and you would not come.

"This city, as you know, is built deep beneath the surface of the earth, with only the vomitories protruding. Having paced the platform outside my own room, I took the lift to the next platform and paced that also, and so with each in turn, until I came to the topmost, above which begins the earth. All the platforms were exactly alike, and all that I gained by visiting them was to develop my sense of space and my muscles. I think I should have been content with this—it is not a little thing—but as I walked and brooded, it occurred to me that our cities had been built in the days when men still breathed the outer air, and that there had been ventilation shafts for the workmen. I could think of nothing but these ventilation shafts. Had they been destroyed by all the food-tubes and medicine-tubes and music-tubes that the Machine has evolved lately? Or did traces of them remain? One thing was certain. If I came upon them anywhere, it would be in the railway-tunnels of the topmost story. Everywhere else, all space was accounted for.

"I am telling my story quickly, but don't think that I was not a coward or that your answers never depressed me. It is not the proper thing, it is not mechanical, it is not decent to walk along a railway-tunnel. I did not fear that I might tread upon a live rail and be killed. I feared something far more intangible—doing what was not contemplated by the Machine. Then I said to myself, 'Man is the measure,' and I went, and after many visits I found an opening.

"The tunnels, of course, were lighted. Everything is light, artificial light; darkness is the exception. So when I saw a black gap in the tiles, I knew that it was an exception, and rejoiced. I put in my arm—I could put in no more at first—and waved it round and round in ecstasy. I loosened another tile, and put in my head, and shouted into the darkness: 'I am coming, I shall do it yet,' and my voice reverberated down endless passages. I seemed to hear the spirits of those dead workmen who had returned each evening to the starlight and to their wives, and all the generations who had lived in the open air called back to me, 'You will do it yet, you are coming.' "

He paused, and, absurd as he was, his last words moved her. For Kuno had lately asked to be a father, and his request had been refused by the Committee. His was not a type that the Machine desired to hand on.

"Then a train passed. It brushed by me, but I thrust my head and arms into the hole. I had done enough for one day, so I crawled back to the platform, went down in the lift, and summoned my bed. Ah, what dreams! And again I called you, and again you refused."

She shook her head and said:

"Don't. Don't talk of these terrible things. You make me miserable. You are throwing civilization away."

"But I had got back the sense of space and a man cannot rest then. I determined to get in at the hole and climb the shaft. And so I exercised my arms. Day after day I went through ridiculous movements, until my flesh ached and I could hang by my hands and hold the pillow of my bed outstretched for many minutes. Then I summoned a respirator, and started.

"It was easy at first. The mortar had somehow rotted, and I soon pushed some more tiles in, and clambered after them into the darkness, and the spirits of the dead comforted me. I don't know what I mean by that. I just say what I felt. I felt, for the first time, that a protest had been lodged against corruption, and that even as the dead were comforting me, so I was comforting the unborn. I felt that humanity existed, and that it existed without clothes. How can I possibly explain this? It was naked, humanity seemed naked, and all these tubes and buttons and machineries neither came into the world with us, nor will they follow us out, nor do they matter supremely while we are here. Had I been strong, I would have torn off every garment I had, and gone out into the outer air unswaddled. But this is not for me, nor perhaps for my generation. I climbed with my respirator and my hygienic clothes and my dietetic tabloids! Better thus than not at all.

"There was a ladder, made of some primeval metal. The light from the railway fell upon its lowest rungs, and I saw that it led straight upwards out of the rubble at the bottom of the shaft. Perhaps our ancestors ran up and down it a dozen times daily, in their building. As I climbed, the rough edges cut through my gloves so that my hands bled. The light helped me for a little, and then came darkness and, worse still, silence which pierced my ears like a sword. The Machine hums! Did you know that? Its hum penetrates our blood, and may even guide our thoughts. Who knows! I was getting beyond its power. Then I thought: 'This silence means that I am doing wrong.' But I heard voices in the silence, and again they strengthened me." He laughed. "I had need of them. The next moment I cracked my head against something."

She sighed.

"I had reached one of those pneumatic stoppers that defend us from the outer air. You may have noticed them on the air-ship. Pitch dark, my feet on the rungs of an invisible ladder, my hands cut; I cannot explain how I lived through this part, but the voices still comforted me, and I felt for fastenings. The stopper, I suppose, was about eight feet across. I passed my hand over it as far as I could reach. It was perfectly smooth. I felt it almost to the center. Not quite to the center, for my arm was too short. Then the voice said: 'Jump. It is worth it. There may be a handle in the center, and you may catch hold of it and so come to us your own way. And if there is no handle, so that you may fall and are dashed to pieces—it is still worth it: you will still come to us your own way.' So I jumped. There was a handle, and—"

He paused. Tears gathered in his mother's eyes. She knew that he was fated. If he did not die today he would die tomorrow. There was not room for such a person in the world. And with her pity disgust mingled. She was ashamed at having borne such a son, she who had always been so respectable and so full of ideas. Was he really the little boy to whom she had taught the use of his stops and buttons, and to whom she had given his first lessons in the Book? The very hair that disfigured his lip showed that he was reverting to some savage type. On atavism the Machine can have no mercy.

"There was a handle, and I did catch it. I hung tranced over the darkness and heard the hum of these workings as the last whisper in a dying dream. All the things I had cared about and all the people I had spoken to through tubes appeared infinitely little. Meanwhile the handle revolved. My weight had set something in motion and I span slowly, and then—

"I cannot describe it. I was lying with my face to the sunshine. Blood poured from my nose and ears and I heard a tremendous roaring. The stopper, with me clinging to it, had simply been blown out of the earth, and the air that we make down here was escaping through the vent into the air above. It burst up like a fountain. I crawled back to it—for the upper air hurts—and, as it were, I took great sips from the edge. My respirator had flown goodness knows where, my clothes were torn. I just lay with my lips close to the hole, and I sipped until the bleeding stopped. You can imagine nothing so curious. This hollow in the grass—I will speak of it in a minute,—the sun shining into it, not brilliantly but through marbled clouds,—the peace, the nonchalance, the sense of space, and, brushing my cheek, the roaring fountain of our artificial air! Soon I spied my respirator, bobbing up and down in the current high above my head, and higher still were many air-ships. But no one ever looks out of air-ships, and in my case they could not have picked me up. There I was, stranded. The sun shone a little way down the shaft, and revealed the topmost rung of the ladder, but it was hopeless trying to reach it. I should either have been tossed up again by the escape, or else have fallen in, and died. I could only lie on the grass, sipping and sipping, and from time to time glancing around me.

"I knew that I was in Wessex, for I had taken care to go to a lecture on the subject before starting. Wessex lies above the room in which we are talking now. It was once an important state. Its kings held all the southern coast from the Andredswald to Cornwall, while the Wansdyke protected them on the north, running over the high ground. The lecturer was only concerned with the rise of Wessex, so I do not know how long it remained an international power, nor would the knowledge have assisted me. To tell the truth I could do nothing but laugh, during this part. There was I, with a pneumatic stopper by my side and a respirator bobbing over my head, imprisoned, all three of us, in a grass-grown hollow that was edged with fern."

Then he grew grave again.

"Lucky for me that it was a hollow. For the air began to fall back into it and to fill it as water fills a bowl. I could crawl about. Presently I stood. I breathed a mixture, in which the air that hurts predominated whenever I tried to climb the sides. This was not so bad. I had not lost my tabloids and remained ridiculously cheerful, and as for the Machine, I forgot about it altogether. My one aim now was to get to the top, where the ferns were, and to view whatever objects lay beyond.

"I rushed the slope. The new air was still too bitter for me and I came rolling back, after a momentary vision of something gray. The sun grew very feeble, and I remembered that he was in Scorpio—I had been to a lecture on that too. If the sun is in Scorpio and you are in Wessex, it means that you must be as quick as you can, or it will get too dark. (This is the first bit of useful information I have ever got from a lecture, and I expect it will be the last.) It made me try frantically to breathe the new air, and to advance as far as I dared out of my pond. The hollow filled so slowly. At times I thought that the fountain played with less vigor. My respirator seemed to dance nearer the earth; the roar was decreasing."

He broke off.

"I don't think this is interesting you. The rest will interest you even less. There are no ideas in it, and I wish that I had not troubled you to come. We are too different, mother."

She told him to continue.

"It was evening before I climbed the bank. The sun had very nearly slipped out of the sky by this time, and I could not get a good view. You, who have just crossed the Roof of the World, will not want to hear an account of the little hills that I saw—low colorless hills. But to me they were living and the turf that covered them was a skin, under which their muscles rippled, and I felt that those hills had called with incalculable force to men in the past, and that men had loved them. Now they sleep—perhaps for ever. They commune with humanity in dreams. Happy the man, happy the woman, who awakes the hills of Wessex. For though they sleep, they will never die."

His voice rose passionately.

"Cannot you see, cannot all your lecturers see, that it is we who are dying, and that down here the only thing that really lives is the Machine? We created the Machine, to do our will, but we cannot make it do our will now. It has robbed us of the sense of space and of the sense of touch, it has blurred every human relation and narrowed down love to a carnal act, it has paralyzed our bodies and our wills, and now it compels us to worship it. The Machine develops—but not on our lines. The Machine proceeds—but not to our goal. We only exist as the blood corpuscles that course through its arteries, and if it could work without us, it would let us die. Oh, I have no remedy— or, at least, only one—to tell men again and again that I have seen the hills of Wessex as Aelfrid saw them when he overthrew the Danes.

"So the sun set. I forgot to mention that a belt of mist lay between my hill and other hills, and that it was the color of pearl."

He broke off for the second time.

"Go on," said his mother wearily.

He shook his head.

"Go on. Nothing that you say can distress me now. I am hardened."

"I had meant to tell you the rest, but I cannot: I know that I cannot: good-bye."

Vashti stood irresolute. All her nerves were tingling with his blasphemies. But she was also inquisitive.

"This is unfair," she complained. "You have called me across the world to hear your story, and hear it I will. Tell me—as briefly as possible, for this is a disastrous waste of time—tell me how you returned to civilization."

"Oh,—that!" he said, starting. "You would like to hear about civilization. Certainly. Had I got to where my respirator fell down?"

"No—but I understand everything now. You put on your respirator, and managed to walk along the surface of the earth to a vomitory, and there your conduct was reported to the Central Committee."

"By no means."

He passed his hand over his forehead, as if dispelling some strong impression. Then, resuming his narrative, he warmed to it again.

"My respirator fell about sunset. I had mentioned that the fountain seemed feebler, had I not?"

"Yes."

"About sunset, it let the respirator fall. As I said, I had entirely forgotten about the Machine, and I paid no great attention at the time, being occupied with other things. I had my pool of air, into which I could dip when the outer keenness became intolerable, and which would possibly remain for days, provided that no wind sprang up to disperse it. Not until it was too late, did I realize what the stoppage of the escape implied. You see—the gap in the tunnel had been mended; the Mending Apparatus, the Mending Apparatus, was after me.

"One other warning I had, but I neglected it. The sky at night was clearer than it had been in the day, and the moon, which was about half the sky behind the sun, shone into the dell at moments quite brightly. I was in my usual place—on the boundary between the two atmospheres—when I thought I saw something dark move across the bottom of the dell, and vanish into the shaft. In my folly, I ran down. I bent over and listened, and I thought I heard a faint scraping noise in the depths.

"At this—but it was too late—I took alarm. I determined to put on my respirator and to walk right out of the dell. But my respirator had gone. I knew exactly where it had fallen—between the stopper and the aperture—and I could even feel the mark that it had made in the turf. It had gone, and I realized that something evil was at work, and I had better escape to the other air, and, if I must die, die running towards the cloud that had been the color of a pearl. I never started. Out of the shaft—it is too horrible. A worm, a long white worm, had crawled out of the shaft and was gliding over the moonlit grass.

"I screamed. I did everything that I should not have done, I stamped upon the creature instead of flying from it, and it at once curled round the ankle. Then we fought. The worm let me run all over the dell, but edged up my leg as I ran. 'Help!' I cried. (That part is too awful. It belongs to the part that you will never know.) 'Help!' I cried. (Why cannot we suffer in silence?) 'Help!' I cried. Then my feet were wound together, I fell, I was dragged away from the dear ferns and the living hills, and past the great metal stopper (I can tell you this part), and I thought it might save me again if I caught hold of the handle. It also was enwrapped, it also. Oh, the whole dell was full of the things. They were searching it in all directions, they were denuding it, and the white snouts of others peeped out of the hole, ready if needed. Everything that could be moved they brought—brushwood, bundles of fern, everything, and down we all went intertwined into hell. The last things that I saw, ere the stopper closed after us, were certain stars, and I felt that a man of my sort lived in the sky. For I did fight, I fought till the very end, and it was only my head hitting against the ladder that quieted me. I woke up in this room. The worms had vanished. I was surrounded by artificial air, artificial light, artificial peace, and my friends were calling to me down speaking-tubes to know whether I had come across any new ideas lately."

Here his story ended. Discussion of it was impossible, and Vashti turned to go.

"It will end in Homelessness," she said quietly.

"I wish it would," retorted Kuno.

"The Machine has been most merciful."

"I prefer the mercy of God."

"By that superstitious phrase, do you mean that you could live in the outer air?"

"Yes."

"Have you ever seen, round the vomitories, the bones of those who were extruded after the Great Rebellion?"

"Yes."

"They were left where they perished for our edification. A few crawled away, but they perished, too—who can doubt it? And so with the Homeless of our own day. The surface of the earth supports life no longer."

"Indeed."

"Ferns and a little grass may survive, but all higher forms have perished. Has any air-ship detected them?"

"No."

"Has any lecturer dealt with them?"

"No."

"Then why this obstinacy?"

"Because I have seen them," he exploded.

"Seen *what?*"

"Because I have seen her in the twilight—because she came to my help when I called—because she, too, was entangled by the worms, and, luckier than I, was killed by one of them piercing her throat."

He was mad. Vashti departed, nor, in the troubles that followed, did she ever see his face again.

3. THE HOMELESS

During the years that followed Kuno's escapade, two important developments took place in the Machine. On the surface they were revolutionary, but in either case men's minds had been prepared beforehand, and they did but express tendencies that were latent already.

The first of these was the abolition of respirators.

Advanced thinkers, like Vashti, had always held it foolish to visit the surface of the earth. Air-ships might be necessary, but what was the good of going out for mere curiosity and crawling along for a mile or two in a terrestrial motor? The habit was vulgar and perhaps faintly improper: it was unproductive of ideas, and had no connection with the habits that really mattered. So respirators were abolished, and with them, of course, the terrestrial motors, and except for a few lecturers, who complained that they were debarred access to their subject-matter, the development was accepted quietly. Those who still wanted to know what the earth was like had after all only to listen to some gramophone, or to look into some cinematophote. And even the lecturers acquiesced when they found that a lecture on the sea was none the less stimulating when compiled out of other lectures that had already been delivered on the same subject. "Beware of first-hand ideas!" exclaimed one of the most advanced of them. "First-hand ideas do not really exist. They are but the physical impressions produced by love and fear, and on this gross foundation who could erect a philosophy? Let your ideas be second-hand, and if possible tenth-hand, for then they will be far removed from that disturbing element—direct observation. Do not learn anything about this subject of mine—the French Revolution. Learn instead what I think that Enicharmon thought Urizen thought Gutch thought Ho-Yung thought Chi-Bo-Sing thought Lafcadio Hearn thought Carlyle thought Mirabeau said about the French Revolution. Through the medium of these eight great minds, the blood that was shed at Paris and the windows that were broken at Versailles will be clarified to an idea which you may employ most profitably in your daily lives. But be sure that the intermediates are many and varied, for in history one authority exists to counteract another. Urizen must counteract the skepticism of Ho-Yung and Enicharmon, I must myself counteract the impetuosity of Gutch. You who listen to me are in a better position to judge about the French Revolution than I am. Your descendants will be even in a better position than you, for they will learn what you think I think, and yet another intermediate will be added to the chain. And in time"—his voice rose—"there will come a generation that has got beyond facts, beyond impressions, a generation absolutely colorless, a generation

'seraphically free
From taint of personality.'

which will see the French Revolution not as it happened, nor as they would like it to have happened, but as it would have happened, had it taken place in the days of the Machine."

Tremendous applause greeted this lecture, which did but voice a feeling already latent in the minds of men—a feeling that terrestrial facts must be ignored, and that the abolition of respirators was a positive gain. It was even suggested that air-ships should be abolished too. This was not done, because air-ships had somehow worked themselves into the Machine's system. But year by year they were used less, and mentioned less by thoughtful men.

The second great development was the reëstablishment of religion.

This, too, had been voiced in the celebrated lecture. No one could mistake the reverent tone in which the peroration had concluded, and it awakened a responsive echo in the heart of each. Those who had long worshiped silently, now began to talk. They described the strange feeling of peace that came over them when they handled the Book of the Machine, the pleasure that it was to repeat certain numerals out of it, however little meaning those numerals conveyed to the outward ear, the ecstasy of touching a button, however unimportant, or of ringing an electric bell, however superfluously.

"The Machine," they exclaimed, "feeds us and clothes us and houses us; through it we speak to one another, through it we see one another, in it we have our being. The Machine is the friend of ideas and the enemy of superstition: the Machine is omnipotent, eternal; blessed is the Machine." And before long this allocution was printed on the first page of the Book, and in subsequent editions the ritual swelled into a complicated system of praise and prayer. The word "religion" was sedulously avoided, and in theory the Machine was still the creation and the implement of man. But in practice all, save a few retrogrades, worshiped it as divine. Nor was it worshiped in unity. One believer would be chiefly impressed by the blue optic plates, through which he saw other believers; another by the mending apparatus, which simple Kuno had compared to worms; another by the lifts; another by the Book. And each would pray to this or to that, and ask it to intercede for him with the Machine as a whole. Persecution—that also was present. It did not break out, for reasons that will be set forward shortly. But it was latent, and all who did not accept the minimum known as "undenominational Mechanism" lived in danger of Homelessness, which means death, as we know.

To attribute these two great developments to the Central Committee, is to take a very narrow view of civilization. The Central Committee announced the developments, it is true, but they were no more the cause of them than were the kings of the imperialistic period the cause of war. Rather did they yield to some invincible pressure, which came no one knew whither, and which, when gratified, was succeeded by some new pressure equally invincible. To such a state of affairs it is convenient to give the name of progress. No one confessed the Machine was out of hand. Year by year it was served with increased efficiency and decreased intelligence. The better a man knew his own duties upon it, the less he understood the duties of his neighbor, and in all the world there was not one who understood the monster as a whole. Those master brains had perished. They had left full directions, it is true, and their successors had each of them mastered a portion of those directions. But Humanity, in its desire for comfort, had overreached itself. It had exploited the riches of nature too far. Quietly and complacently, it was sinking into decadence, and progress had come to mean the progress of the Machine.

As for Vashti, her life went peacefully forward until the final disaster. She made her room dark and slept; she awoke and made the room light. She lectured and attended lectures. She exchanged ideas with her innumerable friends and believed she was growing more spiritual. At times a friend was granted Euthanasia, and left his or her room for the homelessness that is beyond all human conception. Vashti did not much mind. After an unsuccessful lecture, she would sometimes ask for Euthanasia herself. But the death-rate was not permitted to exceed the birth-rate, and the Machine had hitherto refused it to her.

The troubles began quietly, long before she was conscious of them.

One day she was astonished at receiving a message from her son. They never communicated, having nothing in common, and she had only heard indirectly that he was still alive, and had been transferred from the northern hemisphere, where he had behaved so mischievously, to the southern—indeed, to a room not far from her own.

"Does he want me to visit him?" she thought. "Never again, never. And I have not the time."

No, it was madness of another kind.

He refused to visualize his face upon the blue plate, and speaking out of the darkness with solemnity said:

"The Machine stops."

"What do you say?"

"The Machine is stopping, I know it, I know the signs."

She burst into a peal of laughter. He heard her and was angry, and they spoke no more.

"Can you imagine anything more absurd?" she cried to a friend. "A man who was my son believes that the Machine is stopping. It would be impious if it was not mad."

"The Machine is stopping?" her friend replied. "What does that mean? The phrase conveys nothing to me."

"Nor to me."

"He does not refer, I suppose, to the trouble there has been lately with the music?"

"Oh, no, of course not. Let us talk about music."

"Have you complained to the authorities?"

"Yes, and they say it wants mending, and referred me to the Committee of the Mending Apparatus. I complained of those curious gasping sighs that disfigure the symphonies of the Brisbane school. They sound like someone in pain. The Committee of the Mending Apparatus say that it shall be remedied shortly."

Obscurely worried, she resumed her life. For one thing, the defect in the music irritated her. For another thing, she could not forget Kuno's speech. If he had known that the music was out of repair—he could not know it, for he detested music—if he had known that it was wrong, "the Machine stops" was exactly the venomous sort of remark he would have made. Of course he had made it at a venture, but the coincidence annoyed her, and she spoke with some petulance to the Committee of the Mending Apparatus.

They replied, as before, that the defect would be set right shortly.

"Shortly! At once!" she retorted. "Why should I be worried by imperfect music? Things are always put right at once. If you do not mend it at once, I shall complain to the Central Committee."

"No personal complaints are received by the Central Committee," the Committee of the Mending Apparatus replied.

"Through whom am I to make my complaint, then?"

"Through us."

"I complain then."

"Your complaint shall be forwarded in its turn."

"Have others complained?"

This question was unmechanical, and the Committee of the Mending Apparatus refused to answer it.

"It is too bad!" she exclaimed to another of her friends. "There never was such an unfortunate woman as myself. I can never be sure of my music now. It gets worse and worse each time I summon it."

"I too have my troubles," the friend replied. "Sometimes my ideas are interrupted by a slight jarring noise."

"What is it?"

"I do not know whether it is inside my head, or inside the wall."

"Complain, in either case."

"I have complained, and my complaint will be forwarded in its turn to the Central Committee."

Time passed, and they resented the defects no longer. The defects had not been remedied, but the human tissues in that latter day had become so subservient, that they readily adapted themselves to every caprice of the Machine. The sigh at the crisis of the Brisbane symphony no longer irritated Vashti; she accepted it as part of the melody. The jarring noise, whether in the head or in the wall, was no longer resented by her friend. And so with the moldy artificial fruit, so with the bath water that began to stink, so with the defective rhymes that the poetry machine had taken to emit. All were bitterly complained of at first, and then acquiesced in and forgotten. Things went from bad to worse unchallenged.

It was otherwise with the failure of the sleeping apparatus. That was a more serious stoppage. There came a day when over the whole world—in Sumatra, in Wessex, in the innumerable cities of Courland and Brazil—the beds, when summoned by their tired owners, failed to appear. It may seem a ludicrous matter, but from it we may date the collapse of humanity. The Committee responsible for the failure was assailed by complainants, whom it referred, as usual, to the Committee of the Mending Apparatus, who in its turn assured them that their complaints would be forwarded to the Central Committee. But the discontent grew, for mankind was not yet sufficiently adaptable to do without sleeping.

"Someone is meddling with the Machine—" they began.

"Someone is trying to make himself king, to reintroduce the personal element."

"Punish that man with Homelessness."

"To the rescue! Avenge the Machine! Avenge the Machine!"

"War! Kill the man!"

But the Committee of the Mending Apparatus now came forward, and allayed the panic with well-chosen words. It confessed that the Mending Apparatus was itself in need of repair.

The effect of this frank confession was admirable.

"Of course," said a famous lecturer—he of the French Revolution, who gilded each new decay with splendor—"of course we shall not press our complaints now. The Mending Apparatus has treated us so well in the past that we all sympathize with it, and will wait patiently for its recovery. In its own good time it will resume its duties. Meanwhile let us do without our beds, our tabloids, our other little wants. Such, I feel sure, would be the wish of the Machine."

Thousands of miles away his audience applauded. The Machine still linked them. Under the seas, beneath the roots of the mountains, ran the wires through which they saw and heard, the enormous eyes and ears that were their heritage, and the hum of many workings clothed their thoughts in one garment of subserviency. Only the old and the sick remained ungrateful, for it was rumored that Euthanasia, too, was out of order, and that pain had reappeared among men.

It became difficult to read. A blight entered the atmosphere and dulled its luminosity. At times Vashti could scarcely see across her room. The air, too, was foul. Loud were the complaints, impotent the remedies, heroic the tone of the lecturer as he cried: "Courage, courage! What matter so long as the Machine goes on? To it the darkness and the light are one." And though things improved again after a time, the old brilliancy was never recaptured, and humanity never recovered from its entrance into twilight. There was an hysterical talk of "measures," of "provisional dictatorship," and the inhabitants of Sumatra were asked to familiarize themselves with the workings of the central power station, the said power station being situated in France. But for the most part panic reigned, and men spent their strength praying to their Books, tangible proofs of the Machine's omnipotence. There were gradations of terror—at times came rumors of hope—the Mending Apparatus was almost mended—the enemies of the Machine had been got under—new "nerve-centers" were evolving which would do the work even more magnificently than before. But there came a day when, without the slightest warning, without any previous hint of feebleness, the entire communication-system broke down, all over the world, and the world, as they understood it, ended.

Vashti was lecturing at the time and her earlier remarks had been punctuated with applause. As she proceeded the audience became silent, and at the conclusion there was no sound. Somewhat displeased, she called to a friend who was a specialist in sympathy. No sound: doubtless the friend was sleeping. And so with the next friend whom she tried to summon, and so with the next, until she remembered Kuno's cryptic remark, "The Machine stops."

The phrase still conveyed nothing. If Eternity was stopping it would of course be set going shortly.

For example, there was still a little light and air—the atmosphere had improved a few hours previously. There was still the Book, and while there was the Book there was security.

Then she broke down, for with the cessation of activity came an unexpected terror—silence.

She had never known silence, and the coming of it nearly killed her—it did kill many thousands of people outright. Ever since her birth she had been surrounded by the steady hum. It was to the ear what artificial air was to the lungs, and agonizing pains shot across her head. And scarcely knowing what she did, she stumbled forward and pressed the unfamiliar button, the one that opened the door of her cell.

Now the door of the cell worked on a simple hinge of its own. It was not connected with the central power station, dying far away in France. It opened, rousing immoderate hopes in Vashti, for she thought that the Machine had been mended. It opened, and she saw the dim tunnel that curved far away towards freedom. One look, and then she shrank back. For the tunnel was full of people—she was almost the last in that city to have taken alarm.

People at any time repelled her, and these were nightmares from her worst dreams. People were crawling about, people were screaming, whimpering, gasping for breath, touching each other, vanishing in the dark, and ever and anon being pushed off the platform on to the live rail. Some were fighting round the electric bells, trying to summon trains which could not be summoned. Others were yelling for Euthanasia or for respirators, or blaspheming the Machine. Others stood at the doors of their cells fearing, like herself, either to stop in them or to leave them. And behind all the uproar was silence—the silence which is the voice of the earth and of the generations who have gone.

No—it was worse than solitude. She closed the door again and sat down to wait for the end. The disintegration went on, accompanied by horrible cracks and rumbling. The valves that restrained the Medical Apparatus must have been weakened, for it ruptured and hung hideously from the ceiling. The floor heaved and fell and flung her from her chair. A tube oozed towards her serpent fashion. And at last the final horror approached—light began to ebb, and she knew that civilization's long day was closing.

She whirled round, praying to be saved from this, at any rate, kissing the Book, pressing button after button. The uproar outside was increasing, and even penetrated the wall. Slowly the brilliancy of her cell was dimmed, the reflections faded from her metal switches. Now she could not see the reading-stand, now not the Book, though she held it in her hand. Light followed the flight of sound, air was following light, and the original void returned to the cavern from which it had been so long excluded. Vashti continued to whirl, like the devotees of an earlier religion, screaming, praying, striking at the buttons with bleeding hands.

It was thus that she opened her prison and escaped—escaped in the spirit: at least so it seems to me, ere my meditation closes. That she escapes in the body—I cannot perceive that. She struck, by chance, the switch that released the door, and the rush of foul air on her skin, the loud throbbing whispers in her ears, told her that she was facing the tunnel again, and that tremendous platform on which she had seen men fighting. They were not fighting now. Only the whispers remained, and the little whimpering groans. They were dying by hundreds out in the dark.

She burst into tears.

Tears answered her.

They wept for humanity, those two, not for themselves. They could not bear that this should be the end. Ere silence was completed their hearts were opened, and they knew what had been important on the earth. Man, the flower of all flesh, the noblest of all creatures visible, man who had once made god in his image, and had mirrored his strength on the constellations, beautiful naked man was dying, strangled in the garments that he had woven. Century after century had he toiled, and here was his reward. Truly the garment had seemed heavenly at first, shot with the colors of culture, sewn with the threads of self-denial. And heavenly it had been so long as it was a garment and no more, so long as man could shed it at will and live by the essence that is his soul, and the essence, equally divine, that is his body. The sin against the body—it was for that they wept in chief; the centuries of wrong against the muscles and the nerves, and those five portals by which we can alone apprehend—glozing it over with talk of evolution, until the body was white pap, the home of ideas as colorless, last sloshy stirrings of a spirit that had grasped the stars.

"Where are you?" she sobbed.

His voice in the darkness said, "Here."

"Is there any hope, Kuno?"

"None for us."

"Where are you?"

She crawled towards him over the bodies of the dead. His blood spurted over her hands.

"Quicker," he gasped, "I am dying—but we touch, we talk, not through the Machine."

He kissed her.

"We have come back to our own. We die, but we have recaptured life, as it was in Wessex, when Aelfrid overthrew the Danes. We know what they know outside, they who dwelt in the cloud that is the color of a pearl."

"But, Kuno, is it true? Are there still men on the surface of the earth? Is this—this tunnel, this poisoned darkness—really not the end?"

He replied:

"I have seen them, spoken to them, loved them. They are hiding in the mist and the ferns until our civilization stops. Today they are the Homeless—tomorrow—"

"Oh, tomorrow—some fool will start the Machine again, tomorrow."

"Never," said Kuno, "never. Humanity has learnt its lesson."

As he spoke, the whole city was broken like a honeycomb. An air-ship had sailed in through the vomitory into a ruined wharf. It crashed downwards, exploding as it went, rending gallery after gallery with its wings of steel. For a moment they saw the nations of the dead, and, before they joined them, scraps of the untainted sky.

Judas   *Frank O'Connor*

"Sure you won't be late, Jerry?" said the mother and I going out.

"Am I ever late?" said I, and I laughed.

That was all we said, Michael John, but it stuck in my mind. As I was going down the road I was thinking it was months since I'd taken her to the pictures. Of course, you might think that funny, but after the father's death we were thrown together a lot. And I knew she hated being alone in the house after dark.

At the same time I had my own troubles. You see, Michael John, being an only child I never knocked round the way other fellows did. All the fellows in the office went out with girls, or at any rate they let on they did. They said "Who was the old doll I saw you with last night, Jerry? You'd better mind yourself, or you'll be getting into trouble." To hear them you'd imagine there was no sport in the world, only girls, and that they'd always be getting you into trouble. Paddy Kinnane, for instance, talked like that, and he never saw the way it upset me. I think he thought it was a great compliment. It wasn't until years after that I began to suspect that Paddy's acquaintance with girls was about of one kind with my own.

Then I met Kitty Doherty. Kitty was a hospital nurse, and all the chaps in the office said a fellow should never go with hospital nurses. Ordinary girls were bad enough, but nurses were a fright—they knew too much. I knew when I met Kitty that that was a lie. She was a well-educated superior girl; she lived up the river in a posh locality, and her mother was on all sorts of councils and committees. Kitty was small and wiry; a good-looking girl, always in good humour, and when she talked, she hopped from one thing to another like a robin on a frosty morning.

I used to meet her in the evening up the river road, as if I was walking there by accident and very surprised to see her. "Fancy meeting you!" I'd say or "Well, well, isn't this a great surprise!" Mind you, it usually was, for, no matter how much I was expecting her, I was never prepared for the shock of her presence. Then we'd stand talking for half an hour and I'd see her home. Several times she asked me in, but I was too nervous. I knew I'd lose my head, break the china, use some dirty word, and then go home and cut my throat. Of course, I never asked her to come to the pictures or anything of the sort. She was above that. My only hope was that if I waited long enough I might be able to save her from drowning or the white slavers or something else dramatic, which would show in a modest and dignified way how I felt about her. At the same time I had a bad conscience because I knew I should stay at home more with the mother, but the very thought that I might be missing an opportunity of fishing Kitty out of the river would spoil a whole evening on me.

That night in particular I was nearly distracted. It was three weeks since I'd seen Kitty. I was sure that, at the very least, she was dying and asking for me, and that no one knew my address. A week before, I had felt I simply couldn't bear it any longer, so I had made an excuse and gone down to the post office. I rang up the hospital and asked for Kitty. I fully expected them to say in gloomy tones that Kitty had died half an hour before, and got the shock of my life when the girl at the other end asked my name. I lost my head. "I'm afraid I'm a stranger to Miss Doherty," I said with an embarrassed laugh, "but I have a message for her from a friend."

Then I grew completely panic-stricken. What could a girl like Kitty make of a damned, deliberate lie like that? What else was it but a trap laid by an old and cunning hand? I held the receiver out and looked at it as if it was someone whose neck I was going to wring. "Moynihan," I said to it, "you're mad. An asylum, Moynihan, is the only place for you."

I heard Kitty's voice, not in my ear at all, but in the telephone booth as though she were standing before me, and nearly dropped the receiver in terror. Then I raised it and asked in what I thought of as a French accent: "Who is dat speaking, please?" "This is Kitty Doherty," she replied impatiently. "Who are you?"

That was exactly what I was wondering myself. "I am Monsieur Bertrand," I went on cautiously. "I am afraid I have the wrong number. I am so sorry." Then I put down the receiver carefully and thought how nice it would be if only I had a penknife handy to cut my throat with. It's funny, but from the moment I met Kitty I was always coveting sharp things like razors and penknives.

After that an awful idea dawned on me. Of course, I should have thought of it before, but, as you can see, I wasn't exactly knowledgeable where girls were concerned. I began to see that I wasn't meeting Kitty for the very good reason that Kitty didn't want to meet me. What her reason was, I could only imagine, but imagination was my strong point. I examined my conscience to see what I might have said to her. I remembered every remark I had made. The reason was only too clear. Every single remark I had made was either brutal, indecent or disgusting. I had talked of Paddy Kinnane as a fellow who "went with dolls." What could a pure-minded girl think of a chap who naturally used such a phrase except—what unfortunately was quite true—that he had a mind like a cesspit.

But this evening I felt more confident. It was a lovely summer evening with views of hillsides and fields between the gaps in the houses, and it raised my spirits. Perhaps I was wrong; perhaps she hadn't noticed or understood my filthy conversation, perhaps we might meet and walk home together. I walked the full length of the river road and back, and then started to walk it again. The crowds were thinning out as fellows and girls slipped off up the lanes or down to the river-bank, courting. As the streets went out like lamps about me, my hopes sank lower and lower. I saw clearly that she was avoiding me; that she knew I was not the quiet, good-natured fellow I let on to be but a volcano of brutality and lust. "Lust, lust, lust!" I hissed to myself, clenching my fists. I could have forgiven myself anything but the lust.

Then I glanced up and saw her on a tram. I instantly forgot about the lust and smiled and waved my cap to her, but she was looking ahead and didn't see me. I raced after the car, intending to jump onto it, to sit in one of the back seats on top where she would not see me, and then say in astonishment as she got off "Fancy meeting you here!" But as if the driver knew what was in my mind, he put on speed, and the old tram went tossing and screeching down the one straight bit of road in the town, and I stood panting in the roadway, smiling as though missing a tram were the best joke in the world, and wishing all the time that I had a penknife and the courage to use it. My position was hopeless!

Then I must have gone a bit mad—really mad, I mean—for I started to race the tram. There were still lots of people out walking, and they stared after me in an incredulous way, so I lifted my fists to my chest in the attitude of a professional runner and dropped into what I fondly hoped would look like a comfortable stride and delude them into the belief that I was in training for a big race. By the time I was finished, I *was* a runner, and full of indignation against the people who still continued to stare at me.

Between my running and the tram's halts I just managed to keep it in view as far as the other side of town. When I saw Kitty get off and go up a hilly street, I collapsed and was only just able to drag myself after her. When she went into a house on a terrace, I sat on the high curb with my head between my knees until the panting stopped. At any rate I felt safe. I could afford to rest, could walk up and down before the house until she came out, and accost her with an innocent smile and say "Fancy meeting you!"

But my luck was dead out that night. As I was walking up and down, close enough to the house to keep it in view but not close enough to be observed from the windows, I saw a tall man strolling up at the opposite side of the road and my heart sank. It was Paddy Kinnane.

"Hallo, Jerry," he chuckled with that knowing grin he put on whenever he wanted to compliment you on being discovered in a compromising situation. "What are you doing here?"

"Just waiting for a chap I had a date with, Paddy," I said, trying to sound casual.

"Looks more as if you were waiting for an old doll, to me," Paddy said flatteringly. "Still waters run deep. When are you supposed to be meeting him?"

Cripes, I didn't even know what the time was!

"Half eight," I said at random.

"Half eight?" said Paddy. " 'Tis nearly nine now."

"Ah, he's a most unpunctual fellow," I said. "He's always the same. He'll turn up all right."

"I may as well wait with you," said Paddy, leaning against the wall and taking out a packet of cigarettes. "You might find yourself stuck by the end of the evening. There's people in this town that have no consideration for anyone."

That was Paddy all out: a heart of gold; no trouble too much for him if he could do you a good turn—I'd have loved to strangle him.

"Ah, to hell with him!" I said impatiently. "I won't bother waiting. It only struck me this minute that I have another appointment up the Western Road. You'll excuse me now, Paddy. I'll tell you all about it another time."

And away I went hell-for-leather to the tram. I mounted it and went on to the other terminus, near Kitty's house. There, at least, Paddy Kinnane could not get at me. I sat on the river wall in the dusk. The moon was rising, and every quarter of an hour a tram came grunting and squeaking over the old bridge and went black-out while the conductor switched his trolley. Each time I got off the wall and stood on the curb in the moonlight, searching for Kitty among the passengers. Then a policeman came along, and, as he seemed to be watching me, I slunk slowly off up the hill and stood against a wall in shadow. There was a high wall at the other side of the road as well, and behind it the roof of a house was cut out of the sky in moonlight. Every now and then a tram came in and people passed, and the snatches of conversation I caught were like the warmth from an open door to the heart of a homeless man. It was quite clear now that my position was hopeless. If Kitty had walked or been driven she could have reached home from the opposite direction. She could be at home in bed by now. The last tram came and went, and still there was no Kitty, and still I hung on despairingly. While one glimmer of a chance remained I could not go home.

Then I heard a woman's step. I couldn't even pretend to myself that it might be Kitty until she suddenly shuffled past me with that hasty little walk of hers. I started and called her name. She glanced quickly over her shoulder and, seeing a man emerge from the shadow, took fright and ran. I ran too, but she put on speed and began to outdistance me. At that I despaired. I stood on the pavement and shouted after her at the top of my voice.

"Kitty! Kitty, for God's sake, wait!"

She ran a few steps farther and then halted incredulously. She looked back, and then turned and slowly retraced her steps.

"Jerry Moynihan!" she whispered in astonishment. "What are you doing here?"

I was summoning strength to tell her that I had happened to be taking a stroll in that direction and was astonished to see her when I

realized the improbability of it and began to cry instead. Then I
laughed. It was hysteria, I suppose. But Kitty had had a bad fright and,
now she was getting over it, she was as cross as two sticks.

"What's wrong with you, I say?" she snapped. "Are you out of your
mind or what?"

"But I didn't see you for weeks," I burst out.

"I know," she replied. "I wasn't out. What about it?"

"I thought it might be something I said to you," I said desperately.

"What did you say?" she asked in bewilderment, but I couldn't repeat the hideous things I had already said. Perhaps, after all, she hadn't
noticed them!

"How do I know?"

"Oh, it's not that," she said impatiently. "It's just Mother."

"Why?" I asked almost joyously. "Is there something wrong with
her?"

"Ah, no, but she made such a fuss about it. I felt it wasn't worth it."

"A fuss? What did she make a fuss about?"

"About you, of course," Kitty said in exasperation.

"But what did I do?" I asked, clutching my head. This was worse
than anything I had ever imagined. This was terrible!

"You didn't do anything, but people were talking about us. And you
wouldn't come in and be introduced like anyone else. I know she's a
bit of a fool, and her head is stuffed with old nonsense about her
family. I could never see that they were different to anyone else, and
anyway she married a commercial traveller herself, so she has nothing
to talk about. Still, you needn't be so superior."

I felt cold shivers run through me. I had thought of Kitty as a secret
between God, herself, and me and assumed that she only knew the
half of it. Now it seemed I didn't even know the half. People were
talking about us! I was superior! What next?

"But what has she against me?" I asked despairingly.

"She thinks we're doing a tangle, of course," snapped Kitty as if she
was astonished at my stupidity, "and I suppose she imagines you're not
grand enough for a great-great-grandniece of Daniel O'Connell. I told
her you were above that sort of thing, but she wouldn't believe me. She
said I was a deep, callous, crafty little intriguer and I hadn't a drop of
Daniel O'Connell's blood in my veins." Kitty giggled at the thought of
herself as an intriguer, and no wonder.

"That's all she knows," I said despairingly.

"I know," Kitty agreed. "She has no sense. And anyway she has no reason to think I'm telling lies. Cissy and I always had fellows, and we spooned with them all over the shop under her very nose, so I don't see why she thinks I'm trying to conceal anything."

At this I began to laugh like an idiot. This was worse than appalling. This was a nightmare. Kitty, whom I had thought so angelic, talking in cold blood about "spooning" with fellows all over the house. Even the bad women in the books I had read didn't talk about love-making in that cold-blooded way. Madame Bovary herself had at least the decency to pretend that she didn't like it. It was another door opening on the outside world, but Kitty thought I was laughing at her and started to apologize.

"Of course, I had no sense at the time," she said. "You were the first fellow I met that treated me properly. The others only wanted to fool around, and now, because I don't like it, Mother thinks I'm into something ghastly. I told her I liked you better than any fellow I knew, but that I'd grown out of all that sort of thing."

"And what did she say to that?" I asked fiercely. I was beginning to see that imagination wasn't enough; that all round me there was an objective reality that was a thousand times more nightmarish than any fantasy of my own. I couldn't hear enough about it, though at the same time it turned my stomach.

"Ah, I told you she was silly," Kitty said in embarrassment.

"Go on!" I shouted. "I want to know."

"Well," said Kitty with a demure grin, "she said you were a deep, designing guttersnipe who knew exactly how to get round featherpated little idiots like me. . . . You see, it's quite hopeless. The woman is common. She doesn't understand."

"Oh, God!" I said almost in tears. "I only wish she was right."

"Why do you wish she was right?" Kitty asked with real curiosity.

"Because then I'd have some chance of you," I said.

"Oh!" said Kitty, as if this was news to her. "To tell you the truth," she added after a moment, "I thought you were a bit keen at first, but then I wasn't sure. When you didn't kiss me or anything, I mean."

"God," I said bitterly, "when I think what I've been through in the past few weeks!"

"I know," said Kitty, biting her lip. "I was a bit fed up too."

Then we said nothing for a few moments.

"You're sure you mean it?" she asked suspiciously.

"But I tell you I was on the point of committing suicide," I said angrily.

"What good would that be?" she asked with another shrug, and this time she looked at me and laughed outright—the little jade!

I insisted on telling her about my prospects. She didn't want to hear about my prospects; she wanted me to kiss her, but that seemed to me a very sissy sort of occupation, so I told her just the same, in the intervals. It was as if a stone had been lifted off my heart, and I went home in the moonlight, singing. Then I heard the clock strike, and the singing stopped. I remembered the mother's "Sure you won't be late?" and my own "Am I ever late?" This was desperation too, but of a different sort.

The door was ajar and the kitchen in darkness. I saw her sitting before the fire by herself, and just as I was about to throw my arms round her, I smelt Kitty's perfume and was afraid to go near her. God help us, as though that would have told her anything!

"Hello, Mum," I said with a nervous laugh, rubbing my hands. "You're all in darkness."

"You'll have a cup of tea?" she said.

"I might as well."

"What time is it?" she said, lighting the gas. "You're very late."

"I met a fellow from the office," I said, but at the same time I was stung by the complaint in her tone.

"You frightened me," she said with a little whimper. "I didn't know what happened to you. What kept you at all?"

"Oh, what do you think?" I said, goaded by my own sense of guilt. "Drinking and blackguarding as usual."

I could have bitten my tongue off as I said it; it sounded so cruel, as if some stranger had said it instead of me. She turned to me with a frightened stare as if she were seeing the stranger too, and somehow I couldn't bear it.

"God Almighty!" I said. "A fellow can have no life in his own house."

I went hastily upstairs, lit the candle, undressed, and got into bed. A chap could be a drunkard and blackguard and not be made to suffer what I was being made to suffer for being out late one single night. This, I felt, was what you got for being a good son.

"Jerry," she called from the foot of the stairs, "will I bring you up your cup?"

"I don't want it now, thanks," I said.

I heard her sigh and turn away. Then she locked the doors, front and back. She didn't wash up, and I knew that my cup of tea was standing on the table with a saucer on top in case I changed my mind. She came slowly upstairs and her walk was that of an old woman. I blew out the candle before she reached the landing, in case she came in to ask if I wanted anything else, and the moonlight came in the attic window and brought me memories of Kitty. But every time I tried to imagine her face as she grinned up at me, waiting for me to kiss her, it was the mother's face that came up instead, with that look like a child's when you strike him for the first time—as if he suddenly saw the stranger in you. I remembered all our life together from the night my father died; our early Mass on Sunday; our visits to the pictures, and our plans for the future, and Christ! Michael John, it was as if I was inside her mind while she sat by the fire waiting for the blow to fall. And now it had fallen, and I was a stranger to her, and nothing I could ever do would make us the same to one another again. There was something like a cannon-ball stuck in my chest, and I lay awake till the cocks started crowing. Then I could bear it no longer. I went out on the landing and listened.

"Are you awake, Mother?" I asked in a whisper.

"What is it, Jerry?" she replied in alarm, and I knew that she hadn't slept any more than I had.

"I only came to say I was sorry," I said, opening the door of her room, and then as I saw her sitting up in bed under the Sacred Heart lamp, the cannon-ball burst inside me and I began to cry like a kid.

"Oh, child, child, child!" she exclaimed, "what are you crying for at all, my little boy?" She spread out her arms to me. I went to her and she hugged me and rocked me as she did when I was only a nipper. "Oh, oh, oh," she was saying to herself in a whisper, "my storeen bawn, my little man!"—all the names she hadn't called me in years. That was all we said. I couldn't bring myself to tell her what I had done, nor could she confess to me that she was jealous: all she could do was to try and comfort me for the way I'd hurt her, to make up to me for the nature she had given me. "My storeen bawn!" she said. "My little man!"

Two Little Soldiers

Guy de Maupassant

Every Sunday, the moment they were dismissed, the two little soldiers made off. Once outside the barracks, they struck out to the right through Courbevoie, walking with long rapid strides, as though they were on a march.

When they were beyond the last of the houses, they slackened pace along the bare, dusty roadway which goes toward Bézons.

They were both small and thin, and looked quite lost in their coats, which were too big and too long. Their sleeves hung down over their hands, and they found their enormous red breeches, which compelled them to waddle, very much in the way. Under their stiff, high helmets their faces had little character—two poor, sallow Breton faces, simple with an almost animal simplicity, and with gentle and quiet blue eyes.

They never conversed during these walks, but went straight on, each with the same thought in his head. This thought atoned for the lack of conversation; it was this, that just inside the little wood near Les Champioux they had found a place which reminded them of their own country, where they could feel happy again.

When they arrived under the trees where the roads from Colombes and from Chatou cross, they would take off their heavy helmets and wipe their foreheads. They always halted on the Bézons bridge to look at the Seine, and would remain there two or three minutes, bent double, leaning on the parapet.

Sometimes they would gaze out over the great basin of Argenteuil, where the skiffs might be seen scudding, with their white, careening sails, recalling perhaps the look of the Breton waters, the harbor of Vanne, near which they lived, and the fishing-boats standing out across the Morbihan to the open sea.

Just beyond the Seine they bought their provisions from a sausage merchant, a baker, and a wine-seller. A piece of blood-pudding, four sous' worth of bread, and a liter of "petit bleu" constituted the provisions, which they carried off in their handkerchiefs. After they had left Bézons they traveled slowly and began to talk.

In front of them a barren plain studded with clumps of trees led to the wood, to the little wood which had seemed to them to resemble the one at Kermarivan. Grainfields and hayfields bordered the narrow path,

126

which lost itself in the young greenness of the crops, and Jean Kerderen would always say to Luc le Ganidec:

"It looks like it does near Plounivon."

"Yes; exactly."

Side by side they strolled, their souls filled with vague memories of their own country, with awakened images as naïve as the pictures on the colored broadsheets which you buy for a penny. They kept on recognizing, as it were, now a corner of a field, a hedge, a bit of moorland, now a crossroad, now a granite cross. Then, too, they would always stop beside a certain landmark, a great stone, because it looked something like the cromlech at Locneuven.

Every Sunday on arriving at the first clump of trees Luc le Ganidec would cut a switch, a hazel switch, and begin gently to peel off the bark, thinking meanwhile of the folk at home. Jean Kerderen carried the provisions.

From time to time Luc would mention a name, or recall some deed of their childhood in a few brief words, which caused long thoughts. And their own country, their dear, distant country, recaptured them little by little, seizing on their imaginations, and sending to them from afar her shapes, her sounds, her well-known prospects, her odors—odors of the green lands where the salt sea-air was blowing.

No longer conscious of the exhalations of the Parisian stables, on which the earth of the *banlieue*[1] fattens, they scented the perfume of the flowering broom, which the salt breeze of the open sea plucks and bears away. And the sails of the boats from the river banks seemed like the white wings of the coasting vessels seen beyond the great plain which extended from their homes to the very margin of the sea.

They walked with short steps, Luc le Ganidec and Jean Kerderen, content and sad, haunted by a sweet melancholy, by the lingering, ever-present sorrow of a caged animal who remembers his liberty.

By the time that Luc had stripped the slender wand of its bark they reached the corner of the wood where every Sunday they took breakfast. They found the two bricks which they kept hidden in the thicket, and kindled a little fire of twigs, over which to roast the blood-pudding at the end of a bayonet.

When they had breakfasted, eaten their bread to the last crumb, and drunk their wine to the last drop, they remained seated side by side upon the grass, saying nothing, their eyes on the distance, their eyelids

---

[1] Suburbs or outskirts of a town.

drooping, their fingers crossed as at mass, their red legs stretched out beside the poppies of the field. And the leather of their helmets and the brass of their buttons glittered in the ardent sun, making the larks, which sang and hovered above their heads, cease in mid-song.

Toward noon they began to turn their eyes from time to time in the direction of the village of Bézons, because the girl with the cow was coming. She passed by them every Sunday on her way to milk and change the pasture of her cow—the only cow in this district which ever went out of the stable to grass. It was pastured in a narrow field along the edge of the wood a little farther on.

They soon perceived the girl, the only human being within vision, and were gladdened by the brilliant reflections thrown off by the tin milk-pail under the rays of the sun. They never talked about her. They were simply glad to see her, without understanding why.

She was a big strong wench with red hair, burned by the heat of sunny days, a sturdy product of the environs of Paris.

Once, finding them seated in the same place, she said:

"Good morning. You two are always here, aren't you?"

Luc le Ganidec, the bolder, stammered:

"Yes, we come to rest."

That was all. But the next Sunday she laughed on seeing them, laughed with a protecting benevolence and a feminine keenness which knew well enough that they were bashful. And she asked:

"What are you doing there? Are you trying to see the grass grow?"

Luc was cheered up by this, and smiled likewise: "Maybe we are."

"That's pretty slow work," said she.

He answered, still laughing: "Well, yes, it is."

She went on. But coming back with a milk-pail full of milk, she stopped again before them, and said:

"Would you like a little? It will taste like home."

With the instinctive feeling that they were of the same peasant race as she, being herself perhaps also far away from home, she had divined and touched the spot.

They were both touched. Then with some difficulty, she managed to make a little milk run into the neck of the glass bottle in which they carried their wine. And Luc drank first, with little swallows, stopping every minute to see whether he had drunk more than his half. Then he handed the bottle to Jean.

She stood upright before them, her hands on her hips, her pail on the ground at her feet, glad at the pleasure which she had given.

Then she departed, shouting: "*Allons*, adieu! [2] Till next Sunday!"

And as long as they could see her at all, they followed with their eyes her tall silhouette, which faded, growing smaller and smaller, seeming to sink into the verdure of the fields.

When they were leaving the barracks the week after, Jean said to Luc:

"Oughtn't we to buy her something good?"

They were in great embarrassment before the problem of the choice of a delicacy for the girl with the cow. Luc was of the opinion that a little tripe would be the best, but Jean preferred some *berlingots*[3] because he was fond of sweets. His choice fairly made him enthusiastic, and they bought at a grocer's two sous' worth of white and red candies.

They ate their breakfast more rapidly than usual, being nervous with expectation.

Jean saw her first. "There she is!" he cried. Luc added: "Yes, there she is."

While yet some distance off she laughed at seeing them. Then she cried:

"Is everything going as you like it?"

And in unison they asked:

"Are you getting on all right?"

Then she conversed, talked to them of simple things in which they felt an interest—of the weather, of the crops, and of her master.

They were afraid to offer her the candies, which were slowly melting away in Jean's pocket.

At last Luc grew bold, and murmured:

"We have brought you something."

She demanded, "What is it? Tell me!"

Then Jean, blushing up to his ears, managed to get at the little paper cornucopia, and held it out.

She began to eat the little bonbons, rolling them from one cheek to the other where they made little round lumps. The two soldiers, seated before her, gazed at her with emotion and delight.

Then she went to milk her cow, and once more gave them some milk on coming back.

They thought of her all the week; several times they even spoke of her. The next Sunday she sat down with them for a little longer talk;

[2] "Let's say goodbye!"
[3] Sweetmeats made with caramel.

and all three, seated side by side, their eyes lost in the distance, clasping their knees with their hands, told the small doings, the minute details of life in the villages where they had been born, while over there the cow, seeing that the milkmaid had stopped on her way, stretched out toward her its heavy head with its dripping nostrils, and gave a long low to call her.

Soon the girl consented to eat a bit of bread with them and drink a mouthful of wine. She often brought them plums in her pocket, for the season of plums had come. Her presence sharpened the wits of the two little Breton soldiers, and they chattered like two birds.

But, one Tuesday, Luc le Ganidec asked for leave—a thing which had never happened before—and he did not return until ten o'clock at night. Jean racked his brains uneasily for a reason for his comrade's going out in this way.

The next Thursday Luc, having borrowed ten sous from his bed-fellow, again asked and obtained permission to leave the barracks for several hours. When he set off with Jean on their Sunday walk his manner was very queer, quite restless, and quite changed. Kerderen did not understand, but he vaguely suspected something without divining what it could be.

They did not say a word to one another until they reached their usual halting-place, where, from their constant sitting in the same spot the grass was quite worn away. They ate their breakfast slowly. Neither of them felt hungry.

Before long the girl appeared. As on every Sunday, they watched her coming. When she was quite near, Luc rose and made two steps forward. She put her milk-pail on the ground and kissed him. She kissed him passionately, throwing her arms about his neck, without noticing Jean, without remembering that he was there, without even seeing him.

And he sat there desperate, poor Jean, so desperate that he did not understand, his soul quite overwhelmed, but heart bursting, but not yet understanding himself. Then the girl seated herself beside Luc, and they began to chatter.

Jean did not look at them. He now divined why his comrade had gone out twice during the week, and he felt within him a burning grief, a kind of wound, that sense of rending which is caused by treason.

Luc and the girl went off together to change the position of the cow. Jean followed them with his eyes. He saw them departing side by side. The red breeches of his comrade made a bright spot on the road. It was

Luc who picked up the mallet and hammered down the stake to which they tied the beast.

The girl stooped to milk her, while he stroked the cow's sharp spine with a careless hand. Then they left the milk-pail on the grass, and went deep into the wood.

Jean saw nothing but the wall of leaves where they had entered; and he felt himself so troubled that if he had tried to rise he would certainly have fallen. He sat motionless, stupefied by astonishment and suffering, with an agony which was simple but deep. He wanted to cry, to run away, to hide himself, never to see anybody any more.

Soon he saw them issuing from the thicket. They returned slowly, holding each other's hands as in the villages do those who are promised. It was Luc who carried the pail.

They kissed one another again before they separated, and the girl went off after having thrown Jean a friendly "Good evening" and a smile which was full of meaning. Today she no longer thought of offering him any milk.

The two little soldiers sat side by side, motionless as usual, silent and calm, their placid faces betraying nothing of all which troubled their hearts. The sun fell on them. Sometimes the cow lowed, looking at them from afar.

At their usual hour they rose to go back. Luc cut a switch. Jean carried the empty bottle to return it to the wine-seller at Bézons. Then they sallied out upon the bridge, and, as they did every Sunday, stopped several minutes in the middle to watch the water flowing.

Jean leaned, leaned more and more, over the iron railing, as though he saw in the current something which attracted him. Luc said: "Are you trying to drink?" Just as he uttered the last word Jean's head overbalanced his body, his legs described a circle in the air, and the little blue and red soldier fell in a heap, struck the water, and disappeared.

Luc, his tongue paralyzed with anguish, tried in vain to shout. Farther down he saw something stir; then the head of his comrade rose to the surface of the river and sank immediately. Farther still he again perceived a hand, a single hand, which issued from the stream and then disappeared. That was all.

The bargemen who dragged the river did not find the body that day.

Luc set out alone for the barracks, going at a run, his soul filled with despair. He told of the accident, with tears in his eyes, and a husky voice, blowing his nose again and again: "He leaned over—he—he

leaned over—so far—so far that his head turned a somersault; and
—and—so he fell—he fell—"

Choked with emotion, he could say no more. If he had only known!

Adventure   *Sherwood Anderson*

Alice Hindman, a woman of twenty-seven when George Willard [1] was
a mere boy, had lived in Winesburg all her life. She clerked in Winney's
Dry Goods Store and lived with her mother who had married a second
husband.

Alice's step-father was a carriage painter, and given to drink. His
story is an odd one. It will be worth telling some day.

At twenty-seven Alice was tall and somewhat slight. Her head was
large and overshadowed her body. Her shoulders were a little stooped
and her hair and eyes brown. She was very quiet but beneath a placid
exterior a continual ferment went on.

When she was a girl of sixteen and before she began to work in the
store, Alice had an affair with a young man. The young man, named
Ned Currie, was older than Alice. He, like George Willard, was employed on the *Winesburg Eagle* and for a long time he went to see
Alice almost every evening. Together the two walked under the trees
through the streets of the town and talked of what they would do with
their lives. Alice was then a very pretty girl and Ned Currie took her
into his arms and kissed her. He became excited and said things he
did not intend to say and Alice, betrayed by her desire to have something beautiful come into her rather narrow life, also grew excited. She
also talked. The outer crust of her life, all of her natural diffidence and
reserve, was torn away and she gave herself over to the emotions of
love. When, late in the fall of her sixteenth year, Ned Currie went
away to Cleveland where he hoped to get a place on a city newspaper
and rise in the world, she wanted to go with him. With a trembling
voice she told him what was in her mind. "I will work and you can
work," she said. "I do not want to harness you to a needless expense that
will prevent your making progress. Don't marry me now. We will get

---

[1] The central character in Anderson's *Winesburg, Ohio.*

along without that and we can be together. Even though we live in the same house no one will say anything. In the city we will be unknown and people will pay no attention to us."

Ned Currie was puzzled by the determination and abandon of his sweetheart and was also deeply touched. He had wanted the girl to become his mistress but changed his mind. He wanted to protect and care for her. "You don't know what you're talking about," he said sharply; "you may be sure I'll let you do no such thing. As soon as I get a good job I'll come back. For the present you'll have to stay here. It's the only thing we can do."

On the evening before he left Winesburg to take up his new life in the city, Ned Currie went to call on Alice. They walked about through the streets for an hour and then got a rig from Wesley Moyer's livery and went for a drive in the country. The moon came up and they found themselves unable to talk. In his sadness the young man forgot the resolutions he had made regarding his conduct with the girl.

They got out of the buggy at a place where a long meadow ran down to the bank of Wine Creek and there in the dim light became lovers. When at midnight they returned to town they were both glad. It did not seem to them that anything that could happen in the future could blot out the wonder and beauty of the thing that had happened. "Now we will have to stick to each other, whatever happens we will have to do that," Ned Currie said as he left the girl at her father's door.

The young newspaper man did not succeed in getting a place on a Cleveland paper and went west to Chicago. For a time he was lonely and wrote to Alice almost every day. Then he was caught up by the life of the city; he began to make friends and found new interests in life. In Chicago he boarded at a house where there were several women. One of them attracted his attention and he forgot Alice in Winesburg. At the end of a year he had stopped writing letters, and only once in a long time, when he was lonely or when he went into one of the city parks and saw the moon shining on the grass as it had shone that night on the meadow by Wine Creek, did he think of her at all.

In Winesburg the girl who had been loved grew to be a woman. When she was twenty-two years old her father, who owned a harness repair shop, died suddenly. The harness maker was an old soldier, and after a few months his wife received a widow's pension. She used the first money she got to buy a loom and became a weaver of carpets, and Alice got a place in Winney's store. For a number of years nothing could have induced her to believe that Ned Currie would not in the end return to her.

She was glad to be employed because the daily round of toil in the store made the time of waiting seem less long and uninteresting. She began to save money, thinking that when she had saved two or three hundred dollars she would follow her lover to the city and try if her presence would not win back his affections.

Alice did not blame Ned Currie for what had happened in the moonlight in the field, but felt that she could never marry another man. To her the thought of giving to another what she still felt could belong only to Ned seemed monstrous. When other young men tried to attract her attention she would have nothing to do with them. "I am his wife and shall remain his wife whether he comes back or not," she whispered to herself, and for all of her willingness to support herself could not have understood the growing modern idea of a woman's owning herself and giving and taking for her own ends in life.

Alice worked in the dry goods store from eight in the morning until six at night and on three evenings a week went back to the store to stay from seven until nine. As time passed and she became more and more lonely she began to practice the devices common to lonely people. When at night she went upstairs into her own room she knelt on the floor to pray and in her prayers whispered things she wanted to say to her lover. She became attached to inanimate objects, and because it was her own, could not bear to have anyone touch the furniture of her room. The trick of saving money, begun for a purpose, was carried on after the scheme of going to the city to find Ned Currie had been given up. It became a fixed habit, and when she needed new clothes she did not get them. Sometimes on rainy afternoons in the store she got out her bank book and, letting it lie open before her, spent hours dreaming impossible dreams of saving money enough so that the interest would support both herself and her future husband.

"Ned always liked to travel about," she thought. "I'll give him the chance. Some day when we are married and I can save both his money and my own, we will be rich. Then we can travel together all over the world."

In the dry goods store weeks ran into months and months into years as Alice waited and dreamed of her lover's return. Her employer, a grey old man with false teeth and a thin grey mustache that drooped down over his mouth, was not given to conversation, and sometimes, on rainy days and in the winter when a storm raged in Main Street, long hours passed when no customers came in. Alice arranged and rearranged the stock. She stood near the front window where she could look down the deserted street and thought of the evenings when she had walked with Ned Currie and of what he had said. "We will have to stick to each other now." The words echoed and re-echoed through the mind of the maturing woman. Tears came into her eyes. Sometimes when her employer had gone out and she was alone in the store she put her head on the counter and wept. "Oh, Ned, I am waiting," she whispered over and over, and all the time the creeping fear that he would never come back grew stronger within her.

In the spring when the rains have passed and before the long hot days of summer have come, the country about Winesburg is delightful. The town lies in the midst of open fields, but beyond the fields are pleasant patches of woodlands. In the wooded places are many little cloistered nooks, quiet places where lovers go to sit on Sunday afternoons. Through the trees they look out across the fields and see farmers at work about the barns or people driving up and down on the roads. In the town bells ring and occasionally a train passes, looking like a toy thing in the distance.

For several years after Ned Currie went away Alice did not go into the wood with other young people on Sunday, but one day after he had been gone for two or three years and when her loneliness seemed unbearable, she put on her best dress and set out. Finding a little sheltered place from which she could see the town and a long stretch of the fields, she sat down. Fear of age and ineffectuality took possession of her. She could not sit still, and arose. As she stood looking out over the land something, perhaps the thought of never ceasing life as it expresses itself in the flow of the seasons, fixed her mind on the passing years. With a shiver of dread, she realized that for her the beauty and freshness of youth had passed. For the first time she felt that she had been cheated. She did not blame Ned Currie and did not know what to blame. Sadness swept over her. Dropping to her knees, she tried to pray, but instead of prayers words of protest came to her lips. "It is not going to come to me. I will never find happiness. Why do I tell myself lies?" she cried, and an odd sense of relief came with this, her first bold attempt to face the fear that had become a part of her everyday life.

In the year when Alice Hindman became twenty-five two things happened to disturb the dull uneventfulness of her days. Her mother married Bush Milton, the carriage painter of Winesburg, and she herself became a member of the Winesburg Methodist Church. Alice joined the church because she had become frightened by the loneliness of her position in life. Her mother's second marriage had emphasized her isolation. "I am becoming old and queer. If Ned comes he will not want me. In the city where he is living men are perpetually young. There is so much going on that they do not have time to grow old," she told herself with a grim little smile, and went resolutely about the business of becoming acquainted with people. Every Thursday evening when the store had closed she went to a prayer meeting in the basement of the church and on Sunday evening attended a meeting of an organization called The Epworth League.

When Will Hurley, a middle-aged man who clerked in a drug store and who also belonged to the church, offered to walk home with her she did not protest. "Of course I will not let him make a practice of being with me, but if he comes to see me once in a long time there can be no harm in that," she told herself, still determined in her loyalty to Ned Currie.

Without realizing what was happening, Alice was trying feebly at first, but with growing determination, to get a new hold upon life. Beside the drug clerk she walked in silence, but sometimes in the darkness as they went stolidly along she put out her hand and touched softly the folds of his coat. When he left her at the gate before her mother's house she did not go indoors, but stood for a moment by the door. She wanted to call to the drug clerk, to ask him to sit with her in the darkness on the porch before the house, but was afraid he would not understand. "It is not him that I want," she told herself; "I want to avoid being so much alone. If I am not careful I will grow unaccustomed to being with people."

*   *   *

During the early fall of her twenty-seventh year a passionate restlessness took possession of Alice. She could not bear to be in the company of the drug clerk, and when, in the evening, he came to walk with her she sent him away. Her mind became intensely active and when, weary from the long hours of standing behind the counter in the store, she went home and crawled into bed, she could not sleep. With staring eyes she looked into the darkness. Her imagination, like a child awakened from long sleep, played about the room. Deep within her there was something that would not be cheated by phantasies and that demanded some definite answer from life.

Alice took a pillow into her arms and held it tightly against her breasts. Getting out of bed, she arranged a blanket so that in the darkness it looked like a form lying between the sheets and, kneeling beside the bed, she caressed it, whispering words over and over, like a refrain. "Why doesn't something happen? Why am I left here alone?" she muttered. Although she sometimes thought of Ned Currie, she no longer depended on him. Her desire had grown vague. She did not want Ned Currie or any other man. She wanted to be loved, to have something answer the call that was growing louder and louder within her.

And then one night when it rained Alice had an adventure. It frightened and confused her. She had come home from the store at nine and found the house empty. Bush Milton had gone off to town and her mother to the house of a neighbor. Alice went upstairs to her room and undressed in the darkness. For a moment she stood by the window hearing the rain beat against the glass and then a strange desire took possession of her. Without stopping to think of what she intended to do, she ran downstairs through the dark house and out into the rain. As she stood on the little grass plot before the house and felt the cold rain on her body a mad desire to run naked through the streets took possession of her.

She thought that the rain would have some creative and wonderful effect on her body. Not for years had she felt so full of youth and courage. She wanted to leap and run, to cry out, to find some other lonely human and embrace him. On the brick sidewalk before the house a man stumbled homeward. Alice started to run. A wild, desperate mood took possession of her. "What do I care who it is. He is alone, and I will go to him," she thought; and then without stopping to consider the possible result of her madness, called softly. "Wait!" she cried. "Don't go away. Whoever you are, you must wait."

The man on the sidewalk stopped and stood listening. He was an old man and somewhat deaf. Putting his hand to his mouth, he shouted: "What? What say?" he called.

Alice dropped to the ground and lay trembling. She was so frightened at the thought of what she had done that when the man had gone on his way she did not dare get to her feet, but crawled on hands and knees through the grass to the house. When she got to her own room she bolted the door and drew her dressing table across the doorway. Her body shook as with a chill and her hands trembled so that she had difficulty getting into her nightdress. When she got into bed she buried her face in the pillow and wept brokenheartedly. "What is the matter

with me? I will do something dreadful if I am not careful," she thought,
and turning her face to the wall, began trying to force herself to face
bravely the fact that many people must live and die alone, even in
Winesburg.

The Missing One

Ana María Matute
Translation by Gloria Durán

At night they quarreled. They went to bed full of resentment toward
each other. For some time now, this had been the usual pattern. Everybody in town—and especially Maria Laureana, their neighbor—knew
they were a couple who didn't get along. And that, perhaps, was what
made her most bitter. "One shouldn't, after all, wash dirty linen in
public," she repeated to herself, sleeplessly facing the wall. She turned
her back to him, deliberately, ostentatiously. And his body seemed to
slide away like an eel toward the other side of the bed. "He will fall
on the floor," she told herself. Then she heard his snores, and her resentment grew. "He's just a savage, a brute. He has no feelings." She, on the
other hand, was awake. Awake and facing that whitewashed wall, by
her own choice now bound to him.

She was wretched. Yes, why deny it? She was wretched, and she was
paying for her mistake in having married without love. Her mother, a
simple woman, a peasant, had always told her that it was a sin to marry
without love. But she had been proud. It had all been a matter of pride.
It was to get even with Marco that she had married. There was no
other reason. From her childhood she had always been in love with
Marco. Close to the wall in the darkness, tears swelling her eyelids,
Luisa bit her lips as her memory conjured up a happy time, happy in
spite of the poverty of her youth. "The orchards, the harvest of fruit
. . . Marco. . . . Close to the orchard wall, she and Marco . . . the
sun shining, the water murmuring in the trench behind the wall . . .
Marco." How had it all changed? She could hardly bring herself to
recall: Marco had married the eldest daughter of the judge, a girl who
was stupid, dull, ugly and, to cap it all, already getting on in years. But
Marco had married her. "I never thought he would do it. Never." The
realization still hurt her after so many years, though at times she had
forgotten when life, poverty, and daily worries had erased things from

her mind. Down deep the hurt remained.

Then she had married Amadeo, a stranger in town, a miserable worker in the mines, one of those looked down on by even the humblest day laborers. It was a bitter decision, and the very day of the wedding she repented. She didn't love him, nor would she ever love him. There was no way out. "And there you have it: a couple who don't get along. No more, no less. This man has no heart. He doesn't know what tenderness is. One can be poor, but . . . I myself a daughter of a family of sharecroppers . . . well, we villagers have courtesy for each other, consideration. . . . But this man!" Lately her own words surprised her. She was always saying: "This man" instead of Amadeo. "If at least we had had a child. . . ." But they hadn't had one, and they had already been married five long years.

At dawn she heard him get up. Then the sound of his footsteps in the kitchen, the noise of pots and pans. "He's preparing his own breakfast." She felt a childish pleasure. "Let him get it. I'm not going to." A feeling of resentment swept over her. She trembled a little. "Do I really hate him? She closed her eyes, not wanting to think about it. Her mother had always said to her, "To hate is a sin, Luisa." (Since her mother's death, such words, formerly heard mechanically, now seemed sacred, new and terrible.)

Amadeo left for work, just as he did every day. She heard him go out and the door bang. She curled up in her warm bed and slept.

She arose late. Still out of sorts, she cleaned the house. When she went out to feed the hens, the weasel-like face of her neighbor, Maria Laureana, appeared across the yard.

"Gracious, woman, what a racket you made last night! . . ."

Luisa eyed her furiously.

"And what's that to you? It's our business!"

Maria Laureana smiled smugly.

"Don't be like that. . . . We all understand what you're up against, all of us. That man doesn't deserve you," she continued, full of false pity.

Luisa, frowning, wasn't listening. But she heard the sound of that voice, beating on her eardrums like a slow poison. She had known it a long time and grown used to it. "Leave him, woman. Just leave him. Go back to your sisters. Let him get along by himself."

For the first time she began to think about doing just that, and the idea stirred her: "Return home." "Go home, till the soil again. And why not? Wasn't she used to that?" "Get rid of him." And there arose in her a strange sensation like the bitter happiness of triumph, of vengeance. "I must think about that," she said to herself.

But then the unexpected happened. It was he who did not return.

At first she thought it unimportant. "He'll come back soon," she told herself. Two hours passed beyond the time he usually entered the door. Two hours, and she still knew nothing of him. She had supper ready and was sitting at the door shelling beans. In the pale sky the moon was shining, beautiful and poignant. Her anger had given way to an intimate inner sorrow. "I am a forlorn unfortunate woman." Finally she ate alone. She waited a little longer. Then she went to bed.

At dawn she awakened with a strange tremor. At her side the bed was still empty. She got up barefoot and went to look: the hut was silent; Amadeo's supper was untouched. A cold chill ran through her. She shrugged her shoulders, murmuring to herself, "Well, it's his business, him with his black moods." She went back to bed. Then she thought, "He has never stayed out at night before." But did it matter to her? All men stayed away from home some nights; they all drank at the tavern, sometimes more than they should. It was only strange that he had never done it before. Yes, he was a strange man. She tried to sleep but couldn't. She listened to the church clock strike the hours. She thought of the sky full of moonlight, of the river, of herself. "Yes, I am a luckless unhappy woman," she said. "That's what I am."

Day came. Amadeo had not returned. Nor did he come back the following day, nor the one after that.

The weasel face of Maria Laureana appeared again in the frame of the doorway. "Say, woman, what is this? Is it true that Amadeo isn't going to the mine? Just wait and see if the foreman doesn't fire him!"

Luisa was pale. She had not eaten. "I hate her, I hate everyone," she thought, glaring at Maria; but she answered, "I don't know. I don't know, and I don't care." She turned her back and continued working. "Well, that's good," said her neighbor. . . . "It's much better that way. When you think of the life he led you!"

She went away, and Luisa was alone again, absolutely alone, feeling as if she were dead. Her hands let the knife drop on the floor as she shivered in the cold that gripped her. Through the narrow broken windows she could hear the cries of martins, the rushing of the river over the stones. "Marco, you are to blame for everything. . . . You, because Amadeo. . . ." Suddenly a strange fear came over her that made her hands tremble. "Amadeo loved me. Yes, he did love me." How could she have doubted it? Amadeo was coarse, lacking in tenderness, silent, unable to express his feelings. Now she understood him. Amadeo had had a hard childhood, a bitter growing up. Amadeo was poor and earned his livelihood, his own and hers, and would have earned that of the children they might have had, with a thankless job that was wrecking his health. And she, was she tender with him, understanding, affectionate? Suddenly she became aware of his chair, of his clothes lying on it dirty and waiting to be washed, of his boots still covered with mud. A terrible thought came to her mind. "If he loved me, might he even have killed himself?"

Her heart beat wildly. "Killed himself?" Never to find out anything more about him? Never to see him there at her side, lost in thought, his large hands clenched in each other as he sat next to the fire, his long black hair falling over his forehead, tired and sad? Yes, sad. She had never thought of it that way before. He was sad. Tears ran down her cheeks. She thought in a flash about the child they had never had; she saw the bent head of Amadeo. "Sad. He was sad. He's a man of few words, and he was a sad child too. Sad and beaten. And I? What am I for him?"

She got up and went outside. Running, panting, she took the road to the mine. She arrived out of breath and perspiring. No: they knew nothing about him. The men looked at her with a hard and reproachful look. She noticed it and felt guilty. She was desperate when she returned. She threw herself on the bed and cried because she had lost his companionship. "I had only one thing in the world: his companionship." And could it be so important? She looked with childish anxiety for his dirty clothes, his muddy boots. "His company. His silence by my side. Yes, his silence by my side, his bowed head full of memories, his look. His body there by my side at night." His body, large and dark, was filled with a thirst she could not understand. It was she who had not understood; she was the ignorant, the vulgar, the selfish one. "His company. . . . But what about love? Isn't that important? . . . Marco. . . ." The memory came back, but it was a blurred memory like an old-fashioned print, coldly pale and faded. "Well, and what about love? Is it really important?" At last she answered herself, "And what do I know about love? Something out of novels!"

The house was empty, and she was alone.

Amadeo came back. At nightfall of the fourth day she saw him arrive with a heavy step. She rushed to the door. Face to face they were silent, looking at each other. He was dirty, tired, surely hungry. She could think of only one thing: "He wanted to run away from me, to leave me, and he wasn't able to. He couldn't do it. So he came back."

"Come in, Amadeo," she said as softly as she could, "come in. You've had me dangling on a thread. . . ."

Amadeo swallowed something—a blade of grass or some such object he was holding between his teeth. He put one arm around Luisa's shoulders, and they walked into the house together.

The Lady with the Dog   *Anton Chekhov*

I

It was said that a new person had appeared on the sea-front—a lady with a little dog. Dmitri Dmitritch Gurov, who had by then been a fortnight at Yalta, and so was fairly at home there, had begun to take an interest in new arrivals. Sitting in Verney's pavilion, he saw, walking on the sea-front, a fair-haired young lady of medium height, wearing a *béret;* a white Pomeranian dog was running behind her.

And afterwards he met her in the public gardens and in the square several times a day. She was walking alone, always wearing the same *béret,* and always with the same white dog; no one knew who she was, and every one called her simply "the lady with the dog."

"If she is here alone without a husband or friends, it wouldn't be amiss to make her acquaintance," Gurov reflected.

He was under forty, but he had a daughter already twelve years old and two sons at school. He had been married young, when he was a student in his second year, and by now his wife seemed half as old again as he. She was a tall, erect woman with dark eyebrows, staid and dignified, and, as she said of herself, intellectual. She read a great deal, used phonetic spelling, called her husband, not Dmitri, but Dimitri, and he secretly considered her unintelligent, narrow, inelegant, was afraid of her, and did not like to be at home. He had begun being unfaithful to her long ago—had been unfaithful to her often, and, probably on that account, almost always spoke ill of women, and when they were talked about in his presence, used to call them "the lower race."

It seemed to him that he had been so schooled by bitter experience that he might call them what he liked, and yet he could not get on for two days together without "the lower race." In the society of men he was bored and not himself—with them he was cold and uncommunicative; but when he was in the company of women he felt free, and knew what to say to them and how to behave; and he was at ease with them even when he was silent. In his appearance, in his character, in his whole nature, there was something attractive and elusive which allured women and disposed them in his favor; he knew that, and some force seemed to draw him, too, to them.

Experience often repeated, truly bitter experience, had taught him long ago that with decent people, especially Moscow people—always slow to move and irresolute—every intimacy, which at first so agreeably diversifies life and appears a light and charming adventure, inevitably grows into a regular problem of extreme intricacy, and in the long run the situation becomes unbearable. But at every fresh meeting with an interesting woman this experience seemed to slip out of his memory, and he was eager for life, and everything seemed simple and amusing.

One evening he was dining in the gardens, and the lady in the *béret* came up slowly to take the next table. Her expression, her gait, her dress, and the way she did her hair told him that she was a lady, that she was married, that she was in Yalta for the first time and alone, and that she was dull there. . . . The stories told of the immorality in such places as Yalta are to a great extent untrue; he despised them, and knew that such stories were for the most part made up by persons who would themselves have been glad to sin if they had been able; but when the lady sat down at the next table three paces from him, he remembered these tales of easy conquests, of trips to the mountains, and the tempting thought of a swift, fleeting love affair, a romance with an unknown woman whose name he did not know, suddenly took possession of him.

He beckoned coaxingly to the Pomeranian, and when the dog came up to him he shook his finger at it. The Pomeranian growled: Gurov shook his finger at it again.

The lady looked at him and at once dropped her eyes.

"He doesn't bite," she said, and blushed.

"May I give him a bone?" he asked; and when she nodded he asked courteously, "Have you been long in Yalta?"

"Five days."

"And I have already dragged out a fortnight here."

There was a brief silence.

"Time goes fast, and yet it is so dull here!" she said, not looking at him.

"That's only the fashion to say it is dull here. A provincial will live in Belyov or Zhidra and not be dull, and when he comes here it's 'Oh, the dullness! Oh, the dust!' One would think he came from Grenada."

She laughed. Then both continued eating in silence, like strangers, but after dinner they walked side by side; and there sprang up between them the light, jesting conversation of people who are free and satisfied, to whom it does not matter where they go or what they talk about. They walked and talked of the strange light on the sea; the water was of a soft warm lilac hue, and there was a golden streak from the moon upon it. They talked of how sultry it was after a hot day. Gurov told her that he came from Moscow, that he had taken his degree in Arts, but had a post in a bank; that he had trained as an opera singer, but had given it up, that he owned two houses in Moscow. . . . And from her he learnt that she had grown up in Petersburg, but had lived in S—— since her marriage two years before, that she was staying another month in Yalta, and that her husband, who needed a holiday too, might perhaps come and fetch her. She was not sure whether her husband had a post in a Crown Department or under the Provincial Council—and was amused by her own ignorance. And Gurov learnt, too, that she was called Anna Sergeyevna.

Afterwards he thought about her in his room at the hotel—thought she would certainly meet him next day; it would be sure to happen. As he got into bed he thought how lately she had been a girl at school, doing lessons like his own daughter; he recalled the diffidence, the angularity, that was still manifest in her laugh and her manner of talking with a stranger. This must have been the first time in her life she had been alone in surroundings in which she was followed, looked at, and spoken to merely from a secret motive which she could hardly fail to guess. He recalled her slender, delicate neck, her lovely grey eyes.

"There's something pathetic about her, anyway," he thought, and fell asleep.

II

A week had passed since they had made acquaintance. It was a holiday. It was sultry indoors, while in the street the wind whirled the dust round and round and blew people's hats off. It was a thirsty day, and Gurov often went into the pavilion, and pressed Anna Sergeyevna to have syrup and water or an ice. One did not know what to do with oneself.

In the evening when the wind had dropped a little, they went out on the jetty to see the steamer come in. There were a great many people walking about the harbor; they had gathered to welcome someone, bringing bouquets. And two peculiarities of a well-dressed Yalta crowd were very conspicuous: The elderly ladies were dressed like young ones, and there were great numbers of generals.

Owing to the roughness of the sea, the steamer arrived late, after the sun had set, and it was a long time turning about before it reached the jetty. Anna Sergeyevna looked through her lorgnette at the steamer and the passengers as though looking for acquaintances, and when she turned to Gurov her eyes were shining. She talked a great deal and asked disconnected questions, forgetting next moment what she had asked; then she dropped her lorgnette in the crush.

The festive crowd began to disperse; it was too dark to see people's faces. The wind had completely dropped, but Gurov and Anna Sergeyevna still stood as though waiting to see someone else come from the steamer. Anna Sergeyevna was silent now, and sniffed the flowers without looking at Gurov.

"The weather is better this evening," he said. "Where shall we go now? Shall we drive somewhere?"

She made no answer.

Then he looked at her intently, and all at once put his arm round her and kissed her on the lips, and breathed in the moisture and the fragrance of the flowers; and he immediately looked round him, anxiously wondering whether anyone had seen them.

"Let us go to your hotel," he said softly. And both walked quickly.

The room was close and smelt of the scent she had bought at the Japanese shop. Gurov looked at her and thought: "What different people one meets in the world!" From the past he preserved memories of careless, good-natured women, who loved cheerfully and were grateful to him for the happiness he gave them, however brief it might be; and of women like his wife who loved without any genuine feeling, with superfluous phrases, affectedly, hysterically, with an expression that suggested that it was not love nor passion, but something more significant; and of two or three others, very beautiful, cold women, on whose faces he had caught a glimpse of a rapacious expression—an obstinate desire to snatch from life more than it could give, and these were capricious, unreflecting, domineering, unintelligent women not in their first youth, and when Gurov grew cold to them their beauty excited his hatred, and the lace on their linen seemed to him like scales.

But in this case there was still the diffidence, the angularity of inexperienced youth, an awkward feeling; and there was a sense of consternation as though someone had suddenly knocked at the door. The attitude of Anna Sergeyevna—"the lady with the dog"—to what had happened was somehow peculiar, very grave, as though it were her fall —so it seemed, and it was strange and inappropriate. Her face dropped and faded, and on both sides of it her long hair hung down mournfully; she mused in a dejected attitude like "the woman who was a sinner" in an old-fashioned picture.

"It's wrong," she said. "You will be the first to despise me now."

There was a watermelon on the table. Gurov cut himself a slice and began eating it without haste. There followed at least half an hour of silence.

Anna Sergeyevna was touching; there was about her the purity of a good, simple woman who had seen little of life. The solitary candle burning on the table threw a faint light on her face, yet it was clear that she was very unhappy.

"How could I despise you?" asked Gurov. "You don't know what you are saying."

"God forgive me," she said, and her eyes filled with tears. "It's awful."

"You seem to feel you need to be forgiven."

"Forgiven? No. I am a bad, low woman; I despise myself and don't attempt to justify myself. It's not my husband but myself I have deceived. And not only just now; I have been deceiving myself for a long time. My husband may be a good, honest man, but he is a flunkey! I don't know what he does there, what his work is, but I know he is a flunkey! I was twenty when I was married to him. I have been tormented by curiosity; I wanted something better. 'There must be a different sort of life,' I said to myself. I wanted to live! To live, to live! . . . I was fired by curiosity . . . you don't understand it, but, I swear to God, I could not control myself; something happened to me: I could not be restrained. I told my husband I was ill, and came here. . . . And here I have been walking about as though I were dazed, like a mad creature; . . . and now I have become a vulgar, contemptible woman whom anyone may despise."

Gurov felt bored already, listening to her. He was irritated by the naïve tone, by this remorse, so unexpected and inopportune; but for the tears in her eyes, he might have thought she was jesting or playing a part.

"I don't understand," he said softly. "What is it you want?"

She hid her face on his breast and pressed close to him.

"Believe me, believe me, I beseech you . . . ," she said. "I love a pure, honest life, and sin is loathsome to me. I don't know what I am doing. Simple people say: 'The Evil One has beguiled me.' And I may say of myself now that the Evil One has beguiled me."

"Hush, hush! . . ." he muttered.

He looked at her fixed, scared eyes, kissed her, talked softly and affectionately, and by degrees she was comforted, and her gaiety returned; they both began laughing.

Afterwards when they went out there was not a soul on the seafront. The town with its cypresses had quite a deathlike air, but the sea still broke noisily on the shore; a single barge was rocking on the waves, and a lantern was blinking sleepily on it.

They found a cab and drove to Oreanda.

"I found out your surname in the hall just now: it was written on the board—Von Diderits," said Gurov. "Is your husband a German?"

"No; I believe his grandfather was a German, but he is an Orthodox Russian himself."

At Oreanda they sat on a seat not far from the church, looked down at the sea, and were silent. Yalta was hardly visible through the morning mist; white clouds stood motionless on the mountaintops. The leaves did not stir on the trees, grasshoppers chirruped, and the monotonous hollow sound of the sea rising up from below spoke of the peace, of the eternal sleep awaiting us. So it must have sounded when there was no Yalta, no Oreanda here; so it sounds now, and it will sound as indifferently and monotonously when we are all no more. And in this constancy, in this complete indifference to the life and death of each of us, there lies hid, perhaps, a pledge of our eternal salvation, of the unceasing movement of life upon earth, of unceasing progress towards perfection. Sitting beside a young woman who in the dawn seemed so lovely, soothed and spellbound in these magical surroundings—the sea, mountains, clouds, the open sky—Gurov thought how in reality everything is beautiful in this world when one reflects: Everything except what we think or do ourselves when we forget our human dignity and the higher aims of our existence.

A man walked up to them—probably a keeper—looked at them, and walked away. And this detail seemed mysterious and beautiful, too. They saw a steamer come from Theodosia, with its lights out in the glow of dawn.

"There is dew on the grass," said Anna Sergeyevna, after a silence.

"Yes. It's time to go home."

They went back to the town.

Then they met every day at twelve o'clock on the sea-front, lunched and dined together, went for walks, admired the sea. She complained that she slept badly, that her heart throbbed violently; asked the same questions, troubled now by jealousy and now by the fear that he did not respect her sufficiently. And often in the square or gardens, when there was no one near them, he suddenly drew her to him and kissed her passionately. Complete idleness, these kisses in broad daylight while he looked round in dread of someone's seeing them, the heat, the smell of the sea, and the continual passing to and fro before him of idle, well-dressed, well-fed people, made a new man of him; he told Anna Sergeyevna how beautiful she was, how fascinating. He was impatiently passionate, he would not move a step away from her, while she was often pensive and continually urged him to confess that he did not respect her, did not love her in the least, and thought of her as nothing but a common woman. Rather late almost every evening they drove somewhere out of town, to Oreanda or to the waterfall; and the expedition was always a success—the scenery invariably impressed them as grand and beautiful.

They were expecting her husband to come, but a letter came from him, saying that there was something wrong with his eyes, and he entreated his wife to come home as quickly as possible. Anna Sergeyevna made haste to go.

"It's a good thing I am going away," she said to Gurov. "It's the finger of destiny!"

She went by coach and he went with her. They were driving the whole day. When she had got into a compartment of the express, and when the second bell had rung, she said, "Let me look at you once more . . . look at you once again. That's right."

She did not shed tears, but was so sad that she seemed ill, and her face was quivering.

"I shall remember you . . . think of you," she said. "God be with you; be happy. Don't remember evil against me. We are parting for-ever—it must be so, for we ought never to have met. Well, God be with you."

The train moved off rapidly, its lights soon vanished from sight, and a minute later there was no sound of it, as though everything had conspired together to end as quickly as possible that sweet delirium, that madness. Left alone on the platform, and gazing into the dark distance, Gurov listened to the chirrup of the grasshoppers and the hum of the telegraph wires, feeling as though he had only just waked up. And he thought, musing, that there had been another episode or adventure in his life, and it, too, was at an end, and nothing was left of it but a memory. . . . He was moved, sad, and conscious of a slight remorse. This young woman whom he would never meet again had not been happy with him; he was genuinely warm and affectionate with her, but yet in his manner, his tone, and his caresses there had been a shade of light irony, the coarse condescension of a happy man who was, besides, almost twice her age. All the time she had called him kind, exceptional, lofty; obviously he had seemed to her different from what he really was, so he had unintentionally deceived her. . . .

Here at the station was already a scent of autumn; it was a cold evening.

"It's time for me to go north," thought Gurov as he left the platform. "High time!"

III

At home in Moscow everything was in its winter routine; the stoves were heated, and in the morning it was still dark when the children were having breakfast and getting ready for school, and the nurse would light the lamp for a short time. The frosts had begun already. When the first snow had fallen, on the first day of sledge-driving it is pleasant to see the white earth, the white roofs, to draw soft, delicious breath, and the season brings back the days of one's youth. The old limes and birches, white with hoarfrost, have a good-natured expression; they are nearer to one's heart than cypresses and palms, and near them one doesn't want to be thinking of the sea and the mountains.

Gurov was Moscow-born; he arrived in Moscow on a fine frosty day, and when he put on his fur coat and warm gloves, and walked along Petrovka, and when on Saturday evening he heard the ringing of the bells, his recent trip and the places he had seen lost all charm for him. Little by little he became absorbed in Moscow life, greedily read three newspapers a day, and declared he did not read the Moscow papers on principle! He already felt a longing to go to restaurants, clubs, dinner parties, anniversary celebrations, and he felt flattered at entertaining distinguished lawyers and artists and at playing cards with a professor at the doctors' club. He could already eat a whole plateful of salt fish and cabbage. . . .

In another month, he fancied, the image of Anna Sergeyevna would be shrouded in a mist in his memory, and only from time to time would visit him in his dreams with a touching smile, as others did. But more than a month passed, real winter had come, and everything was still clear in his memory as though he had parted with Anna Sergeyevna only the day before. And his memories glowed more and more vividly. When in the evening stillness he heard from his study the voices of his children preparing their lessons, or when he listened to a song or the organ at the restaurant, or the storm howled in the chimney, suddenly everything would rise up in his memory: What had happened on the jetty, and the early morning with the mist on the mountains, and the steamer coming from Theodosia, and the kisses. He would pace a long time about his room, remembering it all and smiling; then his memories passed into dreams, and in his fancy the past was mingled with what was to come. Anna Sergeyevna did not visit him in dreams, but followed him about everywhere like a shadow and haunted him. When he shut his eyes he saw her as though she were living before him, and she seemed to him lovelier, younger, tenderer than she was; and he imagined himself finer than he had been in Yalta. In the evenings she peeped out at him from the bookcase, from the fireplace, from the corner—he heard her breathing, the caressing rustle of her dress. In the street he watched the women, looking for someone like her.

He was tormented by an intense desire to confide his memories to someone. But in his home it was impossible to talk of his love, and he had no one outside; he could not talk to his tenants nor to any one at the bank. And what had he to talk of? Had he been in love, then? Had there been anything beautiful, poetical, or edifying or simply interesting in his relations with Anna Sergeyevna? And there was nothing for him but to talk vaguely of love, of woman, and no one guessed what it meant; only his wife twitched her black eyebrows, and said: "The part of a lady-killer does not suit you at all, Dimitri."

One evening, coming out of the doctors' club with an official with whom he had been playing cards, he could not resist saying, "If only you knew what a fascinating woman I made the acquaintance of in Yalta!"

The official got into his sledge and was driving away, but turned suddenly and shouted, "Dmitri Dmitritch!"

"What?"

"You were right this evening: The sturgeon was a bit too strong!"

These words, so ordinary, for some reason moved Gurov to indignation, and struck him as degrading and unclean. What savage manners, what people! What senseless nights, what uninteresting, uneventful days! The rage for card-playing, the gluttony, the drunkenness, the continual talk always about the same thing. Useless pursuits and conversations always about the same things absorb the better part of one's time, the better part of one's strength, and in the end there is left a life groveling and curtailed, worthless and trivial, and there is no escaping or getting away from it—just as though one were in a madhouse or a prison.

Gurov did not sleep all night, and was filled with indignation. And he had a headache all next day. And the next night he slept badly; he sat up in bed thinking, or paced up and down his room. He was sick of his children, sick of the bank; he had no desire to go anywhere or to talk of anything.

In the holidays in December he prepared for a journey, and told his wife he was going to Petersburg to do something in the interests of a young friend—and he set off for S——. What for? He did not very well know himself. He wanted to see Anna Sergeyevna and to talk with her—to arrange a meeting, if possible.

He reached S—— in the morning and took the best room at the hotel, in which the floor was covered with gray army cloth, and on the table was an inkstand, gray with dust and adorned with a figure on horseback, with its hat in its hand and its head broken off. The hotel porter gave him the necessary information; Von Diderits lived in a house of his own in Old Gontcharny Street—it was not far from the hotel: he was rich and lived in good style, and had his own horses; every one in the town knew him. The porter pronounced the name "Dridirits."

Gurov went without haste to Old Gontcharny Street and found the house. Just opposite the house stretched a long gray fence adorned with nails.

"One would run away from a fence like that," thought Gurov, looking from the fence to the windows of the house and back again.

He considered: Today was a holiday, and the husband would probably be at home. And in any case it would be tactless to go into the house and upset her. If he were to send her a note it might fall into her husband's hands, and then it might ruin everything. The best thing was to trust to chance. And he kept walking up and down the street by the fence, waiting for the chance. He saw a beggar go in at the gate and the dogs fly at him; then an hour later he heard a piano, and the sounds were faint and indistinct. Probably it was Anna Sergeyevna playing. The front door suddenly opened, and an old woman came out, followed by the familiar white Pomeranian. Gurov was on the point of calling to the dog, but his heart began beating violently, and in his excitement he could not remember the dog's name.

He walked up and down, and loathed the gray fence more and more, and by now he thought irritably that Anna Sergeyevna had forgotten him, and was perhaps already amusing herself with someone else, and that that was very natural in a young woman who had nothing to look at from morning till night but that confounded fence. He went back to his hotel room and sat for a long while on the sofa, not knowing what to do, then he had dinner and a long nap.

"How stupid and worrying it is!" he thought when he woke and looked at the dark windows: it was already evening. "Here I've had a good sleep for some reason. What shall I do in the night?"

He sat on the bed, which was covered by a cheap gray blanket, such as one sees in hospitals, and he taunted himself in his vexation, "So much for the lady with the dog . . . so much for the adventure. . . . You're in a nice fix. . . ."

That morning at the station a poster in large letters had caught his eye. "The Geisha" was to be performed for the first time. He thought of this and went to the theatre.

"It's quite possible she may go to the first performance," he thought.

The theatre was full. As in all provincial theatres, there was a fog above the chandelier, the gallery was noisy and restless; in the front row the local dandies were standing up before the beginning of the performance, with their hands behind them; in the Governor's box the Governor's daughter, wearing a boa, was sitting in the front seat, while the Governor himself lurked modestly behind the curtain with only his hands visible; the orchestra was a long time tuning up; the stage curtain swayed. All the time the audience were coming in and taking their seats Gurov looked at them eagerly.

Anna Sergeyevna, too, came in. She sat down in the third row, and when Gurov looked at her his heart contracted, and he understood clearly that for him there was in the whole world no creature so near, so precious, and so important to him; she, this little woman, in no way remarkable, lost in a provincial crowd, with a vulgar lorgnette in her hand, filled his whole life now, was his sorrow and his joy, the one happiness that he now desired for himself; and to the sounds of the inferior orchestra, of the wretched provincial violins, he thought how lovely she was. He thought and dreamed.

A young man with small side-whiskers, tall and stooping, came in with Anna Sergeyevna and sat down beside her; he bent his head at every step and seemed to be continually bowing. Most likely this was the husband whom at Yalta, in a rush of bitter feeling, she had called a flunkey. And there really was in his long figure, his side-whiskers, and the small bald patch on his head, something of the flunkey's obsequiousness; his smile was sugary, and in his buttonhole there was some badge of distinction like the number on a waiter.

During the first interval the husband went away to smoke; she remained alone in her stall. Gurov, who was sitting in the stalls, too, went up to her and said in a trembling voice, with a forced smile, "Good evening."

She glanced at him and turned pale, then glanced again with horror, unable to believe her eyes, and tightly gripped the fan and the lorgnette in her hands, evidently struggling with herself not to faint. Both were silent. She was sitting, he was standing, frightened by her confusion and not venturing to sit down beside her. The violins and the flute began tuning up. He felt suddenly frightened; it seemed as though all the people in the boxes were looking at them. She got up and went quickly to the door; he followed her, and both walked senselessly along passages, and up and down stairs, and figures in legal, scholastic, and civil service uniforms, all wearing badges, flitted before their eyes. They caught glimpses of ladies, of fur coats hanging on pegs; the drafts blew on them, bringing a smell of stale tobacco. And Gurov, whose heart was beating violently, thought, "Oh, heavens! Why are these people here and this orchestra! . . ."

And at that instant he recalled how when he had seen Anna Sergeyevna off at the station he had thought that everything was over and they would never meet again. But how far they were still from the end!

On the narrow, gloomy staircase over which was written "To the Amphitheatre," she stopped.

"How you have frightened me!" she said, breathing hard, still pale and overwhelmed. "Oh, how you have frightened me! I am half-dead. Why have you come? Why?"

"But do understand, Anna, do understand . . . ," he said hastily in a low voice. "I entreat you to understand. . . ."

She looked at him with dread, with entreaty, with love; she looked at him intently, to keep his features more distinctly in her memory.

"I am so unhappy," she went on, not heeding him. "I have thought of nothing but you all the time; I live only in the thought of you. And I wanted to forget, to forget you; but why, oh, why, have you come?"

On the landing above them two schoolboys were smoking and looking down, but that was nothing to Gurov; he drew Anna Sergeyevna to him, and began kissing her face, her cheeks, and her hands.

"What are you doing, what are you doing!" she cried in horror, pushing him away. "We are mad. Go away today; go away at once. . . . I beseech you by all that is sacred, I implore you. . . . There are people coming this way!"

Someone was coming up the stairs.

"You must go away," Anna Sergeyevna went on in a whisper. "Do you hear, Dmitri Dmitritch? I will come and see you in Moscow. I have never been happy; I am miserable now, and I never, never shall be happy, never! Don't make me suffer still more! I swear I'll come to Moscow. But now let us part. My precious, good, dear one, we must part!"

She pressed his hand and began rapidly going downstairs, looking round at him, and from her eyes he could see that she really was unhappy. Gurov stood for a little while, listened, then, when all sound had died away, he found his coat and left the theatre.

IV

And Anna Sergeyevna began coming to see him in Moscow. Once in two or three months she left S——, telling her husband that she was going to consult a doctor about an internal complaint—and her husband believed her, and did not believe her. In Moscow she stayed at the Slaviansky Bazaar hotel, and at once sent a man in a red cap to Gurov. Gurov went to see her, and no one in Moscow knew of it.

Once he was going to see her in this way on a winter morning (the messenger had come the evening before when he was out). With him walked his daughter, whom he wanted to take to school: it was on the way. Snow was falling in big wet flakes.

"It's three degrees above freezing-point, and yet it is snowing," said Gurov to his daughter. "The thaw is only on the surface of the earth; there is quite a different temperature at a greater height in the atmosphere."

"And why are there no thunderstorms in the winter, father?"

He explained that, too. He talked, thinking all the while that he was going to see *her,* and no living soul knew of it, and probably never would know. He had two lives: one, open, seen and known by all who cared to know, full of relative truth and of relative falsehood, exactly like the lives of his friends and acquaintances; and another life running its course in secret. And through some strange, perhaps accidental, conjunction of circumstances, everything that was essential, of interest and of value to him, everything in which he was sincere and did not deceive himself, everything that made the kernel of his life, was hidden from other people; and all that was false in him, the sheath in which he hid himself to conceal the truth—such, for instance, as his work in the bank, his discussions at the club, his "lower race," his presence with his wife at anniversary festivities—all that was open. And he judged of others by himself, not believing in what he saw, and always believing that every man had his real, most interesting life under the cover of secrecy and under the cover of night. All personal life rested on secrecy, and possibly it was partly on that account that civilized man was so nervously anxious that personal privacy should be respected.

After leaving his daughter at school, Gurov went on to the Slaviansky Bazaar. He took off his fur coat below, went upstairs, and softly knocked at the door. Anna Sergeyevna, wearing his favorite gray dress, exhausted by the journey and the suspense, had been expecting him since the evening before. She was pale; she looked at him, and did not smile, and he had hardly come in when she fell on his breast. Their kiss was slow and prolonged, as though they had not met for two years.

"Well, how are you getting on there?" he asked. "What news?"

"Wait; I'll tell you directly. . . . I can't talk."

She could not speak; she was crying. She turned away from him, and pressed her handkerchief to her eyes.

"Let her have her cry out. I'll sit down and wait," he thought, and he sat down in an armchair.

Then he rang and asked for tea to be brought him, and while he drank his tea she remained standing at the window with her back to him. She was crying from emotion, from the miserable consciousness that their life was so hard for them; they could only meet in secret, hiding themselves from people, like thieves! Was not their life shattered?

"Come, do stop!" he said.

It was evident to him that this love of theirs would not soon be over, that he could not see the end of it. Anna Sergeyevna grew more and more attached to him. She adored him, and it was unthinkable to say to her that it was bound to have an end some day; besides, she would not have believed it!

He went up to her and took her by the shoulders to say something affectionate and cheering, and at that moment he saw himself in the looking glass.

His hair was already beginning to turn gray. And it seemed strange to him that he had grown so much older, so much plainer during the last few years. The shoulders on which his hands rested were warm and quivering. He felt compassion for this life, still so warm and lovely, but probably already not far from beginning to fade and wither like his own. Why did she love him so much? He always seemed to women different from what he was, and they loved in him not himself, but the man created by their imagination, whom they had been eagerly seeking all their lives; and afterwards, when they noticed their mistake, they loved him all the same. And not one of them had been happy with him. Time passed, he had made their acquaintance, got on with them, parted, but he had never once loved; it was anything you like, but not love.

And only now when his head was gray he had fallen properly, really in love—for the first time in his life.

Anna Sergeyevna and he loved each other like people very close and akin, like husband and wife, like tender friends; it seemed to them that fate itself had meant them for one another, and they could not understand why he had a wife and she a husband; and it was as though they were a pair of birds of passage, caught and forced to live in different cages. They forgave each other for what they were ashamed of in their past, they forgave everything in the present, and felt that this love of theirs had changed them both.

In moments of depression in the past he had comforted himself with any arguments that came into his mind, but now he no longer cared for arguments; he felt profound compassion, he wanted to be sincere and tender. . . .

"Don't cry, my darling," he said. "You've had your cry; that's enough. . . . Let us talk now, let us think of some plan."

Then they spent a long while taking counsel together, talked of how to avoid the necessity for secrecy, for deception, for living in different towns and not seeing each other for long at a time. How could they be free from the intolerable bondage?

"How? How?" he asked, clutching his head. "How?"

And it seemed as though in a little while the solution would be found, and then a new and splendid life would begin; and it was clear to both of them that they had still a long, long road before them, and that the most complicated and difficult part of it was only just beginning.

The Lottery

Shirley Jackson

The morning of June 27th was clear and sunny, with the fresh warmth of a full-summer day; the flowers were blossoming profusely and the grass was richly green. The people of the village began to gather in the square, between the post office and the bank, around ten o'clock; in some towns there were so many people that the lottery took two days and had to be started on June 26th, but in this village, where there were only about three hundred people, the whole lottery took less than two hours, so it could begin at ten o'clock in the morning and still be through in time to allow the villagers to get home for noon dinner.

The children assembled first, of course. School was recently over for the summer, and the feeling of liberty sat uneasily on most of them; they tended to gather together quietly for a while before they broke into boisterous play, and their talk was still of the classroom and the teacher, of books and reprimands. Bobby Martin had already stuffed his pockets full of stones, and the other boys soon followed his example, selecting the smoothest and roundest stones; Bobby and Harry Jones and Dickie Delacroix—the villagers pronounced this name "Dellacroy"—eventually made a great pile of stones in one corner of the square and guarded it against the raids of the other boys. The girls stood aside, talking among themselves, looking over their shoulders at the boys, and the very small children rolled in the dust or clung to the hands of their older brothers or sisters.

Soon the men began to gather, surveying their own children, speaking of planting and rain, tractors and taxes. They stood together, away from the pile of stones in the corner, and their jokes were quiet and they smiled rather than laughed. The women, wearing faded house dresses and sweaters, came shortly after their menfolk. They greeted one another and exchanged bits of gossip as they went to join their husbands. Soon the women, standing by their husbands, began to call to their children, and the children came reluctantly, having to be called four or five times. Bobby Martin ducked under his mother's grasping hand and ran, laughing, back to the pile of stones. His father spoke up sharply, and Bobby came quickly and took his place between his father and his oldest brother.

The lottery was conducted—as were the square dances, the teen-age club, the Halloween program—by Mr. Summers, who had time and energy to devote to civic activities. He was a round-faced, jovial man and he ran the coal business, and people were sorry for him, because he had no children and his wife was a scold. When he arrived in the square, carrying the black wooden box, there was a murmur of conversation among the villagers, and he waved and called, "Little late today, folks." The postmaster, Mr. Graves, followed him, carrying a three-legged stool, and the stool was put in the center of the square and Mr. Summers set the black box down on it. The villagers kept their distance, leaving a space between themselves and the stool, and when Mr. Summers said, "Some of you fellows want to give me a hand?" there was a hesitation before two men, Mr. Martin and his oldest son, Baxter, came forward to hold the box steady on the stool while Mr. Summers stirred up the papers inside it.

The original paraphernalia for the lottery had been lost long ago, and the black box now resting on the stool had been put into use even before Old Man Warner, the oldest man in town, was born. Mr. Summers spoke frequently to the villagers about making a new box, but no one liked to upset even as much tradition as was represented by the black box. There was a story that the present box had been made with some pieces of the box that had preceded it, the one that had been constructed when the first people settled down to make a village here. Every year, after the lottery, Mr. Summers began talking again about a new box, but every year the subject was allowed to fade off without anything's being done. The black box grew shabbier each year; by now it was no longer completely black but splintered badly along one side to show the original wood color, and in some places faded or stained.

Mr. Martin and his oldest son, Baxter, held the black box securely on the stool until Mr. Summers had stirred the papers thoroughly with his hand. Because so much of the ritual had been forgotten or discarded, Mr. Summers had been successful in having slips of paper substituted for the chips of wood that had been used for generations. Chips of wood, Mr. Summers had argued, had been all very well when the village was tiny, but now that the population was more than three hundred and likely to keep on growing, it was necessary to use something that would fit more easily into the black box. The night before the lottery, Mr. Summers and Mr. Graves made up the slips of paper and put them in the box, and it was then taken to the safe of Mr. Summers' coal company and locked up until Mr. Summers was ready to take it to the square next morning. The rest of the year, the box was put away, sometimes one place, sometimes another; it had spent one year in Mr. Graves's barn and another year underfoot in the post office, and sometimes it was set on a shelf in the Martin grocery and left there.

There was a great deal of fussing to be done before Mr. Summers declared the lottery open. There were the lists to make up—of heads of families, heads of households in each family, members of each household in each family. There was the proper swearing-in of Mr. Summers by the postmaster, as the official of the lottery; at one time, some people remembered, there had been a recital of some sort, performed by the official of the lottery, a perfunctory, tuneless chant that had been rattled off duly each year; some people believed that the official of the lottery used to stand just so when he said or sang it, others believed that he was supposed to walk among the people, but years and years ago this part of the ritual had been allowed to lapse. There had been, also, a ritual salute, which the official of the lottery had had to use in addressing each person who came up to draw from the box, but this also had changed with time, until now it was felt necessary only for the official to speak to each person approaching. Mr. Summers was very good at all this; in his clean white shirt and blue jeans, with one hand resting carelessly on the black box, he seemed very proper and important as he talked interminably to Mr. Graves and the Martins.

Just as Mr. Summers finally left off talking and turned to the assembled villagers, Mrs. Hutchinson came hurriedly along the path to the square, her sweater thrown over her shoulders, and slid into place in the back of the crowd. "Clean forgot what day it was," she said to Mrs. Delacroix, who stood next to her, and they both laughed softly. "Thought my old man was out back stacking wood," Mrs. Hutchinson went on, "and then I looked out the window and the kids was gone, and then I remembered it was the twenty-seventh and came a-running." She dried her hands on her apron, and Mrs. Delacroix said, "You're in time, though. They're still talking away up there."

Mrs. Hutchinson craned her neck to see through the crowd and found her husband and children standing near the front. She tapped Mrs. Delacroix on the arm as a farewell and began to make her way through the crowd. The people separated good-humoredly to let her through; two or three people said, in voices just loud enough to be heard across the crowd, "Here comes your Missus, Hutchinson," and "Bill, she made it after all." Mrs. Hutchinson reached her husband, and Mr. Summers, who had been waiting, said cheerfully, "Thought we were going to have to get on without you, Tessie." Mrs. Hutchinson said, grinning. "Wouldn't have me leave m'dishes in the sink, now, would you, Joe?," and soft laughter ran through the crowd as the people stirred back into position after Mrs. Hutchinson's arrival.

"Well, now," Mr. Summers said soberly, "guess we better get started, get this over with, so's we can go back to work. Anybody ain't here?"

"Dunbar," several people said. "Dunbar, Dunbar."

Mr. Summers consulted his list. "Clyde Dunbar," he said. "That's right. He's broke his leg, hasn't he? Who's drawing for him?"

"Me, I guess," a woman said, and Mr. Summers turned to look at her. "Wife draws for her husband," Mr. Summers said. "Don't you have a grown boy to do it for you, Janey?" Although Mr. Summers and everyone else in the village knew the answer perfectly well, it was the business of the official of the lottery to ask such questions formally. Mr. Summers waited with an expression of polite interest while Mrs. Dunbar answered.

"Horace's not but sixteen yet," Mrs. Dunbar said regretfully. "Guess I gotta fill in for the old man this year."

"Right," Mr. Summers said. He made a note on the list he was holding. Then he asked, "Watson boy drawing this year?"

A tall boy in the crowd raised his hand. "Here," he said. "I'm drawing for m'mother and me." He blinked his eyes nervously and ducked his head as several voices in the crowd said things like "Good fellow, Jack," and "Glad to see your mother's got a man to do it."

"Well," Mr. Summers said, "guess that's everyone. Old Man Warner make it?"

"Here," a voice said, and Mr. Summers nodded.

A sudden hush fell on the crowd as Mr. Summers cleared his throat and looked at the list. "All ready?" he called. "Now, I'll read the names—heads of families first—and the men come up and take a paper out of the box. Keep the paper folded in your hand without looking at it until everyone has had a turn. Everything clear?"

The people had done it so many times that they only half listened to the directions; most of them were quiet, wetting their lips, not looking around. Then Mr. Summers raised one hand high and said, "Adams." A man disengaged himself from the crowd and came forward. "Hi, Steve," Mr. Summers said, and Mr. Adams said, "Hi, Joe." They grinned at one another humorlessly and nervously. Then Mr. Adams reached into the black box and took out a folded paper. He held it firmly by one corner as he turned and went hastily back to his place in the crowd, where he stood a little apart from his family, not looking down at his hand.

"Allen," Mr. Summers said. "Anderson. . . . Bentham."

"Seems like there's no time at all between lotteries anymore," Mrs. Delacroix said to Mrs. Graves in the back row. "Seems like we got through with the last one only last week."

"Time sure goes fast," Mrs. Graves said.

"Clark. . . . Delacroix."

"There goes my old man," Mrs. Delacroix said. She held her breath while her husband went forward.

"Dunbar," Mr. Summers said, and Mrs. Dunbar went steadily to the box while one of the women said, "Go on, Janey," and another said, "There she goes."

"We're next," Mrs. Graves said. She watched while Mr. Graves came around from the side of the box, greeted Mr. Summers gravely, and selected a slip of paper from the box. By now, all through the crowd there were men holding the small folded papers in their large hands, turning them over and over nervously. Mrs. Dunbar and her two sons stood together, Mrs. Dunbar holding the slip of paper.

"Harburt. . . . Hutchinson."

"Get up there, Bill," Mrs. Hutchinson said, and the people near her laughed.

"Jones."

"They do say," Mr. Adams said to Old Man Warner, who stood next to him, "that over in the north village they're talking of giving up the lottery."

Old Man Warner snorted. "Pack of crazy fools," he said. "Listening to the young folks, nothing's good enough for *them*. Next thing you know, they'll be wanting to go back to living in caves, nobody work any more, live *that* way for a while. Used to be a saying about 'Lottery in June, corn be heavy soon.' First thing you know, we'd all be eating stewed chickweed and acorns. There's *always* been a lottery," he added petulantly. "Bad enough to see young Joe Summers up there joking with everybody."

"Some places have already quit lotteries," Mrs. Adams said.

"Nothing but trouble in *that*," Old Man Warner said stoutly. "Pack of young fools."

"Martin." And Bobby Martin watched his father go forward. "Overdyke. . . . Percy."

"I wish they'd hurry," Mrs. Dunbar said to her older son. "I wish they'd hurry."

"They're almost through," her son said.

"You get ready to run tell Dad," Mrs. Dunbar said.

Mr. Summers called his own name and then stepped forward precisely and selected a slip from the box. Then he called, "Warner."

"Seventy-seventh year I been in the lottery," Old Man Warner said as he went through the crowd. "Seventy-seventh time."

"Watson." The tall boy came awkwardly through the crowd. Someone said, "Don't be nervous, Jack," and Mr. Summers said, "Take your time, son."

"Zanini."

After that, there was a long pause, a breathless pause, until Mr. Summers, holding his slip of paper in the air, said, "All right, fellows." For a minute, no one moved, and then all the slips of paper were opened. Suddenly, all the women began to speak at once, saying, "Who is it?," "Who's got it?," "Is it the Dunbars?," "Is it the Watsons?" Then the voices began to say, "It's Hutchinson. It's Bill," "Bill Hutchinson's got it."

"Go tell your father," Mrs. Dunbar said to her older son.

People began to look around to see the Hutchinsons. Bill Hutchinson was standing quiet, staring down at the paper in his hand. Suddenly, Tessie Hutchinson shouted to Mr. Summers, "You didn't give him time enough to take any paper he wanted. I saw you. It wasn't fair!"

"Be a good sport, Tessie," Mrs. Delacroix called, and Mrs. Graves said, "All of us took the same chance."

"Shut up, Tessie," Bill Hutchinson said.

"Well, everyone," Mr. Summers said, "that was done pretty fast, and now we've got to be hurrying a little more to get done in time." He consulted his next list. "Bill," he said, "you draw for the Hutchinson family. You got any other households in the Hutchinsons?"

"There's Don and Eva," Mrs. Hutchinson yelled. "Make *them* take their chance!"

"Daughters draw with their husbands' families, Tessie," Mr. Summers said gently. "You know that as well as anyone else."

"It wasn't *fair,*" Tessie said.

"I guess not, Joe," Bill Hutchinson said regretfully. "My daughter draws with her husband's family, that's only fair. And I've got no other family except the kids."

"Then, as far as drawing for families is concerned, it's you," Mr. Summers said in explanation, "and as far as drawing for households is concerned, that's you, too. Right?"

"Right," Bill Hutchinson said.

"How many kids, Bill?" Mr. Summers asked formally.

"Three," Bill Hutchinson said. "There's Bill, Jr., and Nancy, and little Dave. And Tessie and me."

"All right, then," Mr. Summers said. "Harry, you got their tickets back?"

Mr. Graves nodded and held up the slips of paper. "Put them in the box, then," Mr. Summers directed. "Take Bill's and put it in."

"I think we ought to start over," Mrs. Hutchinson said, as quietly as she could. "I tell you it wasn't *fair.* You didn't give him time enough to choose. *Every*body saw that."

Mr. Graves had selected the five slips and put them in the box, and he dropped all the papers but those onto the ground, where the breeze caught them and lifted them off.

"Listen, everybody," Mrs. Hutchinson was saying to the people around her.

"Ready, Bill?" Mr. Summers asked, and Bill Hutchinson, with one quick glance around at his wife and children, nodded.

"Remember," Mr. Summers said, "take the slips and keep them folded until each person has taken one. Harry, you help little Dave." Mr. Graves took the hand of the little boy, who came willingly with him up to the box. "Take a paper out of the box, Davy," Mr. Summers said. Davy put his hand into the box and laughed. "Take just *one* paper," Mr. Summers said. "Harry, you hold it for him." Mr. Graves took the child's hand and removed the folded paper from the tight fist and held it while little Dave stood next to him and looked up at him wonderingly.

"Nancy next," Mr. Summers said. Nancy was twelve, and her school friends breathed heavily as she went forward, switching her skirt, and took a slip daintily from the box. "Bill, Jr.," Mr. Summers said, and Billy, his face red and his feet overlarge, nearly knocked the box over as he got a paper out. "Tessie," Mr. Summers said. She hesitated for a minute, looking around defiantly, and then set her lips and went up to the box. She snatched a paper out and held it behind her.

"Bill," Mr. Summers said, and Bill Hutchinson reached into the box and felt around, bringing his hand out at last with the slip of paper in it.

The crowd was quiet. A girl whispered, "I hope it's not Nancy," and the sound of the whisper reached the edges of the crowd.

"It's not the way it used to be," Old Man Warner said clearly. "People ain't the way they used to be."

"All right," Mr. Summers said. "Open the papers. Harry, you open little Dave's."

Mr. Graves opened the slip of paper and there was a general sigh through the crowd as he held it up and everyone could see that it was blank. Nancy and Bill, Jr., opened theirs at the same time, and both beamed and laughed, turning around to the crowd and holding their slips of paper above their heads.

"Tessie," Mr. Summers said. There was a pause, and then Mr. Summers looked at Bill Hutchinson, and Bill unfolded his paper and showed it. It was blank.

"It's Tessie," Mr. Summers said, and his voice was hushed. "Show us her paper, Bill."

Bill Hutchinson went over to his wife and forced the slip of paper out of her hand. It had a black spot on it, the black spot Mr. Summers had made the night before with the heavy pencil in the coal-company office. Bill Hutchinson held it up, and there was a stir in the crowd.

"All right, folks," Mr. Summers said. "Let's finish quickly."

Although the villagers had forgotten the ritual and lost the original black box, they still remembered to use stones. The pile of stones the boys had made earlier was ready; there were stones on the ground with the blowing scraps of paper that had come out of the box. Mrs. Delacroix selected a stone so large she had to pick it up with both hands and turned to Mrs. Dunbar. "Come on," she said. "Hurry up."

Mrs. Dunbar had small stones in both hands, and she said, gasping for breath, "I can't run at all. You'll have to go ahead and I'll catch up with you."

The children had stones already, and someone gave little Davy Hutchinson a few pebbles.

Tessie Hutchinson was in the center of a cleared space by now, and she held her hands out desperately as the villagers moved in on her. "It isn't fair," she said. A stone hit her on the side of the head.

Old Man Warner was saying, "Come on, come on, everyone." Steve Adams was in the front of the crowd of villagers, with Mrs. Graves beside him.

"It isn't fair, it isn't right." Mrs. Hutchinson screamed, and then they were upon her.

An Episode of War *Stephen Crane*

The lieutenant's rubber blanket lay on the ground, and upon it he had poured the company's supply of coffee. Corporals and other representatives of the grimy and hot-throated men who lined the breast-work had come for each squad's portion.

The lieutenant was frowning and serious at this task of division. His lips pursed as he drew with his sword various crevices in the heap, until brown squares of coffee, astoundingly equal in size, appeared on the blanket. He was on the verge of a great triumph in mathematics, and the corporals were thronging forward, each to reap a little square, when suddenly the lieutenant cried out and looked quickly at a man near him as if he suspected it was a case of personal assault. The others cried out also when they saw blood upon the lieutenant's sleeve.

He had winced like a man stung, swayed dangerously, and then straightened. The sound of his hoarse breathing was plainly audible. He looked sadly, mystically, over the breastwork at the green face of a wood, where now were many little puffs of white smoke. During this moment the men about him gazed statuelike and silent, astonished and awed by this catastrophe which happened when catastrophes were not expected—when they had leisure to observe it.

As the lieutenant stared at the wood, they too swung their heads, so that for another instant all hands, still silent, contemplated the distant forest as if their minds were fixed upon the mystery of a bullet's journey.

The officer had, of course, been compelled to take his sword into his left hand. He did not hold it by the hilt. He gripped it at the middle of the blade, awkwardly. Turning his eyes from the hostile wood, he looked at the sword as he held it there, and seemed puzzled as to what to do with it, where to put it. In short, this weapon had of a sudden become a strange thing to him. He looked at it in a kind of stupefaction, as if he had been endowed with a trident, a sceptre, or a spade.

Finally he tried to sheathe it. To sheathe a sword held by the left hand, at the middle of the blade, in a scabbard hung at the left hip, is a feat worthy of a sawdust ring. This wounded officer engaged in a desperate struggle with the sword and the wobbling scabbard, and during the time of it he breathed like a wrestler.

But at this instant the men, the spectators, awoke from their stone-like poses and crowded forward sympathetically. The orderly-sergeant took the sword and tenderly placed it in the scabbard. At the time, he leaned nervously backward, and did not allow even his finger to brush the body of the lieutenant. A wound gives strange dignity to him who bears it. Well men shy from this new and terrible majesty. It is as if the wounded man's hand is upon the curtain which hangs before the revelations of all existence—the meaning of ants, potentates, wars, cities, sunshine, snow, a feather dropped from a bird's wing; and the power of it sheds radiance upon a bloody form, and makes the other men understand sometimes that they are little. His comrades look at him with large eyes thoughtfully. Moreover, they fear vaguely that the weight of a finger upon him might send him headlong, precipitate the tragedy, hurl him at once into the dim, grey unknown. And so the orderly-sergeant, while sheathing the sword, leaned nervously backward.

There were others who proffered assistance. One timidly presented his shoulder and asked the lieutenant if he cared to lean upon it, but the latter waved him away mournfully. He wore the look of one who knows he is the victim of a terrible disease and understands his helplessness. He again stared over the breast-work at the forest, and then, turning, went slowly rearward. He held his right wrist tenderly in his left hand as if the wounded arm was made of very brittle glass.

And the men in silence stared at the wood, then at the departing lieutenant; then at the wood, then at the lieutenant.

As the wounded officer passed from the line of battle, he was enabled to see many things which as a participant in the fight were unknown to him. He saw a general on a black horse gazing over the lines of blue infantry at the green woods which veiled his problems. An aide galloped furiously, dragged his horse suddenly to a halt, saluted, and presented a paper. It was, for a wonder, precisely like a historical painting.

To the rear of the general and his staff a group, composed of a bugler, two or three orderlies, and the bearer of the corps standard, all upon maniacal horses, were working like slaves to hold their ground, preserve their respectful interval, while the shells boomed in the air about them, and caused their chargers to make furious quivering leaps.

A battery, a tumultuous and shining mass, was swirling toward the right. The wild thud of hoofs, the cries of the riders shouting blame and praise, menace and encouragement, and, last, the roar of the wheels, the slant of the glistening guns, brought the lieutenant to an intent pause. The battery swept in curves that stirred the heart; it made halts as dramatic as the crash of a wave on the rocks, and when it fled onward this aggregation of wheels, levers, motors had a beautiful unity, as if it were a missile. The sound of it was a war-chorus that reached into the depths of man's emotion.

The lieutenant, still holding his arm as if it were of glass, stood watching this battery until all detail of it was lost, save the figures of the riders, which rose and fell and waved lashes over the black mass.

Later, he turned his eyes toward the battle, where the shooting sometimes crackled like bush-fires, sometimes sputtered with exasperating irregularity, and sometimes reverberated like the thunder. He saw the smoke rolling upward and saw crowds of men who ran and cheered, or stood and blazed away at the inscrutable distance.

He came upon some stragglers, and they told him how to find the field hospital. They described its exact location. In fact, these men, no longer having part in the battle, knew more of it than others. They told the performance of every corps, every division, the opinion of every general. The lieutenant, carrying his wounded arm rearward, looked upon them with wonder.

At the roadside a brigade was making coffee and buzzing with talk like a girls' boarding school. Several officers came out to him and inquired concerning things of which he knew nothing. One, seeing his arm, began to scold. "Why, man, that's no way to do. You want to fix that thing." He appropriated the lieutenant and the lieutenant's wound. He cut the sleeve and laid bare the arm, every nerve of which softly fluttered under his touch. He bound his handkerchief over the wound, scolding away in the meantime. His tone allowed one to think that he was in the habit of being wounded every day. The lieutenant hung his head, feeling, in this presence, that he did not know how to be correctly wounded.

The low white tents of the hospital were grouped around an old schoolhouse. There was here a singular commotion. In the foreground two ambulances interlocked wheels in the deep mud. The drivers were tossing the blame of it back and forth, gesticulating and berating, while from the ambulances, both crammed with wounded, there came an occasional groan. An interminable crowd of bandaged men were coming and going. Great numbers sat under the trees nursing heads or arms or legs. There was a dispute of some kind raging on the steps of the schoolhouse. Sitting with his back against a tree a man with a face as grey as a new army blanket was serenely smoking a corncob pipe. The lieutenant wished to rush forward and inform him that he was dying.

A busy surgeon was passing near the lieutenant. "Good-morning," he said, with a friendly smile. Then he caught sight of the lieutenant's arm, and his face at once changed. "Well, let's have a look at it." He seemed possessed suddenly of a great contempt for the lieutenant. This wound evidently placed the latter on a very low social plane. The doctor cried out impatiently: "What mutton-head had tied it up that way anyhow?" The lieutenant answered, "Oh, a man."

When the wound was disclosed the doctor fingered it disdainfully. "Humph," he said. "You come along with me and I'll 'tend to you." His voice contained the same scorn as if he were saying: "You will have to go to jail."

The lieutenant had been very meek, but now his face flushed, and he looked into the doctor's eyes. "I guess I won't have it amputated," he said.

"Nonsense, man! Nonsense! Nonsense!" cried the doctor. "Come along, now. I won't amputate it. Come along. Don't be a baby."

"Let go of me," said the lieutenant, holding back wrathfully, his glance fixed upon the door of the old schoolhouse, as sinister to him as the portals of death.

And this is the story of how the lieutenant lost his arm. When he reached home, his sisters, his mother, his wife, sobbed for a long time at the sight of the flat sleeve. "Oh, well," he said, standing shame-faced amid these tears, "I don't suppose it matters so much as all that."

War

Luigi Pirandello

The passengers who had left Rome by the night express had had to stop until dawn at the small station of Fabriano in order to continue their journey by the small old-fashioned local joining the main line with Sulmona.

At dawn, in a stuffy and smoky second-class carriage in which five people had already spent the night, a bulky woman in deep mourning was hoisted in—almost like a shapeless bundle. Behind her—puffing and moaning, followed her husband—a tiny man, thin and weakly, his face death-white, his eyes small and bright and looking shy and uneasy.

Having at last taken a seat he politely thanked the passengers who had helped his wife and who had made room for her; then he turned round to the woman trying to pull down the collar of her coat, and politely inquired:

"Are you all right, dear?"

The wife, instead of answering, pulled up her collar again to her eyes, so as to hide her face.

"Nasty world," muttered the husband with a sad smile.

And he felt it his duty to explain to his traveling companions that the poor woman was to be pitied for the war was taking away from her her only son, a boy of twenty to whom both had devoted their entire life, even breaking up their home at Sulmona to follow him to Rome, where he had to go as a student, then allowing him to volunteer for war with an assurance, however, that at least for six months he would not be sent to the front and now, all of a sudden, receiving a wire saying that he was due to leave in three days' time and asking them to go and see him off.

The woman under the big coat was twisting and wriggling, at times growling like a wild animal, feeling certain that all those explanations would not have aroused even a shadow of sympathy from those people who—most likely—were in the same plight as herself. One of them, who had been listening with particular attention, said:

"You should thank God that your son is only leaving now for the front. Mine has been sent there the first day of the war. He has already come back twice wounded and been sent back again to the front."

"What about me? I have two sons and three nephews at the front," said another passenger.

"Maybe, but in our case it is our *only* son," ventured the husband.

"What difference can it make? You may spoil your only son with excessive attentions, but you cannot love him more than you would all your other children if you had any. Paternal love is not like bread that can be broken into pieces and split amongst the children in equal shares. A father gives *all* his love to each one of his children without discrimination, whether it be one or ten, and if I am suffering now for my two sons, I am not suffering half for each of them but double . . ."

"True . . . true . . ." sighed the embarrassed husband, "but suppose (of course we all hope it will never be your case) a father has two sons at the front and he loses one of them, there is still one left to console him . . . while . . ."

"Yes," answered the other, getting cross, "a son left to console him but also a son left for whom he must survive, while in the case of the father of an only son if the son dies the father can die too and put an end to his distress. Which of the two positions is the worse? Don't you see how my case would be worse than yours?"

"Nonsense," interrupted another traveler, a fat, red-faced man with bloodshot eyes of the palest gray.

He was panting. From his bulging eyes seemed to spurt inner violence of an uncontrolled vitality which his weakened body could hardly contain.

"Nonsense," he repeated, trying to cover his mouth with his hand so as to hide the two missing front teeth. "Nonsense. Do we give life to our children for our own benefit?"

The other travelers stared at him in distress. The one who had had his son at the front since the first day of the war sighed: "You are right. Our children do not belong to us, they belong to the Country. . . ."

"Bosh," retorted the fat traveler. "Do we think of the Country when we give life to our children? Our sons are born because . . . well, because they must be born and when they come to life they take our own life with them. This is the truth. We belong to them but they never belong to us. And when they reach twenty they are exactly what we were at their age. We too had a father and mother, but there were so many other things as well . . . girls, cigarettes, illusions, new ties . . . and the Country, of course, whose call we would have answered—when we were twenty—even if father and mother had said no. Now, at our age, the love of our Country is still great, of course, but stronger than it is the love for our children. Is there any one of us here who wouldn't gladly take his son's place at the front if he could?"

There was a silence all round, everybody nodding as to approve.

"Why then," continued the fat man, "shouldn't we consider the feelings of our children when they are twenty? Isn't it natural that at their age they should consider the love for their Country (I am speaking of decent boys, of course) even greater than the love for us? Isn't it natural that it should be so, as after all they must look upon us as upon old boys who cannot move any more and must stay at home? If Country exists, if Country is a natural necessity, like bread, of which each of us must eat in order not to die of hunger, somebody must go to defend it. And our sons go, when they are twenty, and they don't want tears, because if they die, they die inflamed and happy (I am speaking, of course, of decent boys). Now, if one dies young and happy, without having the ugly sides of life, the boredom of it, the pettiness, the bitterness of disillusion . . . what more can we ask for him? Everyone should stop crying; everyone should laugh, as I do . . . or at least thank God—as I do—because my son, before dying, sent me a message saying that he was dying satisfied at having ended his life in the best way he could have wished. That is why, as you see, I do not even wear mourning. . . ."

He shook his light fawn coat as to show it; his livid lip over his missing teeth was trembling, his eyes were watery and motionless, and soon after he ended with a shrill laugh which might well have been a sob.

"Quite so . . . quite so . . ." agreed the others.

The woman who, bundled in a corner under her coat, had been sitting and listening had—for the last three months—tried to find in the words of her husband and her friends something to console her in her deep sorrow, something that might show her how a mother should resign herself to send her son not even to death but to a probable danger of life. Yet not a word had she found amongst the many which had been said . . . and her grief had been greater in seeing that no-body—as she thought—could share her feelings.

But now the words of the traveler amazed and almost stunned her. She suddenly realized that it wasn't the others who were wrong and could not understand her but herself who could not rise up to the same height of those fathers and mothers willing to resign themselves, without crying, not only to the departure of their sons but even to their death.

She lifted her head, she bent over from her corner trying to listen with great attention to the details which the fat man was giving to his companions about the way his son had fallen as a hero, for his King and his Country, happy and without regrets. It seemed to her that she had stumbled into a world she had never dreamt of, a world so far unknown to her and she was so pleased to hear everyone joining in congratulating that brave father who could so stoically speak of his child's death.

Then suddenly, just as if she had heard nothing of what had been said and almost as if waking up from a dream, she turned to the old man, asking him:

"Then . . . is your son really dead?"

Everybody stared at her. The old man, too, turned to look at her, fixing his great, bulging, horribly watery light gray eyes, deep in her face. For some little time he tried to answer, but words failed him. He looked and looked at her, almost as if only then—at that silly, incongru-ous question—he had suddenly realized at last that his son was really dead—gone for ever—for ever. His face contracted, became horribly distorted, then he snatched in haste a handkerchief from his pocket and, to the amazement of everyone, broke into harrowing, heartrending, un-controllable sobs.

Two Soldiers   *William Faulkner*

Me and Pete would go down to Old Man Killegrew's and listen to his radio. We would wait until after supper, after dark, and we would stand outside Old Man Killegrew's parlor window, and we could hear it because Old Man Killegrew's wife was deaf, and so he run the radio as loud as it would run, and so me and Pete could hear it plain as Old Man Killegrew's wife could, I reckon, even standing outside with the window closed.

And that night I said, "What? Japanese? What's a pearl harbor?" and Pete said, "Hush."

And so we stood there, it was cold, listening to the fellow in the radio talking, only I couldn't make no heads nor tails neither out of it. Then the fellow said that would be all for a while, and me and Pete walked back up the road to home, and Pete told me what it was. Because he was nigh twenty and he had done finished the Consolidated last June and he knowed a heap: about them Japanese dropping bombs on Pearl Harbor and that Pearl Harbor was across the water.

"Across what water?" I said. "Across that Government reservoy up at Oxford?"

"Naw," Pete said. "Across the big water. The Pacific Ocean."

We went home. Maw and pap was already asleep, and me and Pete laid in the bed, and I still couldn't understand where it was, and Pete told me again—the Pacific Ocean.

"What's the matter with you?" Pete said. "You're going on nine years old. You been in school now ever since September. Ain't you learned nothing yet?"

"I reckon we ain't got as fer as the Pacific Ocean yet," I said.

We was still sowing the vetch then that ought to been all finished by the fifteenth of November, because pap was still behind, just like he had been ever since me and Pete had knowed him. And we had firewood to git in, too, but every night me and Pete would go down to Old Man Killegrew's and stand outside his parlor window in the cold and listen to his radio; then we would come back home and lay in the bed and Pete would tell me what it was. That is, he would tell me for a while. Then he wouldn't tell me. It was like he didn't want to talk about it no more. He would tell me to shut up because he wanted to go to sleep, but he never wanted to go to sleep.

He would lay there, a heap stiller than if he was asleep, and it would be something, I could feel it coming out of him, like he was mad at me even, only I knowed he wasn't thinking about me, or like he was worried about something, and it wasn't that neither, because he never had nothing to worry about. He never got behind like pap, let alone stayed behind. Pap give him ten acres when he graduated from the Consolidated, and me and Pete both reckoned pap was durn glad to get shut of at least ten acres, less to have to worry with himself; and Pete had them ten acres all sowed to vetch and busted out and bedded for the winter, and so it wasn't that. But it was something. And still we would go down to Old Man Killegrew's every night and listen to his radio, and they was at it in the Philippines now, but General MacArthur was holding um. Then we would come back home and lay in the bed, and Pete wouldn't tell me nothing or talk at all. He would just lay there still as a ambush and when I would touch him, his side or his leg would feel hard and still as iron, until after a while I would go to sleep.

Then one night—it was the first time he had said nothing to me except to jump on me about not chopping enough wood at the wood tree where we was cutting—he said, "I got to go."

"Go where?" I said.

"To that war," Pete said.

"Before we even finish gettin' in the firewood?"

"Firewood, hell," Pete said.

"All right," I said. "When we going to start?"

But he wasn't even listening. He laid there, hard and still as iron in the dark. "I got to go," he said. "I jest ain't going to put up with no folks treating the Unity States that way."

"Yes," I said. "Firewood or no firewood, I reckon we got to go."

This time he heard me. He laid still again, but it was a different kind of still.

"You?" he said. "To a war?"

"You'll whup the big uns and I'll whup the little uns," I said.

Then he told me I couldn't go. At first I thought he just never wanted me tagging after him, like he wouldn't leave me go with him when he went sparking them girls of Tull's. Then he told me the Army wouldn't leave me go because I was too little, and then I knowed he really meant it and that I couldn't go nohow noways. And somehow I hadn't believed until then that he was going himself, but now I knowed he was and that he wasn't going to leave me go with him a-tall.

"I'll chop the wood and tote the water for you-all then!" I said. "You got to have wood and water!"

Anyway, he was listening to me now. He wasn't like iron now.

He turned onto his side and put his hand on my chest because it was me that was laying straight and hard on my back now.

"No," he said. "You got to stay here and help pap."

"Help him what?" I said. "He ain't never caught up nohow. He can't get no further behind. He can sholy take care of this little shirttail of a farm while me and you are whupping them Japanese. I got to go too. If you got to go, then so have I."

"No," Pete said. "Hush now. Hush." And he meant it, and I knowed he did. Only I made sho from his own mouth. I quit.

"So I just can't go then," I said.

"No," Pete said. "You just can't go. You're too little, in the first place, and in the second place ———"

"All right," I said. "Then shut up and leave me go to sleep."

So he hushed then and laid back. And I laid there like I was already asleep, and pretty soon he was asleep and I knowed it was the wanting to go to the war that had worried him and kept him awake, and now that he had decided to go, he wasn't worried any more.

The next morning he told maw and pap. Maw was all right. She cried.

"No," she said, crying, "I don't want him to go. I would rather go myself in his place, if I could. I don't want to save the country. Them Japanese could take it and keep it, so long as they left me and my family and my children alone. But I remember my brother Marsh in that other war. He had to go to that one when he wasn't but nineteen, and our mother couldn't understand it then any more than I can now. But she told Marsh if he had to go, he had to go. And so, if Pete's got to go to this one, he's got to go to it. Jest don't ask me to understand why."

But pap was the one. He was the feller. "To the war?" he said. "Why, I just don't see a bit of use in that. You ain't old enough for the draft, and the country ain't being invaded. Our President in Washington, D. C., is watching the conditions and he will notify us. Besides, in that other war your ma just mentioned, I was drafted and sent clean to Texas and was held there nigh eight months until they finally quit fighting. It seems to me that that, along with your Uncle Marsh who received a actual wound on the battlefields of France, is enough for me and mine to have to do to protect the country, at least in my lifetime. Besides, what'll I do for help on the farm with you gone? It seems to me I'll get mighty far behind."

"You been behind as long as I can remember," Pete said. "Anyway, I'm going. I got to."

"Of course he's got to go," I said. "Them Japanese ———"

"You hush your mouth!" maw said, crying. "Nobody's talking to you! Go and get me a armful of wood! That's what you can do!"

So I got the wood. And all the next day, while me and Pete and pap was getting in as much wood as we could in that time because Pete said how pap's idea of plenty of wood was one more stick laying against the wall that Maw ain't put on the fire yet, Maw was getting Pete ready to go. She washed and mended his clothes and cooked him a shoe box of vittles. And that night me and Pete laid in the bed and listened to her packing his grip and crying, until after a while Pete got up in his nightshirt and went back there, and I could hear them talking, until at last maw said, "You got to go, and so I want you to go. But I don't understand it, and I won't never, and so don't expect me to." And Pete come back and got into the bed again and laid again still and hard as iron on his back, and then he said, and he wasn't talking to me, he wasn't talking to nobody: "I got to go. I just got to."

"Sho you got to," I said. "Them Japanese ——" He turned over hard, he kind of surged over onto his side, looking at me in the dark.

"Anyway, you're all right," he said. "I expected to have more trouble with you than with all the rest of them put together."

"I reckon I can't help it neither," I said. "But maybe it will run a few years longer and I can get there. Maybe someday I will jest walk in on you."

"I hope not," Pete said. "Folks don't go to wars for fun. A man don't leave his maw crying just for fun."

"Then why are you going?" I said.

"I got to," he said. "I just got to. Now you go on to sleep. I got to ketch that early bus in the morning."

"All right," I said. "I hear tell Memphis is a big place. How will you find where the Army's at?"

"I'll ask somebody where to go to join it," Pete said. "Go on to sleep now."

"Is that what you'll ask for? Where to join the Army?" I said.

"Yes," Pete said. He turned onto his back again. "Shut up and go to sleep."

We went to sleep. The next morning we et breakfast by lamplight because the bus would pass at six o'clock. Maw wasn't crying now. She jest looked grim and busy, putting breakfast on the table while we et it. Then she finished packing Pete's grip, except he never wanted to take no grip to the war, but maw said decent folks never went nowhere, not even to a war, without a change of clothes and something to tote them in. She put in the shoe box of fried chicken and biscuits and she put the Bible in, too, and then it was time to go. We didn't know until then that maw wasn't going to the bus. She jest brought Pete's cap and overcoat, and still she didn't cry no more, she jest stood with her hands on Pete's shoulders and she didn't move, but somehow, and just holding Pete's shoulders, she looked as hard and fierce as when Pete had turned toward me in the bed last night and tole me that anyway I was all right.

"They could take the country and keep the country, so long as they never bothered me and mine," she said. Then she said, "Don't never forget who you are. You ain't rich and the rest of the world outside of Frenchman's Bend never heard of you. But your blood is good as any blood anywhere, and don't you never forget it."

Then she kissed him, and then we was out of the house, with pap toting Pete's grip whether Pete wanted him to or not. There wasn't no dawn even yet, not even after we had stood on the highway by the mailbox, a while. Then we seen the lights of the bus coming and I was watching the bus until it come up and Pete flagged it, and then, sho enough, there was daylight—it had started while I wasn't watching. And now me and Pete expected pap to say something else foolish, like he done before, about how Uncle Marsh getting wounded in France and that trip to Texas pap taken in 1918 ought to be enough to save the Unity States in 1942, but he never. He done all right too. He jest said, "Good-by, son. Always remember what your ma told you and write her whenever you find the time." Then he shaken Pete's hand, and Pete looked at me a minute and put his hand on my head and rubbed my head durn nigh hard enough to wring my neck off and jumped into the bus, and the feller wound the door shut and the bus began to hum; then it was moving, humming and grinding and whining louder and louder; it was going fast, with two little red lights behind it that never seemed to get no littler, but just seemed to be running together until pretty soon they would touch and jest be one light. But they never did, and then the bus was gone, and even like it was, I could have pretty nigh busted out crying, nigh to nine years old and all.

Me and pap went back to the house. All that day we worked at the wood tree, and so I never had no good chance until about middle of the afternoon. Then I taken my slingshot and I would have liked to took all my bird eggs, too, because Pete had give me his collection and he holp me with mine, and he would like to git the box out and look at them as good as I would, even if he was nigh twenty years

old. But the box was too big to tote a long ways and have to worry
with, so I just taken the shikepoke egg, because it was the best un,
and wropped it up good into a matchbox and hid it and the slingshot
under the corner of the barn. Then we et supper and went to bed, and
I thought then how if I would 'a' had to stayed in that room and
that bed like that even for one more night, I jest couldn't 'a' stood it.
Then I could hear pap snoring, but I never heard no sound from maw,
whether she was asleep or not, and I don't reckon she was. So I taken
my shoes and drapped them out the window, and then I clumb out
like I used to watch Pete do when he was still jest seventeen and pap
held that he was too young yet to be tomcatting around at night, and
wouldn't leave him out, and I put on my shoes and went to the barn
and got the slingshot and the shikepoke egg and went to the highway.

It wasn't cold, it was jest durn confounded dark, and that highway
stretched on in front of me like, without nobody using it, it had stretched
out half again as fer just like a man does when he lays down, so that
for a time it looked like full sun was going to ketch me before I had
finished them twenty-two miles to Jefferson. But it didn't. Daybreak
was jest starting when I walked up the hill into town. I could smell
breakfast cooking in the cabins and I wished I had thought to brought
me a cold biscuit, but that was too late now. And Pete had told me
Memphis was a piece beyond Jefferson, but I never knowed it was no
eighty miles. So I stood there on that empty square, with daylight coming and coming and the street lights still burning and that Law looking
down at me, and me still eighty miles from Memphis, and it had took
me all night to walk jest twenty-two miles, and so, by the time I got
to Memphis at that rate, Pete would 'a' done already started for Pearl
Harbor.

"Where do you come from?" the Law said.

And I told him again. "I got to get to Memphis. My brother's there."

"You mean you ain't got any folks around here?" the Law said.
"Nobody but that brother? What are you doing way off down here and
your brother in Memphis?"

And I told him again, "I got to get to Memphis. I ain't got no
time to waste talking about it and I ain't got time to walk it. I got to
git there today."

"Come on here," the Law said.

We went down another street. And there was the bus, just like when
Pete got into it yestiddy morning, except there wasn't no lights on it
now and it was empty. There was a regular bus dee-po like a railroad

dee-po, with a ticket counter and a feller behind it, and the Law said, "Set down over there," and I set down on the bench, and the Law said, "I want to use your telephone," and he talked in the telephone a minute and put it down and said to the feller behind the ticket counter, "Keep your eye on him. I'll be back as soon as Mrs. Habersham can arrange to get herself up and dressed." He went out. I got up and went to the ticket counter.

"I want to go to Memphis," I said.

"You bet," the feller said. "You set down on the bench now. Mr. Foote will be back in a minute."

"I don't know no Mr. Foote," I said. "I want to ride that bus to Memphis."

"You got some money?" he said. "It'll cost you seventy-two cents."

I taken out the matchbox and unwropped the shikepoke egg. "I'll swap you this for a ticket to Memphis," I said.

"What's that?" he said.

"It's a shikepoke egg," I said. "You never seen one before. It's worth a dollar. I'll take seventy-two cents fer it."

"No," he said, "the fellers that own that bus insist on a cash basis. If I started swapping tickets for bird eggs and livestock and such, they would fire me. You go and set down on the bench now, like Mr. Foote ——"

I started for the door, but he caught me, he put one hand on the ticket counter and jumped over it and caught up with me and reached his hand out to ketch my shirt. I whupped out my pocketknife and snapped it open.

"You put a hand on me and I'll cut it off," I said.

I tried to dodge him and run at the door, but he could move quicker than any grown man I ever see, quick as Pete almost. He cut me off and stood with his back against the door and one foot raised a little, and there wasn't no other way to get out. "Get back on that bench and stay there," he said.

And there wasn't no other way out. And he stood there with his back against the door. So I went back to the bench. And then it seemed like to me that dee-po was full of folks. There was that Law again, and there was two ladies in fur coats and their faces already painted. But they still looked like they had got up in a hurry and they still never liked it, a old one and a young one, looking down at me.

"He hasn't got a overcoat!" the old one said. "How in the world did he ever get down here by himself?"

"I ask you," the Law said. "I couldn't get nothing out of him except his brother is in Memphis and he wants to get back up there."

"That's right," I said. "I got to git to Memphis today."

"Of course you must," the old one said. "Are you sure you can find your brother when you get to Memphis?"

"I reckon I can," I said. "I ain't got but one and I have knowed him all my life. I reckon I will know him again when I see him."

The old one looked at me. "Somehow he doesn't look like he lives in Memphis," she said.

"He probably don't," the Law said. "You can't tell though. He might live anywhere, overhalls or not. This day and time they get scattered overnight from he—— hope to breakfast; boys and girls, too, almost before they can walk good. He might have been in Missouri or Texas either yestiddy, for all we know. But he don't seem to have any doubt his brother is in Memphis. All I know to do is send him up there and leave him look."

"Yes," the old one said.

The young one set down on the bench by me and opened a hand satchel and taken out a artermatic writing pen and some papers.

"Now, honey," the old one said, "we're going to see that you find your brother, but we must have a case history for our files first. We want to know your name and your brother's name and where you were born and when your parents died."

"I don't need no case history neither," I said. "All I want is to get to Memphis. I got to get there today."

"You see?" the Law said. He said it almost like he enjoyed it. "That's what I told you."

"You're lucky, at that, Mrs. Habersham," the bus feller said. "I don't think he's got a gun on him, but he can open that knife da—— I mean, fast enough to suit any man."

But the old one just stood there looking at me.

"Well," she said. "Well. I really don't know what to do."

"I do," the bus feller said. "I'm going to give him a ticket out of my own pocket, as a measure of protecting the company against riot and bloodshed. And when Mr. Foote tells the city board about it, it will be a civic matter and they will not only reimburse me, they will give me a medal too. Hey, Mr. Foote?"

But never nobody paid him no mind. The old one still stood looking down at me. She said "Well," again. Then she taken a dollar from her purse and give it to the bus feller. "I suppose he will travel on a child's ticket, won't he?"

"Wellum," the bus feller said, "I just don't know what the regulations would be. Likely I will be fired for not crating him and marking the crate Poison. But I'll risk it."

Then they were gone. Then the Law come back with a sandwich and give it to me.

"You're sure you can find that brother?" he said.

"I ain't yet convinced why not," I said. "If I don't see Pete first, he'll see me. He knows me too."

Then the Law went out for good, too, and I et the sandwich. Then more folks come in and bought tickets, and then the bus feller said it was time to go, and I got into the bus just like Pete done, and we was gone.

I seen all the towns. I seen all of them. When the bus got to going good, I found out I was jest about wore out for sleep. But there was too much I hadn't never saw before. We run out of Jefferson and run past fields and woods, then we would run into another town and out of that un and past fields and woods again, and then into another town with stores and gins and water tanks, and we run along by the railroad for a spell and I seen the signal arm move, and then I seen the train and then some more towns, and I was jest about plumb wore out for sleep, but I couldn't resk it. Then Memphis begun. It seemed like, to me, it went on for miles. We would pass a patch of stores and I would think that was sholy it and the bus would even stop. But it wouldn't be Memphis yet and we would go on again past water tanks and smokestacks on top of the mills, and if they was gins and sawmills, I never knowed there was that many and I never seen any that big, and where they got enough cotton and logs to run um I don't know.

Then I see Memphis. I knowed I was right this time. It was standing up into the air. It looked like about a dozen whole towns bigger than Jefferson was set up on one edge in a field, standing up into the air higher than ara hill in all Yoknapatawpha County. Then we was in it, with the bus stopping ever' few feet, it seemed like to me, and cars rushing past on both sides of it and the street crowded with folks from ever'where in town that day, until I didn't see how there could 'a' been nobody left in Mis'sippi a-tall to even sell me a bus ticket, let alone write out no case histories. Then the bus stopped. It was another bus dee-po, a heap bigger than the one in Jefferson. And I said, "All right. Where do folks join the Army?"

"What?" the bus feller said.

And I said it again, "Where do folks join the Army?"

"Oh," he said. Then he told me how to get there. I was afraid at first I wouldn't ketch on how to do in a town big as Memphis. But I caught on all right. I never had to ask but twice more. Then I was there, and I was durn glad to git out of all them rushing cars and shoving folks and all that racket for a spell, and I thought, It won't be long now, and I thought how if there was any kind of a crowd there that had done already joined the Army, too, Pete would likely see me before I seen him. And so I walked into the room. And Pete wasn't there.

He wasn't even there. There was a soldier with a big arrerhead on his sleeve, writing, and two fellers standing in front of him, and there was some more folks there, I reckon. It seems to me I remember some more folks there.

I went to the table where the soldier was writing, and I said, "Where's Pete?" and he looked up and I said, "My brother. Pete Grier. Where is he?"

"What?" the soldier said. "Who?"

And I told him again. "He joined the Army yestiddy. He's going to Pearl Harbor. So am I. I want to ketch him. Where you all got him?" Now they were all looking at me, but I never paid them no mind. "Come on," I said. "Where is he?"

The soldier had quit writing. He had both hands spraddled out on the table. "Oh," he said. "You're going, too, hah?"

"Yes," I said. "They got to have wood and water. I can chop it and tote it. Come on. Where's Pete?"

The soldier stood up. "Who let you in here?" he said. "Go on. Beat it".

"Durn that," I said. "You tell me where Pete ——"

I be dog if he couldn't move faster than the bus feller even. He never come over the table, he come around it, he was on me almost before I knowed it, so that I jest had time to jump back and whup out my pocket-knife and snap it open and hit one lick, and he hollered and jumped back and grabbed one hand with the other and stood there cussing and hollering.

One of the other fellers grabbed me from behind, and I hit at him with the knife, but I couldn't reach him.

Then both of the fellers had me from behind, and then another soldier come out of a door at the back. He had on a belt with a britching strop over one shoulder.

"What the hell is this?" he said.

"That little son cut me with a knife!" the first soldier hollered. When he said that I tried to get at him again, but both them fellers was holding me, two against one, and the soldier with the backing strop said, "Here, here. Put your knife up, feller. None of us are armed. A man don't knife-fight folks that are barehanded." I could begin to hear him then. He sounded jest like Pete talked to me. "Let him go," he said. They let me go. "Now what's all the trouble about?" And I told him. "I see," he said. "And you come up to see if he was all right before he left."

"No," I said. "I came to ———"

But he had already turned to where the first soldier was wropping a handkerchief around his hand.

"Have you got him?" he said. The first soldier went back to the table and looked at some papers.

"Here he is," he said. "He enlisted yestiddy. He's in a detachment leaving this morning for Little Rock." He had a watch stropped on his arm. He looked at it. "The train leaves in about fifty minutes. If I know country boys, they're probably all down there at the station right now."

"Get him up here," the one with the backing strop said. "Phone the station. Tell the porter to get him a cab. And you come with me," he said.

It was another office behind that un, with jes a table and some chairs. We set there while the soldier smoked, and it wasn't long; I knowed Pete's feet soon as I heard them. Then the first soldier opened the door and Pete come in. He never had no soldier clothes on. He looked jest like he did when he got on the bus yestiddy morning, except it seemed to me like it was at least a week, so much had happened, and I had done had to do so much traveling. He come in and there he was, looking at me like he hadn't never left home, except that here we was in Memphis, on the way to Pearl Harbor.

"What in durnation are you doing here?" he said.

And I told him, "You got to have wood and water to cook with. I can chop it and tote it for you-all."

"No," Pete said. "You're going back home."

"No, Pete," I said. "I got to go too. I got to. It hurts my heart, Pete."

"No," Pete said. He looked at the soldier. "I jest don't know what could have happened to him, lootenant," he said. "He never drawed a knife on anybody before in his life." He looked at me. "What did you do it for?"

"I don't know," I said. "I jest had to. I jest had to git here. I jest had to find you."

"Well, don't you never do it again, you hear?" Pete said. "You put that knife in your pocket and you keep it there. If I ever again hear of you drawing it on anybody, I'm coming back from wherever I am at and whup the fire out of you. You hear me?"

"I would pure cut a throat if it would bring you back to stay," I said. "Pete," I said. "Pete."

"No," Pete said. Now his voice wasn't hard and quick no more, it was almost quiet, and I knowed now I wouldn't never change him. "You must go home. You must look after maw, and I am depending on you to look after my ten acres. I want you to go back home. Today. Do you hear?"

"I hear," I said.

"Can he get back home by himself?" the soldier said.

"He come up here by himself," Pete said.

"I can get back, I reckon," I said. "I don't live in but one place. I don't reckon it's moved."

Pete taken a dollar out of his pocket and give it to me. "That'll buy your bus ticket right to our mailbox," he said. "I want you to mind the lootenant. He'll send you to the bus. And you go back home and you take care of maw and look after my ten acres and keep that durn knife in your pocket. You hear me?"

"Yes, Pete," I said.

"All right," Pete said. "Now I got to go." He put his hand on my head again. But this time he never wrung my neck. He just laid his hand on my head a minute. And then I be dog if he didn't lean down and kiss me, and I heard his feet and then the door, and I never looked up and that was all, me setting there, rubbing the place where Pete kissed me and the soldier throwed back in his chair, looking out the window and coughing. He reached into his pocket and handed something to me without looking around. It was a piece of chewing gum.

"Much obliged," I said. "Well, I reckon I might as well start back. I got a right fer piece to go."

"Wait," the soldier said. Then he telephoned again and I said again

I better start back, and he said again, "Wait. Remember what Pete told you."

So we waited, and then another lady come in, old, too, in a fur coat, too, but she smelled all right, she never had no artermatic writing pen nor no case history neither. She come in and the soldier got up, and she looked around quick until she saw me, and come and put her hand on my shoulder light and quick and easy as maw herself might 'a' done it.

"Come on," she said. "Let's go home to dinner."

"Nome," I said. "I got to ketch the bus to Jefferson."

"I know. There's plenty of time. We'll go home and eat dinner first."

She had a car. And now we was right down in the middle of all them other cars. We was almost under the busses, and all them crowds of people on the street close enough to where I could have talked to them if I had knowed who they was. After a while she stopped the car.

"Here we are," she said, and I looked at it, and if all that was her house, she sho had a big family. But all of it wasn't. We crossed a hall with trees growing in it and went into a little room without nothing in it but a nigger dressed up in a uniform a heap shinier than them soldiers had, and the nigger shut the door, and then I hollered, "Look out!" and grabbed, but it was all right; that whole little room jest went right on up and stopped and the door opened and we was in another hall, and the lady unlocked a door and we went in, and there was another soldier, a old feller, with a britching strop, too, and a silver-colored bird on each shoulder.

"Here we are," the lady said. "This is Colonel McKellogg. Now, what would you like for dinner?"

"I reckon I'll jest have some ham and eggs and coffee," I said.

She had done started to pick up the telephone. She stopped. "Coffee?" she said. "When did you start drinking coffee?"

"I don't know," I said. "I reckon it was before I could remember."

"You're about eight, aren't you?" she said.

"Nome," I said. "I'm eight and ten months. Going on eleven months."

She telephoned then. Then we set there and I told them how Pete had jest left that morning for Pearl Harbor and I had aimed to go with him, but I would have to go back home to take care of maw and look after Pete's ten acres, and she said how they had a little boy about my size, too, in a school in the East. Then a nigger, another one, in a short kind of shirttail coat, roled a kind of wheelbarrer in. It had my ham and eggs and a glass of milk and a piece of pie, too, and I thought

I was hungry. But when I taken the first bite I found out I couldn't swallow it, and I got up quick.

"I got to go," I said.

"Wait," she said.

"I got to go," I said.

"Just a minute," she said. "I've already telephoned for the car. It won't be but a minute now. Can't you drink the milk even? Or maybe some of your coffee?"

"Nome," I said. "I ain't hungry. I'll eat when I git home." Then the telephone rung. She never even answered it.

"There," she said. "There's the car." And we went back down in that 'ere little moving room with the dressed-up nigger. This time it was a big car with a soldier driving it. I got into the front with him. She give the soldier a dollar. "He might get hungry," she said. "Try to find a decent place for him."

"O.K., Mrs. McKellogg," the soldier said.

Then we was gone again. And now I could see Memphis good, bright in the sunshine, while we was swinging around it. And first thing I knowed, we was back on the same highway the bus run on this morning—the patches of stores and them big gins and sawmills, and Memphis running on for miles, it seemed like to me, before it begun to give out. Then we was running again between the fields and woods, running fast now, and except for that soldier, it was like I hadn't never been to Memphis a-tall. We was going fast now. At this rate, before I knowed it we would be home again, and I thought about me riding up to Frenchman's Bend in this big car with a soldier running it, and all of a sudden I begun to cry. I never knowed I was fixing to, and I couldn't stop it. I set there by that soldier, crying. We was going fast.

Quality   *John Galsworthy*

I knew him from the days of my extreme youth, because he made my father's boots; inhabiting with his elder brother two little shops let into one, in a small by-street—now no more, but then most fashionably placed in the West End.

That tenement had a certain quiet distinction; there was no sign upon its face that he made for any of the Royal Family—merely his own German name of Gessler Brothers; and in the window a few pairs of boots. I remember that it always troubled me to account for those unvarying boots in the window, for he made only what was ordered, reaching nothing down, and it seemed so inconceivable that what he made could ever have failed to fit. Had he bought them to put there? That, too, seemed inconceivable. He would never have tolerated in his house leather on which he had not worked himself. Besides, they were too beautiful—the pairs of pumps, so inexpressibly slim, the patent leathers with cloth tops, making water come into one's mouth, the tall brown riding-boots with marvelous sooty glow, as if, though new, they had been worn a hundred years. Those pairs could only have been made by one who saw before him the Soul of Boot—so truly were they prototypes, incarnating the very spirit of all footwear. These thoughts, of course, came to me later, though even when I was promoted to him, at the age of perhaps fourteen, some inkling haunted me of the dignity of himself and brother. For to make boots—such boots as he made— seemed to me then, and still seems to me, mysterious and wonderful.

I remember well my shy remark, one day, while stretching out to him my youthful foot:

"Isn't it awfully hard to do, Mr. Gessler?"

And his answer, given with a sudden smile from out of the sardonic redness of his beard: "Id is an Ardt!"

Himself, he was a little as if made of leather, with his yellow crinkly face, and crinkly reddish hair and beard, and neat folds slanting down his cheeks to the corners of his mouth, and his guttural and one-toned voice; for leather is a sardonic substance, and stiff and slow of purpose. And that was the character of his face, save that his eyes, which were gray-blue, had in them the simple gravity of one secretly possessed by the Ideal. His elder brother was so very like him—though watery, paler in every way, with a great industry—that sometimes in early days I was not quite sure of him until the interview was over. Then I knew that it was he, if the words, "I will ask my brudder," had not been spoken, and that, if they had, it was the elder brother.

When one grew old and wild and ran up bills, one somehow never ran them up with Gessler Brothers. It would not have seemed becoming to go in there and stretch out one's foot to that blue iron-spectacled face, owing him for more than—say—two pairs, just the comfortable reassurance that one was still his client.

For it was not possible to go to him very often—his boots lasted terribly, having something beyond the temporary—some, as it were, essence of boot stitched into them.

One went in, not as into most shops, in the mood of: "Please serve me, and let me go!" but restfully, as one enters a church; and, sitting on the single wooden chair, waited—for there was never anybody there. Soon—over the top edge of that sort of well—rather dark, and smelling soothingly of leather—which formed the shop, there would be seen his face, or that of his elder brother, peering down. A guttural sound, and the tip-tap of bast slippers beating the narrow wooden stairs, and he would stand before one without coat, a little bent, in leather apron, with sleeves turned back, blinking—as if awakened from some dream of boots, or like an owl surprised in daylight and annoyed at this interruption.

And I would say: "How do you do, Mr. Gessler? Could you make me a pair of Russia leather boots?"

Without a word he would leave me, retiring whence he came, or into the other portion of the shop, and I would continue to rest in the wooden chair, inhaling the incense of his trade. Soon he would come back, holding in his thin, veined hand a piece of gold-brown leather. With eyes fixed on it, he would remark: "What a beaudiful biece!" When I, too, had admired it, he would speak again: "When do you wand dem?" And I would answer: "Oh! As soon as you conveniently can." And he would say: "Tomorrow fordnighd?" Or if he were his elder brother: "I will ask my brudder!"

Then I would murmur: "Thank you! Good-morning, Mr. Gessler." "Goot-morning!" he would reply, still looking at the leather in his hand. And as I moved to the door, I would hear the tip-tap of his bast slippers restoring him, up the stairs, to his dream of boots. But if it were some new kind of footgear that he had not yet made me, then indeed he would observe ceremony—divesting me of my boot and holding it long in his hand, looking at it with eyes at once critical and loving, as if recalling the glow with which he had created it, and rebuking the way in which one had disorganized this masterpiece. Then, placing my foot on a piece of paper, he would two or three times tickle the outer edges with a pencil and pass his nervous fingers over my toes, feeling himself into the heart of my requirements.

I cannot forget that day on which I had occasion to say to him: "Mr. Gessler, that last pair of town walking-boots creaked, you know."

He looked at me for a time without replying, as if expecting me to withdraw or qualify the statement, then said:

"Id shouldn'd 'ave greaked."

"It did, I'm afraid."

"You goddem wed before dey found demselves?"

"I don't think so."

At that he lowered his eyes, as if hunting for memory of those boots, and I felt sorry I had mentioned this grave thing.

"Zend dem back!" he said; "I will look at dem."

A feeling of compassion for my creaking boots surged up in me, so well could I imagine the sorrowful long curiosity of regard which he would bend on them.

"Zome boods," he said slowly, "are bad from birdt. If I can do noding wid dem, I dake dem off your bill."

Once (once only) I went absentmindedly into his shop in a pair of boots bought in an emergency at some large firm's. He took my order without showing me any leather, and I could feel his eyes penetrating the interior integument of my foot. At last he said:

"Dose are nod my boods."

The tone was not one of anger, nor of sorrow, not even of contempt, but there was in it something quiet that froze the blood. He put his hand down and pressed a finger on the place where the left boot, endeavoring to be fashionable, was not quite comfortable.

"Id 'urds you dere," he said. "Dose big virms 'ave no self-respect. Drash!" And then, as if something had given way within him, he spoke long and bitterly. It was the only time I ever heard him discuss the conditions and hardships of his trade.

"Dey get id all," he said, "dey get id by adverdisement, nod by work. Dey dake id away from us, who lofe our boods. Id gomes to this— bresently I haf no work. Every year id gets less—you will see." And looking at his lined face I saw things I had never noticed before, bitter things and bitter struggle—and what a lot of gray hairs there seemed suddenly in his red beard!

As best I could, I explained the circumstances of the purchase of those ill-omened boots. But his face and voice made a so deep impression that during the next few minutes I ordered many pairs! Nemesis fell! They lasted more terribly than ever. And I was not able conscientiously to go to him for nearly two years.

When at last I went I was surprised that outside one of the two little windows of his shop another name was painted, also that of a bootmaker—making, of course, for the Royal Family. The old familiar boots, no longer in dignified isolation, were huddled in the single win-

dow. Inside, the now contracted well of the one little shop was more
scented and darker than ever. And it was longer than usual, too, before a face peered down, and the tip-tap of the bast slippers began. At
last he stood before me, and, gazing through those rusty iron spectacles, said:

"Mr. ——, isn'd id?"

"Ah! Mr. Gessler," I stammered, "but your boots are really *too* good,
you know! See, these are quite decent still!" And I stretched out to him
my foot. He looked at it.

"Yes," he said, "beople do nod wand good boods, id seems."

To get away from his reproachful eyes and voice I hastily remarked:
"What have you done to your shop?"

He answered quietly: "Id was too exbensif. Do you wand some
boods?"

I ordered three pairs, though I had wanted only two, and quickly
left. I had, I know not quite what feeling of being part, in his mind,
of a conspiracy against him; or not perhaps so much against him as
against his idea of boot. One does not, I suppose, care to feel like that;
for it was again many months before my next visit to his shop, paid,
I remember, with the feeling: "Oh! well, I can't leave the old boy—
so here goes! Perhaps it'll be his elder brother!"

For his elder brother, I knew, had not character enough to reproach
me, even dumbly.

And, to my relief, in the shop there did appear to be his elder
brother, handling a piece of leather.

"Well, Mr. Gessler," I said, "how are you?"

He came close, and peered at me.

"I am breddy well," he said slowly; "but my elder brudder is dead."

And I saw that it was indeed himself—but how aged and wan! And
never before had I heard him mention his brother. Much shocked,
I murmured: "Oh! I am sorry!"

"Yes," he answered, "he was a good man, he made a good bood;
but he is dead." And he touched the top of his head, where the hair
had suddenly gone as thin as it had been on that of his poor brother,
to indicate, I suppose, the cause of death. "He could nod ged over
losing de oder shop. Do you wand any boods?" And he held up the
leather in his hand: "Id's a beaudiful biece."

I ordered several pairs. It was very long before they came—but
they were better than ever. One simply could not wear them out. And
soon after that I went abroad.

It was over a year before I was again in London. And the first shop I went to was my old friend's. I had left a man of sixty, I came back to find one of seventy-five, pinched and worn and tremulous, who genuinely, this time, did not at first know me.

"Oh! Mr. Gessler," I said, sick at heart; "how splendid your boots are! See, I've been wearing this pair nearly all the time I've been abroad; and they're not half worn out, are they?"

He looked long at my boots—a pair of Russia leather, and his face seemed to regain its steadiness. Putting his hand on my instep, he said:

"Do dey vid you here? I 'ad drouble wid dat bair, I remember."

I assured him that they had fitted beautifully.

"Do you wand any boods?" he said. "I can make dem quickly; id is a slack dime."

I answered: "Please, please! I want boots all round—every kind!"

"I vill make a vresh model. You food must be bigger." And with utter slowness, he traced round my foot, and felt my toes, only once looking up to say:

"Did I dell you my brudder was dead?"

To watch him was quite painful, so feeble had he grown; I was glad to get away.

I had given those boots up, when one evening they came. Opening the parcel, I set the four pairs out in a row. Then one by one I tried them on. There was no doubt about it. In shape and fit, in finish and quality of leather, they were the best he had ever made me. And in the mouth of one of the town walking-boots I found his bill. The amount was the same as usual, but it gave me quite a shock. He had never before sent it in until quarter day. I flew downstairs and wrote a check, and posted it at once with my own hand.

A week later, passing the little street, I thought I would go in and tell him how splendidly the new boots fitted. But when I came to where his shop had been, his name was gone. Still there, in the window, were the slim pumps, the patent leathers with cloth tops, the sooty riding-boots.

I went in, very much disturbed. In the two little shops—again made into one—was a young man with an English face.

"Mr. Gessler in?" I said.

He gave me a strange, ingratiating look.

"No, sir," he said, "no. But we can attend to anything with pleasure. We've taken the shop over. You've seen our name, no doubt, next door. We make for some very good people."

"Yes, yes," I said, "but Mr. Gessler?"

"Oh!" he answered; "dead."

"Dead! But I received these boots from him only last Wednesday week."

"Ah!" he said; "a shockin' go. Poor old man starved 'imself."

"Good God!"

"Slow starvation, the doctor called it! You see he went to work in such a way! Would keep the shop on; wouldn't have a soul touch his boots except himself. When he got an order, it took him such a time. People won't wait. He lost everybody. And there he'd sit, goin' on and on—I will say that for him—not a man in London made a better boot! But look at the competition! He never advertised! Would 'ave the best leather, too, and do it all 'imself. Well, there it is. What could you expect with his ideas?"

"But starvation—!"

"That may be a bit flowery, as the sayin' is—but I know myself he was sittin' over his boots day and night, to the very last. You see, I used to watch him. Never gave 'imself time to eat; never had a penny in the house. All went in rent and leather. How he lived so long I don't know. He regular let his fire go out. He was a character. But he made good boots."

"Yes," I said, "he made good boots."

Eveline   *James Joyce*

She sat at the window watching the evening invade the avenue. Her head was leaned against the window curtains and in her nostrils was the odor of dusty cretonne. She was tired.

Few people passed. The man out of the last house passed on his way home; she heard his footsteps clacking along the concrete pavement and afterwards crunching on the cinder path before the new red houses. One time there used to be a field there in which they used to play every evening with other people's children. Then a man from Belfast bought the field and built houses in it—not like their little brown houses but bright brick houses with shining roofs. The children of the avenue used to play together in that field—the Devines, the Waters, the Dunns, little Keogh the cripple, she and her brothers and sisters. Ernest, however, never played: he was too grown up. Her father used often to hunt them in out of the field with his blackthorn stick; but usually little Keogh used to keep *nix* and call out when he saw her father coming. Still they seemed to have been rather happy then. Her father was not so bad then; and besides, her mother was alive. That was a long time ago; she and her brothers and sisters were all grown up; her mother was dead. Tizzie Dunn was dead, too, and the Waters had gone back to England. Everything changes. Now she was going to go away like the others, to leave her home.

Home! She looked round the room, reviewing all its familiar objects which she had dusted once a week for so many years, wondering where on earth all the dust came from. Perhaps she would never see again those familiar objects from which she had never dreamed of being divided. And yet during all those years she had never found out the name of the priest whose yellowing photograph hung on the wall above the broken harmonium beside the colored print of the promises made to Blessed Margaret Mary Alacoque. He had been a school friend of her father. Whenever he showed the photograph to a visitor her father used to pass it with a casual word:

"He is in Melbourne now."

She had consented to go away, to leave her home. Was that wise? She tried to weigh each side of the question. In her home anyway she had shelter and food; she had those whom she had known all her life about her. Of course she had to work hard, both in the house and at business. What would they say of her in the Stores when they found out that she had run away with a fellow? Say she was a fool, perhaps; and her place would be filled up by advertisement. Miss Gavan would be glad. She had always had an edge on her, especially whenever there were people listening.

"Miss Hill, don't you see these ladies are waiting?"

"Look lively, Miss Hill, please."

She would not cry many tears at leaving the Stores.

But in her new home, in a distant unknown country, it would not be like that. Then she would be married—she, Eveline. People would treat her with respect then. She would not be treated as her mother had been. Even now, though she was over nineteen, she sometimes felt herself in danger of her father's violence. She knew it was that that had given her the palpitations. When they were growing up he had never gone for her, like he used to go for Harry and Ernest, because she was a girl; but latterly he had begun to threaten her and say what he would do to her only for her dead mother's sake. And now she had nobody to protect her. Ernest was dead and Harry, who was in the church decorating business, was nearly always down somewhere in the country. Besides, the invariable squabble for money on Saturday nights had begun to weary her unspeakably. She always gave her entire wages—seven shillings—and Harry always sent up what he could but the trouble was to get any money from her father. He said she used to squander the money, that she had no head, that he wasn't going to give her his hardearned money to throw about the streets, and much more, for he was usually fairly bad on Saturday night. In the end he would give her the money and ask her had she any intention of buying Sunday's dinner. Then she had to rush out as quickly as she could and do her marketing, holding her black leather purse tightly in her hand as she elbowed her way through the crowds and returning home late under her load of provisions. She had hard work to keep the house together and to see that the two young children who had been left to her charge went to school regularly and got their meals regularly. It was hard work—a hard life—but now that she was about to leave it she did not find it a wholly undesirable life.

She was about to explore another life with Frank. Frank was very kind, manly, open-hearted. She was to go away with him by the nightboat to be his wife and to live with him in Buenos Ayres where he had a home waiting for her. How well she remembered the first time she had seen him; he was lodging in a house on the main road where she used to visit. It seemed a few weeks ago. He was standing at the gate, his peaked cap pushed back on his head and his hair tumbled forward over a face of bronze. Then they had come to know each other. He used to meet her outside the Stores every evening and see her home. He took her to see *The Bohemian Girl* and she felt elated as she sat in an unaccustomed part of the theater with him. He was awfully fond of music and sang a little. People knew that they were courting and, when he sang about the lass that loves a sailor, she always felt pleasantly confused. He used to call her Poppens out of fun. First of all it had been an excitement for her to have a fellow and then she had begun to like him. He had tales of distant countries. He had started as a deck boy at a pound a month on a ship of the Allan Line going out to Canada. He told her the names of the ships he had been on and the names of the different services. He had sailed through the Straits of Magellan and he told her stories of the terrible Patagonians. He had fallen on his feet in Buenos Ayres, he said, and had come over to the old country just for a holiday. Of

course, her father had found out the affair and had forbidden her to
have anything to say to him.

"I know these sailor chaps," he said.

One day he had quarreled with Frank and after that she had to meet
her lover secretly.

The evening deepened in the avenue. The white of two letters in her
lap grew indistinct. One was to Harry; the other was to her father.
Ernest had been her favorite but she liked Harry too. Her father was
becoming old lately, she noticed; he would miss her. Sometimes he
could be very nice. Not long before, when she had been laid up for a
day, he had read her out a ghost story and made toast for her at the fire.
Another day, when their mother was alive, they had all gone for a picnic to the Hill of Howth. She remembered her father putting on her
mother's bonnet to make the children laugh.

Her time was running out but she continued to sit by the window,
leaning her head against the window curtain, inhaling the odor of dusty
cretonne. Down far in the avenue she could hear a street organ playing.
She knew the air. Strange that it should come that very night to remind
her of the promise to her mother, her promise to keep the home together as long as she could. She remembered the last night of her
mother's illness; she was again in the close dark room at the other side
of the hall and outside she heard a melancholy air of Italy. The organ
player had been ordered to go away and given sixpence. She remembered her father strutting back into the sickroom saying:

"Damned Italians! coming over here!"

As she mused the pitiful vision of her mother's life laid its spell on
the very quick of her being—that life of commonplace sacrifices closing
in final craziness. She trembled as she heard again her mother's voice
saying constantly with foolish insistence:

"Derevaun Seraun! Derevaun Seraun!"

She stood up in a sudden impulse of terror. Escape! She must escape!
Frank would save her. He would give her life, perhaps love, too. But
she wanted to live. Why should she be unhappy? She had a right to
happiness. Frank would take her in his arms, fold her in his arms. He
would save her.

She stood among the swaying crowd in the station at the North Wall.
He held her hand and she knew that he was speaking to her, saying

[1] William York Tindall in *A Reader's Guide to James Joyce*, p. 22, says that
"Patrick Henchy of the National Library in Kildare Street thinks this mad and
puzzling ejaculation corrupt Gaelic for 'the end of pleasure is pain:'"

something about the passage over and over again. The station was full
of soldiers with brown baggage. Through the wide doors of the sheds
she caught a glimpse of the black mass of the boat, lying in beside the
quay wall, with illumined portholes. She answered nothing. She felt her
cheek pale and cold and, out of a maze of distress, she prayed to God to
direct her, to show her what was her duty. The boat blew a long mournful whistle into the mist. If she went, tomorrow she would be on the sea
with Frank, steaming towards Buenos Ayres. Their passage had been
booked. Could she still draw back after all he had done for her? Her
distress awoke a nausea in her body and she kept moving her lips in
silent fervent prayer.

A bell clanged upon her heart. She felt him seize her hand:

"Come!"

All the seas of the world tumbled about her heart. He was drawing
her into them: he would drown her. She gripped with both hands at the
iron railing.

"Come!"

No! No! No! It was impossible. Her hands clutched the iron in
frenzy. Amid the seas she sent a cry of anguish!

"Eveline! Evvy!"

He rushed beyond the barrier and called to her to follow. He was
shouted at to go on but he still called to her. She set her white face to
him, passive, like a helpless animal. Her eyes gave him no sign of love
or farewell or recognition.

A Clod of Soil

Ryunosuke Akutagawa
Translated by Takashi Kojima

It was the beginning of the tea-picking season and Osumi was sorely
grieved by the loss of her son, Nitaro, who had been lying practically
crippled for over eight years. The death of her son did not bring un-
mixed grief to this old widow, whose soul, the neighbors said, would be
born to live a blessed life in the Land of Bliss after her death. When
she burned an incense stick to pray for the peaceful repose of his soul
now laid in his coffin, she felt as if she had at last managed to cross
the steep mountain pass.

一塊ノ土

After the funeral service of Nitaro was over, the first question that came up was what should be done with his wife, Otami, and her little son. This young widow had taken upon herself most of the family farm work from the hands of her husband who was bedridden. If she left, the family would be burdened not only with the care of the little child but would have no means left for earning a living. Osumi had a good mind to seek a husband for the widowed Otami after the lapse of forty-nine[1] days and to have her work for the family as she did when he was living. In her heart she thought that her late son's cousin, Yokichi, might be a suitable husband for the young widow.

"Are you thinking of leaving this child and me already? It's wrong of me to have been silent about a plan for your future," extraordinarily

[1] In Japan a common Buddhist superstition goes that the soul of a dead person departs his house forty-nine days after his death. T. K.

shocked, Osumi asked in a tone of more appeal than reprimand when she saw Otami tidying up the room on the morning of the eighth day after the death of her husband. Osumi was looking after the grandchild on the verandah adjoining the back room. The plaything she gave him was a spray of cherry-blossoms in full bloom which she had taken from the school playground.

"What are you talking about?" Otami answered with a smile, without even looking at her. What a relief it was to Osumi.

"I just imagined so. Sure you're not leaving us, are you?" Osumi kept harping on her solicitous entreaty in a whining voice. Presently her own words made her sentimental, until tears flowed freely down her cheeks.

"Why, really I mean to stay here for good, if you wish." Otami also grew tearful before she was aware of it, and took up her child, Koji, on her lap. "I've got this child. Why should I ever go anywhere else?" Koji, looking strangely shy, appeared attracted to the spray of cherry blossoms lying upon the old mat of the back room.

*   *   *

Otami kept on working as hard as she did while Nitaro was living. However, the problem of her taking a husband could not be as easily settled as had been expected. She did not seem to have any interest at all in this matter. Osumi of course took every opportunity to arouse Otami's interest in her remarriage and to approach her with a proposal. However, Otami gave only evasive answers like "Maybe next year, please." Doubtless this was as much a joy as a worry to Otami, who finally decided to wait for the turn of the year, yielding to her daughter-in-law's wishes. However, she took seriously to heart what other people might think of them.

The following year came and Otami seemed to give no thought to anything but working out in the fields. The old woman began more persistently and even prayerfully to persuade the young widow to take a husband. This was partly because she worried over criticism leveled by her relatives and backbiting by people.

"But you see, you're so young you can't go along without a man for good, I'm afraid," appealed Osumi.

"Good heavens!" answered Otami. "Can't I get along without a man? How can I help it? If you bring in a stranger among us, Hiro will have a hard time, you'll be under pressure, and I'll have no end of cares and troubles."

"This is why I urge you. Take Yokichi for your husband, won't you? He's given up gambling forever, I understand," persuaded Osumi.

"Why, he's a relative of yours, but, after all, he's a stranger to me," replied the younger woman.

"But you'll have to be patient for years and years," Osumi argued.

"Why not? It's for the sake of my dear Hiro. If I only suffer now, the whole of our farm will pass undivided into his hands," Otami thoughtfully replied.

"Well," Osumi said lowering her voice, as she always did when she talked of this matter. "In any case people will talk, you see. I pray you, Otami, tell others exactly what you've just said to me."

How often they had questions and answers like these! But each time only added to the strength of Otami's determination. Really, without the help of a male hand, she worked harder than ever, planting potatoes and reaping barley. Moreover, during the summers she kept cows, and even on rainy days she went out mowing. This hard work was in itself her strong resistance against admitting a stranger into her home. At last Osumi gave up the idea of getting a husband for Otami. However, her resignation was not altogether unpleasant to her.

*   *   *

Otami continued to support the family by her own hands. There was no doubt that her toil was motivated by her whole-hearted desire to work for the sake of her little son, Hiro. Another more inherent cause was traceable to the power of heredity that ran deep in her blood. She was a daughter of a so-called migrant family that had formerly moved into this district from a sterile mountainous province.

"Your Otami is much stronger than she looks," from time to time the old woman next door was heard to say to Osumi. "The other day I saw her carrying four huge bundles of rice-plants on her back."

Osumi tried to translate her thanks to Otami by taking over the management of the daily household chores: looking after her grandson, taking care of the cows, cooking meals, washing clothes, going to the neighbor's house to draw water, etc. Bent with age, she found happiness and pleasure in taking over all sorts of household tasks herself.

One night in the late autumn, Otami came home with difficulty, carrying bulky bundles of pine-needles under her arms. Just then Osumi with Hiroji fastened to her back, was stoking a fire in the furnace in a corner of the small earthen floor.

"You must be cold. You're back late," Osumi said.

"I did a bit of extra work today," Otami replied wearily.

Tossing down the bundles of pine-needles below the sill, without even taking off her muddy straw sandals, she came in and sat down right by the side of the open fireplace, where an oak stump was burning with a cheery flame. Osumi tried to rise to her feet at once, but burdened with Hiroji on her back, she had to hold on to the edge of the bathtub before she could slowly raise herself.

"Have a bath right away, won't you?"

"I'm too hungry for a bath. I'd rather eat sweet potatoes first. You've got some boiled sweet potatoes, haven't you?"

Osumi toddled along to the sill, and brought back the pot of boiled sweet potatoes. "I've had them waiting for you for a long time. I'm afraid they're cold now."

They roasted the sweet potatoes over the fire in the open fireplace.

"Hiro's fast asleep. Lay the tot in bed."

"No, it's so awfully cold tonight and he won't go to sleep," Osumi replied.

While she talked, Otami began cramming her mouth full of the sweet potatoes which had begun to steam. Her manner of eating could only be observed among farmers who come back home after the day's tiresome labors. She ravenously gulped down one sweet potato after another which she had removed from the spit. Osumi, feeling the weight of the faintly snoring Hiroji on her back, busily kept broiling more sweet potatoes.

"Anyway working as hard as you do, you must feel twice as hungry as anyone else." Time and again Osumi looked admiringly into the face of Otami, as she kept cramming the sweet potatoes into her mouth in the dim light of the sooty fire.

*   *   *

Otami toiled on all the harder doing a man's work without sparing herself. Sometimes even at night she walked around, thinning out greens by the light of a lantern. Osumi always had respect for her daughter-in-law. Really it was more a sense of awe than respect. Except for labor in the fields and hills, Otami thrust all work upon her mother-in-law, without washing even her own clothes. Nevertheless, without breathing a word of complaint, Osumi worked on, straightening herself up now and then.

Osumi never saw the old woman next door without extolling her daughter-in-law to the skies, saying, "Anyway Otami's like that. So no matter when I die, my family will have nothing to worry about."

However, Otami's mania for work seemed too far gone to be thrown off. When another year had passed she began to speak of extending the sphere of her labor to the mulberry field across the irrigation ditch. She asserted that it was absurd to tenant out the land covering a quarter of an acre for only ten dollars a year. She went on to reason that if they planted mulberry trees there and raised silkworms at odd times, their labor would be sure to yield them about 150 dollars net yearly, barring fluctuations in the silkworm market. Although money was their greatest consideration, it was more than Osumi could bear to be pressed with extra labor. Above all, raising silkworms would be an exacting demand upon their time and far beyond the limit of her capacity and endurance. At last she offered a querulous remonstrance.

"You see, Otami. I'm not shirking. We haven't got a man—just a little crying child to look after. Even now the work is too much for me. So your idea's too absurd. How could I ever take up raising silkworms? Think of me a little. I pray you!"

In the face of her mother-in-law's plaintive protest, Otami did not have the heart to insist on having her own way. So she gave up the idea of raising silkworms, but insisted on carrying her point in planting the mulberry field.

"Never mind. Only I've got to work out in the fields." Casting a determined look at Osumi, she grumbled out the insinuating remark.

From this time on, Osumi again thought of adopting a son. Formerly she had entertained this idea out of her anxiety over her family's living and out of her regard for what people might think of her family. But now she wished to adopt a son out of her impatience to be released from her painful duty of taking care of the house work. So now how more intense and irresistible than ever before was her desire to receive a son-in-law into her family!

Just at the time when the tangerine fields were tinged with full-blown blossoms, Osumi seated in front of the oil-lamp, ventured to bring up the proposal, eyeing Otami over the rims of her spectacles, which she wore while doing her needlework at night.

"Talking of my taking a husband again! That's no concern of mine," Otami, sitting cross-legged and munching salted peas, turned a deaf ear. Formerly Osumi might, in all probability, have dropped the proposal.

"But you shouldn't altogether say, 'No,' *now*." This particular night she persistently tried her best to persuade Otami. "Tomorrow at the funeral service of the Miyashita family, our family is assigned the duty of digging the grave. At a time like this I wish we had a man."

"Don't worry. I'll do the digging," Otami interjected.

"Surely not. Being a woman, you don't mean it." Osumi thought of laughing it off. But looking into Otami's face, she dared not.

"Granny, you want to retire now, don't you?" Otami, with her hands on the knees of her crossed legs, coldly touched Osumi on her sensitive spot.

"Oh, no, Otami, why should I ever . . . ?" Osumi, who was caught off balance took off her spectacles in spite of herself. But she could not tell why she did so.

"You remember what you said when Hiro's father died, don't you?" persisted Otami. "It would be a sin against our ancestors ever to divide up the estate of our family . . ."

"Well, yes, I said so. But we have to take things as they are. This can't be helped." Osumi tried hard to plead in favor of bringing a man into their family. Nevertheless, her argument did not sound plausible or convincing even to her own ears. First of all, this was because she could not bring up her real underlying motive, that of living an easier life.

"It may be all very well for you, as you'll die earlier than I." Continuing to munch salted peas, Otami, who had discovered Osumi's vulnerability, began taking her severely to task. Her natural glib tongue lent force to her reprimand. "In the situation I'm in, how can I shirk my responsibility? I haven't remained a widow for any show or pride. At nights when my limbs are too painful for me to go to sleep, I often feel that it's no good being stubborn. But I'm doing all this though, thinking it's for the sake of our family and Hiro."

In a stupid daze, Osumi looked Otami in the face. In the course of time, her mind clearly began to grasp a certain fact. It was that struggle as she might, she could never ease up until she closed her eyes forever. After Otami's outburst was over, she put on her spectacles again.

"But Otami," Osumi concluded her talk as if she were talking to herself. "Things in life don't go only according to reason. Think it over carefully, won't you? I won't say anything more about it."

Twenty minutes later some village youngster walked past the house, singing in a tenor voice:

"The young bride's out on her mowing work today,
Grass bend low, scythe be sharp!"

When the singing died away, Osumi gave another glance at Otami's face over the rims of her spectacles. Otami, on the other side of the lamp, was only yawning heavily, with her legs fully outstretched.

"Now I'll get off to bed. I must get up pretty early in the morning." Muttering these words, Otami snatched a handful of salted peas, and stood up languidly by the fireside.

Osumi silently continued to endure her sufferings for the subsequent three or four years. These were the sufferings an old horse experiences when it teams up with a young spirited one. Otami persevered with her arduous work and toiled in the fields like a bee. To outsiders Osumi seemed to be as happy as ever, taking care of the house. But the shadow of the invisible whip constantly harassed her. She was apt to be scolded or indirectly rebuked by the spirited Otami, sometimes for failing to heat the bath, and at others for forgetting to air unhulled rice or letting the cows out. Nevertheless, without answering back, she continued to endure her sufferings. For one thing, it was because her spirit was accustomed to submission; and for another, because her grandson, Hiro, was attached more to her than to his mother.

Actually, to outsiders, Osumi had hardly changed in any way. If she had, it was that she did not praise her son's wife as she had done previously. However, such a trivial change did not attract any special notice from others. At least to the old woman next door, she remained the same blessed woman as ever.

At high noon one summer when the blazing hot sun was beating straight down upon the earth, Osumi was talking with the next door old woman under the shadow of the grape-vine trellis spreading all over in front of the cowshed. The old woman talked while smoking cigarette butts. She had carefully collected the cigarette butts left by her son.

"Hm. Otami-san's out mowing hay. She's so young, and yet she does all work without complaining," observed the old woman.

"Well, housework is best for women," responded Osumi.

"No, there's nothing more enjoyable than farming. My son's wife hasn't ever been out weeding much less farming for even a single day in the seven years since they got married. She spends all her days washing her children's clothes and remaking her own."

"Tidying up your children and keeping yourself neat and attractive is an adornment to life," chimed Osumi.

"But the young today don't like to work in the fields. Oh, dear! What's the noise now?" asked the neighbor.

"That noise? Why, it's just the cow breaking wind."

"Oh, the cow breaking wind! Really? When young, it's awful trying to weed, with your back blistered under the scorching rays of the sun," concluded the neighbor.

The two old women generally chatted like that in a familiar and friendly way.

For more than eight years after the death of Jintaro, Otami continued to support her family single-handed. In the course of time her name had spread all over the village and beyond. In the eyes of the villagers, she was no longer a young widow, who, seized by a mania for work, toiled night and day. Much less was she a young "missus" to the village youngsters. Instead she was an example to all brides. She was a present-day paragon of female virtue and fidelity. Such spontaneous eulogies were upon everyone's lips. As for Osumi, she did not divulge her sufferings or her innermost thoughts to anyone. Nor did she want to. From the depths of her heart she placed her faith in Providence, although she was not clearly conscious of God. Now that her faith was dashed to pieces, her only and last hope was her grandson, Hiro. She desperately poured her love out to her darling twelve-year-old grandson. But this last hope of hers was often blighted.

One fine fall afternoon Hiro came home hurriedly from school in a state of agitation, holding a sheaf of books under his arm. Osumi, sitting in front of the stable, using her knife quite dexterously, was cording persimmons to dry them. He skipped nimbly over one of the mats, on which unhulled millet was airing, and smartly arranged his feet and raised his hand in a crisp salute.

"Granny," he abruptly asked her earnestly, "is Mama a very great woman?"

"Why?" Resting her hand which had just been using the knife, she could not help staring at her grandson's face.

"Because the teacher told us in the morals lesson that she was greater than any other woman in this neighborhood."

"Eh? The teacher? Who?" First she was upset. "Even the school teacher tells my grandson such a shocking lie." Really nothing was a greater surprise to her. After a moment's confusion, she was seized with a fit of anger, and began berating Otami as if she were a changed being.

"That's a lie. A black lie. Your mama works hard only outdoors, so she seems extraordinary and wonderful to others. But she's real wicked at heart. She drives granny hard, and is so headstrong."

Astonished, Hiroji watched his grandmother's face which was livid with anger. In the course of time a reaction must have overtaken her, for she had tears in her eyes.

"So your granny's living with you as her only hope in life. Always keep this in mind. By and by as soon as you're seventeen, get married and let your granny breathe freely. Your mama takes it easy and says you should get married after you're through with your military service. But how could I ever wait that long? You understand. Be doubly kind to granny so as to do your daddy's share of duty, and I'll be very good to you. You shall have everything," Osumi said persuasively.

"Will you give me these persimmons when they're ripe?" Hiro was fingering and coveting a basket of persimmons.

"Yes, why not?" Osumi hiccuped her laughter through her tears. "You're just a little tyke, but you understand everything. Now don't change your mind."

The night following this outburst, Osumi had a rowdy squabble with Otami about a trifling matter which arose from Osumi's alleged eating of Otami's share of boiled sweet potatoes. As they became heated in their argument Otami said with a grin, "If you don't want to work, you have no choice but to die."

This incensed Osumi and unexpectedly she raved like an insane woman.

"Hiro, here, wake up!" Osumi aroused Hiroji, who had been asleep all this while with his head on her lap, and continued to howl with rage. "Hiro, wake up! Hiro,—wake up! Listen to what your mama says. She tells me to die. Do you hear? Listen real well, will you? In mama's days we've got a bit more money, but grandpa and granny cleared our three acres of farm and all by ourselves. And yet mama tells me I should die if I want to take things easy . . . Otami, I'll die. Why should I be afraid of dying? I won't be dictated to by you. Oh, I'll die by all means. I'll die and haunt you . . ."

Osumi continued to rave and revile in a loud voice, holding her grandson who had started to cry in her arms. Otami all this while lay by the fireside, turning a deaf ear to the ravings of Osumi.

* * *

However, Osumi did not die, while on the other hand Otami, who boasted of her excellent health, caught typhoid fever and died a week later. At that time the disease took an appalling toll of life in the village. The day before she fell ill, she took her turn at the task of digging a grave for the funeral of the iron-smith who had fallen victim to the same disease. At the smith's she saw the young apprentice who was to be sent to the isolation hospital on the very day of the funeral.

"You must've caught it then," after the doctor left, Osumi dropped a hint of her censure to the patient, who lay in bed with her face burning with fever.

The day of Otami's funeral it rained heavily. Nevertheless, her funeral was attended by all the villagers including the village mayor. All those who were there mourned the early death of Otami and expressed their sympathy to Osumi and Hiroji who had lost their breadwinner. The village representative told Osumi that the county office had been contemplating an official commendation for Otami shortly. At these words Osumi could do nothing but bow her head.

"Well, Osumi," went on the good-hearted representative, nodding his bald head. "You'd better resign yourself to your great misfortune. To get the official recommendation of Otami-san, we've sent in petitions to the county office, and I've been there to see the county commissioner five times. But we're going to resign ourselves to the tragedy, so you'd better be resigned, too." His preaching adulterated with levity made the grade-school teachers stare at him with a look of obvious displeasure.

The night after the funeral of Otami found Osumi sleeping with Hiroji inside the same mosquito net in the corner of the back room where the Buddhist altar had been erected. At other times they used to sleep in the room with the light out. That night, however, the altar was still lit with candles and the mats seemed to have been permeated with the peculiar odor of disinfectant, which kept Osumi awake in bed for a long time. Without doubt, Otami's death had at last brought her a great happiness. Now it was no longer necessary for her to work. Besides, she was also free from the fear of being rebuked.

She now had a bank deposit of a thousand dollars and three acres of farm land. She and Hiroji would be free from now on, to eat delicious boiled rice together, instead of having to endure the less-appetizing mixture of boiled barley and rice, and she would also be free to purchase her favorite salted cod by the bale. Never in her life had she felt so relieved from cares as at that moment. Presently her memory vividly recalled a certain night nine years ago. On that night she had heaved the same sigh of relief as she did now. That was the night after the funeral of the only son of her flesh and blood. This was the night on which the funeral of her son's wife who bore her only grandson was also just over.

Osumi opened her eyes and found her grandson asleep close by her with his innocent face turned upward. While she was gazing fondly into his relaxed and restful face, it gradually occurred to her that she was a wretched creature and that at the same time both her son, Jintaro, and his wife, Otami, who formed an ill-fated union with her, were also to be pitied. The change in her feelings helped instantly to erase nine years of hatred and bitterness. The parent and her children, all three, were to be pitied. Osumi, who survived the other two to live such a disgraceful life was the most pitiable of them all.

"Otami, why did you die?" she whispered faintly to the departed. Suddenly in spite of herself an endless stream of tears flowed down her cheeks.

After she heard the clock strike four, the sleep of the weary fell upon her, as the sky, over her thatched roof on the eastern horizon was greeting the first chilly grey streaks of dawn.

The Book of Ruth   *The King James Bible*

Now it came to pass in the days when the judges ruled, that there was a famine in the land. And a certain man of Beth-lehem-judah went to sojourn in the country of Moab, he, and his wife, and his two sons. And the name of the man was Elimelech, and the name of his wife Naomi, and the name of his two sons Mahlon and Chilion, Ephrathites of Beth-lehem-judah. And they came into the country of Moab, and continued there.

And Elimelech Naomi's husband died; and she was left, and her two sons. And they took them wives of the women of Moab; the name of the one was Orpah, and the name of the other Ruth: and they dwelled there about ten years. And Mahlon and Chilion died also both of them; and the woman was left of her two sons and her husband.

Then she arose with her daughters-in-law, that she might return from the country of Moab; for she had heard in the country of Moab how that the Lord had visited His people in giving them bread. Wherefore she went forth out of the place where she was, and her two daughters-in-law with her; and they went on the way to return unto the land of Judah. And Naomi said unto her two daughters-in-law, "Go, return each to her mother's house: the Lord deal kindly with you, as ye have dealt with the dead, and with me. The Lord grant you that ye may find rest, each of you in the house of her husband." Then she kissed them; and they lifted up their voice, and wept. And they said unto her, "Surely we will return with thee unto thy people."

And Naomi said, "Turn again, my daughters: why will ye go with me? are there yet any more sons in my womb, that they may be your husbands? Turn again, my daughters, go your way; for I am too old to have an husband. If I should say, I have hope, if I should have an husband also to-night, and should also bear sons; would ye tarry for them till they were grown? would ye stay for them from having husbands? nay, my daughters, for it grieveth me much for your sakes that the hand of the Lord is gone out against me."

And they lifted up their voice, and wept again: and Orpah kissed her mother-in-law; but Ruth clave unto her. And she said, "Behold, thy sister-in-law is gone back unto her people, and unto her gods: return thou after thy sister-in-law." And Ruth said, "Intreat me not to leave thee, or to return from following after thee: for whither thou goest, I will go; and where thou lodgest, I will lodge: thy people shall be my people, and thy God my God: where thou diest, will I die, and there will I be buried: the Lord do so to me, and more also, if ought but death part thee and me."

When she saw that she was steadfastly minded to go with her, then she left speaking unto her. So they two went until they came to Beth-lehem. And it came to pass, when they were come to Beth-lehem, that all the city was moved about them, and they said, "Is this Naomi?" And she said unto them, "Call me not Naomi, call me Mara: for the Almighty hath dealt very bitterly with me. I went out full, and the Lord hath brought me home again empty: why then call ye me Naomi, seeing the Lord hath testified against me, and the Almighty hath afflicted me?"

So Naomi returned, and Ruth the Moabitess, her daughter-in-law, with her, which returned out of the country of Moab: and they came to Beth-lehem in the beginning of barley harvest. And Naomi had a kinsman of her husband's, a mighty man of wealth, of the family of Elimelech; and his name was Boaz. And Ruth the Moabitess said unto Naomi, "Let me now go to the field, and glean ears of corn after him in whose sight I shall find grace." And she said unto her, "Go, my daughter." And she went, and came, and gleaned in the field after the reapers: and her hap was to light on a part of the field belonging unto Boaz, who was of the kindred of Elimelech.

And, behold, Boaz came from Beth-lehem, and said unto the reapers, "The Lord be with you." And they answered him, "The Lord bless thee." Then said Boaz unto his servant that was set over the reapers, "Whose damsel is this?" And the servant that was set over the reapers answered and said, "It is the Moabitish damsel that came back with Naomi out of the country of Moab: and she said, I pray you, let me glean and gather after the reapers among the sheaves: so she came, and hath continued even from the morning until now, that she tarried a little in the house."

Then said Boaz unto Ruth, "Hearest thou not, my daughter? Go not to glean in another field, neither go from hence, but abide here fast by my maidens: let thine eyes be on the field that they do reap, and go thou after them: have I not charged the young men that they shall not touch thee? and when thou art athirst, go unto the vessels, and drink of that which the young men have drawn."

Then she fell on her face, and bowed herself to the ground, and said unto him, "Why have I found grace in thine eyes, that thou shouldest take knowledge of me, seeing I am a stranger?"

And Boaz answered and said unto her, "It hath fully been shewed me, all that thou hast done unto thy mother-in-law since the death of thine husband: and how thou hast left thy father and thy mother, and the land of thy nativity, and art come unto a people which thou knewest not heretofore. The Lord recompense thy work, and a full reward be given thee of the Lord God of Israel, under whose wings thou art come to trust."

Then she said, "Let me find favor in thy sight, my lord; for that thou hast comforted me, and for that thou hast spoken friendly unto thine handmaid, though I be not like unto one of thine handmaidens."

And Boaz said unto her, "At mealtime come thou hither, and eat of the bread, and dip thy morsel in the vinegar." And she sat beside the reapers: and he reached her parched corn, and she did eat, and was sufficed, and left. And when she was risen up to glean, Boaz commanded his young men, saying, "Let her glean even among the sheaves, and reproach her not: and let fall also some of the handfuls of purpose for her, and leave them, that she may glean them, and rebuke her not."

So she gleaned in the field until even, and beat out that she had gleaned: and it was about an ephah[1] of barley. And she took it up, and went into the city: and her mother-in-law saw what she had gleaned: and she brought forth, and gave to her that she had reserved after she was sufficed. And her mother-in-law said unto her, "Where hast thou gleaned to-day? and where wroughtest thou? blessed be he that did take knowledge of thee."

And she shewed her mother-in-law with whom she had wrought, and said, "The man's name with whom I wrought to-day is Boaz." And Naomi said unto her daughter-in-law, "Blessed be he of the Lord, who hath not left off His kindness to the living and to the dead." And Naomi said unto her, "The man is near of kin unto us, one of our next kinsmen."

And Ruth the Moabitess said, "He said unto me also, Thou shall keep fast by my young men, until they have ended all my harvest."

And Naomi said unto Ruth her daughter-in-law, "It is good, my daughter, that thou go out with his maidens, that they meet thee not in any other field." So she kept fast by the maidens of Boaz to glean unto the end of barley harvest and of wheat harvest; and dwelt with her mother-in-law.

Then Naomi her mother-in-law said unto her, "My daughter, shall I not seek rest for thee, that it may be well with thee? And now is not Boaz of our kindred, with whose maidens thou wast? Behold, he winnoweth barley to-night in the threshing-floor. Wash thyself therefore, and anoint thee, and put thy raiment upon thee, and get thee down to the floor: but make not thyself known unto the man, until he shall have done eating and drinking. And it shall be, when he lieth down, that thou shalt mark the place where he shall lie, and thou shalt go in, and uncover his feet, and lay thee down; and he will tell thee what thou shalt do."

And she said unto her, "All that thou sayest unto me I will do."

And she went down unto the floor, and did according to all that her mother-in-law bade her. And when Boaz had eaten and drunk, and his heart was merry, he went to lie down at the end of the heap of corn: and she came softly, and uncovered his feet, and laid her down. And it came to pass at midnight, that the man was afraid, and turned himself: and, behold, a woman lay at his feet. And he said, "Who art

---

[1] A little more than a bushel.

thou?" And she answered, "I am Ruth thine handmaid: spread therefore thy skirt over thine handmaid: for thou art a near kinsman."

And he said, "Blessed be thou of the Lord, my daughter: for thou hast shewed more kindness in the latter end than at the beginning, inasmuch as thou followedst not young men, whether poor or rich. And now, my daughter, fear not; I will do to thee all that thou requirest: for all the city of my people doth know that thou art a virtuous woman. And now it is true that I am thy near kinsman: howbeit there is a kinsman nearer than I. Tarry this night, and it shall be in the morning, that if he will perform unto thee the part of a kinsman, well; let him do the kinsman part: but if he will not do the part of a kinsman to thee, then will I do the part of a kinsman to thee, as the Lord liveth: lie down until the morning."

And she lay at his feet until the morning: and she rose up before one could know another. And he said, "Let it not be known that a woman came into the floor." Also he said, "Bring the vail [2] that thou hast upon thee, and hold it." And when she held it, he measured six measures of barley, and laid it on her: and she went into the city.

And when she came to her mother-in-law, she said, "Who art thou, my daughter?" And she told her all that the man had done to her. And she said, "These six measures of barley gave he me; for he said to me, Go not empty unto thy mother-in-law." Then said she, "Sit still, my daughter, until thou know how the matter will fall: for the man will not be in rest, until he have finished the thing this day."

Then went Boaz up to the gate, and sat him down there: and, behold, the kinsman of whom Boaz spake came by; unto whom he said, "Ho, such a one! turn aside, sit down here." And he turned aside, and sat down. And he took ten men of the elders of the city, and said, "Sit ye down here." And they sat down. And he said unto the kinsman, "Naomi, that is come again out of the country of Moab, selleth a parcel of land, which was our brother Elimelech's: and I thought to advertise thee, saying, Buy it before the inhabitants, and before the elders of my people. If thou wilt redeem it, redeem it: but if thou wilt not redeem it, then tell me, that I may know: for there is none to redeem it beside thee; and I am after thee."

And he said, "I will redeem it."

Then said Boaz, "What day thou buyest the field of the hand of

[2] Veil.

Naomi, thou must buy it also of Ruth the Moabitess, the wife of the dead, to raise up the name of the dead upon his inheritance."

And the kinsman said, "I cannot redeem it for myself, lest I mar mine own inheritance: redeem thou my right to thyself; for I cannot redeem it." Now this was the manner in former time in Israel concerning redeeming and concerning changing, for to confirm all things; a man plucked off his shoe, and gave it to his neighbor: and this was a testimony in Israel. Therefore the kinsman said unto Boaz, "Buy it for thee." So he drew off his shoe.

And Boaz said unto the elders, and unto all the people, "Ye are witnesses this day, that I have bought all that was Elimelech's, and all that was Chilion's and Mahlon's, of the hand of Naomi. Moreover, Ruth the Moabitess, the wife of Mahlon, have I purchased to be my wife, to raise up the name of the dead upon his inheritance, that the name of the dead be not cut off from among his brethren, and from the gate of his place: ye are witnesses this day."

And all the people that were in the gate, and the elders, said, "We are witnesses. The Lord make the woman that is come into thine house like Rachel and like Leah, which two did build the house of Israel: and do thou worthily in Ephratah, and be famous in Bethlehem: and let thy house be like the house of Pharez, whom Tamar bore unto Judah, of the seed which the Lord shall give thee of this young woman."

So Boaz took Ruth, and she was his wife: and when he went in unto her, the Lord gave her conception, and she bare a son. And the women said unto Naomi, "Blessed be the Lord, which hath not left thee this day without a kinsman, that his name may be famous in Israel. And he shall be unto thee a restorer of thy life, and a nourisher of thine old age: for thy daughter-in-law, which loveth thee, which is better to thee than seven sons, hath born him." And Naomi took the child, and laid it in her bosom, and became nurse unto it. And the women her neighbors gave it a name, saying, "There is a son born to Naomi"; and they called his name Obed: he is the father of Jesse, the father of David.

Drama

CHARACTERS

AGNES

THERESE

THE CLERK

THE MAN

THE VICE-PRESIDENT

MR. CRACHETON

MR. LÉPEDURA

MR. RASEMUTTE

MR. SCHULTZ

THE PRESIDENT

CHEVREDENT

THE CHAIRMAN OF THE BOARD

The Apollo of Bellac

Jean Giraudoux
Adapted by Maurice Valency

The MAN *from Bellac is not Apollo.[1] The* MAN *from Bellac is a little shabby fellow who doesn't know where his next meal is coming from. He is a vagabond and a poet, therefore an inventor. He dreams things up, but he does nothing and he has nothing. He was cast very sensibly on the Ford Omnibus television program, when Claude Dauphin played the role—a fine character-actor, not a matinee idol. The* MAN *from Bellac must evoke Apollo, but visually he must remain the shabby little figure throughout the play. The moment he is cast as a big beautiful man with curly ringlets, the play is spoiled.*

SCENE *The reception room of The International Bureau of Inventions, S.A. This is a large, well-appointed room on the second floor of a magnificent office building in Paris. The French windows are open and afford us a view of tree-tops. There is an elaborate crystal chandelier hanging from the ceiling. The morning sun plays upon it. On a pedestal large enough to conceal a man a bust of Archimedes is set. Four doors open off the room. Three of them are marked Private. These lead into the office of the* PRESIDENT, *Right, and the* FIRST VICE-PRESIDENT *rear Right, and the Directors' Conference Room rear Left. The effect is French and very elegant, perhaps a trifle oppressive in its opulence.*

Behind a period desk sits the RECEPTION CLERK. *The desk has an ivory telephone and a row of signal lights. It has also a period blotter on which the clerk is writing something in an appointment book. The* CLERK *is well on in years and his face makes one think of a caricature by Daumier.*

---

[1] In Greek and Roman mythology, one of the great gods of Olympus. Represented in art as the perfection of youthful manhood, he was the god of music, poetry, and medicine, often typifying the sun.

TIME   *Autumn in Paris. The present or shortly before.*

AT RISE   *The* CLERK *is writing with a meticulous air. The outer door opens.* AGNES *comes in timidly from outer door, and stands in front of the desk. The* CLERK *does not look up.*

AGNES   Er—
CLERK   Yes?
AGNES   Is this the International Bureau of Inventions, Incorporated?
CLERK   Yes.
AGNES   Could I please see the Chairman of the Board?
CLERK   (*looks up*)   The Chairman of the Board? No one sees the Chairman of the Board.
AGNES   Oh.

The outer door opens again. THERESE *sweeps into the room. She is blond, shapely, thirty-five, dressed in expensive mink.* CLERK *rises respectfully.*

CLERK   Good morning, Madame.
THERESE   Is the President in?
CLERK   Yes, Madame. Of course.

THERESE *walks haughtily to President's door.* CLERK *opens it for her and closes it behind her. He goes back to his desk where* AGNES *is waiting.*

AGNES   Could I see the President?
CLERK   No one sees the President.
AGNES   But I have—
CLERK   What type of invention? Major? Intermediate? Minor?
AGNES   I beg pardon?
CLERK   Assistant Secretary to the Third Vice-President. Come back Tuesday. Name?
AGNES   My name?
CLERK   You have a name, I presume?

The MAN *from Bellac appears suddenly from outer door. He is nondescript, mercurial, shabby.*

MAN   Yes. The young lady has a name. But what permits you to conclude that the young lady's invention is as minor as all that?
CLERK   Who are you?

MAN   What chiefly distinguishes the inventor is modesty. You should know that by now. Pride is the invention of non-inventors.

A STREET SINGER, *accompanied by violin and accordion, begins "La Seine" outside the windows.* CLERK *crosses to close them.*

AGNES (*to the* MAN)   Thanks very much, but—

MAN   To the characteristic modesty of the inventor, the young lady adds the charming modesty of her sex—(*He smiles at* AGNES.) But—(CLERK *closes one of the windows.*) how can you be sure, you, that she has not brought us at last the invention which is destined to transform the modern world?

CLERK (*closes the other window*)   For world-transformation it's the Second Vice President. Mondays ten to twelve.

MAN   Today is Tuesday.

CLERK   Now how can I help that?

MAN   So! While all humanity awaits with anguish the discovery which will at last utilize the moon's gravitation for the removal of corns, and when we have every reason to believe that in all likelihood Mademoiselle—Mademoiselle?

AGNES   Agnes.

MAN   Mademoiselle Agnes has this discovery in her handbag— You tell her to come back Monday.

CLERK (*nervously*)   There is going to be a Directors' meeting in just a few minutes. The Chairman of the Board is coming. I must beg you to be quiet.

MAN   I will not be quiet. I am quiet Mondays.

CLERK   Now, please. I don't want any trouble.

MAN   And the Universal Vegetable? Five continents are languishing in the hope of the Universal Vegetable which will once and for all put an end to the ridiculous specialization of the turnip, the leek and the string-bean, which will be at one and the same time bread, meat, wine and coffee, and yield with equal facility cotton, potassium, ivory and wool. The Universal Vegetable which Paracelsus[2] could not, and Burbank[3] dared not, imagine! Yes, my friend. And while in this handbag, which with understandable concern she

---

[2] Philippus Aureolus Theophrastus Paracelsus, whose family name was Bombastus, was a famous Swiss physician (1493–1541) who, reportedly, delved deeply into alchemy and kept a small devil prisoner in the pommel of his sword.

[3] Luther Burbank (1849–1926) was an American scientist famed for his experiments in plant breeding.

clutches to her charming bosom, the seeds of the Universal Vegetable await only the signal of your President to burst upon an ex-
pectant world, you say—come back Monday.

AGNES   Really, sir—

CLERK   If you wish an appointment for Monday, Mademoiselle—

MAN   She does not wish an appointment for Monday.

CLERK   (*shrugs*)   Then she can go jump in the lake.

MAN   What did you say?

CLERK   I said: She can go jump in the lake. Is that clear?

MAN   That's clear. Perfectly clear. As clear as it was to Columbus
when—

The BUZZER sounds on the CLERK'S *desk. A LIGHT flashes on.*

CLERK   Excuse me. (*He crosses to the* VICE PRESIDENT'S *door, knocks
and enters.* MAN *smiles.* AGNES *smiles back wanly.*)

AGNES   But I'm not the inventor of the Universal Vegetable.

MAN   I know. I am.

AGNES   I'm just looking for a job.

MAN   Typist?

AGNES   Not really.

MAN   Stenographer?

AGNES   Not at all.

MAN   Copy-reader, translator, bookkeeper, editor, file-clerk—stop me
when I come to it.

AGNES   You could go on like that for years before I could stop you.

MAN   Well then—your specialty? Charm? Coquetry, devotion, se-
duction, flirtation, passion, romance?

AGNES   That's getting warmer.

MAN   Splendid. The best career for a female is to be a woman.

AGNES   Yes, but—men frighten me.

MAN   Men frighten you?

AGNES   They make me feel weak all over.

MAN   That clerk frightens you?

AGNES   Clerks, presidents, janitors, soldiers. All a man has to do is
to look at me, and I feel like a shoplifter caught in the act.

MAN   Caught in what act?

AGNES   I don't know.

MAN   Perhaps it's their clothes that frighten you. Their vests? Their
trousers?

AGNES (*shakes her head*) I feel the same panic on the beach when they don't wear their trousers.

MAN Perhaps you don't like men.

AGNES Oh, no, I like them. I like their dog-like eyes, their hairiness, their big feet. And they have special organs which inspire tenderness in a woman—. Their Adam's apple, for instance, when they eat dinner or make speeches. But the moment they speak to me, I begin to tremble—

MAN (*he looks appraisingly at her a moment*) You would like to stop trembling?

AGNES Oh yes. But— (*She shrugs hopelessly.*)

MAN Would you like me to teach you the secret?

AGNES Secret?

MAN Of not trembling before men. Of getting whatever you want out of them. Of making the directors jump, the presidents kneel and offer you diamonds?

AGNES Are there such secrets?

MAN One only. It is infallible.

AGNES Will you really tell it to me?

MAN Without this secret a girl has a bad time of it on this earth. With it, she becomes Empress of the World.

AGNES Oh tell it to me quickly.

MAN (*peering about the room*) No one is listening?

AGNES (*whispers*) No one.

MAN Tell them they're handsome.

AGNES You mean, flatter them? Tell them they're handsome, intelligent, kind?

MAN No. As for the intelligence and the kindness, they can shift for themselves. Tell them they're handsome.

AGNES All?

MAN All. The foolish, the wise, the modest, the vain, the young, the old. Say it to the professor of philosophy and he will give you a diploma. Say it to the butcher and he will give you a steak. Say it to the president here, and he will give you a job.

AGNES But to say a thing like that, one has to know a person well—

MAN Not at all. Say it right off. Say it before he has a chance even to open his mouth.

AGNES But one doesn't say a thing like that before people.

MAN Before people. Before all the world. The more witnesses, the better.

AGNES   But if they're not handsome—and for the most part they're not, you know—how can I tell them that they are?

MAN   Surely you're not narrow-minded, Agnes?

She shrugs, not quite sure.

The ugly, the pimply, the crippled, the fat. Do you wish to get on in this world? Tell them they're handsome.

AGNES   Will they believe it?

MAN   They will believe it because they've always known it. Every man, even the ugliest, feels in his heart a secret alliance with beauty. When you tell him he's handsome, he will simply hear outwardly the voice he has been listening to inwardly all his life. And those who believe it the least will be the most grateful. No matter how ugly they may have thought themselves, the moment they find a woman who thinks them handsome, they grapple her to their hearts with hooks of steel. For them, she is the magic glass of truth, the princess of an enchanted world. When you see a woman who can go nowhere without a staff of admirers, it is not so much because they think she is beautiful, it is because she has told them they are handsome.

AGNES   There are women then who already know this secret?

MAN   Yes. But they know it without really knowing it. And usually they evade the issue, they go beside the point. They tell the hunchback he is generous, the walleyed that he's strong. There's no profit in that. I've seen a woman throw away a cool million in diamonds and emeralds because she told a clubfooted lover that he walked swiftly, when all he wanted to hear was—you know what. And now—to work. The President is in every day to those who come to tell him he's handsome.

AGNES   I'd better come back another day. I have to have training. I have a cousin who's not at all bad-looking—I'll practice on him tomorrow, and then the next day I'll—

MAN   You can practice right now. On the receptionist.

AGNES   That monster?

MAN   The monster is perfect for your purpose. After that, the Vice President. I know him. He's even better. Then the President.

The VICE PRESIDENT'S *door opens. The* CLERK *comes in.*

CLERK (*into the dorway*)   Very good, sir.

VOICE   And another thing—

CLERK (*turns*)   Yes sir?
VOICE   When the Chairman of the Board—

CLERK *goes back in and closes the door.*

AGNES   No, I can't!
MAN (*indicating the bust of Archimedes[4] at rear*)   Begin with this bust then.
AGNES   Whose is it?
MAN   What does it matter? It's the bust of a man. It's all ears. Speak!
AGNES (*shuddering*)   It has a beard.
MAN   Begin with what you like. With this chair. With this clock.
AGNES   They're not listening.
MAN   This fly, then. See? He's on your glove. He's listening.
AGNES   Is he a male?
MAN   Yes. Speak. Tell him.
AGNES (*with an effort*)   How handsome he is!
MAN   No, no, no. Say it to him.
AGNES   How handsome you are!
MAN   You see? He's twirling his moustache. Go on. More. More. What is a fly especially vain of?
AGNES   His wings? His eyes?
MAN   That's it. Tell him.
AGNES   How beautiful your wings are, beautiful fly! They sparkle in the sun like jewels. And your eyes—so large, so sad, so sensitive!
MAN   Splendid. Shoo him away now. Here comes the clerk.
AGNES   He won't go. He's clinging to me.
MAN   Naturally.
AGNES (*to the fly*)   You're bow-legged. (*She smiles.*) He's gone.
MAN   You see? And now—

The VICE PRESIDENT'S *door opens slowly.*

Here he comes.
AGNES (*in panic*)   What must I say?
MAN   "How handsome you are."

CLERK *comes in and walks to his desk.* MAN *disappears behind the bust of Archimedes.*

AGNES (*after an agony of indecision*)   How handsome you are!

---

[4] Archimedes (287?–212 B.C.) was a Greek mathematician and inventor.

CLERK (*stops dead*)   What?

AGNES   I said, how handsome you are!

CLERK   Do you get this way often?

AGNES   It's the first time in my life that I've ever—

CLERK (*finishing the sentence for her*)   Called a chimpanzee handsome? Thanks for the compliment. But—why?

AGNES   You're right. Handsome is not the word. I should have said beautiful. Because, mind you, I never judge a face by the shape of the nose or the arch of the brow. To me, what counts is the ensemble.

CLERK   So what you're telling me is: your features are ugly, but they go beautifully together. Is that it?

AGNES   It serves me right. Very well— It's the first time I've ever told a man he was handsome. And it's going to be the last.

CLERK   Now don't get excited, please. I know girls. At your age a girl doesn't calculate; she says whatever comes into her head. I know you meant it. Only—why did you say it so badly?

MAN *sticks his head out and makes a face at* AGNES *behind the* CLERK'S *back.*

AGNES (*to the* MAN)   Did I say it badly? (*To the* CLERK, *who thinks it is said to him*) I thought you were handsome. I may have been wrong.

CLERK   Women are blind as bats. Even if there were something good about me, they'd never see it. What's so good about me? My face? God, no. My figure? Not at all. Only my shadow. But of course you didn't notice that.

AGNES   Is that what you think? And when you leaned over to close the window, I suppose your shadow didn't lean over with you? And when you walked into the Vice President's office, did you put your shadow away in a drawer? (*She strokes his shadow with her hand.*) How could I help noticing a shadow like that?

CLERK   You notice it now because I direct your attention to it.

AGNES   Have it your way. I thought I was looking at you, but what I saw was your shadow.

CLERK   Then you shouldn't say, what a handsome man. You should say, what a handsome shadow. (*He opens the window, the room is filled with MUSIC. It is still "La Seine."*)

AGNES   From now on, I shall say no more about it.

CLERK (*returning to desk*)   Don't be angry, my dear. It's only because I'm a man of years and I have a right to warn you. I have a daughter of your age. I know what girls are. One day they see a fine shadow, and at once their heads are turned, the silly geese, and they think the man himself is handsome. Oh, I don't deny it, it's a rare thing, a fine shadow. And believe me it lasts—you don't keep your hair, you don't keep your skin, but your shadow lasts all your life. Even longer, they say. But that's not the point. These little fools invariably insist on confusing the shadow with the man, and if the idiot lets himself be talked into it, in a moment it's all over and they've ruined their lives for nothing, the nitwits. No, my dear. Heed an old man's warning. You can't live your life among shadows.

MAN *sticks out his head and lifts an admonishing finger.*

AGNES   How handsome you are!

CLERK   You know why? It's because when I'm angry I show my teeth. And the fact is, they are rather good. My dentist says they're perfect. It's no credit to me— It's because I eat hard foods. And when you—

The BUZZER sounds again.

Ah—the Vice President needs me again. Wait just a minute, my dear. I'll make sure that he sees you at once. I'll say it's my niece.

AGNES   (*as he bends over to close a drawer*)   How beautiful it is, your shadow, when it leans over. One would say it belonged to Rodin's Thinker![5]

CLERK   (*delighted*)   Come, now, that will do. If you were my daughter, I'd give you a good slap on the——. Sit down a minute. I'll get him for you. (*Crosses to the* VICE PRESIDENT'S *door and goes out.* MAN *comes out from behind the bust. The MUSIC stops.*)

MAN   Well, it's a start.

AGNES   I think I'm better with flies.

MAN   Because in your mind the idea of beauty is inseparable from the idea of the caress. Women have no sense of the abstract—a woman admiring the sky is a woman caressing the sky. In a woman's mind beauty is something she needs to touch. And you didn't want to touch the clerk, not even his shadow.

AGNES   No.

[5] Famous figure by the French sculptor, François Auguste René Rodin (1840–1917).

MAN   With my method, it's not your hands that must speak, nor your cheek, nor your lips—. It's your brain.

AGNES   I had a narrow squeak. I almost lost him.

MAN   Yes, he had you there with his shadow. You're not ready to tackle a Vice President. No. Not yet.

AGNES   But there's no time. What shall I do?

MAN   Practice. Practice on me.

AGNES   You expect me to tell you you're handsome?

MAN   Is it so difficult?

AGNES   Not at all. Only—

MAN   Think. Think before you speak.

AGNES   Oh, you're not bad at all, you know, when you tease one like this.

MAN   Very feeble. Why when I tease one like this? The rest of the time, I'm not handsome?

AGNES   Oh yes. Always. Always.

MAN   Better. Now it's no longer your hands that are speaking.

AGNES   With you, all the same, they murmur a little something.

MAN   Good.

AGNES   The mass of your body is beautiful. The outline is beautiful. The face matters little.

MAN   What nonsense is this? My face matters little?

AGNES   (*recovering quickly*) No more than the face of Rodin's Thinker.

MAN   In his case, doubtless the feet have more importance. Look here, Agnes, these little allusions to famous statues are ingenious. But is Rodin's Thinker the only one you know?

AGNES   Except for the Venus of Milo.[6] But she wouldn't be much use to me with men.

MAN   That remains to be seen. In any case, we'd better extend your repertory. Forget The Thinker. Michelangelo's David is very good. Or his Moses.[7] But best of all—the Apollo of Bellac—

AGNES   The Apollo of Bellac?

MAN   It doesn't exist. It will do perfectly.

AGNES   What does it look like?

---

[6] Statue (c.400 B.C.), now in the Louvre, of the goddess of beauty and love.
[7] David and Moses are famous statues by the Italian painter and sculptor, Michelangelo Buonarrotti (1475–1564). David, a huge statue carved from a single block of marble, is at the Florence Academy. The statue of Moses is at the tomb of Pope Julius II.

MAN   A little like me, I think. I too come from Bellac. It's a little
town in Limousin. I was born there.

AGNES   But they say the men of Limousin are so ugly. How does
it happen that you are so handsome?

MAN   My father was a very handsome man, and he— Oh-oh. Good
for you. (*He applauds.*)

AGNES   (*pursuing her advantage*)   Oh never! Not with you! You
taught me the secret. With you I could be no other than honest.

MAN   At last. You understand.

The VICE PRESIDENT'S *door opens.*

Here we are. (*Goes behind the bust.*)

CLERK   (*comes in, smiling tenderly*)   The Vice President will be out
in a moment, my dear. No need to put yourself out. A shadow like
his, you may see every day—in the zoo. (*He takes some papers
from his desk and goes into where the Directors will meet.*)

AGNES   (*whispers*)   Help! Help!

MAN *thrusts his head out.*

I feel faint!

MAN   Practice. Practice.

AGNES   (*desperately*)   On whom? On what?

MAN   On anything. The telephone.

AGNES   (*she speaks to the telephone*)   How handsome you are, my
little telephone! (*She strokes it gently.*)

MAN   No! Not with the hands.

AGNES   But it's so much easier that way.

MAN   I know. Try the chandelier. That's one thing you can't touch.

AGNES   How handsome you are, my little, my great chandelier!

The MUSIC begins again. Another tune.

Only when you're all lit up? Oh, don't say that. Other chandeliers,
yes. Street lamps, store-fixtures, yes. Not you. See—you are full of
sunshine. You are the chandelier of the sun. A desk lamp needs
to be lit. A planet needs to be lit. But you have radiance of your
own. You are as beautiful as a galaxy of stars, even more beautiful,
for a galaxy is only an imitation chandelier, a cluster of uncertain
lights swinging precariously in the eternal darkness. But you are
a creature of crystal with limbs of ivory and gold, a living miracle!

The chandelier LIGHTS up by itself.

MAN   Bravo!

VICE PRESIDENT   (*The door opens. The* VICE PRESIDENT *comes in. His manner is important. His face is that of a gargoyle.*)[8] My dear young lady, I have exactly two minutes to give you. (*He crosses to close the window.*)

AGNES (*whispering in awe*)   Oh!

VICE PRESIDENT (*stops and turns*)   Why do you stare at me like that? You've seen me before?

AGNES (*in a tone of wonder*)   No! On the contrary.

VICE PRESIDENT   And what does that mean, no, on the contrary?

AGNES   I was expecting to see the usual Vice President, stoop-shouldered, paunchy, bald— And all at once, I see you!

VICE PRESIDENT *freezes in his tracks.* MAN *thrusts out his head. He raises a warning finger. Hastily.*

How handsome you are!

VICE PRESIDENT   What? (*He turns.*)

AGNES   Nothing. I beg your pardon.

VICE PRESIDENT.   I heard you distinctly. You said I was handsome. Don't deny it. (*He steps closer to her. MUSIC swells up*). You know, it gave me rather a shock to hear you say it. However, it can't be true. If I were really—what you said—wouldn't some woman have told me before this?

AGNES   Oh, the fools! The fools!

VICE PRESIDENT   Whom are you calling fools, Mademoiselle? My sister, my mother, my niece?

AGNES (*giving up all at once. In a formal tone*)   Mr. Vice President, the truth is I am looking for a position. And I happened to hear through a friend of one of your directors, Mr. Lepédura—

MAN *thrusts out his head.*

VICE PRESIDENT   Never mind Monsieur Lepédura. We are discussing me. As you probably know, I am one of the world's authorities in the field of dreams. It is I who work with those who are able to invent only while they sleep, and I have been able to extract from their dreams such extraordinary devices as the book that reads itself and the adjustable Martini, wonders of modern science which

---

[8] A waterspout, usually carved in the shape of a grotesque human or animal figure, which projects from roof gutters. The word "gargoyle" is related to "gargle."

without my help would have remained mere figments of the imagination. If you appeared to me in a dream and told me I was handsome, I should have understood at once. But we are in a waking state, or are we? One moment. (*He pinches himself.*) Ow! I am awake. Permit me. (*Pinches her.*)

AGNES Ow!

VICE PRESIDENT We're not dreaming, Mademoiselle. And now, my dear— (*He takes her hand.*) Why did you say I was handsome? To flatter me?—I can see you are incapable of such baseness. To make fun of me? No—your eye is gentle, your lips attract— Why did you say it, Mademoiselle?

AGNES I say you are handsome because you are handsome. If your mother finds you ugly that's not my concern.

VICE PRESIDENT I cannot permit you to form so low an opinion of my mother's taste. Even when I was a boy, my mother used to say I had the hands of an artist.

AGNES If your niece prefers Charles Boyer—

VICE PRESIDENT My niece? Only yesterday at dinner she was saying that my eyebrows could have been drawn by El Greco.[9]

AGNES If your sister—

VICE PRESIDENT My sister has never quite admitted that I am handsome, no, but she has always said that there was something distinctive about my face. A friend of hers, a history teacher, told her it's because in certain lights, I resemble Lodovico Sforza.[10] (*He makes a deprecating gesture.*)

AGNES Lodovico Sforza? Never. The Apollo of Bellac, yes.

VICE PRESIDENT The Apollo of Bellac?

AGNES Wouldn't you say? Quite objectively?

VICE PRESIDENT Well—if you really think so—perhaps just a little. Although Lodovico Sforza, you know—I've seen engravings—

AGNES When I say the Apollo of Bellac, I mean, naturally, the Apollo of Bellac in a beautifully tailored suit. You see, I am frank. I say what I think. Yes, Mr. Vice President. You have the fault of all really handsome men—you dress carelessly.

VICE PRESIDENT (*smiling*) What insolence! And this from a girl who tells every man she meets that he's handsome!

[9] The foremost Spanish painter of the Castilian school of the sixteenth century.
[10] Member of a celebrated Italian family that ruled Milan, Lodovico lived from 1451–1508.

AGNES   I have said that to two men only in all my life. You are the second.

CLERK *comes in.*

VICE PRESIDENT   What is it? Don't you see I'm busy?

CLERK   The Directors are on the way up, sir. It's time for the meeting.

VICE PRESIDENT   I'll be right in.

CLERK *goes into the Directors' room.*

I'm sorry, Mademoiselle. I must go to this meeting. But we must certainly continue this wonderful conversation. Won't you come back and lunch with me? You know, my secretary is impossible. I'm having her transferred to the sales department. Now you're a first-rate typist, I'm told—

AGNES   I don't type. I play the piano.

VICE PRESIDENT   Ah, that's wonderful. And you take dictation?

AGNES   In longhand, yes.

VICE PRESIDENT   That's much the best way. That gives one time to think. Would you like to be my secretary?

AGNES   On one condition.

VICE PRESIDENT   A condition?

AGNES   On condition that you never wear this awful jacket again. When I think of these wonderful shoulders in that ill-fitting suit—!

VICE PRESIDENT   I have a beautiful blue silk suit. But it's for summer— It's a little light for the season.

AGNES   As you please.

VICE PRESIDENT   I'll wear it tomorrow.

AGNES   Good-bye.

VICE PRESIDENT   Don't forget. Lunch. (*He goes out, smiling, by way of the door to the Directors' room. The Street MUSIC stops.* MAN *peers out from behind the bust.*)

AGNES   I kept my hands behind my back the whole time. I pretended I had no hands. Now I can hardly move my fingers.

MAN   Here come the rest of the apes. Go to work.

AGNES   On the first?

MAN   On all. One after the other.

AGNES   But—

CLERK *throws open the doors of the Directors' room. The street MUSIC starts again. We have a glimpse of the Directors' table with*

chairs pulled back ready to receive the Directors. The VICE PRESI-
DENT *is seen inside. He is posturing in front of a bookcase in the
glass door of which he sees himself reflected, and he is trying vainly
to give a smartly tailored appearance to his coat.* CLERK *glances at
him in astonishment, then he stands by the outer door to announce
the Directors as they appear. They come in through the outer door
and cross the length of the reception room, one by one in time to
the music, which is a waltz.*

CLERK   Mr. Cracheton.

MR. CRACHETON *comes in, a lugubrious type, stiff and melancholy.*

AGNES   How handsome he is!

CRACHETON (*he snaps his head about as if shot. His expression changes.
He smiles. In a low voice*)   Charming girl! (*He goes into the Directors' room, looking all the while over his shoulder.*

CLERK   Mr. Lepédura.

LEPÉDURA (*appears. He has a face full of suspicion and worry. As he
passes* AGNES, *he tips his derby perfunctorily, recognizing her*)
Good morning.

AGNES   How handsome you are!

LEPÉDURA (*stops dead*)   Who says so?

AGNES   Your wife's friend, the Baroness Chagrobis. She thinks you're
wonderful.

LEPÉDURA (*a changed man, gallant and charming*)   She thinks I'm
wonderful? Well, well, give her my love when you see her. And tell
her I mean to call her up shortly myself. She has a pretty thin
time of it with the Baron, you know. We have to be nice to her. Is
she still at the same address?

AGNES   Oh, yes. I'll tell her you're as handsome as ever.

LEPÉDURA   Now don't exaggerate, my dear. We don't want to dis-
appoint her. (*He gives her a radiant smile, and goes in, fully six
inches taller and many pounds lighter. To the* CLERK)   Delightful
girl!

CLERK   Mr. Rasemutte and Mr. Schultz.

They enter together, Mutt and Jeff.

AGNES   How handsome he is!

BOTH *stop as if at a signal.*

RASEMUTTE   To which of us, Mademoiselle—
SCHULTZ   Do you refer?
AGNES   Look at each other. You will see.

They look at each other anxiously, and BOTH *smile radiantly.*

RASEMUTTE   Charming creature!
SCHULTZ   Lovely girl! (SCHULTZ *offers* RASEMUTTE *his arm. They walk into the Directors' room arm in arm like characters in "Alt Wien."* [11] CLERK *blows* AGNES *a kiss, follows them in and closes the doors behind them.* MAN *pokes his head out from behind Archimedes. He shakes his head ruefully.*)
AGNES   I'm not doing it well? You're sad?
MAN   You're doing it much too well. I'm frightened.
AGNES   You?
MAN   Like Frankenstein[12]

The door of the Directors' room is flung open.

CLERK   The President!

As the PRESIDENT *enters the room, we catch a glimpse of the* DI-RECTORS. *Each has a mirror in his hand. While one combs his hair into waves, another settles his tie. Another preens his whiskers. The* VICE PRESIDENT *has taken off his jacket.*

PRESIDENT   So you're the cause of it all, Miss— Miss—?
AGNES   Agnes.
PRESIDENT   Miss Agnes, for fifteen years this organization has been steeped in melancholy, jealousy and suspicion. And now suddenly this morning, everything is changed. My reception clerk, ordinarily a species of hyena— (*the* CLERK *smiles affably*) has become so affable he even bows to his own shadow on the wall—

CLERK *contemplates his silhouette in the sunshine with **a** nod of approval. It nods back.*

The First Vice President, whose reputation for stuffiness and formality has never been seriously challenged, insists on sitting at the Directors' Meeting in his shirt-sleeves, God knows why. In the Di-

---

[11] Translation "Old Vienna," an operetta.
[12] The young student in Mary Wollstonecraft Shelley's novel *Frankenstein* who creates a soulless monster and gives it life. Since Mrs. Shelley gave the monster no name, he is frequently called Frankenstein erroneously.

rectors' Room, around the table, mirrors flash like sunbeams in a forest, and my Directors gaze into them with rapture. Mr. Lepédura contemplates with joy the Adam's apple of Mr. Lepédura. Mr. Rasemutte stares with pride at the nose of Mr. Rasemutte. They are all in love with themselves and with each other. How in the world did you bring about this miracle, Miss Agnes? What was it you said to them?

AGNES   How handsome you are!

PRESIDENT   I beg your pardon?

AGNES   I said to them, to each of them, "How handsome you are!"

PRESIDENT   Ah! You conveyed it to them subtly by means of a smile, a wink, a promise—

AGNES   I said it in a loud clear voice. Like this: How handsome you are!

In the Directors' Room, all heads turn suddenly. CLERK *closes the doors.*

PRESIDENT   I see. Like a child winding up a mechanical doll. Well, well! No wonder my mannikins are quivering with the joy of life.

There is a round of applause from the Directors' Room.

Listen to that. It's Mr. Cracheton proposing the purchase of a new three-way mirror for the men's room. Miss Agnes, I thank you. You have made a wonderful discovery.

AGNES   (*modestly*)   Oh, it was nothing.

PRESIDENT   And the President? How does it happen that you don't tell the President?

AGNES   How handsome he is?

PRESIDENT   He's not worth the trouble, is that it?

She looks at him with a smile full of meaning.

You've had enough of masculine vanity for one morning?

AGNES   Oh, Mr. President—you know the reason as well as I.

PRESIDENT   No. I assure you.

AGNES   But—I don't need to tell *you*. You *are* handsome.

PRESIDENT   (*seriously*)   Would you mind repeating that?

AGNES   You are handsome.

PRESIDENT   Think carefully, Miss Agnes. This is a serious matter. Are you quite sure that to you I seem handsome?

AGNES   You don't seem handsome. You are handsome.

PRESIDENT   You would be ready to repeat that before witnesses? Think. Much depends upon your answer. I have grave decisions to make today, and the outcome depends entirely upon you. Have you thought? Are you still of the same opinion?

AGNES   Completely.

PRESIDENT   Thank heaven. (*He goes to his private door, opens it and calls*) Chevredent!

CHEVREDENT *comes in. She is a thin, sour woman with an insolent air. Her nose is pinched. Her chin is high. Her hair is drawn up tightly. When she opens her mouth she appears to be about to bite.*

CHEVREDENT   Yes? (*She looks at* AGNES *and sniffs audibly.*)

PRESIDENT   Cheveredent, how long have you been my private secretary?

CHEVREDENT   Three years and two months. Why?

PRESIDENT   In all that time there has never been a morning when the prospect of finding you in my office has not made me shudder.

CHEVREDENT   Thanks very much. Same to you.

PRESIDENT   I wouldn't have put up with you for ten minutes if it had ever occurred to me that I was handsome.

CHEVREDENT   Ha-ha.

PRESIDENT   But because I thought I was ugly, I tok your meanness for generosity. Because I thought I was ugly, I assumed that your evil temper concealed a good heart. I thought it was kind of you even to look at me. For I am ugly, am I not?

CHEVREDENT *sneers maliciously.*

Thank you. And now listen to me. This young lady seems to be far better equipped to see than you. Her eyelids are not red like yours, her pupils are clear, her glance is limpid. Miss Agnes, look at me. Am I ugly?

AGNES   You are beautiful.

CHEVREDENT *shrugs.*

PRESIDENT   This young lady's disinterested appraisal of my manly charms has no effect on your opinion?

CHEVREDENT   I never heard such rubbish in my life!

PRESIDENT   Quite so. Well, here is the problem that confronts us. I have the choice of spending my working time with an ugly old shrew who thinks I'm hideous or a delightful young girl who thinks I'm handsome. What do you advise?

CHEVREDENT   You intend to replace me with this little fool?

PRESIDENT   At once.

CHEVREDENT   We'll soon see about that, Mr. President. You may have forgotten, but your wife is inside in your office reading your mail. She should know about this.

PRESIDENT   She should. Tell her.

CHEVREDENT   With pleasure. (*She rushes into the* PRESIDENT'S *office, slamming the door after her.*)

AGNES   I'm terribly sorry, Mr. President.

PRESIDENT   My dear, you come like an angel from heaven at the critical moment of my life. Today is my fifteenth wedding anniversary. My wife, with whose fury Chevredent threatens us, is going to celebrate the occasion by lunching with my Directors. I am going to present her with a gift. A diamond. (*He takes out a case and opens it.*) Like it?

AGNES   How handsome it is!

PRESIDENT   Extraordinary! You praised the diamond in exactly the same tone you used for me. Is it yellow, by any chance? Is it flawed?

AGNES   It is beautiful. Like you.

PRESIDENT   (*his door opens*)   We are about to become less so, both of us. (*He puts the case in his pocket.*) Here is my wife.

THERESE   (THERESE, *the blond lady comes in with icy majesty. She looks* AGNES *up and down*)   So.

PRESIDENT   Therese, my dear, permit me to present—

THERESE   Quite unnecessary. That will be all, Mademoiselle. You may go.

PRESIDENT   Agnes is staying, my dear. She is replacing Chevredent.

THERESE   Agnes! So she is already Agnes!

PRESIDENT   Why not?

THERESE   And why is Agnes replacing Chevredent?

PRESIDENT   Because she thinks I'm handsome.

THERESE   Are you mad?

PRESIDENT   No. Handsome.

THERESE   (*to* AGNES)   You think he's handsome?

AGNES   Oh yes.

THERESE   He makes you think of Galahad? [13] Of Lancelot? [14]

AGNES   Oh no. His type is classic. The Apollo of Bellac.

THERESE   The Apollo of Bellac?

PRESIDENT   Have you ever stopped to wonder, Therese, why the good Lord made women? Obviously they were not torn from our ribs in order to make life a torment for us. Women exist in order to tell men they are handsome. And those who say it the most are those who are most beautiful. Agnes tells me I'm handsome. It's because she's beautiful. You tell me I'm ugly. Why?

MAN (*appears. He applauds.*)   Bravo! Bravo!

THERESE   Who is this maniac?

MAN   When one hears a voice which goes to the very heart of humanity, it is impossible to keep silent.

PRESIDENT   My friend—

MAN   From the time of Adam and Eve, of Samson and Delilah, of Antony and Cleopatra,[15] the problem of man and woman has made an impenetrable barrier between man and woman. If, as it seems, we are able to solve this problem once and for all, it will be a work of immeasurable benefit to the human race.

THERESE   And you think we're getting somewhere with it today, is that it?

MAN   Oh, yes.

THERESE   You don't think the final solution could be deferred until tomorrow?

MAN   Till tomorrow? When the President has just posed the problem so beautifully?

AGNES   So beautifully!

THERESE   The beautiful man poses a beautiful problem, eh, Mademoiselle?

AGNES   I didn't say it. But I can say it. I say what I think.

THERESE   Little cheat!

PRESIDENT   I forbid you to insult Agnes!

THERESE   It's she who insults me!

PRESIDENT   When I'm called handsome, it's an insult to you—is that it?

---

[13] The purest and noblest knight of the Round Table in the legends about King Arthur.
[14] The most famous of the knights of the Round Table, who though always portrayed as a model of chivalry and bravery, was the adulterous lover of Guinevere.
[15] Queen of Egypt, mistress of Julius Caesar and Mark Antony, and the heroine of many famous tragedies, including Shakespeare's *Antony and Cleopatra*.

THERESE   I'm no liar.

PRESIDENT   No. You show us the bottom of your heart.

MAN   Agnes is telling the President the truth, Madame. Just as Cleopatra told the truth, just as Isolt[16] told the truth. The truth about men is, they are beautiful, every last one of them; and your husband is right, Madame, the woman who tells it to them never lies.

THERESE   So I am the liar!

MAN   (*gently*)   It's only because you don't see clearly. All you have to do to see the beauty of men is to watch as they breathe and move their limbs. Each has his special grace. His beauty of body. The heavy ones—how powerfully they hold the ground! The light ones —how well they hang from the sky! His beauty of position. A hunchback on the ridge of Notre Dame makes a masterpiece of Gothic sculpture. All you have to do is to get him up there. And, finally, his beauty of function. The steamfitter has the beauty of a steamfitter. The president has the beauty of a president. There is ugliness only when these beauties become confused—when the steamfitter has the beauty of a president, the president the beauty of a steamfitter.

AGNES   But there is no such confusion here.

THERESE   No. He has the beauty of a garbageman.

PRESIDENT   Thanks very much.

THERESE   My dear, I have known you too long to deceive you. You have many good qualities. But you're ugly.

PRESIDENT   Quiet!

THERESE   Yes. Yes. Ugly! This girl, whatever her motives, is just able to force her lips to whisper her lies. But with every part of me— my heart, my lungs, my arms, my eyes—I scream the truth at you. My legs! You're ugly! Do you hear?

PRESIDENT   I've heard nothing else for years.

THERESE   Because it's true.

MAN   There. And at last she's confessed.

THERESE   Confessed what? What have I confessed?

MAN   Your crime, Madame. You have injured this man. How could you expect him to be handsome in an environment that screamed at him constantly that he was ugly?

PRESIDENT   Ah! Now I understand!

---

[16] Two heroines of Arthurian romance were named Isolt. The more important, Isolt the Beautiful, although the wife of King Mark, loved and was beloved by Tristan.

THERESE   What do you understand? What's the matter with you all? What have I done?

PRESIDENT   Now I understand why I am always embarrassed not only in your presence, but in the presence of everything that belongs to you.

THERESE   Do you know what he is talking about?

PRESIDENT   The sight of your skirt on the back of a chair shortens my spine by three inches. Can you expect me to stand up like a man when you come in? Your stockings on the bureau tell me that I'm knock-kneed and thick-ankled. Is it any wonder if I stumble? Your nail file on my desk hisses at me that my fingers are thick and my gestures clumsy. What do you expect of me after that? And your onyx clock with the Dying Gaul[17] on the mantelpiece—no wonder I always shiver when I go near the fire. Imagine—for fifteen years that Dying Gaul has been sneering at me in my own house, and I never realized why I was uncomfortable. Well, at last I understand. And this very evening—

THERESE   Don't you dare!

PRESIDENT   This very evening your Dying Gaul shall die. You will find him in the garbage with the rest of the conspiracy. Your Dresden china shepherd, your Arab sheik, your directoire chairs with their scratchy bottoms—

THERESE   Those chairs belonged to my grandmother!

PRESIDENT   From now on they belong to the garbage. What are your chairs covered with, Agnes?

AGNES   Yellow satin.

PRESIDENT   I knew it. And the statues on your table?

AGNES   There is only a bowl of fresh flowers on my table. Today it is white carnations.

PRESIDENT   Of course. And over your fireplace?

AGNES   A mirror.

PRESIDENT   Naturally

THERESE   I warn you, if you so much as touch my chairs, I'll leave you forever.

PRESIDENT   As you please, my dear.

THERESE   I see. So this is my anniversary gift after fifteen years of devotion. Very well. Only tell me, what have you to complain of? In all these years has it ever happened that your roast was too rare?

---

[17] A famous marble statue in the Capitoline Museum at Rome.

Did I ever give you your coffee too cold, too hot, too light, too sweet? Thanks to me, you are known as a man whose handkerchief is always fresh, whose socks are always new. Have you ever known what it was to have a hole in your toe? Has anyone ever seen a spot on your vest? And yet how you splash in your gravy, my friend! How you go through your socks!

PRESIDENT   Tell me one thing. Do you say I am ugly because you think I am ugly or merely to spite me?

THERESE   Because you are ugly.

PRESIDENT   Thank you, Therese. Go on.

THERESE   Then this woman appears. And at the first glance we can guess the fate of the unhappy creature who marries her. We see it all—the slippers with the inner sole curled up in a scroll. The nightly battle over the newspaper. The pajamas without buttons and always too small. The headaches without aspirin, the soup without salt, the shower without towels—

PRESIDENT   Agnes, one question. Do you tell me I'm handsome because you think I'm handsome or only to make fun of me?

AGNES   Because you're handsome.

PRESIDENT   Thank you, Agnes.

THERESE   You mean because he's rich.

AGNES   If he were the richest man in the world, I'd still say he was handsome.

THERESE   Very well. Marry her if she thinks you're so handsome. Well? What are you waiting for?

PRESIDENT   Nothing.

THERESE   Take him, you, with my compliments. After fifteen years I've had enough. If you like to hear snoring at night—

AGNES   You snore? How wonderful!

THERESE   If you like bony knees—

AGNES   I like legs that have character.

THERESE   Look at that face! Now tell me he has the brow of a Roman Senator.

AGNES   No, Madame.

THERESE   No?

AGNES   The brow of a king.

THERESE   I give up. Good-bye.

PRESIDENT   Good-bye, my love.

THERESE *rushes out through outer door.*

And now, Agnes, in token of a happy future, accept this diamond. For me, one life has ended, and another begins.

CLERK *comes in and signs to him.*

Forgive me just one moment, Agnes. I must address the Directors. The Chairman of the Board is evidently not coming. I'll be right back. (*He crosses to the door. To the* CLERK) Send down to the florist. I want all the white carnations he has. Agnes, you have made me the happiest of men.

AGNES   The handsomest.

The PRESIDENT *goes out by his door, the* CLERK *by outer door.*

MAN   Well, there you are, my dear. You have everything—a job, a husband and a diamond. I can leave?

AGNES   Oh no!

The street MUSIC starts afresh.

MAN   But what more do you want?

AGNES   Look at me. I have changed—haven't I?

MAN   Perhaps just a little. That can't be helped.

AGNES   It's your fault. I have told so many lies! I must tell the truth at last or I shall burst!

MAN   What truth do you want to tell?

AGNES   I want to tell someone who is really beautiful that he is beautiful. I want to tell the most beautiful man in the world that he is the most beautiful man in the world.

MAN   And to caress him, perhaps, just a little?

AGNES   Just a little.

MAN   There is the Apollo of Bellac.

AGNES   He doesn't exist.

MAN   What does it matter whether or not he exists? His beauty is the supreme beauty. Tell him.

AGNES   I can't. Unless I touch a thing I don't see it. You know that. I have no imagination.

MAN   Close your eyes.

AGNES (*closes them*)   Yes?

MAN   Suppose, Agnes, it were the God of Beauty himself who visited you this morning. Don't be astonished. Perhaps it's true. Where else could this terrible power have come from? Or this extraordinary emotion you feel? Or this sense of oppression? And suppose that now the god reveals himself?

AGNES It is you?

MAN Don't open your eyes. Suppose I stand before you now in all my truth and all my splendor.

AGNES I see you.

MAN Call me thou.

AGNES I see thee.

MAN How do I seem?

AGNES You seem—

MAN I am taller than mortal men. My head is small and fringed with golden ringlets. From the line of my shoulders, the geometricians derived the idea of the square. From my eyebrows the bowmen drew the concept of the arc. I am nude and this nudity inspired in the musicians the idea of harmony.

AGNES Your heels are winged, are they not?

MAN They are not. You are thinking of the Hermes[18] of St. Yrieix.

AGNES I don't see your eyes.

MAN As for the eyes, it's as well you don't see them. The eyes of beauty are implacable. My eyeballs are silver. My pupils are graphite. From the eyes of beauty poets derived the idea of death. But the feet of beauty are enchanting. They are not feet that touch the ground. They are never soiled and never captive. The toes are slender, and from them artists derived the idea of symmetry. Do you see me now?

AGNES You dazzle my eyes.

MAN But your heart sees me.

AGNES I'm not so sure. Do not count on me too much, God of Beauty. My life is small. My days are long, and when I come back to my room each evening, there are five flights to climb in the greasy twilight amid smells of cooking. These five flights mark the beginning and the end of every event of my life, and oh, if you knew, Apollo, how lonely I am! Sometimes I find a cat waiting in a doorway. I kneel and stroke it for a moment, we purr together and it fills the rest of my day with joy. Sometimes I see a milk bottle that has fallen on its side. I set it right and the gesture comforts me. If I smell gas

---

[18] In Greek and Roman mythology Hermes, or Mercury, was the god of science and commerce, the patron of travelers, rogues, vagabonds, and thieves. He is represented as a young man with a hat and winged sandals.

in the hallway I run and speak to the janitor. It is so good to speak to someone about something. Between the second story and the third, the steps sag. At this turning one abandons hope. At this turning one loses one's balance, and catches at the banister, gasping with the anguish of those more fortunate ones who clutch at the rail on the heaving deck of a ship. That is my life, Apollo, a thing of shadows and tortured flesh. That is my conscience, Apollo, a staircase full of stale odors. If I hesitate to see you as you are, O beautiful god, it is because I need so much and I have so little and I must defend myself.

MAN   But I have rescued you, Agnes. You possess the secret.

AGNES   I know. From now on, my staircase will be new and full of light, the treads carpeted in velvet and adorned with initials. But to climb it with you would be unthinkable. Go away, God of Beauty. Leave me for always.

MAN   You wish that?

AGNES   If you were merely a handsome man, Apollo, thick and human in your flesh, with what joy I would take you in my arms! How I would love you! But you are too brilliant and too great for my staircase. I would do better to look at my diamond. Go, Apollo. Go away. Before I open my eyes, I implore you, vanish.

MAN   When I vanish, you will see before you an ordinary creature like yourself, covered with skin, covered with clothes.

AGNES   That is my destiny, and I prefer it. Let me kiss your lips, Apollo. And then—

MAN   (*he kisses her*)   Open your eyes, my dear. Apollo is gone. And I am going.

AGNES   How handsome you are!

MAN   Dear Agnes!

AGNES   Don't go. I will make you rich. I will order the President to buy your invention.

MAN   Which one?

AGNES   The Universal Vegetable. There must be a fortune in it.

MAN   I haven't quite got the hang of it yet. The roots don't hold the earth. I'll be back the moment I've perfected it.

AGNES   You promise?

MAN   We shall plant it together. And now—

AGNES   You are really leaving me? You think I shall marry the President?

MAN   No.

AGNES   Why not?

MAN   He's already married. And his wife has learned a lesson. You will see.

AGNES   Then whom shall I marry, if not the President?

CLERK   (*Enters. He crosses to the Directors' Room and throws open the door. Announces*)   The Chairman of the Board!

The CHAIRMAN *enters from outer door.*

MAN   (*whispers*)   He is a bachelor.

AGNES   How handsome he is!

MAN   Yes. (*He vanishes.*)

CHAIRMAN   Mademoiselle—

PRESIDENT   (*The* PRESIDENT *comes in quickly in great excitement.*) Agnes! Agnes! A miracle! My wife has just telephoned. I don't know what has come over her. She has thrown out the Dying Gaul and the china shepherd.

AGNES   Give her this diamond.

PRESIDENT   Thank you, Agnes. Thank you.

CHAIRMAN   (*taking her hand*)   And who is this charming girl who gives away diamonds?

AGNES   Her name is Agnes.

CHAIRMAN   Dear Agnes!

PRESIDENT   But what's happened to our friend? He isn't here?

AGNES   He is gone.

PRESIDENT   Call him back. He must have lunch with us. Do you know his name?

AGNES   His first name only. Apollo.

PRESIDENT   (*runs to the outer door*)   Apollo! Apollo!

The DIRECTORS *come in, all adorned with white carnations.*

Gentlemen, gentlemen, let's call him! We can't let him go like that. Apollo!

(*They each go to a door of a window save* AGNES *and the* CHAIRMAN *who remain standing hand in hand.*)

PRESIDENT *and* DIRECTORS   Apollo! Apollo!

CHAIRMAN   But whom are they shouting at? Is Apollo here?

AGNES   No. He just passed by.

CURTAIN

Pygmalion   *George Bernard Shaw*

PREFACE TO PYGMALION [1]—
(A PROFESSOR OF PHONETICS)

As will be seen later on, Pygmalion needs, not a preface, but a sequel,
which I have supplied in its due place. The English have no respect for
their language, and will not teach their children to speak it. They spell
it so abominably that no man can teach himself what it sounds like. It
is impossible for an Englishman to open his mouth without making some
other Englishman hate or despise him. German and Spanish are accessible to foreigners: English is not accessible even to Englishmen. The
reformer England needs today is an energetic phonetic enthusiast: that
is why I have made such a one the hero of a popular play. There have
been heroes of that kind crying in the wilderness for many years past.
When I became interested in the subject towards the end of the
eighteen-seventies, the illustrious Alexander Melville Bell, the inventor
of Visible Speech, had emigrated to Canada, where his son invented the
telephone; but Alexander J. Ellis was still a London patriarch, with an
impressive head always covered by a velvet skull cap, for which he
would apologize to public meetings in a very courtly manner. He and
Tito Pagliardini, another phonetic veteran, were men whom it was
impossible to dislike. Henry Sweet, then a young man, lacked their
sweetness of character: he was about as conciliatory to conventional
mortals as Ibsen[2] or Samuel Butler.[3] His great ability as a phonetician
(he was, I think, the best of them all at his job) would have entitled

---

[1] Pygmalion was a sculptor and King of Cypress who hated women but fell in
love with his own statue of Aphrodite. In answer to his prayers, the gods gave the
statue life and he married it. See p. 484 for Ovid's account.

[2] Henrik Ibsen (1829–1906) was a Norwegian dramatist whose plays dealt with
social problems and urged reforms. When first produced, they were widely attacked as "immoral."

[3] Samuel Butler (1835–1902) wrote Swiftian satires on the England of his day and
controversial scientific studies attacking Darwinism.

him to high official recognition, and perhaps enabled him to popularize his subject, but for his Satanic contempt for all academic dignitaries and persons in general who thought more of Greek than of phonetics. Once, in the days when the Imperial Institute rose in South Kensington, and Joseph Chamberlain was booming the Empire, I induced the editor of a leading monthly review to commission an article from Sweet on the imperial importance of his subject. When it arrived, it contained nothing but a savagely derisive attack on a professor of language and literature whose chair Sweet regarded as proper to a phonetic expert only. The article, being libellous, had to be returned as impossible; and I had to renounce my dream of dragging its author into the limelight. When I met him afterwards, for the first time for many years, I found to my astonishment that he, who had been a quite tolerably presentable young man, had actually managed by sheer scorn to alter his personal appearance until he had become a sort of walking repudiation of Oxford and all its traditions. It must have been largely in his own despite that he was squeezed into something called a Readership of phonetics there. The future of phonetics rests probably with his pupils, who all swore by him; but nothing could bring the man himself into any sort of compliance with the university to which he nevertheless clung by divine right in an intensely Oxonian way. I daresay his papers, if he has left any, include some satires that may be published without too destructive results fifty years hence. He was, I believe, not in the least an illnatured man: very much the opposite, I should say; but he would not suffer fools gladly.

Those who knew him will recognize in my third act the allusion to the patent shorthand in which he used to write postcards, and which may be acquired from a four and sixpenny manual published by the Clarendon Press. The postcards which Mrs Higgins describes are such as I have received from Sweet. I would decipher a sound which a cockney would represent by *zerr,* and a Frenchman by *seu,* and then write demanding with some heat what on earth it meant. Sweet, with boundless contempt for my stupidity, would reply that it not only meant but obviously was the word Result, as no other word containing that sound, and capable of making sense with the context, existed in any language spoken on earth. That less expert mortals should require fuller indications was beyond Sweet's patience. Therefore, though the whole point of his Current Shorthand is that it can express every sound in the language perfectly, vowels as well as consonants, and that your hand has to make no stroke except the easy and current ones with which you write m, n, and u, l, p, and q, scribbling them at whatever angle comes easiest to you, his unfortunate determination to make this remarkable and quite legible script serve also as a shorthand reduced it in his own practice to the most inscrutable of cryptograms. His true objective was the provision of a full, accurate, legible script for our noble but ill-dressed language; but he was led past that by his contempt for the popular Pitman system of shorthand, which he called the Pitfall system. The triumph of Pitman was a triumph of business organization: there was a weekly paper to persuade you to learn Pitman: there were cheap textbooks and exercise books and transcripts of speeches for you to copy, and schools where experienced teachers coached you up to the necessary proficiency. Sweet could not organize his market in that fashion. He might as well have been the Sybil who tore up the leaves of prophecy that nobody would attend to. The four and sixpenny manual, mostly in his lithographed handwriting, that was never vulgarly advertized, may perhaps some day be taken up by a syndicate and pushed upon the public as The Times pushed the Encyclopædia Britannica; but until then it will certainly not prevail against Pitman. I have bought three copies of it during my lifetime; and I am informed by the publishers that its cloistered existence is still a steady and healthy one. I actually learned the system two several times; and yet the shorthand in which I am writing these lines is Pitman's. And the reason is, that my secretary cannot transcribe Sweet, having been perforce taught in the schools of Pitman. Therefore, Sweet railed at Pitman as vainly as Thersites railed at Ajax: his raillery, however it may have eased his soul, gave no popular vogue to Current Shorthand.

Pygmalion Higgins is not a portrait of Sweet, to whom the adventure of Eliza Doolittle would have been impossible; still, as will be seen, there are touches of Sweet in the play. With Higgins's physique and temperament Sweet might have set the Thames on fire. As it was, he impressed himself professionally on Europe to an extent that made his comparative personal obscurity, and the failure of Oxford to do justice to his eminence, a puzzle of foreign specialists in his subject. I do not blame Oxford, because I think Oxford is quite right in demanding a certain social amenity from its nurslings (heavens knows it is not exorbitant in its requirements!); for although I well know how hard it is for a man of genius with a seriously underrated subject to maintain serene and kindly relations with the men who underrate it, and who keep all the best places for less important subjects which they profess without originality and sometimes without much capacity for them, still, if he overwhelms them with wrath and disdain, he cannot expect them to heap honors on him.

Of the later generations of phoneticians I know little. Among them towers the Poet Laureate, to whom perhaps Higgins may owe his Miltonic sympathies, though here again I must disclaim all portraiture. But if the play makes the public aware that there are such people as phoneticians, and that they are among the most important people in England at present, it will serve its turn.

I wish to boast that Pygmalion has been an extremely successful play all over Europe and North America as well as at home. It is so intensely and deliberately didactic, and its subject is esteemed so dry, that I delight in throwing it at the heads of the wiseacres who repeat the parrot cry that art should never be didactic. It goes to prove my contention that art should never be anything else.

Finally, and for the encouragement of people troubled wtih accents that cut them off from all high employment, I may add that the change wrought by Professor Higgins in the flower girl is neither impossible nor uncommon. The modern concierge's daughter who fulfils her ambition by playing the Queen of Spain in Ruy Blas at the Théâtre Français is only one of many thousands of men and women who have sloughed off their native dialects and acquired a new tongue. But the thing has to be done scientifically, or the last state of the aspirant may be worse than the first. An honest and natural slum dialect is more tolerable than the attempt of a phonetically untaught person to imitate the vulgar dialect of the golf club; and I am sorry to say that in spite of the efforts of our Royal Academy of Dramatic Art, there is still too much sham golfing English on our stage, and too little of the noble English of Forbes Robertson.

ACT I

Covent Garden at 11.15 *p.m. Torrents of heavy summer rain. Cab whistles blowing frantically in all directions. Pedestrians running for shelter into the market and under the portico of St Paul's Church, where there are already several people, among them a lady and her daughter in evening dress. They are all peering out gloomily at the rain, except one man with his back turned to the rest, who seems wholly preoccupied with a notebook in which he is writing busily. The church clock strikes the first quarter.*

THE DAUGHTER (*in the space between the central pillars, close to the one on her left*)   I'm getting chilled to the bone. What can Freddy be doing all this time? He's been gone twenty minutes.

THE MOTHER (*on her daughter's right*)   Not so long. But he ought to have got us a cab by this.

A BYSTANDER (*on the lady's right*)   He wont get no cab not until half-past eleven, missus, when they come back after dropping their theatre fares.

THE MOTHER   But we must have a cab. We cant stand here until half-past eleven. It's too bad.

THE BYSTANDER   Well, it aint my fault, missus.

THE DAUGHTER   If Freddy had a bit of gumption, he would have got one at the theatre door.

THE MOTHER   What could he have done, poor boy?

THE DAUGHTER   Other people got cabs. Why couldnt he?

FREDDY *rushes in out of the rain from the Southampton Street side, and comes between them closing a dripping umbrella. He is a young man of twenty, in evening dress, very wet round the ankles.*

THE DAUGHTER   Well, havent you got a cab?

FREDDY   Theres not one to be had for love or money.

THE MOTHER   Oh, Freddy, there must be one. You cant have tried.

THE DAUGHTER   It's too tiresome. Do you expect us to go and get one ourselves?

FREDDY   I tell you theyre all engaged. The rain was so sudden: nobody was prepared; and everybody had to take a cab. Ive been to Charing Cross one way and nearly to Ludgate Circus the other; and they were all engaged.

THE MOTHER   Did you try Trafalgar Square?

FREDDY   There wasnt one at Trafalgar Square.

THE DAUGHTER   Did you try?

FREDDY   I tried as far as Charing Cross Station. Did you expect me to walk to Hammersmith?

THE DAUGHTER   You havnt tried at all.

THE MOTHER   You really are very helpless, Freddy. Go again; and dont come back until you have found a cab.

FREDDY   I shall simply get soaked for nothing.

THE DAUGHTER   And what about us? Are we to stay here all night in this draught, with next to nothing on? You selfish pig—

FREDDY   Oh, very well: I'll go, I'll go. (*He opens his umbrella and dashes off Strandwards, but comes into collision with a flower girl, who is hurrying in for shelter, knocking her basket out of her hands. A blinding flash af lightning, followed instantly by a rattling peal of thunder, orchestrates the incident.*)

THE FLOWER GIRL   Nah then, Freddy: look wh' y' gowin, deah.

FREDDY   Sorry (*he rushes off*).

THE FLOWER GIRL   (*picking up her scattered flowers and replacing them in the basket*)   Theres menners f' yer! Te-oo banches o voylets trod into the mad. (*She sits down on the plinth of the column, sorting her flowers, on the lady's right. She is not at all an attractive person. She is perhaps eighteen, perhaps twenty, hardly older. She wears a little sailor hat of black straw that has long been exposed to the dust and soot of London and has seldom if ever been brushed. Her hair needs washing rather badly: its mousy color can hardly be natural. She wears a shoddy black coat that reaches nearly to her knees and is shaped to her waist. She has a brown skirt with a coarse apron. Her boots are much the worse for wear. She is no doubt as clean as she can afford to be; but compared to the ladies she is very dirty. Her features are no worse than theirs; but their condition leaves something to be desired; and she needs the services of a dentist.*)

THE MOTHER   How do you know that my son's name is Freddy, pray?

THE FLOWER GIRL   Ow, eez ye-ooa san, is e? Wal, fewd dan y' de-ooty bawmz a mather should, eed now bettern to spawl a pore gel's flahrzn than ran awy athaht pyin. Will ye-oo py me f' them? (*Here, with apologies, this desperate attempt to represent her dialect without a phonetic alphabet must be abandoned as unintelligible outside London.*)

THE DAUGHTER   Do nothing of the sort, mother. The idea!

THE MOTHER   Please allow me, Clara. Have you any pennies?

THE DAUGHTER   No. Ive nothing smaller than sixpence.

THE FLOWER GIRL   (*hopefully*)   I can give you change for a tanner, kind lady.

THE MOTHER   (*to* CLARA)   Give it to me.

CLARA *parts reluctantly.*

Now (*to the* GIRL) this is for your flowers.

THE FLOWER GIRL   Thank you kindly, lady.

THE DAUGHTER   Make her give you the change. These things are only a penny a bunch.

THE MOTHER   Do hold your tongue, Clara. (*To* THE GIRL) You can keep the change.

THE FLOWER GIRL   Oh, thank you, lady.

THE MOTHER   Now tell me how you know that young gentleman's name.

THE FLOWER GIRL   I didnt.

THE MOTHER   I heard you call him by it. Dont try to deceive me.

THE FLOWER GIRL (*protesting*)   Who's trying to deceive you? I called him Freddy or Charlie same as you might yourself if you was talking to a stranger and wished to be pleasant. (*She sits down beside her basket.*)

THE DAUGHTER   Sixpence thrown away! Really, mamma, you might have spared Freddy *that*. (*She retreats in disgust behind the pillar.*)

An elderly GENTLEMAN *of the amiable military type rushes into the shelter, and closes a dripping umbrella. He is in the same plight as* FREDDY, *very wet about the ankles. He is in evening dress, with a light overcoat. He takes the place left vacant by the daughter's retirement.*

THE GENTLEMAN.   Phew!

THE MOTHER (*to* THE GENTLEMAN)   Oh, sir, is there any sign of its stopping?

THE GENTLEMAN   I'm afraid not. It started worse than ever about two minutes ago. (*He goes to the plinth beside the flower girl; puts up his foot on it; and stoops to turn down his trouser ends.*)

THE MOTHER   Oh dear! (*She retires sadly and joins her daughter.*)

THE FLOWER GIRL (*taking advantage of the military gentleman's proximity to establish friendly relations with him*)   If it's worse, it's a sign it's nearly over. So cheer up, Captain; and buy a flower off a poor girl.

THE GENTLEMAN   I'm sorry. I havnt any change.

THE FLOWER GIRL   I can give you change, Captain.

THE GENTLEMAN   For a sovereign! Ive nothing less.

THE FLOWER GIRL   Garn! Oh do buy a flower off me, Captain. I can change half-a-crown. Take this for tuppence.

THE GENTLEMAN   Now dont be troublesome: theres a good girl. (*Trying his pockets*) I really havnt any change—Stop: heres three hapence, if thats any use to you (*he retreats to the other pillar*).

THE FLOWER GIRL (*disappointed, but thinking three halfpence better than nothing*)   Thank you, sir.

THE BYSTANDER (*to the* GIRL)   You be careful: give him a flower for it. Theres a bloke here behind taking down every blessed word youre saying. (*All turn to the man who is taking notes.*)

THE FLOWER GIRL (*springing up terrified*)   I aint done nothing wrong by speaking to the gentleman. Ive a right to sell flowers if I keep off the kerb. (*Hysterically*) I'm a respectable girl: so help me, I never spoke to him except to ask him to buy a flower off me.

General hubbub, mostly sympathetic to the flower girl, but deprecating her excessive sensibility. Cries of Dont start hollerin. Who's hurting you? Nobody's going to touch you. Whats the good of fussing? Steady on. Easy easy, etc., *come from the elderly staid spectators, who pat her comfortingly. Less patient ones bid her shut her head, or ask her roughly what is wrong with her. A remoter group, not knowing what the matter is, crowd in and increase the noise with question and answer:* Whats the row? Whatshe do? Where is he? A tec taking her down. What! him? Yes: him over there: Took money off the gentleman, etc. THE FLOWER GIRL, *distraught and mobbed, breaks through them to* THE GENTLEMAN, *crying wildly.*

Oh, sir, dont let him charge me. You dunno what it means to me. Theyll take away my character and drive me on the streets for speaking to gentlemen. They—

THE NOTE TAKER (*coming forward on her right, the rest crowding after him*)   There, there, there, there! who's hurting you, you silly girl? What do you take me for?

THE BYSTANDER   It's all right: he's a gentleman: look at his boots. (*Explaining to* THE NOTE TAKER)   She thought you was a copper's nark, sir.

THE NOTE TAKER (*with quick interest*)   Whats a copper's nark?

THE BYSTANDER (*inapt at definition*)   It's a—well, it's a copper's nark, as you might say. What else would you call it? A sort of informer.

THE FLOWER GIRL (*still hysterical*)   I take my Bible oath I never said a word—

THE NOTE TAKER (*overbearing but good-humored*)   Oh, shut up, shut up. Do I look like a policeman?

THE FLOWER GIRL (*far from reassured*)   Then what did you take down my words for? How do I know whether you took me down right? You just shew me what youve wrote about me.

THE NOTE TAKER *opens his book and holds it steadily under her nose,
though the pressure of the mob trying to read it over his shoulders
would upset a weaker man.*

Whats that? *That* aint proper writing. I cant read that.

THE NOTE TAKER   I can. (*Reads, reproducing her pronunciation exactly*)"Cheer ap, Keptin; n' baw ya flahr orf a pore gel."

THE FLOWER GIRL (*much distressed*)   It's because I called him Captain. I meant no harm. (*To* THE GENTLEMAN) Oh, sir, dont let him lay a charge agen me for a word like that. You—

THE GENTLEMAN   Charge! I make no charge. (*To* THE NOTE TAKER) Really, sir, if you are a detective, you need not begin protecting me against molestation by young women until I ask you. Anybody could see that the girl meant no harm.

THE BYSTANDERS GENERALLY (*demonstrating against police espionage*) Course they could. What business is it of yours? You mind your own affairs. He wants promotion, he does. Taking down people's words! Girl never said a word to him. What harm if she did? Nice thing a girl cant shelter from the rain without being insulted, etc., etc., etc.

*She is conducted by the more sympathetic demonstrators back to her
plinth, where she resumes her seat and struggles with her emotion.*

THE BYSTANDER   He aint a tec. He's a blooming busybody: thats what he is. I tell you, look at his boots.

THE NOTE TAKER (*turning on him genially*)   And how are all your people down at Selsey?

THE BYSTANDER (*suspiciously*)   Who told you my people come from Selsey?

THE NOTE TAKER   Never you mind. They did. (*To* THE GIRL) How do you come to be up so far east? You were born in Lisson Grove.

THE FLOWER GIRL (*appalled*)   Oh, what harm is there in my leaving Lisson Grove? It wasnt fit for a pig to live in; and I had to pay four-and-six a week. (*In tears*) Oh, boo—hoo—oo—

THE NOTE TAKER   Live where you like; but stop that noise.

THE GENTLEMAN (*to* THE GIRL)   Come, come! he cant touch you: you have a right to live where you please.

A SARCASTIC BYSTANDER (*thrusting himself between* THE NOTE TAKER *and* THE GENTLEMAN)   Park Lane, for instance. I'd like to go into the Housing Question with you, I would.

THE FLOWER GIRL (*subsiding into a brooding melancholy over her*

basket, and talking very low-spiritedly to herself)   I'm a good girl,
I am.

THE SARCASTIC BYSTANDER (*not attending to her*)   Do you know
where *I* come from?

THE NOTE TAKER (*promptly*)   Hoxton.

Titterings. Popular interest in THE NOTE TAKER'S *performance in-
creases.*

THE SARCASTIC ONE (*amazed*)   Well, who said I didnt? Bly me! You
know everything, you do.

THE FLOWER GIRL (*still nursing her sense of injury*)   Aint no call to
meddle with me, he aint.

THE BYSTANDER (*to her*)   Of course he aint. Dont you stand it from
him. (*To* THE NOTE TAKER) See here: what call have you to know
about people what never offered to meddle with you? Where's your
warrant?

SEVERAL BYSTANDERS (*encouraged by this seeming point of law*)   Yes:
wheres your warrant?

THE FLOWER GIRL   Let him say what he likes. I dont want to have no
truck with him.

THE BYSTANDER   You take us for dirt under your feet, dont you?
Catch you taking liberties with a gentleman!

THE SARCASTIC BYSTANDER   Yes: tell *him* where he come from if you
want to go fortune-telling.

THE NOTE TAKER   Cheltenham, Harrow, Cambridge, and India.

THE GENTLEMAN   Quite right.

Great laughter. Reaction in THE NOTE TAKER'S *favor. Exclamations
of* He knows all about it. Told him proper. Hear him tell the toff
where he come from? etc.

May I ask, sir, do you do this for your living at a music hall?

THE NOTE TAKER   Ive thought of that. Perhaps I shall some day.

*The rain has stopped; and the persons on the outside of the crowd
begin to drop off.*

THE FLOWER GIRL (*resenting the reaction*)   He's no gentleman, he
aint, to interfere with a poor girl.

THE DAUGHTER (*out of patience, pushing her way rudely to the front
and displacing* THE GENTLEMAN, *who politely retires to the other side*

of the pillar)   What on earth is Freddy doing? I shall get pneumonia if I stay in this draught any longer.

THE NOTE TAKER (*to himself, hastily making a note of her pronunciation of "monia"*)   Earlscourt.

THE DAUGHTER (*violently*)   Will you please keep your impertinent remarks to yourself.

THE NOTE TAKER   Did I say that out loud? I didnt mean to. I beg your pardon. Your mother's Epsom, unmistakably.

THE MOTHER (*advancing between her daughter and* THE NOTE TAKER)   How very curious! I was brought up in Largelady Park, near Epsom.

THE NOTE TAKER (*uproariously amused*)   Ha! ha! What a devil of a name! Excuse me. (*To* THE DAUGHTER) You want a cab, do you?

THE DAUGHTER   Dont dare speak to me.

THE MOTHER   Oh please, please, Clara.

Her daughter repudiates her with an angry shrug and retires haughtily.

We should be so grateful to you, sir, if you found us a cab.

THE NOTE TAKER *produces a whistle.*

Oh, thank you. (*She joins her daughter.*)

THE NOTE TAKER *blows a piercing blast.*

THE SARCASTIC BYSTANDER   There! I knowed he was a plain-clothes copper.

THE BYSTANDER   That aint a police whistle: thats a sporting whistle.

THE FLOWER GIRL (*still preoccupied with her wounded feelings*)   He's no right to take away my character. My character is the same to me as any lady's.

THE NOTE TAKER   I dont know whether youve noticed it; but the rain stopped about two minutes ago.

THE BYSTANDER   So it has. Why didnt you say so before? and us losing our time listening to your silliness! (*He walks off towards the Strand.*)

THE SARCASTIC BYSTANDER   I can tell where you come from. You come from Anwell. Go back there.

THE NOTE TAKER (*helpfully*)   *H*anwell.

THE SARCASTIC BYSTANDER (*affecting great distinction of speech*)   Thenk you, teacher. Haw haw! So long (*he touches his hat with mock respect and strolls off*).

THE FLOWER GIRL   Frightening people like that! How would he like it himself?

THE MOTHER   It's quite fine now, Clara. We can walk to a motor bus. Come. (*She gathers her skirts above her ankles and hurries off towards the Strand.*)

THE DAUGHTER   But the cab—(*her mother is out of hearing*). Oh, how tiresome! (*She follows angrily.*)

All the rest have gone except THE NOTE TAKER, THE GENTLEMAN, *and* THE FLOWER GIRL, *who sits arranging her basket and still pitying herself in murmurs.*

THE FLOWER GIRL   Poor girl! Hard enough for her to live without being worrited and chivied.

THE GENTLEMAN (*returning to his former place on* THE NOTE TAKER'S *left*)   How do you do it, if I may ask?

THE NOTE TAKER   Simply phonetics. The science of speech. Thats my profession: also my hobby. Happy is the man who can make a living by his hobby! You can spot an Irishman or a Yorkshireman by his brogue. *I* can place any man within six miles. I can place him within two miles in London. Sometimes within two streets.

THE FLOWER GIRL   Ought to be ashamed of himself, unmanly coward.

THE GENTLEMAN   But is there a living in that?

THE NOTE TAKER   Oh yes. Quite a fat one. This is an age of upstarts. Men begin in Kentish Town with £80 a year, and end in Park Lane with a hundred thousand. They want to drop Kentish Town; but they give themselves away every time they open their mouths. Now I can teach them—

THE FLOWER GIRL   Let him mind his own business and leave a poor girl—

THE NOTE TAKER (*explosively*)   Woman: cease this detestable boo-hooing instantly; or else seek the shelter of some other place of worship.

THE FLOWER GIRL (*with feeble defiance*)   Ive a right to be here if I like, same as you.

THE NOTE TAKER   A woman who utters such depressing and disgusting sounds has no right to be anywhere—no right to live. Remember that you are a human being with a soul and the divine gift of articulate speech: that your native language is the language of Shakespear and Milton and The Bible: and dont sit there crooning like a bilious pigeon.

THE FLOWER GIRL (*quite overwhelmed, looking up at him in mingled wonder and deprecation without daring to raise her head*)   Ah-ah-ah-ow-ow-ow-oo!

THE NOTE TAKER (*whipping out his book*)   Heavens! what a sound! (*He writes; then holds out the book and reads, reproducing her vowels exactly.*) Ah-ah-ah-ow-ow-ow-oo!

THE FLOWER GIRL (*tickled by the performance, and laughing in spite of herself*)   Garn!

THE NOTE TAKER   You see this creature with her kerbstone English: the English that will keep her in the gutter to the end of her days. Well, sir, in three months I could pass that girl off as a duchess at an ambassador's garden party. I could even get her a place as lady's maid or shop assistant, which requires better English. Thats the sort of thing I do for commercial millionaires. And on the profits of it I do genuine scientific work in phonetics, and a little as a poet on Miltonic lines.

THE GENTLEMAN   I am myself a student of Indian dialects; and—

THE NOTE TAKER (*eagerly*)   Are you? Do you know Colonel Pickering, the author of Spoken Sanscrit?

THE GENTLEMAN   I *am* Colonel Pickering. Who are you?

THE NOTE TAKER   Henry Higgins, author of Higgins's Universal Alphabet.

PICKERING (*with enthusiasm*)   I came from India to meet you.

HIGGINS   I was going to India to meet you.

PICKERING   Where do you live?

HIGGINS   27A Wimpole Street. Come and see me tomorrow.

PICKERING.   I'm at the Carlton. Come with me now and lets have a jaw over some supper.

HIGGGINS   Right you are.

THE FLOWER GIRL (*to* PICKERING, *as he passes her*)   Buy a flower, kind gentleman. I'm short for my lodging.

PICKERING   I really havnt any change. I'm sorry (*he goes away*).

HIGGINS (*shocked at the girl's mendacity*)   Liar. You said you could change half-a-crown.

THE FLOWER GIRL (*rising in desperation*)   You ought to be stuffed with nails, you ought. (*Flinging the basket at his feet*) Take the whole blooming basket for sixpence.

The church clock strikes the second quarter.

HIGGINS (*hearing in it the voice of God, rebuking him for his Pharisaic want of charity to the poor girl)*   A reminder. (*He raises his hat solemnly; then throws a handful of money into the basket and follows* PICKERING.)

THE FLOWER GIRL (*picking up a half-crown*)   Ah-ow-ooh! (*Picking up a couple of florins*) Aaah-ow-ooh! (*Picking up several coins*) Aaaaaah-ow-ooh! (*Picking up a half-sovereign*) Aaaaaaaaaaaa-ow-ooh!!!

FREDDY (*springing out of a taxicab*)   Got one at last. Hallo! (*To* THE GIRL) Where are the two ladies that were here?

THE FLOWER GIRL   They walked to the bus when the rain stopped.

FREDDY   And left me with a cab on my hands! Damnation!

THE FLOWER GIRL (*with grandeur*)   Never mind, young man. I'm going home in a taxi. (*She sails off to the cab. The driver puts his hand behind him and holds the door firmly shut against her. Quite understanding his mistrust, she shews him her handful of money.*) Eightpence aint no object to me, Charlie.

He grins and opens the door.

Angel Court, Drury Lane, round the corner of Micklejohn's oil shop. Lets see how fast you can make her hop it. (*She gets in and pulls the door to with a slam as the taxicab starts.*)

FREDDY   Well, I'm dashed!

ACT II

Next day at 11 a.m. Higgins's laboratory in Wimpole Street. It is a room on the first floor, looking on the street, and was meant for the drawing room. The double doors are in the middle of the back wall; and persons entering find in the corner to their right two tall file cabinets at right angles to one another against the walls. In this corner stands a flat writing-table, on which are a phonograph, a laryngoscope, a row of tiny organ pipes with bellows, a set of lamp chimneys for singing flames with burners attached to a gas plug in the wall by an indiarubber tube, several tuning-forks of different sizes, a life-size image of half a human head, shewing in section the vocal organs, and a box containing a supply of wax cylinders for the phonograph.

Further down the room, on the same side, is a fireplace, with a comfortable leather-covered easy-chair at the side of the hearth nearest the door, and a coal-scuttle. There is a clock on the mantelpiece. Between the fireplace and the phonograph table is a stand for newspapers.

On the other side of the central door, to the left of the visitor, is a cabinet of shallow drawers. On it is a telephone and the telephone directory. The corner beyond, and most of the side wall, is occupied by a grand piano, with the keyboard at the end furthest from the door, and a bench for the player extending the full length of the keyboard. On the piano is a dessert dish heaped with fruit and sweets, mostly chocolates.

The middle of the room is clear. Besides the easy-chair, the piano bench, and two chairs at the phonograph table, there is one stray chair. It stands near the fireplace. On the walls, engravings: mostly Piranesi[4] and mezzotint portraits. No paintings.

PICKERING *is seated at the table, putting down some cards and a tuning-fork which he has been using.* HIGGINS *is standing up near him, closing two or three file drawers which are hanging out. He appears in the morning light as a robust, vital, appetizing sort of man of forty or thereabouts, dressed in a professional-looking black frock-coat with a white linen collar and black silk tie. He is of the energetic, scientific type, heartily, even violently interested in everything that can be studied as a scientific subject, and careless about himself and other people, including their feelings. He is, in fact, but for his years and size, rather like a very impetuous baby "taking notice" eagerly and loudly, and requiring almost as much watching to keep him out of unintended mischief. His manner varies from genial bullying when he is in a good humor to stormy petulance when anything goes wrong; but he is so entirely frank and void of malice that he remains likeable even in his least reasonable moments.*

HIGGINS (*as he shuts the last drawer*)   Well, I think thats the whole show.

PICKERING   It's really amazing. I havnt taken half of it in, you know.

HIGGINS   Would you like to go over any of it again?

PICKERING (*rising and coming to the fireplace, where he plants himself*

---

[4] Giambattista Piranesi (1720–78) was an Italian architect, painter, and engraver, whose copperplate engravings are used as source material for the investigation of Louis XIV, Adam, and Empire styles of architecture.

with his back to the fire)   No, thank you; not now. I'm quite done up for this morning.

HIGGINS (*following him, and standing beside him on his left*)   Tired of listening to sounds?

PICKERING   Yes. It's a fearful strain. I rather fancied myself because I can pronounce twenty-four distinct vowel sounds; but your hundred and thirty beat me. I cant hear a bit of difference between most of them.

HIGGINS (*chuckling, and going over to the piano to eat sweets*)   Oh, that comes with practice. You hear no difference at first; but you keep on listening, and presently you find theyre all as different as A from B.

MRS PEARCE *looks in: she is Higgins's housekeeper.*

Whats the matter?

MRS PEARCE (*hesitating, evidently perplexed*)   A young woman wants to see you, sir.

HIGGINS   A young woman! What does she want?

MRS PEARCE   Well, sir, she says youll be glad to see her when you know what she's come about. She's quite a common girl, sir. Very common indeed. I should have sent her away, only I thought perhaps you wanted her to talk into your machines. I hope Ive not done wrong; but really you see such queer people sometimes—youll excuse me, I'm sure, sir—

HIGGINS   Oh, thats all right, Mrs Pearce. Has she an interesting accent?

MRS PEARCE   Oh, something dreadful, sir, really. I dont know how you can take an interest in it.

HIGGINS (*to* PICKERING)   Lets have her up. Shew her up, Mrs. Pearce (*he rushes across to his working table and picks out a cylinder to use on the phonograph*).

MRS PEARCE (*only half resigned to it*)   Very well, sir. It's for you to say. (*She goes downstairs.*)

HIGGINS   This is rather a bit of luck. I'll shew you how I make records. We'll set her talking; and I'll take it down first in Bell's Visible Speech; then in broad Romic; and then we'll get her on the phonograph so that you can turn her on as often as you like with the written transcript before you.

MRS PEARCE (*returning*)   This is the young woman, sir.

THE FLOWER GIRL *enters in state. She has a hat with three ostrich feathers, orange, sky-blue, and red. She has a nearly clean apron, and the shoddy coat has been tidied a little. The pathos of this deplorable figure, with its innocent vanity and consequential air, touches* PICKERING, *who has already straightened himself in the presence of Mrs Pearce. But as to* HIGGINS, *the only distinction he makes between men and women is that when he is neither bullying nor exclaiming to the heavens against some feather-weight cross, he coaxes women as a child coaxes its nurse when it wants to get anything out of her.*

HIGGINS (*brusquely, recognizing her with unconcealed disappointment, and at once, baby-like, making an intolerable grievance of it*). Why, this is the girl I jotted down last night. She's no use: Ive got all the records I want of the Lisson Grove lingo; and I'm not going to waste another cylinder on it. (*To* THE GIRL) Be off with you: I dont want you.

THE FLOWER GIRL   Dont you be so saucy. You aint heard what I come for yet. (*To* MRS PEARCE, *who is waiting at the door for further instructions*) Did you tell him I come in a taxi?

MRS PEARCE   Nonsense, girl! what do you think a gentleman like Mr Higgins cares what you came in?

THE FLOWER GIRL   Oh, we are proud! He aint above giving lessons, not him: I heard him say so. Well, I aint come here to ask for any compliment; and if my money's not good enough I can go elsewhere.

HIGGINS   Good enough for what?

THE FLOWER GIRL   Good enough for ye-oo. Now you know, dont you? I'm come to have lessons, I am. And to pay for em too: make no mistake.

HIGGINS (*stupent*)   Well!!! (*Recovering his breath with a gasp*) What do you expect me to say to you?

THE FLOWER GIRL   Well, if you was a gentleman, you might ask me to sit down, I think. Dont I tell you I'm bringing you business?

HIGGINS   Pickering: shall we ask this baggage to sit down, or shall we throw her out of the window?

THE FLOWER GIRL (*running away in terror to the piano, where she turns at bay*) Ah-ah-oh-ow-ow-ow-oo! (*Wounded and whimpering*) I wont be called a baggage when Ive offered to pay like any lady.

Motionless, the two men stare at her from the other side of the room, amazed.

PICKERING (*gently*)   What is it you want, my girl?

THE FLOWER GIRL   I want to be a lady in a flower shop stead of selling at the corner of Tottenham Court Road. But they wont take me unless I can talk more genteel. He said he could teach me. Well, here I am ready to pay him—not asking any favor—and he treats me as if I was dirt.

MRS PEARCE   How can you be such a foolish ignorant girl as to think you could afford to pay Mr Higgins?

THE FLOWER GIRL   Why shouldnt I? I know what lessons cost as well as you do; and I'm ready to pay.

HIGGINS   How much?

THE FLOWER GIRL (*coming back to him, triumphant*)   Now youre talking! I thought youd come off it when you saw a chance of getting back a bit of what you chucked at me last night. (*Confidentially*) Youd had a drop in, hadnt you?

HIGGINS (*peremptorily*)   Sit down.

THE FLOWER GIRL   Oh, if youre going to make a compliment of it—

HIGGINS (*thundering at her*)   Sit down.

MRS PEARCE (*severely*)   Sit down, girl. Do as youre told. (*She places the stray chair near the hearthrug between* HIGGINS *and* PICKERING, *and stands behind it waiting for the girl to sit down.*)

THE FLOWER GIRL   Ah-ah-ah-ow-ow-oo! (*She stands, half rebellious, half bewildered.*)

PICKERING (*very courteous*)   Wont you sit down?

THE FLOWER GIRL (*coyly*)   Dont mind if I do. (*She sits down.* PICKERING *returns to the hearthrug.*)

HIGGINS   Whats your name?

THE FLOWER GIRL   Liza Doolittle.

HIGGINS (*declaiming gravely*)
> Eliza, Elizabeth, Betsy and Bess,
> They went to the woods to get a bird's nes':

PICKERING   They found a nest with four eggs in it:

HIGGINS   They took one apiece, and left three in it.

They laugh heartily at their own wit.

LIZA   Oh, dont be silly.

MRS PEARCE   You mustnt speak to the gentleman like that.

LIZA Well, why wont he speak sensible to me?

HIGGINS Come back to business. How much do you propose to pay me for the lessons?

LIZA Oh. I know whats right. A lady friend of mine gets French lessons for eighteenpence an hour from a real French gentleman. Well, you wouldnt have the face to ask me the same for teaching me my own language as you would for French; so I wont give more than a shilling. Take it or leave it.

HIGGINS (*walking up and down the room, rattling his keys and his cash in his pockets*) You know, Pickering, if you consider a shilling, not as a simple shilling, but as a percentage of this girl's income, it works out as fully equivalent to sixty or seventy guineas from a millionaire.

PICKERING How so?

HIGGINS Figure it out. A millionaire has about £150 a day. She earns about half-a-crown.

LIZA (*haughtily*) Who told you I only—

HIGGINS (*continuing*) She offers me two-fifths of her day's income for a lesson. Two-fifths of a millionaire's income for a day would be somewhere about £60. It's handsome. By George, it's enormous! It's the biggest offer I ever had.

LIZA (*rising, terrified*) Sixty pounds! What are you talking about? I never offered you sixty pounds. Where would I get—

HIGGINS Hold your tongue.

LIZA (*weeping*) But I aint got sixty pounds. Oh—

MRS PEARCE Dont cry, you silly girl. Sit down. Nobody is going to touch your money.

HIGGINS Somebody is going to touch you, with a broomstick, if you dont stop snivelling. Sit down.

LIZA (*obeying slowly*) Ah-ah-ah-ow-oo-o! One would think you was my father.

HIGGINS If I decide to teach you, I'll be worse than two fathers to you. Here (*he offers her his silk handkerchief*)!

LIZA Whats this for?

HIGGINS To wipe your eyes. To wipe any part of your face that feels moist. Remember: thats your handkerchief; and thats your sleeve. Dont mistake the one for the other if you wish to become a lady in a shop.

LIZA, *utterly bewildered, stares helplessly at him.*

MRS PEARCE It's no use talking to her like that, Mr Higgins: she doesnt understand you. Besides, youre quite wrong: she doesnt do it that way at all (*she takes the handkerchief*).

LIZA (*snatching it*) Here! You give me that handkerchief. He give it to me, not to you.

PICKERING (*laughing*) He did. I think it must be regarded as her property, Mrs Pearce.

MRS PEARCE (*resigning herself*). Serve you right, Mr Higgins.

PICKERING Higgins: I'm interested. What about the ambassador's garden party? I'll say youre the greatest teacher alive if you make that good. I'll bet you all the expenses of the experiment you cant do it. And I'll pay for the lessons.

LIZA Oh, you are real good. Thank you, Captain.

HIGGINS (*tempted, looking at her*) It's almost irresistible. She's so deliciously low—so horribly dirty—

LIZA (*protesting extremely*) Ah-ah-ah-ah-ow-ow-oo-oo!!! I aint dirty: I washed my face and hands afore I come, I did.

PICKERING Youre certainly not going to turn her head with flattery, Higgins.

MRS PEARCE (*uneasy*) Oh, dont say that, sir: theres more ways than one of turning a girl's head; and nobody can do it better than Mr Higgins, though he may not always mean it. I do hope, sir, you wont encourage him to do anything foolish.

HIGGINS (*becoming excited as the idea grows on him*) What is life but a series of inspired follies? The difficulty is to find them to do. Never lose a chance: it doesnt come every day. I shall make a duchess of this draggletailed guttersnipe.

LIZA (*strongly deprecating this view of her*) Ah-ah-ah-ow-ow-oo!

HIGGINS (*carried away*) Yes: in six months—in three if she has a good ear and a quick tongue—I'll take her anywhere and pass her off as anything. We'll start today: now! this moment! Take her away and clean her, Mrs Pearce. Monkey Brand, if it wont come off any other way. Is there a good fire in the kitchen?

MRS PEARCE (*protesting*) Yes; but—

HIGGINS (*storming on*) Take all her clothes off and burn them. Ring up Whiteley or somebody for new ones. Wrap her up in brown paper til they come.

LIZA Youre no gentleman, youre not, to talk of such things. I'm a good girl, I am; and I know what the like of you are, I do.

HIGGINS We want none of your Lisson Grove prudery here, young woman. Youve got to learn to behave like a duchess. Take her away, Mrs Pearce. If she gives you any trouble, wallop her.

LIZA (*springing up and running between* PICKERING *and* MRS PEARCE *for protection*)   No! I'll call the police, I will.

MRS PEARCE   But Ive no place to put her.

HIGGINS   Put her in the dustbin.

LIZA   Ah-ah-ah-ow-ow-oo!

PICKERING   Oh come, Higgins! be reasonable.

MRS PEARCE (*resolutely*)   You *must* be reasonable, Mr Higgins: really you must. You cant walk over everybody like this.

HIGGINS, *thus scolded, subsides. The hurricane is succeeded by a zephyr of amiable surprise.*

HIGGINS (*with professional exquisiteness of modulation*)   *I* walk over everybody! My dear Mrs Pearce, my dear Pickering, I never had the slightest intention of walking over anyone. All I propose is that we should be kind to this poor girl. We must help her to prepare and fit herself for her new station in life. If I did not express myself clearly it was because I did not wish to hurt her delicacy, or yours.

LIZA, *reassured, steals back to her chair.*

MRS PEARCE (*to* PICKERING)   Well, did you ever hear anything like that, sir?

PICKERING (*laughing heartily*)   Never, Mrs Pearce: never.

HIGGINS (*patiently*)   Whats the matter?

MRS PEARCE   Well, the matter is, sir, that you cant take a girl up like that as if you were picking up a pebble on the beach.

HIGGINS   Why not?

MRS PEARCE   Why not! But you dont know anything about her. What about her parents? She may be married.

LIZA   Garn!

HIGGINS   There! As the girl very properly says, Garn! Married indeed! Dont you know that a woman of that class looks a worn out drudge of fifty a year after she's married?

LIZA   Whood marry me?

HIGGINS (*suddenly resorting to the most thrillingly beautiful low tones in his best elocutionary style*)   By George, Eliza, the streets will be strewn with the bodies of men shooting themselves for your sake before Ive done with you.

MRS PEARCE   Nonsense, sir. You mustnt talk like that to her.

LIZA (*rising and squaring herself determinedly*)   I'm going away. He's off his chump, he is. I dont want no balmies teaching me.

HIGGINS (*wounded in his tenderest point by her insensibility to his elocution*)   Oh, indeed! I'm mad, am I? Very well, Mrs Pearce: you neednt order the new clothes for her. Throw her out.

LIZA (*whimpering*)   Nah-ow. You got no right to touch me.

MRS PEARCE   You see now what comes of being saucy. (*Indicating the door*) This way, please.

LIZA (*almost in tears*)   I didnt want no clothes. I wouldnt have taken them (*she throws away the handkerchief*). I can buy my own clothes.

HIGGINS (*deftly retrieving the handkerchief and intercepting her on her reluctant way to the door*)   Youre an ungrateful wicked girl. This is my return for offering to take you out of the gutter and dress you beautifully and make a lady of you.

MRS PEARCE   Stop, Mr Higgins. I wont allow it. It's you that are wicked. Go home to your parents, girl; and tell them to take better care of you.

LIZA   I ain't got no parents. They told me I was big enough to earn my own living and turned me out.

MRS PEARCE   Wheres your mother?

LIZA   I aint got no mother. Her that turned me out was my sixth step-mother. But I done without them. And I'm a good girl, I am.

HIGGINS   Very well, then, what on earth is all this fuss about? The girl doesnt belong to anybody—is no use to anybody but me. (*He goes to* MRS PEARCE *and begins coaxing.*) You can adopt her, Mrs Pearce: I'm sure a daughter would be a great amusement to you. Now dont make any more fuss. Take her downstairs; and—

MRS PEARCE   But whats to become of her? Is she to be paid anything? Do be sensible, sir.

HIGGINS   Oh, pay her whatever is necessary: put it down in the housekeeping book. (*Impatiently*) What on earth will she want with money? She'll have her food and her clothes. She'll only drink if you give her money.

LIZA (*turning on him*)   Oh you *are* a brute. It's a lie: nobody ever saw the sign of liquor on me. (*She goes back to her chair and plants herself there defiantly.*)

PICKERING (*in good-humored remonstrance*)   Does it occur to you, Higgins, that the girl has some feelings?

HIGGINS (*looking critically at her*)   Oh no, I dont think so. Not any feelings that we need bother about. (*Cheerily*) Have you, Eliza?

LIZA   I got my feelings same as anyone else.

HIGGINS (*to* PICKERING, *reflectively*)   You see the difficulty?

PICKERING.   Eh? What difficulty?

HIGGINS   To get her to talk grammar. The mere pronunciation is easy enough.

LIZA   I dont want to talk grammar. I want to talk like a lady.

MRS PEARCE   Will you please keep to the point, Mr Higgins? I want to know on what terms the girl is to be here. Is she to have any wages? And what is to become of her when youve finished your teaching? You must look ahead a little.

HIGGINS (*impatiently*)   Whats to become of her if I leave her in the gutter? Tell me that, Mrs Pearce.

MRS PEARCE   Thats her own business, not yours, Mr Higgins.

HIGGINS   Well, when Ive done with her, we can throw her back into the gutter; and then it will be her own business again; so thats all right.

LIZA   Oh, youve no feeling heart in you: you dont care for nothing but yourself (*she rises and takes the floor resolutely*). Here! Ive had enough of this. I'm going (*making for the door*). You ought to be ashamed of yourself, you ought.

HIGGINS (*snatching a chocolate cream from the piano, his eyes suddenly beginning to twinkle with mischief*)   Have some chocolates, Eliza.

LIZA (*halting, tempted*)   How do I know what might be in them? Ive heard of girls being drugged by the like of you.

HIGGINS *whips out his penknife; cuts a chocolate in two; puts one half into his mouth and bolts it; and offers her the other half.*

HIGGINS   Pledge of good faith, Eliza. I eat one half: you eat the other. (LIZA *opens her mouth to retort: he pops the half chocolate into it.*) You shall have boxes of them, barrels of them, every day. You shall live on them. Eh?

LIZA (*who has disposed of the chocolate after being nearly choked by it*)   I wouldnt have ate it, only I'm too ladylike to take it out of my mouth.

HIGGINS   Listen, Eliza. I think you said you came in a taxi.

LIZA   Well, what if I did? Ive as good a right to take a taxi as anyone else.

HIGGINS   You have, Eliza; and in future you shall have as many taxis as you want. You shall go up and down and round the town in a taxi every day. Think of that, Eliza.

MRS PEARCE   Mr Higgins: youre tempting the girl. It's not right. She should think of the future.

HIGGINS   At her age! Nonsense! Time enough to think of the future when you havnt any future to think of. No, Eliza: do as this lady does: think of other people's futures; but never think of your own. Think of chocolates, and taxis, and gold, and diamonds.

LIZA   No: I dont want no gold and no diamonds. I'm a good girl, I am. (*She sits down again, with an attempt at dignity.*)

HIGGINS   You shall remain so, Eliza, under the care of Mrs Pearce. And you shall marry an officer in the Guards, with a beautiful moustache: the son of a marquis, who will disinherit him for marrying you, but will relent when he sees your beauty and goodness—

PICKERING   Excuse me, Higgins; but I really must interfere. Mrs Pearce is quite right. If this girl is to put herself in your hands for six months for an experiment in teaching, she must understand thoroughly what she's doing.

HIGGINS   How can she? She's incapable of understanding anything. Besides, do any of us understand what we are doing? If we did, would we ever do it?

PICKERING   Very clever, Higgins; but not sound sense. (*To* ELIZA) Miss Doolittle—

LIZA (*overwhelmed*)   Ah-ah-ow-oo!

HIGGINS   There! Thats all youll get out of Eliza. Ah-ah-ow-oo! No use explaining. As a military man you ought to know that. Give her her orders: thats what she wants. Eliza: you are to live here for the next six months, learning how to speak beautifully, like a lady in a florist's shop. If youre good and do whatever youre told, you shall sleep in a proper bedroom, and have lots to eat, and money to buy chocolates and take rides in taxis. If youre naughty and idle you will sleep in the back kitchen among the black beetles, and be walloped by Mrs Pearce with a broomstick. At the end of six months you shall go to Buckingham Palace in a carriage, beautifully dressed. If the King finds out youre not a lady, you will be taken by the police to the Tower of London, where your head will be cut off as a warning to other presumptuous flower girls. If you are not found out, you shall have a present of seven-and-sixpence to start life with as a lady in a shop. If you refuse this offer you will be a most ungrateful and wicked girl; and the angels will weep for you. (*To* PICKERING) Now are you satisfied, Pickering? (*To* MRS PEARCE) Can I put it more plainly and fairly, Mrs Pearce?

MRS PEARCE (*patiently*) I think youd better let me speak to the girl properly in private. I dont know that I can take charge of her or consent to the arrangement at all. Of course I know you dont mean her any harm; but when you get what you call interested in people's accents, you never think or care what may happen to them or you. Come with me, Eliza.

HIGGINS Thats all right. Thank you, Mrs Pearce. Bundle her off to the bathroom.

LIZA (*rising reluctantly and suspiciously*) Youre a great bully, you are. I wont stay here if I dont like. I wont let nobody wallop me. I never asked to go to Bucknam Palace, I didnt. I was never in trouble with the police, not me. I'm a good girl—

MRS PEARCE Dont answer back, girl. You dont understand the gentleman. Come with me. (*She leads the way to the door, and holds it open for* ELIZA.)

LIZA (*as she goes out*) Well, what I say is right. I wont go near the King, not if I'm going to have my head cut off. If I'd known what I was letting myself in for, I wouldnt have come here. I always been a good girl; and I never offered to say a word to him; and I dont owe him nothing; and I dont care; and I wont be put upon; and I have my feelings the same as anyone else—

MRS PEARCE *shuts the door; and* ELIZA'S *plaints are no longer audible. PICKERING comes from the hearth to the chair and sits astride it with his arms on the back.*

PICKERING Excuse the straight question, Higgins. Are you a man of good character where women are concerned?

HIGGINS (*moodily*) Have you ever met a man of good character where women are concerned?

PICKERING Yes: very frequently.

HIGGINS (*dogmatically, lifting himself on his hands to the level of the piano, and sitting on it with a bounce*) Well, I havnt. I find that the moment I let a woman make friends with me, she becomes jealous, exacting, suspicious, and a damned nuisance. I find that the moment I let myself make friends with a woman, I become selfish and tyrannical. Women upset everything. When you let them into your life, you find that the woman is driving at one thing and youre driving at another.

PICKERING   At what, for example?

HIGGINS (*coming off the piano restlessly*)   Oh, Lord knows! I suppose the woman wants to live her own life; and the man wants to live his; and each tries to drag the other on to the wrong track. One wants to go north and the other south; and the result is that both have to go east, though they both hate the east wind. (*He sits down on the bench at the keyboard.*) So here I am, a confirmed old bachelor, and likely to remain so.

PICKERING (*rising and standing over him gravely*)   Come, Higgins! You know what I mean. If I'm to be in this business I shall feel responsible for that girl. I hope it's understood that no advantage is to be taken of her position.

HIGGINS   What! That thing! Sacred, I assure you. (*Rising to explain*) You see, she'll be a pupil; and teaching would be impossible unless pupils were sacred. Ive taught scores of American millionairesses how to speak English: the best looking women in the world. I'm seasoned. They might as well be blocks of wood. *I* might as well be a block of wood. It's—

MRS PEARCE *opens the door. She has Eliza's hat in her hand.* PICKERING *retires to the easy chair at the hearth and sits down.*

HIGGINS (*eagerly*)   Well, Mrs Pearce: is it all right?

MRS PEARCE (*at the door*)   I just wish to trouble you with a word, if I may, Mr Higgins.

HIGGINS   Yes, certainly. Come in. (*She comes forward.*) Dont burn that, Mrs Pearce. I'll keep it as a curiosity. (*He takes the hat.*)

MRS PEARCE   Handle it carefully, sir, *please*. I had to promise her not to burn it; but I had better put it in the oven for a while.

HIGGINS (*putting it down hastily on the piano*)   Oh! thank you. Well, what have you to say to me?

PICKERING   Am I in the way?

MRS PEARCE   Not at all, sir. Mr. Higgins: will you please be very particular what you say before the girl?

HIGGINS (*sternly*)   Of course. I'm always particular about what I say. Why do you say this to me?

MRS PEARCE (*unmoved*)   No, sir: youre not at all particular when youve mislaid anything or when you get a little impatient. Now it doesnt matter before me: I'm used to it. But you really must not swear before the girl.

HIGGINS (*indignantly*) *I* swear! (*Most emphatically*) I never swear. I detest the habit. What the devil do you mean?

MRS PEARCE (*stolidly*) Thats what I mean, sir. You swear a great deal too much. I dont mind your damning and blasting, and *what* the devil and *where* the devil and *who* the devil—

HIGGINS Mrs Pearce: this language from your lips! Really!

MRS PEARCE (*not to be put off*) —but there is a certain word I must ask you not to use. The girl has just used it herself because the bath was too hot. It begins with the same letter as bath. She knows no better: she learnt it at her mother's knee. But she must not hear it from *your* lips.

HIGGINS (*loftily*) I cannot charge myself with having ever uttered it, Mrs Pearce.

She looks at him steadfastly. He adds, hiding an uneasy conscience with a judicial air

Except perhaps in a moment of extreme and justifiable excitement.

MRS PEARCE Only this morning, sir, you applied it to your boots, to the butter, and to the brown bread.

HIGGINS Oh, that! Mere alliteration, Mrs Pearce, natural to a poet.

MRS PEARCE Well, sir, whatever you choose to call it, I beg you not to let the girl hear you repeat it.

HIGGINS Oh, very well, very well. Is that all?

MRS PEARCE No, sir. We shall have to be very particular with this girl as to personal cleanliness.

HIGGINS Certainly. Quite right. Most important.

MRS PEARCE I mean not to be slovenly about her dress or untidy in leaving things about.

HIGGINS (*going to her solemnly*) Just so. I intended to call your attention to that. (*He passes on to* PICKERING, *who is enjoying the conversation immensely.*) It is these little things that matter, Pickering. Take care of the pence and the pounds will take care of themselves is as true of personal habits as of money. (*He comes to anchor on the hearthrug, with the air of a man in an unassailable position.*)

MRS PEARCE Yes, sir. Then might I ask you not to come down to breakfast in your dressing-gown, or at any rate not to use it as a napkin to the extent you do, sir. And if you would be so good as not to eat everything off the same plate, and to remember not to put the porridge saucepan out of your hand on the clean tablecloth, it would be a better example to the girl. You know you nearly choked yourself with a fishbone in the jam only last week.

HIGGINS (*routed from the hearthrug and drifting back to the piano*) I may do these things sometimes in absence of mind; but surely I dont do them habitually. (*Angrily*) By the way: my dressing-gown smells most damnably of benzine.

MRS PEARCE No doubt it does, Mr Higgins. But if you *will* wipe your fingers—

HIGGINS (*yelling*) Oh very well, very well: I'll wipe them in my hair in future.

MRS PEARCE I hope youre not offended, Mr Higgins.

HIGGINS (*shocked at finding himself thought capable of an unamiable sentiment*) Not at all, not at all. Youre quite right, Mrs. Pearce: I shall be particularly careful before the girl. Is that all?

MRS PEARCE No, sir. Might she use some of those Japanese dresses you brought from abroad? I really cant put her back into her old things.

HIGGINS Certainly. Anything you like. Is *that* all?

MRS PEARCE Thank you, sir. Thats all. (*She goes out.*)

HIGGINS You know, Pickering, that woman has the most extraordinary ideas about me. Here I am, a shy, diffident sort of man. Ive never been able to feel really grown-up and tremendous, like other chaps. And yet she's firmly persuaded that I'm an arbitrary overbearing bossing kind of person. I cant account for it.

MRS PEARCE *returns.*

MRS PEARCE If you please, sir, the trouble's beginning already. Theres a dustman downstairs, Alfred Doolittle, wants to see you. He says you have his daughter here.

PICKERING (*rising*) ——Phew! I say! (*He retreats to the hearthrug.*)

HIGGINS (*promptly*) Send the blackguard up.

MRS PEARCE Oh, very well, sir. (*She goes out.*)

PICKERING He may not be a blackguard, Higgins.

HIGGINS Nonsense. Of course he's a blackguard.

PICKERING Whether he is or not, I'm afraid we shall have some trouble with him.

HIGGINS (*confidently*) Oh no: I think not. If theres any trouble he shall have it with me, not I with him. And we are sure to get something interesting out of him.

PICKERING   About the girl?

HIGGINS   No. I mean his dialect.

PICKERING   Oh!

MRS PEARCE (*at the door*)   Doolittle, sir. (*She admits* DOOLITTLE *and retires.*)

ALFRED DOOLITTLE *is an elderly but vigorous dustman, clad in the costume of his profession, including a hat with a black brim covering his neck and shoulders. He has well marked and rather interesting features, and seems equally free from fear and conscience. He has a remarkably expressive voice, the result of a habit of giving vent to his feelings without reserve. His present pose is that of wounded honor and stern resolution.*

DOOLITTLE (*at the door, uncertain which of the two gentlemen is his man*)   Professor Higgins?

HIGGINS   Here. Good morning. Sit down.

DOOLITTLE   Morning, Governor. (*He sits down magisterially.*) I come about a very serious matter, Governor.

HIGGINS (*to* PICKERING)   Brought up in Hounslow. Mother Welsh, I should think. (DOOLITTLE *opens his mouth, amazed.* HIGGINS *continues*) What do you want, Doolittle?

DOOLITTLE (*menacingly*)   I want my daughter: thats what I want. See?

HIGGINS   Of course you do. Youre her father, arnt you? You dont suppose anyone else wants her, do you? I'm glad to see you have some spark or family feeling left. She's upstairs. Take her away at once.

DOOLITTLE (*rising, fearfully taken aback*)   What!

HIGGINS   Take her away. Do you suppose I'm going to keep your daughter for you?

DOOLITTLE (*remonstrating*)   Now, now, look here, Governor. Is this reasonable? Is it fairity to take advantage of a man like this? The girl belongs to me. You got her. Where do I come in? (*He sits down again.*)

HIGGINS   Your daughter had the audacity to come to my house and ask me to teach her how to speak properly so that she could get a place in a flower shop. This gentleman and my housekeeper have been here all the time. (*Bullying him*) How dare you come here and attempt to blackmail me? You sent her here on purpose.

DOOLITTLE (*protesting*)   No, Governor.

HIGGINS   You must have. How else could you possibly know that she is here?

DOOLITTLE   Dont take a man up like that, Governor.

HIGGINS   The police shall take you up. This is a plant—a plot to extort money by threats. I shall telephone for the police. (*He goes resolutely to the telephone and opens the directory.*)

DOOLITTLE   Have I asked you for a brass farthing? I leave it to the gentleman here: have I said a word about money?

HIGGINS   (*throwing the book aside and marching down on* DOOLITTLE *with a poser*)   What else did you come for?

DOOLITTLE   (*sweetly*)   Well, what *would* a man come for? Be human, Governor.

HIGGINS   (*disarmed*)   Alfred: did you put her up to it?

DOOLITTLE   So help me, Governor, I never did. I take my Bible oath I aint seen the girl these two months past.

HIGGINS   Then how did you know she was here?

DOOLITTLE   (*"most musical, most melancholy"*)   I'll tell you, Governor, if youll only let me get a word in. I'm willing to tell you. I'm wanting to tell you. I'm waiting to tell you.

HIGGINS   Pickering: this chap has a certain natural gift of rhetoric. Observe the rhythm of his native woodnotes wild. "I'm willing to tell you: I'm wanting to tell you: I'm waiting to tell you." Sentimental rhetoric! thats the Welsh strain in him. It also accounts for his mendacity and dishonesty.

PICKERING   Oh, *please,* Higgins: I'm west country myself. (*To* DOOLITTLE)   How did you know the girl was here if you didnt send her?

DOOLITTLE   It was like this, Governor. The girl took a boy in the taxi to give him a jaunt. Son of her landlady, he is. He hung about on the chance of her giving him another ride home. Well, she sent him back for her luggage when she heard you was willing for her to stop here. I met the boy at the corner of Long Acre and Endell Street.

HIGGINS   Public house. Yes?

DOOLITTLE   The poor man's club, Governor: why shouldnt I?

PICKERING   Do let him tell his story, Higgins.

DOOLITTLE   He told me what was up. And I ask you, what was my feelings and my duty as a father? I says to the boy, "You bring me the luggage," I says—

PICKERING   Why didnt you go for it yourself?

DOOLITTLE Landlady wouldnt have trusted me with it, Governor. She's that kind of woman: you know. I had to give the boy a penny afore he trusted me with it, the little swine. I brought it to her just to oblige you like, and make myself agreeable. Thats all.

HIGGINS How much luggage?

DOOLITTLE Musical instrument, Governor. A few pictures, a trifle of jewelry, and a bird-cage. She said she didnt want no clothes. What was I to think from that, Governor? I ask you as a parent what was I to think?

HIGGINS So you came to rescue her from worse than death, eh?

DOOLITTLE (*appreciatively: relieved at being so well understood*) Just so, Governor. Thats right.

PICKERING But why did you bring her luggage if you intended to take her away?

DOOLITTLE Have I said a word about taking her away? Have I now?

HIGGINS (*determinedly*) Youre going to take her away, double quick. (*He crosses to the hearth and rings the bell.*)

DOOLITTLE (*rising*) No, Governor. Dont say that. I'm not the man to stand in my girl's light. Heres a career opening for her, as you might say; and—

MRS PEARCE *opens the door and awaits orders.*

HIGGINS Mrs Pearce: this is Eliza's father. He has come to take her away. Give her to him. (*He goes back to the piano, with an air of washing his hands of the whole affair.*)

DOOLITTLE No. This is a misunderstanding. Listen here—

MRS PEARCE He cant take her away, Mr Higgins: how can he? You told me to burn her clothes.

DOOLITTLE Thats right. I cant carry the girl through the streets like a blooming monkey, can I? I put it to you.

HIGGINS You have put it to me that you want your daughter. Take your daughter. If she has no clothes go out and buy her some.

DOOLITTLE (*desperate*) Wheres the clothes she come in? Did I burn them or did your missus here?

MRS PEARCE I am the housekeeper, if you please. I have sent for some clothes for your girl. When they come you can take her away. You can wait in the kitchen. This way, please.

DOOLITTLE, *much troubled, accompanies her to the door; then hesitates; finally turns confidently to* HIGGINS.

DOOLITTLE   Listen here, Governor. You and me is men of the world, aint we?

HIGGINS   Oh! Men of the world, are we? Youd better go, Mrs Pearce.

MRS PEARCE   I think so, indeed, sir. (*She goes, with dignity.*)

PICKERING   The floor is yours, Mr Doolittle.

DOOLITTLE   (*to* PICKERING) I thank you, Governor. (*To* HIGGINS, *who takes refuge on the piano bench, a little overwhelmed by the proximity of his visitor; for* DOOLITTLE *has a professional flavor of dust about him*) Well, the truth is, Ive taken a sort of fancy to you, Governor; and if you want the girl, I'm not so set on having her back home again but what I might be open to an arrangement. Regarded in the light of a young woman, she's a fine handsome girl. As a daughter she's not worth her keep; and so I tell you straight. All I ask is my rights as a father; and youre the last man alive to expect me to let her go for nothing; for I can see youre one of the straight sort, Governor. Well, whats a five-pound note to you? And whats Eliza to me? (*He returns to his chair and sits down judicially.*)

PICKERING   I think you ought to know, Doolittle, that Mr Higgins's intentions are entirely honorable.

DOOLITTLE   Course they are, Governor. If I thought they wasnt, I'd ask fifty.

HIGGINS   (*revolted*) Do you mean to say, you callous rascal, that you would sell your daughter for £50?

DOOLITTLE   Not in a general way I wouldnt; but to oblige a gentleman like you I'd do a good deal, I do assure you.

PICKERING   Have you no morals, man?

DOOLITTLE   (*unabashed*) Cant afford them, Governor. Neither could you if you was as poor as me. Not that I mean any harm, you know. But if Liza is going to have a bit out of this, why not me too?

HIGGINS   (*troubled*) I dont know what to do, Pickering. There can be no question that as a matter of morals it's a positive crime to give this chap a farthing. And yet I feel a sort of rough justice in his claim.

DOOLITTLE   Thats it, Governor. Thats all I say. A father's heart, as it were.

PICKERING   Well, I know the feeling; but really it seems hardly right—

DOOLITTLE   Dont say that, Governor. Dont look at it that way. What am I, Governors both? I ask you, what am I? I'm one of the undeserving poor: thats what I am. Think of what that means to a man. It means that he's up agen middle class morality all the time. If theres anything going, and I put in for a bit of it, it's always the same story: "Youre undeserving; so you cant have it." But my needs is as great as the most deserving widow's that ever got money out of six different charities in one week for the death of the same husband. I dont need less than a deserving man: I need more. I dont eat less hearty than him; and I drink a lot more. I want a bit of amusement, cause I'm a thinking man. I want cheerfulness and a song and a band when I feel low. Well, they charge me just the same for everything as they charge the deserving. What is middle class morality? Just an excuse for never giving me anything. Therefore, I ask you, as two gentlemen, not to play that game on me. I'm playing straight with you. I aint pretending to be deserving. I'm undeserving; and I mean to go on being undeserving. I like it; and thats the truth. Will you take advantage of a man's nature to do him out of the price of his own daughter what he's brought up and fed and clothed by the sweat of his brow until she's growed big enough to be interesting to you two gentlemen? Is five pounds unreasonable? I put it to you; and I leave it to you.

HIGGINS (*rising, and going over to* PICKERING) Pickering: if we were to take this man in hand for three months, he could choose between a seat in the Cabinet and a popular pulpit in Wales.

PICKERING What do you say to that, Doolittle?

DOOLITTLE Not me, Governor, thank you kindly. Ive heard all the preachers and all the prime ministers—for I'm a thinking man and game for politics or religion or social reform same as all the other amusements—and I tell you it's a dog's life any way you look at it. Undeserving poverty is my line. Taking one station in society with another, it's—it's—well, it's the only one that has any ginger in it, to my taste.

HIGGINS I suppose we must give him a fiver.

PICKERING He'll make a bad use of it, I'm afraid.

DOOLITTLE Not me, Governor, so help me I wont. Dont you be afraid that I'll save it and spare it and live idle on it. There wont be a penny of it left by Monday: I'll have to go to work same as if I'd never had it. It wont pauperize me, you bet. Just one good spree for myself and the missus, giving pleasure to ourselves and employment to others, and satisfaction to you to think it's not been throwed away. You couldnt spend it better.

HIGGINS (*taking out his pocket book and coming between* DOOLITTLE *and the piano*) This is irresistible. Lets give him ten. (*He offers two notes to the dustman.*)

DOOLITTLE   No, Governor. She wouldnt have the heart to spend ten; and perhaps I shouldnt neither. Ten pounds is a lot of money: it makes a man feel prudent like; and then goodbye to happiness. You give me what I ask you, Governor: not a penny more, and not a penny less.

PICKERING   Why dont you marry that missus of yours? I rather draw the line at encouraging that sort of immorality.

DOOLITTLE   Tell her so, Governor: tell her so. I'm willing. It's me that suffers by it. Ive no hold on her. I got to be agreeable to her. I got to give her presents. I got to buy her clothes something sinful. I'm a slave to that woman, Governor, just because I'm not her lawful husband. And she knows it too. Catch her marrying me! Take my advice, Governor: marry Eliza while she's young and dont know no better. If you dont youll be sorry for it after. If you do, *she'll* be sorry for it after; but better her than you, because youre a man, and she's only a woman and dont know how to be happy anyhow.

HIGGINS   Pickering: if we listen to this man another minute, we shall have no convictions left. (*To* DOOLITTLE) Five pounds I think you said.

DOOLITTLE   Thank you kindly, Governor.

HIGGINS   Youre sure you wont take ten?

DOOLITTLE   Not now. Another time, Governor.

HIGGINS (*handing him a five-pound note*) Here you are.

DOOLITTLE   Thank you, Governor. Good morning. (*He hurries to the door, anxious to get away with his booty. When he opens it he is confronted with a dainty and exquisitely clean young Japanese lady in a simple blue cotton kimono printed cunningly with small white jasmine blossoms.* MRS PEARCE *is with her. He gets out of her way deferentially and apologizes.*) Beg pardon, miss.

THE JAPANESE LADY   Garn! Dont you know your own daughter?

DOOLITTLE
HIGGINS   (*exclaiming simultaneously*)
PICKERING

Bly me! it's Eliza!
Whats that! This!
By Jove!

LIZA   Dont I look silly?

HIGGINS   Silly?

MRS PEARCE (*at the door*) Now, Mr Higgins, please dont say anything to make the girl conceited about herself.

HIGGINS (*conscientiously*) Oh! Quite right, Mrs Pearce. (*To* ELIZA) Yes: damned silly.

MRS PEARCE Please, sir.

HIGGINS (*correcting himself*) I mean extremely silly.

LIZA I should look all right with my hat on. (*She takes up her hat; puts it on; and walks across the room to the fireplace with a fashionable air.*)

HIGGINS A new fashion, by George! And it ought to look horrible!

DOOLITTLE (*with fatherly pride*) Well, I never thought she'd clean up as good looking as that, Governor. She's a credit to me, aint she?

LIZA I tell you, it's easy to clean up here. Hot and cold water on tap, just as much as you like, there is. Woolly towels, there is; and a towel horse so hot, it burns your fingers. Soft brushes to scrub yourself, and a wooden bowl of soap smelling like primroses. Now I know why ladies is so clean. Washing's a treat for them. Wish they saw what it is for the like of me!

HIGGINS I'm glad the bathroom met with your approval.

LIZA It didnt: not all of it; and I dont care who hears me say it. Mrs Pearce knows.

HIGGINS What was wrong, Mrs Pearce?

MRS PEARCE (*blandly*) Oh, nothing, sir. It doesnt matter.

LIZA I had a good mind to break it. I didnt know which way to look. But I hung a towel over it, I did.

HIGGINS Over what?

MRS PEARCE Over the looking glass, sir.

HIGGINS Doolittle: you have brought your daughter up too strictly.

DOOLITTLE Me! I never brought her up at all, except to give her a lick of a strap now and again. Dont put it on me, Governor. She aint accustomed to it, you see: thats all. But she'll soon pick up your free-and-easy ways.

LIZA I'm a good girl, I am; and I wont pick up no free-and-easy ways.

HIGGINS Eliza: if you say again that youre a good girl, your father shall take you home.

LIZA Not him. You dont know my father. All he come here for was to touch you for some money to get drunk on.

DOOLITTLE Well, what else would I want money for? To put into the plate in church, I suppose.

She puts out her tongue at him. He is so incensed by this that PICKERING *presently finds it necessary to step between them.*

Dont you give me none of your lip; and dont let me hear you giving this gentleman any of it neither, or youll hear from me about it. See?

HIGGINS   Have you any further advice to give her before you go, Doolittle? Your blessing, for instance.

DOOLITTLE   No, Governor: I aint such a mug as to put up my children to all I know myself. Hard enough to hold them in without that. If you want Eliza's mind improved, Governor, you do it yourself with a strap. So long, gentlemen. (*He turns to go.*)

HIGGINS (*impressively*)   Stop. Youll come regularly to see your daughter. It's your duty, you know. My brother is a clergyman; and he could help you in your talks with her.

DOOLITTLE (*evasively*)   Certainly. I'll come, Governor. Not just this week, because I have a job at a distance. But later on you may depend on me. Afternoon, gentlemen. Afternoon, maam. (*He takes off his hat to* MRS PEARCE, *who disdains the salutation and goes out. He winks at* HIGGINS, *thinking him probably a fellow-sufferer from* MRS PEARCE'S *difficult disposition, and follows her.*)

LIZA   Dont you believe that old liar. He'd as soon you set a bull-dog on him as a clergyman. You wont see him again in a hurry.

HIGGINS   I dont want to, Eliza. Do you?

LIZA   Not me. I dont want never to see him again, I dont. He's a disgrace to me, he is, collecting dust, instead of working at his trade.

PICKERING   What is his trade, Eliza?

LIZA   Taking money out of other people's pockets into his own. His proper trade's a navvy; and he works at it sometimes too—for exercise—and earns good money at it. Aint you going to call me Miss Doolittle any more?

PICKERING   I beg your pardon, Miss Doolittle. It was a slip of the tongue.

LIZA   Oh, I dont mind; only it sounded so genteel. I *should* just like to take a taxi to the corner of Tottenham Court Road and get out there and tell it to wait for me, just to put the girls in their place a bit. I wouldn't speak to them, you know.

PICKERING   Better wait till we get you something really fashionable.

HIGGINS   Besides, you shouldnt cut your old friends now that you have risen in the world. Thats what we call snobbery.

LIZA   You dont call the like of them my friends now, I should hope. Theyve took it out of me often enough with their ridicule when they had the chance; and now I mean to get a bit of my own back. But if I'm to have fashionable clothes, I'll wait. I should like to have some. Mrs Pearce says youre going to give me some to wear in bed at night different to what I wear in the daytime; but it do seem a waste of money when you could get something to shew. Besides, I never could fancy changing into cold things on a winter night.

MRS PEARCE (*coming back*)   Now, Eliza. The new things have come for you to try on.

LIZA   Ah-ow-oo-ooh! (*She rushes out.*)

MRS PEARCE (*following her*)   Oh, dont rush about like that, girl. (*She shuts the door behind her.*)

HIGGINS   Pickering: we have taken on a stiff job.

PICKERING (*with conviction*)   Higgins: we have.

ACT III

It is MRS HIGGINS'S *at-home day. Nobody has yet arrived. Her draw-ing room, in a flat on Chelsea Embankment, has three windows look-ing on the river; and the ceiling is not so lofty as it would be in an older house of the same pretension. The windows are open, giving ac-cess to a balcony with flowers in pots. If you stand with your face to the windows, you have the fireplace on your left and the door in the right-hand wall close to the corner nearest the windows.*

MRS HIGGINS *was brought up on Morris*[5] *and Burne Jones;*[6] *and her room, which is very unlike her son's room in Wimpole Street, is not crowded with furniture and little tables and nicknacks. In the middle of the room there is a big ottoman; and this, with the carpet, the Morris wall-papers, and the Morris chintz window curtains and brocade covers of the ottoman and its cushions, supply all the orna-ment, and are much too handsome to be hidden by odds and ends of useless things. A few good oil-paintings from the exhibitions in the Grosvenor Gallery thirty years ago (the Burne Jones, not the Whistler side of them) are on the walls. The only landscape is a Cecil Lawson on the scale of a Rubens. There is a portrait of* MRS HIGGINS *as she was when she defied fashion in her youth in one of*

---

[5] William Morris (1834–96) English art-lover and author, who, in an effort to help improve the taste of the Victorian middle class, helped to found a firm which manufactured furniture, carpets, tapestries, and the like.

[6] Sir Edward Coley Burne-Jones (1833–98) was an English painter whose literary, religious, and symbolic scenes were emotional, mystic, and exotic.

*the beautiful Rosettian costumes which, when caricatured by people
who did not understand, led to the absurdities of popular estheticism
in the eighteen-seventies.*

In the corner diagonally opposite the door MRS HIGGINS, *now over
sixty and long past taking the trouble to dress out of the fashion, sits
writing at an elegantly simple writing-table with a bell button within
reach of her hand. There is a Chippendale chair further back in the
room between her and the window nearest her side. At the other side
of the room, further forward, is an Elizabethan chair roughly carved
in the taste of Inigo Jones. On the same side a piano in a decorated
case. The corner between the fireplace and the window is occupied
by a divan cushioned in Morris chintz.*

It is between four and five in the afternoon.

The door is opened violently; and HIGGINS *enters with his hat on.*

MRS HIGGINS (*dismayed*)   Henry (*scolding him*)! What are you doing
here today? It is my at-home day: you promised not to come. (*As
he bends to kiss her, she takes his hat off, and presents it to him.*)

HIGGINS   Oh bother! (*He throws the hat down on the table.*)

MRS HIGGINS   Go home at once.

HIGGINS (*kissing her*)   I know, mother. I came on purpose.

MRS HIGGINS   But you mustnt. I'm serious, Henry. You offend all my
friends: they stop coming whenever they meet you.

HIGGINS   Nonsense! I know I have no small talk; but people dont mind.
(*He sits on the settee.*)

MRS HIGGINS   Oh! dont they? Small talk indeed! What about your large
talk? Really, dear, you mustnt stay.

HIGGINS   I must. Ive a job for you. A phonetic job.

MRS HIGGINS   No use, dear. I'm sorry; but I cant get round your vowels;
and though I like to get pretty postcards in your patent shorthand, I
always have to read the copies in ordinary writing you so thoughtfully
send me.

HIGGINS   Well, this isnt a phonetic job.

MRS HIGGINS   You said it was.

HIGGINS   Not your part of it. Ive picked up a girl.

MRS HIGGINS   Does that mean that some girl has picked you up?

HIGGINS   Not at all. I dont mean a love affair.

MRS HIGGINS   What a pity.

HIGGINS   Why?

MRS HIGGINS   Well, you never fall in love with anyone under forty-five.

When will you discover that there are some rather nice-looking young women about?

HIGGINS   Oh, I cant be bothered with young women. My idea of a lovable woman is something as like you as possible. I shall never get into the way of seriously liking young women: some habits lie too deep to be changed. (*Rising abruptly and walking about jingling his money and his keys in his trouser pockets*) Besides, theyre all idiots.

MRS HIGGINS   Do you know what you would do if you really loved me, Henry?

HIGGINS   Oh bother! What? Marry, I suppose?

MRS HIGGINS   No. Stop fidgeting and take your hands out of your pockets. (*With a gesture of despair, he obeys and sits down again.*) Thats a good boy. Now tell me about the girl.

HIGGINS   She's coming to see you.

MRS HIGGINS   I dont remember asking her.

HIGGINS   You didnt. *I* asked her. If youd known her you wouldnt have asked her.

MRS HIGGINS   Indeed! Why?

HIGGINS   Well, it's like this. She's a common flower girl. I picked her off the kerbstone.

MRS HIGGINS   And invited her to my at-home!

HIGGINS   (*rising and coming to her to coax her*)   Oh, thatll be all right. Ive taught her to speak properly; and she has strict orders as to her behavior. She's to keep to two subjects; the weather and everybody's health—Fine day and How do you do, you know—and not to let herself go on things in general. That will be safe.

MRS HIGGINS   Safe! To talk about our health! about our insides! perhaps about our outsides! How could you be so silly, Henry?

HIGGINS   (*impatiently*)   Well, she must talk about something. (*He controls himself and sits down again.*) Oh, she'll be all right: dont you fuss. Pickering is in it with me. Ive a sort of bet on that I'll pass her off as a duchess in six months. I started on her some months ago; and she's getting on like a house on fire. I shall win my bet. She has a quick ear; and she's been easier to teach than my middle class pupils because she's had to learn a complete new language. She talks English almost as you talk French.

MRS HIGGINS   That's satisfactory, at all events.

HIGGINS   Well, it is and it isnt.

MRS HIGGINS   What does that mean?

HIGGINS   You see, Ive got her pronunciation all right; but you have to consider not only *how* a girl pronounces, but *what* she pronounces; and thats where—

They are interrupted by THE PARLOR-MAID, *announcing guests.*

THE PARLOR-MAID   Mrs and Miss Eynsford Hill. (*She withdraws.*)

HIGGINS   Oh Lord! (*He rises; snatches his hat from the table; and makes for the door; but before he reaches it his mother introduces him.*)

MRS *and* MISS EYNSFORD HILL *are the mother and daughter who sheltered from the rain in Covent Garden. The mother is well bred, quiet, and has the habitual anxiety of straitened means. The daughter has acquired a gay air of being very much at home in society: the bravado of genteel poverty.*

MRS EYNSFORD HILL (*to* MRS HIGGINS)   How do you do? (*They shake hands.*)

MISS EYNSFORD HILL   How d'you do? (*She shakes.*)

MRS HIGGINS (*introducing*)   My son Henry.

MRS EYNSFORD HILL   Your celebrated son! I have so longed to meet you, Professor Higgins.

HIGGINS (*glumly, making no movement in her direction*)   Delighted. (*He backs against the piano and bows brusquely.*)

MISS EYNSFORD HILL (*going to him with confident familiarity*)   How do you do?

HIGGINS (*staring at her*)   Ive seen you before somewhere. I havnt the ghost of a notion where; but Ive heard your voice. (*Drearily*) It doesn't matter. Youd better sit down.

MRS HIGGINS   I'm sorry to say that my celebrated son has no manners. You mustnt mind him.

MISS EYNSFORD HILL (*gaily*)   I dont. (*She sits in the Elizabethan chair.*)

MRS EYNSFORD HILL (*a little bewildered*)   Not at all. (*She sits on the ottoman between her daughter and* MRS HIGGINS, *who has turned her chair away from the writing-table.*)

HIGGINS   Oh, have I been rude? I didnt mean to be. (*He goes to the central window, through which, with his back to the company, he contemplates the river and the flowers in Battersea Park on the opposite bank as if they were a frozen desert.*)

THE PARLOR-MAID *returns, ushering in* PICKERING.

THE PARLOR-MAID   Colonel Pickering. (*She withdraws.*)

PICKERING   How do you do, Mrs Higgins?

MRS HIGGINS   So glad youve come. Do you know Mrs Eynsford Hill—Miss Eynsford Hill? (*Exchange of bows.* THE COLONEL *brings the Chippendale chair a little forward between* MRS HILL *and* MRS HIGGINS, *and sits down.*)

PICKERING   Has Henry told you what weve come for?

HIGGINS (*over his shoulder*)   We were interrupted: damn it!

MRS HIGGINS   Oh Henry, Henry, really!

MRS EYNSFORD HILL (*half rising*)   Are we in the way?

MRS HIGGINS (*rising and making her sit down again*)   No, no. You couldnt have come more fortunately: we want you to meet a friend of ours.

HIGGINS (*turning hopefully*)   Yes, by George! We want two or three people. Youll do as well as anybody else.

THE PARLOR-MAID *returns, ushering* FREDDY.

THE PARLOR-MAID   Mr Eynsford Hill.

HIGGINS (*almost audibly, past endurance*)   God of Heaven! another of them.

FREDDY (*shaking hands with* MRS HIGGINS)   Ahdedo?

MRS HIGGINS   Very good of you to come. (*Introducing*) Colonel Pickering.

FREDDY (*bowing*)   Ahdedo?

MRS HIGGINS   I dont think you know my son, Professor Higgins.

FREDDY (going to HIGGINS)   Ahdedo?

HIGGINS (*looking at him much as if he were a pickpocket*)   I'll take my oath Ive met *you* before somewhere. Where was it?

FREDDY   I dont think so.

HIGGINS (*resignedly*)   It don't matter, anyhow. Sit down. (*He shakes* FREDDY'S *hand, and almost slings him on to the ottoman with his face to the windows; then comes round to the other side of it.*)

HIGGINS   Well, here we are, anyhow! (*He sits down on the ottoman next* MRS EYNSFORD HILL, *on her left.*) And now, what the devil are we going to talk about until Eliza comes?

MRS HIGGINS   Henry: you are the life and soul of the Royal Society's soirées; but really youre rather trying on more commonplace occasions.

HIGGINS   Am I? Very sorry. (*Beaming suddenly*) I suppose I am, you know. (*Uproariously*) Ha, ha!

MISS EYNSFORD HILL (*who considers* HIGGINS *quite eligible matrimonially*)   I sympathize. *I* havnt any small talk. If people would only be frank and say what they really think!

HIGGINS (*relapsing into gloom*)   Lord forbid!

MRS EYNSFORD HILL (*taking up her daughter's cue*)   But why?

HIGGINS   What they think they ought to think is bad enough, Lord knows; but what they really think would break up the whole show. Do you suppose it would be really agreeable if I were to come out now with what *I* really think?

MISS EYNSFORD HILL (*gaily*)   Is it so very cynical?

HIGGINS   Cynical! Who the dickens said it was cynical? I mean it wouldnt be decent.

MRS EYNSFORD HILL (*seriously*)   Oh! I'm sure you dont mean that, Mr Higgins.

HIGGINS   You see, we're all savages, more or less. We're supposed to be civilized and cultured—to know all about poetry and philosophy and art and science, and so on; but how many of us know even the meanings of these names? (*To* MISS HILL) What do *you* know of poetry? (*To* MRS HILL) What do *you* know of science? (*Indicating* FREDDY) What does *he* know of art or science or anything else? What the devil do you imagine I know of philosophy?

MRS HIGGINS (*warningly*)   Or of manners, Henry?

THE PARLOR-MAID (*opening the door*)   Miss Doolittle. (*She withdraws.*)

HIGGINS (*rising hastily and running to* MRS HIGGINS)   Here she is, mother. (*He stands on tiptoe and makes signs over his mother's head to* ELIZA *to indicate to her which lady is her hostess.*)

LIZA, *who is exquisitely dressed, produces an impression of such remarkable distinction and beauty as she enters that they all rise, quite fluttered. Guided by* HIGGINS's *signals, she comes to* MRS HIGGINS *with studied grace.*

LIZA (*speaking with pedantic correctness of pronunciation and great beauty of tone*)   How do you do, Mrs Higgins? (*She gasps slightly in making sure of the H in Higgins, but is quite successful.*) Mr Higgins told me I might come.

MRS HIGGINS (*cordially*)   Quite right: I'm very glad indeed to see you.

PICKERING   How do you do, Miss Doolittle?

LIZA (*shaking hands with him*)   Colonel Pickering, is it not?

MRS EYNSFORD HILL   I feel sure we have met before, Miss Doolittle. I remember your eyes.

LIZA   How do you do? (*She sits down on the ottoman gracefully in the place just left vacant by* HIGGINS.)

MRS EYNSFORD HILL (*introducing*)   My daughter Clara.

LIZA   How do you do?

CLARA (*impulsively*)   How do you do? (*She sits down on the ottoman beside* ELIZA, *devouring her with her eyes.*)

FREDDY (*coming to their side of the ottoman*)   Ive certainly had the pleasure.

MRS EYNSFORD HILL (*introducing*)   My son Freddy.

LIZA   How do you do?

FREDDY *bows and sits down in the Elizabethan chair, infatuated.*

HIGGINS (*suddenly*)   By George, yes: it all comes back to me! (*They stare at him.*) Covent Garden! (*Lamentably*) What a damned thing!

MRS HIGGINS   Henry, please! (*He is about to sit on the edge of the table.*) Dont sit on my writing-table: youll break it.

HIGGINS (*sulkily*)   Sorry. (*He goes to the divan, stumbling into the fender and over the fire-irons on his way; extricating himself with muttered imprecations; and finishing his disastrous journey by throwing himself so impatiently on the divan that he almost breaks it.* MRS. HIGGINS *looks at him, but controls herself and says nothing.*
   A long and painful pause ensues.)

MRS HIGGINS (*at last, conversationally*)   Will it rain, do you think?

LIZA   The shallow depression in the west of these islands is likely to move slowly in an easterly direction. There are no indications of any great change in the barometrical situation.

FREDDY   Ha! ha! how awfully funny!

LIZA   What is wrong with that, young man? I bet I got it right.

FREDDY   Killing!

MRS EYNSFORD HILL   I'm sure I hope it wont turn cold. Theres so much influenza about. It runs right through our whole family regularly every spring.

LIZA (*darkly*)   My aunt died of influenza: so they said.

MRS EYNSFORD HILL (*clicks her tongue sympathetically*)!!!

LIZA (*in the same tragic tone*)   But it's my belief they done the old woman in.

MRS HIGGINS (*puzzled*)   Done her in?

LIZA   Y-e-e-e-es, Lord love you! Why should *she* die of influenza? She come through diphtheria right enough the year before. I saw her with my own eyes. Fairly blue with it, she was. They all thought she was dead; but my father he kept ladling gin down her throat til she came to so sudden that she bit the bowl off the spoon.

MRS EYNSFORD HILL (*startled*)   Dear me!

LIZA (*piling up the indictment*)   What call would a woman with that strength in her have to die of influenza? What become of her new straw hat that should have come to me? Somebody pinched it; and what I say is, them as pinched it done her in.

MRS EYNSFORD HILL   What does doing her in mean?

HIGGINS (*hastily*)   Oh, thats the new small talk. To do a person in means to kill them.

MRS EYNSFORD HILL (*to* ELIZA, *horrified*)   You surely don't believe that your aunt was killed?

LIZA   Do I not! Them she lived with would have killed her for a hat-pin, let alone a hat.

MRS EYNSFORD HILL   But it cant have been right for your father to pour spirits down her throat like that. It might have killed her.

LIZA   Not her. Gin was mother's milk to her. Besides, he'd poured so much down his own throat that he knew the good of it.

MRS EYNSFORD HILL   Do you mean that he drank?

LIZA   Drank! My word! Something chronic.

MRS EYNSFORD HILL   How dreadful for you!

LIZA   Not a bit. It never did him no harm what I could see. But then he did not keep it up regular. (*Cheerfully*) On the burst, as you might say, from time to time. And always more agreeable when he had a drop in. When he was out of work, my mother used to give him fourpence and tell him to go out and not come back until he'd drunk himself cheerful and loving-like. Theres lots of women has to make their husbands drunk to make them fit to live with. (*Now quite at her ease*) You see, it's like this. If a man has a bit of a conscience, it always takes him when he's sober; and then it makes him low-spirited. A drop of booze just takes that off and makes him happy. (*To* FREDDY, *who is in convulsions of suppressed laughter*) Here! what are you sniggering at?

FREDDY   The new small talk. You do it so awfully well.

LIZA   If I was doing it proper, what was you laughing at? (*To* HIGGINS) Have I said anything I oughtn't?

MRS HIGGINS (*interposing*)   Not at all, Miss Doolittle.

LIZA   Well, thats a mercy, anyhow. (*Expansively*) What I always say is—

HIGGINS (*rising and looking at his watch*)   Ahem!

LIZA (*looking round at him; taking the hint; and rising*)   Well: I must go. (*They all rise.* FREDDY *goes to the door.*) So pleased to have met you. Goodbye. (*She shakes hands with* MRS HIGGINS.)

MRS HIGGINS   Goodbye.

LIZA   Goodbye, Colonel Pickering.

PICKERING   Goodbye, Miss Doolittle. (*They shake hands.*)

LIZA (*nodding to the others*)   Goodbye, all.

FREDDY (*opening the door for her*)   Are you walking across the Park, Miss Doolittle? If so—

LIZA   Walk! Not bloody likely. (*Sensation.*) I am going in a taxi. (*She goes out.*)

PICKERING *gasps and sits down.* FREDDY *goes out on the balcony to catch another glimpse of* ELIZA.

MRS EYNSFORD HILL (*suffering from shock*).   Well, I really cant get used to the new ways.

CLARA (*throwing herself discontentedly into the Elizabethan chair*)   Oh, it's all right, mamma, quite right. People will think we never go anywhere or see anybody if you are so old-fashioned.

MRS EYNSFORD HILL   I daresay I am very old-fashioned; but I do hope you wont begin using that expression, Clara. I have got accustomed to hear you talking about men as rotters, and calling everything filthy and beastly; though I do think it horrible and unladylike. But this last is really too much. Dont you think so, Colonel Pickering?

PICKERING   Dont ask me. Ive been away in India for several years; and manners have changed so much that I sometimes dont know whether I'm at a respectable dinner-table or in a ship's forecastle.

CLARA   It's all a matter of habit. Theres no right or wrong in it. Nobody means anything by it. And it's so quaint, and gives such a smart emphasis to things that are not in themselves very witty. I find the new small talk delightful and quite innocent.

MRS EYNSFORD HILL (*rising*)   Well, after that, I think it's time for us to go.

PICKERING *and* HIGGINS *rise*.

CLARA (*rising*)   Oh yes: we have three at-homes to go to still. Goodbye, Mrs Higgins. Goodbye, Colonel Pickering. Goodbye, Professor Higgins.

HIGGINS (*coming grimly at her from the divan, and accompanying her to the door*)   Goodbye. Be sure you try on that small talk at the three at-homes. Dont be nervous about it. Pitch it in strong.

CLARA (*all smiles*)   I will. Goodbye. Such nonsense, all this early Victorian prudery!

HIGGINS (*tempting her*)   Such damned nonsense!

CLARA   Such bloody nonsense!

MRS EYNSFORD HILL (*convulsively*)   Clara!

CLARA   Ha! ha! (*She goes out radiant, conscious of being thoroughly up to date, and is heard descending the stairs in a stream of silvery laughter.*)

FREDDY (*to the heavens at large*)   Well, I ask you— (*He gives it up, and comes to* MRS HIGGINS.) Goodbye.

MRS HIGGINS (*shaking hands*)   Goodbye. Would you like to meet Miss Doolittle again?

FREDDY (*eagerly*)   Yes, I should, most awfully.

MRS HIGGINS   Well, you know my days.

FREDDY   Yes. Thanks awfully. Goodbye. (*He goes out.*)

MRS EYNSFORD HILL   Goodbye, Mr Higgins.

HIGGINS   Goodbye. Goodbye.

MRS EYNSFORD HILL (*to* PICKERING)   Its no use. I shall never be able to bring myself to use that word.

PICKERING   Dont. It's not compulsory, you know. Youll get on quite well without it.

MRS EYNSFORD HILL   Only, Clara is so down on me if I am not positively reeking with the latest slang. Goodbye.

PICKERING.   Goodbye. (*They shake hands.*)

MRS EYNSFORD HILL (*to* MRS HIGGINS)   You mustnt mind Clara. (PICKERING, *catching from her lowered tone that this is not meant for him to hear, discreetly joins* HIGGINS *at the window.*) We're so poor! and she gets so few parties, poor child! She doesn't quite know. (MRS HIGGINS, *seeing that her eyes are moist, takes her hand sympathetically and goes with her to the door.*) But the boy is nice. Dont you think so?

MRS HIGGINS   Oh, quite nice. I shall always be delighted to see him.

MRS EYNSFORD HILL   Thank you, dear. Goodbye. (*She goes out.*)

HIGGINS (*eagerly*)   Well? Is Eliza presentable? (*He swoops on his*

mother and drags her to the ottoman, where she sits down in ELIZA'S
place with her son on her left.)

PICKERING *returns to his chair on her right.*

MRS HIGGINS   You silly boy, of course she's not presentable. She's a
triumph of your art and of her dressmaker's; but if you suppose for
a moment that she doesnt give herself away in every sentence she
utters, you must be perfectly cracked about her.

PICKERING   But dont you think something might be done? I mean
something to eliminate the sanguinary element from her conversation.

MRS HIGGINS   Not as long as she is in Henry's hands.

HIGGINS (*aggrieved*)   Do you mean that my language is improper?

MRS HIGGINS   No, dearest: it would be quite proper—say on a canal
barge; but it would not be proper for her at a garden party.

HIGGINS (*deeply injured*)   Well I must say—

PICKERING (*interrupting him*)   Come, Higgins: you must learn to
know yourself. I havnt heard such language as yours since we used
to review the volunteers in Hyde Park twenty years ago.

HIGGINS (*sulkily*)   Oh, well, if *you* say so, I suppose I dont always
talk like a bishop.

MRS HIGGINS (*quieting* HENRY *with a touch*)   Colonel Pickering: will
you tell me what is the exact state of things in Wimpole Street?

PICKERING (*cheerfully: as if this completely changed the subject*)
Well, I have come to live there with Henry. We work together at my
Indian Dialects; and we think it more convenient—

MRS HIGGINS   Quite so. I know all about that: it's an excellent arrangement. But where does this girl live?

HIGGINS   With us, of course. Where *should* she live?

MRS HIGGINS   But on what terms? Is she a servant? If not, what is she?

PICKERING (*slowly*)   I think I know what you mean, Mrs. Higgins.

HIGGINS   Well, dash me if *I* do. Ive had to work at the girl every day
for months to get her to her present pitch. Besides, she's useful.
She knows where my things are, and remembers my appointments
and so forth.

MRS HIGGINS   How does your housekeeper get on with her?

HIGGINS   Mrs. Pearce? Oh, she's jolly glad to get so much taken off
her hands; for before Eliza came, *she* used to have to find things and
remind me of my appointments. But she's got some silly bee in her

bonnet about Eliza. She keeps saying "You dont *think,* sir": doesnt she, Pick?

PICKERING   Yes: thats the formula. "You dont *think,* sir." Thats the end of every conversation about Eliza.

HIGGINS   As if I ever stop thinking about the girl and her confounded vowels and consonants. I'm worn out, thinking about her, and watching her lips and her teeth and her tongue, not to mention her soul, which is the quaintest of the lot.

MRS HIGGINS   You certainly are a pretty pair of babies, playing with your live doll.

HIGGINS   Playing! The hardest job I ever tackled: make no mistake about that, mother. But you have no idea how frightfully interesting it is to take a human being and change her into a quite different human being by creating a new speech for her. It's filling up the deepest gulf that separates class from class and soul from soul.

PICKERING   (*drawing his chair closer to* MRS HIGGINS *and bending over to her eagerly*)   Yes: it's enormously interesting. I assure you, Mrs Higgins, we take Eliza very seriously. Every week—every day almost —there is some new change. (*Closer again*) We keep records of every stage—dozens of gramaphone disks and photographs—

HIGGINS   (*assailing her at the other ear*)   Yes, by George: it's the most absorbing experiment I ever tackled. She regularly fills our lives up: doesnt she, Pick?

PICKERING   We're always talking Eliza.

HIGGINS   Teaching Eliza.

PICKERING   Dressing Eliza.

MRS HIGGINS   What!

HIGGINS   Inventing new Elizas.

HIGGINS	(*speaking together*)	You know, she has the most extraordinary quickness of ear:
PICKERING		I assure you, my dear Mrs Higgins, that girl
HIGGINS		just like a parrot. Ive tried her with every
PICKERING		is a genius. She can play the piano quite beautifully.
HIGGINS		possible sort of sound that a human being can make—
PICKERING		We have taken her to classical concerts and to music

HIGGINS	Continental dialects, African dialects, Hottentot
PICKERING	halls; and it's all the same to her: she plays everything
HIGGINS	clicks, things it took me years to get hold of; and
PICKERING	she hears right off when she comes home, whether
HIGGINS	she picks them up like a shot, right away, as if she had
PICKERING	it's Beethoven and Brahms or Lehar and Lionel Monckton;
HIGGINS	been at it all her life.
PICKERING	though six months ago, she'd never as much as touched a piano—

MRS HIGGINS (*putting her fingers in her ears, as they are by this time shouting one another down with an intolerable noise*) Sh-sh-sh—sh! (*They stop.*)

PICKERING I beg your pardon. (*He draws his chair back apologetically.*)

HIGGINS Sorry. When Pickering starts shouting nobody can get a word in edgeways.

MRS HIGGINS Be quiet, Henry. Colonel Pickering: dont you realize that when Eliza walked into Wimpole Street, something walked in with her.

PICKERING Her father did. But Henry soon got rid of him.

MRS HIGGINS It would have been more to the point if her mother had. But as her mother didnt something else did.

PICKERING But what?

MRS HIGGINS (*unconsciously dating herself by the word*) A problem.

PICKERING Oh, I see. The problem of how to pass her off as a lady.

HIGGINS I'll solve that problem. Ive half solved it already.

MRS HIGGINS No, you two infinitely stupid male creatures: the problem of what is to be done with her afterwards.

HIGGINS I dont see anything in that. She can go her own way, with all the advantages I have given her.

MRS HIGGINS The advantages of that poor woman who was here just now! The manners and habits that disqualify a fine lady from earning her own living without giving her a fine lady's income! Is that what you mean?

PICKERING (*indulgently, being rather bored*)   Oh, that will be all right, Mrs Higgins. (*He rises to go.*)

HIGGINS (*rising also*)   We'll find her some light employment.

PICKERING   She's happy enough. Dont you worry about her. Goodbye. (*He shakes hands as if he were consoling a frightened child, and makes for the door.*)

HIGGINS   Anyhow, theres no good bothering now. The thing's done. Goodbye, mother. (*He kisses her, and follows* PICKERING.)

PICKERING (*turning for a final consolation*)   There are plenty of openings. We'll do whats right. Goodbye.

HIGGINS (*to* PICKERING *as they go out together*)   Let's take her to the Shakespear exhibition at Earlscourt.

PICKERING   Yes: lets. Her remarks will be delicious.

HIGGINS   She'll mimic all the people for us when we get home.

PICKERING   Ripping. (*Both are heard laughing as they go downstairs.*)

MRS HIGGINS (*rises with an impatient bounce, and returns to her work at the writing-table. She sweeps a litter of disarranged papers out of her way; snatches a sheet of paper from her stationery case; and tries resolutely to write. At the third line she gives it up; flings down her pen; grips the table angrily and exclaims*)   Oh, men! men!! men!!!

ACT IV

The Wimpole Street laboratory. Midnight. Nobody in the room. The clock on the mantelpiece strikes twelve. The fire is not alight: it is a summer night.

Presently HIGGINS *and* PICKERING *are heard on the stairs.*

HIGGINS (*calling down to* PICKERING)   I say, Pick: lock up, will you? I shant be going out again.

PICKERING   Right. Can Mrs Pearce go to bed? We dont want anything more, do we?

HIGGINS   Lord, no!

ELIZA *opens the door and is seen on the lighted landing in opera cloak, brilliant evening dress, and diamonds, with fan, flowers, and all acces-*

sories. She comes to the hearth, and switches on the electric lights there. She is tired: her pallor contrasts strongly with her dark eyes and hair; and her expression is almost tragic. She takes off her cloak; puts her fan and flowers on the piano; and sits down on the bench, brooding and silent. HIGGINS, *in evening dress, with overcoat and hat, comes in, carrying a smoking jacket which he has picked up downstairs. He takes off the hat and overcoat; throws them carelessly on the newspaper stand; disposes of his coat in the same way; puts on the smoking jacket; and throws himself wearily into the easy-chair at the hearth.* PICKERING, *similarly attired, comes in. He also takes off his hat and overcoat, and is about to throw them on* HIGGINS'S *when he hesitates.*

PICKERING   I say: Mrs Pearce will row if we leave these things lying about in the drawing room.

HIGGINS   Oh, chuck them over the bannisters into the hall. She'll find them there in the morning and put them away all right. She'll think we were drunk.

PICKERING   We are, slightly. Are there any letters?

HIGGINS   I didnt look. (PICKERING *takes the overcoats and hats and goes downstairs.* HIGGINS *begins half singing half yawning an air from La Fanciulla del Golden West. Suddenly he stops and exclaims.*) I wonder where the devil my slippers are!

ELIZA *looks at him darkly; then rises suddenly and leaves the room.*

HIGGINS *yawns again, and resumes his song.*

PICKERING *returns, with the contents of the letter-box in his hand.*

PICKERING   Only circulars, and this coroneted billet-doux for you. (*He throws the circulars into the fender, and posts himself on the hearthrug, with his back to the grate.*)

HIGGINS (*glancing at the billet-doux*)   Money-lender. (*He throws the letter after the circulars.*)

ELIZA *returns with a pair of large down-at-heel slippers. She places them on the carpet before* HIGGINS, *and sits as before without a word.*

HIGGINS (*yawning again*)   Oh Lord! What an evening! What a crew! What a silly tomfoolery! (*He raises his shoe to unlace it, and catches sight of the slippers. He stops unlacing and looks at them as if they had appeared there of their own accord.*) Oh! theyre there, are they?

PICKERING (*stretching himself*)   Well, I feel a bit tired. It's been a long day. The garden party, a dinner party, and the opera! Rather too much of a good thing. But youve won your bet, Higgins. Eliza did the trick, and something to spare, eh?

HIGGINS (*fervently*)   Thank God it's over!

LIZA *flinches violently; but they take no notice of her; and she recovers herself and sits stonily as before.*

PICKERING   Were you nervous at the garden party? *I* was. Eliza didnt seem a bit nervous.

HIGGINS   Oh, *she* wasnt nervous. I knew she'd be all right. No: it's the strain of putting the job through all these months that has told on me. It was interesting enough at first, while we were at the phonetics; but after that I got deadly sick of it. If I hadnt backed myself to do it I should have chucked the whole thing up two months ago. It was a silly notion: the whole thing has been a bore.

PICKERING   Oh come! the garden party was frightfully exciting. My heart began beating like anything.

HIGGINS   Yes, for the first three minutes. But when I saw we were going to win hands down, I felt like a bear in a cage, hanging about doing nothing. The dinner was worse: sitting gorging there for over an hour, wtih nobody but a damned fool of a fashionable woman to talk to! I tell you, Pickering, never again for me. No more artificial duchesses. The whole thing has been simple purgatory.

PICKERING   Youve never been broken in properly to the social routine. (*Strolling over to the piano*) I rather enjoy dipping into it occasionally myself: it makes me feel young again. Anyhow, it was a great success: an immense success. I was quite frightened once or twice because Eliza was doing it so well. You see, lots of real people cant do it at all: theyre such fools that they think style comes by nature to people in their position; and so they never learn. Theres always something professional about doing a thing superlatively well.

HIGGINS   Yes: thats what drives me mad: the silly people dont know their own silly busines. (*Rising*) However, it's over and done with; and now I can go to bed at last without dreading tomorrow.

LIZA'S *beauty becomes murderous.*

PICKERING   I think I shall turn in too. Still, it's been a great occasion: a triumph for you. Goodnight. (*He goes.*)

HIGGINS (*following him*)   Goodnight. (*Over his shoulder, at the door*) Put out the lights, Eliza; and tell Mrs Pearce not to make coffee for me in the morning: I'll take tea. (*He goes out.*)

LIZA *tries to control herself and feel indifferent as she rises and walks across to the hearth to switch off the lights. By the time she gets there she is on the point of screaming. She sits down in Higgins's chair and holds on hard to the arms. Finally she gives way and flings herself furiously on the floor, raging.*

HIGGINS (*in despairing wrath outside*)   What the devil have I done with my slippers? (*He appears at the door.*)

LIZA (*snatching up the slippers, and hurling them at him one after the other with all her force*)   There are your slippers. And there. Take your slippers; and may you never have a day's luck with them!

HIGGINS (*astounded*)   What on earth—! (*He comes to her.*) Whats the matter? Get up. (*He pulls her up.*) Anything wrong?

LIZA (*breathless*)   Nothing wrong—with you. Ive won your bet for you, havnt I? Thats enough for you. *I* dont matter, I suppose.

HIGGINS   *You* won my bet! You! Presumptuous insect! *I* won it. What did you throw those slippers at me for?

LIZA   Because I wanted to smash your face. I'd like to kill you, you selfish brute. Why didnt you leave me where you picked me out of— in the gutter? You thank God it's all over, and that now you can throw me back again there, do you? (*She crisps her fingers frantically.*)

HIGGINS (*looking at her in cool wonder*)   The creature is nervous, after all.

LIZA (*gives a suffocated scream of fury, and instinctively darts her nails at his face*)!!

HIGGINS (*catching her wrists*)   Ah! would you? Claws in, you cat. How dare you shew your temper to me? Sit down and be quiet. (*He throws her roughly into the easy-chair.*)

LIZA (*crushed by superior strength and weight*)   Whats to become of me? Whats to become of me?

HIGGINS   How the devil do I know whats to become of you? What does it matter what becomes of you?

LIZA   You dont care. I know you dont care. You wouldnt care if I was dead. I'm nothing to you—not so much as them slippers.

HIGGINS (*thundering*)   *Those* slippers.

LIZA (*with bitter submission*)   Those slippers. I didnt think it made any difference now.

A pause. ELIZA *hopeless and crushed.* HIGGINS *a little uneasy.*

HIGGINS (*in his loftiest manner*)   Why have you begun going on like this? May I ask whether you complain of your treatment here?

LIZA   No.

HIGGINS   Has anybody behaved badly to you? Colonel Pickering? Mrs Pearce? Any of the servants?

LIZA   No.

HIGGINS   I presume you dont pretend that *I* have treated you badly?

LIZA   No.

HIGGINS   I am glad to hear it. (*He moderates his tone.*) Perhaps youre tired after the strain of the day. Will you have a glass of champagne? (*He moves towards the door.*)

LIZA   No. (*Recollecting her manners*) Thank you.

HIGGINS (*good-humored again*)   This has been coming on you for some days. I suppose it was natural for you to be anxious about the garden party. But thats all over now. (*He pats her kindly on the shoulder. She writhes.*) Theres nothing more to worry about.

LIZA   No. Nothing more for *you* to worry about. (*She suddenly rises and gets away from him by going to the piano bench, where she sits and hides her face.*) Oh God! I wish I was dead.

HIGGINS (*staring after her in sincere surprise*)   Why? In heaven's name, why? (*Reasonably, going to her*) Listen to me, Eliza. All this irritation is purely subjective.

LIZA   I dont understand. I'm too ignorant.

HIGGINS   It's only imagination. Low spirits and nothing else. Nobody's hurting you. Nothing's wrong. You go to bed like a good girl and sleep it off. Have a little cry and say your prayers: that will make you comfortable.

LIZA   I heard your prayers. "Thank God it's all over!"

HIGGINS (*impatiently*)   Well, *dont* you thank God it's all over? Now you are free and can do what you like.

LIZA (*pulling herself together in desperation*)   What am I fit for? What have you left me fit for? Where am I to go? What am I to do? Whats to become of me?

HIGGINS (*enlightened, but not at all impressed*)   Oh thats whats worrying you, is it? (*He thrusts his hands into his pockets, and walks about in his usual manner, rattling the contents of his pockets, as if condescending to a trivial subject out of pure kindness.*) I shouldn't bother about it if I were you. I should imagine you wont have much difficulty in settling yourself somewhere or other, though I hadn't quite realized that you were going away.

(*She looks quickly at him: he does not look at her, but examines the dessert stand on the piano and decides that he will eat an apple.*)

You might marry, you know. (*He bites a large piece out of the apple and munches it noisily.*) You see, Eliza, all men are not confirmed old bachelors like me and the Colonel. Most men are the marrying sort (poor devils!); and youre not bad-looking: it's quite a pleasure to look at you sometimes—not now, of course, because youre crying and looking as ugly as the very devil; but when youre all right and quite yourself, youre what I should call attractive. That is, to the people in the marrying line, you understand. You go to bed and have a good nice rest; and then get up and look at yourself in the glass; and you wont feel so cheap.

LIZA *again looks at him, speechless, and does not stir.*

The look is quite lost on him: he eats his apple with a dreamy expression of happiness, as it is quite a good one.

HIGGINS (*a genial afterthought occurring to him*)   I daresay my mother could find some chap or other who would do very well.

LIZA   We were above that at the corner of Tottenham Court Road.

HIGGINS (*waking up*)   What do you mean?

LIZA   I sold flowers. I didn't sell myself. Now youve made a lady of me I'm not fit to sell anything else. I wish youd left me where you found me.

HIGGINS (*slinging the core of the apple decisively into the grate*)   Tosh, Eliza. Dont you insult human relations by dragging all this cant about buying and selling into it. You neednt marry the fellow if you dont like him.

LIZA   What else am I to do?

HIGGINS   Oh, lots of things. What about your old idea of a florist's shop? Pickering could set you up in one: he's lots of money. (*Chuckling*) He'll have to pay for all those togs you have been wearing today; and that, with the hire of the jewellery, will make a big hole in two hundred pounds. Why, six months ago you would have thought it the millennium to have a flower shop of your own. Come! youll be all right. I must clear off to bed: I'm devilish sleepy. By the way, I came down for something: I forget what it was.

LIZA   Your slippers.

HIGGINS   Oh yes, of course. You shied them at me. (*He picks them up, and is going out when she rises and speaks to him.*)

LIZA   Before you go, sir—

HIGGINS (*dropping the slippers in his surprise at her calling him Sir*) Eh?

LIZA   Do my clothes belong to me or to Colonel Pickering?

HIGGINS (*coming back into the room as if her question were the very climax of unreason*)   What the devil use would they be to Pickering?

LIZA   He might want them for the next girl you pick up to experiment on.

HIGGINS (*shocked and hurt*)   Is *that* the way you feel towards us?

LIZA   I dont want to hear anything more about that. All I want to know is whether anything belongs to me. My own clothes were burnt.

HIGGINS   But what does it matter? Why need you start bothering about that in the middle of the night?

LIZA   I want to know what I may take away with me. I dont want to be accused of stealing.

HIGGINS (*now deeply wounded*)   Stealing! You shouldnt have said that, Eliza. That shews a want of feeling.

LIZA   I'm sorry. I'm only a common ignorant girl; and in *my* station I have to be careful. There cant be any feelings between the like of you and the like of me. Please will you tell me what belongs to me and what doesnt?

HIGGINS (*very sulky*)   You may take the whole damned houseful if you like. Except the jewels. Theyre hired. Will that satisfy you? (*He turns on his heel and is about to go in extreme dudgeon.*)

LIZA (*drinking in his emotion like nectar, and nagging him to provoke a further supply*)   Stop, please. (*She takes off her jewels.*) Will you take these to your room and keep them safe? I dont want to run the risk of their being missing.

HIGGINS (*furious*)   Hand them over.

She puts them into his hands.

If these belonged to me instead of to the jeweller, I'd ram them down your ungrateful throat. (*He perfunctorily thrusts them into his pockets, unconsciously decorating himself with the protruding ends of the chains.*)

LIZA (*taking a ring off*)   This ring isnt the jeweller's: it's the one you bought me in Brighton. I dont want it now.

HIGGINS *dashes the ring violently into the fireplace, and turns on her so threateningly that she crouches over the piano with her hands over her face, and exclaims*   Dont you hit me.

HIGGINS   Hit you! You infamous creature, how dare you accuse me of such a thing? It is you who have hit me. You have wounded me to the heart.

LIZA (*thrilling with hidden joy*)   I'm glad. I've got a little of my own back, anyhow.

HIGGINS (*with dignity, in his finest professional style*)   You have caused me to lose my temper: a thing that has hardly ever happened to me before. I prefer to say nothing more tonight. I am going to bed.

LIZA (*pertly*)   Youd better leave a note for Mrs Pearce about the coffee; for she wont be told by me.

HIGGINS (*formally*)   Damn Mrs Pearce; and damn the coffee; and damn you; and damn my own folly in having lavished hard-earned knowledge and the treasure of my regard and intimacy on a heartless guttersnipe. (*He goes out with impressive decorum, and spoils it by slamming the door savagely.*)

ELIZA *smiles for the first time; expresses her feelings by a wild pantomime in which an imitation of* HIGGINS'S *exit is confused with her own triumph; and finally goes down on her knees on the hearthrug to look for the ring.*

ACT V

MRS HIGGINS'S *drawing room. She is at her writing-table as before.* THE PARLOR-MAID *comes in.*

THE PARLOR-MAID (*at the door*)   Mr Henry, maam, is downstairs with Colonel Pickering.

MRS HIGGINS   Well, shew them up.

THE PARLOR-MAID   Theyre using the telephone, maam. Telephoning to the police, I think.

MRS HIGGINS   What!

THE PARLOR-MAID (*coming further in and lowering her voice*)   Mr Henry is in a state, maam. I thought I'd better tell you.

MRS HIGGINS   If you had told me that Mr Henry was not in a state it would have been more surprising. Tell them to come up when theyve finished with the police. I suppose he's lost something.

THE PARLOR-MAID   Yes, maam (*going*).

MRS HIGGINS   Go upstairs and tell Miss Doolittle that Mr Henry and the Colonel are here. Ask her not to come down til I send for her.

THE PARLOR-MAID   Yes, maam.

HIGGINS *bursts in. He is, as* THE PARLOR-MAID *has said, in a state.*

HIGGINS Look here, mother: heres a confounded thing!
MRS HIGGINS Yes, dear. Good morning.

He checks his impatience and kisses her, whilst THE PARLOR-MAID *goes out.*

What is it?
HIGGINS Eliza's bolted.
MRS HIGGINS (*calmly continuing her writing*) You must have frightened her.
HIGGINS Frightened her! nonsense! She was left last night, as usual, to turn out the lights and all that; and instead of going to bed she changed her clothes and went right off: her bed wasnt slept in. She came in a cab for her things before seven this morning; and that fool Mrs Pearce let her have them without telling me a word about it. What am I to do?
MRS HIGGINS Do without, I'm afraid, Henry. The girl has a perfect right to leave if she chooses.
HIGGINS (*wandering distractedly across the room*) But I cant find anything. I dont know what appointments Ive got. I'm—

PICKERING *comes in.* MRS HIGGINS *puts down her pen and turns away from the writing-table.*

PICKERING (*shaking hands*) Good morning, Mrs Higgins. Has Henry told you? (*He sits down on the ottoman.*)
HIGGINS What does that ass of an inspector say? Have you offered a reward?
MRS HIGGINS (*rising in indignant amazement*) You dont mean to say you have set the police after Eliza.
HIGGINS Of course. What are the police for? What else could we do? (*He sits in the Elizabethan chair.*)
PICKERING The inspector made a lot of difficulties. I really think he suspected us of some improper purpose.
MRS HIGGINS Well, of course he did. What right have you to go to the police and give the girl's name as if she were a thief, or a lost umbrella, or something? Really! (*She sits down again, deeply vexed.*)
HIGGINS But we want to find her.

PICKERING We cant let her go like this, you know, Mrs Higgins. What were we to do?

MRS HIGGINS You have no more sense, either of you, than two children. Why—

THE PARLOR-MAID (*comes in and breaks off the conversation*) Mr Henry: a gentleman wants to see you very particular. He's been sent on from Wimpole Street.

HIGGINS Oh, bother! I cant see anyone now. Who is it?

THE PARLOR-MAID A Mr Doolittle, sir.

PICKERING Doolittle! Do you mean the dustman?

THE PARLOR-MAID Dustman! Oh no, sir: a gentleman.

HIGGINS (*springing up excitedly*) By George, Pick, it's some relative of hers that she's gone to. Somebody we know nothing about. (*To* THE PARLOR-MAID) Send him up, quick.

THE PARLOR-MAID Yes, sir. (*She goes.*)

HIGGINS (*eagerly, going to his mother*) Genteel relatives! now we shall hear something. (*He sits down in the Chippendale chair.*)

MRS HIGGINS Do you know any of her people?

PICKERING Only her father: the fellow we told you about.

THE PARLOR-MAID (*announcing*) Mr Doolittle. (*She withdraws.*)

DOOLITTLE *enters. He is brilliantly dressed in a new fashionable frock-coat, with white waistcoat and grey trousers. A flower in his button-hole, a dazzling silk hat, and patent leather shoes complete the effect. He is too concerned with the business he has come on to notice* MRS HIGGGINS. *He walks straight to* HIGGINS, *and accosts him with vehement reproach.*

DOOLITTLE (*indicating his own person*) See here! Do you see this? You done this.

HIGGINS Done what, man?

DOOLITTLE This, I tell you. Look at it. Look at this hat. Look at this coat.

PICKERING Has Eliza been buying you clothes?

DOOLITTLE Eliza! not she. Not half. Why would she buy me clothes?

MRS HIGGINS Good morning, Mr. Doolittle. Wont you sit down?

DOOLITTLE (*taken aback as he becomes conscious that he has forgotten his hostess*) Asking your pardon, maam. (*He approaches her and shakes her proffered hand.*) Thank you. (*He sits down on the otto-*

man, on PICKERING'S *right.*) I am that full of what has happened
to me that I cant think of anything else.

HIGGINS   What the dickens *has* happened to you?

DOOLITTLE   I shouldnt mind if it had only happened to me: anything
might happen to anybody and nobody to blame but Providence, as
you might say. But this is something that you done to me: yes, you,
Henry Higgins.

HIGGINS   Have you found Eliza? Thats the point.

DOOLITTLE   Have you lost her?

HIGGINS   Yes.

DOOLITTLE   You have all the luck, you have. I aint found her; but
she'll find me quick enough now after what you done to me.

MRS HIGGINS   But what has my son done to you, Mr Doolittle?

DOOLITTLE   Done to me! Ruined me. Destroyed my happiness. Tied
me up and delivered me into the hands of middle class morality.

HIGGINS (*rising intolerantly and standing over* DOOLITTLE)   Youre
raving. Youre drunk. Youre mad. I gave you five pounds. After that
I had two conversations with you, at half-a-crown an hour. Ive
never seen you since.

DOOLITTLE   Oh! Drunk! am I? Mad? am I? Tell me this. Did you or
did you not write a letter to an old blighter in America that was
giving five millions to found Moral Reform Societies all over the
world, and that wanted you to invent a universal language for him?

HIGGINS   What! Ezra D. Wannafeller! He's dead. (*He sits down again
carelessly.*)

DOOLITTLE   Yes: he's dead; and I'm done for. Now did you or did
you not write a letter to him to say that the most original moralist
at present in England, to the best of your knowledge, was Alfred
Doolittle, a common dustman?

HIGGINS   Oh, after your last visit I remember making some silly joke
of the kind.

DOOLITTLE   Ah! you may well call it a silly joke. It put the lid on
me right enough. Just give him the chance he wanted to shew that
Americans is not like us: that they recognize and respect merit in
every class of life, however humble. Them words is in his blooming
will, in which, Henry Higgins, thanks to your silly joking, he leaves
me a share in his Predigested Cheese Trust worth three thousand
a year on condition that I lecture for his Wannafeller Moral Reform World League as often as they ask me up to six times a year.

HIGGINS   The devil he does! Whew! (*Brightening suddenly*) What a lark!

PICKERING   A safe thing for you, Doolittle. They wont ask you twice.

DOOLITTLE   It aint the lecturing I mind. I'll lecture them blue in the face, I will, and not turn a hair. It's making a gentleman of me that I object to. Who asked him to make a gentleman of me? I was happy. I was free. I touched pretty nigh everybody for money when I wanted it, same as I touched you, Henry Higgins. Now I am worrited; tied neck and heels; and everybody touches me for money. It's a fine thing for you, says my solicitor. Is it? says I. You mean it's a good thing for you, I says. When I was a poor man and had a solicitor once when they found a pram in the dust cart, he got me off, and got shut of me and got me shut of him as quick as he could. Same with the doctors: used to shove me out of the hospital before I could hardly stand on my legs, and nothing to pay. Now they finds out that I'm not a healthy man and cant live unless they looks after me twice a day. In the house I'm not let do a hand's turn for myself: somebody else must do it and touch me for it. A year ago I hadnt a relative in the world except two or three that wouldnt speak to me. Now Ive fifty, and not a decent week's wages among the lot of them. I have to live for others and not for myself: thats middle class morality. You talk of losing Eliza. Dont you be anxious: I bet she's on my doorstep by this: she that could support herself easy by selling flowers if I wasnt respectable. And the next one to touch me will be you, Henry Higgins. I'll have to learn to speak middle class language from you, instead of speaking proper English. Thats where youll come in; and I daresay thats what you done it for.

MRS HIGGINS   But, my dear Mr Doolittle, you need not suffer all this if you are really in earnest. Nobody can force you to accept this bequest. You can repudiate it. Isnt that so, Colonel Pickering?

PICKERING   I believe so.

DOOLITTLE   (*softening his manner in deference to her sex*) Thats the tragedy of it, maam. It's easy to say chuck it; but I havnt the nerve. Which of us has? We're all intimidated. Intimidated, maam: thats what we are. What is there for me if I chuck it but the workhouse in my old age? I have to dye my hair already to keep my job as a dustman. If I was one of the deserving poor, and had put by a bit, I could chuck it; but then why should I, acause the deserving poor might as well be millionaires for all the happiness they ever has. They dont know what happiness is. But I, as one of the undeserving poor, have nothing between me and the pauper's uniform but this here blasted three thousand a year that shoves me into the middle class. (*Excuse the expression, maam: youd use it yourself if you had my provocation.*) Theyve got you every way you turn: it's a choice between the Skilly of the workhouse and the Char Bydis of the middle class; and I havnt the nerve for the workhouse. Intimidated: thats what I am. Broke. Brought up. Happier men than me will call for my dust, and touch me for their tip; and I'll look on helpless, and envy them. And thats what your son has brought me to. (*He is overcome by emotion.*)

MRS HIGGINS   Well, I'm very glad youre not going to do anything foolish, Mr Doolittle. For this solves the problem of Eliza's future. You can provide for her now.

DOOLITTLE (*with melancholy resignation*)   Yes, maam: I'm expected to provide for everyone now, out of three thousand a year.

HIGGINS (*jumping up*)   Nonsense! he cant provide for her. He shant provide for her. She doesnt belong to him. I paid him five pounds for her. Doolittle: either youre an honest man or a rogue.

DOOLITTLE (*tolerantly*)   A little of both, Henry, like the rest of us: a little of both.

HIGGINS   Well, you took that money for the girl; and you have no right to take her as well.

MRS HIGGINS   Henry: dont be absurd. If you want to know where Eliza is, she is upstairs.

HIGGINS (*amazed*)   Upstairs!!! Then I shall jolly soon fetch her downstairs. (*He makes resolutely for the door.*)

MRS HIGGINS (*rising and following him*)   Be quiet, Henry. Sit down.

HIGGINS   I—

MRS HIGGINS   Sit down, dear; and listen to me.

HIGGINS   Oh, very well, very well, very well. (*He throws himself ungraciously on the ottoman, with his face towards the windows.*) But I think you might have told us this half an hour ago.

MRS HIGGINS   Eliza came to me this morning. She passed the night partly walking about in a rage, partly trying to throw herself into the river and being afraid to, and partly in the Carlton Hotel. She told me of the brutal way you two treated her.

HIGGINS (*bounding up again*)   What!

PICKERING (*rising also*)   My dear Mrs Higgins, she's been telling you stories. We didnt treat her brutally. We hardly said a word to her; and we parted on particularly good terms. (*Turning on* HIGGINS) Higgins: did you bully her after I went to bed?

HIGGINS   Just the other way about. She threw my slippers in my face. She behaved in the most outrageous way. I never gave her the slightest provocation. The slippers came bang into my face the moment I entered the room—before I had uttered a word. And used perfectly awful language.

PICKERING (*astonished*)   But why? What did we do to her?

MRS HIGGINS   I think I know pretty well what you did. The girl is naturally rather affectionate, I think. Isnt she, Mr Doolittle?

DOOLITTLE   Very tender-hearted, maam. Takes after me.

MRS HIGGINS   Just so. She had become attached to you both. She worked very hard for you, Henry! I dont think you quite realize what anything in the nature of brain work means to a girl like that. Well, it seems that when the great day of trial came, and she did this wonderful thing for you without making a single mistake, you two sat there and never said a word to her, but talked together of how glad you were that it was all over and how you had been bored with the whole thing. And then you were surprised because she threw your slippers at you! *I* should have thrown the fire-irons at you.

HIGGINS   We said nothing except that we were tired and wanted to go to bed. Did we, Pick?

PICKERING (*shrugging his shoulders*)   That was all.

MRS HIGGINS (*ironically*)   Quite sure?

PICKERING   Absolutely. Really, that was all.

MRS HIGGINS   You didnt thank her, or pet her, or admire her, or tell her how splendid she'd been.

HIGGINS (*impatiently*)   But she knew all about that. We didnt make speeches to her, if thats what you mean.

PICKERING (*conscience stricken*)   Perhaps we were a little inconsiderate. Is she very angry?

MRS HIGGINS (*returning to her place at the writing-table*)   Well, I'm afraid she wont go back to Wimpole Street, especially now that Mr Doolittle is able to keep up the position you have thrust on her; but she says she is quite willing to meet you on friendly terms and to let bygones be bygones.

HIGGINS (*furious*)   Is she, by George? Ho!

MRS HIGGINS   If you promise to behave yourself, Henry, I'll ask her to come down. If not, go home; for you have taken up quite enough of my time.

HIGGINS   Oh, all right. Very well. Pick: you behave yourself. Let us put on our best Sunday manners for this creature that we picked out of the mud. (*He flings himself sulkily into the Elizabethan chair.*)

DOOLITTLE (*remonstrating*)   Now, now, Henry Higgins! have some consideration for my feelings as a middle class man.

MRS HIGGINS   Remember your promise, Henry. (*She presses the bell-button on the writing-table.*) Mr Doolittle: will you be so good as to step out on the balcony for a moment. I dont want Eliza to have the shock of your news until she has made it up with these two gentlemen. Would you mind?

DOOLITTLE   As you wish, lady. Anything to help Henry to keep her off my hands. (*He disappears through the window.*)

THE PARLOR-MAID *answers the bell.* PICKERING *sits down in* DOOLITTLE'S *place.*

MRS HIGGINS   Ask Miss Doolittle to come down, please.

THE PARLOR-MAID   Yes, maam. (*She goes out.*)

MRS HIGGINS   Now, Henry: be good.

HIGGINS   I am behaving myself perfectly.

PICKERING   He is doing his best, Mrs Higgins.

A pause. HIGGINS *throws back his head; stretches out his legs; and begins to whistle.*

MRS HIGGINS   Henry, dearest, you dont look at all nice in that attitude.

HIGGINS (*pulling himself together*)   I was not trying to look nice, mother.

MRS HIGGINS   It doesnt matter, dear. I only wanted to make you speak.

HIGGINS   Why?

MRS HIGGINS   Because you cant speak and whistle at the same time.

HIGGINS *groans. Another very trying pause.*

HIGGINS (*springing up, out of patience*)   Where the devil is that girl? Are we to wait here all day?

ELIZA *enters, sunny, self-possessed, and giving a staggeringly convincing exhibition of ease of manner. She carries a little work-basket, and is very much at home.* PICKERING *is too much taken aback to rise.*

LIZA   How do you do, Professor Higgins? Are you quite well?

HIGGINS (*choking*)   Am I— (*He can say no more.*)

LIZA   But of course you are: you are never ill. So glad to see you again, Colonel Pickering. (*He rises hastily; and they shake hands.*) Quite chilly this morning, isnt it? (*She sits down on his left. He sits beside her.*)

HIGGINS   Dont you dare try this game on me. I taught it to you; and it doesnt take me in. Get up and come home; and dont be a fool.

ELIZA *takes a piece of needlework from her basket, and begins to stitch at it, without taking the least notice of this outburst.*

MRS HIGGINS   Very nicely put, indeed, Henry. No woman could resist such an invitation.

HIGGINS   You let her alone, mother. Let her speak for herself. You will jolly soon see whether she has an idea that I havnt put into her head or a word that I havnt put into her mouth. I tell you I have created this thing out of the squashed cabbage leaves of Covent Garden; and now she pretends to play the fine lady with me.

MRS HIGGINS (*placidly*)   Yes, dear, but youll sit down, wont you?

HIGGINS *sits down again, savagely.*

LIZA (*to* PICKERING, *taking no apparent notice of* HIGGINS, *and working away deftly*)   Will *you* drop me altogether now that the experiment is over, Colonel Pickering?

PICKERING   Oh dont. You mustnt think of it as an experiment. It shocks me, somehow.

LIZA   Oh, I'm only a squashed cabbage leaf—

PICKERING (*impulsively*)   No.

LIZA (*continuing quietly*)   —but I owe so much to you that I should be very unhappy if you forgot me.

PICKERING   It's very kind of you to say so, Miss Doolittle.

LIZA   It's not because you paid for my dresses. I know you are generous to everybody with money. But it was from you that I learnt really nice manners; and that is what makes one a lady, isnt it? You see it was so very difficult for me with the example of Professor Higgins always before me. I was brought up to be just like him, unable to control myself, and using bad language on the slightest

provocation. And I should never have known that ladies and gentlemen didnt behave like that if you hadnt been there.

HIGGINS   Well!!

PICKERING   Oh, thats only his way, you know. He doesnt mean it.

LIZA   Oh, *I* didnt mean it either, when I was a flower girl. It was only
my way. But you see I did it; and thats what makes the difference
after all.

PICKERING   No doubt. Still, he taught you to speak; and I couldnt
have done that, you know.

LIZA (*trivially*)   Of course: that is his profession.

HIGGINS   Damnation!

LIZA (*continuing*)   It was just like learning to dance in the fashionable way: there was nothing more than that in it. But do you know
what began my real education?

PICKERING   What?

LIZA (*stopping her work for a moment*)   Your calling me Miss Doolittle that day when I first came to Wimpole Street. That was the
beginning of self-respect for me. (*She resumes her stitching.*) And
there were a hundred little things you never noticed, because they
came naturally to you. Things about standing up and taking off your
hat and opening doors—

PICKERING   Oh, that was nothing.

LIZA   Yes: things that shewed you thought and felt about me as if I
were something better than a scullery-maid; though of course I
know you would have been just the same to a scullery-maid if she
had been let into the drawing room. You never took off your boots
in the dining room when I was there.

PICKERING   You mustnt mind that. Higgins takes off his boots all
over the place.

LIZA   I know. I am not blaming him. It is his way, isnt it? But it made
such a difference to me that you didnt do it. You see, really and
truly, apart from the things anyone can pick up (the dressing and
the proper way of speaking, and so on), the difference between a
lady and a flower girl is not how she behaves, but how she's treated.
I shall always be a flower girl to Professor Higgins, because he
always treats me as a flower girl, and always will; but I know I can
be a lady to you, because you always treat me as a lady, and always
will.

MRS HIGGINS   Please dont grind your teeth, Henry.

PICKERING   Well, this is really very nice of you, Miss Doolittle.

LIZA   I should like you to call me Eliza, now, if you would.

PICKERING   Thank you. Eliza, of course.

LIZA   And I should like Professor Higgins to call me Miss Doolittle.

HIGGINS   I'll see you damned first.

MRS HIGGINS   Henry! Henry!

PICKERING (*laughing*)   Why dont you slang back at him? Dont stand it. It would do him a lot of good.

LIZA   I cant. I could have done it once; but now I cant go back to it. Last night, when I was wandering about, a girl spoke to me; and I tried to get back into the old way with her; but it was no use. You told me, you know, that when a child is brought to a foreign country, it picks up the language in a few weeks, and forgets its own. Well, I am a child in your country. I have forgotten my own language, and can speak nothing but yours. Thats the real break-off with the corner of Tottenham Court Road. Leaving Wimpole Street finishes it.

PICKERING (*much alarmed*)   Oh! but youre coming back to Wimpole Street, arnt you? Youll forgive Higgins?

HIGGINS (*rising*)   Forgive! Will she, by George! Let her go. Let her find out how she can get on without us. She will relapse into the gutter in three weeks without me at her elbow.

DOOLITTLE *appears at the centre window. With a look of dignified reproach at* HIGGINS, *he comes slowly and silently to his daughter, who, with her back to the window, is unconscious of his approach.*

PICKERING   He's incorrigible, Eliza. You wont relapse, will you?

LIZA   No: not now. Never again. I have learnt my lesson. I dont believe I could utter one of the old sounds if I tried. (DOOLITTLE *touches her on her left shoulder. She drops her work, losing her self-possession utterly at the spectacle of her father's splendor.*) A-a-a-a-ah-ow-ooh!

HIGGINS (*with a crow of triumph*)   Aha! Just so. A-a-a-a-ahowooh! A-a-a-a-ahowooh! A-a-a-a-ahowooh! Victory! Victory! (*He throws himself on the divan, folding his arms, and spraddling arrogantly.*)

DOOLITTLE   Can you blame the girl? Dont look at me like that, Eliza. It aint my fault. Ive come into some money.

LIZA   You must have touched a millionaire this time, dad.

DOOLITTLE   I have. But I'm dressed something special today. I'm going to St George's, Hanover Square. Your stepmother is going to marry me.

LIZA (*angrily*)   Youre going to let yourself down to marry that low common woman!

PICKERING (*quietly*)   He ought to, Eliza. (*To* DOOLITTLE) Why has she changed her mind?

DOOLITTLE (*sadly*)   Intimidated, Governor. Intimidated. Middle class morality claims its victim. Wont you put on your hat, Liza, and come and see me turned off?

LIZA   If the Colonel says I must, I—I'll (*almost sobbing*) I'll demean myself. And get insulted for my pains, like enough.

DOOLITTLE   Dont be afraid: she never comes to words with anyone now, poor woman! respectability has broke all the spirit out of her.

PICKERING (*squeezing* ELIZA's *elbow gently*).   Be kind to them, Eliza. Make the best of it.

LIZA (*forcing a little smile for him through her vexation*)   Oh well, just to shew theres no ill feeling. I'll be back in a moment. (*She goes out.*)

DOOLITTLE (*sitting down beside* PICKERING)   I feel uncommon nervous about the ceremony, Colonel. I wish youd come and see me through it.

PICKERING   But youve been through it before, man. You were married to Eliza's mother.

DOOLITTLE   Who told you that, Colonel?

PICKERING   Well, nobody told me. But I concluded—naturally—

DOOLITTLE   No: that aint the natural way, Colonel: it's only the middle class way. My way was always the undeserving way. But dont say nothing to Eliza. She dont know: I always had a delicacy about telling her.

PICKERING   Quite right. We'll leave it so, if you dont mind.

DOOLITTLE   And youll come to the church, Colonel, and put me through straight?

PICKERING   With pleasure. As far as a bachelor can.

MRS HIGGINS   May I come, Mr Doolittle? I should be very sorry to miss your wedding.

DOOLITTLE   I should indeed be honored by your condescension, maam; and my poor old woman would take it as a tremenjous compliment. She's been very low, thinking of the happy days that are no more.

MRS HIGGINS (*rising*)   I'll order the carriage and get ready. (*The men rise, except* HIGGINS.) I shant be more than fifteen minutes. (*As she goes to the door* ELIZA *comes in, hatted and buttoning her gloves.*) I'm going to the church to see your father married, Eliza. You had

better come in the brougham with me. Colonel Pickering can go
on with the bridegroom.

MRS HIGGINS *goes out.* ELIZA *comes to the middle of the room between
the centre window and the ottoman.* PICKERING *joins her.*

DOOLITTLE   Bridegroom! What a word! It makes a man realize his
position, somehow. (*He takes up his hat and goes towards the door.*)

PICKERING   Before I go, Eliza, do forgive him and come back to us.

LIZA   I dont think papa would allow me. Would you, dad?

DOOLITTLE (*sad but magnanimous*)   They played you off very cunning, Eliza, them two sportsmen. If it had been only one of them,
you could have nailed him. But you see, there was two; and one of
them chaperoned the other, as you might say. (*To* PICKERING) It
was artful of you, Colonel; but I bear no malice: I should have done
the same myself. I been the victim of one woman after another all
my life; and I dont grudge you two getting the better of Eliza. I
shant interfere. It's time for us to go, Colonel. So long, Henry. See
you in St George's, Eliza. (*He goes out.*)

PICKERING (*coaxing*)   Do stay with us, Eliza. (*He follows* DOOLIT-
TLE.)

ELIZA *goes out on the balcony to avoid being alone with* HIGGINS. *He
rises and joins her there. She immediately comes back into the room
and makes for the door; but he goes along the balcony quickly and
gets his back to the door before she reaches it.*

HIGGINS   Well, Eliza, youve had a bit of your own back, as you call
it. Have you had enough? and are you going to be reasonable? Or
do you want any more?

LIZA   You want me back only to pick up your slippers and put up
with your tempers and fetch and carry for you.

HIGGINS   I havnt said I wanted you back at all.

LIZA   Oh, indeed. Then what are we talking about?

HIGGINS   About you, not about me. If you come back I shall treat you
just as I have always treated you. I cant change my nature; and I
dont intend to change my manners. My manners are exactly the same
as Colonel Pickering's.

LIZA   Thats not true. He treats a flower girl as if she was a duchess.

HIGGINS   And I treat a duchess as if she was a flower girl.

LIZA   I see. (*She turns away composedly, and sits on the ottoman,
facing the window.*) The same to everybody.

HIGGINS.   Just so.

LIZA   Like father.

HIGGINS (*grinning, a little taken down*)   Without accepting the comparison at all points, Eliza, it's quite true that your father is not a snob, and that he will be quite at home in any station of life to which his eccentric destiny may call him. (*Seriously*) The great secret, Eliza, is not having bad manners or good manners or any other particular sort of manners, but having the same manner for all human souls: in short, behaving as if you were in Heaven, where there are no third-class carriages, and one soul is as good as another.

LIZA   Amen. You are a born preacher.

HIGGINS (*irritated*)   The question is not whether I treat you rudely, but whether you ever heard me treat anyone else better.

LIZA (*with sudden sincerity*)   I dont care how you treat me. I dont mind your swearing at me. I dont mind a black eye: Ive had one before this. But (*standing up and facing him*) I wont be passed over.

HIGGINS   Then get out of my way; for I wont stop for you. You talk about me as if I were a motor bus.

LIZA   So you are a motor bus: all bounce and go, and no consideration for anyone. But I can do without you: dont think I cant.

HIGGINS   I know you can. I told you you could.

LIZA (*wounded, getting away from him to the other side of the ottoman with her face to the hearth*)   I know you did, you brute. You wanted to get rid of me.

HIGGINS   Liar.

LIZA   Thank you. (*She sits down with dignity.*)

HIGGINS   You never asked yourself, I suppose, whether *I* could do without you.

LIZA (*earnestly*)   Dont you try to get round me. Youll *have* to do without me.

HIGGINS (*arrogant*)   I can do without anybody. I have my own soul: my own spark of divine fire. But (*with sudden humility*) I shall miss you, Eliza. (*He sits down near her on the ottoman.*) I have learnt something from your idiotic notions: I confess that humbly and gratefully. And I have grown accustomed to your voice and appearance. I like them, rather.

LIZA   Well, you have both of them on your gramophone and in your book of photographs. When you feel lonely without me, you can turn the machine on. It's got no feelings to hurt.

HIGGINS   I cant turn your soul on. Leave me those feelings; and you can take away the voice and the face. They are not you.

LIZA   Oh, you *are* a devil. You can twist the heart in a girl as easy as some could twist her arms to hurt her. Mrs Pearce warned me. Time and again she has wanted to leave you; and you always got round her at the last minute. And you dont care a bit for her. And you dont care a bit for me.

HIGGINS   I care for life, for humanity; and you are a part of it that has come my way and been built into my house. What more can you or anyone ask?

LIZA   I wont care for anybody that doesnt care for me.

HIGGINS   Commercial principles, Eliza. Like (*reproducing her Covent Garden pronunciation with professional exactness*) s'yollin voylets (*selling violets*), isnt it?

LIZA   Dont sneer at me. It's mean to sneer at me.

HIGGINS   I have never sneered in my life. Sneering doesnt become either the human face or the human soul. I am expressing my righteous contempt for Commercialism. I dont and wont trade in affection. You call me a brute because you couldnt buy a claim on me by fetching my slippers and finding my spectacles. You were a fool: I think a woman fetching a man's slippers is a disgusting sight: did I ever fetch *your* slippers? I think a good deal more of you for throwing them in my face. No use slaving for me and then saying you want to be cared for: who cares for a slave? If you come back, come back for the sake of good fellowship; for youll get nothing else. Youve had a thousand times as much out of me as I have out of you; and if you dare to set up your little dog's tricks of fetching and carrying slippers against my creation of a Duchess Eliza, I'll slam the door in your silly face.

LIZA   What did you do it for if you didnt care for me?

HIGGINS   (*heartily*)   Why, because it was my job.

LIZA   You never thought of the trouble it would make for me.

HIGGINS   Would the world ever have been made if its maker had been afraid of making trouble? Making life means making trouble. Theres only one way of escaping trouble; and thats killing things. Cowards, you notice, are always shrieking to have troublesome people killed.

LIZA   I'm no preacher: I dont notice things like that. I notice that you dont notice me.

HIGGINS (*jumping up and walking about intolerantly*) Eliza: youre an idiot. I waste the treasures of my Miltonic mind by spreading them before you. Once for all, understand that I go my way and do my work without caring twopence what happens to either of us. I am not intimidated, like your father and your stepmother. So you can come back or go to the devil: which you please.

LIZA What am I to come back for?

HIGGINS (*bouncing up on his knees on the ottoman and leaning over it to her*). For the fun of it. Thats why I took you on.

LIZA (*with averted face*). And you may throw me out to-morrow if I dont do everything you want me to?

HIGGINS Yes; and you may walk out to-morrow if I dont do everything *you* want me to.

LIZA And live with my stepmother?

HIGGINS Yes, or sell flowers.

LIZA Oh! if I only *could* go back to my flower basket! I should be independent of both you and father and all the world! Why did you take my independence from me? Why did I give it up? I'm a slave now, for all my fine clothes.

HIGGINS Not a bit. I'll adopt you as my daughter and settle money on you if you like. Or would you rather marry Pickering?

LIZA (*looking fiercely round at him*) I wouldnt marry *you* if you asked me; and youre nearer my age than what he is.

HIGGINS (*gently*) Than he is: not "than what he is."

LIZA (*losing her temper and rising*) I'll talk as I like. Youre not my teacher now.

HIGGINS (*reflectively*) I dont suppose Pickering would, though. He's as confirmed an old bachelor as I am.

LIZA Thats not what I want; and dont you think it. Ive always had chaps enough wanting me that way. Freddy Hill writes to me twice and three times a day, sheets and sheets.

HIGGINS (*disagreeably surprised*) Damn his impudence! (*He recoils and finds himself sitting on his heels.*)

LIZA He has a right to if he likes, poor lad. And he does love me.

HIGGINS (*getting off the ottoman*) You have no right to encourage him.

LIZA Every girl has a right to be loved.

HIGGINS What! By fools like that?

LIZA Freddy's not a fool. And if he's weak and poor and wants me, may be he'd make me happier than my betters that bully me and dont want me.

HIGGINS   Can he *make* anything of you? Thats the point.

LIZA   Perhaps I could make something of him. But I never thought of us making anything of one another; and you never think of anything else. I only want to be natural.

HIGGINS   In short, you want me to be as infatuated about you as Freddy? Is that it?

LIZA   No I dont. Thats not the sort of feeling I want from you. And dont you be too sure of yourself or of me. I could have been a bad girl if I'd liked. Ive seen more of some things than you, for all your learning. Girls like me can drag gentlemen down to make love to them easy enough. And they wish each other dead the next minute.

HIGGINS   Of course they do. Then what in thunder are we quarrelling about?

LIZA   (*much troubled*)   I want a little kindness. I know I'm a common ignorant girl, and you a book-learned gentleman; but I'm not dirt under your feet. What I done (*correcting herself*) what I did was not for the dresses and the taxis: I did it because we were pleasant together and I come—came—to care for you; not to want you to make love to me, and not forgetting the difference between us, but more friendly like.

HIGGINS   Well, of course. Thats just how I feel. And how Pickering feels. Eliza: youre a fool.

LIZA   Thats not a proper answer to give me. (*She sinks on the chair at the writing-table in tears.*)

HIGGINS   It's all youll get until you stop being a common idiot. If youre going to be a lady, youll have to give up feeling neglected if the men you know dont spend half their time snivelling over you and the other half giving you black eyes. If you cant stand the coldness of my sort of life, and the strain of it, go back to the gutter. Work til you are more a brute than a human being; and then cuddle and squabble and drink til you fall asleep. Oh, it's a fine life, the life of the gutter. It's real: it's warm: it's violent: you can feel it through the thickest skin: you can taste it and smell it without any training or any work. Not like Science and Literature and Classical Music and Philosophy and Art. You find me cold, unfeeling, selfish, dont you? Very well: be off with you to the sort of people you like. Marry some sentimental hog or other with lots of money, and a thick pair of lips to kiss you with and a thick pair of boots to kick you with. If you cant appreciate what youve got, youd better get what you can appreciate.

LIZA (*desperate*) Oh, you *are* a cruel tyrant. I cant talk to you: you turn everything against me: I'm always in the wrong. But you know very well all the time that youre nothing but a bully. You know I cant go back to the gutter, as you call it, and that I have no real friends in the world but you and the Colonel. You know well I couldnt bear to live with a low common man after you two; and it's wicked and cruel of you to insult me by pretending I could. You think I must go back to Wimpole Street because I have nowhere else to go but father's. But dont you be too sure that you have me under your feet to be trampled on and talked down. I'll marry Freddy, I will, as soon as he's able to support me.

HIGGINS (*sitting down beside her*) Rubbish! You shall marry an ambassador. You shall marry the Governor-General of India or the Lord-Lieutenant of Ireland, or somebody who wants a deputy-queen. I'm not going to have my masterpiece thrown away on Freddy.

LIZA You think I like you to say that. But I havnt forgot what you said a minute ago; and I wont be coaxed round as if I was a baby or a puppy. If I cant have kindness, I'll have independence.

HIGGINS Independence? Thats middle class blasphemy. We are all dependent on one another, every soul of us on earth.

LIZA (*rising determinedly*) I'll let you see whether I'm dependent on you. If you can preach, I can teach. I'll go and be a teacher.

HIGGINS Whatll you teach, in heaven's name?

LIZA What you taught me. I'll teach phonetics.

HIGGINS Ha! ha! ha!

LIZA I'll offer myself as an assistant to Professor Nepean.

HIGGINS (*rising in a fury*) What! That impostor! that humbug! that toadying ignoramus! Teach him *my* methods! *my* discoveries! You take one step in his direction and I'll wring your neck. (*He lays hands on her.*) Do you hear?

LIZA (*defiantly non-resistant*) Wring away. What do I care? I knew youd strike me some day.

He lets her go, stamping with rage at having forgotten himself, and recoils so hastily that he stumbles back into his seat on the ottoman.

Aha! Now I know how to deal with you. What a fool I was not to think of it before! You cant take away the knowledge you gave me.

You said I had a finer ear than you. And I can be civil and kind to people, which is more than you can. Aha! Thats done you, Henry Higgins, it has. Now I dont care *that* (*snapping her fingers*) for your bullying and your big talk. I'll advertize it in the papers that your duchess is only a flower girl that you taught, and that she'll teach anybody to be a duchess just the same in six months for a thousand guineas. Oh, when I think of myself crawling under your feet and being trampled on and called names, when all the time I had only to lift up my finger to be as good as you, I could just kick myself.

HIGGINS (*wondering at her*) You damned impudent slut, you! But it's better than snivelling; better than fetching slippers and finding spectacles, isnt it? (*Rising*) By George, Eliza, I said I'd make a woman of you; and I have. I like you like this.

LIZA Yes: you turn round and make up to me now that I'm not afraid of you, and can do without you.

HIGGINS Of course I do, you little fool. Five minutes ago you were like a millstone round my neck. Now youre a tower of strength: a consort battleship. You and I and Pickering will be three old bachelors together instead of only two men and a silly girl.

MRS HIGGINS *returns, dressed for the wedding.* ELIZA *instantly becomes cool and elegant.*

MRS HIGGINS The carriage is waiting, Eliza. Are you ready?

LIZA Quite. Is the Professor coming?

MRS HIGGINS Certainly not. He cant behave himself in church. He makes remarks out loud all the time on the clergyman's pronunciation.

LIZA Then I shall not see you again, Professor. Goodbye. (*She goes to the door.*)

MRS HIGGGINS (*coming to* HIGGINS) Goodbye, dear.

HIGGINS Goodbye, mother. (*He is about to kiss her, when he recollects something.*) Oh, by the way, Eliza, order a ham and a Stilton cheese, will you? And buy me a pair of reindeer gloves, number eights, and a tie to match that new suit of mine, at Eale & Binman's. You can choose the color. (*His cheerful, careless, vigorous voice shows that he is incorrigible.*)

LIZA (*disdainfully*) Buy them yourself. (*She sweeps out.*)

MRS HIGGINS I'm afraid youve spoiled that girl, Henry. But never mind, dear: I'll buy you the tie and gloves.

HIGGINS (*sunnily*) Oh, dont bother. She'll buy em all right enough. Goodbye.

They kiss. MRS HIGGINS *runs out.* HIGGINS, *left alone, rattles his cash in his pocket; chuckles; and disports himself in a highly self-satisfied manner.*

The rest of the story need not be shewn in action, and indeed, would hardly need telling if our imaginations were not so enfeebled by their lazy dependence on the ready-mades and reach-me-downs of the rag-shop in which Romance keeps its stock of "happy endings" to misfit all stories. Now, the history of Eliza Doolittle, though called a romance because the transfiguration it records seems exceedingly improbable, is common enough. Such transfigurations have been achieved by hundreds of resolutely ambitious young women since Nell Gwynne[7] set them the example by playing queens and fascinating kings in the theatre in which she began by selling oranges. Nevertheless, people in all directions have assumed, for no other reason than that she became the heroine of a romance, that she must have married the hero of it. This is unbearable, not only because her little drama, if acted on such a thoughtless assumption, must be spoiled, but because the true sequel is patent to anyone with a sense of human nature in general, and of feminine instinct in particular.

Eliza, in telling Higgins she would not marry him if he asked her, was not coquetting: she was announcing a well-considered decision. When a bachelor interests, and dominates, and teaches, and becomes important to a spinster, as Higgins with Eliza, she always, if she has character enough to be capable of it, considers very seriously indeed whether she will play for becoming that bachelor's wife, especially if he is so little interested in marriage that a determined and devoted woman might capture him if she set herself resolutely to do it. Her decision will depend a good deal on whether she is really free to choose; and that, again, will depend on her age and income. If she is at the end of her youth, and has no security for her livelihood, she will marry him because she must marry anybody who will provide for her. But at Eliza's age a good-looking girl does not feel that pressure: she feels free to pick and choose. She is therefore guided by her instinct in the matter. Eliza's instinct tells her not to marry Hig-

---

[7] Nell Gwynne or Gwyn (1652–87), English actress and mistress of Charles II, was a great favorite with the public as well.

gins. It does not tell her to give him up. It is not in the slightest doubt as to his remaining one of the strongest personal interests in her life. It would be very sorely strained if there was another woman likely to supplant her with him. But as she feels sure of him on that last point, she has no doubt at all as to her course, and would not have any, even if the difference of twenty years in age, which seems so great to youth, did not exist between them.

As our own instincts are not appealed to by her conclusion, let us see whether we cannot discover some reason in it. When Higgins excused his indifference to young women on the ground that they had an irresistible rival in his mother, he gave the clue to his inveterate old-bachelordom. The case is uncommon only to the extent that remarkable mothers are uncommon. If an imaginative boy has a sufficiently rich mother who has intelligence, personal grace, dignity of character without harshness, and a cultivated sense of the best art of her time to enable her to make her house beautiful, she sets a standard for him against which very few women can struggle, besides effecting for him a disengagement of his affections, his sense of beauty, and his idealism from his specifically sexual impulses. This makes him a standing puzzle to the huge number of uncultivated people who have been brought up in tasteless homes by commonplace or disagreeable parents, and to whom, consequently, literature, painting, sculpture, music, and affectionate personal relations come as modes of sex if they come at all. The word passion means nothing else to them; and that Higgins could have a passion for phonetics and idealize his mother instead of Eliza, would seem to them absurd and unnatural. Nevertheless, when we look round and see that hardly anyone is too ugly or disagreeable to find a wife or a husband if he or she wants one, whilst many old maids and bachelors are above the average in quality and culture, we cannot help suspecting that the disentanglement of sex from the associations with which it is so commonly confused, a disentanglement which persons of genius achieve by sheer intellectual analysis, is sometimes produced or aided by parental fascination.

Now, though Eliza was incapable of thus explaining to herself Higgins's formidable powers of resistance to the charm that prostrated Freddy at the first glance, she was instinctively aware that she could never obtain a complete grip of him, or come between him and his mother (the first necessity of the married woman). To put it shortly, she knew that for some mysterious reason he had not the makings of a married man in him, according to her conception of a husband as one to whom she would be his nearest and fondest and warmest interest. Even had there been no mother-rival, she would still have refused to accept an interest in herself that was secondary to philosophic interests. Had Mrs Higgins died, there would still have been Milton and the Universal Alphabet. Landor's[8] remark that to those who have the greatest power of loving, love is a secondary affair, would not have recommended Landor to Eliza. Put that along with her resentment of Higgins's domineering superiority, and her mistrust of his coaxing cleverness in getting round her and evading her wrath when he had gone too far with his impetuous bullying, and you will see that Eliza's instinct had good grounds for warning her not to marry her Pygmalion.

And now, whom did Eliza marry? For if Higgins was a predestinate old bachelor, she was most certainly not a predestinate old maid. Well, that can be told very shortly to those who have not guessed it from the indications she has herself given them.

Almost immediately after Eliza is stung into proclaiming her considered determination not to marry Higgins, she mentions the fact that young Mr Frederick Eynsford Hill is pouring out his love for her daily through the post. Now Freddy is young, practically twenty years younger than Higgins: he is a gentleman (or, as Eliza would qualify him, a toff), and speaks like one; he is nicely dressed, is treated by the Colonel as an equal, loves her unaffectedly, and is not her master, nor ever likely to dominate her in spite of his advantage of social standing. Eliza has no use for the foolish romantic tradition that all women love to be mastered, if not actually bullied and beaten. "When you go to women," says Nietzsche,[9] "take your whip with you." Sensible despots have never confined that precaution to women: they have taken their whips with them when they have dealt with men, and been slavishly idealized by the men over whom they have flourished the whip much more than by women. No doubt there are slavish women as well as slavish men: and women, like men, admire those that are stronger than themselves. But to admire a strong person and to live under that strong person's thumb are two different things. The weak may not be admired and hero-worshipped; but they are by no means disliked or shunned; and they never seem to have the least difficulty in marrying

[8] Presumably Walter Savage Landor (1775–1864), an English poet, critic, and prose writer.
[9] Frederick Wilhelm Nietzsche (1844–1900) was a German philosopher and poet whose ideal conception of man made him despise the weak and the rabble, defy Christianity, and demand the training of a race of "supermen."

people who are too good for them. They may fail in emergencies; but life is not one long emergency: it is mostly a string of situations for which no exceptional strength is needed, and with which even rather weak people can cope if they have a stronger partner to help them out. Accordingly, it is a truth everywhere in evidence that strong people, masculine or feminine, not only do not marry stronger people, but do not shew any preference for them in selecting their friends. When a lion meets another with a louder roar "the first lion thinks the last a bore." The man or woman who feels strong enough for two, seeks for every other quality in a partner than strength.

The converse is also true. Weak people want to marry strong people who do not frighten them too much; and this often leads them to make the mistake we describe metaphorically as "biting off more than they can chew." They want too much for too little; and when the bargain is unreasonable beyond all bearing, the union becomes impossible: it ends in the weaker party being either discarded or borne as a cross, which is worse. People who are not only weak, but silly or obtuse as well, are often in these difficulties.

This being the state of human affairs, what is Eliza fairly sure to do when she is placed between Freddy and Higgins? Will she look forward to a lifetime of fetching Higgins's slippers or to a lifetime of Freddy fetching hers? There can be no doubt about the answer. Unless Freddy is biologically repulsive to her, and Higgins biologically attractive to a degree that overwhelms all her other instincts, she will, if she marries either of them, marry Freddy.

And that is just what Eliza did.

Complications ensued; but they were economic, not romantic. Freddy had no money and no occupation. His mother's jointure, a last relic of the opulence of Largelady Park, had enabled her to struggle along in Earlscourt with an air of gentility, but not to procure any serious secondary education for her children, much less give the boy a profession. A clerkship at thirty shillings a week was beneath Freddy's dignity, and extremely distasteful to him besides. His prospects consisted of a hope that if he kept up appearances somebody would do something for him. The something appeared vaguely to his imagination as a private secretaryship or a sinecure of some sort. To his mother it perhaps appeared as a marriage to some lady of means who could not resist her boy's niceness. Fancy her feelings when he married a flower girl who had become déclassée under extraordinary circumstances which were now notorious!

It is true that Eliza's situation did not seem wholly ineligible. Her father, though formerly a dustman, and now fantastically disclassed, had become extremely popular in the smartest society by a social talent which triumphed over every prejudice and every disadvantage. Rejected by the middle class, which he loathed, he had shot up at once into the highest circles by his wit, his dustmanship (which he carried like a banner), and his Nietzschean transcendence of good and evil. At intimate ducal dinners he sat on the right hand of the Duchess; and in country houses he smoked in the pantry and was made much of by the butler when he was not feeding in the dining room and being consulted by cabinet ministers. But he found it almost as hard to do all this on four thousand a year as Mrs Eynsford Hill to live in Earlscourt on an income so pitiably smaller that I have not the heart to disclose its exact figure. He absolutely refused to add the last straw to his burden by contributing to Eliza's support.

Thus Freddy and Eliza, now Mr and Mrs Eynsford Hill, would have spent a penniless honeymoon but for a wedding present of £500 from the Colonel to Eliza. It lasted a long time because Freddy did not know how to spend money, never having had any to spend, and Eliza, socially trained by a pair of old bachelors, wore her clothes as long as they held together and looked pretty, without the least regard to their being many months out of fashion. Still, £500 will not last two young people for ever; and they both knew, and Eliza felt as well, that they must shift for themselves in the end. She could quarter herself on Wimpole Street because it had come to be her home; but she was quite aware that she ought not to quarter Freddy there, and that it would not be good for his character if she did.

Not that the Wimpole Street bachelors objected. When she consulted them, Higgins declined to be bothered about her housing problem when that solution was so simple. Eliza's desire to have Freddy in the house with her seemed of no more importance than if she had wanted an extra piece of bedroom furniture. Pleas as to Freddy's character, and the moral obligation on him to earn his own living, were lost on Higgins. He denied that Freddy had any character, and declared that if he tried to do any useful work some competent person would have the trouble of undoing it: a procedure involving a net loss to the community, and great unhappiness to Freddy himself, who was obviously intended by Nature for such light work as amusing Eliza, which, Higgins declared, was a much more useful and honorable occupation than working in the city. When Eliza referred again to her project of teaching phonetics, Higgins abated not a jot of his violent opposition to it. He said she was not within ten years of being qualified to meddle with his pet subject; and as it was evident that the Colonel agreed with him, she felt she could not go against them in this grave matter, and that she had no right, without Higgins's consent, to exploit the knowledge he had given her; for his knowledge seemed to her as much his private property as his watch: Eliza was no communist. Besides, she was superstitiously devoted to them both, more entirely and frankly after her marriage than before it.

It was the Colonel who finally solved the problem, which had cost him much perplexed cogitation. He one day asked Eliza, rather shyly, whether she had quite given up her notion of keeping a flower shop. She replied that she had thought of it, but had put it out of her head, because the Colonel had said, that day at Mrs Higgins's, that it would never do. The Colonel confessed that when he said that, he had not quite recovered from the dazzling impression of the day before. They broke the matter to Higgins that evening. The sole comment vouchsafed by him very nearly led to a serious quarrel with Eliza. It was to the effect that she would have in Freddy an ideal errand boy.

Freddy himself was next sounded on the subject. He said he had been thinking of a shop himself; though it had presented itself to his pennilessness as a small place in which Eliza should sell tobacco at one counter whilst he sold newspapers at the opposite one. But he agreed that it would be extraordinarily jolly to go early every morning with Eliza to Covent Garden and buy flowers on the scene of their first meeting: a sentiment which earned him many kisses from his wife. He added that he had always been afraid to propose anything of the sort, because Clara would make an awful row about a step that must damage her matrimonial chances, and his mother could not be expected to like it after clinging for so many years to that step of the social ladder on which retail trade is impossible.

This difficulty was removed by an event highly unexpected by Freddy's mother. Clara, in the course of her incursions into those artistic circles which were the highest within her reach, discovered that her conversational qualifications were expected to include a grounding on the novels of Mr H. G. Wells.[10] She borrowed them in various directions so energetically that she swallowed them all within two months. The result was a conversion of a kind quite common today.

[10] His criticisms of twentieth-century society and his predictions for the future, such as air warfare and atomic bombs, aroused much controversy.

A modern Acts of the Apostles would fill fifty whole Bibles if anyone were capable of writing it.

Poor Clara, who appeared to Higgins and his mother as a disagreeable and ridiculous person, and to her own mother as in some inexplicable way a social failure, had never seen herself in either light; for, though to some extent ridiculed and mimicked in West Kensington like everybody else there, she was accepted as a rational and normal—or shall we say inevitable?—sort of human being. At worst they called her The Pusher; but to them no more than to herself had it ever occurred that she was pushing the air, and pushing it in a wrong direction. Still, she was not happy. She was growing desperate. Her one asset, the fact that her mother was what the Epsom greengrocer called a carriage lady, had no exchange value, apparently. It had prevented her from getting educated, because the only education she could have afforded was education with the Earlscourt greengrocer's daughter. It had led her to seek the society of her mother's class; and that class simply would not have her, because she was much poorer than the greengrocer, and, far from being able to afford a maid, could not afford even a housemaid, and had to scrape along at home with an illiberally treated general servant. Under such circumstances nothing could give her an air of being a genuine product of Largelady Park. And yet its tradition made her regard a marriage with anyone within her reach as an unbearable humiliation. Commercial people and professional people in a small way were odious to her. She ran after painters and novelists; but she did not charm them; and her bold attempts to pick up and practice artistic and literary talk irritated them. She was, in short, an utter failure, an ignorant, incompetent, pretentious, unwelcome, penniless, useless little snob; and though she did not admit these disqualifications (for nobody ever faces unpleasant truths of this kind until the possibility of a way out dawns on them) she felt their effects too keenly to be satisfied with her position.

Clara had a startling eyeopener when, on being suddenly wakened to enthusiasm by a girl of her own age who dazzled her and produced in her a gushing desire to take her for a model, and gain her friendship, she discovered that this exquisite apparition had graduated from the gutter in a few months time. It shook her so violently, that when Mr H. G. Wells lifted her on the point of his puissant pen, and placed her at the angle of view from which the life she was leading and the society to which she clung appeared in its true relation to real human needs and worthy social structure, he effected a conversion and a conviction of sin comparable to the most sensational feats of General Booth[11] or Gypsy Smith.[12] Clara's snobbery went bang. Life suddenly began to move with her. Without knowing how or why, she began to make friends and enemies. Some of the acquaintances to whom she had been a tedious or indifferent or ridiculous affliction, dropped her: others became cordial. To her amazement she found that some "quite nice" people were saturated with Wells, and that this accessibility to ideas was the secret of their niceness. People she had thought deeply religious, and had tried to conciliate on that tack with disastrous results, suddenly took an interest in her, and revealed a hostility to conventional religion which she had never conceived possible except among the most desperate characters. They made her read Galsworthy,[13] and Galsworthy exposed the vanity of Largelady Park and finished her. It exasperated her to think that the dungeon in which she had languished for so many unhappy years had been unlocked all the time, and that the impulses she had so carefully struggled with and stifled for the sake of keeping well with society, were precisely those by which alone she could have come into any sort of sincere human contact. In the radiance of these discoveries, and the tumult of their reaction, she made a fool of herself as freely and conspicuously as when she so rashly adopted Eliza's expletive in Mrs Higgins's drawing room; for the newborn Wellsian had to find her bearings almost as ridiculously as a baby; but nobody hates a baby for its ineptitudes, or thinks the worse of it for trying to eat the matches; and Clara lost no friends by her follies. They laughted at her to her face this time; and she had to defend herself and fight it out as best she could.

When Freddy paid a visit to Earlscourt (which he never did when he could possibly help it) to make the desolating announcement that he and his Eliza were thinking of blackening the Largelady scutcheon by opening a shop, he found the little household already convulsed by a prior announcement from Clara that she also was going to work in an old furniture shop in Dover Street, which had been started by a fellow Wellsian. This appointment Clara owed, after all, to her old social accomplishment of Push. She had made up her mind that, cost what it might, she would see Mr Wells in the flesh; and she had achieved her end at a garden party. She had better luck than so rash an enter-

---

[11] William Booth (1829–1912) was an English Methodist preacher who founded the Salvation Army in 1865.
[12] English evangelist (1860–1947).
[13] See Biographical Notes.

prise deserved. Mr Wells came up to her expectations. Age had not withered him, nor could custom stale his infinite variety in half an hour. His pleasant neatness and compactness, his small hands and feet, his teeming ready brain, his unaffected accessibility, and a certain fine apprehensiveness which stamped him as susceptible from his topmost hair to his tipmost toe, proved irresistible. Clara talked of nothing else for weeks and weeks afterwards. And as she happened to talk to the lady of the furniture shop, and that lady also desired above all things to know Mr Wells and sell pretty things to him, she offered Clara a job on the chance of achieving that end through her.

And so it came about that Eliza's luck held, and the expected opposition to the flower shop melted away. The shop is in the arcade of a railway station not very far from the Victoria and Albert Museum; and if you live in that neighborhood you may go there any day and buy a buttonhole from Eliza.

Now here is a last opportunity for romance. Would you not like to be assured that the shop was an immense success, thanks to Eliza's charms and her early business experience in Covent Garden? Alas! the truth is the truth: the shop did not pay for a long time, simply because Eliza and her Freddy did not know how to keep it. True, Eliza had not to begin at the very beginning: she knew the names and prices of the cheaper flowers; and her elation was unbounded when she found that Freddy, like all youths educated at cheap, pretentious, and thoroughly inefficient schools, knew a little Latin. It was very little, but enough to make him appear to her a Porson[14] or Bentley,[15] and to put him at his ease with botanical nomenclature. Unfortunately he knew nothing else; and Eliza, though she could count money up to eighteen shillings or so, and had acquired a certain familiarity with the language of Milton from her struggles to qualify herself for winning Higgins's bet, could not write out a bill without utterly disgracing the establishment. Freddy's power of stating in Latin that Balbus built a wall and that Gaul was divided into three parts did not carry with it the slightest knowledge of accounts or business: Colonel Pickering had to explain to him what a cheque book and a bank account meant. And the pair were by no means easily teachable. Freddy backed up Eliza in her obstinate refusal to believe that they could save money by engaging a

[14] Richard Porson (1759–1808) was an English classical scholar who was Regius Professor of Greek at Cambridge in 1792.
[15] Richard Bentley (1662–1742) was a famous English scholar, whom Swift satirized in *The Battle of the Books*.

bookkeeper with some knowledge of the business. How, they argued, could you possibly save money by going to extra expense when you already could not make both ends meet? But the Colonel, after making the ends meet over and over again, at last gently insisted; and Eliza, humbled to the dust by having to beg from him so often, and stung by the uproarious derision of Higgins, to whom the notion of Freddy succeeding at anything was a joke that never palled, grasped the fact that business, like phonetics, has to be learned.

On the piteous spectacle of the pair spending their evenings in short-hand schools and polytechnic classes, learning bookkeeping and type-writing with incipient junior clerks, male and female, from the ele-mentary schools, let me not dwell. There were even classes at the London School of Economics, and a humble personal appeal to the director of that institution to recommend a course bearing on the flower business. He, being a humorist, explained to them the method of the celebrated Dickensian essay on Chinese Metaphysics by the gentleman who read an article on China and an article on Metaphysics and combined the information. He suggested that they should combine the London School with Kew Gardens. Eliza, to whom the procedure of the Dickensian gentleman seemed perfectly correct (as in fact it was) and not in the least funny (which was only her ignorance), took his advice with entire gravity. But the effort that cost her the deepest hu-miliation was a request to Higgins, whose pet artistic fancy, next to Milton's verse, was calligraphy, and who himself wrote a most beautiful Italian hand, that he would teach her to write. He declared that she was congenitally incapable of forming a single letter worthy of the least of Milton's words; but she persisted; and again he suddenly threw himself into the task of teaching her with a combination of stormy intensity, concentrated patience, and occasional bursts of interesting disquisition on the beauty and nobility, the august mission and destiny, of human handwriting. Eliza ended by acquiring an extremely uncom-mercial script which was a positive extension of her personal beauty, and spending three times as much on stationery as anyone else because certain qualities and shapes of paper became indispensable to her. She could not even address an envelope in the usual way because it made the margins all wrong.

Their commercial schooldays were a period of disgrace and despair for the young couple. They seemed to be learning nothing about flower shops. At last they gave it up as hopeless, and shook the dust of the shorthand schools, and the polytechnics, and the London School of

Economics from their feet for ever. Besides, the business was in some mysterious way beginning to take care of itself. They had somehow forgotten their objections to employing other people. They came to the conclusion that their own way was the best, and that they had really a remarkable talent for business. The Colonel, who had been compelled for some years to keep a sufficient sum on current account at his bankers to make up their deficits, found that the provision was unnecessary: the young people were prospering. It is true that there was not quite fair play between them and their competitors in trade. Their week-ends in the country cost them nothing, and saved them the price of their Sunday dinners; for the motor car was the Colonel's; and he and Higgins paid the hotel bills. Mr F. Hill, florist and greengrocer (they soon discovered that there was money in asparagus; and asparagus led to other vegetables), had an air which stamped the business as classy; and in private life he was still Frederick Eynsford Hill, Esquire. Not that there was any swank about him: nobody but Eliza knew that he had been christened Frederick Challoner. Eliza herself swanked like anything.

That is all. That is how it has turned out. It is astonishing how much Eliza still manages to meddle in the housekeeping at Wimpole Street in spite of the shop and her own family. And it is notable that though she never nags her husband, and frankly loves the Colonel as if she were his favorite daughter, she has never got out of the habit of nagging Higgins that was established on the fatal night when she won his bet for him. She snaps his head off on the faintest provocation, or on none. He no longer dares to tease her by assuming an abysmal inferiority of Freddy's mind to his own. He storms and bullies and derides: but she stands up to him so ruthlessly that the Colonel has to ask her from time to time to be kinder to Higgins; and it is the only request of his that brings a mulish expression into her face. Nothing but some emergency or calamity great enough to break down all likes and dislikes, and throw them both back on their common humanity—and may they be spared any such trial!—will ever alter this. She knows that Higgins does not need her, just as her father did not need her. The very scrupulousness with which he told her that day that he had become used to having her there, and dependent on her for all sorts of little services, and that he should miss her if she went away (it would never have occurred to Freddy or the Colonel to say anything of the sort) deepens her inner certainty that she is "no more to him than them slippers"; yet she has a sense, too, that his indifference is deeper than the infatuation of commoner souls. She is immensely interested in him. She has even secret mischievous moments in which she wishes she could get him alone, on a desert island, away from all ties and with nobody else in the world to consider, and just drag him off his pedestal and see him making love like any common man. We all have private imaginations of that sort. But when it comes to business, to the life that she really leads as distinguished from the life of dreams and fancies, she likes Freddy and she likes the Colonel; and she does not like Higgins and Mr Doolittle. Galatea[16] never does quite like Pygmalion; his relation to her is too godlike to be altogether agreeable.

[16] In a Greek legend, a statue made by Pygmalion that was imbued with life but caused so much mischief, because of her lack of worldly knowledge, that she returned to her original state.

CHARACTERS

MICKEY MALOY

JAMIE CREGAN

SARA MELODY

NORA MELODY

CORNELIUS MELODY

DEBORAH (*Mrs. Henry Harford*)

DAN ROCHE

PADDY O'DOWD

PATCH RILEY

NICHOLAS GADSBY

SCENES

ACT 1   *Dining room of Melody's Tavern morning of July 27, 1828*

ACT 2   *The same, later that morning*

ACT 3   *The same, that evening*

ACT 4   *The same, that night*

A Touch of the Poet

Eugene O'Neill

ACT ONE

SCENE   *The dining room of Melody's Tavern, in a village a few miles from Boston. The tavern is over a hundred years old. It had once been prosperous, a breakfast stop for the stagecoach, but the stage line had been discontinued and for some years now the tavern has fallen upon neglected days.*

The dining room and barroom were once a single spacious room, low-ceilinged, with heavy oak beams and paneled walls—the taproom of the tavern in its prosperous days, now divided into two rooms by a flimsy partition, the barroom being off left. The partition is painted to imitate the old paneled walls but this only makes it more of an eyesore.

At left front, two steps lead up to a closed door opening on a flight of stairs to the floor above. Farther back is the door to the bar. Between these doors hangs a large mirror. Beyond the bar door a small cabinet is fastened to the wall. At rear are four windows. Between the middle two is the street door. At right front is another door, open, giving on a hallway and the main stairway to the second floor, and leading to the kitchen. Farther front at right, there is a high schoolmaster's desk with a stool.

In the foreground are two tables. One, with four chairs, at left center; a larger one, seating six, at right center. At left and right, rear, are two more tables, identical with the ones at right center. All these tables are set with white tablecloths, etc., except the small ones in the foreground at left.

It is around nine in the morning of July 27, 1828. Sunlight shines in through the windows at rear.

MICKEY MALOY *sits at the table at left front, facing right. He is glancing through a newspaper. Maloy is twenty-six, with a sturdy physique and an amiable, cunning face, his mouth usually set in a half-leering grin.*

JAMIE CREGAN *peers around the half-open door to the bar. Seeing Maloy, he comes in. As obviously Irish as Maloy, he is middle-aged, tall, with a lantern-jawed face. There is a scar of a saber cut over one cheekbone. He is dressed neatly but in old, worn clothes. His eyes are bloodshot, his manner sickly, but he grins as he greets Maloy sardonically.*

CREGAN   God bless all here—even the barkeep.

MALOY   (*with an answering grin*)   Top o' the mornin'.

CREGAN   Top o' me head. (*He puts his hand to his head and groans.*) Be the saints, there's a blacksmith at work on it!

MALOY   Small wonder. You'd the divil's own load when you left at two this mornin'.

CREGAN   I must have. I don't remember leaving. (*He sits at right of table.*) Faix, you're takin' it aisy.

MALOY   There's no trade this time o' day.

CREGAN   It was a great temptation, when I saw no one in the bar, to make off with a bottle. A hair av the dog is what I need, but I've divil a penny in my pantaloons.

MALOY   Have one on the house. (*He goes to the cupboard and takes out a decanter of whiskey and a glass.*)

CREGAN   Thank you kindly. Sure, the good Samaritan was a crool haythen beside you.

MALOY   (*putting the decanter and glass before him*)   It's the same you was drinking last night—his private dew. He keeps it here for emergencies when he don't want to go in the bar.

CREGAN   (*pours out a big drink*)   Lave it to Con never to be caught dry. (*Raising his glass*) Your health and inclinations—if they're virtuous! (*He drinks and sighs with relief.*) God bless you, Whiskey, it's you can rouse the dead! Con hasn't been down yet for his morning's morning?

MALOY   No. He won't be till later.

CREGAN   It's like a miracle, me meeting him again. I came to these parts looking for work. It's only by accident I heard talk of a Con Melody and come here to see was it him. Until last night, I'd not seen hide nor hair of him since the war with the French in Spain— after the battle of Salamanca in '12. I was a corporal in the Seventh Dragoons and he was major. (*Proudly*) I got this cut from a saber at

Talavera, bad luck to it!—serving under him. He was a captain then.

MALOY   So you told me last night.

CREGAN   (*with a quick glance at him*)   Did I now? I must have said more than my prayers, with the lashings of whiskey in me.

MALOY   (*with a grin*)   More than your prayers is the truth. (*Cregan glances at him uneasily. Maloy pushes the decanter toward him.*) Take another taste.

CREGAN   I don't like sponging. Sure, my credit ought to be good in this shebeen! Ain't I his cousin?

MALOY   You're forgettin' what himself told you last night as he went up to bed. You could have all the whiskey you could pour down you, but not a penny's worth of credit. This house, he axed you to remember, only gives credit to gentlemen.

CREGAN   Divil mend him!

MALOY   (*with a chuckle*)   You kept thinking about his insults after he'd gone out, getting madder and madder.

CREGAN   God pity him, that's like him. He hasn't changed much. (*He pours out a drink and gulps it down—with a cautious look at Maloy.*) If I was mad at Con, and me blind drunk, I must have told you a power of lies.

MALOY   (*winks slyly*)   Maybe they wasn't lies.

CREGAN   If I said any wrong of Con Melody—

MALOY   Arrah, are you afraid I'll gab what you said to him? I won't, you can take my oath.

CREGAN   (*his face clearing*)   Tell me what I said and I'll tell you if it was lies.

MALOY   You said his father wasn't of the quality of Galway like he makes out, but a thievin' shebeen keeper who got rich by money-lendin' and squeezin' tenants and every manner of trick. And when he'd enough he married, and bought an estate with a pack of hounds and set up as one of the gentry. He'd hardly got settled when his wife died givin' birth to Con.

CREGAN   There's no lie there.

MALOY   You said none of the gentry would speak to auld Melody, but he had a tough hide and didn't heed them. He made up his mind he'd bring Con up a true gentleman, so he packed him off to Dublin to school, and after that to the College with sloos of money to prove himself the equal of any gentleman's son. But Con found, while there was plenty to drink on him and borrow money, there was few didn't sneer behind his back at his pretensions.

CREGAN   That's the truth, too. But Con wiped the sneer off their mugs when he called one av thim out and put a bullet in his hip. That was his first duel. It gave his pride the taste for revenge and after that he was always lookin' for an excuse to challenge someone.

MALOY   He's done a power av boastin' about his duels, but I thought he was lyin'.

CREGAN   There's no lie in it. It was that brought disgrace on him in the end, right after he'd been promoted to major. He got caught by a Spanish noble making love to his wife, just after the battle of Salamanca, and there was a duel and Con killed him. The scandal was hushed up but Con had to resign from the army. If it wasn't for his fine record for bravery in battle, they'd have court-martialed him. (*Then guiltily*) But I'm sayin' more than my prayers again.

MALOY   It's no news about his women. You'd think, to hear him when he's drunk, there wasn't one could resist him in Portugal and Spain.

CREGAN   If you'd seen him then, you wouldn't wonder. He was as strong as an ox, and on a thoroughbred horse, in his uniform, there wasn't a handsomer man in the army. And he had the chance he wanted in Portugal and Spain where a British officer was welcome in the gentry's houses. At home, the only women he'd known was whores. (*He adds hastily*) Except Nora, I mean. (*Lowering his voice*) Tell me, has he done any rampagin' wid women here?

MALOY   He hasn't. The damned Yankee gentry won't let him come near them, and he considers the few Irish around here to be scum beneath his notice. But once in a while there'll be some Yankee stops overnight wid his wife or daughter and then you'd laugh to see Con, if he thinks she's gentry, sidlin' up to her, playin' the great gentleman and makin' compliments, and then boasting afterward he could have them in bed if he'd had a chance at it, for all their modern Yankee airs.

CREGAN   And maybe he could. If you'd known him in the auld days, you'd nivir doubt any boast he makes about fightin' and women, and gamblin' or any kind av craziness. There nivir was a madder divil.

MALOY   (*lowering his voice*)   Speakin' av Nora, you nivir mentioned her last night, but I know all about it without you telling me. I used to have my room here, and there's nights he's madder drunk than most when he throws it in her face he had to marry her because— Mind you, I'm not saying anything against poor Nora. A sweeter woman never lived. And I know you know all about it.

CREGAN   (*reluctantly*)   I do. Wasn't I raised on his estate?

MALOY   He tells her it was the priests tricked him into marrying her. He hates priests.

CREGAN   He's a liar, then. He may like to blame it on them but it's little Con Melody cared what they said. Nothing ever made him do anything, except himself. He married her because he'd fallen in love with her, but he was ashamed of her in his pride at the same time because her folks were only ignorant peasants on his estate, as poor as poor. Nora was as pretty a girl as you'd find in a year's travel, and he'd come to be bitter lonely, with no woman's company but the whores was helpin' him ruin the estate. (*He shrugs his shoulders.*) Well, anyways, he married her and then went off to the war, and left her alone in the castle to have her child, and nivir saw her again till he was sent home from Spain. Then he raised what money he still was able, and took her and Sara here to America where no one would know him.

MALOY   (*thinking this over for a moment*)   It's hard for me to believe he ever loved her. I've seen the way he treats her now. Well, thank you for telling me, and I take my oath I'll nivir breathe a word of it —for Nora's sake, not his.

CREGAN   (*grimly*)   You'd better kape quiet for fear of him, too. If he's one-half the man he was, he could bate the lights out of the two av us.

MALOY   He's strong as a bull still for all the whiskey he's drunk. (*He pushes the bottle toward* CREGAN.) Have another taste. (CREGAN *pours out a drink.*) Drink hearty.

CREGAN   Long life. (*He drinks.* MALOY *puts the decanter and glass back on the cupboard. A girl's voice is heard from the hall at right.* CREGAN *jumps up—hastily.*) That's Sara, isn't it? I'll get out. She'll likely blame me for Con getting so drunk last night. I'll be back after Con is down. (*He goes out.* MALOY *starts to go in the bar, as if he too wanted to avoid* SARA. *Then he sits down defiantly.*)

MALOY   Be damned if I'll run from her. (*He takes up the paper as* SARA MELODY *comes in from the hall at right.*)

SARA *is twenty, an exceedingly pretty girl with a mass of black hair, fair skin with rosy cheeks, and beautiful, deep-blue eyes. There is a curious blending in her of what are commonly considered aristocratic and peasant characteristics. She has a fine forehead. Her nose is thin and straight. She has small ears set close to her well-shaped head, and a slender neck. Her mouth, on the other hand, has a touch of coarseness and sensuality and her jaw is too heavy. Her figure is strong and graceful, with full, firm breasts and hips, and a slender waist. But she has large feet and broad, ugly hands with stubby fingers. Her voice is soft and musical, but her speech has at times a self-conscious, stilted quality about it, due to her restraining a tendency to lapse into brogue. Her everyday working dress is of cheap material, but she wears it in a way that gives a pleasing effect of beauty unadorned.*

SARA (*with a glance at* MALOY, *sarcastically*)   I'm sorry to interrupt you when you're so busy, but have you your bar book ready for me to look over?

MALOY (*surlily*)   I have. I put it on your desk.

SARA   Thank you. (*She turns her back on him, sits at the desk, takes a small account book from it, and begins checking figures.*)

MALOY (*watches her over his paper*)   If it's profits you're looking for, you won't find them—not with all the drinks himself's been treating to. (*She ignores this. He becomes resentful.*) You've got your airs of a grand lady this morning, I see. There's no talkin' to you since you've been playin' nurse to the young Yankee upstairs. (*She makes herself ignore this, too.*) Well, you've had your cap set for him ever since he came to live by the lake, and now's your chance, when he's here sick and too weak to defend himself.

SARA (*turns on him—with quiet anger*)   I warn you to mind your own business, Mickey, or I'll tell my father of your impudence. He'll teach you to keep your place, and God help you.

MALOY (*doesn't believe this threat but is frightened by the possibility*)   Arrah, don't try to scare me. I know you'd never carry tales to him. (*Placatingly*) Can't you take a bit of teasing, Sara?

SARA (*turns back to her figuring*)   Leave Simon out of your teasing.

MALOY   Oho, he's Simon to you now, is he? Well, well. (*He gives her a cunning glance.*) Maybe, if you'd come down from your high horse, I could tell you some news.

SARA   You're worse than an old woman for gossip. I don't want to hear it.

MALOY   When you was upstairs at the back taking him his breakfast, there was a grand carriage with a nigger coachman stopped at the corner and a Yankee lady got out and came in here. I was sweeping and Nora was scrubbing the kitchen.

SARA *has turned to him, all attention now.*

She asked me what road would take her near the lake—

SARA (*starts*)   Ah.

MALOY   So I told her, but she didn't go. She kept looking around, and said she'd like a cup of tea, and where was the waitress. I knew she must be connected someway with Harford or why would she want to go to the lake, where no one's ever lived but him. She didn't want tea at all, but only an excuse to stay.

SARA   (*resentfully*)   So she asked for the waitress, did she? I hope you told her I'm the owner's daughter, too.

MALOY   I did. I don't like Yankee airs any more than you. I was short with her. I said you was out for a walk, and the tavern wasn't open yet, anyway. So she went out and drove off.

SARA   (*worriedly now*)   I hope you didn't insult her with your bad manners. What did she look like, Mickey?

MALOY   Pretty, if you like that kind. A pale, delicate wisp of a thing with big eyes.

SARA   That fits what he's said of his mother. How old was she?

MALOY   It's hard to tell, but she's too young for his mother, I'd swear. Around thirty, I'd say. Maybe it's his sister.

SARA   He hasn't a sister.

MALOY   (*grinning*)   Then maybe she's an old sweetheart looking for you to scratch your eyes out.

SARA   He's never had a sweetheart.

MALOY   (*mockingly*)   Is that what he tells you, and you believe him? Faix, you must be in love!

SARA   (*angrily*)   Will you mind your own business? I'm not such a fool! (*Worried again*)   Maybe you ought to have told her he's here sick to save her the drive in the hot sun and the walk through the woods for nothing.

MALOY   Why would I tell her, when she never mentioned him?

SARA   Yes, it's her own fault. But—— Well, there's no use thinking of it now—or bothering my head about her, anyway, whoever she was. (*She begins checking figures again. Her mother appears in the doorway at right.*)

NORA MELODY *is forty, but years of overwork and worry have made her look much older. She must have been as pretty as a girl as* SARA *is now. She still has the beautiful eyes her daughter has inherited. But she has become too worn out to take care of her appearance. Her black hair, streaked with gray, straggles in untidy wisps about her face. Her body is dumpy, with sagging breasts, and her old clothes are like a bag covering it, tied around the middle. Her red hands are knotted by rheumatism. Cracked working shoes, run down at the heel, are on her bare feet. Yet in spite of her slovenly appearance there is a spirit which shines through and makes her lovable, a simple sweetness and charm, something gentle and sad and, somehow, dauntless.*

MALOY (*jumps to his feet, his face lighting up with affection*)   God bless you, Nora, you're the one I was waitin' to see. Will you keep an eye on the bar while I run to the store for a bit av 'baccy?

SARA (*sharply*)   Don't do it, Mother.

NORA (*smiles—her voice is soft, with a rich brogue*)   Why wouldn't I? "Don't do it, Mother."

MALOY   Thank you, Nora. (*He goes to the door at rear and opens it, burning for a parting shot at* SARA.) And the back o' my hand to you, your Ladyship! (*He goes out, closing the door.*)

SARA   You shouldn't encourage his laziness. He's always looking for excuses to shirk.

NORA   Ah, nivir mind, he's a good lad. (*She lowers herself painfully on the nearest chair at the rear of the table at center front.*) Bad cess to the rheumatism. It has me destroyed this mornin'.

SARA (*still checking figures in the book—gives her mother an impatient but at the same time worried glance. Her habitual manner toward her is one of mingled love and pity and exasperation.*)   I've told you a hundred times to see the doctor.

NORA   We've no money for doctors. They're bad luck, anyway. They bring death with them. (*A pause.* NORA *sighs.*) Your father will be down soon. I've some fine fresh eggs for his breakfast.

SARA (*Her face becomes hard and bitter.*)   He won't want them.

NORA (*defensively*)   You mean he'd a drop too much taken last night? Well, small blame to him, he hasn't seen Jamie since—

SARA   *Last* night? What night hasn't he?

NORA   Ah, don't be hard on him. (*A pause—worriedly*) Neilan sent round a note to me about his bill. He says we'll have to settle by the end of the week or we'll get no more groceries. (*With a sigh*) I can't blame him. How we'll manage, I dunno. There's the intrist on the mortgage due the first. But that I've saved, God be thanked.

SARA (*exasperatedly*)   If you'd only let me take charge of the money.

NORA (*with a flare of spirit*)   I won't. It'd mean you and himself would be at each other's throats from dawn to dark. It's bad enough between you as it is.

SARA   Why didn't you pay Neilan the end of last week? You told me you had the money put aside.

NORA   So I did. But Dickinson was tormentin' your father with his feed bill for the mare.

SARA (*angrily*)   I might have known! The mare comes first, if she takes the bread out of our mouths! The grand gentleman must have his thoroughbred to ride out in state!

NORA (*defensively*)   Where's the harm? She's his greatest pride. He'd be heartbroken if he had to sell her.

SARA   Oh yes, I know well he cares more for a horse than for us!

NORA   Don't be saying that. He has great love for you, even if you do be provokin' him all the time.

SARA   Great love for me! Arrah, God pity you, Mother!

NORA (*sharply*)   Don't put on the brogue, now. You know how he hates to hear you. And I do, too. There's no excuse not to cure yourself. Didn't he send you to school so you could talk like a gentleman's daughter?

SARA (*resentfully, but more careful of her speech*)   If he did, I wasn't there long.

NORA   It was you insisted on leavin'.

SARA   Because if he hadn't the pride or love for you not to live on your slaving your heart out, I had that pride and love!

NORA (*tenderly*)   I know, Acushla. I know.

SARA (*with bitter scorn*)   We can't afford a waitress, but he can afford to keep a thoroughbred mare to prance around on and show himself off! And he can afford a barkeep when, if he had any decency, he'd do his part and tend the bar himself.

NORA (*indignantly*)   Him, a gentleman, tend bar!

SARA   A gentleman! Och, Mother, it's all right for the two of us, out of our own pride, to pretend to the world we believe that lie, but it's crazy for you to pretend to me.

NORA (*stubbornly*)   It's no lie. He *is* a gentleman. Wasn't he born rich in a castle on a grand estate and educated in college, and wasn't he an officer in the Duke of Wellington's army—

SARA   All right, Mother. You can humor his craziness, but he'll never make me pretend to him I don't know the truth.

NORA   Don't talk as if you hated him. You ought to be shamed—

SARA   I do hate him for the way he treats you. I heard him again last night, raking up the past, and blaming his ruin on his having to marry you.

NORA (*protests miserably*)   It was the drink talkin', not him.

SARA (*exasperated*)   It's you ought to be ashamed, for not having more pride! You bear all his insults as meek as a lamb! You keep on slaving for him when it's that has made you old before your time! (*Angrily*) You can't much longer, I tell you! He's getting worse. You'll have to leave him.

NORA (*aroused*)   I'll never! Howld your prate!

SARA   You'd leave him today, if you had any pride!

NORA   I've pride in my love for him! I've loved him since the day I set eyes on him, and I'll love him till the day I die! (*With a strange superior scorn*) It's little you know of love, and you never will, for there's the same divil of pride in you that's in him, and it'll kape you from ivir givin' all of yourself, and that's what love is.

SARA   I could give all of myself if I wanted to, but—

NORA   If! Wanted to! Faix, it proves how little of love you know when you prate about if's and want-to's. It's when you don't give a thought for all the if's and want-to's in the world! It's when, if all the fires of hell was between you, you'd walk in them gladly to be with him, and sing with joy at your own burnin', if only his kiss was on your mouth! That's love, and I'm proud I've known the great sorrow and joy of it!

SARA (*cannot help being impressed—looks at her mother with wondering respect*)   You're a strange woman, Mother. (*She kisses her impulsively.*) And a grand woman! (*Defiant again, with an arrogant toss of her head*) I'll love—but I'll love where it'll gain me freedom and not put me in slavery for life.

NORA   There's no slavery in it when you love! (*Suddenly her exultant expression crumbles and she breaks down.*) For the love of God, don't take the pride of my love from me, Sara, for without it what am I at all but an ugly, fat woman gettin' old and sick!

SARA (*puts her arm around her—soothingly*)   Hush, Mother. Don't mind me. (*Briskly, to distract her mother's mind*) I've got to finish the bar book. Mickey can't put two and two together without making five. (*She goes to the desk and begins checking figures again.*)

NORA (*dries her eyes—after a pause she sighs worriedly*)   I'm worried about your father. Father Flynn stopped me on the road yesterday and tould me I'd better warn him not to sneer at the Irish around here and call thim scum, or he'll get in trouble. Most of thim is in a rage at him because he's come out against Jackson and the Democrats and says he'll vote with the Yankees for Quincy Adams.

SARA (*contemptuously*)   Faith, they can't see a joke, then, for it's a great joke to hear him shout against mob rule, like one of the Yankee gentry, when you know what he came from. And after the way the Yanks swindled him when he came here, getting him to buy this inn by telling him a new coach line was going to stop here. (*She laughs with bitter scorn.*) Oh, he's the easiest fool ever came to America! It's that I hold against him as much as anything, that when he came here the chance was before him to make himself all his lies pretended to be. He had education above most Yanks, and he had money enough to start him, and this is a country where you can rise as high as you like, and no one but the fools who envy you care what you rose from, once you've the money and the power goes with it. (*Passionately*) Oh, if I was a man with the chance he had, there wouldn't be a dream I'd not make come true! (*She looks at her mother, who is staring at the floor dejectedly and hasn't been listening. She is exasperated for a second—then she smiles pityingly.*) You're a fine one to talk to, Mother. Wake up. What's worrying you now?

NORA   Father Flynn tould me again I'd be damned in hell for lettin' your father make a haythen of me and bring you up a haythen, too.

SARA (*with an arrogant toss of her head*)   Let Father Flynn mind his own business, and not frighten you with fairy tales about hell.

NORA   It's true, just the same.

SARA   True, me foot! You ought to tell the good Father we aren't the ignorant shanty scum he's used to dealing with. (*She changes the subject abruptly—closing* MICKEY'S *bar book.*) There. That's done. (*She puts the book in the desk.*) I'll take a walk to the store and have a talk with Neilan. Maybe I can blarney him to let the bill go another month.

NORA (*gratefully*)   Oh, you can. Sure, you can charm a bird out of a tree when you want to. But I don't like you beggin' to a Yankee. It's all right for me but I know how you hate it.

SARA (*puts her arms around her mother—tenderly*)   I don't mind at all, if I can save you a bit of the worry that's killing you. (*She kisses her.*) I'll change to my Sunday dress so I can make a good impression.

NORA (*with a teasing smile*)   I'm thinkin' it isn't on Neilan alone you want to make an impression. You've changed to your Sunday best a lot lately.

SARA (*coquettishly*)   Aren't you the sly one! Well, maybe you're right.

NORA   How was he when you took him his breakfast?

SARA   Hungry, and that's a good sign. He had no fever last night. Oh, he's on the road to recovery now, and it won't be long before he'll be back in his cabin by the lake.

NORA   I'll never get it clear in my head what he's been doing there the past year, living like a tramp or a tinker, and him a rich gentleman's son.

SARA (*with a tender smile*)   Oh, he isn't like his kind, or like anyone else at all. He's a born dreamer with a raft of great dreams, and he's very serious about them. I've told you before he wanted to get away from his father's business, where he worked for a year after he graduated from Harvard College, because he didn't like being in trade, even if it is a great company that trades with the whole world in its own ships.

NORA (*approvingly*)   That's the way a true gentleman would feel—

SARA   He wanted to prove his independence by living alone in the wilds, and build his own cabin, and do all the work, and support himself simply, and feel one with Nature, and think great thoughts about what life means, and write a book about how the world can be changed so people won't be greedy to own money and land and get the best of each other but will be content with little and live in peace and freedom together, and it will be like heaven on earth. (*She laughs fondly—and a bit derisively.*) I can't remember all of it. It seems crazy to me, when I think of what people are like. He hasn't written any of it yet, anyway—only the notes for it. (*She smiles coquettishly.*) All he's written the last few months are love poems.

NORA   That's since you began to take long walks by the lake. (*She smiles.*) It's you are the sly one.

SARA (*laughing*)   Well, why shouldn't I take walks on our own property? (*Her tone changes to a sneer.*) The land our great gentleman was swindled into buying when he came here with grand ideas of owning an American estate!—a bit of farm land no one would work any more, and the rest all wilderness! You couldn't give it away.

NORA (*soothingly*)   Hush, now. (*Changing the subject*) Well, it's easy to tell young Master Harford has a touch av the poet in him—(*She adds before she thinks*) the same as your father.

SARA (*scornfully*)   God help you, Mother! Do you think Father's a poet because he shows off reciting Lord Byron?

NORA (*with an uneasy glance at the door at left front*)   Whist, now. Himself will be down any moment. (*Changing the subject*) I can see the Harford lad is falling in love with you.

SARA (*Her face lights up triumphantly.*) Falling? He's fallen head over heels. He's so timid, he hasn't told me yet, but I'll get him to soon.

NORA I know you're in love with him.

SARA (*simply*) I am, Mother. (*She adds quickly*) But not too much. I'll not let love make me any man's slave. I want to love him just enough so I can marry him without cheating him, or myself. (*Determinedly*) For I'm going to marry him, Mother. It's my chance to rise in the world and nothing will keep me from it.

NORA (*admiringly*) Musha, but you've boastful talk! What about his fine Yankee family? His father'll likely cut him off widout a penny if he marries a girl who's poor and Irish.

SARA He may at first, but when I've proved what a good wife I'll be— He can't keep Simon from marrying me. I know that. Simon doesn't care what his father thinks. It's only his mother I'm afraid of. I can tell she's had great influence over him. She must be a queer creature, from all he's told me. She's very strange in her ways. She never goes out at all but stays home in their mansion, reading books, or in her garden. (*She pauses.*) Did you notice a carriage stop here this morning, Mother?

NORA (*preoccupied—uneasily*) Don't count your chickens before they're hatched. Young Harford seems a dacent lad. But maybe it's not marriage he's after.

SARA (*angrily*) I won't have you wronging him, Mother. He has no thought— (*Bitterly*) I suppose you're bound to suspect— (*She bites her words back, ashamed.*) Forgive me, Mother. But it's wrong of you to think badly of Simon. (*She smiles.*) You don't know him. Faith, if it came to seducing, it'd be me that'd have to do it. He's that respectful you'd think I was a holy image. It's only in his poems, and in the diary he keeps— I had a peek in it one day I went to tidy up the cabin for him. He's terribly ashamed of his sinful inclinations and the insult they are to my purity. (*She laughs tenderly.*)

NORA (*smiling, but a bit shocked*) Don't talk so bould. I don't know if it's right, you to be in his room so much, even if he is sick. There's a power av talk about the two av you already.

SARA Let there be, for all I care! Or all Simon cares, either. When it comes to not letting others rule him, he's got a will of his own behind his gentleness. Just as behind his poetry and dreams I feel he has it in him to do anything he wants. So even if his father cuts him off, with me to help him we'll get on in the world. For I'm no fool, either.

NORA   Glory be to God, you have the fine opinion av yourself!

SARA (*laughing*)   Haven't I, though! (*Then bitterly*) I've had need to have, to hold my head up, slaving as a waitress and chambermaid so my father can get drunk every night like a gentleman!

The door at left front is slowly opened and CORNELIUS MELODY *appears in the doorway above the two steps. He and* SARA *stare at each other. She stiffens into hostility and her mouth sets in scorn. For a second his eyes waver and he looks guilty. Then his face becomes expressionless. He decends the steps and bows—pleasantly.*

MELODY   Good morning, Sara.

SARA (*curtly*)   Good morning. (*Then, ignoring him*) I'm going up and change my dress, Mother. (*She goes out right.*)

CORNELIUS MELODY *is forty-five, tall, broad-shouldered, deep-chested, and powerful, with long muscular arms, big feet, and large hairy hands. His heavy-boned body is still firm, erect, and soldierly. Beyond shaky nerves, it shows no effects of hard drinking. It has a bull-like, impervious strength, a tough peasant vitality. It is his face that reveals the ravages of dissipation—a ruined face, which was once extraordinarily handsome in a reckless, arrogant fashion. It is still handsome—the face of an embittered Byronic hero, with a finely chiseled nose over a domineering, sensual mouth set in disdain, pale, hollow-cheeked, framed by thick, curly iron-gray hair. There is a look of wrecked distinction about it, of brooding, humiliated pride. His bloodshot gray eyes have an insulting cold stare which anticipates insult. His manner is that of a polished gentleman. Too much so. He overdoes it and one soon feels that he is overplaying a role which has become more real than his real self to him. But in spite of this, there is something formidable and impressive about him. He is dressed with foppish elegance in old, expensive, finely tailored clothes of the style worn by English aristocracy in Peninsular War days.*

MELODY (*advancing into the room—bows formally to his wife*)   Good morning, Nora. (*His tone condescends. It addresses a person of inferior station.*)

NORA (*stumbles to her feet—timidly*)   Good mornin', Con. I'll get your breakfast.

MELODY   No. Thank you. I want nothing now.

NORA (*coming toward him*)   You look pale. Are you sick, Con, darlin'?

MELODY   No.

NORA (*puts a timid hand on his arm*)   Come and sit down.

He moves his arm away with instinctive revulsion and goes to the table at center front, and sits in the chair she had occupied. NORA *hovers round him.*

I'll wet a cloth in cold water to put round your head.

MELODY   No! I desire nothing—except a little peace in which to read the news. (*He picks up the paper and holds it so it hides his face from her.*)

NORA (*meekly*)   I'll lave you in peace. (*She starts to go to the door at right but turns to stare at him worriedly again. Keeping the paper before his face with his left hand, he reaches out with his right and pours a glass of water from the carafe on the table. Although he cannot see his wife, he is nervously conscious of her. His hand trembles so violently that when he attempts to raise the glass to his lips the water sloshes over his hand and he sets the glass back on the table with a bang. He lowers the paper and explodes nervously.*)

MELODY   For God's sake, stop your staring!

NORA   I—I was only thinkin' you'd feel better if you'd a bit av food in you.

MELODY   I told you once—! (*Controlling his temper*) I am not hungry, Nora. (*He raises the paper again. She sighs, her hands fiddling with her apron. A pause.*)

NORA (*dully*)   Maybe it's a hair av the dog you're needin'.

MELODY (*as if this were something he had been waiting to hear, his expression loses some of its nervous strain. But he replies virtuously*) No, damn the liquor. Upon my conscience, I've about made up my mind I'll have no more of it. Besides, it's a bit early in the day.

NORA   If it'll give you an appetite—

MELODY   To tell the truth, my stomach is out of sorts. (*He licks his lips.*) Perhaps a drop wouldn't come amiss.

NORA *gets the decanter and glass from the cupboard and sets them before him. She stands gazing at him with a resigned sadness.* MELODY, *his eyes on the paper, is again acutely conscious of her. His nerves cannot stand it. He throws his paper down and bursts out in bitter anger.*

Well? I know what you're thinking! Why haven't you the courage to say it for once? By God, I'd have more respect for you! I hate the damned meek of this earth! By the rock of Cashel, I sometimes believe you have always deliberately encouraged me to— It's the one point of superiority you can lay claim to, isn't it?

NORA (*bewilderedly—on the verge of tears*)   I don't— It's only your comfort— I can't bear to see you—

MELODY (*His expression changes and a look of real affection comes into his eyes. He reaches out a shaking hand to pat her shoulder with an odd, guilty tenderness. He says quietly and with genuine contrition.*) Forgive me, Nora. That was unpardonable.

Her face lights up. Abruptly he is ashamed of being ashamed. He looks away and grabs the decanter. Despite his trembling hand he manages to pour a drink and get it to his mouth and drain it. Then he sinks back in his chair and stares at the table, waiting for the liquor to take effect. After a pause he sighs with relief.

I confess I needed that as medicine. I begin to feel more myself. (*He pours out another big drink and this time his hand is steadier, and he downs it without much difficulty. He smacks his lips.*) By the Immortal, I may have sunk to keeping an inn but at least I've a conscience in my trade. I keep liquor a gentleman can drink. (*He starts looking over the paper again—scowls at something—disdainfully, emphasizing his misquote of the line from Byron.*) "There shall he rot—Ambition's *dis*honored fool!" The paper is full of the latest swindling lies of that idol of the riffraff, Andrew Jackson. Contemptible, drunken scoundrel! But he will be the next President, I predict, for all we others can do to prevent. There is a cursed destiny in these decadent times. Everywhere the scum rises to the top. (*His eyes fasten on the date and suddenly he strikes the table with his fist.*) Today is the 27th! By God, and I would have forgotten!

NORA   Forgot what?

MELODY   The anniversary of Talavera!

NORA (*hastily*)   Oh, ain't I stupid not to remember.

MELODY (*bitterly*)   I had forgotten myself and no wonder. It's a far cry from this dunghill on which I rot to that glorious day when the Duke of Wellington—Lord Wellesley, then—did me the honor before all the army to commend my bravery. (*He glances around the room with loathing.*) A far cry, indeed! It would be better to forget!

NORA (*rallying him*)   No, no, you mustn't. You've never missed celebratin' it and you won't today. I'll have a special dinner for you like I've always had.

MELODY (*with a quick change of manner—eagerly*) Good, Nora. I'll invite Jamie Cregan. It's a stroke of fortune he is here. He served under me at Talavera, as you know. A brave soldier, if he isn't a gentleman. You can place him on my right hand. And we'll have Patch Riley to make music, and O'Dowd and Roche. If they are rabble, they're full of droll humor at times. But put them over there. (*He points to the table at left front.*) I may tolerate their presence out of charity, but I'll not sink to dining at the same table.

NORA I'll get your uniform from the trunk, and you'll wear it for dinner like you've done each year.

MELODY Yes, I must confess I still welcome an excuse to wear it. It makes me feel at least the ghost of the man I was then.

NORA You're so handsome in it still, no woman could take her eyes off you.

MELODY (*with a pleased smile*) I'm afraid you've blarney on your tongue this morning, Nora. (*Then boastfully*) But it's true, in those days in Portugal and Spain— (*He stops a little shamefacedly, but NORA gives no sign of offense. He takes her hand and pats it gently— avoiding her eyes.*) You have the kindest heart in the world, Nora. And I— (*His voice breaks.*)

NORA (*instantly on the verge of grateful tears*) Ah, who wouldn't, Con darlin', when you— (*She brushes a hand across her eyes— hastily.*) I'll go to the store and get something tasty. (*Her face drops as she remembers.*) But, God help us, where's the money?

MELODY (*stiffens—haughtily*) Money? Since when has my credit not been good?

NORA (*hurriedly*) Don't fret, now. I'll manage. (*He returns to his newspaper, disdaining further interest in money matters.*)

MELODY Ha. I see work on the railroad at Baltimore is progressing. (*Lowering his paper*) By the Eternal, if I had not been a credulous gull and let the thieving Yankees swindle me of all I had when we came here, that's how I would invest my funds now. And I'd become rich. This country, with its immense territory cannot depend solely on creeping canal boats, as shortsighted fools would have us believe. We must have railroads. Then you will see how quickly America will become rich and great? (*His expression changes to one of bitter hatred.*) Great enough to crush England in the next war between them, which I know is inevitable! Would I could live to celebrate that victory! If I have one regret for the past—and there are few things in it that do not call for bitter regret—it is that I shed my blood for a country that thanked me with disgrace. But I will be avenged. This country—my country, now—will drive the English from the face of the earth their shameless perfidy has dishonored!

NORA   Glory be to God for that! And we'll free Ireland!

MELODY (*contemptuously*)   Ireland? What benefit would freedom be to her unless she could be freed from the Irish? (*Then irritably*) But why do I discuss such things with you?

NORA (*humbly*)   I know. I'm ignorant.

MELODY   Yet I tried my best to educate you, after we came to America —until I saw it was hopeless.

NORA   You did, surely. And I tried, too, but—

MELODY   You won't even cure yourself of that damned peasant's brogue. And you daughter is becoming as bad.

NORA   She only puts on the brogue to tease you. She can speak as fine as any lady in the land if she wants.

MELODY (*is not listening—sunk in bitter brooding*)   But, in God's name, who am I to reproach anyone with anything? Why don't you tell me to examine my own conduct?

NORA   You know I'd never.

MELODY (*Stares at her—again he is moved—quietly*)   No. I know you would not, Nora. (*He looks away—after a pause.*) I owe you an apology for what happened last night.

NORA   Don't think of it.

MELODY (*with assumed casualness*)   Faith, I'd a drink too many, talking over old times with Jamie Cregan.

NORA   I know.

MELODY   I am afraid I may have— The thought of old times— I become bitter. But you understand, it was the liquor talking, if I said anything to wound you.

NORA   I know it.

MELODY (*deeply moved, puts his arm around her*)   You're a sweet, kind woman, Nora—too kind. (*He kisses her.*)

NORA (*with blissful happiness*)   Ah, Con darlin', what do I care what you say when the black thoughts are on you? Sure, don't you know I love you?

MELODY (*A sudden revulsion of feeling convulses his face. He bursts out with disgust, pushing her away from him.*)   For God's sake, why don't you wash your hair? It turns my stomach with its stink of onions and stew! (*He reaches for the decanter and shakingly pours a drink.* NORA *looks as if he had struck her.*)

NORA (*dully*) I do be washin' it often to plaze you. But when you're standin' over the stove all day, you can't help—

MELODY Forgive me, Nora. Forget I said that. My nerves are on edge. You'd better leave me alone.

NORA (*her face brightening a little*) Will you ate your breakfast now? I've fine fresh eggs—

MELODY (*grasping at this chance to get rid of her—impatiently*) Yes! In a while. Fifteen minutes, say. But leave me alone now.

She goes out right. MELODY *drains his drink. Then he gets up and paces back and forth, his hands clasped behind him. The third drink begins to work and his face becomes arrogantly self-assured. He catches his reflection in the mirror on the wall at left and stops before it. He brushes a sleeve fastidiously, adjusts the set of his coat, and surveys himself.*

Thank God, I still bear the unmistakable stamp of an officer and a gentleman. And so I will remain to the end, in spite of all fate can do to crush my spirit! (*He squares his shoulders defiantly. He stares into his eyes in the glass and recites from Byron's "Childe Harold," as if it were an incantation by which he summons pride to justify his life to himself.*)

"I have not loved the World, nor the World me;
I have not flattered its rank breath, nor bowed
To its idolatries a patient knee,
Nor coined my cheek to smiles,—nor cried aloud
In worship of an echo: in the crowd
They could not deem me one of such—I stood
Among them, but not of them . . ."

(*He pauses, then repeats:*)

"Among them, but not of them."

By the Eternal, that expresses it! Thank God for you, Lord Byron—poet and nobleman who made of his disdain immortal music!

SARA *appears in the doorway at right. She has changed to her Sunday dress, a becoming blue that brings out the color of her eyes. She draws back for a moment—then stands watching him contemptuously.* MELODY *senses her presence. He starts and turns quickly away from the mirror. For a second his expression is guilty and confused, but he immediately assumes an air of gentlemanly urbanity and bows to her.*

Ah, it's you, my dear. Are you going for a morning stroll? You've a beautiful day for it. It will bring fresh roses to your cheeks.

SARA   I don't know about roses, but it will bring a blush of shame to my cheeks. I have to beg Neilan to give us another month's credit, because you made Mother pay the feed bill for your fine thoroughbred mare! (*He gives no sign he hears this. She adds scathingly*) I hope you saw something in the mirror you could admire!

MELODY (*in a light tone*)   Faith, I suppose I must have looked a vain peacock, preening himself, but you can blame the bad light in my room. One cannot make a decent toilet in that dingy hole in the wall.

SARA   You have the best room in the house, that we ought to rent to guests.

MELODY   Oh, I've no complaints. I was merely explaining my seeming vanity.

SARA   Seeming!

MELODY (*keeping his tone light*)   Faith, Sara, you must have risen the wrong side of the bed this morning, but it takes two to make a quarrel and I don't feel quarrelsome. Quite the contrary. I was about to tell you how exceedingly charming and pretty you look, my dear.

SARA (*with a mocking, awkward, servant's curtsy—in broad brogue*) Oh, thank ye, yer Honor.

MELODY   Every day you resemble your mother more, as she looked when I first knew her.

SARA   Musha, but it's you have the blarneyin' tongue, God forgive you!

MELODY (*in spite of himself, this gets under his skin—angrily*)   Be quiet! How dare you talk to me like a common, ignorant— You're my daughter, damn you. (*He controls himself and forces a laugh.*) A fair hit! You're a great tease, Sara. I shouldn't let you score so easily. Your mother warned me you only did it to provoke me. (*Unconsciously he reaches out for the decanter on the table—then pulls his hand back.*)

SARA (*contemptuously—without brogue now*)   Go on and drink. Surely you're not ashamed before me, after all these years.

MELODY (*haughtily*)   Ashamed? I don't understand you. A gentleman drinks as he pleases—provided he can hold his liquor as he should.

SARA   A gentleman!

MELODY (*pleasantly again*)   I hesitated because I had made a good resolve to be abstemious today. But if you insist— (*He pours a drink —a small one—his hand quite steady now.*) To your happiness, my dear.

She stares at him scornfully. He goes on graciously.

Will you do me the favor to sit down? I have wanted a quiet chat with you for some time. (*He holds out a chair for her at rear of the table at center.*)

SARA (*eyes him suspiciously—then sits down*)   What is it you want?

MELODY (*with a playfully paternal manner*)   Your happiness, my dear, and what I wish to discuss means happiness to you, unless I have grown blind. How is our patient, young Simon Harford, this morning?

SARA (*curtly*)   He's better.

MELODY   I am delighted to hear it. (*Gallantly*) How could he help but be with such a charming nurse? (*She stares at him coldly. He goes on.*) Let us be frank. Young Simon is in love with you. I can see that with half an eye—and, of course, you know it. And you return his love, I surmise.

SARA   Surmise whatever you please.

MELODY   Meaning you do love him? I am glad, Sara. (*He becomes sentimentally romantic.*) Requited love is the greatest blessing life can bestow on us poor mortals; and first love is the most blessed of all. As Lord Byron has it: (*He recites.*)

"But sweeter still than this, than these, than all,

Is first and passionate Love—it stands alone,

Like Adam's recollection of his fall . . ."

SARA (*interrupts him rudely*)   Was it to listen to you recite Byron—?

MELODY (*concealing discomfiture and resentment—pleasantly*)   No. What I was leading up to is that you have my blessing, if that means anything to you. Young Harford is, I am convinced, an estimable youth. I have enjoyed my talks with him. It has been a privilege to be able to converse with a cultured gentleman again. True, he is a bit on the sober side for one so young, but by way of compensation, there is a romantic touch of the poet behind his Yankee phlegm.

SARA   It's fine you approve of him!

MELODY   In your interest I have had some enquiries made about his family.

SARA (*angered—with taunting brogue*)   Have you, indade? Musha, that's cute av you! Was it auld Patch Riley, the Piper, made them?

Or was it Dan Roche or Paddy O'Dowd, or some other drunken sponge—

MELODY (*as if he hadn't heard—condescendingly*)   I find his people will pass muster.

SARA   Oh, do you? That's nice!

MELODY   Apparently, his father is a gentleman—that is, by Yankee standards, insofar as one in trade can lay claim to the title. But as I've become an American citizen myself, I suppose it would be downright snobbery to hold to old-world standards.

SARA   Yes, wouldn't it be!

MELODY   Though it is difficult at times for my pride to remember I am no longer the master of Melody Castle and an estate of three thousand acres of as fine pasture and woodlands as you'd find in the whole United Kingdom, with my stable of hunters, and—

SARA (*bitterly*)   Well, you've a beautiful thoroughbred mare now, at least—to prove you're still a gentleman!

MELODY (*stung into defiant anger*)   Yes, I've the mare! And by God, I'll keep her if I have to starve myself so she may eat.

SARA   You mean, make Mother slave to keep her for you, even if she has to starve!

MELODY (*controls his anger—and ignores this*)   But what was I saying? Oh, yes, young Simon's family. His father will pass muster, but it's through his mother, I believe, he comes by his really good blood. My information is, she springs from generations of well-bred gentlefolk.

SARA   It would be a great pride to her, I'm sure, to know you found her suitable!

MELODY   I suppose I may expect the young man to request an interview with me as soon as he is up and about again?

SARA   To declare his honorable intentions and ask you for my hand, is that what you mean?

MELODY   Naturally. He is a man of honor. And there are certain financial arrangements Simon's father or his legal representative will wish to discuss with me. The amount of your settlement has to be agreed upon.

SARA (*stares at him as if she could not believe her ears*)   My settlement! Simon's father! God pity you—!

MELODY (*firmly*)   Your settlement, certainly. You did not think, I hope, that I would give you away without a penny to your name as if you were some poverty-stricken peasant's daughter? Please remember

I have my own position to maintain. Of course, it is a bit difficult at present. I am temporarily hard pressed. But perhaps a mortgage on the inn—

SARA   It's mortgaged to the hilt already, as you very well know.

MELODY   If nothing else, I can always give my note at hand for whatever amount—

SARA   You can give it, sure enough! But who'll take it?

MELODY   Between gentlemen, these matters can always be arranged.

SARA   God help you, it must be a wonderful thing to live in a fairy tale where only dreams are real to you. (*Then sharply*) But you needn't waste your dreams worrying about my affairs. I'll thank you not to interfere. Attend to your drinking and leave me alone.

He gives no indication that he has heard a word she has said. She stares at him and a look almost of fear comes into her eyes. She bursts out with a bitter exasperation in which there is a strong undercurrent of entreaty.

Father! Will you never let yourself wake up—not even now when you're sober, or nearly? Is it stark mad you've gone, so you can't tell any more what's dead and a lie, and what's the living truth?

MELODY   (*His face is convulsed by a spasm of pain as if something vital had been stabbed in him—with a cry of tortured appeal.*) Sara! (*But instantly his pain is transformed into rage. He half rises from his chair threateningly.*) Be quiet, damn you! How dare you—!

She shrinks away and rises to her feet. He forces control on himself and sinks back in his chair, his hands gripping the arms.

The street door at rear is flung open and DAN ROCHE, PADDY O'DOWD, *and* PATCH RILEY *attempt to pile in together and get jammed for a moment in the doorway. They all have hangovers, and* ROCHE *is talking boisterously.* DAN ROCHE *is middle-aged, squat, bowlegged, with a potbelly and short arms lumpy with muscle. His face is flat with a big mouth, protruding ears, and red-rimmed little pig's eyes. He is dressed in dirty, patched clothes.* PADDY O'DOWD *is thin, round-shouldered, flat-chested, with a pimply complexion, bulgy eyes, and a droopy mouth. His manner is oily and fawning, that of a born sponger and parasite. His clothes are those of a cheap sport.* PATCH RILEY *is an old man with a thatch of dirty white hair. His washed-out blue eyes have a wandering, half-witted expression. His skinny body is clothed in rags and there is nothing under his tattered coat but his bare skin. His mouth is sunken in, toothless. He carries an Irish bagpipe under his arm.*

ROCHE   (*His back is half turned as he harangues* O'DOWD *and* RILEY, *and he does not see* MELODY *and* SARA.) And I says, it's Andy Jackson will put you in your place, and all the slave-drivin' Yankee skin-flints like you! Take your damned job, I says, and—

O'DOWD (*warningly, his eyes on* MELODY)   Whist! Whist! Hold your prate!

ROCHE *whirls around to face* MELODY, *and his aggressiveness oozes from him, changing to a hangdog apprehension. For* MELODY *has sprung to his feet, his eyes blazing with an anger which is increased by the glance of contempt* SARA *casts from him to the three men.* O'DOWD *avoids* MELODY's *eyes, busies himself in closing the door.* PATCH RILEY *stands gazing at* SARA *with a dreamy, admiring look, lost in a world of his own fancy, oblivious to what is going on.*

ROCHE (*placatingly*)   Good mornin' to ye, Major.

O'DOWD (*fawning*)   Good mornin', yer Honor.

MELODY   How dare you come tramping in here in that manner! Have you mistaken this inn for the sort of dirty shebeen you were used to in the old country where the pigs ran in and out the door?

O'DOWD   We ask pardon, yer Honor.

MELODY (*to* ROCHE—*an impressive menace in his tone*)   You, Paddy. Didn't I forbid you ever to mention that scoundrel Jackson's name in my house or I'd horsewhip the hide off your back? (*He takes a threatening step toward him.*) Perhaps you think I cannot carry out that threat.

ROCHE (*backs away frightenedly*)   No, no, Major. I forgot— Good mornin' to ye, Miss.

O'DOWD   Good mornin', Miss Sara.

She ignores them. PATCH RILEY *is still gazing at her with dreamy admiration, having heard nothing, his hat still on his head.* O'DOWD *officiously snatches it off for him—rebukingly.*

Where's your wits, Patch? Didn't ye hear his Honor?

RILEY (*unheeding—addresses* SARA)   Sure it's you, God bless you, looks like a fairy princess as beautiful as a rose in the mornin' dew. I'll raise a tune for you. (*He starts to arrange his pipes.*)

SARA (*curtly*)   I want none of your tunes. (*Then, seeing the look of wondering hurt in the old man's eyes, she adds kindly*) That's sweet of you, Patch. I know you'd raise a beautiful tune, but I have to go out. (*Consoled, the old man smiles at her gratefully.*)

MELODY   Into the bar, all of you, where you belong! I told you not to use this entrance! (*With disdainful tolerance*) I suppose it's a free drink you're after. Well, no one can say of me that I turned away anyone I knew thirsty from my door.

O'DOWD   Thank ye, yer Honor. Come along, Dan. (*He takes* RILEY'S *arm.*) Come on, Patch. (*The three go into the bar and* O'DOWD *closes the door behind them.*)

SARA (*in derisive brogue*)   Sure, it's well trained you've got the poor retainers on your American estate to respect the master! (*Then as he ignores her and casts a furtive glance at the door to the bar, running his tongue over his dry lips, she says acidly, with no trace of brogue*) Don't let me keep you from joining the gentlemen! (*She turns her back on him and goes out the street door at rear.*)

MELODY   (*His face is again convulsed by a spasm of pain—pleadingly.*) Sara!

NORA *enters from the hall at right, carrying a tray with toast, eggs, bacon, and tea. She arranges his breakfast on the table at front center, bustling garrulously.*

NORA   Have I kept you waitin'? The divil was in the toast. One lot burned black as a naygur when my back was turned. But the bacon is crisp, and the eggs not too soft, the way you like them. Come and sit down now.

MELODY *does not seem to hear her. She looks at him worriedly.*

What's up with you, Con? Don't you hear me?

O'DOWD (*pokes his head in the door from the bar*)   Mickey won't believe you said we could have a drink, yer Honor, unless ye tell him.

MELODY (*licking his lips*)   I'm coming. (*He goes to the bar door.*)

NORA   Con! Have this in your stomach first! It'll all get cauld.

MELODY (*without turning to her—in his condescendingly polite tone*)   I find I am not the least hungry, Nora. I regret your having gone to so much trouble. (*He goes into the bar, closing the door behind him.* NORA *slumps on a chair at the rear of the table and stares at the breakfast with a pitiful helplessness. She begins to sob quietly.*)

CURTAIN

ACT TWO

SCENE   *Same as Act One. About half an hour has elapsed. The bar-room door opens and* MELODY *comes in. He has had two more drinks and still no breakfast, but this has had no outward effect except that his face is paler and his manner more disdainful. He turns to give orders to the spongers in the bar.*

MELODY   Remember what I say. None of your loud brawling. And you, Riley, keep your bagpipe silent, or out you go. I wish to be alone in quiet for a while with my memories. When Corporal Cregan returns, Mickey, send him in to me. He, at least, knows Talavera is not the name of a new brand of whiskey. (*He shuts the door contemptuously on* MICKEY's "Yes, Major" *and the obedient murmur of the others. He sits at rear of the table at left front. At first, he poses to himself, striking an attitude—a Byronic hero, noble, embittered, disdainful, defying his tragic fate, brooding over past glories. But he has no audience and he cannot keep it up. His shoulders sag and he stares at the table top, hopelessness and defeat bringing a trace of real tragedy to his ruined, handsome face.*)

The street door is opened and SARA *enters. He does not hear the click of the latch, or notice her as she comes forward. Fresh from the humiliation of cajoling the storekeeper to extend more credit, her eyes are bitter. At sight of her father they become more so. She moves toward the door at right, determined to ignore him, but something unusual in his attitude strikes her and she stops to regard him searchingly. She starts to say something bitter—stops—finally, in spite of herself, she asks with a trace of genuine pity in her voice.*

SARA   What's wrong with you, Father? Are you really sick or is it just—

He starts guiltily, ashamed of being caught in such a weak mood.

MELODY   (*gets to his feet politely and bows*)   I beg your pardon, my dear. I did not hear you come in. (*With a deprecating smile*) Faith, I was far away in spirit, lost in memories of a glorious battle in Spain, nineteen years ago today.

SARA   (*Her face hardens.*) Oh. It's the anniversary of Talavera, is it?

Well, I know what that means—a great day for the spongers and a bad day for this inn!

MELODY (*coldly*)   I don't understand you. Of course I shall honor the occasion.

SARA   You needn't tell me. I remember the other celebrations—and this year, now Jamie Cregan has appeared, you've an excuse to make it worse.

MELODY   Naturally, an old comrade in arms will be doubly welcome—

SARA   Well, I'll say this much. From the little I've seen of him, I'd rather have free whiskey go down his gullet than the others'. He's a relation, too.

MELODY (*stiffly*)   Merely a distant cousin. That has no bearing. It's because Corporal Cregan fought by my side—

SARA   I suppose you've given orders to poor Mother to cook a grand feast for you, as usual, and you'll wear your beautiful uniform, and I'll have the honor of waiting on table. Well, I'll do it just this once more for Mother's sake, or she'd have to, but it'll be the last time. (*She turns her back on him and goes to the door at right.*) You'll be pleased to learn your daughter had almost to beg on her knees to Neilan before he'd let us have another month's credit. He made it plain it was to Mother he gave it because he pities her for the husband she's got. But what do you care about that, as long as you and your fine thoroughbred mare can live in style!

MELODY *is shaken for a second. He glances toward the bar as if he longed to return there to escape her. Then he gets hold of himself. His face becomes expressionless. He sits in the same chair and picks up the paper, ignoring her. She starts to go out just as her mother appears in the doorway.* NORA *is carrying a glass of milk.*

NORA   Here's the milk the doctor ordered for the young gentleman. It's time for it, and I knew you'd be going upstairs.

SARA (*takes the milk*)   Thank you, Mother. (*She nods scornfully toward her father.*) I've just been telling him I begged another month's credit from Neilan, so he needn't worry.

NORA   Ah, thank God for that. Neilan's a kind man.

MELODY (*explodes*)   Damn his kindness! By the Eternal, if he'd refused, I'd have—! (*He controls himself, meeting* SARA'S *contemptuous eyes. He goes on quietly, a bitter, sneering antagonism underneath.*) Don't let me detain you, my dear. Take his milk to our Yankee guest, as your mother suggests. Don't miss any chance to play the ministering angel. (*Vindictively*) Faith, the poor young devil hasn't a chance to escape with you two scheming peasants laying snares to trap him!

SARA   That's a lie! And leave Mother out of your insults!

MELODY   And if all other tricks fail, there's always one last trick to get him through his honor!

SARA (*tensely*)   What trick do you mean?

NORA *grabs her arm.*

NORA   Hould your prate, now! Why can't you leave him be? It's your fault, for provoking him.

SARA (*quietly*)   All right, Mother. I'll leave him to look in the mirror, like he loves to, and remember what he said, and be proud of himself.

MELODY *winces.* SARA *goes out right.*

MELODY (*after a pause—shakenly*)   I— She mistook my meaning— It's as you said. She goads me into losing my temper, and I say things—

NORA (*sadly*)   I know what made you say it. You think maybe she's like I was, and you can't help remembering my sin with you.

MELODY (*guiltily vehement*)   No! No! I tell you she mistook my meaning, and now you— (*Then exasperatedly*) Damn your priests' prating about your sin! (*With a strange, scornful vanity*) To hear you tell it, you'd think it was you who seduced me! That's likely, isn't it? —remembering the man I was then!

NORA   I remember well. Sure, you was that handsome, no woman could resist you. And you are still.

MELODY (*pleased*)   None of your blarney, Nora. (*With Byronic gloom*) I am but a ghost haunting a ruin. (*Then gallantly but without looking at her*) And how about you in those days? Weren't you the prettiest girl in all Ireland? (*Scornfully*) And be damned to your lying, pious shame! You had no shame then, I remember. It was love and joy and glory in you and you were proud!

NORA (*her eyes shining*)   I'm still proud and will be to the day I die!

MELODY (*gives her an approving look which turns to distaste at her appearance—looks away irritably*)   Why do you bring up the past? I do not wish to discuss it.

NORA (*after a pause—timidly*)   All the same, you shouldn't talk to Sara as if you thought she'd be up to anything to catch young Harford.

MELODY   I did not think that! She is my daughter—

NORA   She is surely. And he's a dacent lad. (*She smiles a bit scornfully.*) Sure, from all she's told me, he's that shy he's never dared even to kiss her hand!

MELODY (*with more than a little contempt*)   I can well believe it. When it comes to making love the Yankees are clumsy, fish-blooded louts. They lack savoir-faire. They have no romantic fire! They know nothing of women. (*He snorts disdainfully.*) By the Eternal, when I was his age— (*Then quickly*) Not that I don't approve of young Harford, mind you. He is a gentleman. When he asks me for Sara's hand I will gladly give my consent, provided his father and I can agree on the amount of her settlement.

NORA (*hastily*)   Ah, there's no need to think of that yet. (*Then lapsing into her own dream*) Yes, she'll be happy because she loves him dearly, a lot more than she admits. And it'll give her a chance to rise in the world. We'll see the day when she'll live in a grand mansion, dressed in silks and satins, and riding in a carriage with coachman and footman.

MELODY   I desire that as much as you do, Nora. I'm done—finished— no future but the past. But my daughter has the looks, the brains— ambition, youth— She can go far. (*Then sneeringly*) That is, if she can remember she's a gentlewoman and stop acting like a bog-trotting peasant wench! (*He hears* SARA *returning downstairs.*) She's coming back. (*He gets up—bitterly.*) As the sight of me seems to irritate her, I'll go in the bar a while. I've had my fill of her insults for one morning. (*He opens the bar door. There is a chorus of eager, thirsty welcome from inside. He goes in, closing the door.* SARA *enters from right. Her face is flushed and her eyes full of dreamy happiness.*)

NORA (*rebukingly*)   Himself went in the bar to be out of reach of your tongue. A fine thing! Aren't you ashamed you haven't enough feeling not to torment him, when you know it's the anniversary—

SARA   All right, Mother. Let him take what joy he can out of the day. I'll even help you get his uniform out of the trunk in the attic and brush and clean it for you.

NORA   Ah, God bless you, that's the way— (*Then, astonished at this unexpected docility*) Glory be, but you've changed all of a sudden. What's happened to you?

SARA   I'm so happy now—I can't feel bitter against anyone. (*She hesitates—then shyly*) Simon kissed me. (*Having said this, she goes on triumphantly*) He got his courage up at last, but it was me made him. I was freshening up his pillows and leaning over him, and he couldn't help it, if he was human. (*She laughs tenderly.*) And then you'd have laughed to see him. He near sank through the bed with shame at his boldness. He began apologizing as if he was afraid I'd be so insulted I'd never speak to him again.

NORA (*teasingly*)   And what did you do? I'll wager you wasn't as brazen as you pretend.

SARA (*ruefully*)   It's true, Mother. He made me as bashful as he was. I felt a great fool.

NORA   And was that all? Sure, kissing is easy. Didn't he ask you if you'd marry—?

SARA   No. (*Quickly*) But it was my fault he didn't. He was trying to be brave enough. All he needed was a word of encouragement. But I stood there, dumb as a calf, and when I did speak it was to say I had to come and help you, and the end was I ran from the room, blushing as red as a beet— (*She comes to her mother.* NORA *puts her arms around her.* SARA *hides her face on her shoulder, on the verge of tears.*) Oh, Mother, ain't it crazy to be such a fool?

NORA   Well, when you're in love—

SARA (*breaking away from her—angrily*)   That's just it! I'm too much in love and I don't want to be! I won't let my heart rule my head and make a slave of me! (*Suddenly she smiles confidently.*) Ah well, he loves me as much, and more, I know that, and the next time I'll keep my wits. (*She laughs happily.*) You can consider it as good as done, Mother. I'm Mrs. Simon Harford, at your pleasure. (*She makes a sweeping bow.*)

NORA (*smiling*)   Arrah, none of your airs and graces with me! Help me, now, like you promised, and we'll get your father's uniform out of the trunk. It won't break your back in the attic, like it does me.

SARA (*gaily puts her arm around her mother's waist*)   Come along then.

NORA (*as they go out right*)   I disremember which trunk—and you'll have to help me find the key.

There is a pause. Then the bar door is opened and MELODY *enters again in the same manner as he did at the beginning of the act. There is the same sound of voices from the bar but this time* MELODY *gives no parting orders but simply shuts the door behind him. He scowls with disgust.*

MELODY   Cursed ignorant cattle. (*Then with a real, lonely yearning*)
I wish Jamie Cregan would come. (*Bitterly*) Driven from pillar to
post in my own home! Everywhere ignorance—or the scorn of my
own daughter! (*Then defiantly*) But by the Eternal God, no power
on earth, nor in hell itself, can break me! (*His eyes are drawn irre-
sistibly to the mirror. He moves in front of it, seeking the satisfying
reassurance of his reflection there. What follows is an exact repetition
of his scene before the mirror in Act One. There is the same squaring of his shoulders, arrogant lifting of his head, and then the favorite
quote from Byron, recited aloud to his own image.*

"I have not loved the World, nor the World me;
I have not flattered its rank breath, nor bowed
To its idolatries a patient knee,
Nor coined my cheek to smiles,—nor cried aloud
In the worship of an echo: in the crowd
They could not deem me one of such—I stood
Among them, but not of them . . ."

(*He stands staring in the mirror and does not hear the latch of the
street door click. The door opens and* DEBORAH [*Mrs. Henry Harford*], *Simon's mother, enters, closing the door quietly behind her.*
MELODY *continues to be too absorbed to notice anything. For a
moment, blinded by the sudden change from the bright glare of the
street, she does not see him. When she does, she stares incredulously.
Then she smiles with an amused and mocking relish.*)

DEBORAH *is forty-one, but looks to be no more than thirty. She is small,
a little over five feet tall, with a fragile, youthful figure. One would
never suspect that she is the middle-aged mother of two grown sons.
Her face is beautiful—that is, it is beautiful from the standpoint of
the artist with an eye for bone structure and unusual character. It is
small, with high cheekbones, wedge-shaped, narrowing from a broad
forehead to a square chin, framed by thick, wavy, red-brown hair.
The nose is delicate and thin, a trifle aquiline. The mouth, with full
lips and even, white teeth, is too large for her face. So are the long-
lashed, green-flecked brown eyes, under heavy, angular brows. These
would appear large in any face, but in her they seem enormous and
are made more startling by the pallor of her complexion. She has
tiny, high-arched feet and thin, tapering hands. Her slender, fragile
body is dressed in white with calculated simplicity. About her whole
personality is a curious atmosphere of deliberate detachment, the*

*studied aloofness of an ironically amused spectator. Something per-
versely assertive about it too, as if she consciously carried her originality to the point of whimsical eccentricity.*

DEBORAH   I beg your pardon.

MELODY *jumps and whirls around. For a moment his face has an ab-
surdly startled, stupid look. He is shamed and humiliated and furious
at being caught for the second time in one morning before the mirror. His revenge is to draw himself up haughtily and survey her
insolently from head to toe. But at once, seeing she is attractive and
a lady, his manner changes. Opportunity beckons and he is confident
of himself, put upon his mettle. He bows, a gracious, gallant gentleman. There is seductive charm in his welcoming smile and in his
voice.*

MELODY   Good morning, Mademoiselle. It is an honor to welcome
you to this unworthy inn. (*He draws out a chair at rear of the larger
table in the foreground—bowing again.*) If I may presume. You will
find it comfortable here, away from the glare of the street.

DEBORAH (*regards him for a second puzzledly. She is impressed in spite
of herself by his bearing and distinguished, handsome face.*)   Thank
you. (*She comes forward.* MELODY *makes a gallant show of holding
her chair and helping her be seated. He takes in all her points with
sensual appreciation. It is the same sort of pleasure a lover of horse-
flesh would have in the appearance of a thoroughbred horse. Meanwhile he speaks with caressing courtesy.*)

MELODY   Mademoiselle— (*He sees her wedding ring.*) Pray forgive
me, I see it is Madame— Permit me to say again, how great an honor
I will esteem it to be of any service. (*He manages, as he turns away,
as if by accident to brush his hand against her shoulder. She is startled
and caught off guard. She shrinks and looks up at him. Their eyes
meet and at the nakedly physical appraisement she sees in his, a
fascinated fear suddenly seizes her. But at once she is reassured as
he shifts his gaze, satisfied by her reactions to his first attack, and
hastens to apologize.*) I beg your pardon, Madame. I am afraid my
manners have grown clumsy with disuse. It is not often a lady comes
here now. This inn, like myself, has fallen upon unlucky days.

DEBORAH (*curtly ignoring this*)   I presume you are the innkeeper,
Melody?

MELODY (*a flash of anger in his eyes—arrogantly*)   I am *Major* Cornelius Melody, one time of His Majesty's Seventh Dragoons, at your service. (*He bows with chill formality.*)

DEBORAH (*is now an amused spectator again—apologetically*)   Oh. Then it is I who owe you an apology, Major Melody.

MELODY (*encouraged—gallantly*)   No, no, dear lady, the fault is mine. I should not have taken offense. (*With the air of one frankly admitting a praiseworthy weakness*) Faith, I may as well confess my besetting weakness is that of all gentlemen who have known better days. I have a pride unduly sensitive to any fancied slight.

DEBORAH (*playing up to him now*)   I assure you, sir, there was no intention on my part to slight you.

MELODY (*His eyes again catch hers and hold them—his tone insinuatingly caressing.*)   You are as gracious as you are beautiful, Madame.

DEBORAH's *amusement is gone. She is again confused and, in spite of herself, frightened and fascinated.* MELODY *proceeds with his attack, full of confidence now, the successful seducer of old. His voice takes on a calculated melancholy cadence. He becomes a romantic, tragic figure, appealing for a woman's understanding and loving compassion.*

I am a poor fool, Madame. I would be both wiser and happier if I could reconcile myself to being the proprietor of a tawdry tavern, if I could abjure pride and forget the past. Today of all days it is hard to forget, for it is the anniversary of the battle of Talavera. The most memorable day of my life, Madame. It was on that glorious field I had the honor to be commended for my bravery by the great Duke of Wellington, himself—Sir Arthur Wellesley,[1] then. So I am sure you can find it in your heart to forgive—(*His tone more caressing*) One so beautiful must understand the hearts of men full well, since so many must have given their hearts to you. (*A coarse passion comes into his voice.*) Yes, I'll wager my all against a penny that even among the fish-blooded Yankees there's not a man whose heart doesn't catch flame from your beauty! (*He puts his hand over one of her hands on the table and stares into her eyes ardently.*) As mine does now!

DEBORAH (*feeling herself borne down weakly by the sheer force of his physical strength, struggles to release her hand. She stammers, with*

---

[1] British general and statesmen who defeated Napoleon at Waterloo and later served as prime minister (1828–30).

an attempt at lightness)   Is this—what the Irish call blarney, sir?

MELODY (*with a fierce, lustful sincerity*)   No! I take my oath by the living God, I would charge a square of Napoleon's Old Guard single-handed for one kiss of your lips. (*He bends lower, while his eyes hold hers. For a second it seems he will kiss her and she cannot help herself. Then abruptly the smell of whiskey on his breath brings her to herself, shaken with disgust and coldly angry. She snatches her hand from his and speaks with withering contempt.*)

DEBORAH   Pah! You reek of whiskey! You are drunk, sir! You are insolent and disgusting! I do not wonder your inn enjoys such meager patronage, if you regale all your guests of my sex with this absurd performance!

MELODY *straightens up with a jerk, taking a step back as though he had been slapped in the face.* DEBORAH *rises to her feet, ignoring him disdainfully. At this moment* SARA *and her mother enter through the doorway at right. They take in the scene at a glance.* MELODY *and* DEBORAH *do not notice their entrance.*

NORA (*half under her breath*)   Oh, God help us!

SARA (*guesses at once this must be the woman* MICKEY *had told her about. She hurries toward them quickly, trying to hide her apprehension and anger and shame at what she knows must have happened*)   What is it, Father? What does the lady wish?

Her arrival is a further blow for MELODY, *seething now in a fury of humiliated pride.* DEBORAH *turns to face* SARA.

DEBORAH (*coolly self-possessed—pleasantly*)   I came here to see you, Miss Melody, hoping you might know the present whereabouts of my son, Simon.

This is a bombshell for MELODY.

MELODY (*blurts out with no apology in his tone but angrily, as if she had intentionally made a fool of him*)   You're his mother? In God's name, Madame, why didn't you say so!

DEBORAH (*ignoring him—to* SARA)   I've been out to his hermit's cabin, only to find the hermit flown.

SARA (*stammers*)   He's here, Mrs. Harford—upstairs in bed. He's been sick—

DEBORAH   Sick? You don't mean seriously?

SARA (*recovering a little from her confusion*)   Oh, he's over it now, or almost. It was only a spell of chills and fever he caught from the damp of the lake. I found him there shivering and shaking and made him come here where there's a doctor handy and someone to nurse him.

DEBORAH (*pleasantly*)   The someone being you, Miss Melody?

SARA   Yes, me and—my mother and I.

DEBORAH (*graciously*)   I am deeply grateful to you and your mother for your kindness.

NORA (*who has remained in the background, now comes forward— with her sweet, friendly smile*)   Och, don't be thankin' us, ma'am. Sure, your son is a gentle, fine lad, and we all have great fondness for him. He'd be welcome here if he never paid a penny—(*She stops embarrassedly, catching a disapproving glance from* SARA. DEBORAH *is repelled by* NORA'S *slovenly appearance, but she feels her simple charm and gentleness, and returns her smile.*)

SARA (*with embarrassed stiffness*)   This is my mother, Mrs. Harford.

DEBORAH *inclines her head graciously.* NORA *instinctively bobs in a peasant's curtsy to one of the gentry.* MELODY, *snubbed and seething, glares at her.*

NORA   I'm pleased to make your acquaintance, ma'am.

MELODY   Nora! For the love of God, stop— (*Suddenly he is able to become the polished gentleman again—considerately and even a trifle condescendingly.*) I am sure Mrs. Harford is waiting to be taken to her son. Am I not right, Madame?

DEBORAH *is so taken aback by his effrontery that for a moment she is speechless. She replies coldly, obviously doing so only because she does not wish to create further embarrassment.*

DEBORAH   That is true, sir. (*She turns her back on him.*) If you will be so kind, Miss Melody. I've wasted so much of the morning and I have to return to the city. I have only time for a short visit—

SARA   Just come with me, Mrs. Harford. (*She goes to the door at right, and steps aside to let* DEBORAH *precede her.*) What a pleasant surprise this will be for Simon. He'd have written you he was sick, but he didn't want to worry you. (*She follows* DEBORAH *into the hall.*)

MELODY   Damned fool of a woman! If I'd known— No, be damned if I regret! Cursed Yankee upstart! (*With a sneer*) But she didn't fool me with her insulted airs! I've known too many women— (*In a rage*) "Absurd performance," was it? God damn her!

NORA (*timidly*)   Don't be cursing her and tormenting yourself. She seems a kind lady. She won't hold it against you, when she stops to think, knowing you didn't know who she is.

MELODY (*tensely*)   Be quiet!

NORA   Forget it now, do, for Sara's sake. Sure, you wouldn't want anything to come between her and the lad. (*He is silent. She goes on comfortingly.*) Go on up to your room now and you'll find something to take your mind off. Sara and I have your uniform brushed and laid out on the bed.

MELODY (*harshly*)   Put it back in the trunk! I don't want it to remind me— (*With humiliated rage again*) By the Eternal, I'll wager she believed what I told her of Talavera and the Great Duke honoring me was a drunken liar's boast!

NORA   No, she'd never, Con. She couldn't.

MELODY (*seized by an idea*)   Well, seeing would be believing, eh, my fine lady? Yes, by God, that will prove to her— (*He turns to* NORA, *his self-confidence partly restored.*) Thank you for reminding me of my duty to Sara. You are right. I do owe it to her interests to forget my anger and make a formal apology to Simon's mother for our little misunderstanding. (*He smiles condescendingly.*) Faith, as a gentleman, I should grant it is a pretty woman's privilege to be always right even when she is wrong. (*He goes to the door at extreme left front and opens it.*) If the lady should come back, kindly keep her here on some excuse until I return. (*This is a command. He disappears, closing the door behind him.*)

NORA (*sighs*)   Ah well, it's all right. He'll be on his best behavior now, and he'll feel proud again in his uniform. (*She sits at the end of center table right and relaxes wearily. A moment later* SARA *enters quickly from right and comes to her.*)

SARA   Where's Father?

NORA   I got him to go up and put on his uniform. It'll console him.

SARA (*bitterly*)   Console *him*? It's me ought to be consoled for having such a great fool for a father!

NORA   Hush now! How could he know who—?

SARA (*with a sudden reversal of feeling—almost vindictively*)   Yes, it serves her right. I suppose she thinks she's such a great lady anyone in America would pay her respect. Well, she knows better now. And she didn't act as insulted as she might. Maybe she liked it, for all her pretenses. (*Again with an abrupt reversal of feeling*) Ah, how can I talk such craziness! Him and his drunken love-making! Well, he got put in his place, and aren't I glad! He won't forget in a hurry how she snubbed him, as if he was no better than dirt under her feet!

NORA   She didn't. She had the sense to see he'd been drinking and not to mind him.

SARA   (*dully*)   Maybe. But isn't that bad enough? What woman would want her son to marry the daughter of a man like— (*She breaks down.*) Oh, Mother, I was feeling so happy and sure of Simon, and now— Why did she have to come today? If she'd waited till tomorrow, even, I'd have got him to ask me to marry him, and once he'd done that no power on earth could change him.

NORA   If he loves you no power can change him, anyway. (*Proudly*) Don't I know! (*Reassuringly*) She's his mother, and she loves him and she'll want him to be happy, and she'll see he loves you. What makes you think she'll try to change him?

SARA   Because she hates me, Mother—for one reason.

NORA   She doesn't. She couldn't.

SARA   She does. Oh, she acted as nice as nice, but she didn't fool me. She's the kind would be polite to the hangman, and her on the scaffold. (*She lowers her voice.*) It isn't just to pay Simon a visit she came. It's because Simon's father got a letter telling him about us, and he showed it to her.

NORA   Who did a dirty trick like that?

SARA   It wasn't signed, she said. I suppose someone around here that hates Father—and who doesn't?

NORA   Bad luck to the blackguard, whoever it was!

SARA   She said she'd come to warn Simon his father is wild with anger and he's gone to see his lawyer— But that doesn't worry me. It's only her influence I'm afraid of.

NORA   How do you know about the letter?

SARA   (*avoiding her eyes*)   I sneaked back to listen outside the door.

NORA   Shame on you! You should have more pride!

SARA   I was ashamed, Mother, after a moment or two, and I came away. (*Then defiantly*) No, I'm not ashamed. I wanted to learn what tricks she might be up to, so I'll be able to fight them. I'm not ashamed at all. I'll do anything to keep him. (*Lowering her voice*) She started talking the second she got in the door. She had only a few minutes because she has to be home before dinner so her husband won't suspect she came here. He's forbidden her to see Simon ever since Simon came out here to live.

NORA   Well, doesn't her coming against her husband's orders show she's on Simon's side?

SARA   Yes, but it doesn't show she wants him to marry me. (*Impatiently*) Don't be so simple, Mother. Wouldn't she tell Simon that anyway, even if the truth was her husband sent her to do all she could to get him away from me?

NORA   Don't look for trouble before it comes. Wait and see, now. Maybe you'll find—

SARA   I'll find what I said, Mother—that she hates me. (*Bitterly*) Even if she came here with good intentions, she wouldn't have them now, after our great gentleman has insulted her. Thank God, if he's putting on his uniform, he'll be hours before the mirror, and she'll be gone before he can make a fool of himself again. (NORA *starts to tell her the truth—then thinks better of it.* SARA *goes on, changing her tone.*) But I'd like her to see him in his uniform, at that, if he was sober. She'd find she couldn't look down on him—(*Exasperatedly*) Och! I'm as crazy as he is. As if she hadn't the brains to see through him.

NORA (*wearily*)   Leave him be, for the love of God.

SARA (*after a pause—defiantly*)   Let her try whatever game she likes. I have brains too, she'll discover. (*Then uneasily*) Only, like Simon's told me, I feel she's strange and queer behind her lady's airs, and it'll be hard to tell what she's really up to. (*They both hear a sound from upstairs.*) That's her, now. She didn't waste much time. Well, I'm ready for her. Go in the kitchen, will you, Mother? I want to give her the chance to have it out with me alone.

NORA *gets up—then, remembering* MELODY'S *orders, glances toward the door at left front uneasily and hesitates.* SARA *says urgently*

Don't you hear me? Hurry, Mother!

NORA *sighs and goes out quickly, right.* SARA *sits at rear of the center table and waits, drawing herself up in an unconscious imitation of her father's grand manner.* DEBORAH *appears in the doorway at right. There is nothing in her expression to betray any emotion resulting from her interview with her son. She smiles pleasantly at* SARA, *who rises graciously from her chair.*

DEBORAH (*coming to her*)   I am glad to find you here, Miss Melody. It gives me another opportunity to express my gratitude for your kindness to my son during his illness.

SARA   Thank you, Mrs. Harford. My mother and I have been only too happy to do all we could. (*She adds defiantly*) We are very fond of Simon.

DEBORAH   (*a glint of secret amusement in her eyes*)   Yes, I feel you are. And he has told me how fond he is of you. (*Her manner becomes reflective. She speaks rapidly in a remote, detached way, lowering her voice unconsciously as if she were thinking aloud to herself.*) This is the first time I have seen Simon since he left home to seek self-emancipation at the breast of Nature. I find him not so greatly changed as I had been led to expect from his letters. Of course, it is some time since he has written. I had thought his implacably honest discovery that the poetry he hoped the pure freedom of Nature would inspire him to write is, after all, but a crude imitation of Lord Byron's would have more bitterly depressed his spirit. (*She smiles.*) But evidently he has found a new romantic dream by way of recompense. As I might have known he would. Simon is an inveterate dreamer—a weakness he inherited from me, I'm afraid, although I must admit the Harfords have been great dreamers, too, in their way. Even my husband has a dream—a conservative, material dream, naturally. I have just been reminding Simon that his father is rigidly unforgiving when his dream is flouted, and very practical in his methods of defending it. (*She smiles again.*) My warning was the mechanical gesture of a mother's duty, merely. I realized it would have no effect. He did not listen to what I said. For that matter, neither did I. (*She laughs a little detached laugh, as if she were secretly amused.*)

SARA   (*stares at her, unable to decide what is behind all this and how she should react—with an undercurrent of resentment*)   I don't think Simon imitates Lord Byron. I hate Lord Byron's poetry. And I know there's a true poet in Simon.

DEBORAH   (*vaguely surprised—speaks rapidly again*)   Oh, in feeling, of course. It is natural you should admire that in him—now. But I warn you it is a quality difficult for a woman to keep on admiring in a Harford, judging from what I know of the family history. Simon's great-grandfather, Jonathan Harford, had it. He was killed at Bunker Hill, but I suspect the War for Independence was merely a symbolic opportunity for him. His was a personal war, I am sure—for pure freedom. Simon's grandfather, Evan Harford, had the quality too. A fanatic in the cause of pure freedom, he became scornful of our Revolution. It made too many compromises with the ideal to free him. He went to France and became a rabid Jacobin, a worshiper of Robespierre.[2] He would have liked to have gone to the guillotine with his incorruptible Redeemer, but he was too unimportant. They simply forgot to kill him. He came home and lived in a little temple of Liberty he had built in a corner of what is now my garden. It is still there. I remember him well. A dry, gentle, cruel, indomitable, futile old idealist who used frequently to wear his old uniform of the French Republican National Guard. He died wearing it. But the point is, you can have no idea what revengeful hate the Harford pursuit of freedom imposed upon the women who shared their lives. The three daughters-in-law of Jonathan, Evan's half-sisters, had to make a large, greedy fortune out of privateering and the Northwest trade, and finally were even driven to embrace the profits of the slave trade —as a triumphant climax, you understand, of their long battle to escape the enslavement of freedom by enslaving it. Evan's wife, of course, was drawn into this conflict, and became their tool and accomplice. They even attempted to own me, but I managed to escape because there was so little of me in the flesh that aged, greedy fingers could clutch. I am sorry they are dead and cannot know you. They would approve of you, I think. They would see that you are strong and ambitious and determined to take what you want. They would have smiled like senile, hungry serpents and welcomed you into their coils. (*She laughs.*) Evil old witches! Detestable, but I could not help admiring them—pitying them, too—in the end. We had a bond in common. They idolized Napoleon. They used to say he was the only man they would ever have married. And I used to dream I was Josephine—even after my marriage, I'm afraid. The Sisters, as everyone called them, and all of the family accompanied my husband and me on our honeymoon—to Paris to witness the Emperor's coronation. (*She pauses, smiling at her memories.*)

SARA (*against her will, has become a bit hypnotized by* DEBORAH'S *rapid, low, musical flow of words, as she strains to grasp the implication for her. She speaks in a low, confidential tone herself, smiling naturally*)   I've always admired him too. It's one of the things I've held against my father, that he fought against him and not for him.

DEBORAH (*starts, as if awakening—with a pleasant smile*)   Well, Miss Melody, this is tiresome of me to stand here giving you a discourse on Harford family history. I don't know what you must think of

---

[2] French revolutionist (1758–94).

me—but doubtless Simon has told you I am a bit eccentric at times. (*She glances at* SARA'S *face—amusedly.*) Ah, I can see he has. Then I am sure you will make allowances. I really do not know what inspired me—except perhaps, that I wish to be fair and warn you, too.

SARA (*stiffens*)   Warn me about what, Mrs. Harford?

DEBORAH   Why, that the Harfords never part with their dreams even when they deny them. They cannot. That is the family curse. For example, this book Simon plans to write to denounce the evil of greed and possessive ambition, and uphold the virtue of freeing oneself from the lust for power and saving our souls by being content with little. I cannot imagine you taking that seriously. (*She again flashes a glance at* SARA.) I see you do not. Neither do I. I do not even believe Simon will ever write this book on paper. But I warn you it is already written on his conscience and— (*She stops with a little disdaining laugh.*) I begin to resemble Cassandra with all my warnings. And I continue to stand here boring you with words. (*She holds out her hand graciously.*) Goodbye, Miss Melody.

SARA (*takes her hand mechanically*)   Goodbye, Mrs. Harford.

DEBORAH *starts for the door at rear.* SARA *follows her, her expression confused, suspicious, and at the same time hopeful. Suddenly she blurts out impulsively.*

Mrs. Harford, I—

DEBORAH (*turns on her, pleasantly*)   Yes, Miss Melody? (*But her eyes have become blank and expressionless and discourage any attempt at further contact.*)

SARA (*silenced—with stiff politeness*)   Isn't there some sort of cooling drink I could get you before you go? You must be parched after walking from the road to Simon's cabin and back on this hot day.

DEBORAH   Nothing, thank you. (*Then talking rapidly again in her strange detached way*) Yes, I did find my walk alone in the woods a strangely overpowering experience. Frightening—but intoxicating, too. Such a wild feeling of release and fresh enslavement. I have not ventured from my garden in many years. There, nature is tamed, constrained to obey and adorn. I had forgotten how compelling the brutal power of primitive, possessive nature can be—when suddenly one is attacked by it. (*She smiles.*) It has been a most confusing morning for a tired, middle-aged matron, but I flatter myself I have preserved a philosophic poise, or should I say, pose, as well as may be. Nevertheless, it will be a relief to return to my garden and books and meditations and listen indifferently again while the footsteps of life pass and recede along the street beyond the high wall. I shall never venture forth again to do my duty. It is a noble occupation, no doubt, for those who can presume they know what their duty to others is; but I— (*She laughs.*) Mercy, here I am chattering on again. (*She turns to the door.*) Cato will be provoked at me for keeping him waiting. I've already caused his beloved horses to be half-devoured by flies. Cato is our black coachman. He also is fond of Simon, although since Simon became emancipated he has embarrassed Cato acutely by shaking his hand whenever they meet. Cato was always a self-possessed free man even when he was a slave. It astonishes him that Simon has to prove that he—I mean Simon—is free. (*She smiles.*) Goodbye again, Miss Melody. This time I really am going.

SARA *opens the door for her. She walks past* SARA *into the street, turns left, and, passing before two windows, disappears.* SARA *closes the door and comes back slowly to the head of the table at center. She stands thinking, her expression puzzled, apprehensive, and resentful.* NORA *appears in the doorway at right.*

NORA   God forgive you, Sara, why did you let her go? Your father told me—

SARA   I can't make her out, Mother. You'd think she didn't care, but she does care. And she hates me. I could feel it. But you can't tell— She's crazy, I think. She talked on and on as if she couldn't stop— queer blather about Simon's ancestors, and herself, and Napoleon, and Nature, and her garden and freedom, and God knows what— but letting me know all the time she had a meaning behind it, and was warning and threatening me. Oh, she may be daft in some ways, but she's no fool. I know she didn't let Simon guess she'd rather have him dead than married to me. Oh, no, I'm sure she told him if he was sure he loved me and I meant his happiness— But then she'd say he ought to wait and prove he's sure—anything to give her time. She'd make him promise to wait. Yes, I'll wager that's what she's done!

NORA   (*who has been watching the door at left front, preoccupied by her own worry—frightenedly*)   Your father'll be down any second. I'm going out in the garden. (*She grabs* SARA'S *arm.*) Come along with me, and give him time to get over his rage.

SARA (*shakes off her hand—exasperatedly*)   Leave me be, Mother. I've enough to worry me without bothering about him. I've got to plan the best way to act when I see Simon. I've got to be as big a liar as she was. I'll have to pretend I liked her and I'd respect whatever advice she gave him. I mustn't let him see— But I won't go to him again today, Mother. You can take up his meals and his milk, if you will. Tell him I'm too busy. I want to get him anxious and afraid maybe I'm mad at him for something, that maybe his mother said something. If he once has the idea maybe he's lost me—that ought to help, don't you think, Mother?

NORA (*sees the door at left front begin to open—in a whisper*)   Oh, God help me! (*She turns in panicky flight and disappears through the doorway, right.*)

The door at left front slowly opens—slowly because MELODY, *hearing voices in the room and hoping* DEBORAH *is there, is deliberately making a dramatic entrance. And in spite of its obviousness, it is effective. Wearing the brilliant scarlet full-dress uniform of a major in one of Wellington's dragoon regiments, he looks extraordinarily handsome and distinguished—a startling, colorful, romantic figure, possessing now a genuine quality he has not had before, the quality of the formidably strong, disdainfully fearless cavalry officer he really had been. The uniform has been preserved with the greatest care. Each button is shining and the cloth is spotless. Being in it has notably restored his self-confident arrogance. Also, he has done everything he can to freshen up his face and hide any effect of his morning's drinks. When he discovers* DEBORAH *is not in the room, he is mildly disappointed and, as always when he first confronts* SARA *alone, he seems to shrink back guiltily within himself.* SARA'S *face hardens and she gives no sign of knowing he is there. He comes slowly around the table at left front, until he stands at the end of the center table facing her. She still refuses to notice him and he is forced to speak. He does so with the air of one who condescends to be amused by his own foibles.*

MELODY   I happened to go to my room and found you and your mother had laid out my uniform so invitingly that I could not resist the temptation to put it on at once instead of waiting until evening.

SARA (*turns on him. In spite of herself she is so struck by his appearance that the contempt is forced back and she can only stammer a bit foolishly*) Yes, I—I see you did. (*There is a moment's pause. She stares at him fascinatedly—then blurts out with impulsive admiration*) You look grand and handsome, Father.

MELODY (*as pleased as a child*) Why, it is most kind of you to say that, my dear Sara. (*Preening himself*) I flatter myself I do not look too unworthy of the man I was when I wore this uniform with honor.

SARA (*an appeal forced out of her that is both pleading and a bitter reproach*) Oh, Father, why can't you ever be the thing you can seem to be? (*A sad scorn comes into her voice.*) The man you were. I'm sorry I never knew that soldier. I think he was the only man who wasn't just a dream.

MELODY (*His face becomes a blank disguise—coldly.*) I don't understand you. (*A pause. He begins to talk in an arrogantly amused tone.*) I suspect you are still holding against me my unfortunate blunder with your future mother-in-law. I would not blame you if you did. (*He smiles.*) Faith, I did put my foot in it. (*He chuckles.*) The devil of it is, I can never get used to these Yankee ladies. I do them the honor of complimenting them with a bit of harmless flattery and, lo and behold, suddenly my lady acts as if I had insulted her. It must be their damned narrow Puritan background. They can't help seeing sin hiding under every bush, but this one need not have been alarmed. I never had an eye for skinny, pale snips of women— (*Hastily*) But what I want to tell you is I am sorry it happened, Sara, and I will do my best, for the sake of your interests, to make honorable amends. I shall do the lady the honor of tendering her my humble apologies when she comes downstairs. (*With arrogant vanity*) I flatter myself she will be graciously pleased to make peace. She was not as outraged by half as her conscience made her pretend, if I am any judge of feminine frailty.

SARA (*who has been staring at him with scorn until he says this last— impulsively, with a sneer of agreement*) I'll wager she wasn't for all her airs. (*Then furious at herself and him*) Ah, will you stop telling me your mad dreams! (*Controlling herself—coldly*) You'll have no chance to make bad worse by trying to fascinate her with your beautiful uniform. She's gone.

MELODY (*stunned*) Gone? (*Furiously*) You're lying, damn you!

SARA I'm not. She left ten minutes ago, or more.

MELODY (*before he thinks*) But I told your mother to keep her here until— (*He stops abruptly.*)

SARA   So that's why Mother is so frightened. Well, it was me let her go, so don't take out your rage on poor Mother.

MELODY   Rage? My dear Sara, all I feel is relief. Surely you can't believe I could have looked forward to humbling my pride, even though it would have furthered your interests.

SARA   Furthered my interests by giving her another reason to laugh up her sleeve at your pretenses? (*With angry scorn, lapsing into broad brogue*) Arrah, God pity you! (*She turns her back on him and goes off, right.* MELODY *stands gripping the back of the chair at the foot of the table in his big, powerful hands in an effort to control himself. There is a crack as the chair back snaps in half. He stares at the fragments in his hands with stupid surprise. The door to the bar is shoved open and* MICKEY *calls in.*)

MALOY   Here's Cregan back to see you, Major.

MELODY   (*startled, repeats stupidly*)   Cregan? (*Then his face suddenly lights up with pathetic eagerness and his voice is full of welcoming warmth as he calls.*) Jamie! My old comrade in arms! (*As* CREGAN *enters, he grips his hand.*) By the Powers, I'm glad you're here, Jamie.

CREGAN *is surprised and pleased by the warmth of his welcome.* MELODY *draws him into the room.*

Come. Sit down. You'll join me in a drink, I know. (*He gets* CREGAN *a glass from the cupboard. The decanter and* MELODY'S *glass are already on the table.*)

CREGAN   (*admiringly*)   Be God, it's the old uniform, no less, and you look as fine a figure in it as ever you did in Spain. (*He sits at right of table at left front as* MELODY *sits at rear.*)

MELODY   (*immensely pleased—deprecatingly*)   Hardly, Jamie—but not a total ruin yet, I hope. I put it on in honor of the day. I see you've forgotten. For shame, you dog, not to remember Talavera.

CREGAN   (*excitedly*)   Talavera, is it? Where I got my saber cut. Be the mortal, I remember it, and you've a right to celebrate. You was worth any ten men in the army that day!

MELODY *has shoved the decanter toward him. He pours a drink.*

MELODY   (*This compliment completely restores him to his arrogant self.*) Yes, I think I may say I did acquit myself with honor. (*Patronizingly*) So, for that matter, did you. (*He pours a drink and raises his glass.*) To the day and your good health, Corporal Cregan.

CREGAN (*enthusiastically*)   To the day and yourself, God bless you, Con! (*He tries to touch brims with* MELODY'S *glass, but* MELODY *holds his glass away and draws himself up haughtily.*)

MELODY (*with cold rebuke*)   I said, to the day and your good health, *Corporal Cregan.*

CREGAN (*for a second is angry—then he grins and mutters admiringly*) Be God, it's you can bate the world and never let it change you! (*Correcting his toast with emphasis*) To the day and yourself, *Major Melody.*

MELODY (*touches his glass to* CREGAN'S—*graciously condescending*) Drink hearty, Corporal. (*They drink.*)

CURTAIN

ACT THREE

SCENE—*The same. The door to the bar is closed. It is around eight that evening and there are candles on the center table.* MELODY *sits at the head of this table. In his brilliant uniform he presents more than ever an impressively colorful figure in the room, which appears smaller and dingier in the candlelight.* CREGAN *is in the chair on his right. The other chairs at this table are unoccupied.* RILEY, O'DOWD, *and* ROCHE *sit at the table at left front.* RILEY *is at front, but his chair is turned sideways so he faces right.* O'DOWD *has the chair against the wall, facing right, with* ROCHE *across the table from him, his back to* MELODY. *All five are drunk,* MELODY *more so than any of them, but except for the glazed glitter in his eyes and his deathly pallor, his appearance does not betray him. He is holding his liquor like a gentleman.*

CREGAN *is the least drunk.* O'DOWD *and* ROCHE *are boisterous. The effect of the drink on* RILEY *is merely to sink him deeper in dreams. He seems oblivious to his surroundings.*

An empty and a half-empty bottle of port are on the table before MELODY *and* CREGAN, *and their glasses are full. The three at the table have a decanter of whiskey.*

SARA, *wearing her working dress and an apron, is removing dishes and the remains of the dinner. Her face is set. She is determined to ignore them, but there is angry disgust in her eyes.* MELODY *is arranging forks, knives, spoons, saltcellar, etc., in a plan of battle on the table before him.* CREGAN *watches him.* PATCH RILEY *gives a few tuning-up quavers on his pipes.*

MELODY   Here's the river Tagus. And here, Talavera. This would be the French position on a rise of ground with the plain between our lines and theirs. Here is our redoubt with the Fourth Division and the Guards. And here's our cavalry brigade in a valley toward our left, if you'll remember, Corporal Cregan.

CREGAN (*excitedly*)   Remember? Sure I see it as clear as yesterday!

RILEY (*bursts into a rollicking song, accompanying himself on the pipes, his voice the quavering ghost of a tenor but still true—to the tune of "Baltiorum."*)

"She'd a pig and boneens,
She'd a bed and a dresser,
And a nate little room
For the father confessor;
With a cupboard and curtains, and something, I'm towld,
That his riv'rance liked when the weather was cowld.
And it's hurroo, hurroo! Biddy O'Rafferty!"

ROCHE *and* O'DOWD *roar after him, beating time on the table with their glasses*—"Hurroo, hurroo! Biddy O'Rafferty!"—*and laugh drunkenly.* CREGAN, *too, joins in this chorus.* MELODY *frowns angrily at the interruption, but at the end he smiles with lordly condescension, pleased by the irreverence of the song.*

O'DOWD (*after a cunning glance at* MELODY'S *face to see what his reaction is—derisively*)   Och, lave it to the priests, divil mend them! Ain't it so, Major?

MELODY   Ay, damn them all! A song in the right spirit, Piper. Faith, I'll have you repeat it for my wife's benefit when she joins us. She still has a secret fondness for priests. And now, less noise, you blackguards. Corporal Cregan and I cannot hear each other with your brawling.

O'DOWD (*smirkingly obedient*)   Quiet it is, yer Honor. Be quiet, Patch. (*He gives the old man, who is lost in dreams, a shove that almost knocks him off his chair.* RILEY *stares at him bewilderedly.* O'DOWD *and* ROCHE *guffaw.*)

MELODY (*scowls at them, then turns to* CREGAN)   Where was I, Corporal? Oh, yes, we were waiting in the valley. We heard a trumpet from the French lines and saw them forming for the attack. An aide-de-camp galloped down the hill to us—

SARA (*who has been watching him disdainfully, reaches out to take his plate—rudely in mocking brogue*)   I'll have your plate, av ye plaze, Major, before your gallant dragoons charge over it and break it.

MELODY (*holds his plate on the table with one hand so she cannot take it, and raises his glass of wine with the other—ignoring her*)   Wet your lips, Corporal. Talavera was a devilish thirsty day, if you'll remember. (*He drinks.*)

CREGAN (*glances uneasily at* SARA)   It was that. (*He drinks.*)

MELODY (*smacking his lips*)   Good wine, Corporal. Thank God, I still have wine in my cellar fit for a gentleman.

SARA (*angrily*)   Are you going to let me take your plate?

MELODY (*ignoring her*)   No, I have no need to apologize for the wine. Nor for the dinner, for that matter. Nora is a good cook when she forgets her infernal parsimony and buys food that one can eat without disgust. But I do owe you an apology for the quality of the service. I have tried to teach the waitress not to snatch plates from the table as if she were feeding dogs in a kennel but she cannot learn. (*He takes his hand from the plate—to* SARA.) There. Now let me see you take it properly.

She stares at him for a moment, speechless with anger—then snatches the plate from in front of him.

CREGAN (*hastily recalls* MELODY *to the battlefield*)   You were where the aide-de-camp galloped up to us, Major. It was then the French artillery opened on us.

SARA *goes out right, carrying a tray laden with plates.*

MELODY   We charged the columns on our left—here— (*he marks the tablecloth*) that were pushing back the Guards. I'll never forget the blast of death from the French squares. And then their chasseurs and lancers were on us! By God, it's a miracle any of us came through!

CREGAN   You wasn't touched except you'd a bullet through your coat, but I had this token on my cheek to remember a French saber by.

MELODY   Brave days, those! By the Eternal, then one lived! Then one forgot! (*He stops—when he speaks again it is bitterly.*) Little did I dream then the disgrace that was to be my reward later on.

CREGAN (*consolingly*)   Ah well, that's the bad luck of things. You'd have been made a colonel soon, if you'd left the Spanish woman alone and not fought that duel.

MELODY (*arrogantly threatening*) Are you presuming to question my conduct in that affair, Corporal Cregan?

CREGAN (*hastily*) Sorra a bit! Don't mind me, now.

MELODY (*stiffly*) I accept your apology. (*He drinks the rest of his wine, pours another glass, then stares moodily before him.* CREGAN *drains his glass and refills it.*)

O'DOWD (*peering past* ROCHE *to watch* MELODY, *leans across to* ROCHE —*in a sneering whisper*) Ain't he the lunatic, sittin' like a play-actor in his red coat, lyin' about his battles with the French!

ROCHE (*sullenly—but careful to keep his voice low*) He'd ought to be shamed he ivir wore the bloody red av England, God's curse on him!

O'DOWD Don't be wishin' him harm, for it's thirsty we'd be without him. Drink long life to him, and may he always be as big a fool as he is this night! (*He sloshes whiskey from the decanter into both their glasses.*)

ROCHE (*with a drunken leer*) Thrue for you! I'll toast him on that. (*He twists round to face* MELODY, *holds up his glass and bawls.*) To the grandest gintleman ivir come from the shores av Ireland! Long life to you, Major!

O'DOWD Hurroo! Long life, yer Honor!

RILEY (*awakened from his dream, mechanically raises his glass*) And to all that belong to ye.

MELODY (*startled from his thoughts, becomes at once the condescending squire—smiling tolerantly*) I said, less noise, you dogs. All the same, I thank you for your toast. (*They drink. A pause. Abruptly* MELODY *begins to recite from Byron. He reads the verse well, quietly, with a bitter eloquence.*

"But midst the crowd, the hum, the shock of men,
To hear, to see, to feel, and to possess,
And roam along, the World's tired denizen,
With none who bless us, none whom we can bless;
Minions of Splendour shrinking from distress!
None that, with kindred consciousness endued,
If we were not, would seem to smile the less,
Of all that flattered—followed—sought, and sued;
This is to be alone—This, this is Solitude!"

(*He stops and glances from one face to another. Their expressions are all blank. He remarks with insulting derisiveness.*) What? You do not understand, my lads? Well, all the better for you. So may you go on fooling yourselves that I am fooled in you. (*Then with a quick change of mood, heartily*) Give us a hunting song, Patch. You've not forgotten "Modideroo," I'll be bound.

RILEY (*roused to interest immediately*)   Does a duck forget wather? I'll show ye! (*He begins the preliminary quavers on his pipes.*)

O'DOWD   Modideroo!

ROCHE   Hurroo!

RILEY (*accompanying himself, sings with wailing melancholy the first verse that comes to his mind of an old hunting song.*)

"And the fox set him down and looked about,
And many were feared to follow;
'Maybe I'm wrong,' says he, 'but I doubt
That you'll be as gay tomorrow.
For loud as you cry, and high as you ride,
And little you feel my sorrow,
I'll be free on the mountainside
While you'll lie low tomorrow.'
Oh, Modideroo, aroo, aroo!"

MELODY, *excited now, beats time on the table with his glass along with* CREGAN, ROCHE, *and* O'DOWD, *and all bellow the refrain,* "Oh, Modideroo, aroo, aroo!"

MELODY (*his eyes alight, forgetting himself, a strong lilt of brogue coming into his voice*)   Ah, that brings it back clear as life! Melody Castle in the days that's gone! A wind from the south, and a sky gray with clouds—good weather for the hounds. A true Irish hunter under me that knows and loves me and would raise to a jump over hell if I gave the word! To hell with men, I say!—and women, too!—with their cowardly hearts rotten and stinking with lies and greed and treachery! Give me a horse to love and I'll cry quits to men! And then away, with the hounds in full cry, and after them! Off with divil a care for your neck, over ditches and streams and stone walls and fences, the fox doubling up the mountainside through the furze and the heather—!

SARA *has entered from right as he begins this longing invocation of old hunting days. She stands behind his chair, listening contemptuously.*

He suddenly feels her presence and turns his head. When he catches the sneer in her eyes, it is as if cold water were dashed in his face. He addresses her as if she were a servant.

Well? What is it? What are you waiting for now?

SARA (*roughly, with coarse brogue*)   What would I be waitin' for but for you to get through with your blather about lovin' horses, and give me a chance to finish my work? Can't you—and the other gintlemen—finish gettin' drunk in the bar and lave me clear the tables?

O'DOWD *conceals a grin behind his hand;* ROCHE *stifles a malicious guffaw.*

CREGAN (*with an apprehensive glance at* MELODY, *shakes his head at her admonishingly*)   Now, Sara, be aisy.

But MELODY *suppresses any angry reaction. He rises to his feet, a bit stiffly and carefully, and bows.*

MELODY (*coldly*)   I beg your pardon if we have interfered with your duties. (*To* O'DOWD *and his companions*) Into the bar, you louts!

O'DOWD   The bar it is, sorr. Come, Dan. Wake up, Patch. (*He pokes the piper. He and* ROCHE *go into the bar, and* RILEY *stumbles vaguely after them.* CREGAN *waits for* MELODY.)

MELODY   Go along, Corporal. I'll join you presently. I wish to speak to my daughter.

CREGAN   All right, Major. (*He again shakes his head at* SARA, *as if to say, don't provoke him. She ignores him. He goes into the bar, closing the door behind him. She stares at her father with angry disgust.*)

SARA   You're drunk. If you think I'm going to stay here and listen to—

MELODY (*his face expressionless, draws out his chair at the head of the center table for her—politely*)   Sit down, my dear.

SARA   I won't. I have no time. Poor Mother is half dead on her feet. I have to help her. There's a pile of dishes to wash after your grand anniversary feast! (*With bitter anger*) Thank God it's over, and it's the last time you'll ever take satisfaction in having me wait on table for drunken scum like O'Dowd and—

MELODY (*quietly*)   A daughter who takes satisfaction in letting even the scum see that she hates and despises her father! (*He shrugs his shoulders.*) But no matter. (*Indicating the chair again*) Won't you sit down, my dear?

SARA   If you ever dared face the truth, you'd hate and despise yourself! (*Passionately*) All I pray to God is that someday when you're admiring yourself in the mirror something will make you see at last what you really are! That will be revenge in full for all you've done to Mother and me! (*She waits defiantly, as if expecting him to lose his temper and curse her. But* MELODY *acts as if he had not heard her.*)

MELODY (*his face expressionless, his manner insistently bland and polite*)   Sit down, my dear. I will not detain you long, and I think you will find what I have to tell you of great interest.

She searches his face, uneasy now, feeling a threat hidden behind his cold, quiet, gentlemanly tone. She sits down and he sits at rear of table, with an empty chair separating them.

SARA   You'd better think well before you speak, Father. I know the devil that's in you when you're quiet like this with your brain mad with drink.

MELODY I don't understand you. All I wish is to relate something which happened this afternoon.

SARA   (*giving way to bitterness at her humiliation again—sneeringly*) When you went riding on your beautiful thoroughbred mare while Mother and I were sweating and suffocating in the heat of the kitchen to prepare your Lordship's banquet? Sure, I hope you didn't show off and jump your beauty over a fence into somebody's garden, like you've done before, and then have to pay damages to keep out of jail!

MELODY (*roused by mention of his pet—disdainfully*)   The damned Yankee yokels should feel flattered that she deigns to set her dainty hooves in their paltry gardens! She's a truer-born, well-bred lady than any of their women—than the one who paid us a visit this morning, for example.

SARA   Mrs. Harford was enough of a lady to put you in your place and make a fool of you.

MELODY (*seemingly unmoved by this taunt—calmly*)   You are very simple-minded, my dear, to let yourself be taken in by such an obvious bit of clever acting. Naturally, the lady was a bit discomposed when she heard you and your mother coming, after she had just allowed me to kiss her. She had to pretend—

SARA   (*eagerly*)   She let you kiss her? (*Then disgustedly*) It's a lie, but I don't doubt you've made yourself think it's the truth by now.

(*Angrily*) I'm going. I don't want to listen to the whiskey in you boasting of what never happened—as usual! (*She puts her hands on the table and starts to rise.*)

MELODY (*with a quick movement pins hers down with one of his*) Wait! (*A look of vindictive cruelty comes into his eyes—quietly.*) Why are you so jealous of the mare, I wonder? Is it because she has such slender ankles and dainty feet? (*He takes his hand away and stares at her hands—with disgust, commandingly.*) Keep your thick wrists and ugly, peasant paws off the table in my presence, if you please! They turn my stomach! I advise you never to let Simon get a good look at them—

SARA (*instinctively jerks her hands back under the table guiltily. She stammers*)   You—you cruel devil! I knew you'd—

MELODY (*for a second is ashamed and really contrite*)   Forgive me, Sara. I didn't mean—the whiskey talking—as you said. (*He adds in a forced tone, a trace of mockery in it*) An absurd taunt, when you really have such pretty hands and feet, my dear.

She jumps to her feet, so hurt and full of hatred her lips tremble and she cannot speak. He speaks quietly.

Are you going? I was about to tell you of the talk I had this afternoon with young Harford.

She stares at him in dismay. He goes on easily.

It was after I returned from my ride. I cantered the mare by the river and she pulled up lame. So I dismounted and led her back to the barn. No one noticed my return and when I went upstairs it occurred to me I would not find again such an opportunity to have a frank chat with Harford—free from interruptions. (*He pauses, as if he expects her to be furious, but she remains tensely silent, determined not to let him know her reaction.*) I did not beat about the bush. I told him he must appreciate, as a gentleman, it was my duty as your father to demand he lay his cards on the table. I said he must realize that even before you began nursing him here and going alone to his bedroom, there was a deal of gossip about your visits to his cabin, and your walks in the woods with him. I put it to him that such an intimacy could not continue without gravely compromising your reputation.

SARA (*stunned—weakly*)   God forgive you! And what did he say?

MELODY   What could he say? He is a man of honor. He looked damn embarrassed and guilty for a moment, but when he found his tongue, he agreed with me most heartily. He said his mother had told him the same thing.

SARA   Oh, she did, did she? I suppose she did it to find out by watching him how far—

MELODY   (*coldly*)   Well, why not? Naturally, it was her duty as his mother to discover all she could about you. She is a woman of the world. She would be bound to suspect that you might be his mistress.

SARA   (*tensely*)   Oh, would she!

MELODY   But that's beside the point. The point is, my bashful young gentleman finally blurted out that he wanted to marry you.

SARA   (*forgetting her anger—eagerly*)   He told you that?

MELODY   Yes, and he said he had told his mother, and she had said all she wanted was his happiness but she felt in fairness to you and to himself—and I presume she also meant to both families concerned—he should test his love and yours by letting a decent interval of time elapse before your marriage. She mentioned a year, I believe.

SARA   (*angrily*)   Ah! Didn't I guess that would be her trick!

MELODY   (*lifting his eyebrows—coldly*)   Trick? In my opinion, the lady displayed more common sense and knowledge of the world than I thought she possessed. The reasons she gave him are sound and show a consideration for your good name which ought to inspire gratitude in you and not suspicion.

SARA   Arrah, don't tell me she's made a fool of you again! A lot of consideration she has for me!

MELODY   She pointed out to him that if you were the daughter of some family in their own little Yankee clique, there would be no question of a hasty marriage, and so he owed it to you—

SARA   I see. She's the clever one!

MELODY   Another reason was—and here your Simon stammered so embarrassedly I had trouble making him out—she warned him a sudden wedding would look damnably suspicious and start a lot of evil-minded gossip.

SARA   (*tensely*)   Oh, she's clever, all right! But I'll beat her.

MELODY   I told him I agreed with his mother. It is obvious that were there a sudden wedding without a suitable period of betrothal, everyone would believe—

SARA   I don't care what they believe! Tell me this! Did she get him to promise her he'd wait? (*Before he can answer—bitterly*) But of course she did! She'd never have left till she got that out of him!

MELODY (*ignores this*)   I told him I appreciated the honor he did me in asking for your hand, but he must understand that I could not commit myself until I had talked to his father and was assured the necessary financial arrangements could be concluded to our mutual satisfaction. There was the amount of settlement to be agreed upon, for instance.

SARA   That dream, again! God pity you! (*She laughs helplessly and a bit hysterically.*) And God help Simon. He must have thought you'd gone out of your mind! What did he say?

MELODY   He said nothing, naturally. He is well bred and he knows this is a matter he must leave to his father to discuss. There is also the equally important matter of how generous an allowance Henry Harford is willing to settle on his son. I did not mention this to Simon, of course, not wishing to embarrass him further with talk of money.

SARA   Thank God for that, at least! (*She giggles hysterically.*)

MELODY (*quietly*)   May I ask what you find so ridiculous in an old established custom? Simon is an elder son, the heir to his father's estate. No matter what their differences in the past may have been, now that Simon has decided to marry and settle down his father will wish to do the fair thing by him. He will realize, too, that although there is no more honorable calling than that of poet and philosopher, which his son has chosen to pursue, there is no decent living to be gained by its practice. So naturally he will settle an allowance on Simon, and I shall insist it be a generous one, befitting your position as my daughter. I will tolerate no niggardly trader's haggling on his part.

SARA (*stares at him fascinatedly, on the edge of helpless, hysterical laughter*)   I suppose it would never occur to you that old Harford might not think it an honor to have his son marry your daughter.

MELODY (*calmly*)   No, it would never occur to me—and if it should occur to him, I would damned soon disabuse his mind. Who is he but a money-grubbing trader? I would remind him that I was born in a castle and there was a time when I possessed wealth and position, and an estate compared to which any Yankee upstart's home in this country is but a hovel stuck in a cabbage patch. I would remind him that you, my daughter, were born in a castle!

SARA (*impulsively, with a proud toss of her head*)   Well, that's no more than the truth. (*Then furious with herself and him*) Och, what crazy blather! (*She springs to her feet.*) I've had enough of your mad dreams!

MELODY   Wait! I haven't finished yet. (*He speaks quietly, but as he goes on there is an increasing vindictiveness in his tone.*) There was another reason why I told young Harford I could not make a final decision. I wished time to reflect on a further aspect of this proposed marriage. Well, I have been reflecting, watching you and examining your conduct, without prejudice, trying to be fair to you and make every possible allowance— (*He pauses.*) Well, to be brutally frank, my dear, all I can see in you is a common, greedy, scheming, cunning peasant girl, whose only thought is money and who has shamelessly thrown herself at a young man's head because his family happens to possess a little wealth and position.

SARA   (*trying to control herself*)   I see your game, Father. I told you when you were drunk like this— But this time, I won't give you the satisfaction— (*Then she bursts out angrily*) It's a lie! I love Simon, or I'd never—

MELODY   (*as if she hadn't spoken*)   So, I have about made up my mind to decline for you Simon Harford's request for your hand in marriage.

SARA   (*jeers angrily now*)   Oh, you have, have you? As if I cared a damn what you—!

MELODY   As a gentleman, I feel I have a duty, in honor, to Simon. Such a marriage would be a tragic misalliance for him—and God knows I know the sordid tragedy of such a union.

SARA   It's Mother has had the tragedy!

MELODY   I hold young Harford in too high esteem. I cannot stand by and let him commit himself irrevocably to what could only bring him disgust and bitterness, and ruin to all his dreams.

SARA   So I'm not good enough for him, you've decided now?

MELODY   That is apparent from your every act. No one, no matter how charitably inclined, could mistake you for a lady. I have tried to make you one. It was an impossible task. God Himself cannot transform a sow's ear into a silk purse!

SARA   (*furiously*)   Father!

MELODY   Young Harford needs to be saved from himself. I can understand his physical infatuation. You are pretty. So was your mother pretty once. But marriage is another matter. The man who would be the ideal husband for you, from a standpoint of conduct and character, is Mickey Maloy, my bartender, and I will be happy to give him my parental blessing—

SARA   Let you stop now, Father!

MELODY   You and he would be congenial. You can match tongues together. He's a healthy animal. He can give you a raft of peasant brats to squeal and fight with the pigs on the mud floor of your hovel.

SARA   It's the dirty hut in which your father was born and raised you're remembering, isn't it?

MELODY   (*stung to fury, glares at her with hatred. His voice quivers but is deadly quiet.*)   Of course, if you trick Harford into getting you with child, I could not refuse my consent. (*Letting go, he bangs his fist on the table.*) No, by God, even then, when I remember my own experience, I'll be damned if I could with a good conscience advise him to marry you!

SARA   (*glaring back at him with hatred*)   You drunken devil! (*She makes a threatening move toward him, raising her hand as if she were going to slap his face—then she controls herself and speaks with quiet, biting sarcasm.*) Consent or not, I want to thank you for your kind fatherly advice on how to trick Simon. I don't think I'll need it but if the worst comes to the worst I promise you I'll remember—

MELODY   (*coldly, his face expressionless*)   I believe I have said all I wished to say to you. (*He gets up and bows stiffly.*) If you will excuse me, I shall join Corporal Cregan. (*He goes to the bar door.* SARA *turns and goes quietly out right, forgetting to clear the few remaining dishes on the center table. His back turned, he does not see her go. With his hand on the knob of the bar door, he hesitates. For a second he breaks—torturedly.*) Sara! (*Then quietly*) There are things I said which I regret—even now. I—I trust you will overlook— As your mother knows, it's the liquor talking, not—I must admit that, due to my celebrating the anniversary, my brain is a bit addled by whiskey—as you said. (*He waits, hoping for a word of forgiveness. Finally, he glances over his shoulder. As he discovers she is not there and has not heard him, for a second he crumbles, his soldierly erectness sags and his face falls. He looks sad and hopeless and bitter and old, his eyes wandering dully. But, as in the two preceding acts, the mirror attracts him, and as he moves from the bar door to stand before it he assumes his arrogant, Byronic pose again. He repeats in each detail his pantomime before the mirror. He speaks proudly.*) Myself to the bitter end! No weakening, so help me God! (*There is a knock on the street door but he does not hear it. He starts his familiar incantation quotes from Byron.*)

"I have not loved the World, nor the World me;

I have not flattered its rank breath, nor bowed
To its idolatries a patient knee . . ."

(*The knock on the door is repeated more loudly.* MELODY *starts guiltily and steps quickly away from the mirror. His embarrassment is transformed into resentful anger. He calls.*) Come in, damn you! Do you expect a lackey to open the door for you?

The door opens and NICHOLAS GADSBY *comes in.* GADSBY *is in his late forties, short, stout, with a big, bald head, round, florid face, and small, blue eyes. A rigidly conservative, best-family attorney, he is stiffly correct in dress and manner, dryly portentous in speech, and extremely conscious of his professional authority and dignity. Now, however, he is venturing on unfamiliar ground and is by no means as sure of himself as his manner indicates. The unexpected vision of* MELODY *in his uniform startles him and for a second he stands, as close to gaping as he can be, impressed by* MELODY'S *handsome distinction.* MELODY, *in his turn, is surprised. He had not thought the intruder would be a gentleman. He unbends, although his tone is still a bit curt. He bows a bit stiffly, and* GADSBY *finds himself returning the bow.*

Your pardon, sir. When I called, I thought it was one of the damned riffraff mistaking the barroom door. Pray be seated, sir.

GADSBY *comes forward and takes the chair at the head of the center table, glancing at the few dirty dishes on it with distaste.* MELODY *says*

Your pardon again, sir. We have been feasting late, which accounts for the disarray. I will summon a servant to inquire your pleasure.

GADSBY (*beginning to recover his aplomb—shortly*)   Thank you, but I want nothing, sir. I came here to seek a private interview with the proprietor of this tavern, by name, Melody. (*He adds a bit hesitantly*) Are you, by any chance, he?

MELODY (*stiffens arrogantly*)   I am not, sir. But if you wish to see Major Cornelius Melody, one time of His Majesty's Seventh Dragoons, who served with honor under the Duke of Wellington in Spain, I am he.

GADSBY (*dryly*)   Very well, sir. Major Melody, then.

MELODY (*does not like his tone—insolently sarcastic*)   And whom have I the *honor* of addressing?

As GADSBY *is about to reply,* SARA *enters from right, having remembered the dishes.* MELODY *ignores her as he would a servant.* GADSBY *examines her carefully as she gathers up the dishes. She notices him staring at her and gives him a resentful, suspicious glance. She carries the dishes out, right, to the kitchen, but a moment later she can be seen just inside the hall at right, listening. Meanwhile, as soon as he thinks she has gone,* GADSBY *speaks.*

GADSBY (*with affected casualness*)   A pretty young woman. Is she your daughter, sir? I seemed to detect a resemblance—

MELODY (*angrily*)   No! Do I look to you, sir, like a man who would permit his daughter to work as a waitress? Resemblance to me? You must be blind, sir. (*Coldly*) I am still waiting for you to inform me who you are and why you should wish to see me.

GADSBY (*hands him a card—extremely nettled by* MELODY'S *manner—curtly*)   My card, sir.

MELODY (*glances at the card*)   Nicholas Gadsby. (*He flips it aside disdainfully.*) Attorney, eh? The devil take all your tribe, say I. I have small liking for your profession, sir, and I cannot imagine what business you can have with me. The damned thieves of the law did their worst to me many years ago in Ireland. I have little left to tempt you. So I do not see—(*Suddenly an idea comes to him. He stares at* GADSBY, *then goes on in a more friendly tone.*) That is, unless— Do you happen by any chance to represent the father of young Simon Harford?

GADSBY (*indignant at* MELODY'S *insults to his profession—with a thinly veiled sneer*)   Ah, then you were expecting— That makes things easier. We need not beat about the bush. I do represent Mr. Henry Harford, sir.

MELODY (*thawing out, in his total misunderstanding of the situation*) Then accept my apologies, sir, for my animadversions against your profession. I am afraid I may be prejudiced. In the army, we used to say we suffered more casualties from your attacks at home than the French ever inflicted. (*He sits down on the chair on* GADSBY'S *left, at rear of table—remarking with careless pride*) A word of explanation as to why you find me in uniform. It is the anniversary of the battle of Talavera, sir, and—

GADSBY (*interrupts dryly*)   Indeed, sir? But I must tell you my time is short. With your permission, we will proceed at once to the matter in hand.

MELODY (*controlling his angry discomfiture—coldly*) I think I can hazard a guess as to what that matter is. You have come about the settlement?

GADSBY (*misunderstanding him, replies in a tone almost openly contemptuous*) Exactly, sir. Mr. Harford was of the opinion, and I agreed with him, that a settlement would be foremost in your mind.

MELODY (*scowls at his tone but, as he completely misunderstands* GADSBY'S *meaning, he forces himself to bow politely*) It does me honor, sir, that Mr. Harford appreciates he is dealing with a gentleman and has the breeding to know how these matters are properly arranged.

GADSBY *stares at him, absolutely flabbergasted by what he considers a piece of the most shameless effrontery.* MELODY *leans toward him confidentially.*

I will be frank with you, sir. The devil of it is, this comes at a difficult time for me. Temporary, of course, but I cannot deny I am pinched at the moment—devilishly pinched. But no matter. Where my only child's happiness is at stake, I am prepared to make every possible effort. I will sign a note of hand, no matter how ruinous the interest demanded by the scoundrelly moneylenders. By the way, what amount does Mr. Harford think proper? Anything in reason—

GADSBY (*listening in utter confusion, finally gets the idea* MELODY *is making him the butt of a joke—fuming*) I do not know what you are talking about, sir, unless you think to make a fool of me! If this is what is known as Irish wit—

MELODY (*bewildered for a second—then in a threatening tone*) Take care, sir, and watch your words or I warn you you will repent them, no matter whom you represent! No damned pettifogging dog can insult me with impunity! (*As* GADSBY *draws back apprehensively, he adds with insulting disdain*) As for making a fool of you, sir, I would be the fool if I attempted to improve on God's handiwork!

GADSBY (*ignoring the insults, forces a placating tone*) I wish no quarrel with you, sir. I cannot for the life of me see— I fear we are dealing at cross-purposes. Will you tell me plainly what you mean by your talk of settlement?

MELODY Obviously, I mean the settlement I am prepared to make on my daughter. (*As* GADSBY *only looks more dumfounded, he continues sharply*) Is not your purpose in coming here to arrange, on

Mr. Harford's behalf, for the marriage of his son with my daughter?

GADSBY   Marriage? Good God, no! Nothing of the kind!

MELODY (*dumfounded*)   Then what have you come for?

GADSBY (*feeling he has now the upper hand—sharply*)   To inform you that Mr. Henry Harford is unalterably opposed to any further relationship between his son and your daughter, whatever the nature of that relationship in the past.

MELODY (*leans forward threateningly*)   By the Immortal, sir, if you dare insinuate—!

GADSBY (*draws back again, but he is no coward and is determined to carry out his instructions*)   I insinuate nothing, sir. I am here on Mr. Harford's behalf, to make you an offer. That is what I thought you were expecting when you mentioned a settlement. Mr. Harford is prepared to pay you the sum of three thousand dollars—provided, mark you, that you and your daughter sign an agreement I have drawn up which specifies that you relinquish all claims, of whatever nature. And also provided you agree to leave this part of the country at once with your family. Mr. Harford suggests it would be advisable that you go West—to Ohio, say.

MELODY (*so overcome by a rising tide of savage, humiliated fury, he can only stammer hoarsely*)   So Henry Harford does me the honor —to suggest that, does he?

GADSBY (*watching him uneasily, attempts a reasonable, persuasive tone*)   Surely you could not have spoken seriously when you talked of marriage. There is such a difference in station. The idea is preposterous. If you knew Mr. Harford, you would realize he would never countenance—

MELODY (*his pent-up rage bursts out—smashing his fist on the table*)   Know him? By the Immortal God, I'll know him soon! And he'll know me! (*He springs to his feet.*) But first, you Yankee scum, I'll deal with you! (*He draws back his fist to smash* GADSBY *in the face, but* SARA *has run from the door at right and she grabs his arm. She is almost as furious as he is and there are tears of humiliated pride in her eyes.*)

SARA   Father! Don't! He's only a paid lackey. Where is your pride that you'd dirty your hands on the like of him?

While she is talking the door from the bar opens and ROCHE, O'DOWD, *and* CREGAN *crowd into the room.* MICKEY *stands in the doorway.* NORA *follows* SARA *in from right.*

ROCHE (*with drunken enthusiasm*)   It's a fight! For the love of God, clout the damned Yankee, Major!

MELODY (*controls himself—his voice shaking*)   You are right, Sara. It would be beneath me to touch such a vile lickspittle. But he won't get off scot-free. (*Sharply, a commander ordering his soldiers*) Here you, Roche and O'Dowd! Get hold of him!

They do so with enthusiasm and yank GADSBY *from his chair.*

GADSBY   You drunken ruffians! Take your hands off me!

MELODY (*addressing him—in his quiet, threatening tone now*)   You may tell the swindling trader, Harford, who employs you that he'll hear from me! (*To* ROCHE *and* O'DOWD) Throw this thing out! Kick it down to the crossroads!

ROCHE   Hurroo! (*He and* O'DOWD *run* GADSBY *to the door at rear.* CREGAN *jumps ahead, grinning, and opens the door for them.*)

GADSBY (*struggling futilely as they rush him through the door*)   You scoundrels! Take your hands off me! Take—

MELODY *looks after them. The two women watch him,* NORA *frightened,* SARA *with a strange look of satisfied pride.*

CREGAN (*in the doorway, looking out—laughing*)   Oh, it'd do your heart good, Con, to see the way they're kicking his butt down the street! (*He comes in and shuts the door.*)

MELODY (*his rage welling again, as his mind dwells on his humiliation —starting to pace up and down*)   It's with his master I have to deal, and, by the Powers, I'll deal with him! You'll come with me, Jamie. I'll want you for a witness. He'll apologize to me—more than that, he'll come back here this very night and apologize publicly to my daughter, or else he meets me in the morning! By God, I'll face him at ten paces or across a handkerchief! I'll put a bullet through him, so help me, Christ!

NORA (*breaks into a dirgelike wail*)   God forgive you, Con, is it a duel again—murtherin' or gettin' murthered?

MELODY   Be quiet, woman! Go back to your kitchen! Go, do you hear me!

NORA *turns obediently toward the door at right, beginning to cry.*

SARA (*puts an arm around her mother. She is staring at* MELODY *apprehensively now.*)   There, Mother, don't worry. Father knows that's all foolishness. He's only talking. Go on now in the kitchen and sit down and rest, Mother.

NORA *goes out right.* SARA *closes the door after her and comes back.*

MELODY (*turns on her with bitter anger*) Only talking, am I? It's the first time in my life I ever heard anyone say Con Melody was a coward! It remains for my own daughter—!

SARA (*placatingly*) I didn't say that, Father. But can't you see— you're not in Ireland in the old days now. The days of duels are long past and dead, in this part of America anyway. Harford will never fight you. He—

MELODY He won't, won't he? By God, I'll make him! I'll take a whip. I'll drag him out of his house and lash him down the street for all his neighbors to see! He'll apologize, or he'll fight, or I'll brand him a craven before the world!

SARA (*frightened now*) But you'll never be let see him! His servants will keep you out! He'll have the police arrest you, and it'll be in the papers about another drunken Mick raising a crazy row! (*She appeals to* CREGAN.) Tell him I'm telling the truth, Jamie. You've still got some sober sense in you. Maybe he'll listen to you.

CREGAN (*glances at* MELODY *uneasily*) Maybe Sara's right, Major.

MELODY When I want your opinion, I'll ask for it! (*Sneeringly*) Of course, if you've become such a coward you're afraid to go with me—

CREGAN (*stung*) Coward, is ut? I'll go, and be damned to you!

SARA Jamie, you fool! Oh, it's like talking to crazy men! (*She grabs her father's arm—pleadingly.*) Don't do it, Father, for the love of God! Have I ever asked you anything? Well, I ask you to heed me now! I'll beg you on my knees, if you like! Isn't it me you'd fight about, and haven't I a right to decide? You punished that lawyer for the insult. You had him thrown out of here like a tramp. Isn't that your answer to old Harford that insults him? It's for him to challenge you, if he dares, isn't it? Why can't you leave it at that and wait—

MELODY (*shaking off her hand—angrily*) You talk like a scheming peasant! It's a question of my honor!

SARA No! It's a question of my happiness, and I won't have your mad interfering—! (*Desperately forcing herself to reason with him again*) Listen, Father! If you'll keep out of it, I'll show you how I'll make a fool of old Harford! Simon won't let anything his father does keep him from marrying me. His mother is the only one who might have the influence over him to come between us. She's only watching for a good excuse to turn Simon against marrying me, and if you go raising a drunken row at their house, and make a public scandal, shouting you want to murder his father, can't you see what a chance that will give her?

MELODY (*raging*)   That damned, insolent Yankee bitch! She's all the more reason. Marry, did you say? You dare to think there can be any question now of your marrying the son of a man who has insulted my honor—and yours?

SARA (*defiantly*)   Yes, I dare to think it! I love Simon and I'm going to marry him!

MELODY   And I say you're not! If he wasn't sick, I'd— But I'll get him out of here tomorrow! I forbid you ever to see him again! If you dare disobey me I'll—! (*Beginning to lose all control of himself*) If you dare defy me—for the sake of the dirty money you think you can beg from his family, if you're his wife—!

SARA (*fiercely*)   You lie! (*Then with quiet intensity*) Yes. I defy you or anyone who tries to come between us!

MELODY   You'd sell your pride as my daughter—! (*His face convulsed by fury*) You filthy peasant slut! You whore! I'll see you dead first—! By the living God, I'd kill you myself! (*He makes a threatening move toward her.*)

SARA (*shrinks back frightenedly*)   Father! (*Then she stands and faces him defiantly.*)

CREGAN (*steps between them*)   Con! In the name of God!

MELODY's *fit of insane fury leaves him. He stands panting for breath, shuddering with the effort to regain some sort of poise.* CREGAN *speaks, his only thought to get him away from* SARA.

If we're going after old Harford, Major, we'd better go. That thief of a lawyer will warn him—

MELODY (*seizing on this—hoarsely*)   Yes, let's go. Let's go, Jamie. Come along, Corporal. A stirrup cup, and we'll be off. If the mare wasn't lame, I'd ride alone—but we can get a rig at the livery stable. Don't let me forget to stop at the barn for my whip. (*By the time he finishes speaking, he has himself in hand again and his ungovernable fury has gone. There is a look of cool, menacing vengefulness in his face. He turns toward the bar door.*)

SARA (*helplessly*)   Father! (*Desperately, as a last, frantic threat*) You'll force me to go to Simon—and do what you said!

If he hears this, he gives no sign of it. He strides into the bar. CREGAN *follows him, closing the door.* SARA *stares before her, the look of defiant desperation hardening on her face. The street door is flung open and* O'DOWD *and* ROCHE *pile in, laughing uproariously.*

ROCHE   Hurroo!

O'DOWD   The army is back, Major, with the foe flying in retreat. (*He sees* MELODY *is not there—to* SARA) Where's himself?

SARA *appears not to see or hear him.*

ROCHE (*after a quick glance at her*)   Lave her be. He'll be in the bar. Come on. (*He goes to the bar.*)

O'DOWD (*following him, speaks over his shoulder to* SARA)   You should have seen the Yank! His coachman had to help him in his rig at the corner—and Roche gave the coachman a clout too, for good measure! (*He disappears, laughing, slamming the door behind him.* NORA *opens the door at right and looks in cautiously. Seeing* SARA *alone, she comes in.*)

NORA   Sara. (*She comes over to her.*) Sara. (*She takes hold of her arm —whispers uneasily*) Where's himself?

SARA (*dully*)   I couldn't stop him.

NORA   I could have told you you was wastin' breath. (*With a queer pride*) The divil himself couldn't kape Con Melody from a duel! (*Then mournfully*) It's like the auld times come again, and the same worry and sorrow. Even in the days before ivir I'd spoke a word to him, or done more than make him a bow when he'd ride past on his hunter, I used to lie awake and pray for him when I'd hear he was fightin' a duel in the mornin'. (*She smiles a shy, gentle smile.*) I was in love with him even then.

SARA *starts to say something bitter but what she sees in her mother's face stops her.* NORA *goes on, with a feeble attempt at boastful confidence.*

But I'll not worry this time, and let you not, either. There wasn't a man in Galway was his equal with a pistol, and what chance will this auld stick av a Yankee have against him? (*There is a noise of boisterous farewells from the bar and the noise of an outer door shutting.* NORA *starts.*) That's him leavin'! (*Her mouth pulls down pitiably. She starts for the bar with a sob.*) Ah, Con darlin', don't—! (*She stops, shaking her head helplessly.*) But what's the good? (*She sinks on a chair with a weary sigh.*)

SARA (*bitterly, aloud to herself more than to her mother*)   No good.
Let him go his way—and I'll go mine. (*Tensely*) I won't let him
destroy my life with his madness, after all the plans I've made and
the dreams I've dreamed. I'll show him I can play at the game of
gentleman's honor too!

NORA *has not listened. She is sunk in memories of old fears and her
present worry about the duel.* SARA *hesitates—then, keeping her face
turned away from her mother, touches her shoulder.*

I'm going upstairs to bed, Mother.

NORA (*starts—then indignantly*)   To bed, is it? You can think of
sleepin' when he's—

SARA   I didn't say sleep, but I can lie down and try to rest. (*Still avoiding looking at her mother*) I'm dead tired, Mother.

NORA (*tenderly solicitous now, puts an arm around her*)   You must be,
darlin'. It's been the divil's own day for you, with all— (*With sudden
remorse*) God forgive me, darlin'. I was forgettin' about you and the
Harford lad. (*Miserably*) Oh, God help us! (*Suddenly with a flash
of her strange, fierce pride in the power of love*) Never mind! If
there's true love between you, you'll not let a duel or anything in the
world kape you from each other, whatever the cost! Don't I know!

SARA (*kisses her impulsively, then looks away again*)   You're going to
sit up and wait down here?

NORA   I am. I'd be destroyed with fear lying down in the dark. Here,
the noise of them in the bar kapes up my spirits, in a way.

SARA   Yes, you'd better stay here. Good night, Mother.

NORA   Good night, darlin'.

SARA *goes out at right, closing the door behind her.*

CURTAIN

ACT FOUR

SCENE   *The same. It is around midnight. The room is in darkness except for one candle on the table, center. From the bar comes the
sound of* PATCH RILEY'S *pipes playing a reel and the stamp of dancing feet.*

NORA *sits at the foot of the table at center. She is hunched up in
an old shawl, her arms crossed over her breast, hugging herself as if*

*she were cold. She looks on the verge of collapse from physical
fatigue and hours of worry. She starts as the door from the bar is
opened. It is* MICKEY. *He closes the door behind him, shutting out an
uproar of music and drunken voices. He has a decanter of whiskey
and a glass in his hand. He has been drinking, but is not drunk.*

NORA (*eagerly*) There's news of himself?

MALOY (*putting the decanter and glass on the table*) Sorra a bit.
Don't be worryin' now. Sure, it's not so late yet.

NORA (*dully*) It's aisy for you to say—

MALOY I came in to see how you was, and bring you a taste to put
heart in you. (*As she shakes her head*) Oh, I know you don't indulge,
but I've known you once in a while, and you need it this night. (*As
she again shakes her head—with kindly bullying*) Come now, don't
be stubborn. I'm the doctor and I highly recommend a drop to drive
out black thoughts and rheumatism.

NORA Well—maybe—a taste, only.

MALOY That's the talkin'. (*He pours a small drink and hands it to
her.*) Drink hearty, now.

NORA (*takes a sip, then puts the glass on the table and pushes it away
listlessly*) I've no taste for anything. But I thank you for the
thought. You're a kind lad, Mickey.

MALOY Here's news to cheer you. The word has got round among the
boys, and they've all come in to wait for Cregan and himself. (*With
enthusiasm*) There'll be more money taken over the bar than any
night since this shebeen started!

NORA That's good.

MALOY If they do hate Con Melody, he's Irish, and they hate the
Yanks worse. They're all hopin' he's bate the livin' lights out of
Harford.

NORA (*with belligerent spirit*) And so he has, I know that!

MALOY (*grins*) That's the talk. I'm glad to see you roused from your
worryin'. (*Turning away*) I'd better get back. I left O'Dowd to tend
bar and I'll wager he has three drinks stolen already. (*He hesitates.*)
Sara's not been down?

NORA No.

MALOY (*resentfully*) It's a wonder she wouldn't have more thought for
you than to lave you sit up alone.

NORA (*stiffens defensively*) I made her go to bed. She was droppin'
with tiredness and destroyed with worry. She must have fallen
asleep, like the young can. None of your talk against Sara, now!

MALOY (*starts an exasperated retort*)   The divil take— (*He stops and grins at her with affection.*) There's no batin' you, Nora. Sure, it'd be the joy av me life to have a mother like you to fight for me—or, better still, a wife like you.

NORA   (*A sweet smile of pleased coquetry lights up her drawn face.*) Arrah, save your blarney for the young girls!

MALOY   The divil take young girls. You're worth a hundred av thim.

NORA (*with a toss of her head*)   Get along with you!

MICKEY *grins with satisfaction at having cheered her up and goes in the bar, closing the door. As soon as he is gone, she sinks back into apprehensive brooding.*

SARA *appears silently in the doorway at right. She wears a faded old wrapper over her nightgown, slippers on her bare feet. Her hair is down over her shoulders, reaching to her waist. There is a change in her. All the bitterness and defiance have disappeared from her face. It looks gentle and calm and at the same time dreamily happy and exultant. She is much prettier than she has ever been before. She stands looking at her mother, and suddenly she becomes shy and uncertain—as if, now that she'd come this far, she had half a mind to retreat before her mother discovered her. But NORA senses her presence and looks up.*

NORA (*dully*)   Ah, it's you, darlin'! (*Then gratefully*) Praise be, you've come at last! I'm sick with worry and I've got to the place where I can't bear waitin' alone, listenin' to drunks dancin' and celebratin'.

SARA *comes to her.* NORA *breaks. Tears well from her eyes.*

It's cruel, it is! There's no heart or thought for himself in divil a one av thim. (*She starts to sob.* SARA *hugs her and kisses her cheek gently. But she doesn't speak. It is as if she were afraid her voice would give her away.* NORA *stops sobbing. Her mood changes to resentment and she speaks as if* SARA *had spoken.*) Don't tell me not to worry. You're as bad as Mickey. The Yankee didn't apologize or your father'd been back here long since. It's a duel, that's certain, and he must have taken a room in the city so he'll be near the ground. I hope he'll sleep, but I'm feared he'll stay up drinkin', and at the dawn he'll have had too much to shoot his best and maybe— (*Then defiantly self-reassuringly*) Arrah, I'm the fool! It's himself can keep his head clear and his eyes sharp, no matter what he's taken! (*Pushing* SARA *away—with nervous peevishness*) Let go of me. You've hardened not to care. I'd rather stay alone. (*She grabs* SARA's *hand.*) No. Don't heed me. Sit down, darlin'.

SARA *sits down on her left at rear of table. She pats her mother's hand, but remains silent, her expression dreamily happy, as if she heard* NORA's *words but they had no meaning for her.* NORA *goes on worriedly again.*

But if he's staying in the city, why hasn't he sent Jamie Cregan back for his duelin' pistols? I know he'd nivir fight with any others. (*Resentful now at* MELODY) Or you'd think he'd send Jamie or someone back with a word for me. He knows well how tormented I'd be waiting. (*Bitterly*) Arrah, don't talk like a loon! Has he ever cared for anyone except himself and his pride? Sure, he'd never stoop to think of me, the grand gentleman in his red livery av bloody England! His pride, indade! What is it but a lie? What's in his veins, God pity him, but the blood of thievin' auld Ned Melody who kept a dirty shebeen? (*Then is horrified at herself as if she had blasphemed*) No! I won't say it! I've nivir! It would break his heart if he heard me! I'm the only one in the world he knows nivir sneers at his dreams! (*Working herself to rebellion again*) All the same, I won't stay here the rist of the night worryin' my heart out for a man who—it isn't only fear over the duel. It's because I'm afraid it's God punishment, all the sorrow and trouble that's come on us, and I have the black tormint in my mind that it's the fault of the mortal sin I did with him unmarried, and the promise he made me make to leave the Church that's kept me from ever confessin' to a priest. (*She pauses—dully.*) Go to a doctor, you say, to cure the rheumatism. Sure, what's rheumatism but a pain in your body? I could bear ten of it. It's the pain of guilt in my soul. Can a doctor's medicine cure that? No, only a priest of Almighty God— (*With a roused rebellion again*) It would serve Con right if I took the chance now and broke my promise and woke up the priest to hear my confession and give me God's forgiveness that'd bring my soul peace and comfort so I wouldn't feel the three of us were damned. (*Yearningly*) Oh, if I only had the courage! (*She rises suddenly from her chair—with brave defiance.*) I'll do it, so I will! I'm going to the priest's, Sara. (*She starts for the street door—gets halfway to it and stops.*)

SARA (*a strange, tenderly amused smile on her lips—teasingly*)   Well, why don't you go, Mother?

NORA (*defiantly*)   Ain't I goin'? (*She takes a few more steps toward the door—stops again—she mutters beatenly*) God forgive me, I can't. What's the use pretendin'?

SARA (*as before*)   No use at all, Mother. I've found that out.

NORA (*as if she hadn't heard, comes back slowly*)   He'd feel I'd betrayed him and my word and my love for him—and for all his scorn, he knows my love is all he has in the world to comfort him. (*Then spiritedly, with a proud toss of her head*) And it's my honor, too! It's not for his sake at all! Divil mend him, he always prates as if he had all the honor there is, but I've mine, too, as proud as his. (*She sits down in the same chair.*)

SARA (*softly*)   Yes, the honor of her love to a woman. I've learned about that too, Mother.

NORA (*as if this were the first time she was really conscious of SARA speaking, and even now had not heard what she said—irritably*)   So you've found your tongue, have you? Thank God. You're cold comfort, sitting silent like a statue, and me making talk to myself. (*Regarding her as if she hadn't really seen her before—resentfully*) Musha but it's pleased and pretty you look, as if there wasn't a care in the world, while your poor father—

SARA (*dreamily amused, as if this no longer had any importance or connection with her*)   I know it's no use telling you there won't be any duel, Mother, and it's crazy to give it a thought. You're living in Ireland long ago, like Father. But maybe you'll take Simon's word for it, if you won't mine. He said his father would be paralyzed with indignation just at the thought he'd ever fight a duel. It's against the law.

NORA (*scornfully*)   Och, who cares for the law? He must be a coward. (*She looks relieved.*) Well, if the young lad said that, maybe it's true.

SARA   Of course it's true, Mother.

NORA   Your father'd be satisfied with Harford's apology and that'd end it.

SARA (*helplessly*)   Oh, Mother! (*Then quickly*) Yes, I'm sure it ended hours ago.

NORA (*intent on her hope*)   And you think what's keeping him out is he and Jamie would take a power av drinks to celebrate.

SARA   They'd drink, that's sure, whatever happened. (*She adds dreamily*) But that doesn't matter now at all.

NORA (*stares at her—wonderingly*) You've a queer way of talking, as if you'd been asleep and was still half in a dream.

SARA In a dream right enough, Mother, and it isn't half of me that's in it but all of me, body and soul. And it's a dream that's true, and always will be to the end of life, and I'll never wake from it.

NORA Sure, what's come over you at all?

SARA (*gets up impulsively and comes around in back of her mother's chair and slips to her knees and puts her arms about her—giving her a hug*) Joy. That's what's come over me. I'm happy, Mother. I'm happy because I know now Simon is mine, and no one can ever take him from me.

NORA (*At first her only reaction is pleased satisfaction.*) God be thanked! It was a great sorrow tormentin' me that the duel would come between you. (*Defiantly*) Honor or not, why should the children have their lives and their love destroyed!

SARA I was a great fool to fear his mother could turn him against me, no matter what happened.

NORA You've had a talk with the lad?

SARA I have. That's where I've been.

NORA You've been in his room ever since you went up?

SARA Almost. After I'd got upstairs it took me a while to get up my courage.

NORA (*rebukingly*) All this time—in the dead of the night!

SARA (*teasingly*) I'm his nurse, aren't I? I've a right.

NORA That's no excuse!

SARA (*her face hardening*) Excuse? I had the best in the world. Would you have me do nothing to save my happiness and my chance in life, when I thought there was danger they'd be ruined forever? Don't you want me to have love and be happy, Mother?

NORA (*melting*) I do, darlin'. I'd give my life— (*Then rebuking again*) Were you the way you are, in only a nightgown and wrapper?

SARA (*gaily*) I was—and Simon liked my costume, if you don't, although he turned red as a beet when I came in.

NORA Small wonder he did! Shame on you!

SARA He was trying to read a book of poetry, but he couldn't he was that worried hoping I'd come to say goodnight, and being frightened I wouldn't. (*She laughs tenderly.*) Oh, it was the cutest thing I've ever done, Mother, not to see him at all since his mother left. He kept waiting for me and when I didn't come, he got scared

to death that his kissing me this morning had made me angry. So
he was wild with joy to see me—

NORA   In your bare legs with only your nightgown and wrapper to
cover your nakedness! Where's your modesty?

SARA (*gaily teasing*)   I had it with me, Mother, though I'd tried hard
to leave it behind. I got as red as he was. (*She laughs.*) Oh, Mother,
it's a great joke on me. Here I'd gone to his room with my mind
made up to be as bold as any street woman and tempt him because I
knew his honor would make him marry me right away if— (*She
laughs.*) And then all I could do was stand and gape at him and
blush!

NORA   Oh. (*Rebukingly*) I'm glad you had the dacency to blush.

SARA   It was Simon spoke first, and once he started, all he'd been
holding back came out. The waiting for me, and the fear he'd had
made him forget all his shyness, and he said he loved me and asked
me to marry him the first day we could. Without knowing how it
happened, there I was with his arms around me and mine around
him and his lips on my lips and it was heaven, Mother.

NORA (*moved by the shining happiness in* SARA's *face*)   God bless the
two av you.

SARA   Then I was crying and telling him how afraid I'd been his
mother hated me, Father's madness about the duel would give her
a good chance to come between us; Simon said no one could ever
come between us and his mother would never try to, now she knew
he loved me, which was what she came over to find out. He said
all she wanted was for him to be free to do as he pleased, and she
only suggested he wait a year, she didn't make him promise. And
Simon said I was foolish to think she would take the duel craziness
serious. She'd only be amused at the joke it would on his father,
after he'd been so sure he could buy us off, if he had to call the
police to save him.

NORA (*aroused at the mention of police*)   Call the police, is it? The
coward!

SARA (*goes on, unheedingly*)   Simon was terribly angry at his father
for that. And at Father too when I told how he threatened he'd kill
me. But we didn't talk of it much. We had better things to discuss.
(*She smiles tenderly.*)

NORA (*belligerently*)   A lot Con Melody cares for police, and him in
a rage! Not the whole dirty force av thim will dare interfere with
him!

SARA (*goes on as if she hadn't heard*)   And then Simon told me how scared he'd been I didn't love him and wouldn't marry him. I was so beautiful, he said, and he wasn't handsome at all. So I kissed him and told him he was the handsomest in the world, and he is. And he said he wasn't worthy because he had so little to offer, and was a failure at what he'd hoped he could be, a poet. So I kissed him and told him he was too a poet, and always would be, and it was what I loved most about him.

NORA   The police! Let one av thim lay his dirty hand on Con Melody, and he'll knock him senseless with one blow.

SARA   Then Simon said how poor he was, and he'd never accept a penny from his father, even if he offered it. And I told him never mind, that if we had to live in a hut, or sleep in the grass of a field without a roof to our heads, and work our hands to the bone, or starve itself, I'd be in heaven and sing with the joy of our love! (*She looks up at her mother.*) And I meant it, Mother! I meant every word of it from the bottom of my heart!

NORA (*answers vaguely from her preoccupation with the police—patting* SARA's *hair mechanically*)   Av course you did, darlin'.

SARA   But he kissed me and said it wouldn't be as bad as that, he'd been thinking and he'd had an offer from an old college friend who'd inherited a cotton mill and who wants Simon to be equal partners if he'll take complete charge of it. It's only a small mill and that's what tempts Simon. He said maybe I couldn't believe it but he knows from his experience working for his father he has the ability for trade, though he hates it, and he could easily make a living for us from this mill—just enough to be comfortable, and he'd have time over to write his book, and keep his wisdom, and never let himself become a slave to the greed for more than enough that is the curse of mankind. Then he said he was afraid maybe I'd think it was weakness in him, not wisdom, and could I be happy with enough and no more. So I kissed him and said all I wanted in life was his love, and whatever meant happiness to him would be my only ambition. (*She looks up at her mother again—exultantly.*) And I meant it, Mother! With all my heart and soul!

NORA (*as before, patting her hair*)   I know, darlin'.

SARA   Isn't that a joke on me, with all my crazy dreams of riches and a grand estate and me a haughty lady riding around in a carriage with coachman and footman! (*She laughs at herself.*) Wasn't I the fool to think that had any meaning at all when you're in love?

You were right, Mother. I knew nothing of love, or the pride a woman can take in giving everything—the pride in her own love! I was only an ignorant, silly girl boasting, but I'm a woman now, Mother, and I know.

NORA (*as before, mechanically*)   I'm sure you do, darlin'. (*She mutters fumingly to herself.*) Let the police try it! He'll whip them back to their kennels, the dirty curs!

SARA (*lost in her happiness*)   And then we put out the light and talked about how soon we'd get married, and how happy we'd be the rest of our lives together, and we'd have children—and he forgot whatever shyness was left in the dark and said he meant all the bold things he'd written in the poems I'd seen. And I confessed that I was up to every scheme to get him, because I loved him so much there wasn't anything I wouldn't do to make sure he was mine. And all the time we were kissing each other, wild with happiness. And— (*She stops abruptly and looks down guiltily.*)

NORA (*as before*)   Yes, darlin', I know.

SARA (*guiltily, keeping her eyes down*)   You—know, Mother?

NORA (*abruptly comes out of her preoccupation, startled and uneasy*) I know what? What are you sayin'? Look up at me! (*She pulls* SARA's *head back so she can look down in her face—falteringly.*) I can see— You let him! You wicked, sinful girl!

SARA (*defiantly and proudly*)   There was no letting about it, only love making the two of us!

NORA (*helplessly resigned already but feeling it her duty to rebuke*) Ain't you ashamed to boast—?

SARA   No! There was no shame in it! (*Proudly*) Ashamed? You know I'm not! Haven't you told me of the pride in your love? Were you ashamed?

NORA (*weakly*)   I was. I was dead with shame.

SARA   You were not! You were proud like me!

NORA   But it's a mortal sin. God will punish you—

SARA   Let Him! If He'd say to me, for every time you kiss Simon you'll have a thousand years in hell, I wouldn't care, I'd wear out my lips kissing him!

NORA (*frightenedly*)   Whist, now! He might hear you.

SARA   Wouldn't you have said the same—?

NORA (*distractedly*)   Will you stop! Don't torment me with your sinful questions! I won't answer you!

SARA (*hugging her*)   All right. Forgive me, Mother. (*A pause*—

smilingly) It was Simon who felt guilty and repentant. If he'd had his way, he'd be out of bed now, and the two of us would be walking around in the night, trying to wake up someone who could marry us. But I was so drunk with love, I'd lost all thought or care about marriage. I'd got to the place where all you know or care is that you belong to love, and you can't call your soul your own any more, let alone your body, and you're proud you've given them to love. (*She pauses—then teasing lovingly*) Sure, I've always known you're the sweetest woman in the world, Mother, but I never suspected you were a wise woman too, until I knew tonight the truth of what you said this morning, that a woman can forgive whatever the man she loves could do and still love him, because it was through him she found the love in herself; that, in one way, he doesn't count at all, because it's love, your own love, you love in him, and to keep that your pride will do anything. (*She smiles with a self-mocking happiness.*) It's love's slaves we are, Mother, not men's—and wouldn't it shame their boasting and vanity if we ever let them know our secret? (*She laughs—then suddenly looks guilty.*) But I'm talking great nonsense. I'm glad Simon can't hear me. (*She pauses.* NORA *is worrying and hasn't listened.* SARA *goes on.*) Yes, I can even understand now—a little anyway—how you can still love Father and be proud of it, in spite of what he is.

NORA (*at the mention of* MELODY, *comes out of her brooding*) Hush, now! (*Miserably*) God help us, Sara, why doesn't he come, what's happened to him?

SARA (*gets to her feet exasperatedly*) Don't be a fool, Mother. (*Bitterly*) Nothing's happened except he's made a public disgrace of himself, for Simon's mother to sneer at. If she wanted revenge on him, I'm sure she's had her fill of it. Well, I don't care. He deserves it. I warned him and I begged him, and got called a peasant slut and a whore for my pains. All I hope now is that whatever happened wakes him from his lies and mad dreams so he'll have to face the truth of himself in that mirror. (*Sneeringly*) But there's devil a chance he'll ever let that happen. Instead, he'll come home as drunk as two lords, boasting of his glorious victory over old Harford, whatever the truth is!

But NORA *isn't listening. She has heard the click of the latch on the street door at rear.*

NORA (*excitedly*) Look, Sara!

The door is opened slowly and JAMIE CREGAN *sticks his head in cautiously to peer around the room. His face is battered, nose red and swollen, lips cut and puffed, and one eye so blackened it is almost closed.* NORA'S *first reaction is a cry of relief.*

Praise be to the Saints, you're back, Jamie!

CREGAN (*puts a finger to his lips—cautioningly*)   Whist!

NORA (*frightenedly*)   Jamie! Where's himself?

CREGAN (*sharply*)   Whist, I'm telling you! (*In a whisper*) I've got him in a rig outside, but I had to make sure no one was here. Lock the bar door, Sara, and I'll bring him in.

She goes and turns the key in the door, her expression contemptuous. CREGAN *then disappears, leaving the street door half open.*

NORA   Did you see Jamie's face? They've been fightin' terrible. Oh, I'm afraid, Sara.

SARA   Afraid of what? It's only what I told you to expect. A crazy row—and now he's paralyzed drunk.

CREGAN *appears in the doorway at rear. He is half leading, half supporting* MELODY. *The latter moves haltingly and woodenly. But his movements do not seem those of drunkenness. It is more as if a sudden shock or stroke had shattered his coordination and left him in a stupor. His scarlet uniform is filthy and torn and pulled awry. The pallor of his face is ghastly. He has a cut over his left eye, a blue swelling on his left cheekbone, and his lips are cut and bloody. From a big raw bruise on his forehead, near the temple, trickles of dried blood run down to his jaw. Both his hands are swollen, with skinned knuckles, as are* CREGAN'S. *His eyes are empty and lifeless. He stares at his wife and daughter as if he did not recognize them.*

NORA (*rushes and puts her arm around him*)   Con, darlin'! Are you hurted bad?

He pushes her away without looking at her. He walks dazedly to his chair at the head of the center table. NORA *follows him, breaking into lamentation.*

Con, don't you know me? Oh, God help us, look at his head!

SARA   Be quiet, Mother. Do you want them in the bar to know he's come home—the way he is. (*She gives her father a look of disgust.*)

CREGAN   Ay, that's it, Sara. We've got to rouse him first. His pride'd nivir forgive us if we let thim see him dead bate like this.

There is a pause. They stare at him and he stares sightlessly at the table top. NORA *stands close by his side, behind the table, on his right,* SARA *behind her on her right,* CREGAN *at right of* SARA.

SARA He's drunk, isn't that all it is, Jamie?

CREGAN (*sharply*) He's not. He's not taken a drop since we left here. It's the clouts on the head he got, that's what ails him. A taste of whiskey would bring him back, if he'd only take it, but he won't.

SARA (*gives her father a puzzled, uneasy glance*) He won't?

NORA (*gets the decanter and a glass and hands them to* CREGAN) Here. Try and make him.

CREGAN (*pours out a big drink and puts it before* MELODY—*coaxingly*) Drink this now, Major, and you'll be right as rain!

MELODY *does not seem to notice. His expression remains blank and dead.* CREGAN *scratches his head puzzledly.*

He won't. That's the way he's been all the way back when I tried to persuade him. (*Then irritably*) Well, if he won't, I will, be your leave. I'm needin' it bad. (*He downs the whiskey, and pours out another—to* NORA *and* SARA.) It's the divil's own rampage we've had.

SARA (*quietly contemptuous, but still with the look of puzzled uneasiness at her father*) From your looks it must have been.

CREGAN (*indignantly*) You're takin' it cool enough, and you seein' the marks av the batin' we got! (*He downs his second drink—boastfully.*) But if we're marked, there's others is marked worse and some av them is police!

NORA God be praised! The dirty cowards!

SARA Be quiet, Mother. Tell us what happened, Jamie.

CREGAN Faix, what didn't happen? Be the rock av Cashel, I've nivir engaged in a livelier shindy! We had no trouble findin' where Harford lived. It's a grand mansion, with a big walled garden behind it, and we wint to the front door. A flunky in livery answered wid two others behind. A big black naygur one was. That pig av a lawyer must have warned Harford to expect us. Con spoke wid the airs av a lord. "Kindly inform your master," he says, "that Major Cornelius Melody, late of His Majesty's Seventh Dragoons, respectfully requests a word with him." Well, the flunky put an insolent sneer on him. "Mr. Harford won't see you," he says. I could see Con's rage risin' but he kept polite. "Tell him," he says, "if he knows what's good for him he'll see me. For if he don't, I'll come in and see him." "Ye will, will ye?" says the flunky, "I'll have you know Mr. Harford don't allow drunken Micks to come here disturbing him. The police have been informed," he says, "and you'll be arrested if you make trouble." Then he started to shut the door. "Anyway, you've come to the wrong door," he says, "the place for the loiks av you is the servants' entrance."

NORA (*angrily*)   Och, the impident divil!

SARA (*in spite of herself her temper has been rising. She looks at* MELODY *with angry scorn.*)   You let Harford's servants insult you! (*Then quickly*) But it serves you right! I knew what would happen! I warned you!

CREGAN   Let thim be damned! Kape your mouth shut, and lave me tell it, and you'll see if we let them! When he'd said that, the flunky tried to slam the door in our faces, but Con was too quick. He pushed it back on him and lept in the hall, roarin' mad, and hit the flunky a cut with his whip across his ugly mug that set him screaming like a stuck pig!

NORA (*enthusiastically*)   Good for you, Con darlin'!

SARA (*humiliatedly*)   Mother! Don't! (*To* MELODY *with biting scorn*) The famous duelist—in a drunken brawl with butlers and coachmen!

But he is staring sightlessly at the table top as if he didn't see her or know her.

CREGAN (*angrily, pouring himself another drink*)   Shut your mouth, Sara, and don't be trying to plague him. You're wastin' breath anyway, the way he is. He doesn't know you or hear you. And don't put on lady's airs about fighting when you're the whole cause of it.

SARA (*angrily*)   It's a lie! You know I tried to stop—

CREGAN (*gulps down his drink, ignoring this, and turns to* NORA— *enthusiastically*)   Wait till you hear, Nora! (*He plunges into the midst of battle again.*) The naygur hit me a clout that had my head dizzy. He'd have had me down only Con broke the butt av the whip over his black skull and knocked him to his knees. Then the third man punched Con and I gave him a kick where it'd do him least good, and he rolled on the floor, grabbin' his guts. The naygur was in again and grabbed me, but Con came at him and knocked him down. Be the mortal, we had the three av thim licked, and we'd have dragged auld Harford from his burrow and tanned his Yankee hide if the police hadn't come!

NORA (*furiously*)   Arrah, the dirthy cowards! Always takin' sides with the rich Yanks against the poor Irish!

SARA (*more and more humiliated and angry and torn by conflicting emotions—pleadingly*)   Mother! Can't you keep still?

CREGAN   Four av thim wid clubs came behind us. They grabbed us before we knew it and dragged us into the street. Con broke away and hit the one that held him, and I gave one a knee in his belly. And then, glory be, there was a fight! Oh, it'd done your heart good to see himself! He was worth two men, lettin' out right and left, roarin' wid rage and cursin' like a trooper—

MELODY (*without looking up or any change in his dazed expression, suddenly speaks in a jeering mumble to himself*)   Bravely done, Major Melody! The Commander of the Forces honors your exceptional gallantry! Like the glorious field of Talavera! Like the charge on the French square! Cursing like a drunken, foul-mouthed son of a thieving shebeen keeper who sprang from the filth of a peasant hovel, with pigs on the floor—with that pale Yankee bitch watching from a window, sneering with disgust!

NORA (*frightenedly*)   God preserve us, it's crazed he is!

SARA (*stares at him startled and wondering. For a second there is angry pity is her eyes. She makes an impulsive move toward him.*)   Father! (*Then her face hardening*) He isn't crazed, Mother. He's come to his senses for once in his life! (*To* MELODY) So she was sneering, was she? I don't blame her! I'm glad you've been taught a lesson! (*Then vindictively*) But I've taught her one, too. She'll soon sneer from the wrong side of her mouth!

CREGAN (*angrily*)   Will you shut your gab, Sara! Lave him be and don't heed him. It's the same crazy blather he's talked every once in a while since they brought him to—about the Harford woman—and speakin' av the pigs and his father one minute, and his pride and honor and his mare the next. (*He takes up the story again.*) Well, anyways, they was too much for us, the four av thim wid clubs. The last thing I saw before I was knocked senseless was three av thim clubbing Con. But, be the Powers, we wint down fightin' to the last for the glory av auld Ireland!

MELODY (*in a jeering mutter to himself*)   Like a rum-soaked trooper, brawling before a brothel on a Saturday night, puking in the gutter!

SARA (*strickenly*)   Don't, Father!

CREGAN (*indignantly to* MELODY)   We wasn't in condition. If we had been—but they knocked us senseless and rode us to the station and locked us up. And we'd be there yet if Harford hadn't made thim turn us loose, for he's rich and has influence. Small thanks to him! He was afraid the row would get in the paper and put shame on him.

MELODY *laughs crazily and springs to his feet. He sways dizzily, clutching his head—then goes toward the door at left front.*

NORA   Con! Where are you goin'? (*She starts after him and grabs his arm. He shakes her hand off roughly as if he did not recognize her.*)

CREGAN   He don't know you. Don't cross him now, Nora. Sure, he's only goin' upstairs to bed. (*Wheedlingly*) You know what's best for you, don't you, Major?

MELODY *feels his way gropingly through the door and disappears, leaving it open.*

SARA (*uneasy, but consoling her mother*)   Jamie's right, Mother. If he'll fall asleep, that's the best thing— (*Abruptly she is terrified*) Oh God, maybe he'll take revenge on Simon—(*She rushes to the door and stands listening—with relief.*) No, he's gone to his room. (*She comes back—a bit ashamed.*) I'm a fool. He'd never harm a sick man, no matter—(*She takes her mother's arm—gently.*) Don't stand there, Mother. Sit down. You're tired enough—

NORA (*frightenedly*)   I've never heard him talk like that in all the years—with that crazy dead look in his eyes. Oh, I'm afeered, Sara. Lave go of me. I've got to make sure he's gone to bed. (*She goes quickly to the door and disappears.* SARA *makes a move to follow her.*)

CREGAN (*roughly*)   Stay here, unless you're a fool, Sara. He might come to all av a sudden and give you a hell av a thrashin'. Troth, you deserve one. You're to blame for what's happened. Wasn't he fightin' to revenge the insults to you? (*He sprawls on a chair at rear of the table at center.*)

SARA (*Sitting down at rear of the small table at left front—angrily*)   I'll thank you to mind your own business, Jamie Cregan. Just because you're a relation—

CREGAN (*harshly*)   Och, to hell with your airs! (*He pours out a drink and downs it. He is becoming drunk again.*)

SARA   I can revenge my own insults, and I have! I've beaten the Harfords—and he's only made a fool of himself for her to sneer at.

But I've beaten her and I'll sneer last! (*She pauses, a hard, triumphant smile on her lips. It fades. She gives a little bewildered laugh.*) God forgive me, what a way to think of—I must be crazy, too.

CREGAN (*drunkenly*)   Ah, don't be talkin'! Didn't the two of us lick them all! And Con's all right. He's all right, I'm sayin'! It's only the club on the head makes him quare a while. I've seen it often before. Ay, and felt it meself. I remember at a fair in the auld country I was clouted with the butt av a whip and I didn't remember a thing for hours, but they told me after I never stopped gabbin' but went around tellin' every stranger all my secrets. (*He pauses.* SARA *hasn't listened. He goes on uneasily.*) All the same, it's no fun listening to his mad blather about the pale bitch, as he calls her, like she was a ghost, haunting and scorning him. And his gab about his beautiful thoroughbred mare is madder still, raving what a grand, beautiful lady she is, with her slender ankles and dainty feet, sobbin' and beggin' her forgiveness and talkin' of dishonor and death— (*He shrinks superstitiously—then angrily, reaching for the decanter.*) Och, be damned to this night!

Before he can pour a drink, NORA *comes hurrying in from the door at left front.*

NORA (*breathless and frightened*)   He's come down! He pushed me away like he didn't see me. He's gone out to the barn. Go after him, Jamie.

CREGAN (*drunkenly*)   I won't. He's all right. Lave him alone.

SARA (*jeeringly*)   Sure, he's only gone to pay a call on his sweetheart, the mare, Mother, and hasn't he slept in her stall many a time when he was dead drunk, and she never even kicked him?

NORA (*distractedly*)   Will you shut up, the two av you! I heard him openin' the closet in his room where he keeps his auld set of duelin' pistols, and he was carryin' the box when he came down—

CREGAN (*scrambles hastily to his feet*)   Oh, the lunatic!

NORA   He'll ride the mare back to Harford's! He'll murther someone! For the love av God, stop him, Jamie!

CREGAN (*drunkenly belligerent*)   Be Christ, I'll stop him for you, Nora, pistols or no pistols! (*He walks a bit unsteadily out the door at left front.*)

SARA (*stands tensely—bursts out with a strange triumphant pride*)   Then he's not beaten! (*Suddenly she is overcome by a bitter, tortured revulsion of feeling.*) Merciful God, what am I thinking? As if he hadn't done enough to destroy— (*Distractedly*) Oh, the mad fool! I wish he was—

From the yard, off left front, there is the muffled crack of a pistol shot hardly perceptible above the noise in the barroom. But SARA *and* NORA *both hear it and stand frozen with horror.* SARA *babbles hysterically.*

I didn't mean it, Mother! I didn't!

NORA (*numb with fright—mumbles stupidly*)   A shot!

SARA   You know I didn't mean it, Mother!

NORA   A shot! God help us, he's kilt Jamie!

SARA (*stammers*)   No—not Jamie— (*Wildly*) Oh, I can't bear waiting! I've got to know— (*She rushes to the door at left front—then stops frightenedly.*) I'm afraid to know! I'm afraid—

NORA (*mutters stupidly*)   Not Jamie? Then who else? (*She begins to tremble—in a horrified whisper.*) Sara! You think— Oh, God have mercy!

SARA   Will you hush, Mother! I'm trying to hear— (*She retreats quickly into the room and backs around the table at left front until she is beside her mother.*) Someone's at the yard door. It'll be Jamie coming to tell us—

NORA   It's a lie! He'd nivir. He'd nivir!

They stand paralyzed by terror, clinging to each other, staring at the open door. There is a moment's pause in which the sound of drunken roistering in the bar seems louder. Then MELODY *appears in the doorway with* CREGAN *behind him.* CREGAN *has him by the shoulder and pushes him roughly into the room, like a bouncer handling a drunk.* CREGAN *is shaken by the experience he has just been through and his reaction is to make him drunkenly angry at* MELODY. *In his free hand is a dueling pistol.* MELODY'S *face is like gray wax. His body is limp, his feet drag, his eyes seem to have no sight. He appears completely possessed by a paralyzing stupor.*

SARA (*impulsively*)   Father! Oh, thank God! (*She takes one step toward him—then her expression begins to harden.*)

NORA (*sobs with relief*)   Oh, praise God you're alive! Sara and me was dead with fear— (*She goes toward them.*) Con! Con, darlin'!

CREGAN (*dumps* MELODY *down on the nearest chair at left of the small table—roughly, his voice trembling*) Let you sit still now, Con Melody, and behave like a gintleman! (*To* NORA) Here he is for ye, Nora, and you're welcome, bad luck to him! (*He moves back as* NORA *comes and puts her arms around* MELODY *and hugs him tenderly.*)

NORA Oh, Con, Con, I was so afeered for you!

He does not seem to hear or see her, but she goes on crooning to him comfortingly as if he were a sick child.

CREGAN He was in the stable. He'd this pistol in his hand, with the mate to it on the floor beside the mare. (*He shudders and puts the pistol on the table shakenly.*) It's mad he's grown entirely! Let you take care av him now, his wife and daughter! I've had enough. I'm no damned keeper av lunatics! (*He turns toward the barroom.*)

SARA Wait, Jamie. We heard a shot. What was it?

CREGAN (*angrily*) Ask him, not me! (*Then with bewildered horror*) He kilt the poor mare, the mad fool!

SARA *stares at him in stunned amazement.*

I found him on the floor with her head in his lap, and her dead. He was sobbing like a soul in hell— (*He shudders.*) Let me get away from the sight of him where there's men in their right senses laughing and singing! (*He unlocks the barroom door.*) And don't be afraid, Sara, that I'll tell the boys a word av this. I'll talk of our fight in the city only, because it's all I want to remember. (*He jerks open the door and goes in the bar, slamming the door quickly behind him. A roar of welcome is heard as the crowd greets his arrival.* SARA *locks the door again. She comes back to the center table, staring at* MELODY, *an hysterical, sneering grin making her lips quiver and twitch.*)

SARA What a fool I was to be afraid! I might know you'd never do it as long as a drink of whiskey was left in the world! So it was the mare you shot? (*She bursts into uncontrollable, hysterical laughter. It penetrates* MELODY'S *stupor and he stiffens rigidly on his chair, but his eyes remain fixed on the table top.*)

NORA Sara! Stop! For the love av God, how can you laugh—!

SARA I can't—help it, Mother. Didn't you hear—Jamie? It was the mare he shot! (*She gives way to laughter again.*)

NORA (*distractedly*) Stop it, I'm sayin'!

SARA *puts her hand over her mouth to shut off the sound of her laughing, but her shoulders still shake.* NORA *sinks on the chair at rear of the table. She mutters dazedly.*

Kilt his beautiful mare? He must be mad entirely.

MELODY (*suddenly speaks, without looking up, in the broadest brogue, his voice coarse and harsh*)   Lave Sara laugh. Sure, who could blame her? I'm roarin' meself inside me. It's the damnedest joke a man ivir played on himself since time began.

They stare at him. SARA'S *laughter stops. She is startled and repelled by his brogue. Then she stares at him suspiciously, her face hardening.*

SARA   What joke? Do you think murdering the poor mare a good joke?

MELODY *stiffens for a second, but that is all. He doesn't look up or reply.*

NORA (*frightened*)   Look at the dead face on him, Sara. He's like a corpse. (*She reaches out and touches one of his hands on the table top with a furtive tenderness—pleadingly.*) Con, darlin'. Don't!

MELODY (*looks up at her. His expression changes so that his face loses all its remaining distinction and appears vulgar and common, with a loose, leering grin on his swollen lips.*)   Let you not worry, Allanah. Sure, I'm no corpse, and with a few drinks in me, I'll soon be lively enough to suit you.

NORA (*miserably confused*)   Will you listen to him, Sara—puttin' on the brogue to torment us.

SARA (*growing more uneasy but sneering*)   Pay no heed to him, Mother. He's play-acting to amuse himself. If he's that cruel and shameless after what he's done—

NORA (*defensively*)   No, it's the blow on the head he got fightin' the police.

MELODY (*vulgarly*)   The blow, me foot! That's Jamie Cregan's blather. Sure, it'd take more than a few clubs on the head to darken my wits long. Me brains, if I have any, is clear as a bell. And I'm not puttin' on brogue to tormint you, me darlint. Nor play-actin', Sara. That was the Major's game. It's quare, surely, for the two av ye to object when I talk in me natural tongue, and yours, and don't put on airs loike the late lamented auld liar and lunatic, Major Cornelius Melody, av His Majesty's Seventh Dragoons, used to do.

NORA   God save us, Sara, will you listen!

MELODY   But he's dead now, and his last bit av lyin' pride is murthered and stinkin'. (*He pats* NORA's *hand with what seems to be genuine comforting affection.*) So let you be aisy, darlint. He'll nivir again hurt you with his sneers, and his pretindin' he's a gintleman, blatherin' about pride and honor, and his boastin' av duels in the days that's gone, and his showin' off before the Yankees, and thim laughin' at him, prancing around drunk on his beautiful thoroughbred mare— (*He gulps as if he were choking back a sob.*) For she's dead, too, poor baste.

SARA   (*This is becoming unbearable for her—tensely.*) Why—why did you kill her?

MELODY   Why did the Major, you mean! Be Christ, you're stupider than I thought you, if you can't see that. Wasn't she the livin' reminder, so to spake, av all his lyin' boasts and dreams? He meant to kill her first wid one pistol, and then himself wid the other. But faix, he saw the shot that killed her had finished him, too. There wasn't much pride left in the auld lunatic, anyway, and seeing her die made an end av him. So he didn't bother shooting himself, because it'd be a mad thing to waste a good bullet on a corpse! (*He laughs coarsely.*)

SARA (*tensely*)   Father! Stop it!

MELODY   Didn't I tell you there was a great joke in it? Well, that's the joke. (*He begins to laugh again but he chokes on a stifled sob. Suddenly his face loses the coarse, leering, brutal expression and is full of anguished grief. He speaks without brogue, not to them but aloud to himself.*) Blessed Christ, the look in her eyes by the lantern light with life ebbing out of them—wondering and sad, but still trustful, not reproaching me—with no fear in them—proud, understanding pride—loving me—she saw I was dying with her. She understood! She forgave me! (*He starts to sob but wrenches himself out of it and speaks in broad, jeering brogue.*) Begorra, if that wasn't the mad Major's ghost speakin'! But be damned to him, he won't haunt me long, if I know it! I intind to live at my ease from now on and not let the dead bother me, but enjoy life in my proper station as auld Nick Melody's son. I'll bury his Major's damned red livery av bloody England deep in the ground and he can haunt its grave if he likes, and boast to the lonely night av Talavera and the ladies of Spain and fightin' the French! (*With a leer*) Troth, I think the boys is right when they say he stole the uniform and he nivir fought under Wellington at all. He was a terrible liar, as I remember him.

NORA   Con, darlin', don't be grievin' about the mare. Sure, you can get another. I'll manage—

SARA   Mother! Hush! (*To* MELODY, *furiously*) Father, will you stop this mad game you're playing—?

MELODY (*roughly*)   Game, is it? You'll find it's no game. It was the Major played a game all his life, the crazy auld loon, and cheated only himself. But I'll be content to stay meself in the proper station I was born to, from this day on. (*With a cunning leer at* SARA) And it's meself feels it me duty to give you a bit av fatherly advice, Sara darlint, while my mind is on it. I know you've great ambition, so remember it's to hell wid honor if ye want to rise in this world. Remember the blood in your veins and be your grandfather's true descendent. There was an able man for you! Be Jaysus, he nivir felt anything beneath him that could gain him something, and for lyin' tricks to swindle the bloody fools of gintry, there wasn't his match in Ireland, and he ended up wid a grand estate, and a castle, and a pile av gold in the bank.

SARA (*distractedly*)   Oh, I hate you!

NORA   Sara!

MELODY (*goes on as if he hadn't heard*)   I know he'd advise that to give you a first step up, darlint, you must make the young Yankee gintleman have you in his bed, and afther he's had you, weep great tears and appeal to his honor to marry you and save yours. Be God, he'll nivir resist that, if I know him, for he's a young fool, full av dacency and dreams, and looney, too, wid a touch av the poet in him. Oh, it'll be aisy for you—

SARA (*goaded beyond bearing*)   I'll make you stop your dirty brogue and your play-acting! (*She leans toward him and speaks with taunting vindictiveness, in broad brogue herself.*) Thank you kindly but I've already taken your wise advice, Father. I made him have me in his bed, while you was out drunk fightin' the police!

NORA (*frightenedly*)   Sara! Hault your brazen tongue!

MELODY (*His body stiffens on his chair and the coarse leer vanishes from his face. It becomes his old face. His eyes fix on her in a threatening stare. He speaks slowly, with difficulty keeping his words in brogue.*)   Did you now, God bless you! I might have known you'd not take any chance that the auld loon av a Major, going out to revenge an insult to you, would spoil your schemes. (*He forces a horrible grin.*) Be the living God, it's me should be proud this night that one av the Yankee gintry has stooped to be seduced by my slut av a daughter! (*Still keeping his eyes fixed on hers, he begins to rise from his chair, his right hand groping along the table top until it clutches the dueling pistol. He aims it at* SARA'S *heart, like an automaton, his eyes as cold, deadly, and merciless as they must have been in his duels of long ago.* SARA *is terrified but she stands unflinchingly.*)

NORA (*horror-stricken, lunges from her chair and grabs his arm*) Con! For the love av God! Would you be murthering Sara?

A dazed look comes over his face. He grows limp and sinks back on his chair and lets the pistol slide from his fingers on the table. He draws a shuddering breath—then laughs hoarsely.

MELODY (*with a coarse leer*) Murtherin' Sara, is it? Are ye daft, Nora? Sure, all I want is to congratulate her!

SARA (*hopelessly*) Oh! (*She sinks down on her chair at rear of the center table and covers her face with her hands.*)

NORA (*with pitifully well-meant reassurance*) It's all right, Con. The young lad wants to marry her as soon as can be, she told me, and he did before.

MELODY Musha, but that's kind of him! Be God, we ought to be proud av our daughter, Nora. Lave it to her to get what she wants by hook or crook. And won't we be proud watchin' her rise in the world till she's a grand lady!

NORA (*simply*) We will, surely.

SARA Mother!

MELODY She'll have some trouble, rootin' out his dreams. He's set in his proud, noble ways, but she'll find the right trick! I'd lay a pound, if I had one, to a shilling she'll see the day when she'll wear fine silks and drive in a carriage wid a naygur coachman behind spankin' thoroughbreds, her nose in the air; and she'll live in a Yankee mansion, as big as a castle, on a grand estate av stately woodland and soft green meadows and a lake. (*With a leering chuckle*) Be the Saints, I'll start her on her way by making her a wedding present av the Major's place where he let her young gintleman build his cabin—the land the Yankees swindled him into buyin' for his American estate, the mad fool! (*He glances at the dueling pistol—jeeringly.*) Speakin' av the departed, may his soul roast in hell, what am I doin' wid his pistol? Be God, I don't need pistols. Me fists, or a club if it's handy, is enough. Didn't me and Jamie lick a whole regiment av police this night?

NORA (*stoutly*)   You did, and if there wasn't so many av thim—

MELODY (*turns to her—grinningly*)   That's the talk, darlint! Sure, there's divil a more loyal wife in the whole world— (*He pauses, staring at her—then suddenly kisses her on the lips, roughly but with a strange real tenderness.*) *and I love you.*

NORA (*with amazed, unthinking joy*)   Oh, Con!

MELODY (*grinning again*)   I've meant to tell you often, only the Major, damn him, had me under his proud thumb. (*He pulls her over and kisses her hair.*)

NORA   Is it kissin' my hair—!

MELODY   I am. Why wouldn't I? You have beautiful hair, God bless you! And don't remember what the Major used to tell you. The gintleman's sneers he put on is buried with him. I'll be a real husband to you, and help ye run this shebeen, instead of being a sponge. I'll fire Mickey and tend the bar myself, like my father's son ought to.

NORA   You'll not! I'll nivir let you!

MELODY (*leering cunningly*)   Well, I offered, remember. It's you refused. Sure, I'm not in love with work, I'll confess, and maybe you're right not to trust me too near the whiskey. (*He licks his lips.*) Be Jaysus, that reminds me. I've not had a taste for hours. I'm dyin' av thirst.

NORA (*starts to rise*)   I'll get you—

MELODY (*pushes her back on her chair*)   Ye'll not. I want company and singin' and dancin' and great laughter. I'll join the boys in the bar and help Cousin Jamie celebrate our wonderful shindy wid the police. (*He gets up. His old soldierly bearing is gone. He slouches and his movements are shambling and clumsy, his big hairy hands dangling at his sides. In his torn, disheveled, dirt-stained uniform, he looks like a loutish, grinning clown.*)

NORA   You ought to go to bed, Con darlin', with your head hurted.

MELODY   Me head? Faix, it was nivir so clear while the Major lived to tormint me, makin' me tell mad lies to excuse his divilments. (*He grins.*) And I ain't tired a bit. I'm fresh as a man new born. So I'll say goodnight to you, darlint. (*He bends and kisses her.* SARA *has lifted her tear-stained face from her hands and is staring at him with a strange, anguished look of desperation. He leers at her.*) And you go to bed, too, Sara. Troth, you deserve a long, dreamless slape after all you've accomplished this day.

SARA   Please! O, Father, I can't bear— Won't you be yourself again?

MELODY (*threatening her good-humoredly*) Let you kape your mouth closed, ye slut, and not talk like you was ashamed of me, your father. I'm not the Major who was too much of a gintleman to lay hand on you. Faix, I'll give you a box on the ear that'll teach you respect, if ye kape on trying to raise the dead!

She stares at him, sick and desperate. He starts toward the bar door.

SARA (*springs to her feet*) Father! Don't go in with those drunken scum! Don't let them hear and see you! You can drink all you like here. Jamie will come and keep you company. He'll laugh and sing and help you celebrate Talavera—

MELODY (*roughly*) To hell wid Talavera! (*His eyes are fastened on the mirror. He leers into it.*) Be Jaysus, if it ain't the mirror the auld loon was always admirin' his mug in while he spouted Byron to pretend himself was a lord wid a touch av the poet— (*He strikes a pose which is a vulgar burlesque of his old before-the-mirror one and recites in mocking brogue.*)

"I have not loved the World, nor the World me;
 I have not flatthered uts rank breath, nor bowed
 To uts idolatries a pashunt knee,
 Nor coined me cheek to smiles,—nor cried aloud
 In worship av an echo: in the crowd
 They couldn't deem me one av such—I stood
 Among thim, but not av thim . . ."

(*He guffaws contemptuously.*)
Be Christ, if he wasn't the joke av the world, the Major. He should have been a clown in a circus. God rest his soul in the flames av tormint! (*Roughly*) But to hell wid the dead.

The noise in the bar rises to an uproar of laughter as if JAMIE *had just made some climactic point in his story.* MELODY *looks away from the mirror to the bar door.*

Be God, *I'm* alive and in the crowd they *can* deem me one av such! I'll be among thim and av thim, too—and make up for the lonely dog's life the Major led me. (*He goes to the bar door.*)

SARA (*starts toward him—beseechingly*) Father! Don't put this final shame on yourself. You're not drunk now. There's no excuse you can give yourself. You'll be as dead to yourself after, as if you'd shot yourself along with the mare!

MELODY (*leering—with a wink at* NORA) Listen to her, Nora, reproachin' me because I'm not drunk. Troth, that's a condition soon mended. (*He puts his hand on the knob of the door.*)

SARA   Father!

NORA (*has given way to such complete physical exhaustion, she hardly hears, much less comprehends what is said—dully*)   Lave him alone, Sara. It's best.

MELODY (*as another roar is heard from the bar*)   I'm missin' a lot av fun. Be God, I've a bit of news to tell the boys that'll make them roar the house down. The Major's passin' to his eternal rest has set me free to jine the Democrats, and I'll vote for Andy Jackson, the friend av the common men like me, God bless him! (*He grins with anticipation.*) Wait till the boys hear that! (*He starts to turn the knob.*)

SARA (*rushes to him and grabs his arm*)   No! I won't let you! It's my pride, too! (*She stammers.*) Listen! Forgive me, Father! I know it's my fault—always sneering and insulting you—but I only meant the lies in it. The truth—Talavera—the Duke praising your bravery— an officer in his army—even the ladies in Spain—deep down that's been my pride, too—that I was your daughter. So don't— I'll do anything you ask— I'll even tell Simon—that after his father's insult to you—I'm too proud to marry a Yankee coward's son!

MELODY (*has been visibly crumbling as he listens until he appears to have no character left in which to hide and defend himself. He cries wildly and despairingly, as if he saw his last hope of escape suddenly cut off.*)   Sara! For the love of God, stop—let me go—!

NORA (*dully*)   Lave your poor father be. It's best.

In a flash MELODY *recovers and is the leering peasant again.*

SARA (*with bitter hopelessness*)   Oh, Mother! Why couldn't you be still!

MELODY (*roughly*)   Why can't you, ye mean. I warned ye what ye'd get if ye kept on interferin' and tryin' to raise the dead. (*He cuffs her on the side of the head. It is more of a playful push than a blow, but it knocks her off balance back to the end of the table at center.*)

NORA (*aroused—bewilderedly*)   God forgive you, Con! (*Angrily*) Don't you be hittin' Sara now. I've put up with a lot but I won't—

MELODY (*with rough good nature*)   Shut up, darlint. I won't have to again. (*He grins leeringly at* SARA.) That'll teach you, me proud Sara! I know you won't try raisin' the dead any more. And let me hear no more gab out of you about not marryin' the young lad upstairs. Be Jaysus, haven't ye any honor? Ye seduced him and ye'll make an honest gentleman av him if I have to march ye both by the scruff av the neck to the nearest church. (*He chuckles—then leeringly*) And now with your permission, ladies both, I'll join me good friends in the bar. (*He opens the door and passes into the bar, closing the door behind him. There is a roar of welcoming drunken shouts, pounding of glasses on bar and tables, then quiet as if he had raised a hand for silence, followed by his voice greeting them and ordering drinks, and other roars of acclaim mingled with the music of* RILEY'S *pipes.* SARA *remains standing by the side of the center table, her shoulders bowed, her head hanging, staring at the floor.*)

NORA (*overcome by physical exhaustion again, sighs*)   Don't mind his giving you a slap. He's still quare in his head. But he'll sing and laugh and drink a power av whiskey and slape sound after, and tomorrow he'll be himself again—maybe.

SARA (*dully—aloud to herself rather than to her mother*)   No. He'll never be. He's beaten at last and he wants to stay beaten. Well, I did my best. Though why I did, I don't know. I must have his crazy pride in me. (*She lifts her head, her face hardening—bitterly.*) I mean, the late Major Melody's pride. I mean, I did have it. Now it's dead—thank God—and I'll make a better wife for Simon.

There is a sudden lull in the noise from the bar, as if someone had called for silence—then MELODY'S *voice is plainly heard in the silence as he shouts a toast:* "Here's to our next President, Andy Jackson! Hurroo for Auld Hickory, God bless him!" *There is a drunken chorus of answering* "hurroos" *that shakes the walls.*

NORA   Glory be to God, cheerin' for Andy Jackson! Did you hear him, Sara?

SARA (*her face hard*)   I heard someone. But it wasn't anyone I ever knew or want to know.

NORA (*as if she hadn't heard*)   Ah well, that's good. They won't all be hatin' him now. (*She pauses—her tired, worn face becomes suddenly shy and tender.*) Did you hear him tellin' me he loved me, Sara? Did you see him kiss me on the mouth—and then kiss my hair? (*She gives a little, soft laugh.*) Sure, he must have gone mad altogether!

SARA (*stares at her mother. Her face softens.*)   No, Mother, I know he meant it. He'll keep on meaning it, too, Mother. He'll be free to, now. (*She smiles strangely.*) Maybe I deserved the slap for interfering.

NORA (*preoccupied with her own thoughts*)   And if he wants to kape on makin' game of everyone, puttin' on the brogue and actin' like one av thim in there—(*She nods toward the bar.*) Well, why shouldn't he if it brings him peace and company in his loneliness? God pity him, he's had to live all his life alone in the hell av pride. (*Proudly*) And I'll play any game he likes and give him love in it. Haven't I always? (*She smiles.*) Sure, I have no pride at all—except that.

SARA (*stares at her—moved*)   You're a strange, noble woman, Mother. I'll try and be like you. (*She comes over and hugs her—then she smiles tenderly.*) I'll wager Simon never heard the shot or anything. He was sleeping like a baby when I left him. A cannon wouldn't wake him.

In the bar, RILEY *starts playing a reel on his pipes and there is the stamp of dancing feet. For a moment* SARA'S *face becomes hard and bitter again. She tries to be mocking.*

Faith, Patch Riley don't know it but he's playing a requiem for the dead. (*Her voice trembles.*) May the hero of Talavera rest in peace! (*She breaks down and sobs, hiding her face on her mother's shoulder —bewilderedly.*) But why should I cry, Mother? Why do I mourn for him?

NORA (*at once forgetting her own exhaustion, is all tender, loving help and comfort*)   Don't, darlin', don't. You're destroyed with tiredness, that's all. Come on to bed, now, and I'll help you undress and tuck you in. (*Trying to rouse her—in a teasing tone*) Shame on you to cry when you have love. What would the young lad think of you?

CURTAIN

Picnic on the Battlefield

Fernando Arrabal

Translation by James Hewitt

CHARACTERS

ZAPO, *a soldier*
MONSIEUR TÉPAN, *the soldier's father*
MADAME TÉPAN, *the soldier's mother*
ZÉPO, *an enemy soldier*
FIRST CORPSMAN
SECOND CORPSMAN

SCENE   *A battlefield. Barbed wire stretches from one end of the stage to the other, with sandbags piled against it.*
    Battle is in full swing. We hear bombs bursting, rifle shots and machine-gun fire.
    Alone on stage, hidden flat on his belly among the sandbags, ZAPO *is very frightened.*
    The fighting stops. Silence.
    From a knitting-bag, ZAPO *takes out a ball of wool, knitting needles, and starts knitting a sweater that is already quite well along. The field telephone beside him suddenly rings.*

ZAPO   Hello . . . hello . . . yes, sir, Captain. . . . Yes, this is the sentry in Section 47. . . . Nothing new, Captain. . . . Excuse me, Captain, when are we going to start fighting again? . . . And what am I supposed to do with the grenades? Should I send them on up front or to the rear? . . . Don't get annoyed, I didn't say that to upset you. . . . And, Captain, I'm really feeling pretty lonesome. Couldn't you send me a companion out here? . . . Even the goat.

423

(*Evidently the Captain gives him a good dressing down.*) Yes sir, Captain, yes sir! (ZAPO *hangs up. We hear him grumbling to himself. Silence.*)

Enter MONSIEUR *and* MADAME TÉPAN, *carrying baskets as though they are off on a picnic. Their son, who is sitting with his back turned, does not see them arriving.*

M. TÉPAN (*ceremoniously*) My boy, get up and kiss your mother on the forehead.

Taken by surprise, ZAPO *gets up and, with a great deal of respect, gives his mother a kiss on the forehead. He is about to speak, but his father beats him to it.*

Now give *me* a kiss.

ZAPO   My dear sweet parents, how did you ever dare come all the way out to a dangerous spot like this? You must leave here right away.

M. TÉPAN   Are you trying to tell your father what war and danger are all about? For me, all this is only a game. How many times do you think I've jumped off the subway while it was still moving?

MME. TÉPAN   We thought you were probably bored, so we came to pay you a little visit. After all, this war business must get pretty tiresome.

ZAPO   It all depends.

M. TÉPAN   I know perfectly well what goes on. In the beginning, it's all new and exciting. You enjoy the killing and throwing grenades and wearing a helmet; it's quite the thing, but you end up bored as hell. In my day, you'd have really seen something. Wars were a lot livelier, much more colorful. And then best of all, there were horses, lots of horses. It was a real pleasure: if the captain said "Attack!" before you could shake a stick we were all assembled on horseback in our red uniforms. That was something to see. And then we'd go galloping forward, sword in hand, and suddenly find ourselves hard against the enemy. And they'd be at their finest too, with their horses—there were always loads and loads of beautifully round-bottomed horses and their polished boots, and their green uniforms.

MME. TÉPAN   No, the enemy uniform wasn't green. It was blue. I remember perfectly well it was blue.

M. TÉPAN   And I say it was green.

MME. TÉPAN   When I was little I went out on the balcony any number of times to watch the battle, and I'd say to the little boy next door,

"I'll bet you a gumdrop the Blues win." And the Blues were our enemies.

M. TÉPAN   All right, so you win.

MME. TÉPAN   I always loved battles. When I was little, I always said that when I grew up I wanted to be a Colonel in the Dragoons. But Mama didn't want me to. You know what a stickler she is.

M. TÉPAN   Your mother's a real nincompoop.

ZAPO   Forgive me, but you've got to leave. You just can't go walking into a war when you're not a soldier.

M. TÉPAN   I don't give a damn. We're here to have a picnic with you in the country and spend a nice Sunday.

MME. TÉPAN   I even made a lovely meal. Sausage, hard-boiled eggs, I know how much you like them! Ham sandwiches, red wine, some salad and some little cakes.

ZAPO   O.K., we'll do whatever you say. But if the Captain comes along he'll throw a fit. Plus the fact that he doesn't much go for the idea of visiting the battlefront. He keeps telling us: "War calls for discipline and grenades, but no visits."

M. TÉPAN   Don't you worry about it, I'll have a few words with your Captain.

ZAPO   And what if we have to start fighting again?

M. TÉPAN   You think that scares me, I've seen worse. Now if it was only cavalry battles! Times have changed, that's something you don't understand. (*A pause.*) We came on motorcycle. Nobody said anything.

ZAPO   They probably thought you were arbitrators.

M. TÉPAN   We did have some trouble getting through, though. With all those jeeps and tanks.

MME. TÉPAN   And the very minute we arrived, you remember that bottleneck because of the cannon?

M. TÉPAN   During wartime, you've got to be prepared for anything. Everybody knows that.

MME. TÉPAN   Well now, we're ready to start eating.

M. TÉPAN   Right you are, I could eat a horse. It's the smell of gunpowder that does it.

MME. TÉPAN   We'll eat sitting down on the blanket.

ZAPO   All right to eat with my rifle?

MME. TÉPAN   Let your rifle alone. It's bad manners to bring your rifle to the table. (*A pause.*) Why, child, you're filthy as a little pig. How did you manage to get in such a mess? Let's see your hands.

ZAPO   (*Ashamed, he shows them.*) I had to crawl along the ground during maneuvers.

MME. TÉPAN   How about your ears?

ZAPO   I washed them this morning.

MME. TÉPAN   That should do then. Now how about you teeth? (*He shows them.*) Very good. Now who's going to give his little boy a great big kiss for brushing his teeth so nicely? (*To her husband*) Well, give your son a kiss for brushing his teeth so nicely.

M. TÉPAN *gives his son a kiss.*

Because, you know, one thing I just won't allow is not washing, and blaming it on the war.

ZAPO   Yes, Mama. (*They eat.*)

M. TÉPAN   Well, my boy, have you been keeping up a good shooting score?

ZAPO   When?

M. TÉPAN   Why, the last few days.

ZAPO   Where?

M. TÉPAN   Right here and now. After all, you *are* fighting a war.

ZAPO   No, no great shakes. I haven't kept up a very good score. Practically no bull's-eyes.

M. TÉPAN   Well, what have you been scoring best with in your shooting, enemy horses or soldiers?

ZAPO   No, no horses. There aren't any horses any more.

M. TÉPAN   Well, soldiers then?

ZAPO   Could be.

M. TÉPAN   Could be? Aren't you sure?

ZAPO   It's just that I . . . I fire without taking aim (*a pause*) and when I fire I say an *Our Father* for the guy I shot.

M. TÉPAN   You've got to show more courage. Like your father.

MME. TÉPAN   I'm going to put a record on the phonograph. (*She puts on a record: a Spanish pasodoble. Sitting on the ground, they all three listen.*)

M. TÉPAN   Now that's real music. Yes, ma'am. I tell you. *Olé!*

As the music continues, an enemy soldier, ZÉPO *enters. He is dressed like* ZAPO. *Only the color of his uniform is different.* ZÉPO *wears green;* ZAPO *wears gray.*

Standing unseen behind the family, his mouth agape, ZÉPO *listens to the music. The record comes to an end.* ZAPO, *getting up, spots* ZÉPO.

Both raise their hands in the air, while M. *and* MME. TÉPAN *look at them, startled.*

M. TÉPAN   What's going on?

ZAPO *seems about to act, but hesitates. Then, very decisively, he points his rifle at* ZÉPO.

ZAPO   Hands up!

ZÉPO, *more terrified than ever, raises his hands still higher.* ZAPO *doesn't know what to do. All of a sudden, he hurriedly runs toward* ZÉPO *and taps him gently on the shoulder, saying*

ZAPO   You're it! (*Pleased as punch, to his father*) There you are! A prisoner!
M. TÉPAN   That's fine. Now what are you going to do with him?
ZAPO   I don't know. But could be they'll make me a corporal.
M. TÉPAN   In the meantime, tie him up.
ZAPO   Tie him up? What for?
M. TÉPAN   That's what you do with prisoners, you tie 'em up!
ZAPO   How?
M. TÉPAN   By his hands.
MME. TÉPAN   Oh yes, you've definitely got to tie his hands. That's the way I've always seen it done.
ZAPO   All right. (*To the prisoner*) Please put your hands together.
ZÉPO   Don't do it too hard.
ZAPO   Oh, no.
ZÉPO   Ouch! You're hurting me.
M. TÉPAN   Come on now, don't mistreat your prisoner.
MME. TÉPAN   Is that the way I brought you up? Haven't I told you over and over again that you've got to be considerate of your fellow man?
ZAPO   I didn't do it on purpose. (*To* ZÉPO) Does it hurt the way it is now?
ZÉPO   No, like this it doesn't hurt.
M. TÉPAN   Speak right up and tell him if it does. Just pretend we're not here.
ZÉPO   This way it's O.K.
M. TÉPAN   Now his feet.
ZAPO   His feet too? How long does this go on?
M. TÉPAN   Didn't they teach you the rules?

ZAPO   Sure.

M. TÉPAN   Well?

ZAPO   (*to* ZÉPO, *very politely*)   Would you kindly be good enough to please sit down on the ground?

ZÉPO   All right, but don't hurt me.

MME. TÉPAN   See! Now he's taking a dislike to you.

ZAPO   No. No he's not. I'm not hurting you, am I?

ZÉPO   No, this is fine.

ZAPO   (*out of nowhere*)   Papa, suppose you took a snapshot with the prisoner down there on the ground and me standing with my foot on his stomach?

M. TÉPAN   Say, yes! That'll look classy.

ZÉPO   Oh, no you don't. Not that.

MME. TÉPAN   Let him. Don't be so stubborn.

ZÉPO   No. I said no and I mean no.

MME. TÉPAN   Just a little old snip of a snapshot. What difference could that possibly make to you? Then we could put it in the dining room right next to the Lifesaving Certificate my husband got thirteen years ago.

ZÉPO   No, you'll never talk me into it.

ZAPO   But why should you refuse?

ZÉPO   I've got a fiancée. And if she ever sees the snapshot, she'll say I don't know how to fight a war.

ZAPO   No, all you have to do is tell her it isn't you at all, it's a panther.

MME. TÉPAN   C'mon, say yes.

ZÉPO   All right, but I'm only doing it to please you.

ZAPO   Stretch all the way out.

ZÉPO *stretches all the way out.* ZAPO *puts one foot on his stomach and grabs his rifle with a military air.*

MME. TÉPAN   Throw your chest out more.

ZAPO   Like this?

MME. TÉPAN   Yes, that's it. Don't breathe.

M. TÉPAN   Make like a hero.

ZAPO   How do you mean a hero, like this?

M. TÉPAN   It's a cinch. Make like the butcher when he was telling us what a lady-killer he is.

ZAPO   Like so?

M. TÉPAN   Yes, that's it.

MME. TÉPAN Just be sure your chest is puffed way out, and don't breathe.

ZÉPO Are you about finished?

M. TÉPAN Have a little patience. One . . . two . . . three.

ZAPO I hope I'll come out all right.

MME. TÉPAN Oh yes, you looked very military.

M. TÉPAN You were fine.

MME. TÉPAN That makes me want to have my picture taken, too.

M. TÉPAN Now there's a good idea.

ZAPO All right. I'll take it if you want me to.

MME. TÉPAN Give me your helmet so I'll look like a soldier.

ZÉPO I don't want any more pictures. Even one was too much.

ZAPO Don't feel that way. Come right down to it, what difference could it make?

ZÉPO That's my final say.

M. TÉPAN (*to his wife*) Don't push him. Prisoners are always very touchy. If we keep it up, he'll get mad and spoil all our fun.

ZAPO Well now, what are we going to do with him?

MME. TÉPAN We could ask him to eat with us. What do you think?

M. TÉPAN I don't see any reason why not.

ZAPO (*to* ZÉPO) All right then, how'd you like to eat with us?

ZÉPO Uh . . .

M. TÉPAN We brought along a nice bottle of wine.

ZÉPO Well, in that case O.K.

MME. TÉPAN Make yourself right at home. Don't be afraid to ask for things.

ZÉPO Fine.

M. TÉPAN Well now, how about you, have you been keeping up a good shooting score?

ZÉPO When?

M. TÉPAN Why, the last few days.

ZÉPO Where?

M. TÉPAN Right here and now. After all, you *are* fighting a war.

ZÉPO No, no great shakes. I haven't kept up a very good score. Practically no bull's-eyes.

M. TÉPAN Well, what have you been scoring best with in your shooting, enemy horses or soldiers?

ZÉPO No, no horses. There aren't any horses any more.

M. TÉPAN Well, soldiers then?

ZÉPO   Could be.

M. TÉPAN   Could be? Aren't you sure?

ZÉPO   It's just that I . . . I fire without taking aim (*a pause*) and when I fire I say a *Hail Mary* for the guy I shot.

ZAPO   A *Hail Mary*? I'd have thought you'd say an *Our Father*.

ZÉPO   No. Always a *Hail Mary*. (*A pause.*) It's shorter.

M. TÉPAN   Come, my boy, you have to be courageous.

MME. TÉPAN (*to* ZÉPO)   If you like, we can untie you.

ZÉPO   No, leave me this way. It doesn't matter.

M. TÉPAN   You're not going to start putting on airs with us? If you want us to untie you, just say the word.

MME. TÉPAN   Please feel free.

ZÉPO   Well, if you really mean it, untie my feet. But it's just to please you people.

M. TÉPAN   Zapo, untie him. (ZAPO *unties him.*)

MME. TÉPAN   Well now, feel better?

ZÉPO   Sure do. But listen, maybe I'm causing you too much trouble.

M. TÉPAN   Not at all. Make yourself right at home. And if you want us to undo your hands, just say so.

ZÉPO   No, not my hands, too. I don't want to overdo it.

M. TÉPAN   Not at all, my boy, not at all. I tell you, you don't disturb us one bit.

ZÉPO   All right, go ahead and untie my hands then. But just while we eat, huh? I don't want you to think when you give me an inch I'm going to take a mile.

M. TÉPAN   Untie his hands, sonny.

MME. TÉPAN   Well, since our honorable prisoner is so nice, we're going to have a lovely day out here in the country.

ZÉPO   Don't call me "honorable" prisoner. Just say "prisoner" plain and simple.

MME. TÉPAN   You're sure that won't make you feel bad?

ZÉPO   No, not at all.

M. TÉPAN   Well, you're certainly unpretentious, anyway.

Sound of airplanes.

ZAPO   Airplanes. They're going to bomb us for sure. (ZAPO *and* ZÉPO *dive for the sandbags and hide.*)

ZAPO (*to his parents*)   Run for cover! The bombs are going to land right on you.

The sound of the planes drowns out everything. Immediately bombs start falling. Shells explode nearby. Deafening racket. ZAPO *and* ZÉPO *are crouching among the sandbags.* M. TÉPAN *goes on calmly talking to his wife, who answers him with equal calm. Because of the bombardment we cannot hear their conversation.*

MME. TÉPAN *heads for one of the picnic baskets, from which she takes an umbrella. She opens it. The* TÉPANS *take shelter under the umbrella as though it were raining. Standing there, they shift from one foot to the other, in rhythm, all the while discussing personal matters. The bombardment continues.*

At last, the airplanes take off. Silence.

M. TÉPAN *stretches one arm out from under the umbrella to make certain there is no longer anything coming down from the sky.*

M. TÉPAN   You can close your umbrella now. (MME TÉPAN *closes it. Together they go over to their son and prod him on the behind a couple of times with the umbrella.*)

M. TÉPAN   All right, come on out. The bombing's over.

ZAPO *and* ZÉPO *come out of their hiding place.*

ZAPO   They didn't get you?

M. TÉPAN   You don't expect anything to happen to your father, do you? (*Proudly*) Little bombs like that? Don't make me laugh.

From the left, a pair of Red Cross CORPSMEN *enter, carrying a stretcher.*

1ST CORPSMAN   Any bodies?

ZAPO   No, none here.

1ST CORPSMAN   You're sure you took a good look?

ZAPO   Absolutely.

1ST CORPSMAN   And there's not one single body?

ZAPO   Didn't I just say so?

1ST CORPSMAN   Not even someone wounded?

ZAPO   Not even.

2ND CORPSMAN   Well, we're really up the creek! (*To* ZAPO, *persuasively*) Take a good look all around here, see if you don't turn up a stiff someplace.

1ST CORPSMAN   Don't press the issue. They told you once and for all there aren't any.

2ND CORPSMAN   What a lousy deal!

ZAPO   I'm really very sorry. I swear I didn't plan it that way.

2ND CORPSMAN   That's what they all say. That there aren't any corpses, and that they didn't plan it that way.

1ST CORPSMAN   So let the man alone!

M. TÉPAN (*obligingly*)   If we can help you at all, we'd be delighted to. At your service.

2ND CORPSMAN   Well, I don't know. If we keep on like this, I really don't know what the Captain's going to say to us.

M. TÉPAN   What seems to be the trouble?

2ND CORPSMAN   Just that the others are all getting sore wrists carrying out the dead and wounded, while we still haven't come up with anything. And it's not because we haven't been looking.

M. TÉPAN   I see. That really is a bore. (*To* ZAPO) You're quite sure there are no corpses?

ZAPO   Obviously, Papa.

M. TÉPAN   You looked under the sandbags?

ZAPO   Yes, Papa.

M. TÉPAN (*angrily*)   Why don't you come right out and say you don't want to have any part in helping these good gentlemen?

1ST CORPSMAN   Don't jump on him like that. Leave him alone. We'll just hope we have better luck in some other trench where maybe everybody'll be dead.

M. TÉPAN   I'd be delighted for you.

MME. TÉPAN   So would I. Nothing pleases me more than to see people who take their work seriously.

M. TÉPAN (*indignantly, to anyone within hearing*)   Well, isn't anyone going to do anything for these gentlemen?

ZAPO   If it was up to me, it'd be good as done.

ZÉPO   Same here.

M. TÉPAN   Look here now, isn't one of you at least wounded?

ZAPO (*ashamed*)   No, not me.

M. TÉPAN (*to* ZÉPO)   What about you?

ZÉPO (*ashamed*)   Me either. I never was lucky.

MME. TÉPAN (*delighted*)   I just remembered! This morning, while I was peeling onions, I cut my finger. How's that?

M. TÉPAN   Why of course! (*Really in the swing of things*)   They'll put you on the stretcher and carry you right off!

1ST CORPSMAN   Sorry, it's no good. Women don't count.

M. TÉPAN   Well, that didn't get us anywhere.

1ST CORPSMAN   It doesn't matter.

2ND CORPSMAN   Maybe we can get our fill in the other trenches. (*They start to go off.*)

M. TÉPAN   Don't you worry, if we find a corpse, we'll hang onto it for you. There's not a chance we'd give it to anybody but you.

2ND CORPSMAN   Thank you very much, sir.

M. TÉPAN   It's nothing, my boy. It's the very least I could do.

The CORPSMEN *make their goodbyes. All four of the others reply in kind. The* CORPSMEN *exit.*

MME. TÉPAN   That's what's so pleasant about spending Sunday out in the battlefield. You always run into such nice folks. (*A pause.*) Come to think of it, why is it you're enemies?

ZÉPO   I don't know. I'm not too well educated.

MME. TÉPAN   I mean is it from birth, or did you become enemies after?

ZÉPO   I don't know. I don't know a thing about it.

M. TÉPAN   Well then, how did you come to go to war?

ZÉPO   One day I was home fixing my mother's iron and a man came by and said to me: "Are you Zépo?" . . . "Yes." . . . "Good, you've got to go to war." So I asked him, "What war?" And he said to me: "Don't you read the newspapers? You *are* a hick!" So I told him yes I did, but not all that war stuff . . .

ZAPO   That's just what happened to me; exactly what happened to me.

M. TÉPAN   Sure, they came after you, too.

MME. TÉPAN   No, it's not the same. You weren't fixing the iron that day, you were repairing the car.

M. TÉPAN   I was talking about the rest of it (*To* ZÉPO) Go on. Then what happened?

ZÉPO   Well then I told him that I had a fiancée, and if I didn't take her to the movies on Sunday, she wouldn't know what to do with herself. He said that that didn't matter.

ZAPO   Same as me. Exactly the same as me.

ZÉPO   Well, then my father came down and he said I couldn't go to war because I didn't have a horse.

ZAPO   Like my father said.

ZÉPO   The man said they didn't use horses any more, and I asked him if I could take along my fiancée. He said no. Then I asked him could I take along my aunt to make me custard every Thursday. I like custard.

MME. TÉPAN (*realizing that she has forgotten something*)   Oh! The custard!

ZÉPO   Again he said no.

ZAPO   The way he did to me.

ZÉPO   And ever since then, here I am, nearly always all alone in the trench here.

MME. TÉPAN   As long as you're so much alike, and both so bored, I think you and your honorable prisoner might play together this afternoon.

ZAPO   Oh no, Mama! I'm too scared. He's an enemy.

M. TÉPAN   Oh come on now, don't be scared.

ZAPO   If you knew what the general told us about the enemy.

MME. TÉPAN   What did he tell you?

ZAPO   He said the enemy soldiers are very mean. When they take prisoners, they put pebbles in their socks so it hurts when they walk.

MME. TÉPAN   How horrible! What savages!

M. TÉPAN (*indignantly, to* ZÉPO)   Aren't you ashamed to be part of an army of criminals?

ZÉPO   I didn't do anything. I'm not mad at anybody.

MME. TÉPAN   He's trying to put one over on us, acting like a little saint.

M. TÉPAN   We should never have untied him. Probably all we have to do is have our backs turned for him to go putting pebbles in our socks.

ZÉPO   Don't be so mean to me.

M. TÉPAN   How do you expect us to be? I'm shocked. I know just what I'm going to do. I'm going to find the Captain and ask him to let me go into battle.

ZAPO   He won't let you. You're too old.

M. TÉPAN   Well then I'll go buy a horse and a saber and I'll go to war on my own.

ZÉPO   Please, madame, don't treat me like this. Besides, I was just going to tell you, *our* general said the same thing about you people.

MME. TÉPAN   How could he dare tell such a lie?

ZAPO   The very same thing, honest?

ZÉPO   Yes, the very same thing.

M. TÉPAN   Maybe it's the same one who talked to both of you.

MME. TÉPAN   Well, if it is the same general, the least he could do is use a different speech. Imagine telling everybody the same thing.

M. TÉPAN (*to* ZÉPO, *changing his tone*)   Can I fill your glass again?

MME. TÉPAN   I hope you enjoyed our little lunch.

M. TÉPAN   It was better than last Sunday, anyway.

ZÉPO   What happened then?

M. TÉPAN   Well, we went out to the country and laid all our chow out on the blanket. While we had our backs turned, a cow came along and ate the whole lunch, including the napkins.

ZÉPO   What a glutton, that cow!

M. TÉPAN   Yes, but then to get even, we ate the cow. (*They laugh.*)

ZAPO (*to* ZÉPO)   I bet they weren't hungry after that.

M. TÉPAN   To your health! (*They all drink.*)

MME. TÉPAN (*to* ZÉPO)   Tell me something, what do you do for amusement in the trenches?

ZÉPO   Just to pass the time and keep myself amused, I take odds and ends of rags and make little flowers out of them. See, I get bored a lot.

MME. TÉPAN   And what do you do with these rag flowers?

ZÉPO   At first I used to send them to my fiancée, but one day she told me that the cellar and the greenhouse were already filled with them, that she didn't know what to do with them any more, and would I mind sending her something else for a change?

MME. TÉPAN   And what did you do?

ZÉPO   I tried learning something else, but I couldn't do it. So, to pass the time, I just go on making my rag flowers.

MME. TÉPAN   And then do you throw them away?

ZÉPO   No, now I've found a way to make use of them: I furnish one flower for each of my buddies who dies. That way, I know that even if I make a whole lot, there'll never be enough.

M. TÉPAN   You found a good way out.

ZÉPO (*timidly*)   Yes.

ZAPO   Well, you know what I do so's not to get bored is knit.

MME. TÉPAN   But tell me, do all the soldiers get bored the way you two do?

ZÉPO   That depends on what they do for relaxation.

ZAPO   Same thing over on our side.

M. TÉPAN   Well then, let's stop the war.

ZÉPO   But how?

M. TÉPAN   Very easy. You tell your buddies that the enemy doesn't want to fight, and you tell the same thing to your comrades. And everybody goes home.

ZAPO   Terrific!

MME. TÉPAN   That way you can finish fixing the iron.

ZAPO   How come nobody ever thought of that before?

MME. TÉPAN   It takes your father to come up with ideas like that. Don't forget he's a Normal School graduate, and a philatelist, too.

ZÉPO   But what will all the field-marshals and the corporals do?

M. TÉPAN   We'll give 'em guitars and castanets to keep 'em quiet.

ZÉPO   Excellent idea.

M. TÉPAN   See how easy it is? It's all settled.

ZÉPO   We'll wow 'em.

ZAPO   Boy, will my buddies be glad!

MME. TÉPAN   What do you say we celebrate and put on that pasodoble we were listening to before?

ZÉPO   Wonderful!

ZAPO   Yes, put on the record, Mama.

MME. TÉPAN *puts on the record. She winds the phonograph and waits. Not a sound is heard.*

M. TÉPAN   You can't hear anything.

MME. TÉPAN (*going to the phonograph*)   Oh! . . . I made a boo-boo! Instead of putting on a record, I put on a beret.

She puts the record on. A lively pasodoble is heard. ZAPO *dances with* ZÉPO; MME. TÉPAN *with her husband.*

The field telephone rings. None of the group hears it. They go on dancing in a lively manner.

The phone rings again. The dancing continues. Battle breaks out once more with a great din of bombs, rifle fire and the crackle of machine-guns. Having noticed nothing, the two couples keep on dancing gaily.

A sudden machine-gun blast mows them all down. They fall to the ground, stone dead. One bullet seems to have nicked the phonograph: the music keeps repeating the same strain over and over, like a record with a scratch in it. We hear this repeated strain for the remainder of the play.

From the left, the two CORPSMEN *enter, carrying the empty stretcher.*

FAST CURTAIN

Antigonê

Sophocles

*Translation by Dudley Fitts
and Robert Fitzgerald*

CHARACTERS

ANTIGONÊ, *daughter of Oedipus and Iocastê*
ISMENÊ, *her sister*
CREON, *the new King of Thebes, brother of Iocastê*
EURYDICÊ, *his wife*
HAIMON, *their son, betrothed to Antigonê*

TEIRESIAS, *an old, blind seer*
SENTRY
MESSENGER
CHORUS OF THEBAN ELDERS
CHORAGOS, *leader of the Chorus*

SCENE *Before the palace of* CREON, *King of Thebes. A central double door, and two lateral doors. A platform extends the length of the façade, and from this platform three steps lead down into the "orchestra," or chorus-ground.*

TIME *Dawn of the day after the repulse of the Argive army from the assault on Thebes.*

PROLOGUE

ANTIGONÊ *and* ISMENÊ *enter from the central door of the Palace.*

ANTIGONÊ Ismenê, dear sister,
You would think that we had already suffered enough

For the curse on Oedipus:[1]
I cannot imagine any grief
That you and I have not gone through. And now—
Have they told you of the new decree of our King Creon?

ISMENÊ   I have heard nothing: I know
That two sisters lost two brothers, a double death
In a single hour; and I know that the Argive army

10   Fled in the night; but beyond this, nothing.

ANTIGONÊ   I thought so. And that is why I wanted you
To come out here with me. There is something we must do.

ISMENÊ   Why do you speak so strangely?

ANTIGONÊ   Listen, Ismenê:
Creon buried our brother Eteoclês
With military honors, gave him a soldier's funeral,
And it was right that he should; but Polyneicês,
Who fought as bravely and died as miserably,—
They say that Creon has sworn

---

[1] When Oedipus was born, he was left on Mount Cithaeron to die because it had been predicted that this baby would grow up to kill his father and marry his mother. (His feet were bound, hence the name Oedipus which means swollen feet.) He was rescued by a Corinthian shepherd, and adopted by Polybus, the king of Corinth. An oracle of Apollo gave the young man Oedipus this same prediction, and Oedipus left Corinth in an attempt to escape his fate. On his journey he killed an aged traveler in a violent roadside quarrel. This stranger was his father, Laïos.

Oedipus then went on to Thebes where a monster, the Sphinx, was terrorizing the people and devouring all who tried unsuccessfully to solve her riddle:

What goes on four feet, on two feet, and three,
But the more feet it goes on the weaker it be?

When Oedipus replied that a man crawls on four feet as an infant, walks on two feet as he matures, then uses a staff in his old age, the riddle was solved, and the Sphinx slew herself. Oedipus was made king of Thebes and married the widowed queen, Iocastê who bore him two daughters, Antigone and Ismemê, and two sons, Eteoclês and Polyneicês. Subsequently a terrible plague ravished Thebes and the Oracle declared that the murderer of the former king, Laïos, must be banished if the Thebans wished to be cleansed. The search for the murderer revealed to Oedipus and Iocastê that he was her son. Iocastê then hanged herself. Oedipus put out his eyes and, expelled from Thebes and accompanied only by his daughter, Antigone, wandered from place to place until his death.

The two brothers, Eteoclês and Polyneicês quarreled. Polyneicês was driven out of Thebes and joined the Argive army in an assault on his native city. During the battle the brothers killed each other in single combat. Creon, their uncle, who had become King, ordered that Eteoclês be buried with full military honors, but decreed that Polyneicês, a traitor, be left unburied on the battlefield. Since the Greeks believed that the Gods denied peace forever to the unburied dead, this decree was a dreadful fate for Polyneicês. At this point the play, *Antigone,* begins.

20 No one shall bury him, no one mourn for him,
But his body must lie in the fields, a sweet treasure
For carrion birds to find as they search for food.
That is what they say, and our good Creon is coming here
To announce it publicly; and the penalty—
Stoning to death in the public square!
                                    There it is,
And now you can prove what you are:
A true sister, or a traitor to your family.
ISMENÊ   Antigonê, you are mad! What could I possibly do?
ANTIGONÊ   You must decide whether you will help me or not.
30 ISMENÊ   I do not understand you. Help you in what?
ANTIGONÊ   Ismenê, I am going to bury him. Will you come?
ISMENÊ   Bury him! You have just said the new law forbids it.
ANTIGONÊ   He is my brother. And he is your brother, too.
ISMENÊ   But think of the danger! Think what Creon will do!
ANTIGONÊ   Creon is not strong enough to stand in my way.
ISMENÊ   Ah sister!
Oedipus died, everyone hating him
For what his own search brought to light, his eyes
Ripped out by his own hand; and Iocastê died,
40 His mother and wife at once: she twisted the cords
That strangled her life; and our two brothers died,
Each killed by the other's sword. And we are left:
But oh, Antigonê,
Think how much more terrible than these
Our own death would be if we should go against Creon
And do what he has forbidden! We are only women,
We cannot fight with men, Antigonê!
The law is strong, we must give in to the law
In this thing, and in worse. I beg the Dead
50   To forgive me, but I am helpless: I must yield
To those in authority. And I think it is dangerous business
To be always meddling.
ANTIGONÊ   If that is what you think,
I should not want you, even if you asked to come.
You have made your choice, you can be what you want to be.
But I will bury him; and if I must die,
I say that this crime is holy: I shall lie down

With him in death, and I shall be as dear
To him as he to me.

                  It is the dead,
Not the living, who make the longest demands:
⁶⁰ We die for ever . . .

                      You may do as you like,
Since apparently the laws of the gods mean nothing to you.

ISMENÊ   They mean a great deal to me; but I have no strength
To break laws that were made for the public good.

ANTIGONÊ   That must be your excuse, I suppose. But as for me,
I will bury the brother I love.

ISMENÊ   Antigonê,
I am so afraid for you!

ANTIGONÊ   You need not be:
You have yourself to consider, after all.

ISMENÊ   But no one must hear of this, you must tell no one!
I will keep it a secret, I promise!

ANTIGONÊ   Oh tell it! Tell everyone!
⁷⁰ Think how they'll hate you when it all comes out
If they learn that you knew about it all the time!

ISMENÊ   So fiery! You should be cold with fear.

ANTIGONÊ   Perhaps. But I am doing only what I must.

ISMENÊ   But can you do it? I say that you cannot.

ANTIGONÊ   Very well: when my strength gives out, I shall do no
    more.

ISMENÊ   Impossible things should not be tried at all.

ANTIGONÊ   Go away, Ismenê:
I shall be hating you soon, and the dead will too,
For your words are hateful. Leave me my foolish plan:
⁸⁰ I am not afraid of the danger; if it means death,
It will not be the worst of deaths—death without honor.

ISMENÊ   Go then, if you feel that you must.
   You are unwise,
But a loyal friend indeed to those who love you.

Exit into the Palace. ANTIGONÊ *goes off, left. Enter the* CHORUS.

PÁRODOS [2]

STROPHE 1

CHORUS   Now the long blade of the sun, lying
   Level east to west, touches with glory
   Thebes of the Seven Gates. Open, unlidded
   Eye of golden day! O marching light
   Across the eddy and rush of Dircê's [3] stream,
   Striking the white shields of the enemy
   Thrown headlong backward from the blaze of morning!
CHORAGOS [4]   Polyneicês their commander
   Roused them with windy phrases,
10   He the wild eagle screaming
   Insults above our land,
   His wings their shields of snow,
   His crest their marshalled helms.

ANTISTROPHE 1

CHORUS   Against our seven gates in a yawning ring
  The famished spears came onward in the night;
   But before his jaws were sated with our blood,
   Or pinefire took the garland of our towers,
   He was thrown back; and as he turned, great Thebes—
   No tender victim for his noisy power—
20   Rose like a dragon behind him, shouting war.
CHORAGOS   For God hates utterly
   The bray of bragging tongues;
   And when he beheld their smiling,
   Their swagger of golden helms,
   The frown of his thunder blasted
   Their first man from our walls. [5]

---

[2] The párodos was the choral entry song. The choral song or ode usually consisted of three parts: the strophe, the antistrophe, and the epode or after-song. The word strophe means "a turn" and was, originally, that part of the ode which was sung by the chorus as it moved in one direction on the stage. The antistrophe which followed was chanted or sung as the chorus reversed the direction of its movement.

[3] Dircê was the name of a spring or river west of Thebes.

[4] The choragos was the leader of the chorus.

[5] Capaneus, one of the seven captains of the Argives who assaulted Thebes, had boasted that not even Zeus could prevent his climbing the Theban walls. When he made the attempt, he was killed by Zeus' weapon, the thunderbolt.

STROPHE 2

CHORUS   We heard his shout of triumph high in the air
      Turn to a scream; far out in a flaming arc
      He fell with his windy torch, and the earth struck him.
30   And others storming in fury no less than his
      Found shock of death in the dusty joy of battle.

CHORAGOS   Seven captains at seven gates
      Yielded their clanging arms to the god
      That bends the battle-line and breaks it.
      These two only, brothers in blood,
      Face to face in matchless rage,
      Mirroring each the other's death,
      Clashed in long combat.

ANTISTROPHE 2

CHORUS   But now in the beautiful morning of victory
40   Let Thebes of the many chariots sing for joy!
      With hearts for dancing we'll take leave of war:
      Our temples shall be sweet with hymns of praise,
      And the long night shall echo with our chorus.

SCENE I

CHORAGOS   But now at last our new King is coming:
      Creon of Thebes, Menoikeus' son.
      In this auspicious dawn of his reign
      What are the new complexities
      That shifting Fate has woven for him?
      What is his counsel? Why has he summoned
      The old men to hear him?

Enter CREON *from the Palace, center. He addresses the* CHORUS
from the top step.

CREON   Gentlemen: I have the honor to inform you that our Ship
      of State, which recent storms have threatened to destroy, has
10   come safely to harbor at last, guided by the merciful wisdom
      of Heaven. I have summoned you here this morning because
      I know that I can depend upon you: your devotion to King Laïos
      was absolute; you never hesitated in your duty to our late ruler

Oedipus; and when Oedipus died, your loyalty was transferred to his children. Unfortunately, as you know, his two sons, the princes Eteoclês and Polyneicês, have killed each other in battle; and I, as the next in blood, have succeeded to the full power of the throne.

20 I am aware, of course, that no Ruler can expect complete loyalty from his subjects until he has been tested in office. Nevertheless, I say to you at the very outset that I have nothing but contempt for the kind of Governor who is afraid, for whatever reason, to follow the course that he knows is best for the State; and as for the man who sets private friendship above the public welfare,—I have no use for him, either. I call God to witness that if I saw my country headed for ruin, I should not be afraid to speak out plainly; and I need hardly remind you that I would never have any dealings with an enemy of the people. No one values friendship more highly than I; but we must remember

30 that friends made at the risk of wrecking our Ship are not real friends at all.

These are my principles, at any rate, and that is why I have made the following decision concerning the sons of Oedipus: Eteoclês, who died as a man should die, fighting for his country, is to be buried with full military honors, with all the ceremony that is usual when the greatest heroes die; but his brother Polyneicês, who broke his exile to come back with fire and sword against his native city and the shrines of his fathers' gods, whose one idea was to spill the blood of his blood and sell his own

40 people into slavery—Polyneicês, I say, is to have no burial: no man is to touch him or say the least prayer for him; he shall lie on the plain, unburied; and the birds and the scavenging dogs can do with him whatever they like.

This is my command, and you can see the wisdom behind it. As long as I am King, no traitor is going to be honored with the loyal man. But whoever shows by word and deed that he is on the side of the State,—he shall have my respect while he is living, and my reverence when he is dead.

CHORAGOS If that is your will, Creon son of Menoikeus,

50 You have the right to enforce it: we are yours.

CREON That is my will. Take care that you do your part.

CHORAGOS We are old men: let the younger ones carry it out.

CREON I do not mean that: the sentries have been appointed.

CHORAGOS   Then what is it that you would have us do.

CREON   You will give no support to whoever breaks this law.

CHORAGOS   Only a crazy man is in love with death!

CREON   And death it is; yet money talks, and the wisest
Have sometimes been known to count a few coins too many.

Enter SENTRY *from left.*

SENTRY   I'll not say that I'm out of breath from running, King,
60   because every time I stopped to think about what I have to tell
you, I felt like going back. And all the time a voice kept saying,
"You fool, don't you know you're walking straight into trouble?";
and then another voice: "Yes, but if you let somebody else get
the news to Creon first, it will be even worse than that for you!"
But good sense won out, at least I hope it was good sense, and
here I am with a story that makes no sense at all; but I'll tell it
anyhow, because, as they say, what's going to happen's going
to happen, and—

CREON   Come to the point. What have you to say?

70   SENTRY   I did not do it. I did not see who did it. You must not
punish me for what someone else has done.

CREON   A comprehensive defense! More effective, perhaps,
If I knew its purpose. Come: what is it?

SENTRY   A dreadful thing . . . I don't know how to put it—

CREON   Out with it!

SENTRY   Well, then;
The dead man—
                    Polyneicês—

Pause. The SENTRY *is overcome, fumbles for words.* CREON *waits impassively.*

out there—
                    someone,—

New dust on the slimy flesh!

Pause. No sign from CREON.

Someone has given it burial that way, and
Gone . . .

Long pause. CREON *finally speaks with deadly control:*

⁸⁰ CREON   And the man who dared do this?

SENTRY   I swear I
Do not know! You must believe me!

                                                  Listen:
The ground was dry, not a sign of digging, no,
Not a wheeltrack in the dust, no trace of anyone.
It was when they relieved us this morning: and one of them,
The corporal, pointed to it.

                                          There it was,
The strangest—

                    Look:
The body, just mounded over with light dust: you see?
Not buried really, but as if they'd covered it
Just enough for the ghost's peace. And no sign

⁹⁰ Of dogs or any wild animal that had been there.

And then what a scene there was! Every man of us
Accusing the other: we all proved the other man did it,
We all had proof that we could not have done it.
We were ready to take hot iron in our hands,
Walk through fire, swear by all the gods,
It was not I!
I do not know who it was, but it was not I!

CREON'S *rage has been mounting steadily, but the* SENTRY *is too*
intent upon his story to notice it.

And then, when this came to nothing, someone said
A thing that silenced us and made us stare

¹⁰⁰ Down at the ground: you had to be told the news,
And one of us had to do it! We threw the dice,
And the bad luck fell to me. So here I am,
No happier to be here than you are to have me:
Nobody likes the man who brings bad news.

CHORAGOS   I have been wondering, King: can it be that the gods
    have done this?

CREON (*Furiously*)   Stop!
Must you doddering wrecks
Go out of your heads entirely? "The gods!"
Intolerable!

110   The gods favor this corpse? Why? How had he served them?
Tried to loot their temples, burn their images,
Yes, and the whole State, and its laws with it!
Is it your senile opinion that the gods love to honor bad men?
A pious thought!—

                 No, from the very beginning
There have been those who have whispered together,
Stiff-necked anarchists, putting their heads together,
Scheming against me in alleys. These are the men,
And they have bribed my own guard to do this thing.

Money!   (*Sententiously*)
120   There's nothing in the world so demoralizing as money.
Down go your cities,
Homes gone, men gone, honest hearts corrupted,
Crookedness of all kinds, and all for money!

(*To* SENTRY)   But you—!
I swear by God and by the throne of God,
The man who has done this thing shall pay for it!
Find that man, bring him here to me, or your death
Will be the least of your problems: I'll string you up
Alive, and there will be certain ways to make you
Discover your employer before you die;
130   And the process may teach you a lesson you seem to have missed:
The dearest profit is sometimes all too dear:
That depends on the source. Do you understand me?
A fortune won is often misfortune.

SENTRY   King, may I speak?
CREON   Your very voice distresses me.
SENTRY   Are you sure that it is my voice, and not your conscience?
CREON   By God, he wants to analyze me now!
SENTRY   It is not what I say, but what has been done, that hurts
    you.
CREON   You talk too much.
SENTRY   Maybe; but I've done nothing.
CREON   Sold your soul for some silver: that's all you've done.
140   SENTRY   How dreadful it is when the right judge judges wrong!
CREON   Your figures of speech
May entertain you now; but unless you bring me the man,
You will get little profit from them in the end.

Exit CREON *into the Palace.*

SENTRY   "Bring me the man"—!
  I'd like nothing better than bringing him the man!
  But bring him or not, you have seen the last of me here.
  At any rate, I am safe!

Exit SENTRY.

ODE I

STROPHE 1
CHORUS   Numberless are the world's wonders, but none
  More wonderful than man; the stormgray sea
  Yields to his prows, the huge crests bear him high;
  Earth, holy and inexhaustible, is graven
  With shining furrows where his plows have gone
  Year after year, the timeless labor of stallions.

ANTISTROPHE 1
  The lightboned birds and beasts that cling to cover,
  The lithe fish lighting their reaches of dim water,
  All are taken, tamed in the net of his mind;
10 The lion on the hill, the wild horse windy-maned,
  Resign to him; and his blunt yoke has broken
  The sultry shoulders of the mountain bull.

STROPHE 2
  Words also, and thought as rapid as air,
  He fashions to his good use; statecraft is his,
  And his the skill that deflects the arrows of snow,
  The spears of winter rain: from every wind
  He has made himself secure—from all but one:
  In the late wind of death he cannot stand.

ANTISTROPHE 2
  O clear intelligence, force beyond all measure!
20 O fate of man, working both good and evil!
  When the laws are kept, how proudly his city stands!
  When the laws are broken, what of his city then?
  Never may the anárchic man find rest at my hearth,
  Never be it said that my thoughts are his thoughts.

SCENE II

Re-enter SENTRY *leading* ANTIGONÊ.

CHORAGOS   What does this mean? Surely this captive woman
  Is the Princess, Antigonê. Why should she be taken?
SENTRY   Here is the one who did it! We caught her
  In the very act of burying him.—Where is Creon?
CHORAGOS   Just coming from the house.

Enter CREON, *center.*

                                                    What has happened?
  Why have you come back so soon?
SENTRY (*expansively*)   O King,
  A man should never be too sure of anything:
  I would have sworn
  That you'd not see me here again: your anger
10 Frightened me so, and the things you threatened me with;
  But how could I tell then
  That I'd be able to solve the case so soon?

  No dice-throwing this time: I was only too glad to come!

  Here is this woman. She is the guilty one:
  We found her trying to bury him.
  Take her, then; question her; judge her as you will.
  I am through with the whole thing now, and glad of it.
CREON   But this is Antigonê! Why have you brought her here?
SENTRY   She was burying him, I tell you!
CREON (*severely*)   Is this the truth?
20 SENTRY   I saw her with my own eyes. Can I say more?
CREON   The details: come, tell me quickly!
SENTRY   It was like this:
  After those terrible threats of yours, King,
  We went back and brushed the dust away from the body.
  The flesh was soft by now, and stinking,
  So we sat on a hill to windward and kept guard.
  No napping this time! We kept each other awake.
  But nothing happened until the white round sun
  Whirled in the center of the round sky over us:

Then, suddenly,

30 A storm of dust roared up from the earth, and the sky
Went out, the plain vanished with all its trees
In the stinging dark. We closed our eyes and endured it.
The whirlwind lasted a long time, but it passed;
And then we looked, and there was Antigonê!
I have seen
A mother bird come back to a stripped nest, heard
Her crying bitterly a broken note or two
For the young ones stolen. Just so, when this girl
Found the bare corpse, and all her love's work wasted,
40 She wept, and cried on heaven to damn the hands
That had done this thing.

                    And then she brought more dust
And sprinkled wine three times for her brother's ghost.

We ran and took her at once. She was not afraid,
Not even when we charged her with what she had done.
She denied nothing.

             And this was a comfort to me,
And some uneasiness: for it is a good thing
To escape from death, but it is no great pleasure
To bring death to a friend.

                  Yet I always say
There is nothing so comfortable as your own safe skin!
50 CREON (*slowly, dangerously*)   And you, Antigonê,
You with your head hanging,—do you confess this thing?
ANTIGONÊ I do. I deny nothing.
CREON (*to* SENTRY)   You may go.

Exit SENTRY.

(*To* ANTIGONÊ) Tell me, tell me briefly:
Had you heard my proclamation touching this matter?
ANTIGONÊ It was public. Could I help hearing it?
CREON And yet you dared defy the law
ANTIGONÊ   I dared.
It was not God's proclamation. That final Justice
That rules the world below makes no such laws.

Your edict, King, was strong,
60 But all your strength is weakness itself against

The immortal unrecorded laws of God.
They are not merely now: they were, and shall be,
Operative for ever, beyond man utterly.

I knew I must die, even without your decree:
I am only mortal. And if I must die
Now, before it is my time to die,
Surely this is no hardship: can anyone
Living, as I live, with evil all about me,
Think Death less than a friend? This death of mine
70   Is of no importance; but if I had left my brother
Lying in death unburied, I should have suffered.
Now I do not.
                    You smile at me. Ah Creon,
Think me a fool, if you like; but it may well be
That a fool convicts me of folly.

CHORAGOS   Like father, like daughter: both headstrong, deaf to
    reason!
She has never learned to yield.

CREON   She has much to learn
The inflexible heart breaks first, the toughest iron
Cracks first, and the wildest horses bend their necks
At the pull of the smallest curb.
                              Pride? In a slave?
80   This girl is guilty of a double insolence,
Breaking the given laws and boasting of it.
Who is the man here,
She or I, if this crime goes unpunished?
Sister's child, or more than sister's child,
Or closer yet in blood—she and her sister
Win bitter death for this!
(*To* SERVANTS)   Go, some of you,
Arrest Ismenê. I accuse her equally.
Bring her: you will find her sniffling in the house there.

Her mind's a traitor: crimes kept in the dark
90   Cry for light, and the guardian brain shudders;
But how much worse than this
Is brazen boasting of barefaced anarchy!

ANTIGONÊ   Creon, what more do you want than my death?

CREON   Nothing.

That gives me everything.

ANTIGONÊ   Then I beg you: kill me.
This talking is a great weariness: your words
Are distasteful to me, and I am sure that mine
Seem so to you. And yet they should not seem so:
I should have praise and honor for what I have done.
All these men here would praise me

100 Were their lips not frozen shut with fear of you.

(*Bitterly*) Ah the good fortune of kings,
Licensed to say and do whatever they please!

CREON   You are alone here in that opinion.

ANTIGONÊ   No, they are with me. But they keep their tongues in
leash.

CREON   Maybe. But you are guilty, and they are not.

ANTIGONÊ   There is no guilt in reverence for the dead.

CREON   But Eteoclês—was he not your brother too?

ANTIGONÊ   My brother too.

CREON   And you insult his memory?

ANTIGONÊ (*softly*)   The dead man would not say that I insult it.

110 CREON   He would: for you honor a traitor as much as him.

ANTIGONÊ   His own brother, traitor or not, and equal in blood.

CREON   He made war on his country. Eteoclês defended it.

ANTIGONÊ   Nevertheless, there are honors due all the dead.

CREON   But not the same for the wicked as for the just.

ANTIGONÊ   Ah Creon, Creon,
Which of us can say what the gods hold wicked?

CREON   An enemy is an enemy, even dead.

ANTIGONÊ   It is my nature to join in love, not hate.

CREON (*finally losing patience*)   Go join them, then; if you must
have your love,

120 Find it in hell!

CHORAGOS   But see, Ismenê comes:

Enter ISMENÊ, *guarded.*

Those tears are sisterly, the cloud
That shadows her eyes rains down gentle sorrow.

CREON   You too, Ismenê,
Snake in my ordered house, sucking my blood
Stealthily—and all the time I never knew

That these two sisters were aiming at my throne!

                                                  Ismenê,

Do you confess your share in this crime, or deny it?

Answer me.

130 ISMENÊ   Yes, if she will let me say so. I am guilty.

ANTIGONÊ (*coldly*)   No, Ismenê. You have no right to say so.

    You would not help me, and I will not have you help me.

ISMENÊ   But now I know what you meant; and I am here

    To join you, to take my share of punishment.

ANTIGONÊ   The dead man and the gods who rule the dead

    Know whose act this was. Words are not friends.

ISMENÊ   Do you refuse me, Antigonê? I want to die with you:

    I too have a duty that I must discharge to the dead.

ANTIGONÊ   You shall not lessen my death by sharing it.

140 ISMENÊ   What do I care for life when you are dead?

ANTIGONÊ   Ask Creon. You're always hanging on his opinions.

ISMENÊ   You are laughing at me. Why, Antigonê?

ANTIGONÊ   It's a joyless laughter, Ismenê.

ISMENÊ   But can I do nothing?

ANTIGONÊ   Yes. Save yourself. I shall not envy you.

    There are those who will praise you; I shall have honor, too.

ISMENÊ   But we are equally guilty!

ANTIGONÊ   No more, Ismenê.

    You are alive, but I belong to Death.

CREON (*to the* CHORUS)   Gentlemen, I beg you to observe these

    girls:

    One has just now lost her mind; the other,

150   It seems, has never had a mind at all.

ISMENÊ   Grief teaches the steadiest minds to waver, King.

CREON   Yours certainly did, when you assumed guilt with the

    guilty!

ISMENÊ   But how could I go on living without her?

CREON   You are.

    She is already dead.

ISMENÊ   But your own son's bride!

CREON   There are places enough for him to push his plow.

    I want no wicked women for my sons!

ISMENÊ   O dearest Haimon, how your father wrongs you!

CREON   I've had enough of your childish talk of marriage!

CHORAGOS   Do you really intend to steal this girl from your son?

160 CREON   No; Death will do that for me.
    CHORAGOS   Then she must die?
    CREON (*ironically*)   You dazzle me.
                  —But enough of this talk!
    (*To* GUARDS) You, there, take them away and guard them well:
    For they are but women, and even brave men run
    When they see Death coming.

    Exeunt ISMENÊ, ANTIGONÊ, *and* GUARDS.

ODE II

CHORAGOS   Fortunate is the man who has never tasted God's ven-
    geance!
    Where once the anger of heaven has struck, that house is shaken
    For ever: damnation rises behind each child
    Like a wave cresting out of the black northeast,
    When the long darkness under sea roars up
    And bursts drumming death upon the wind-whipped sand.

ANTISTROPHE 1
    I have seen this gathering sorrow from time long past
    Loom upon Oedipus' children: generation from generation
    Takes the compulsive rage of the enemy god.
10   So lately this last flower of Oedipus' line
    Drank the sunlight! but now a passionate word
    And a handful of dust have closed up all its beauty.

STROPHE 2
        What mortal arrogance
        Transcends the wrath of Zeus? [6]
    Sleep cannot lull him, nor the effortless long months
    Of the timeless gods: but he is young for ever,
    And his house is the shining day of high Olympos.[7]
        All that is and shall be,
        And all the past, is his.
20   No pride on earth is free of the curse of heaven.

ANTISTROPHE 2
        The straying dreams of men

[6] Zeus was the king of the gods (the Roman Jupiter).
[7] Olympos was a mountain in northern Greece where the gods lived.

May bring tehm ghosts of joy:
But as they drowse, the waking embers burn them;
Or they walk with fixed eyes, as blind men walk.
But the ancient wisdom speaks for our own time:
  Fate works most for woe
  With Folly's fairest show.
Man's little pleasure is the spring of sorrow.

SCENE III

CHORAGOS   But here is Haimon, King, the last of all your sons.
Is it grief for Antigonê that brings him here,
And bitterness at being robbed of his bride?

Enter HAIMON.

CREON   We shall soon see, and no need of diviners.

—Son,

You have heard my final judgment on that girl:
Have you come here hating me, or have you come
With deference and with love, whatever I do?
HAIMON   I am your son, father. You are my guide.
You make things clear for me, and I obey you.
10   No marriage means more to me than your continuing wisdom.
CREON   Good. That is the way to behave: subordinate
Everything else, my son, to your father's will.
This is what a man prays for, that he may get
Sons attentive and dutiful in his house,
Each one hating his father's enemies,
Honoring his father's friends. But if his sons
Fail him, if they turn out unprofitably,
What has he fathered but trouble for himself
And amusement for the malicious?

So you are right
20   Not to lose your head over this woman.
Your pleasure with her would soon grow cold, Haimon,
And then you'd have a hellcat in bed and elsewhere.
Let her find her husband in Hell!
Of all the people in this city, only she
Has had contempt for my law and broken it.

Do you want me to show myself weak before the people?
Or to break my sworn word? No, and I will not.
The woman dies.

I suppose she'll plead "family ties." Well, let her.
30   If I permit my own family to rebel,
How shall I earn the world's obedience?
Show me the man who keeps his house in hand,
He's fit for public authority.

                             I'll have no dealings
With law-breakers, critics of the government:
Whoever is chosen to govern should be obeyed—
Must be obeyed, in all things, great and small,
Just and unjust! O Haimon,
The man who knows how to obey, and that man only,
Knows how to give commands when the time comes.
40   You can depend on him, no matter how fast
The spears come: he's a good soldier, he'll stick it out.

Anarchy, anarchy! Show me a greater evil!
This is why cities tumble and the great houses rain down,
This is what scatters armies!

No, no: good lives are made so by discipline.
We keep the laws then, and the lawmakers,
And no woman shall seduce us. If we must lose,
Let's lose to a man, at least! Is a woman stronger than we?
CHORAGOS   Unless time has rusted my wits,
50   What you say, King, is said with point and dignity.
HAIMON (*boyishly earnest*)   Father:
Reason is God's crowning gift to man, and you are right
To warn me against losing mine. I cannot say—
I hope that I shall never want to say!—that you
Have reasoned badly. Yet there are other men
Who can reason, too; and their opinions might be helpful.
You are not in a position to know everything
That people say or do, or what they feel:
Your temper terrifies them—everyone
60   Will tell you only what you like to hear.
But I, at any rate, can listen; and I have heard them
Muttering and whispering in the dark about this girl.

They say no woman has ever, so unreasonably,
Died so shameful a death for a generous act:
"She covered her brother's body. Is this indecent?
She kept him from dogs and vultures. Is this a crime?
Death?—She should have all the honor that we can give her!"

This is the way they talk out there in the city.

You must believe me.
70   Nothing is closer to me than your happiness.
What could be closer? Must not any son
Value his father's fortune as his father does his?
I beg you, do not be unchangeable:
Do not believe that you alone can be right.
The man who thinks that,
That man who maintains that only he has the power
To reason correctly, the gift to speak, the soul—
A man like that, when you know him, turns out empty.

It is not reason never to yield to reason!
80   In flood time you can see how some trees bend,
And because they bend, even their twigs are safe,
While stubborn trees are torn up, roots and all.
And the same thing happens in sailing:
Make your sheet fast, never slacken,—and over you go,
Head over heels and under: and there's your voyage.
Forget you are angry! Let yourself be moved!
I know I am young; but please let me say this:
The ideal condition
Would be, I admit, that men should be right by instinct;
90   But since we are all too likely to go astray,
The reasonable thing is to learn from those who can teach.
CHORAGOS   You will do well to listen to him, King,
If what he says is sensible. And you, Haimon,
Must listen to your father.—Both speak well.
CREON   You consider it right for a man of my years and experience
To go to school to a boy?
HAIMON   It is not right
If I am wrong. But if I am young, and right,
What does my age matter?

CREON   You think it right to stand up for an anarchist?

100 HAIMON   Not at all. I pay no respect to criminals.

CREON   Then she is not a criminal?

HAIMON   The City would deny it, to a man.

CREON   And the City proposes to teach me how to rule?

HAIMON   Ah. Who is it that's talking like a boy now?

CREON   My voice is the one voice giving orders in this City!

HAIMON   It is no City if it takes orders from one voice.

CREON   The State is the King!

HAIMON   Yes, if the State is a desert.

Pause.

CREON   This boy, it seems, has sold out to a woman.

HAIMON   If you are a woman: my concern is only for you.

110 CREON   So? Your "concern"! In a public brawl with your father!

HAIMON   How about you, in a public brawl with justice?

CREON   With justice, when all that I do is within my rights?

HAIMON   You have no right to trample on God's right.

CREON (*completely out of control*)   Fool, adolescent fool! Taken
      in by a woman!

HAIMON   You'll never see me taken in by anything vile.

CREON   Every word you say is for her!

HAIMON (*quietly, darkly*)   And for you.
      And for me. And for the gods under the earth.

CREON   You'll never marry her while she lives.

HAIMON   Then she must die.—But her death will cause another.

120 CREON   Another?
      Have you lost your senses? Is this an open threat?

HAIMON   There is no threat in speaking to emptiness.

CREON   I swear you'll regret this superior tone of yours!
      You are the empty one!

HAIMON   If you were not my father,
      I'd say you were perverse.

CREON   You girlstruck fool, don't play at words with me!

HAIMON   I am sorry. You prefer silence.

CREON   Now, by God—!
      I swear, by all the gods in heaven above us,
      You'll watch it, I swear you shall!
      (*To the* SERVANTS)   Bring her out!

130   Bring the woman out! Let her die before his eyes!

Here, this instant, with her bridegroom beside her!
HAIMON   Not here, no; she will not die here, King.
And you will never see my face again.
Go on raving as long as you've a friend to endure you.

Exit HAIMON.

CHORAGOS   Gone, gone.
Creon, a young man in a rage is dangerous!
CREON   Let him do, or dream to do, more than a man can.
He shall not save these girls from death.
CHORAGOS   These girls?
You have sentenced them both?
CREON   No, you are right.
140   I will not kill the one whose hands are clean.
CHORAGOS   But Antigonê?
CREON (*somberly*)   I will carry her far away
Out there in the wilderness, and lock her
Living in a vault of stone. She shall have food,
As the custom is, to absolve the State of her death,[8]
And there let her pray to the gods of hell:
They are her only gods:
Perhaps they will show her an escape from death,
Or she may learn,
                        though late,
That piety shown the dead is pity in vain.

Exit CREON.

ODE III

STROPHE
CHORUS   Love, unconquerable
Waster of rich men, keeper
Of warm lights and all-night vigil
In the soft face of a girl:
Sea-wanderer, forest-visitor!
Even the pure Immortals cannot escape you,
And mortal man, in his one day's dusk,
Trembles before your glory.

---

[8] If food were left with a criminal who was buried alive, the Greeks believed his death might be attributed to natural causes.

ANTISTROPHE
10   Surely you swerve upon ruin
      The just man's consenting heart,
      As here you have made bright anger
      Strike between father and son—
      And none has conquered but Love!
      A girl's glance working the will of heaven:
      Pleasure to her alone who mocks us,
      Merciless Aphroditê.[9]

SCENE IV

As ANTIGONÊ *enters guarded*

CHORAGOS   But I can no longer stand in awe of this,
      Nor, seeing what I see, keep back my tears.
      Here is Antigonê, passing to that chamber
      Where all find sleep at last.

STROPHE 1
ANTIGONÊ   Look upon me, friends, and pity me
      Turning back at the night's edge to say
      Good-by to the sun that shines for me no longer;
      Now sleepy Death
      Summons me down to Acheron,[10] that cold shore:
10   There is no bridesong there, nor any music.
   CHORUS   Yet not unpraised, not without a kind of honor,
      You walk at last into the underworld;
      Untouched by sickness, broken by no sword.
      What woman has ever found your way to death?

ANTISTROPHE 1
ANTIGONÊ   How often I have heard the story of Niobê,[11]
      Tantalos'[12] wretched daughter, how the stone
      Clung fast about her, ivy-close: and they say

[9] Aphrodite was the goddess of love (the Roman Venus).
[10] Acheron was the river of the underworld, the infernal regions.
[11] Niobê, an earlier Queen of Thebes, was the mother of seven sons and seven daughters. In retribution for her boast that she had more children than Leto, the mother of Apollo, all fourteen children were destroyed. Niobê was turned into a stone on Mount Sipylus, whose streams are her tears.
[12] Tantalos, Niobê's father, was a son of Zeus.

The rain falls endlessly
And sifting soft snow; her tears are never done.
20   I feel the loneliness of her death in mine.
  CHORUS   But she was born of heaven, and you
        Are woman, woman-born. If her death is yours,
        A mortal woman's, is this not for you
        Glory in our world and in the world beyond?

STROPHE 2

ANTIGONÊ   You laugh at me. Ah, friends, friends,
        Can you not wait until I am dead? O Thebes,
        O men many-charioted, in love with Fortune,
        Dear springs of Dircê, sacred Theban grove,
        Be witnesses for me, denied all pity,
30   Unjustly judged! and think a word of love
        For her whose path turns
        Under dark earth, where there are no more tears.
  CHORAGOS   You have passed beyond human daring and come at
        last
        Into a place of stone where Justice sits.
        I cannot tell
        What shape of your father's guilt appears in this.

ANTISTROPHE 2

ANTIGONÊ   You have touched it at last: that bridal bed
        Unspeakable, horror of son and mother mingling:
        Their crime, infection of all our family!
40   O Oedipus, father and brother!
        Your marriages strikes from the grave to murder mine.
        I have been a stranger here in my own land:
        All my life
        The blasphemy of my birth has followed me.
  CHORUS   Reverence is a virtue, but strength
        Lives in established law: that must prevail.
        You have made your choice,
        Your death is the doing of your conscious hand.

EPODE

ANTIGONÊ   Then let me go, since all your words are bitter,
50   And the very light of the sun is cold to me.
        Lead me to my vigil, where I must have
        Neither love nor lamentation; no song, but silence.

CREON (*interrupts impatiently*)   If dirges and planned lamenta-
tions could put off death,
Men would be singing for ever.

(*To the* SERVANTS)   Take her, go!
You know your orders: take her to the vault
And leave her alone there. And if she lives or dies,
That's her affair, not ours: our hands are clean.

ANTIGONÊ   O tomb, vaulted bride-bed in eternal rock,
Soon I shall be with my own again

60 Where Persephonê[13] welcomes the thin ghosts underground:
And I shall see my father again, and you, mother,
And dearest Polyneicês—
                         dearest indeed
To me, since it was my hand
That washed him clean and poured the ritual wine:
And my reward is death before my time!

[*Passage omitted.*] [14]

And yet, as men's hearts know, I have done no wrong,
I have not sinned before God. Or if I have,
I shall know the truth in death. But if the guilt
Lies upon Creon who judged me, then, I pray,
May his punishment equal my own.

70 CHORAGOS   O passionate heart,
Unyielding, tormented still by the same winds!

CREON   Her guards shall have good cause to regret their delaying.

ANTIGONÊ   Ah! That voice is like the voice of death!

CREON   I can give you no reason to think you are mistaken.

ANTIGONÊ   Thebes, and you my fathers' gods,
And rulers of Thebes, you see me now, the last
Unhappy daughter of a line of kings,
Your kings, led away to death. You will remember
What things I suffer, and at what men's hands,

80 Because I would not transgress the laws of heaven.

(*To the* GUARDS, *simply*)   Come: let us wait no longer.

Exit ANTIGONÊ, *left, guarded.*

---

[13] Persephone was the wife of Pluto, who ruled the underworld.
[14] The translators omitted a passage here, which is present in all extant manu-
scripts, because they believe it to be spurious.

ODE IV

STROPHE 1

CHORUS   All Danaê's[15] beauty was locked away
In a brazen cell where the sunlight could not come:
A small room, still as any grave, enclosed her.
Yet she was a princess too,
And Zeus in a rain of gold poured love upon her.
O child, child,
No power in wealth or war
Or tough sea-blackened ships
Can prevail against untiring Destiny!

ANTISTROPHE 1

10   And Dryas'[16] son also, that furious king,
Bore the god's prisoning anger for his pride:
Sealed up by Dionysos in deaf stone,
His madness died among echoes.
So at the last he learned what dreadful power
His tongue had mocked:
For he had profaned the revels,
And fired the wrath of the nine
Implacable Sisters[17] that love the sound of the flute.

STROPHE 2

And old men tell a half-remembered tale
20   Of horror done where a dark ledge splits the sea
And a double surf beats on the gray shores:
How a king's new woman,[18] sick
With hatred for the queen he had imprisoned,
Ripped out his two sons' eyes with her bloody hands

[15] Danâe was imprisoned by her father, Acrisius, who had been warned by an oracle that should she bear a child, that child would kill him. Zeus came to her prison in a shower of gold and begat Perseus, who later accidentally killed Acrisius with a discus in an athletic festival.

[16] Dryas' son, Lycurgus, opposed the wild revelry of the god Dionysos (the Roman Bacchus). For punishment, Lycurgus was driven mad and shut up in a rocky prison where he went blind and died.

[17] The nine sisters were the Muses, the nine daughters of Zeus and Mnemosyne. Originally goddesses of memory only, they were later identified with individual arts and sciences.

[18] Eidotheo, the second wife of King Phineus, blinded her stepsons. Their mother, Cleopatra of Thrace—daughter of Boreas, god of the north wind—had been imprisoned in a cave.

While grinning Arês[19] watched the shuttle plunge
Four times: four blind wounds crying for revenge,

ANTISTROPHE

Crying, tears and blood mingled.—Piteously born,
Those sons whose mother was of heavenly birth!
Her father was the god of the North Wind

30   And she was cradled by gales,
She raced with young colts on the glittering hills
And walked untrammeled in the open light:
But in her marriage deathless Fate found means
To build a tomb like yours for all her joy.

SCENE V

Enter blind TEIRESIAS, *led by a boy. The opening speeches of*
TEIRESIAS *should be in singsong contrast to the realistic lines of*
CREON

TEIRESIAS   This is the way the blind man comes, Princes, Princes,
   Lock-step, two heads lit by the eyes of one.
CREON   What new thing have you to tell us, old Teiresias?
TEIRESIAS   I have much to tell you: listen to the prophet, Creon.
CREON   I am not aware that I have ever failed to listen.
TEIRESIAS   Then you have done wisely, King, and ruled well.
CREON   I admit my debt to you. But what have you to say?
TEIRESIAS   This, Creon: you stand once more on the edge of fate.
CREON   What do you mean? Your words are a kind of dread.
10   TEIRESIAS   Listen, Creon:
   I was sitting in my chair of augury, at the place
   Where the birds gather about me. They were all a-chatter,
   As is their habit, when suddenly I heard
   A strange note in their jangling, a scream, a
   Whirring fury; I knew that they were fighting,
   Tearing each other, dying
   In a whirlwind of wings clashing. And I was afraid.
   I began the rites of burnt-offering at the altar,
   But Hephaistos[20] failed me: instead of bright flame,

---

[19] Arês was the god of war (the Roman Mars).
[20] Hephaistos was the god of fire (the Roman Vulcan).

20   There was only the sputtering slime of the fat thigh-flesh
      Melting: the entrails dissolved in gray smoke,
      The bare bone burst from the welter. And no blaze!

      This was a sign from heaven. My boy described it,
      Seeing for me as I see for others.

      I tell you, Creon, you yourself have brought
      This new calamity upon us. Our hearths and altars
      Are stained with the corruption of dogs and carrion birds
      That glut themselves on the corpse of Oedipus' son.
      The gods are deaf when we pray to them, their fire
30   Recoils from our offering, their birds of omen
      Have no cry of comfort, for they are gorged
      With the thick blood of the dead.
                                    Oh my son,
      These are no trifles! Think: all men make mistakes,
      But a good man yields when he knows his course is wrong,
      And repairs the evil. The only crime is pride.
      Give in to the dead man, then: do not fight with a corpse—
      What glory is it to kill a man who is dead?
      Think, I beg you:
      It is for your own good that I speak as I do.
40   You should be able to yield for your own good.

    CREON   It seems that prophets have made me their especial
          province
      All my life long
      I have been a kind of butt for the dull arrows
      Of doddering fortune-tellers!
                              No, Teiresias:
      If your birds—if the great eagles of God himself
      Should carry him stinking bit by bit to heaven,
      I would not yield. I am not afraid of pollution:
      No man can defile the gods.
                              Do what you will,
      Go into business, make money, speculate
50   In India gold or that synthetic gold from Sardis,
      Get rich otherwse than by my consent to bury him.
      Teiresias, it is a sorry thing when a wise man
      Sells his wisdom, lets out his words for hire!

    TEIRESIAS   Ah Creon! Is there no man left in the world—

CREON   To do what?—Come, let's have the aphorism!

TEIRESIAS   No man who knows that wisdom outweighs any wealth?

CREON   As surely as bribes are baser than any baseness.

TEIRESIAS   You are sick, Creon! You are deathly sick!

CREON   As you say: it is not my place to challenge a prophet.

60 TEIRESIAS   Yet you have said my prophecy is for sale.

CREON   The generation of prophets has always loved gold.

TEIRESIAS   The generation of kings has always loved brass.

CREON   You forget yourself! You are speaking to your King.

TEIRESIAS   I know it. You are a king because of me.

CREON   You have a certain skill; but you have sold out.

TEIRESIAS   King, you will drive me to words that—

CREON   Say them, say
   them!
   Only remember: I will not pay you for them.

TEIRESIAS   No, you will find them too costly.

CREON   No doubt. Speak:
   Whatever you say, you will not change my will.

70 TEIRESIAS   Then take this, and take it to heart!
   The time is not far off when you shall pay back
   Corpse for corpse, flesh of your own flesh.
   You have thrust the child of this world into living night,
   You have kept from the gods below the child that is theirs:
   The one in a grave before her death, the other,
   Dead, denied the grave. This is your crime:
   And the Furies[21] and the dark gods of Hell
   Are swift with terrible punishment for you.

   Do you want to buy me now, Creon?

                                                     Not many days,
80   And your house will be full of men and women weeping,
   And curses will be hurled at you from far
   Cities grieving for sons unburied, left to rot
   Before the walls of Thebes.

   These are my arrows, Creon: they are all for you.

   (*To* BOY)   But come, child: lead me home.
   Let him waste his fine anger upon younger men.

---

[21] The Furies were avenging spirits.

Maybe he will learn at last
To control a wiser tongue in a better head.

Exit TEIRESIAS.

CHORAGOS   The old man is gone, King, but his words
90   Remain to plague us. I am old, too,
But I cannot remember that he was ever false.
CREON   That is true. . . . It troubles me.
Oh it is hard to give in! but it is worse
To risk everything for stubborn pride.
CHORAGOS   Creon: take my advice.
CREON   What shall I do?
CHORAGOS   Go quickly: free Antigonê from her vault
And build a tomb for the body of Polyneicês.
CREON   You would have me do this?
CHORAGOS   Creon, yes!
And it must be done at once: God moves
100   Swiftly to cancel the folly of stubborn men.
CREON   It is hard to deny the heart! But I
Will do it: I will not fight with destiny.
CHORAGOS   You must go yourself, you cannot leave it to others.
CREON   I will go.
                    —Bring axes, servants:
Come with me to the tomb. I buried her, I
Will set her free.
                    Oh quickly!
My mind misgives—
The laws of the gods are mighty, and a man must serve them
To the last day of his life!

Exit CREON.

PAEAN [22]

STROPHE 1
CHORAGOS   God of many names

---

[22] The chorus sings to Dionysos, also called Iacchos and other names. His father was Zeus, his mother Sémelê, the daughter of Kadmos who founded Thebes. God of wine and fertility, Dionysos was the patron of Thebes. His worshippers were the Maenads.

CHORUS   O Iacchos
                                 son
of Kadmeian Sémelê
                     O born of the Thunder!
Guardian of the West
                   Regent
of Eleusis' [23] plain
                   O Prince of maenad Thebes
and the Dragon Field [24] by rippling Ismenos: [25]

ANTISTROPHE 1
CHORAGOS   God of many names
CHORUS   the flame of torches
flares on our hills
                the nymphs of Iacchos
dance at the spring of Castalia: [26]

from the vine-close mountain
                     come ah come in ivy: [27]
10   *Evoché evohé!* [28] sings through the streets of Thebes.

STROPHE 2
CHORAGOS   God of many names
CHORUS   Iacchos of Thebes
heavenly Child
                of Sémelê bride of the Thunderer!
The shadow of plague is upon us:
                     come
with clement feet
                oh come from Parnasos
down the long slopes
                   across the lamenting water.

ANTISTROPHE 2
CHORAGOS   Iô Fire! Chorister of the throbbing stars!

---

[23] Eleusis, a city near Athens, was the center of a religious cult.
[24] Kadmos killed a dragon on the site that became Thebes. He sowed the dragon's teeth, from which a race of warriors, the ancestors of the Theban nobility, grew.
[25] Ismenos was a river east of Thebes.
[26] Castalia was a spring on Mount Parnasus, a sacred mountain in Greece on which the Delphic Oracle was located.
[27] Ivy was sacred to Dionysos.
[28] *"Evohé"* and *"Iô"* (line 17) were cries of Dionysos' worshippers.

O purest among the voices of the night!
Thou son of God, blaze for us!
CHORUS   Come with choric rapture of circling Maenads
20   Who cry *Iô Iacche!*
                    God of many names!

ÉXODOS [29]

Enter MESSENGER, *left.*

MESSENGER   Men of the line of Kadmos, you who live Near
    Amphion's[30] citadel:
                            I cannot say
Of any condition of human life "This is fixed,
This is clearly good, or bad." Fate raises up,
And Fate casts down the happy and unhappy alike:
No man can foretell his Fate.
                        Take the case of Creon:
Creon was happy once, as I count happiness:
Victorious in battle, sole governor of the land,
Fortunate father of children nobly born.
10   And now it has all gone from him! Who can say
That a man is still alive when his life's joy fails?
He is a walking dead man. Grant him rich,
Let him live like a king in his great house:
If his pleasure is gone, I would not give
So much as the shadow of smoke for all he owns.
CHORAGOS   Your words hint at sorrow: what is your news for us?
MESSENGER   They are dead. The living are guilty of their death.
CHORAGOS   Who is guilty? Who is dead? Speak!
MESSENGER   Haimon.
Haimon is dead; and the hand that killed him
Is his own hand.
20 CHORAGOS   His father's? or his own?
MESSENGER   His own, driven mad by the murder his father had
    done.

---

[29] The Éxodos is the conclusion.
[30] Amphion, son of Zeus and Antiope and husband of Niobe, played so sweetly
on his lyre that the stones moved of their own accord to form a wall around
Thebes.

CHORAGOS   Teiresias, Teiresias, how clearly you saw it all!

MESSENGER   This is my news: you must draw what conclusions
you can from it.

CHORAGOS   But look: Eurydicê, our Queen:
Has she overheard us?

Enter EURYDICÊ *from the Palace, center.*

EURYDICÊ   I have heard something, friends:
As I was unlocking the gate of Pallas' [31] shrine,
For I needed her help today, I heard a voice
Telling of some new sorrow. And I fainted
30   There at the temple with all my maidens about me.
But speak again: whatever it is, I can bear it:
Grief and I are no strangers.

MESSENGER   Dearest Lady,
I will tell you plainly all that I have seen.
I shall not try to comfort you: what is the use,
Since comfort could lie only in what is not true?
The truth is always best.

                         I went with Creon
To the outer plain where Polyneicês was lying,
No friend to pity him, his body shredded by dogs.
We made our prayers in that place to Hecatê [32]
40   And Pluto, [33] that they would be merciful. And we bathed
The corpse with holy water, and we brought
Fresh-broken branches to burn what was left of it,
And upon the urn we heaped up a towering barrow
Of the earth of his own land.

                         When we were done, we ran
To the vault where Antigonê lay on her couch of stone.
One of the servants had gone ahead,
And while he was yet far off he heard a voice
Grieving within the chamber, and he came back
And told Creon. And as the King went closer,
50   The air was full of wailing, the words lost,
And he begged us to make all haste. "Am I a prophet?"
He said, weeping, "And must I walk this road,
The saddest of all that I have gone before?

[31] Pallas Athene was the goddess of wisdom (the Roman Minerva).
[32] Hecatê, a goddess of the underworld, was associated with sorcery and ghosts.
[33] Pluto was the king of the underworld, the abode of the dead.

My son's voice calls me on. Oh quickly, quickly!
Look through the crevice there, and tell me
If it is Haimon, or some deception of the gods!"

We obeyed; and in the cavern's farthest corner
We saw her lying:
She had made a noose of her fine linen veil
60 And hanged herself. Haimon lay beside her,
His arms about her waist, lamenting her,
His love lost under ground, crying out
That his father had stolen her away from him.

When Creon saw him the tears rushed to his eyes
And he called to him: "What have you done, child? Speak to me.
What are you thinking that makes your eyes so strange?
O my son, my son, I come to you on my knees!"
But Haimon spat in his face. He said not a word,
Staring—
            And suddenly drew his sword
70 And lunged. Creon shrank back, the blade missed; and the boy,
Desperate against himself, drove it half its length
Into his own side, and fell. And as he died
He gathered Antigonê close in his arms again,
Choking, his blood bright red on her white cheek.
And now he lies dead with the dead, and she is his
At last, his bride in the houses of the dead.

Exit EURYDICÊ *into the Palace.*

CHORAGOS   She has left us without a word. What can this mean?
MESSENGER   It troubles me, too; yet she knows what is best,
Her grief is too great for public lamentation,
80 And doubtless she has gone to her chamber to weep
For her dead son, leading her maidens in his dirge.
CHORAGOS   It may be so: but I fear this deep silence.

Pause.

MESSENGER   I will see what she is doing. I will go in.

Exit MESSENGER *into the Palace.*

Enter CREON *with attendants, bearing* HAIMON's *body.*

CHORAGOS   But here is the King himself: oh look at him,
Bearing his own damnation in his arms.

CREON Nothing you say can touch me any more.
My own blind heart has brought me
From darkness to final darkness. Here you see
The father murdering, the murdered son—
90 And all my civic wisdom!

Haimon my son, so young, so young to die,
I was the fool, not you; and you died for me.
CHORAGOS That is the truth; but you were late in learning it.
CREON This truth is hard to bear. Surely a god
Has crushed me beneath the hugest weight of heaven,
And driven me headlong a barbaric way
To trample out the thing I held most dear.

The pains that men will take to come to pain!

Enter MESSENGER *from the Palace.*

MESSENGER The burden you carry in your hands is heavy,
100 But it is not all: you will find more in your house.
CREON What burden worse than this shall I find there?
MESSENGER The Queen is dead.
CREON O port of death, deaf world,
Is there no pity for me? And you, Angel of evil,
I was dead, and your words are death again.
Is it true, boy? Can it be true?
Is my wife dead? Has death bred death?
MESSENGER You can see for yourself.

The doors are opened, and the body of EURYDICÊ *is disclosed within.*

CREON Oh pity!
110 All true, all true, and more than I can bear!
O my wife, my son!
MESSENGER She stood before the altar, and her heart
Welcomed the knife her own hand guided,
And a great cry burst from her lips for Megareus[34] dead,
And for Haimon dead, her sons; and her last breath
Was a curse for their father, the murderer of her sons.
And she fell, and the dark flowed in through her closing eyes.
CREON O God, I am sick with fear.

[34] Megareus, Haimon's brother, had died defending Thebes in battle.

Are there no swords here? Has no one a blow for me?

¹²⁰ MESSENGER   Her curse is upon you for the deaths of both.

CREON   It is right that it should be. I alone am guilty.
I know it, and I say it. Lead me in,
Quickly, friends.
I have neither life nor substance. Lead me in.

CHORAGOS   You are right, if there can be right in so much wrong.
The briefest way is best in a world of sorrow.

CREON   Let it come,
Let death come quickly, and be kind to me.
I would not ever see the sun again.

¹³⁰ CHORAGOS   All that will come when it will; but we, meanwhile,
Have much to do. Leave the future to itself.

CREON   All my heart was in that prayer!

CHORAGOS   Then do not pray any more: the sky is deaf.

CREON   Lead me away. I have been rash and foolish.
I have killed my son and my wife.
I look for comfort; my comfort lies here dead.
Whatever my hands have touched has come to nothing.
Fate has brought all my pride to a thought of dust.

As CREON *is being led into the house, the* CHORAGOS *advances
and speaks directly to the audience.*

CHORAGOS   There is no happiness where there is no wisdom;
¹⁴⁰   No wisdom but in submission to the gods.
Big words are always punished,
And proud men in old age learn to be wise.

Poetry

Barbra Allen[1]

Anonymous

Arr. by William Wilson

In Lon - don City where I once did dwell, There's
where I got my learn - ing, I
fell in love with a pretty young girl, Her
name was Bar - bra Al - len.

1. In London City where I once did dwell, there's where I got
   my learning,
   I fell in love with a pretty young girl, her name was Barbra
   Allen.
   I courted for for seven long years, she said she would not
   have me;
   Then straightway home as I could go and liken to a dying.

2. I wrote her a letter on my death bed, I wrote it slow and
   moving;
   "Go take this letter to my old true love and tell her I am
   dying."

[1] Ballads and folk songs have preserved the oral traditions of the people. Five types are represented here: the love ballad, the work song, the Negro spiritual, the lullaby, and the cowboy song.

She took the letter in her lily-white hand, she read it slow
and moving;
"Go take this letter back to him, and tell him I am coming."

3. As she passed by his dying bed she saw his pale lips
quivering;
"No better, no better I'll ever be until I get Barbra Allen."
As she passed by his dying bed; "You're very sick and
almost dying,
No better, no better you will ever be, for you can't get
Barbra Allen."

4. As she went down the long stair steps she heard the death
bell toning,
And every bell appeared to say, "Hard-hearted Barbra
Allen!"
As she went down the long piney walk she heard some small
birds singing,
And every bird appeared to say, "Hard-hearted Barbra
Allen!"

5. She looked to the East, she looked to the West, she saw the
pale corpse coming
"Go bring them pale corpse unto me, and let me gaze upon
them.
Oh, mama, mama, go make my bed, go make it soft and
narrow!
Sweet Willie died today for me, I'll die for him tomorrow!"

6. They buried Sweet Willie in the old church yard, they
buried Miss Barbra beside him;
And out of his grave there sprang a red rose, and out of
hers a briar.
They grew to the top of the old church tower, they could
not grow any higher,
They hooked, they tied in a true love's knot, red rose around
the briar.

John Henry

Anonymous

Arr. by Judy Fendall

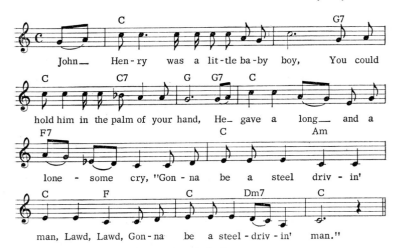

John— Hen-ry was a lit-tle ba-by boy, You could hold him in the palm of your hand, He— gave a long— and a lone - some cry, "Gon - na be a steel driv - in' man, Lawd, Lawd, Gon-na be a steel - driv - in' man."

1. John Henry was a little baby boy,
   You could hold him in the palm of your hand,
   He gave a long and a lonesome cry,
   "Gonna be a steel-drivin' man, Lawd, Lawd,
   Gonna be a steel drivin' man."

2. They took John Henry to the tunnel,
   Put him in the lead to drive,
   The rock was so tall, John Henry so small,
   That he lied down his hammer and he cried, "Lawd, Lawd,"
   Lied down his hammer and he cried.

3. John Henry started on the right hand,
   The steam drill started on the left,
   "Fo' I'd let that steamdrill beat me down,
   I'd hammer my fool self to death, Lawd, Lawd," *etc.*

4. John Henry told his captain,
   "A man ain't nothin' but a man,
   'Fo' I let your steamdrill beat me down
   I'll die with this hammer in my hand, Lawd, Lawd," *etc.*

5. John Henry had a little woman
    Her name were Polly Anne,
    John Henry took sick and he had to go to bed,
    Polly Anne drove steel like a man, Lawd, Lawd, *etc.*

6. Now the Captain told John Henry,
    "I b'lieve my tunnel's sinkin' in."
    "Stand back, Captain, and doncha be afraid,
    That's nothin' but my hammer catchin' wind, Lawd, Lawd,"
        etc.

7. John Henry he told his shaker,
    "Now shaker, why don't you sing?
    I'm throwin' nine pounds from my hips on down,
    Just listen to the cold steel ring, Lawd, Lawd," *etc.*

8. John Henry he told his shaker,
    "Now shaker, why don't you pray?
    For if I miss this six-foot steel
    Tomorrow'll be your buryin' day, Lawd, Lawd," *etc.*

9. John Henry he told his Cap'n,
    "Looky yonder, boy, what do I see?
    Your drill's done broke and your hole's done choke,
    And you can't drive steel like me, Lawd, Lawd," *etc.*

10. John Henry hammerin' in the mountain
    Till the handle of his hammer caught on fire,
    He drove so hard till he broke his po' heart,
    Then he lied down his hammer and he died, Lawd, Lawd,
        etc.

11. Women in the west heard of John Henry's death
    They couldn' hardly stay in bed,
    Stood in the rain, flagged that east-bound train
    "Goin' where that man fell dead, Lawd, Lawd," *etc.*

12. They took John Henry to the tunnel,
    And they buried him in the sand,
    An' every locomotive come rollin' by
    Say, "There lays a steel-driven' man, Lawd, Lawd," *etc.*

13. Now some say he come from England,
    And some say he come from Spain,

But I say he's nothin' but a Lou'siana man,
Leader of a steel-drivin' gang, Lawd, Lawd, *etc.*

Go Down, Moses

Anonymous

Arr. by Joseph Lonon

When Is-rael was in E-gypt land, Let my peo-ple go, Op-pressed so hard they could not stand, Let my peo-ple go.

Chorus

Go down, Mos-es, Way down in E-gypt land.

Tell old_ Pha-roah,_ To let my peo-ple go.

1. When Israel was in Egypt land,
   Let my people go,
   Oppressed so hard they could not stand,
   Let my people go.
   Go down, Moses,
   Way down in Egypt land,
   Tell old Pharaoh
   To let my people go.

2. "Thus spoke the Lord" bold Moses said,
   "Let my people go,
   If not, I'll smite your first-born dead,
   Let my people go." (*Chorus*)

3. "Your foes shall not before you stand,
   Let my people go,

And you'll possess fair Canaan's land,
Let my people go." (*Chorus*)

4. "You'll not get lost in the wilderness,
    Let my people go,
    With a lighted candle in your breast,
    Let my people go." (*Chorus*)

Hush, Little Baby

Anonymous

Arr. by Judy Fendall

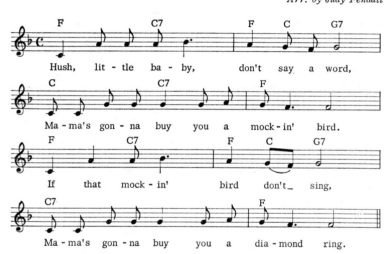

Hush, lit - tle ba - by, don't say a word,
Ma - ma's gon - na buy you a mock - in' bird.
If that mock - in' bird don't sing,
Ma - ma's gon - na buy you a dia - mond ring.

1. Hush, little baby, don't say a word,
    Mama's gonna buy you a mockin' bird.

2. If that mockin' bird don't sing,
    Mama's gonna buy you a diamond ring.

3. If that diamond ring turns brass,
    Mama's gonna buy you a lookin' glass.

4. If that lookin' glass gets broke,
    Mama's gonna buy you a billy-goat.

5. If that billy-goat won't pull,
    Mama's gonna buy you a cart and bull.

6. If that cart and bull turn over,
    Mama's gonna buy you a dog named Rover.

7. If that dog named Rover don't bark,
    Mama's gonna buy you a horse and cart.

8. If that horse and cart fall down,
    You'll be the sweetest little girl in town.

Red River Valley   *Anonymous*

Arr. by Joseph Lonon

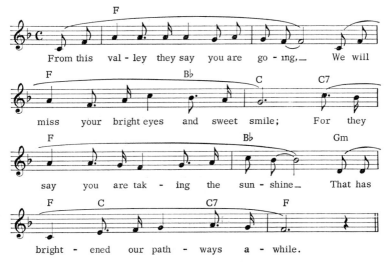

From this   val - ley they say   you are   go - ing,—   We will
miss   your   bright eyes   and   sweet   smile;   For   they
say   you   are tak - ing   the   sun - shine—   That has
bright - ened   our   path - ways   a - while.

1. From this valley they say you are going,
    We will miss your bright eyes and sweet smile;
    For they say you are taking the sunshine
    That has brightened our pathways awhile.

    Chorus:
    Come and sit by my side, if you love me,
    Do not hasten to bid me adieu

Just remember the Red River Valley,
And the cowboy who loved you so true.

2. I've been thinking a long time my darling,
Of the sweet words you never would say,
Now alas must my fond hopes all vanish?
For they say you are going away.
Chorus:

3. Do you think of the valley you're leaving?
Oh how lonely and dreary it will be
Do you think of the kind hearts you are breaking,
And the pain you are causing to me?
Chorus:

4. They will bury me where you have wandered,
Near the hills where the daffodils grow,
When you're gone from the Red River Valley,
For I can't live without you I know.
Chorus:

Psalm 1   *The King James Bible*

1. Blessed *is* the man that walketh not in the counsel of the
ungodly, nor standeth in the way of sinners, nor sitteth in
the seat of the scornful.

2. But his delight *is* in the law of the LORD; and in his law doth
he meditate day and night.

3. And he shall be like a tree planted by the rivers of water,
that bringeth forth his fruit in his season; his leaf also shall
not wither; and whatsoever he doeth shall prosper.

4. The ungodly *are* not so: but *are* like the chaff which the
wind driveth away.

5. Therefore the ungodly shall not stand in the judgment, nor
sinners in the congregation of the righteous.

6. For the LORD knoweth the way of the righteous: but the
way of the ungodly shall perish.

GREEK LYRICS [1]

Appearance of Wisdom *Phocylides*

Translation by Willis Barnstone

Many empty-headed clods pass by like sages
when they walk with chin erect and stern eyes.

Inscription for a Monument *Simonides*
for the Spartan Soldiers
Who Died at Thermopylae *Translation by Chester Bowles*

Go tell the Spartans, thou that passest by,
That here obedient to their laws we lie.

On Magical Whiskers *Lucian*

Translation by Willis Barnstone

If by growing a goatee you hope to come upon wisdom,
then, O wise friend, any smelly goat in
a handsome beard
is at once Plato.

---

[1] These lyrics appeared in *The Greek Anthology,* a collection of several thousand
poems, songs, epigrams, epitaphs, and the like by numerous Greek writers from
the fifth century B.C. to the sixth century A.D.

Pygmalion[1]

Ovid (Publius Ovidius Naso)

Translation by John Dryden

Pygmalion, loathing their lascivious life,
Abhorred all womankind, but most a wife;
So single chose to live, and shunned to wed,
Well pleased to want a consort of his bed;
Yet fearing idleness, the nurse of ill,
In sculpture exercised his happy skill,
And carved in ivory such a maid, so fair,
As Nature could not with his art compare,
Were she to work; but, in her own defence,
10 Must take her pattern here, and copy hence.
Pleased with his idol, he commends, admires,
Adores, and last, the thing adored desires:
A very virgin in her face was seen,
And had she moved, a living maid had been:
One would have thought she could have stirred, but strove
With modesty, and was ashamed to move:
Art hid with art, so well performed the cheat,
It caught the carver with his own deceit:
He knows 'tis madness, yet he must adore,
20 And still the more he knows it, loves the more.
The flesh, or what so seems, he touches oft,
Which feels so smooth that he believes it soft;
Fired with this thought, at once he strained the breast,
And on the lips a burning kiss impressed.
'Tis true, the hardened breast resists the gripe,
And the cold lips return a kiss unripe:
But when, retiring back, he looked again,
To think it ivory was a thought too mean;
With flattery now he seeks her mind to move,
30 And now with gifts (the powerful bribes of love):
He furnishes her closet first, and fills
The crowded shelves with rarities of shells;
Adds orient pearls, which from the conchs he drew,

---

[1] Pygmalion is from *Metamorphoses,* Book X.

And all the sparkling stones of various hue;
And parrots, imitating human tongue,
And singing birds, in silver cages hung;
And every fragrant flower and odorous green
Were sorted well, with lumps of amber laid between:
Rich fashionable robes her person deck,
40 Pendants her ears, and pearls adorn her neck:
Her tapered fingers too with rings are graced,
And an embroidered zone surrounds her slender waist.
Thus like a queen arrayed, so richly dressed,
Beauteous she showed, but unadorned the best.
Then from the floor he raised a royal bed,
With coverings of Sidonian purple spread.
    The feast of Venus came, a solemn day,
To which the Cypriots due devotion pay;
With gilded horns the milk white heifers led,
50 Slaughtered before the sacred altars bled.
    Pygmalion offering, first approached the shrine,
And then with prayers implored the powers divine:
Almighty gods, if all we mortals want,
If all we can require, be yours to grant,
Make this fair statue mine, he would have said,
But changed his words for shame, and only prayed,
"Give me the likeness of my ivory maid."
    The golden goddess, present at the prayer,
Well knew he meant the inanimated fair,
60 And gave the sign of granting his desire;
For thrice in cheerful flames ascends the fire.
The youth, returning to his mistress hies,
And, impudent in hope, with ardent eyes,
And beating breast, by the dear statue lies.
He kisses her white lips, renews the bliss,
And looks, and thinks they redden at the kiss;
He thought them warm before, nor longer stays,
But next his hand on the hard substance lays;
Hard as it was, beginning to relent,
70 It seemed the block beneath his fingers bent:
He felt again—his fingers made a print,
'Twas flesh, but flesh so firm, it rose against the dint:
The pleasing task he fails not to renew—

Soft, and more soft, at every touch it grew;
Like pliant wax, when chafing hands reduce
The former mass to form, and frame for use.
He would believe, but yet is still in pain,
And tries his argument of sense again—
Presses the pulse, and feels the leaping vein:
80 Convinced, o'erjoyed, his studied thanks and praise,
To her who made the miracle, he pays:
Then lips to lips he joined; now freed from fear,
He found the savor of the kiss sincere.
At this the wakened image oped her eyes,
And viewed at once the light and lover with surprise.
The goddess, present at the match she made,
So blessed the bed, such fruitfulness conveyed,
That ere ten months had sharpened either horn,
To crown their bliss, a lovely boy was born:
90 Paphos his name, who, grown to manhood, walled
The city **Paphos**, from the founder called.

**Let Me Not to the Marriage
of True Minds**   *William Shakespeare*

CXVI

Let me not to the marriage of true minds
Admit impediments. Love is not love
Which alters when it alteration finds,
Or bends with the remover to remove:
Oh, no! it is an ever-fixed mark
That looks on tempests and is never shaken;
It is the star to every wandering bark,
Whose worth's unknown, although his height be taken.
Love's not Time's fool, though rosy lips and cheeks
10 Within his bending sickle's compass come;
Love alters not with his brief hours and weeks,
But bears it out even to the edge of doom.
If this be error and upon me proved,
I never writ, nor no man ever loved.

My Mistress' Eyes

William Shakespeare

CXXX

My mistress' eyes are nothing like the sun;
Coral is far more red than her lips' red;
If snow be white, why then her breasts are dun;
If hairs be wires, black wires grow on her head.
I have seen roses demasked, red and white,
But no such roses see I in her cheeks;
And in some perfumes is there more delight
Than in the breath that from my mistress reeks.
I love to hear her speak, yet well I know
10 That music hath a far more pleasing sound;
I grant I never saw a goddess go:
My mistress, when she walks, treads on the ground.
   And yet, by heaven, I think my love as rare
   As any she belied with false compare.

Polonius' Speech to Laertes[1]

William Shakespeare

And these few precepts in thy memory
See thou character. Give thy thoughts no tongue,
Nor any unproportioned thought his act.
Be thou familiar, but by no means vulgar
Those friends thou hast, and their adoption tried,
Grapple them to thy soul with hoops of steel,
But do not dull thy palm with entertainment
Of each new-hatched unfledged comrade. Beware
Of entrance to a quarrel; but being in,
10 Bear't, that the opposed may beware of thee.
Give every man thy ear, but few thy voice:
Take each man's censure, but reserve thy judgment.

[1] From *Hamlet,* I. iii. 58–80.

Costly thy habit as thy purse can buy,
But not expressed in fancy; rich, not gaudy:
For the apparel oft proclaims the man;
And they in France of the best rank and station
Are of a most select and generous chief in that.
Neither a borrower nor a lender be:
For loan oft loses both itself and friend,
20 And borrowing dulls the edge of husbandry.
This above all: to thine own self be true,
And it must follow, as the night the day,
Thou canst not then be false to any man.

There Is a Garden in Her Face   *Thomas Campion*

There is a garden in her face
Where roses and white lilies grow;
    A heav'nly paradise is that place,
Wherein all pleasant fruits do flow.
        There cherries grow which none may buy
        Till cherry-ripe themselves do cry.

Those cherries fairly do enclose
Of orient pearl a double row,
    Which when her lovely laughter shows,
10 They look like rosebuds filled with snow.
        Yet them nor peer nor prince can buy,
        Till cherry-ripe themselves do cry.

Her eyes like angels watch them still;
Her brows like bended bows do stand,
    Threat'ning with piercing frowns to kill
All that attempt with eye or hand
        Those sacred cherries to come nigh,
        Till cherry-ripe themselves do cry.

Song, to Celia

Ben Jonson

Drink to me only with thine eyes,
    And I will pledge with mine;
Or leave a kiss but in the cup
    And I'll not look for wine.
The thirst that from the soul doth rise
    Doth ask a drink divine;
But might I of Jove's nectar sup,
    I would not change for thine.

I sent thee late a rosy wreath,
10   Not so much honoring thee
As giving it a hope that there
    It could not withered be;
But thou thereon didst only breathe,
    And sent'st it back to me;
Since when it grows, and smells, I swear,
    Not of itself but thee!

Come, My Celia

Ben Jonson

Come, my Celia, let us prove,
While we can, the sports of love;
Time will not be ours for ever—
He, at length, our goods will sever.
Spend not then his gifts in vain:
Suns that set may rise again;
But if once we lose this light,
'Tis with us perpetual night.
Why should we defer our joys?
10 Fame and rumor are but toys.
Cannot we delude the eyes
Of a few poor household spies?
Or his easier ears beguile,

So removed by our wile?
'Tis no sin love's fruits to steal,
But the sweet theft to reveal,
To be taken, to be seen,
These have crimes accounted been.

To My Book   *Ben Jonson*

It will be looked for, book, when some but see
Thy title, "Epigrams," and named of me,
Thou should'st be bold, licentious, full of gall,
Wormwood, and sulphur, sharp and toothed withal;
Become a petulant thing, hurl ink and wit,
As madmen stones, not caring whom they hit.
Deceive their malice, who could wish it so.
And by thy wiser temper, let men know
Thou art not covetous of least self-fame,
10 Made from the hazard of another's shame;
Much less with lewd, profane, and beastly phrase,
To catch the world's loose laughter or vain gaze.
He that departs with his own honesty
For vulgar praise, doth it too dearly buy.

Song   *John Donne*

Go and catch a falling star,
    Get with child a mandrake root,
Tell me where all past years are,
    Or who cleft the devil's foot,
Teach me to hear mermaids singing,
Or to keep off envy's stinging,
            And find
            What wind
Serves to advance an honest mind.

¹⁰ If thou be'st born to strange sights,
    Things invisible to see,
Ride ten thousand days and nights,
    Till age snow white hairs on thee.
Thou, when thou return'st, wilt tell me,
All strange wonders that befell thee,
        And swear,
        No where
Lives a woman true and fair.

If thou find'st one, let me know;
²⁰   Such a pilgrimage were sweet.
Yet do not, I would not go,
    Though at next door we might meet:
Though she were true when you met her,
And last till you write your letter,
        Yet she
        Will be
False, ere I come, to two or three.

Love's Deity

John Donne

I long to talk with some old lover's ghost,
    Who died before the god of love was born.
I cannot think that he, who then loved most,
    Sunk so low as to love one which did scorn.

But since this god produced a destiny,
And that vice-nature, custom, lets it be,
    I must love her that loves not me.

Sure, they which made him god, meant not so much,
    Nor he in his young godhead practised it:
¹⁰ But when an even flame two hearts did touch,
    His office was indulgently to fit
Actives to passives. Correspondency
Only his subject was; it cannot be
    Love, till I love her, that loves me.

But every modern god will now extend
  His vast prerogative as far as Jove.
To rage, to lust, to write to, to commend,
  All is the purlieu of the god of love.
O! were we wakened by this tyranny
20 To ungod this child again, it could not be
  I should love her, who loves not me.

Rebel and atheist too, why murmur I,
  As though I felt the worst that love could do?
Love might make me leave loving, or might try
  A deeper plague, to make her love me too;
Which, since she loves before, I'm loth to see.
Falsehood is worse than hate; and that must be,
  If she whom I love, should love me.

Death, Be Not Proud   *John Donne*

x

Death, be not proud, though some have called thee
Mighty and dreadful, for thou art not so,
For those whom thou think'st thou dost overthrow
Die not, poor Death, nor yet canst thou kill me.
From rest and sleep, which but thy picture be,
Much pleasure, then from thee much more must flow;
And soonest our best men with thee do go—
Rest of their bones and souls' delivery!
Thou'rt slave to fate, chance, kings and desperate men,
10 And dost with poison, war, and sickness dwell,
And poppy or charms can make us sleep as well,
And better than thy stroke; why swell'st thou then?
One short sleep past, we wake eternally,
And death shall be no more: Death, thou shalt die!

When I Consider How My Light Is Spent   *John Milton*

When I consider how my light is spent
Ere half my days in this dark world and wide,
And that one talent which is death to hide
Lodged with me useless, though my soul more bent
To serve therewith my Maker, and present
My true account, lest He returning chide,
"Doth God exact day-labor, light denied?"
I fondly ask. But Patience, to prevent
That murmur, soon replies, "God doth not need
10 Either man's work or his own gifts. Who best
Bear His mild yoke, they serve Him best. His state
Is kingly: thousands at His bidding speed,
And post o'er land and ocean without rest;
They also serve who only stand and wait."

Methought I Saw My Late Espousèd Saint   *John Milton*

Methought I saw my late espoused Saint
Brought to me like Alcestis[1] from the grave,
Whom Jove's great son to her glad husband gave,
Rescued from death by force though pale and faint.
Mine as whom washt from spot of child-bed taint,
Purification in the old Law[2] did save,
And such, as yet once more I trust to have
Full sight of her in Heaven without restraint,
Came vested all in white, pure as her mind:
10 Her face was veiled; yet to my fancied sight,
Love, sweetness, goodness, in her person shined

[1] The wife of Admetus, who volunteered to die in his place when he provoked the gods on their wedding day. Hercules brought her back from the world of shadows.
[2] The rules for purification of women after childbirth are set forth in Leviticus, 12.

So clear, as in no face with more delight.
But O as to embrace me she enclined
I waked, she fled, and day brought back my night.

The Constant Lover   *Sir John Suckling*

Out upon it, I have loved
   Three whole days together!
And am like to love three more,
   If it prove fair weather.

Time shall moult away his wings
   Ere he shall discover
In the whole wide world again
   Such a constant lover.

But the spite on't is, no praise
10   Is due at all to me:
Love with me had made no stays,
   Had it been but she.

Had it any been but she,
   And that very face,
There had been at least ere this
   A dozen in her place.

To Lucasta, on Going to the Wars   *Richard Lovelace*

Tell me not, Sweet, I am unkind
   That from the nunnery
Of thy chaste breast and quiet mind,
   To war and arms I fly.

True, a new mistress now I chase,
   The first foe in the field;

And with a stronger faith embrace
    A sword, a horse, a shield.

Yet this inconstancy is such
10   As you too shall adore;
I could not love thee, dear, so much,
    Loved I not honor more.

To His Coy Mistress

Andrew Marvell

Had we but world enough, and time,
This coyness, lady, were no crime.
We would sit down, and think which way
To walk, and pass our long love's day.
Thou by the Indian Ganges' side
Shouldst rubies find: I by the tide
Of Humber[1] would complain. I would
Love you ten years before the Flood:
And you should if you please refuse
10 Till the conversion of the Jews.
My vegetable love should grow
Vaster than empires, and more slow.
An hundred years should go to praise
Thine eyes, and on thy forehead gaze.
Two hundred to adore each breast:
But thirty thousand to the rest.
An age at least to every part,
And the last age should show your heart.
For, lady, you deserve this state;
20 Nor would I love at lower rate.
    But at my back I always hear
Times wingèd chariot hurrying near:
And yonder all before us lie
Deserts of vast eternity.
Thy beauty shall no more be found,
Nor, in thy marble vault, shall sound

[1] A river in England.

My echoing song; then worms shall try
That long preserved virginity:
And your quaint honour turn to dust;
30 And into ashes all my lust.
The grave's a fine and private place,
But none, I think, do there embrace.
    Now therefore, while the youthful hue
Sits on thy skin like morning dew,
And while thy willing soul transpires
At every pore with instant fires,
Now let us sport us while we may;
And now, like am'rous birds of prey,
Rather at once our time devour,
40 Than languish in his slow-chapped[2] pow'r.
Let us roll all our strength, and all
Our sweetness, up into one ball:
And tear our pleasures with rough strife,
Thorough the iron gates of life.
Thus, though we cannot make our sun
Stand still, yet we will make him run.

An Epitaph   *Matthew Prior*

Interred beneath this marble stone
Lie sauntering Jack and idle Joan.
While rolling threescore years and one
Did round this globe their courses run,
If human things went ill or well,
If changing empires rose or fell,
The morning passed, the evening came,
And found this couple still the same.
They walked and eat, good folks—what then?
10 Why then they walked and eat again.
They soundly slept the night away;
They did just nothing all the day;

[2] Slow-jawed.

And having buried children four,
Would not take pains to try for more.
Nor sister either had, nor brother;
They seemed just tallied for each other.
   Their moral and economy
Most perfectly they made agree;
Each virtue kept its proper bound,
20 Nor trespassed on the other's ground.
Nor fame nor censure they regarded;
They neither punished nor rewarded.
He cared not what the footmen did;
Her maids she neither praised nor chid;
So every servant took his course,
And bad at first, they all grew worse.
Slothful disorder filled his stable.
And sluttish plenty decked her table.
Their beer was strong; their wine was port;
30 Their meal was large; their grace was short.
They gave the poor the remnant-meat,
Just when it grew not fit to eat.
   They paid the church and parish rate,
And took, but read not the receipt;
For which they claimed their Sunday's due
Of slumbering in an upper pew.
   No man's defects sought they to know,
So never made themselves a foe.
No man's good deeds did they commend,
40 So never raised themselves a friend.
Nor cherished they relations poor,
That might decrease their present store;
Nor barn nor house did they repair,
That might oblige their future heir.
   They neither added nor confounded;
They neither wanted nor abounded.
Each Christmas they accompts did clear,
And wound their bottom round the year.
Nor tear nor smile did they employ
50 At news of public grief or joy.
When bells were rung and bonfires made,
If asked, they ne'er denied their aid.

Their jug was to the ringers carried,
Whoever either died or married.
Their billet at the fire was found,
Whoever was deposed or crowned.
    Nor good, nor bad, nor fools, nor wise,
They would not learn, nor could advise.
Without love, hatred, joy, or fear,
60 They led—a kind of—as it were,
Nor wished, nor cared, nor laughed, nor cried.
And so they lived; and so they died.

O God, Our Help in Ages Past   *Isaac Watts*

O God, our help in ages past,
    Our hope for years to come,
Our shelter from the stormy blast,
    And our eternal home:

Under the shadow of Thy throne,
    Thy saints have dwelt secure;
Sufficient is Thine arm alone,
    And our defense is sure.

Before the hills in order stood,
10   Or earth received her frame,
From everlasting Thou art God,
    To endless years the same.

A thousand ages in Thy sight
    Are like an evening gone;
Short as the watch that ends the night
    Before the rising sun.

Time, like an ever-rolling stream,
    Bears all its sons away;
They fly forgotten, as a dream
20   Dies at the op'ning day.

O God, our help in ages past;
    Our hope for years to come;

Be Thou our guard while troubles last,
   And our eternal home!

FROM **An Essay on Man**   *Alexander Pope*

Hope humbly then; with trembling pinions soar;
Wait the great teacher, Death, and God adore.
What future bliss, he gives not thee to know,
But gives that hope to be thy blessing now;
Hope springs eternal in the human breast—
Man never is, but always to be blessed.
The soul, uneasy and confined from home,
Rests and expatiates in a life to come.
Lo, the poor Indian! whose untutored mind
¹⁰ Sees God in clouds, or hears him in the wind;
His soul proud science never taught to stray
Far as the solar walk, or milky way,
Yet simple nature to his hope has given,
Behind the cloud-topped hill, an humbler heaven.

Know then thyself, presume not God to scan,
The proper study of mankind is man.
Placed on this isthmus of a middle state,
A being darkly wise, and rudely great:
With too much knowledge for the sceptic side,
²⁰ With too much weakness for the stoic's pride,
He hangs between; in doubt to act, or rest;
In doubt to deem himself a god, or beast;
In doubt his mind or body to prefer;
Born but to die, and reasoning but to err;
Alike in ignorance, his reason such,
Whether he thinks too little or too much:
Chaos of thought and passion, all confused;
Still by himself abused or disabused;
Created half to rise and half to fall;
³⁰ Great lord of all things, yet a prey to all;
Sole judge of truth, in endless error hurled:
The glory, jest, and riddle of the world!

Whate'er the passion—knowledge, fame, or pelf,
Not one will change his neighbor with himself.
The learned is happy nature to explore,
The fool is happy that he knows no more;
The rich is happy in the plenty given,
The poor contents him with the care of Heaven.
See the blind beggar dance, the cripple sing,
40 The sot a hero, lunatic a king;
The starving chemist in his golden views
Supremely blest, the poet in his muse.
See some strange comfort every state attend,
And pride bestowed on all, a common friend;
See some fit passion every age supply,
Hope travels through nor quits us when we die.
   Behold the child, by nature's kindly law,
Pleased with a rattle, tickled with a straw:
Some livelier plaything gives his youth delight,
50 A little louder, but as empty quite:
Scarfs, garters, gold, amuse his riper stage,
And beads and prayer-books are the toys of age:
Pleased with this bauble still, as that before;
Till tired he sleeps, and life's poor play is o'er.

Ode Written in the Beginning of the Year 1746

William Collins

How sleep the brave, who sink to rest,
By all their country's wishes blest!
When Spring, with dewy fingers cold,
Returns to deck their hallowed mold,
She there shall dress a sweeter sod
Than Fancy's feet have ever trod.

By fairy hands their knell is rung;
By forms unseen their dirge is sung;
There Honor comes, a pilgrim gray,
10 To bless the turf that wraps their clay,

And Freedom shall awhile repair,
To dwell a weeping hermit there!

Walking with God   *William Cowper*

Oh! for a closer walk with God,
    A calm and heav'nly frame;
A light to shine upon the road
    That leads me to the Lamb!

Where is the blessedness I knew
    When first I saw the Lord?
Where is the soul-refreshing view
    Of Jesus, and his word?

What peaceful hours I once enjoyed!
10   How sweet their memory still!
But they have left an aching void,
    The world can never fill.

Return, O holy Dove, return,
    Sweet messenger of rest;
I hate the sins that made Thee mourn,
    And drove Thee from my breast.

The dearest idol I have known,
    Whate'er that idol be,
Help me to tear it from Thy throne,
20   And worsip only Thee.

So shall my walk be close with God,
    Calm and serene my frame;
So purer light shall mark the road
    That leads me to the Lamb.

The Little Black Boy

William Blake

My mother bore me in the southern wild,
And I am black, but O! my soul is white
White as an angel is the English child,
But I am black, as if bereaved of light.

My mother taught me underneath a tree,
And, sitting down before the heat of day,
She took me on her lap and kissed me,
And, pointing to the east, began to say:

"Look on the rising sun—there God does live,
10 And gives his light, and gives his heat away;
And flowers and trees and beasts and men receive
Comfort in morning, joy in the noon day.

"And we are put on earth a little space,
That we may learn to bear the beams of love;
And these black bodies and this sunburnt face
Is but a cloud, and like a shady grove.

"For when our souls have learned the heat to bear,
The cloud will vanish, we shall hear his voice,
Saying: 'Come out from the grove, my love and care,
20 And round my golden tent like lambs rejoice.' "

Thus did my mother say, and kissed me;
And thus I say to little English boy.
When I from black, and he from white cloud free,
And round the tent of God like lambs we joy,

I'll shade him from the heat, till he can bear
To lean in joy upon our father's knee;
And then I'll stand and stroke his silver hair,
And be like him, and he will then love me.

The Clod and the Pebble
William Blake

"Love seeketh not itself to please,
    Nor for itself hath any care,
But for another gives its ease,
    And builds a Heaven in Hell's despair."

So sung a little Clod of Clay
    Trodden with the cattle's feet,
But a Pebble of the brook
    Warbled out these metres meet:

"Love seeketh only self to please,
10   To bind another to its delight,
Joys in another's loss of ease,
    And builds a Hell in Heaven's despite."

A Poison Tree
William Blake

I was angry with my friend:
I told my wrath, my wrath did end.
I was angry with my foe:
I told it not, my wrath did grow.

And I water'd it in fears,
Night & morning with my tears;
And I sunned it with smiles,
And with soft deceitful wiles.

And it grew both day and night,
10 Till it bore an apple bright;
And my foe beheld it shine,
And he knew that it was mine,

And into my garden stole
When the night had veil'd the pole:

In the morning glad I see
My foe outstretch'd beneath the tree.

To a Louse   *Robert Burns*

On Seeing One on a Lady's Bonnet at Church

Ha! wh'are ye gaun, ye crowlin ferlie? [1]
Your impudence protects you sairly;
I canna say but ye strunt rarely,
    Owre gauze and lace,
Tho' faith! I fear ye dine but sparely
    On sic a place.

Ye ugly, creepin, blastit wonner,
Detested, shunned by saunt an' sinner,
How dare ye set your fit upon her,
10   Sae fine a lady?
Gae somewhere else, and seek your dinner
    On some poor body.

Swith,[2] in some beggar's hauffet[3] squattle;[4]
There ye may creep, and sprawl, and sprattle[5]
Wi' ither kindred jumping cattle,
    In shoals and nations;
Whare horn nor bane[6] ne'er dare unsettle
    Your thick plantations.

Now haud[7] you there! ye're out o' sight,
20 Below the fatt'rils,[8] snug an' tight;
Na, faith ye yet! ye'll no be right
    Till ye've got on it,
The very tapmost tow'ring height
    O' Miss's bonnet.

My sooth! right bauld ye set your nose out,
As plump an' gray as onie grozet;[9]

---

[1] Wonder.   [2] Hurry.   [3] Lock of hair.   [4] Squat.   [5] Scramble.   [6] Bone.   [7] Hide.
[8] Ribbon ends.   [9] Gooseberry.

O for some rank mercurial rozet,[10]
      Or fell red smeddum! [11]
I'd gie you sic a hearty dose o't,
30   Wad dress your droddum! [12]

I wad na been surprised to spy
You on an auld wife's flainen toy;[13]
Or aiblins[14] some bit duddie boy,[15]
      On's wyliecoat;[16]
But Miss's fine Lunardi! fie,
      How daur ye do't?

O Jenny, dinna toss your head,
An' set your beauties a' abread!
Ye little ken what cursed speed
40   The blastie's makin!
Thae winks and finger-ends, I dread,
      Are notice takin!

O wad some Power the giftie gie us
To see oursels as ithers see us!
It wad frae monie a blunder free us,
      An' foolish notion:
What airs in dress an' gait wad lea'e us,
      An' ev'n devotion!

She Was a Phantom of Delight   *William Wordsworth*

She was a phantom of delight
When first she gleamed upon my sight;
A lovely apparition, sent
To be a moment's ornament;
Her eyes as stars of twilight fair;
Like twilight's, too, her dusky hair;
But all things else about her drawn
From May-time and the cheerful dawn;

[10] Resin.   [11] Powder.   [12] Breeches.   [13] Flannel scarf.   [14] Perhaps.   [15] Ragged.
[16] Undervest.

A dancing shape, an image gay,
10 To haunt, to startle, and waylay.

I saw her upon nearer view,
A spirit, yet a woman too!
Her household motions light and free,
And steps of virgin-liberty;
A countenance in which did meet
Sweet records, promises as sweet;
A creature not too bright or good
For human nature's daily food;
For transient sorrows, simple wiles,
20 Praise, blame, love, kisses, tears, and smiles.

And now I see with eye serene
The very pulse of the machine;
A being breathing thoughtful breath,
A traveller between life and death;
To reason firm, the temperate will,
Endurance, foresight, strength, and skill;
A perfect woman, nobly planned,
To warn, to comfort, and command;
And yet a spirit still, and bright
30 With something of angelic light.

The World Is Too Much with Us   *William Wordsworth*

The world is too much with us; late and soon,
Getting and spending, we lay waste our powers:
Little we see in Nature that is ours;
We have given our hearts away, a sordid boon!
The Sea that bares her bosom to the moon;
The winds that will be howling at all hours,
And are up-gathered now like sleeping flowers;
For this, for everything, we are out of tune;
It moves us not.—Great God! I'd rather be
10 A Pagan, suckled in a creed outworn,
So might I, standing on this pleasant lea,

Have glimpses that would make me less forlorn;
Have sight of Proteus[1] rising from the sea;
Or hear old Triton[2] blow his wreathed horn.

She Walks in Beauty   *George Gordon, Lord Byron*

She walks in beauty, like the night
Of cloudless climes and starry skies,
And all that's best of dark and bright
Meet in her aspect and her eyes;
Thus mellowed to that tender light
Which heaven to gaudy day denies.

One shade the more, one ray the less,
Had half impaired the nameless grace
Which waves in every raven tress
10 Or softly lightens o'er her face,
Where thoughts serenely sweet express
How pure, how dear their dwelling-place.

And on that cheek and o'er that brow
So soft, so calm, yet eloquent,
The smiles that win, the tints that glow
But tell of days in goodness spent,
A mind at peace with all below,
A heart whose love is innocent.

When We Two Parted   *George Gordon, Lord Byron*

When we two parted
In silence and tears,

[1] Neptune was the Roman god of the sea. His herdsman, Proteus, was an old man and a prophet, who could assume different shapes at will.
[2] The son of Neptune, who makes the roaring of the sea by blowing through his shell, was represented as a fish with a human head.

Half broken-hearted
    To sever for years,
Pale grew thy cheek and cold,
    Colder thy kiss;
Truly that hour foretold
    Sorrow to this.

The dew of the morning
10   Sunk chill on my brow—
It felt like the warning
    Of what I feel now.
Thy vows are all broken,
    And light is thy fame:
I hear thy name spoken,
    And share in its shame.

They name thee before me,
    A knell to mine ear;
A shudder comes o'er me—
20   Why wert thou so dear?
They know not I knew thee,
    Who knew thee too well:—
Long, long shall I rue thee,
    Too deeply to tell.

In secret we met—
    In silence I grieve,
That thy heart could forget,
    Thy spirit deceive.
If I should meet thee
30   After long years,
How should I greet thee?—
    With silence and tears.

The Destruction of Sennacherib   *George Gordon, Lord Byron*

The Assyrian came down like the wolf on the fold,
And his cohorts were gleaming in purple and gold;

And the sheen of their spears was like stars on the sea,
When the blue wave rolls nightly on deep Galilee.

Like the leaves of the forest when summer is green,
That host with their banners at sunset were seen:
Like the leaves of the forest when autumn hath blown,
That host on the morrow lay wither'd and strown.

For the Angel of Death spread his wings on the blast,
10   And breathed in the face of the foe as he pass'd;
And the eyes of the sleepers wax'd deadly and chill,
And their hearts but once heaved, and forever grew still!

And there lay the steed with his nostril all wide,
But through it there roll'd not the breath of his pride;
And the foam of his gasping lay white on the turf,
And cold as the spray of the rock-beating surf.

And there lay the rider distorted and pale,
With the dew on his brow, and the rust on his mail:
And the tents were all silent, the banners alone,
20   The lances unlifted, the trumpet unblown.

And the widows of Ashur[1] are loud in their wail,
And the idols are broke in the temple of Baal;[2]
And the might of the Gentile, unsmote by the sword,
Hath melted like snow in the glance of the Lord!

Ozymandias   *Percy Bysshe Shelley*

I met a traveller from an antique land
Who said: Two vast and trunkless legs of stone
Stand in the desert. Near them, on the sand,
Half sunk, a shattered visage lies, whose frown,
And wrinkled lip, and sneer of cold command,
Tell that its sculptor well those passions read
Which yet survive, stamped on these lifeless things,

[1] In Assyrian mythology, the god of war and empire.
[2] A general name for several ancient semitic gods.

The hand that mocked them and the heart that fed:
And on the pedestal these words appear:
10   "My name is Ozymandias, king of kings:
Look at my works, ye Mighty, and despair!"
Nothing beside remains. Round the decay
Of that colossal wreck, boundless and bare
The lone and level sands stretch far away.

One Word Is Too Often Profaned   *Percy Bysshe Shelley*

One word is too often profaned
      For me to profane it,
One feeling too falsely disdain'd
      For thee to disdain it;
One hope is too like despair
      For prudence to smother,
And Pity from thee more dear
      Than that from another.

I can give not what men call love;
10   But wilt thou accept not
The worship the heart lifts above
      And the Heavens reject not,—
The desire of the moth for the star,
      Of the night for the morrow,
The devotion to something afar
      From the sphere of our sorrow?

On First Looking into Chapman's Homer[1]   *John Keats*

Much have I travelled in the realms of gold,
      And many goodly states and kingdoms seen;

[1] George Chapman (c. 1559–1634) published translations of *The Iliad* in 1611 and *The Odyssey* in 1616.

Round many western islands have I been
Which bards in fealty to Apollo hold.
Oft of one wide expanse had I been told
That deep-browed Homer ruled as his demesne;[2]
Yet did I never breathe its pure serene
Till I heard Chapman speak out loud and bold:
Then felt I like some watcher of the skies
10 When a new planet swims into his ken;
Or like stout Cortez[3] when with eagle eyes
He stared at the Pacific—and all his men
Looked at each other with a wild surmise—
Silent, upon a peak in Darien.

La Belle Dame sans Merci

John Keats

O what can ail thee, knight-at-arms,
    Alone and palely loitering?
The sedge has wither'd from the lake,
    And no birds sing.

O what can ail thee, knight-at-arms,
    So haggard and so woe-begone?
The squirrel's granary is full,
    And the harvest's done.

I see a lily on thy brow
    With anguish moist and fever
10   dew,
And on thy cheek a fading rose
    Fast withereth too.

I met a lady in the meads,
    Full beautiful—a faery's child,

[2] Domain.
[3] Hernando Cortez (1485–1547), Spanish conqueror of Mexico. Vasco Núñez de Balboa (1457–1517), however, first sighted the Pacific from Darien, a region in eastern Panama.

Her hair was long, her foot was light,
    And her eyes were wild.

I made a garland for her head,
    And bracelets too, and fragrant zone;
She look'd at me as she did love,
20   And made sweet moan.

I set her on my pacing steed,
    And nothing else saw all day long,
For sidelong would she bend, and sing
    A faery's song.

She found me roots of relish sweet,
    And honey wild, and manna dew,
And sure in language strange she said—
    "I love thee true."

She took me to her elfin grot,
30 And there she wept, and sigh'd full sore.
And there I shut her wild wild eyes
    With kisses four.

And there she lulled me asleep,
    And there I dream'd—Ah! woe betide!
The latest dream I ever dream'd
    On the cold hill side.

I saw pale kings and princes too,
    Pale warriors, death-pale were they all;
They cried—"La Belle Dame sans Merci
40   Hath thee in thrall!"

I saw their starved lips in the gloam,
    With horrid warning gaped wide,
And I awoke and found me here,
    On the cold hill's side.

And this is why I sojourn here,
    Alone and palely loitering,
Though the sedge is wither'd from the lake,
    And no birds sing.

Ode to a Nightingale

John Keats

My heart aches, and a drowsy numbness pains
    My sense, as though of hemlock[1] I had drunk,
Or emptied some dull opiate to the drains
    One minute past, and Lethe-wards[2] had sunk:
'Tis not through envy of thy happy lot,
    But being too happy in thine happiness,—
        That thou, light-wingèd Dryad [3] of the trees,
        In some melodious plot
    Of beechen green, and shadows numberless,
10   Singest of summer in full-throated ease.

O, for a draught of vintage! that hath been
Cooled a long age in the deep-delved earth,
Tasting of Flora[4] and the country green,
    Dance, and Provençal [5] song, and sunburnt mirth!
O for a beaker full of the warm South,
    Full of the true, the blushful Hippocrene,[6]
        With beaded bubbles winking at the brim,
        And purple-stained mouth;
    That I might drink, and leave the world unseen,
20   And with thee fade away into the forest dim:

Fade far away, dissolve, and quite forget
    What thou among the leaves hast never known,
The weariness, the fever, and the fret
    Here, where men sit and hear each other groan;
Where palsy shakes a few, sad, last gray hairs,
    Where youth grows pale, and spectre-thin, and dies;

[1] A poison made from an herb.
[2] Lethe is the river of forgetfulness in Hades, the underground kingdom of the dead.
[3] Wood nymph.
[4] Goddess of flowers.
[5] Provençe is a French province noted for its minstrelsy.
[6] A fountain on Mt. Helicon in Greece, said to have sprung from a stroke of Pegasus' foot, and traditionally sacred to the muses.

513

Where but to think is to be full of sorrow
    And leaden-eyed despairs,
Where Beauty cannot keep her lustrous eyes,
30   Or new Love pine at them beyond to-morrow.

Away! away! for I will fly to thee,
    Not charioted by Bacchus[7] and his pards,[8]
But on the viewless wings of Poesy,
    Though the dull brain perplexes and retards:
Already with thee! tender is the night,
    And haply the Queen-Moon is on her throne,
      Clustered around by all her starry Fays;[9]
        But here is no light,
Save what from heaven is with the breezes blown
40   Through verdurous glooms and winding mossy ways.

I cannot see what flowers are at my feet,
    Nor what soft incense hangs upon the boughs,
But, in embalmed darkness, guess each sweet
    Wherewith the seasonable month endows
The grass, the thicket, and the fruit-tree wild;
    White hawthorn, and the pastoral eglantine;
      Fast fading violets covered up in leaves;
        And mid-May's eldest child,
The coming musk-rose, full of dewy wine,
50   The murmurous haunt of flies on summer eves.

Darkling I listen; and, for many a time
    I have been half in love with easeful Death,
Called him soft names in many a mused rhyme,
    To take into the air my quiet breath;
Now more than ever seems it rich to die,
    To cease upon the midnight with no pain,
      While thou art pouring forth thy soul abroad
        In such an ecstasy!
Still wouldst thou sing, and I have ears in vain—
60   To thy high requiem become a sod.

[7] God of wine and revelry.
[8] Leopards.
[9] Fairies.

Thou wast not born for death, immortal Bird!
No hungry generations tread thee down;
The voice I hear this passing night was heard
In ancient days by emperor and clown:
Perhaps the self-same song that found a path
Through the sad heart of Ruth,[10] when, sick for home,
She stood in tears amid the alien corn;
The same that oft-times hath
Charmed magic casements, opening on the foam
70   Of perilous seas, in faery lands forlorn.

Forlorn! the very word is like a bell
To toll me back from thee to my sole self!
Adieu! the fancy cannot cheat so well
As she is famed to do, deceiving elf.
Adieu! adieu! thy plaintive anthem fades
Past the near meadows, over the still stream,
Up the hill-side; and now 'tis buried deep
In the next valley-glades:
Was it a vision, or a waking dream?
80   Fled is that music:—Do I wake or sleep?

There Was a Child Went Forth   *Walt Whitman*

There was a child went forth every day,
And the first object he looked upon, that object he became,
And that object became part of him for the day or a certain part of
the day,
Or for many years or stretching cycles of years.

The early lilacs became part of this child,
And grass and white and red morning-glories, and white and red
clover, and the song of the phoebe-bird,
And the Third-month lambs and the sow's pink-faint litter, and the
mare's foal and the cow's calf,

[10] Young widow in the Book of Ruth who went with her mother-in-law to an alien
land. See p. 207.

And the noisy brood of the barnyard or by the mire of the pond-side,
And the fish suspending themselves so curiously below there, and the
beautiful curious liquid,
10 And the water-plants with their graceful flat heads, all became part
of him.

The field-sprouts of Fourth-month and Fifth-month became part of
him,
Winter-grain sprouts and those of the light-yellow corn, and the
esculent roots of the garden,
And the apple-trees covered with blossoms and the fruit afterward,
and wood-berries, and the commonest weeds by the road,
And the old drunkard staggering home from the outhouse of the
tavern whence he had lately risen,
And the schoolmistress that passed on her way to the school,
And the friendly boys that passed, and the quarrelsome boys,
And the tidy and fresh-cheeked girls, and the barefoot negro boy and
girl,
And all the changes of city and country wherever he went.

His own parents, he that had fathered him and she that had conceived him in her womb and birthed him,
20 They gave this child more of themselves than that,
They gave him afterward every day, they became part of him.

The mother at home quietly placing the dishes on the supper-table,
The mother with mild words, clean her cap and gown, a wholesome
odor falling off her person and clothes as she walks by,
The father, strong, self-sufficient, manly, mean, angered, unjust,
The blow, the quick loud word, the tight bargain, the crafty lure,
The family usages, the language, the company, the furniture, the
yearning and swelling heart,
Affection that will not be gainsayed, the sense of what is real, the
thought if after all it should prove unreal,
The doubts of day-time and the doubts of night-time, the curious
whether and how,
Whether that which appears so is so, or is it all flashes and specks?
30 Men and women crowding fast in the streets, if they are not flashes
and specks what are they?
The streets themselves and the façades of houses, and goods in the
windows,

Vehicles, teams, the heavy-planked wharves, the huge crossing at the ferries,

The village on the highland seen from afar at sunset, the river between,

Shadows, aureola and mist, the light falling on roofs and gables of white or brown two miles off,

The schooner near by sleepily dropping down the tide, the little boat slack-towed astern,

The hurrying tumbling waves, quick-broken crests, slapping,

The strata of colored clouds, the long bar of maroon-tint away solitary by itself, the spread of purity it lies motionless in,

The horizon's edge, the flying sea-crow, the fragrance of salt marsh and shore mud,

These became part of that child who went forth every day, and who now goes, and will always go forth every day.

Beginning My Studies   *Walt Whitman*

Beginning my studies the first step pleas'd me so much,
The mere fact consciousness, these forms, the power of motion,
The least insect or animal, the senses, eyesight, love,
The first step I say awed me and pleas'd me so much,
I have hardly gone and hardly wish'd to go any farther,
But stop and loiter all the time to sing it in ecstatic songs.

When I Heard the Learn'd Astronomer   *Walt Whitman*

When I heard the learn'd astronomer,
When the proofs, the figures, were ranged in columns before me,
When I was shown the charts and diagrams, to add, divide, and measure them,
When I sitting heard the astronomer where he lectured with much applause in the lecture-room,

How soon unaccountable I became tired and sick,
Till rising and gliding out I wandered off by myself,
In the mystical moist night-air, and from time to time
Looked up in perfect silence at the stars.

When Lilacs Last in the Dooryard Bloom'd

Walt   Whitman

I

When lilacs last in the dooryard bloom'd,
And the great star early droop'd in the western sky in the night,
I mourn'd, and yet shall mourn with ever-returning spring.

Ever-returning spring, trinity sure to me you bring,
Lilac blooming perennial and drooping star in the west,
And thought of him[1] I love.

II

O powerful western fallen star!
O shades of night—O moody, tearful night!
O great star disappear'd—O the black murk that hides the star!
10   O cruel hands that hold me powerless—O helpless soul of me!
O harsh surrounding cloud that will not free my soul.

III

In the dooryard fronting an old farm-house near the white-wash'd
    palings,
Stands the lilac-bush tall-growing with heart-shaped leaves of rich
    green,
With many a pointed blossom rising delicate, with the perfume
    strong I love,
With every leaf a miracle—and from this bush in the dooryard,
With delicate-color'd blossoms and heart-shaped leaves of rich
    green,
A sprig with its flower I break.

---

[1] The slain President, Abraham Lincoln.

IV

In the swamp in secluded recesses,
A shy and hidden bird is warbling a song.

20 Solitary the thrush,
The hermit withdrawn to himself, avoiding the settlements,
Sings by himself a song.

Song of the bleeding throat,
Death's outlet song of life, (for well dear brother I know,
If thou wast not granted to sing thou would'st surely die.)

V

Over the breast of the spring, the land, amid cities,
Amid lanes and through old woods, where lately the violets
    peep'd from the ground, spotting the gray débris,
Amid the grass in the fields each side of the lanes, passing the
    endless grass,
Passing the yellow-spear'd wheat, every grain from its shroud in
    the dark-brown fields uprisen,
30 Passing the apple-tree blows of white and pink in the orchards,
Carrying a corpse to where it shall rest in the grave,
Night and day journeys a coffin.

VI

Coffin that passes through lanes and streets,
Through day and night with the great cloud darkening the land,
With the pomp of the inloop'd flags with the cities draped in black,
With the show of the States themselves as of crape-veil'd women
    standing,
With processions long and winding and the flambeaus of the night,
With the countless torches lit, with the silent sea of faces and the
    unbared heads,
With the waiting depot, the arriving coffin, and the somber faces,
40 With dirges through the night, with the thousand voices rising
    strong and solemn,
With all the mournful voices of the dirges pour'd around the coffin,
The dim-lit churches and the shuddering organs—where amid these
    you journey,
With the tolling tolling bells' perpetual clang,

Here, coffin that slowly passes,
I give you my sprig of lilac.

VII

(Nor for you, for one alone,
Blossoms and branches green to coffins all I bring,
For fresh as the morning, thus would I chant a song for you O
sane and sacred death.

All over bouquets of roses,
50 O death, I cover you over with roses and early lilies,
But mostly and now the lilac that blooms the first,
Copious I break, I break the sprigs from the bushes,
With loaded arms I come, pouring for you,
For you and the coffins all of you O death.)

VIII

O western orb sailing the heaven,
Now I know what you must have meant as a month since I walk'd,
As I walk'd in silence the transparent shadowy night,
As I saw you had something to tell as you bent to me night after
night,
As you droop'd from the sky low down as if to my side, (while
the other stars all look'd on,)
60 As we wander'd together the solemn night, (for something I know
not what kept me from sleep,)
As the night advanced, and I saw on the rim of the west how full
you were of woe,
As I stood on the rising ground in the breeze in the cool trans-
parent night,
As I watch'd where you pass'd and was lost in the netherward
black of the night,
As my soul in its trouble dissatisfied sank, as where you sad orb,
Concluded, dropt in the night, and was gone.

IX

Sing on there in the swamp,
O singer bashful and tender, I hear your notes, I hear your call,
I hear, I come presently, I understand you,
But a moment I linger, for the lustrous star has detain'd me,
70 The star my departing comrade holds and detains me

X

O how shall I warble myself for the dead one there I loved?
And how shall I deck my song for the large sweet soul that has
   gone?
And what shall my perfume be for the grave of him I love?

Sea-winds blown from east and west,
Blown from the Eastern sea and blown from the Western sea, till
   there on the prairies meeting,
These and with these and the breath of my chant,
I'll perfume the grave of him I love.

XI

O what shall I hang on the chamber walls?
And what shall the pictures be that I hang on the walls,
80 To adorn the burial-house of him I love?
Pictures of growing spring and farms and homes,
With the Fourth-month eve at sundown, and the gray smoke lucid
   and bright,
With floods of the yellow gold of the gorgeous, indolent, sinking
   sun, burning, expanding the air,
With the fresh sweet herbage under foot, and the pale green leaves
   of the trees prolific,
In the distance the flowing glaze, the breast of the river, with a
   wind-dapple here and there,
With ranging hills on the banks, with many a line against the sky,
   and shadows,
And the city at hand, with dwellings so dense, and stacks of chimneys,
And all the scenes of life and the workshops, and the workmen
   homeward returning.

XII

Lo, body and soul—this land,
90 My own Manhattan with spires, and the sparkling and hurrying
   tides, and the ships,
The varied and ample land, the South and the North in the light,
   Ohio's shores and flashing Missouri,
And ever the far-spreading prairies cover'd with grass and corn.

Lo, the most excellent sun so calm and haughty,
The violet and purple morn with just-felt breezes,
The gentle soft-born measureless light,
The miracle spreading bathing all, the fulfill'd noon,
The coming eve delicious, the welcome night and the stars,
Over my cities shining all, enveloping man and land.

XIII

Sing on, sing on you gray-brown bird,
100 Sing from the swamps, the recesses, pour your chant from the
bushes,
Limitless out of the dusk, out of the cedars and pines.
Sing on dearest brother, warble your reedy song,
Loud human song, with voice of uttermost woe.

O liquid and free and tender!
O wild and loose to my soul—O wondrous singer!
You only I hear—yet the star holds me, (but will soon depart,)
Yet the lilac with mastering odor holds me.

XIV

Now while I sat in the day and look'd forth,
In the close of the day with its light and the fields of spring, and
the farmers preparing their crops,
110 In the large unconscious scenery of my land with its lakes and
forests,
In the heavenly aerial beauty, (after the perturb'd winds and the
storms,)
Under the arching heavens of the afternoon swift passing, and the
voices of children and women,
The many-moving sea-tides, and I saw the ships how they sail'd,
And the summer approaching with richness, and the fields all busy
with labor,
And the infinite separate houses, how they all went on, each with
its meals and minutia of daily usages,
And the streets how their throbbings throbb'd, and the cities pent
—lo, then and there,
Falling upon them all and among them all, enveloping me with the
rest,
Appear'd the cloud, appear'd the long black trail,
And I knew death, its thought, and the sacred knowledge of death.

120 Then with the knowledge of death as walking one side of me,
And the thought of death close-walking the other side of me,
And I in the middle as with companions, and as holding the hands
of companions,
I fled forth to the hiding receiving night that talks not,
Down to the shores of the water, the path by the swamp in the
dimness,
To the solemn shadowy cedars and ghostly pines so still.

And the singer so shy to the rest receiv'd me,
The gray-brown bird I know receiv'd us comrades three,
And he sang the carol of death, and a verse for him I love.

From deep secluded recesses,
130 From the fragrant cedars and the ghostly pines so still,
Came the carol of the bird.
And the charm of the carol rapt me
As I held as if by their hands my comrades in the night,
And the voice of my spirit tallied the song of the bird.

Come lovely and soothing death,
Undulate round the world, serenely arriving, arriving,
In the day, in the night, to all, to each,
Sooner or later delicate death.

Prais'd be the fathomless universe,
140 *For life and joy, and for objects and knowledge curious,*
And for love, sweet love—but praise! praise! praise!
For the sure-enwinding arms of cool-enfolding death.

Dark mother always gliding near with soft feet,
Have none chanted for thee a chant of fullest welcome?
Then I chant it for thee, I glorify thee above all,
I bring thee a song that when thou must indeed come, come un-
falteringly.

Approach strong deliveress,
When it is so, when thou hast taken them I joyously sing the dead,
Lost in the loving floating ocean of thee,
150 *Laved in the flood of thy bliss O death.*

From me to thee glad serenades,
Dances for thee I propose saluting thee, adornments and feastings
for thee,

*And the sights of the open landscape and the high-spread sky are
  fitting,*
And life and the fields, and the huge and thoughtful night.

The night in silence under many a star,
*The ocean shore and the husky whispering wave whose voice I
  know,*
And the soul turning to thee O vast and well-veil'd death,
And the body gratefully nestling close to thee.

Over the tree-tops I float thee a song,
160 *Over the rising and sinking waves, over the myriad fields and the
  prairies wide,*
Over the dense-pack'd cities all and the teeming wharves and ways,
I float this carol with joy, with joy to thee O death.

XV

To the tally of my soul,
Loud and strong kept up the gray-brown bird,
With pure deliberate notes spreading filling the night.
Loud in the pines and cedars dim,
Clear in the freshness moist and the swamp-perfume,
And I with my comrades there in the night.

While my sight that was bound in my eyes unclosed,
170 As to long panoramas of visions.

And I saw askant the armies,
I saw as in noiseless dreams hundreds of battle-flags,
Borne through the smoke of the battles and pierc'd with missiles I
  saw them,
And carried hither and yon through the smoke, and torn and
  bloody,
And at last but a few shreds left on the staffs, (and all in silence,)
And the staffs all splinter'd and broken.

I saw battle-corpses, myriads of them,
And the white skeletons of young men, I saw them,
I saw the débris and débris of all the slain soldiers of the war,
180 But I saw they were not as was thought,
They themselves were fully at rest, they suffer'd not,
The living remain'd and suffer'd, the mother suffer'd,

And the wife and the child and the musing comrade suffer'd,
And the armies that remain'd suffer'd.

XVI

Passing the visions, passing the night,
Passing, unloosing the hold of my comrades' hands,
Passing the song of the hermit bird and the tallying song of my
    soul,
Victorious song, death's outlet song, yet varying ever-altering song,
As low and wailing, yet clear the notes, rising and falling, flooding
    the night,
190 Sadly sinking and fainting, as warning and warning, and yet again
    bursting with joy,
Covering the earth and filling the spread of the heaven,
As that powerful psalm in the night I heard from recesses,
Passing, I leave thee lilac with heart-shaped leaves,
I leave thee there in the dooryard, blooming, returning with spring.

I cease from my song for thee,
From my gaze on thee in the west, fronting the west, communing
    with thee,
O comrade lustrous with silver face in the night.

Yet each to keep and all, retrievements out of the night,
The song, the wondrous chant of the gray-brown bird,
200 And the tallying chant, the echo arous'd in my soul,
With the lustrous and drooping star with the countenance full of
    woe,
With the holders holding my hand nearing the call of the bird,
Comrades mine and I in the midst, and their memory ever to keep,
    for the dead I loved so well,
For the sweetest, wisest soul of all my days and lands—and this
    for his dear sake,
Lilac and star and bird twined with the chant of my soul,
There in the fragrant pines and the cedars dusk and dim.

I Sit and Look Out
Walt Whitman

I sit and look out upon all the sorrows of the world, and upon all
oppression and shame,
I hear secret convulsive sobs from young men at anguish with
themselves, remorseful after deeds done,
I see in low life the mother misused by her children, dying, neglected, gaunt, desperate,
I see the wife misused by her husband, I see the treacherous seducer of young women,
I mark the ranklings of jealousy and unrequited love attempted to
be hid, I see these sights on the earth,
I see the working of battle, pestilence, tyranny, I see martyrs and
prisoners,
I observe a famine at sea, I observe the sailors casting lots who
shall be kill'd to preserve the lives of the rest,
I observe the slights and degradations cast by arrogant persons
upon laborers, the poor, and upon negroes, and the like;
All these—all the meanness and agony without end I sitting look
out upon,
10 See, hear, and am silent.

Ulysses[1]
Alfred, Lord Tennyson

It little profits that an idle king,
By this still hearth, among these barren crags,
Matched with an aged wife,[2] I mete and dole
Unequal laws unto a savage race,
That hoard, and sleep, and feed, and know not me.
I cannot rest from travel; I will drink
Life to the lees. All times I have enjoyed
Greatly, have suffered greatly, both with those

[1] The hero of *The Odyssey*.   [2] Penelope.

That loved me, and alone; on shore, and when
10 Thro' scudding drifts the rainy Hyades[3]
Vext the dim sea. I am become a name;
For always roaming with a hungry heart
Much have I seen and known,—cities of men
And manners, climates, councils, governments,
Myself not least, but honored of them all,—
And drunk delight of battle with my peers,
Far on the ringing plains of windy Troy.
I am a part of all that I have met;
Yet all experience is an arch wherethro'
20 Gleams that untravelled world whose margin fades
For ever and for ever when I move.
How dull it is to pause, to make an end,
To rust unburnished, not to shine in use!
As tho' to breathe were life! Life piled on life
Were all too little, and of one to me
Little remains; but every hour is saved
From that eternal silence, something more,
A bringer of new things; and vile it were
For some three suns to store and hoard myself,
30 And this gray spirit yearning in desire
To follow knowledge like a sinking star,
Beyond the utmost bound of human thought.
       This is my son, mine own Telemachus,
To whom I leave the sceptre and the isle,[4]
Well-loved of me, discerning to fulfill
This labor, by slow prudence to make mild
A rugged people, and thro' soft degrees
Subdue them to the useful and the good.
Most blameless is he, centered in the sphere
40 Of common duties, decent not to fail
In offices of tenderness, and pay
Meet adoration to my household gods,
When I am gone. He works his work, I mine.
       There lies the port; the vessel puffs her sail;

[3] In Greek mythology, the five daughters of Atlas whom Zeus set among the stars, forming a constellation whose rising at the same time as the sun was believed to bring rain.
[4] Ithaca.

There gloom the dark, broad seas. My mariners,
Souls that have toiled, and wrought, and thought with me,—
That ever with a frolic welcome took
The thunder and the sunshine, and opposed
Free hearts, free foreheads,—you and I are old;
50 Old age hath yet his honor and his toil.
Death closes all; but something ere the end,
Some work of noble note, may yet be done,
Not unbecoming men that strove with Gods.
The lights begin to twinkle from the rocks;
The long day wanes; the slow moon climbs; the deep
Moans round with many voices. Come, my friends.
'Tis not too late to seek a newer world.
Push off, and sitting well in order smite
The sounding furrows; for my purpose holds
60 To sail beyond the sunset, and the baths
Of all the western stars, until I die.
It may be that the gulfs will wash us down;
It may be we shall touch the Happy Isles,
And see the great Achilles,[5] whom we knew.
Tho' much is taken, much abides; and tho'
We are not now that strength which in old days
Moved earth and heaven, that which we are, we are,—
One equal temper of heroic hearts,
Made weak by time and fate, but strong in will
70 To strive, to seek, to find, and not to yield.

Tithonus[1]   *Alfred, Lord Tennyson*

The woods decay, the woods decay and fall,
The vapors weep their burthen to the ground,
Man comes and tills the field and lies beneath,
And after many a summer dies the swan.

[5] The hero of *The Iliad*, a prototype of manly valor, who was fatally wounded with an arrow shot by Paris.
[1] A handsome Trojan loved by Aurora, goddess of the dawn, who granted him immortality but not eternal youth, which he forgot to request.

Me only cruel immortality
Consumes; I wither slowly in thine arms,
Here at the quiet limit of the world,
A white-haired shadow roaming like a dream
The ever-silent spaces of the East,
10 Far-folded mists, and gleaming halls of morn.
    Alas! for this gray shadow, once a man—
So glorious in his beauty and thy choice,
Who madest him thy chosen, that he seemed
To his great heart none other than a God!
I asked thee, "Give me immortality."
Then didst thou grant mine asking with a smile,
Like wealthy men who care not how they give.
But thy strong Hours indignant worked their wills,
And beat me down and marred and wasted me,
20 And tho' they could not end me, left me maimed
To dwell in presence of immortal youth,
Immortal age beside immortal youth,
And all I was in ashes. Can thy love,
Thy beauty, make amends, tho' even now,
Close over us, the silver star, thy guide,
Shines in those tremulous eyes that fill with tears
To hear me? Let me go; take back thy gift.
Why should a man desire in any way
To vary from the kindly race of men,
30 Or pass beyond the goal of ordinance
Where all should pause, as is most meet for all?
    A soft air fans the cloud apart; there comes
A glimpse of that dark world where I was born.
Once more the old mysterious glimmer steals
From thy pure brows, and from thy shoulders pure,
And bosom beating with a heart renewed.
Thy cheek begins to redden thro' the gloom,
Thy sweet eyes brighten slowly close to mine,
Ere yet they blind the stars, and the wild team
40 Which love thee, yearning for thy yoke, arise
And shake the darkness from their loosened manes,
And beat the twilight into flakes of fire.
    Lo! ever thus thou growest beautiful
In silence, then before thine answer given

Departest, and thy tears are on my cheek.
   Why wilt thou ever scare me with thy tears,
And make me tremble lest a saying learnt,
In days far-off, on that dark earth, be true?
"The Gods themselves cannot recall their gifts."
⁵⁰   Ay me! ay me! with what another heart
In days far-off, and with what other eyes
I used to watch—if I be he that watched—
The lucid outline forming round thee; saw
The dim curls kindle into sunny rings;
Changed with thy mystic change, and felt my blood
Glow with the glow that slowly crimsoned all
Thy presence and thy portals, while I lay,
Mouth, forehead, eyelids, growing dewy-warm
With kisses balmier than half-opening buds
⁶⁰ Of April, and could hear the lips that kissed
Whispering I knew not what of wild and sweet,
Like that strange song I heard Apollo sing,
While Ilion[2] like a mist rose into towers.
   Yet hold me not for ever in thine East;
How can my nature longer mix with thine?
Coldly thy rosy shadows bathe me, cold
Are all thy lights, and cold my wrinkled feet
Upon thy glimmering thresholds, when the steam
Floats up from those dim fields about the homes
⁷⁰ Of happy men that have the power to die,
And grassy barrows of the happier dead.
Release me, and restore me to the ground.
Thou seest all things, thou wilt see my grave;
Thou wilt renew thy beauty morn by morn,
I earth in earth forget these empty courts,
And thee returning on thy silver wheels.

[2] Troy, whose walls Apollo built as he sang.

Porphyria's Lover

Robert Browning

The rain set early in tonight,
   The sullen wind was soon awake,
It tore the elm-tops down for spite,
   And did its worst to vex the lake:
I listened with heart fit to break.
When glided in Porphyria; straight
   She shut the cold out and the storm,
And kneeled and made the cheerless grate
   Blaze up, and all the cottage warm;
¹⁰ Which done, she rose, and from her form
Withdrew the dripping cloak and shawl,
   And laid her soiled gloves by, untied
Her hat and let the damp hair fall,
   And, last, she sat down by my side
And called me. When no voice replied,
She put my arm about her waist,
   And made her smooth white shoulder bare
And all her yellow hair displaced,
   And, stooping, made my cheek lie there,
²⁰ And spread, o'er all, her yellow hair,
Murmuring how she loved me—she
   Too weak, for all her heart's endeavor,
To set its struggling passion free
   From pride, and vainer ties dissever,
And give herself to me forever.
But passion sometimes would prevail,
   Nor could tonight's gay feast restrain
A sudden thought of one so pale
   For love of her, and all in vain:
³⁰ So, she was come through wind and rain.
Be sure I looked up at her eyes
   Happy and proud; at last I knew
Porphyria worshipped me; surprise
   Made my heart swell, and still it grew
While I debated what to do.

That moment she was mine, mine, fair,
　　Perfectly pure and good: I found
A thing to do, and all her hair
　　In one long yellow string I wound
40　Three times her little throat around,
And strangled her. No pain felt she;
　　I am quite sure she felt no pain.
As a shut bud that holds a bee,
　　I warily oped her lids: again
Laughed the blue eyes without a stain.
And I untightened next the tress
　　About her neck; her cheek once more
Blushed bright beneath my burning kiss:
　　I propped her head up as before,
50　Only, this time my shoulder bore
Her head, which droops upon it still:
　　The smiling rosy little head,
So glad it has its utmost will,
　　That all it scorned at once is fled,
And I, its love, am gained instead!
Porphyria's love: she guessed not how
　　Her darling one wish would be heard.
And thus we sit together now,
　　And all night long we have not stirred,
60　And yet God has not said a word!

The Laboratory　　　　　　　　　　　　*Robert Browning*

(ANCIEN REGIME [1])

Now that I, tying thy glass mask tightly,
May gaze through these faint smokes curling whitely,
As thou pliest thy trade in this devil's-smithy—
Which is the poison to poison her, prithee?

He is with her; and they know that I know
Where they are, what they do: they believe my tears flow

[1] The period before the French Revolution.

While they laugh, laugh at me, at me fled to the drear
Empty church, to pray God in, for them!—I am here.

Grind away, moisten and mash up thy paste,
10 Pound at thy powder,—I am not in haste!
Better sit thus, and observe thy strange things,
Than go where men wait me and dance at the King's.

That in the mortar—you'll call it a gum?
Ah, the brave tree whence such gold oozings come!
And yonder soft phial, the exquisite blue,
Sure to taste sweetly—is that poison too?

Had I but all of them, thee and thy treasures,
What a wild crowd of invisible pleasures!
To carry pure death in an earring, a casket,
20 A signet, a fan-mount, a filigree-basket!

Soon, at the King's a mere lozenge to give
And Pauline should have just thirty minutes to live!
But to light a pastille, and Elise, with her head
And her breast and her arms and her hands, should drop
   dead!

Quick—is it finished? The color's too grim!
Why not soft like the phial's, enticing and dim?
Let it brighten her drink, let her turn it and stir,
And try it and taste, ere she fix and prefer!

What a drop! She's not little, no minion like me—
30 That's why she ensnared him: this never will free
The soul from those masculine eyes—say, 'No'!
To that pulse's magnificent come-and-go.

For only last night, as they whispered, I brought
My own eyes to bear on her so, that I thought
Could I keep them one half minute fixed she would fall,
Shrivelled; she fell not; yet this does it all!

Not that I bid you spare her the pain!
Let death be felt and the proof remain;
Brand, burn up, bite into its grace—
40 He is sure to remember her dying face!

Is it done? Take my mask off! Nay, be not morose;
It kills her, and this prevents seeing it close:
The delicate droplet, my whole fortune's fee—
If it hurts her, beside, can it ever hurt me?

Now, take all my jewels, gorge gold to your fill,
You may kiss me, old man, on my mouth if you will!
But brush this dust off me, lest horror it brings
Ere I know it—next moment I dance at the King's!

Say Not, the Struggle   *Arthur Hugh Clough*
Nought Availeth

Say not, the struggle nought availeth,
    The labour and the wounds are vain,
The enemy faints not, nor faileth,
    And as things have been they remain.

If hopes were dupes, fears may be liars;
    It may be, in yon smoke concealed,
Your comrades chase e'en now the fliers,
    And, but for you, possess the field.

For while the tired waves, vainly breaking,
10   Seem here no painful inch to gain,
Far back, through creeks and inlets making,
    Comes silent, flooding in, the main,

And not by eastern windows only,
    When daylight comes, comes in the light,
In front, the sun climbs slow, how slowly,
    But westward, look, the land is bright.

The Latest Decalogue   *Arthur Hugh Clough*

Thou shalt have one God only; who
Would be at the expense of two?

No graven images may be
Worshipped, except the currency:
Swear not at all; for, for thy curse
Thine enemy is none the worse:
At church on Sunday to attend
Will serve to keep the world thy friend:
Honour thy parents; that is, all
10 From whom advancement may befall:
Thou shalt not kill; but need'st not strive
Officiously to keep alive:
Do not adultery commit;
Advantage rarely comes of it:
Thou shalt not steal; an empty feat,
When 'tis so lucrative to cheat:
Bear not false witness; let the lie
Have time on its own wings to fly:
Thou shalt not covet, but tradition
20 Approves all forms of competition.

Dover Beach   *Matthew Arnold*

The sea is calm to-night,
The tide is full, the moon lies fair
Upon the straits;—on the French coast the light
Gleams and is gone; the cliffs of England stand,
Glimmering and vast, out in the tranquil bay.
Come to the window, sweet is the night-air!
Only, from the long line of spray
Where the sea meets the moon-blanched land,
Listen! you hear the grating roar
10 Of pebbles which the waves draw back, and fling,
At their return, up the high strand,
Begin, and cease, and then again begin,
With tremulous cadence slow, and bring
The eternal note of sadness in.

Sophocles[1] long ago
Heard it on the Ægean, and it brought
Into his mind the turbid ebb and flow
Of human misery; we
Find also in the sound a thought,
20 Hearing it by this distant northern sea.

The Sea of Faith
Was once, too, at the full, and round earth's shore
Lay like the folds of a bright girdle furled.
But now I only hear
Its melancholy, long, withdrawing roar,
Retreating, to the breath
Of the night-wind, down the vast edges drear
And naked shingles of the world.
Ah, love, let us be true
30 To one another! for the world, which seems
To lie before us like a land of dreams,
So various, so beautiful, so new,
Hath really neither joy, nor love, nor light,
Nor certitude, nor peace, nor help for pain;
And we are here as on a darkling plain
Swept with confused alarms of struggle and flight,
Where ignorant armies clash by night.

I Like to See It   *Emily Dickinson*
Lap the Miles

I like to see it lap the miles,
And lick the valleys up,
And stop to feed itself at tanks;
And then, prodigious, step

Around a pile of mountains,
And, supercilious, peer

[1] See Biographical Notes. In *Antigone* Sophocles compares the curse of heaven to the ebb and flow of the sea.

In shanties by the sides of roads;
And then a quarry pare

To fit its sides, and crawl between,
10 Complaining all the while
In horrid, hooting stanza;
Then chase itself down hill

And neigh like Boanerges;[1]
Then, punctual as a star,
Stop—docile and omnipotent—
At its own stable door.

There Is No Frigate Like a Book   *Emily Dickinson*

There is no frigate like a book
    To take us lands away,
Nor any coursers like a page
    Of prancing poetry.

This traverse may the poorest take
    Without oppress of toll;
How frugal is the chariot
    That bears a human soul!

The Grass So Little Has to Do   *Emily Dickinson*

The Grass so little has to do—
A Sphere of simple Green—
With only Butterflies to brood
And Bees to entertain—

---

[1] Literally, sons of thunder; the name was given to James and John, the sons of Zebedee, because they wanted to call down the "fire from heaven" on the Samaritans for not receiving the Lord Jesus.

And stir all day to pretty Tunes
The Breezes fetch along—
And hold the Sunshine in its lap
And bow to everything—

And thread the Dews, all night, like Pearls—
10 And make itself so fine
A Duchess were too common
For such a noticing—

And even when it dies—to pass
In Odors so divine—
Like Lowly spices, lain to sleep—
Or Spikenards,[1] perishing—

And then, in Sovereign Barns to dwell—
And dream the Days away,
The Grass so little has to do
20 I wish I were a Hay—

After Great Pain,   *Emily Dickinson*
a Formal Feeling Comes

After great pain, a formal feeling comes.
The nerves sit ceremonious, like tombs.
The stiff heart questions was it he that bore,
And yesterday, or centuries before?

The feet, mechanical, go round,
Of ground, or air, or ought,
A wooden way
Regardless grown,
A quartz contentment, like a stone.

[1] A fragrant and costly ointment of ancient times, supposedly prepared from an eastern herb; also, an American perennial herb with an aromatic root.

Because I Could Not Stop for Death

Emily Dickinson

Because I could not stop for Death—
He kindly stopped for me—
The Carriage held but just Ourselves—
And Immortality.

We slowly drove—He knew no haste
And I had put away
My labor and my leisure too,
For His Civility—

We passed the School, where Children strove
10 At Recess—in the Ring—
We passed the Fields of Gazing Grain—
We passed the Setting Sun—

Or rather—He passed Us—
The Dews drew quivering and chill—
For only Gossamer,[1] my Gown—
My Tippet[2]—only Tulle[3]—

We paused before a House that seemed
A Swelling of the Ground—
The Roof was scarcely visible—
20 The Cornice—in the Ground—

Since then—'tis Centuries—and yet
Feels shorter than the Day
I first surmised the Horses' Heads
Were toward Eternity—

[1] A filmy, gauzelike fabric.
[2] Scarf.
[3] A fine open-meshed material.

Apparently with No Surprise

Emily Dickinson

Apparently with no surprise
To any happy Flower
The Frost beheads it at its play—
In accidental power—
The blonde Assassin passes on—
The Sun proceeds unmoved
To measure off another Day
For an Approving God.

The Man He Killed

Thomas Hardy

"Had he and I but met
By some old ancient inn,
We should have sat us down to wet
Right many a nipperkin!

"But ranged as infantry,
And staring face to face,
I shot at him as he at me,
And killed him in his place.

"I shot him dead because—
10 Because he was my foe,
Just so: my foe of course he was;
That's clear enough; although

"He thought he'd 'list, perhaps,
Off-hand like—just as I—
Was out of work—had sold his traps—
No other reason why.

"Yes; quaint and curious war is!
You shoot a fellow down
You'd treat if met where any bar is,
20 Or help to half-a-crown."

Ah, Are You Digging on My Grave? *Thomas Hardy*

"Ah, are you digging on my grave
   My loved one?—planting rue?"
     —"No: yesterday he went to wed
     One of the brightest wealth has bred.
     'It cannot hurt her now,' he said,
     'That I should not be true.' "

"Then who is digging on my grave?
   My nearest, dearest kin?"
     —"Ah, no: they sit and think, 'What use!
10   *What good will planting flowers produce?*
     No tendance of her mound can loose
     Her spirit from Death's gin.' "

"But someone digs upon my grave?
   My enemy?—prodding sly?"
     —"Nay: when she heard you had passed the Gate
     That shuts on all flesh soon or late,
     She thought you no more worth her hate,
     She cares not where you lie."

"Then, who is digging on my grave?
20   Say—since I have not guessed!"
     —"O it is I, my mistress dear,
     Your little dog, who still lives near,
     And much I hope my movements here
     Have not disturbed your rest?"

"Ah, yes! *You* dig upon my grave. . . .
   Why flashed it not on me
That one true heart was left behind!
What feeling do we ever find
To equal among human kind
30   A dog's fidelity!"

     "Mistress, I dug upon your grave
     To bury a bone, in case
     I should be hungry near this spot

When passing on my daily trot.
I am sorry, but I quite forgot
It was your resting-place."

At the Draper's[1]   *Thomas Hardy*

"I stood at the back of the shop, my dear,
But you did not perceive me.
Well, when they deliver what you were shown
I shall know nothing of it, believe me!"
And he coughed and coughed as she paled and said,
"Oh, I didn't see you come in there—
Why couldn't you speak?"—"Well, I didn't. I left
That you should not notice I'd been there.

"You were viewing some lovely things.
10 *'Soon required for a widow of latest fashion';*
And I knew 'twould upset you to meet the man
Who had to be cold and ashen,

And screwed in a box before they could dress you
'In the last new note in mourning,'
As they defined it. So, not to distress you,
I left you to your adorning."

The Oxen   *Thomas Hardy*

Christmas Eve, and twelve of the clock.
   "Now they are all on their knees,"
An elder said as we sat in a flock
   By the embers in hearthside ease.

We pictured the meek mild creatures where
   They dwelt in their strawy pen,

[1] A dealer in cloth or drygoods.

Nor did it occur to one of us there
    To doubt they were kneeling then.

So fair a fancy few would weave
10   In these years! Yet, I feel,
If someone said on Christmas Eve,
    "Come; see the oxen kneel

"In the lonely barton[1] by yonder coomb[2]
    Our childhood used to know,"
I should go with him in the gloom,
    Hoping it might be so.

God's Grandeur   *Gerard Manley Hopkins*

The world is charged with the grandeur of God.
    It will flame out, like shining from shook foil;
    It gathers to a greatness, like the ooze of oil
Crushed. Why do men then now not reck his rod?
Generations have trod, have trod, have trod;
    And all is seared with trade; bleared, smeared with toil;
    And wears man's smudge and shares man's smell: the soil
Is bare now, nor can foot feel, being shod.

And for all this, nature is never spent;
10   There lives the dearest freshness deep down things;
And though the last lights off the black West went
    Oh, morning, at the brown brink eastward, springs—
Because the Holy Ghost over the bent
    World broods with warm breast and with ah! bright wings.

[1] Farmyard.
[2] Valley.

When I Was One-and-Twenty   *A. E. Housman*

When I was one-and-twenty
  I heard a wise man say,
"Give crowns and pounds and guineas
  But not your heart away;
Give pearls away and rubies
  But keep your fancy free."
But I was one-and-twenty,
  No use to talk to me.

When I was one-and-twenty
10 I heard him say again,
"The heart out of the bosom
  Was never given in vain;
'Tis paid with sighs a-plenty
  And sold for endless rue."
And I am two-and-twenty,
  And oh, 'tis true, 'tis true.

To an Athlete Dying Young   *A. E. Housman*

The time you won your town the race
We chaired you through the market-place;
Man and boy stood cheering by,
And home we brought you shoulder-high.

Today, the road all runners come,
Shoulder-high we bring you home,
And set you at your threshold down,
Townsman of a stiller town.

Smart lad, to slip betimes away
30 From fields where glory does not stay,
And early though the laurel grows
It withers quicker than the rose.

Eyes the shady night has shut
Cannot see the record cut,
And silence sounds no worse than cheers
After earth has stopped the ears:

Now you will not swell the rout
Of lads that wore their honors out,
Runners whom renown outran
20 And the name died before the man.

So set, before its echoes fade,
The fleet foot on the sill of shade,
And hold to the low lintel up
The still-defended challenge-cup.

And round that early-laureled head
Will flock to gaze the strengthless dead,
And find unwithered on its curls
The garland briefer than a girl's.

Is My Team Ploughing?   *A. E. Housman*

"Is my team ploughing,
    That I was used to drive
And hear the harness jingle
    When I was man alive?"

Ay, the horses trample,
    The harness jingles now;
No change though you lie under
    The land you used to plough.

"Is football playing
10   Along the river shore,
With lads to chase the leather,
    Now I stand up no more?"

Ay, the ball is flying,
    The lads play heart and soul;

The goal stands up, the keeper
   Stands up to keep the goal.

"Is my girl happy,
   That I thought hard to leave,
And has she tired of weeping
20   As she lies down at eve?"

Ay, she lies down lightly,
   She lies not down to weep:
Your girl is well contented.
   Be still, my lad, and sleep.

"Is my friend hearty,
   Now I am thin and pine,
And has he found to sleep in
   A better bed than mine?"

Yes, lad, I lie easy,
30   I lie as lads would choose;
I cheer a dead man's sweetheart,
   Never ask me whose.

"Terence, This Is Stupid Stuff"   *A. E. Housman*

"Terence, this is stupid stuff:
You eat your victuals fast enough;
There can't be much amiss, 'tis clear,
To see the rate you drink your beer.
But oh, good Lord, the verse you make,
It gives a chap the belly-ache.
The cow, the old cow, she is dead;
It sleeps well, the horned head:
We poor lads, 'tis our turn now
10 To hear such tunes as killed the cow.
Pretty friendship 'tis to rhyme
Your friends to death before their time
Moping melancholy mad:
Come, pipe a tune to dance to, lad."

Why, if 'tis dancing you would be,
There's brisker pipes than poetry.
Say, for what were hop-yards meant,
Or why was Burton built on Trent? [1]
Oh, many a peer of England brews
20 Livelier liquor than the Muse,
And malt does more than Milton can
To justify God's ways to man. [2]
Ale, man, ale's the stuff to drink
For fellows whom it hurts to think:
Look into the pewter pot
To see the world as the world's not.
And faith, 'tis pleasant till 'tis past:
The mischief is that 'twill not last.
Oh, I have been to Ludlow [3] fair
30 And left my necktie God knows where,
And carried half-way home, or near,
Pints and quarts of Ludlow beer:
Then the world seemed none so bad,
And I myself a sterling lad;
And down in lovely muck I've lain,
Happy till I woke again.
Then I saw the morning sky:
Heigho, the tale was all a lie;
The world, it was the old world yet,
40 I was I, my things were wet,
And nothing now remained to do
But begin the game anew.

Therefore, since the world has still
Much good, but much less good than ill,
And while the sun and moon endure
Luck's a chance, but trouble's sure,
I'd face it as a wise man would,
And train for ill and not for good.
'Tis true, the stuff I bring for sale
50 Is not so brisk a brew as ale:

[1] City in Staffordshire noted for its breweries.
[2] Milton's purpose in *Paradise Lost*.
[3] Town in Shropshire.

Out of a stem that scored the hand
I wrung it in a weary land.
But take it: if the smack is sour,
The better for the embittered hour;
It should do good to heart and head
When your soul is in my soul's stead;
And I will friend you, if I may,
In the dark and cloudy day.
   There was a king[4] reigned in the East:
60 There, when kings will sit to feast,
They get their fill before they think
With poisoned meat and poisoned drink.
He gathered all that springs to birth
From the many-venomed earth;
First a little, thence to more,
He sampled all her killing store;
And easy, smiling, seasoned sound,
Sate the king when healths went round.
They put arsenic in his meat
70 And stared aghast to watch him eat;
They poured strychnine in his cup
And shook to see him drink it up:
They shook, they stared as white's their shirt:
Them it was their poison hurt.
—I tell the tale that I heard told.
Mithridates, he died old.

My Dreams Are of a Field Afar   *A. E. Housman*

My dreams are of a field afar
  And blood and smoke and shot.
There in their graves my comrades are,
  In my grave I am not.
I too was taught the trade of man

---

[4] Mithridates VI, King of Pontus (c. 133 B.C.–63 B.C.), who was called the Great but was defeated by Pompey, is the subject of the legend Housman tells here.

And spelt the lesson plain;
But they, when I forgot and ran,
Remembered and remain.

A Prayer for My Daughter   *William Butler Yeats*

Once more the storm is howling, and half hid
Under this cradle-hood and coverlid
My child sleeps on. There is no obstacle
But Gregory's wood and one bare hill
Whereby the haystack- and roof-levelling wind,
Bred on the Atlantic, can be stayed;
And for an hour I have walked and prayed
Because of the great gloom that is in my mind.

I have walked and prayed for this young child an hour
10 And heard the sea-wind scream upon the tower,
And under the arches of the bridge, and scream
In the elms above the flooded stream;
Imagining in excited reverie
That the future years had come,
Dancing to a frenzied drum,
Out of the murderous innocence of the sea.

May she be granted beauty and yet not
Beauty to make a stranger's eye distraught,
Or hers before a looking-glass, for such,
20 Being made beautiful overmuch,
Consider beauty a sufficient end,
Lose natural kindness and maybe
The heart-revealing intimacy
That chooses right, and never find a friend.

Helen[1] being chosen found life flat and dull
And later had much trouble from a fool,
While that great Queen,[2] that rose out of the spray,

---

[1] Wife of Menelaus, King of Sparta, Helen eloped with Paris and brought about the siege and destruction of Troy.
[2] Venus, the goddess of love, was married to Vulcan who forged thunderbolts for Jove.

Being fatherless could have her way
Yet chose a bandy-legged smith for man.
30 It's certain that fine women eat
A crazy salad with their meat
Whereby the Horn of Plenty is undone.

In courtesy I'd have her chiefly learned;
Hearts are not had as a gift but hearts are earned
By those that are not entirely beautiful;
Yet many, that have played the fool
For beauty's very self, has charm made wise,
And many a poor man that has roved,
Loved and thought himself beloved,
40 From a glad kindness cannot take his eyes.

May she become a flourishing hidden tree
That all her thoughts may like the linnet be,
And have no business but dispensing round
Their magnanimities of sound,
Nor but in merriment begin a chase,
Nor but in merriment a quarrel.
O may she live like some green laurel
Rooted in one dear perpetual place.

My mind, because the minds that I have loved,
50 The sort of beauty that I have approved,
Prosper but little, has dried up of late,
Yet knows that to be choked with hate
May well be of all evil chances chief.
If there's no hatred in a mind
Assault and battery of the wind
Can never tear the linnet from the leaf.

An intellectual hatred is the worst,
So let her think opinions are accursed.
Have I not seen the loveliest woman born
60 Out of the mouth of Plenty's horn,
Because of her opinionated mind
Barter that horn and every good
By quiet natures understood
For an old bellows full of angry wind?

Considering that, all hatred driven hence,
The soul recovers radical innocence
And learns at last that it is self-delighting,
Self-appeasing, self-affrighting,
And that its own sweet will is Heaven's will;
70 She can, though every face should scowl
And every windy quarter howl
Or every bellows burst, be happy still.

And may her bridegroom bring her to a house
Where all's accustomed, ceremonious;
For arrogance and hatred are the wares
Peddled in the thoroughfares.
How but in custom and in ceremony
Are innocence and beauty born?
Ceremony's a name for the rich horn,
80 And custom for the spreading laurel tree.

Why Should Not Old Men Be Mad?   *William Butler Yeats*

Why should not old men be mad?
Some have known a likely lad
That had a sound fly-fisher's wrist
Turn to a drunken journalist;
A girl that knew all Dante once
Live to bear children to a dunce;
A Helen of social welfare dream,
Climb on a wagonette to scream.
Some think it a matter of course that chance
10 Should starve good men and bad advance,
That if their neighbours figured plain,
As though upon a lighted screen,
No single story would they find
Of an unbroken happy mind,
A finish worthy of the start.
Young men know nothing of this sort,

Observant old men know it well;
And when they know what old books tell,
And that no better can be had,
20 Know why an old man should be mad.

To a Friend
Whose Work Has Come to Nothing

William Butler Yeats

Now all the truth is out,
Be secret and take defeat
From any brazen throat,
For how can you compete,
Being honour bred, with one
Who, were it proved he lies,
Were neither shamed in his own
Nor in his neighbours' eyes?
Bred to a harder thing
10 Than Triumph, turn away
And like a laughing string
Whereon mad fingers play
Amid a place of stone,
Be secret and exult,
Because of all things known
That is most difficult.

Richard Cory

Edwin Arlington Robinson

Whenever Richard Cory went down town,
We people on the pavement looked at him:
He was a gentleman from sole to crown,
Clean favored, and imperially slim.

And he was always quietly arrayed,
And he was always human when he talked;

But still he fluttered pulses when he said,
"Good-morning," and he glittered when he walked.

And he was rich—yes, richer than a king—
10 And admirably schooled in every grace:
In fine, we thought that he was everything
To make us wish that we were in his place.

So on we worked, and waited for the light,
And went without the meat, and cursed the bread;
And Richard Cory, one calm summer night,
Went home and put a bullet through his head.

How Annandale Went Out   *Edwin Arlington Robinson*

"They called it Annandale—and I was there
To flourish, to find words, and to attend:
Liar, physician, hypocrite, and friend,
I watched him; and the sight was not so fair
As one or two that I had seen elsewhere:
An apparatus not for me to mend—
A wreck, with hell between him and the end,
Remained of Annandale; and I was there.
I knew the ruin as I knew the man;
10 So put the two together, if you can,
Remembering the worst you know of me.
Now view yourself as I was, on the spot—
With a slight kind of engine. Do you see?
Like this . . . . You wouldn't hang me?
    I thought not."

Mr. Flood's Party   *Edwin Arlington Robinson*

Old Eben Flood, climbing alone one night
Over the hill between the town below

And the forsaken upland hermitage
That held as much as he should ever know
On earth again of home, paused warily.
The road was his with not a native near;
And Eben, having leisure, said aloud,
For no man else in Tilbury Town[1] to hear:

"Well, Mr. Flood, we have the harvest moon
10 Again, and we may not have many more;
The bird is on the wing, the poet says,
And you and I have said it here before.
Drink to the bird." He raised up to the light
The jug that he had gone so far to fill,
And answered huskily: "Well, Mr. Flood,
Since you propose it, I believe I will."

Alone, as if enduring to the end
A valiant armor of scarred hopes outworn,
He stood there in the middle of the road
20 Like Roland's[2] ghost winding a silent horn.
Below him, in the town among the trees,
Where friends of other days had honored him,
A phantom salutation of the dead
Rang thinly till old Eben's eyes were dim.

Then, as a mother lays her sleeping child
Down tenderly, fearing it may awake,
He set the jug down slowly at his feet
With trembling care, knowing that most things break;
And only when assured that on firm earth
30 It stood, as the uncertain lives of men
Assuredly did not, he paced away,
And with his hand extended paused again:

"Well, Mr. Flood, we have not met like this
In a long time; and many a change has come
To both of us, I fear, since last it was

---

[1] See Biographical Notes.
[2] Hero of the eleventh century *Song of Roland*, who blew his horn so mightily to summon aid for his rearguard, as they covered Charlemagne's retreat from Spain, that the veins of his neck burst. Charlemagne heard the horn, but came too late and Roland died of his wounds.

We had a drop together. Welcome home!"
Convivially returning with himself,
Again he raised the jug up to the light;
And with an acquiescent quaver said:
40 "Well, Mr. Flood, if you insist, I might.

"Only a very little, Mr. Flood—
For auld lang syne. No more, sir; that will do."
So, for the time, apparently it did,
And Eben evidently thought so too;
For soon amid the silver loneliness
Of night he lifted up his voice and sang,
Secure, with only two moons listening,
Until the whole harmonious landscape rang—

"For auld lang syne." The weary throat gave out,
50 The last word wavered; and the song being done,
He raised again the jug regretfully
And shook his head, and was again alone.
There was not much that was ahead of him,
And there was nothing in the town below—
Where strangers would have shut the many doors
That many friends had opened long ago.

Lucinda Matlock   *Edgar Lee Masters*

I went to the dances at Chandlerville,
And played snap-out at Winchester.
One time we changed partners,
Driving home in the moonlight of middle June,
And then I found Davis.
We were married and lived together for seventy years,
Enjoying, working, raising the twelve children,
Eight of whom we lost
Ere I had reached the age of sixty.
10 I spun, I wove, I kept the house, I nursed the sick,
I made the garden, and for holiday

Rambled over the fields where sang the larks,
And by Spoon River gathering many a shell,
And many a flower and medicinal weed—
Shouting to the wooded hills, singing to the green valleys.
At ninety-six I had lived enough, that is all,
And passed to a sweet repose.
What is this I hear of sorrow and weariness,
Anger, discontent and drooping hopes?
20 Degenerate sons and daughters,
Life is too strong for you—
It takes life to love Life.

Knowlt Hoheimer   *Edgar Lee Masters*

I was the first fruits of the battle of Missionary Ridge.
When I felt the bullet enter my heart
I wished I had staid at home and gone to jail
For stealing the hogs of Curl Trenary,
Instead of running away and joining the army.
Rather a thousand times the county jail
Than to lie under this marble figure with wings,
And this granite pedestal
Bearing the words, *"Pro Patria."* [1]
10 What do they mean, anyway?

A Youth in Apparel That Glittered   *Stephen Crane*

A youth in apparel that glittered
Went to walk in a grim forest.
There he met an assassin
Attired all in garb of old days;
He, scowling through the thickets,

[1] For one's country.

And dagger poised quivering,
Rushed upon the youth.
"Sir," said the latter,
"I am enchanted, believe me,
10 To die, thus,
In this mediæval fashion,
According to the best legends;
Ah, what joy!"
Then took he the wound, smiling,
And died, content.

War Is Kind   *Stephen Crane*

Do not weep, maiden, for war is kind.
Because your lover threw wild hands toward the sky
And the affrighted steed ran on alone,
Do not weep.
War is kind.

Hoarse, booming drums of the regiment,
Little souls who thirst for fight,
These men were born to drill and die.
The unexplained glory flies above them,
10 Great is the battle-god, great, and his kingdom—
A field where a thousand corpses lie.

Do not weep, babe, for war is kind.
Because your father tumbled in the yellow trenches,
Raged at his breast, gulped and died,
Do not weep.
War is kind

Swift blazing flag of the regiment,
Eagle with crest of red and gold,
These men were born to drill and die.
20 Point for them the virtue of slaughter,
Make plain to them the excellence of killing
And a field where a thousand corpses lie.

Mother whose heart hung humble as a button
On the bright splendid shroud of your son,
Do not weep.
War is kind.

A Man Said to the Universe   *Stephen Crane*

A man said to the universe:
"Sir, I exist!"
"However," replied the universe,
"The fact has not created in me
A sense of obligation."

Stopping by Woods on a Snowy Evening   *Robert Frost*

Whose woods these are I think I know.
His house is in the village though;
He will not see me stopping here
To watch his woods fill up with snow.

My little horse must think it queer
To stop without a farmhouse near
Between the woods and frozen lake
The darkest evening of the year.

He gives his harness bells a shake
10 To ask if there is some mistake.
The only other sound's the sweep
Of easy wind and downy flake.

The woods are lovely, dark and deep.
But I have promises to keep,
And miles to go before I sleep,
And miles to go before I sleep.

Mending Wall

Robert Frost

Something there is that doesn't love a wall,
That sends the frozen-ground-swell under it,
And spills the upper boulders in the sun;
And makes gaps even two can pass abreast.
The work of hunters is another thing:
I have come after them and made repair
Where they have left not one stone on a stone,
But they would have the rabbit out of hiding,
To please the yelping dogs. The gaps I mean,
10 No one has seen them made or heard them made,
But at spring mending-time we find them there.
I let my neighbor know beyond the hill;
And on a day we meet to walk the line
And set the wall between us once again.
We keep the wall between us as we go.
To each the boulders that have fallen to each.
And some are loaves and some so nearly balls
We have to use a spell to make them balance:
"Stay where you are until our backs are turned!"
20 We wear our fingers rough with handling them.
Oh, just another kind of out-door game,
One on a side. It comes to little more:
There where it is we do not need the wall:
He is all pine and I am apple orchard.
My apple trees will never get across
And eat the cones under his pines, I tell him.
He only says, "Good fences make good neighbors."
Spring is the mischief in me, and I wonder
If I could put a notion in his head:
30 "Why do they make good neighbors? Isn't it
Where there are cows? But here there are no cows.
Before I built a wall I'd ask to know
What I was walling in or walling out,
And to whom I was like to give offence.
Something there is that doesn't love a wall,

That wants it down." I could say "Elves" to him,
But it's not elves exactly, and I'd rather
He said it for himself. I see him there
Bringing a stone grasped firmly by the top
40   In each hand, like an old-stone savage armed.
He moves in darkness as it seems to me,
Not of woods only and the shade of trees.
He will not go behind his father's saying,
And he likes having thought of it so well
He says again, "Good fences make good neighbors."

A Semi-Revolution   *Robert Frost*

I advocate a semi-revolution.
The trouble with a total revolution
(Ask any reputable Rosicrucian[1])
Is that it brings the same class up on top.
Executives of skillful execution
Will therefore plan to go halfway and stop.
Yes, revolutions are the only salves,
But they're one thing that should be done by halves.

Design   *Robert Frost*

I found a dimpled spider, fat and white,
On a white heal-all,[2] holding up a moth
Like a white piece of rigid satin cloth—
Assorted characters of death and blight
Mixed ready to begin the morning right,
Like the ingredients of a witches' broth—

---

[1] A member of a secret society devoted to the practical application of an occult philosophy to human affairs.
[2] A flower, normally blue.

A snow-drop spider, a flower like froth,
And dead wings carried like a paper kite.

What had that flower to do with being white,
10 The wayside blue and innocent heal-all?
What brought the kindred spider to that height,
Then steered the white moth thither in the night?
What but design of darkness to appall?—
If design govern in a thing so small.

---

warty bliggens, the toad   *Don Marquis*

i met a toad
the other day by the name
of warty bliggens
he was sitting under
a toadstool
feeling contented
he explained that when the cosmos
was created
that toadstool was especially
10 planned for his personal
shelter from sun and rain
thought out and prepared
for him

do not tell me
said warty bliggens
that there is not a purpose
in the universe
the thought is blasphemy
a little more
20 conversation revealed
that warty bliggens
considers himself to be
the center of the said
universe
the earth exists

especially planned for his personal shelter

to grow toadstools for him
to sit under
the sun to give him light
by day and the moon
³⁰ and wheeling constellations
to make beautiful
the night for the sake of
warty bliggens

to what act of yours
do you impute
this interest on the part
of the creator
of the universe

          i asked him
40   why is it that you
          are so greatly favored
          ask rather
          said warty bliggens
          what the universe
          has done to deserve me
          if i were a
          human being i would
          not laugh
          too complacently
50   at poor warty bliggens
          for similar
          absurdities
          have only too often
          lodged in the crinkles
          of the human cerebrum
                              archy

---

the song of mehitabel   *Don Marquis*

          this is the song of mehitabel
          of mehitabel the alley cat
          as i wrote you before boss
          mehitabel is a believer
          in the pythagorean
          theory of the transmigration
          of the soul and she claims
          that formerly her spirit
          was incarnated in the body
10   of cleopatra

          that was a long time ago
          and one must not be
          surprised if mehitabel
          has forgotten some of her
          more regal manners

i have had my ups and downs
but wotthehell wotthehell
yesterday sceptres and crowns
fried oysters and velvet gowns
20   and today i herd with bums
but wotthehell wotthehell
i wake the world from sleep
as i caper and sing and leap
when i sing my wild free tune
wotthehell wotthehell
under the blear eyed moon
i am pelted with cast off shoon
but wotthehell wotthehell

do you think that i would change
30   my present freedom to range
for a castle or moated grange
wotthehell wotthehell
cage me and i d go frantic
my life is so romantic
capricious and corybantic
and i m toujours gai toujours gai[1]

i know that i am bound
for a journey down the sound
in the midst of a refuse mound
40   but wotthehell wotthehell
oh I should worry and fret
death and i will coquette
there s a dance in the old dame yet
toujours gai toujours gai

i once was an innocent kit
wotthehell wotthehell
with a ribbon my neck to fit
and bells tied onto it
o wotthehell wotthehell
50   but a maltese cat came by
with a come hither look in his eye

---

[1] Always gay.

i followed adown the street
the pad of his rhymical Feet

and a song that soared to the sky
and wotthehell wotthehell
and i followed adown the street
the pad of his rhythmical feet
o permit me again to repeat
wotthehell wotthehell

my youth i shall never forget
but there s nothing i really regret
60 wotthehell wotthehell
there s a dance in the old dame yet
toujours gai toujours gai

the things that i had not ought to
i do because i ve gotto

wotthehell wotthehell
and i end with my favorite motto
toujours gai toujours gai

boss sometimes i think
that our friend mehitabel
70 is a trifle too gay

Sunday Morning

I

Complacencies of the peignoir, and late
Coffee and oranges in a sunny chair,
And the green freedom of a cockatoo
Upon a rug mingle to dissipate
The holy hush of ancient sacrifice.
She dreams a little, and she feels the dark
Encroachment of that old catastrophe,
As a calm darkens among water-lights.
The pungent oranges and bright, green wings
10 Seem things in some procession of the dead,
Winding across wide water, without sound.
The day is like wide water, without sound,
Stilled for the passing of her dreaming feet
Over the seas, to silent Palestine,
Dominion of the blood and sepulchre.

II

Why should she give her bounty to the dead?
What is divinity if it can come
Only in silent shadows and in dreams?
Shall she not find in comforts of the sun,
20 In pungent fruit and bright, green wings, or else
In any balm or beauty of the earth,
Things to be cherished like the thought of heaven?
Divinity must live within herself:
Passions of rain, or moods in falling snow;

Grievings in loneliness, or unsubdued
Elations when the forest blooms; gusty
Emotions on wet roads on autumn nights;
All pleasures and all pains, remembering
The bough of summer and the winter branch.
30   These are the measures destined for her soul.

III

Jove in the clouds had his inhuman birth.
No mother suckled him, no sweet land gave
Large-mannered emotions to his mythy mind.
He moved among us, as a muttering king,
Magnificent, would move among his hinds,
Until our blood, commingling, virginal,
With heaven, brought such requital to desire
The very hinds discerned it, in a star.
Shall our blood fail? Or shall it come to be
40   The blood of paradise? And shall the earth
Seem all of paradise that we shall know?
The sky will be much friendlier then than now,
A part of labor and a part of pain,
And next in glory to enduring love,
Not this dividing and indifferent blue.

IV

She says, 'I am content when wakened birds,
Before they fly, test the reality
Of misty fields, by their sweet questionings;
But when the birds are gone, and their warm fields
50   Return no more, where, then, is paradise?'
There is not any haunt of prophecy,
Nor any old chimera of the grave,
Neither the golden underground, nor isle
Melodious, where spirits gat them home,
Nor visionary south, nor cloudy palm
Remote on heaven's hill, that has endured
As April's green endures; or will endure
Like her remembrance of awakened birds,
Or her desire for June and evening, tipped
60   By the consummation of the swallow's wings.

V

She says, 'But in contentment I still feel
The need of some imperishable bliss.'
Death is the mother of beauty; hence from her,
Alone, shall come fulfilment to our dreams
And our desires. Although she strews the leaves
Of sure obliteration on our paths,
The path sick sorrow took, the many paths
Where triumph rang its brassy phrase, or love
Whispered a little out of tenderness,
70 She makes the willow shiver in the sun
For maidens who were wont to sit and gaze
Upon the grass, relinquished to their feet.
She causes boys to pile new plums and pears
On disregarded plate. The maidens taste
And stray impassioned in the littering leaves.

VI

Is there no change of death in paradise?
Does ripe fruit never fall? Or do the boughs
Hang always heavy in that perfect sky,
Unchanging, yet so like our perishing earth,
80 With rivers like our own that seek for seas
They never find, the same receding shores
That never touch with inarticulate pang?
Why set the pear upon those river-banks
Or spice the shores with odors of the plum?
Alas, that they should wear our colors there,
The silken weavings of our afternoons,
And pick the strings of our insipid lutes!
Death is the mother of beauty, mystical,
Within whose burning bosom we devise
90 Our earthly mothers waiting, sleeplessly.

VII

Supple and turbulent, a ring of men
Shall chant in orgy on a summer morn
Their boisterous devotion to the sun,
Not as a god, but as a god might be,

Naked among them, like a savage source.
Their chant shall be a chant of paradise,
Out of their blood, returning to the sky;
And in their chant shall enter, voice by voice,
The windy lake wherein their lord delights,
100 The trees, like serafin, and echoing hills,
That choir among themselves long afterward.
They shall know well the heavenly fellowship
Of men that perish and of summer morn.
And whence they came and whither they shall go
The dew upon their feet shall manifest.

VIII

She hears, upon that water without sound,
A voice that cries, 'The tomb in Palestine
Is not the porch of spirits lingering.
It is the grave of Jesus, where he lay.'
110 We live in an old chaos of the sun,
Or old dependency of day and night,
Our island solitude, unsponsored, free,
Of that wide water, inescapable.
Deer walk upon our mountains, and the quail
Whistle about us their spontaneous cries;
Sweet berries ripen in the wilderness;
And, in the isolation of the sky,
At evening, casual flocks of pigeons make
Ambiguous undulations as they sink,
120 Downward to darkness, on extended wings.

A Pact   *Ezra Pound*

I make a pact with you, Walt Whitman—
I have detested you long enough.
I come to you as a grown child
Who has had a pig-headed father;
I am old enough now to make friends.
It was you that broke the new wood,

Now is a time for carving.
We have one sap and one root—
Let there be commerce between us.

The River Merchant's Wife: A Letter

Rihaku
Translation by Ezra Pound

While my hair was still cut straight across my forehead
I played about the front gate, pulling flowers.
You came by on bamboo stilts, playing horse,
You walked about my seat, playing with blue plums.
And we went on living in the village of Chokan:
Two small people, without dislike or suspicion.
At fourteen I married My Lord you.
I never laughed, being bashful.
Lowering my head, I looked at the wall.
10 Called to, a thousand times, I never looked back.

At fifteen I stopped scowling,
I desired my dust to be mingled with yours
Forever and forever and forever.
Why should I climb the look out?

At sixteen you departed,
You went into far Ku-to-yen, by the river of swirling eddies,
And you have been gone five months.
The monkeys make sorrowful noise overhead.

You dragged your feet when you went out.
20 By the gate now, the moss is grown, the different mosses,
Too deep to clear them away!
The leaves fall early this autumn, in wind.
The paired butterflies are already yellow with August
Over the grass in the West garden;
They hurt me. I grow older.
If you are coming down through the narrows of the river
      Kiang,

Please let me know beforehand,
And I will come out to meet you
                              As far as Cho-fu-Sa.

Macavity: the Mystery Cat   *T. S. Eliot*

Macavity's a Mystery Cat: he's called the Hidden Paw—
For he's the master criminal who can defy the Law.
He's the bafflement of Scotland Yard, the Flying Squad's despair:
For when they reach the scene of crime—*Macavity's not there!*

Macavity, Macavity, there's no-one like Macavity,
He's broken every human law, he breaks the law of gravity.
His powers of levitation would make a fakir stare,
And when you reach the scene of crime—*Macavity's not there!*
You may seek him in the basement, you may look up in the air—
10 But I tell you once and once again, *Macavity's not there!*

Macavity's a ginger cat, he's very tall and thin;
You would know him if you saw him, for his eyes are sunken in.
His brow is deeply lined with thought, his head is highly domed;
His coast is dusty from neglect, his whiskers are uncombed.
He sways his head from side to side, with movements like a snake;
And when you think he's half asleep, he's always wide awake.

Macavity, Macavity, there's no-one like Macavity,
For he's a fiend in feline shape, a monster of depravity.
You may meet him in a by-street, you may see him in the square—
20 But when a crime's discovered, then *Macavity's not there!*

He's outwardly respectable. (They say he cheats at cards.)
And his footprints are not found in any file of Scotland Yard's.
And when the larder's looted, or the jewel-case is rifled,
Or when the milk is missing, or another Peke's been stifled,
Or the greenhouse glass is broken, and the trellis past repair—
Ay, there's the wonder of the thing! *Macavity's not there!*

And when the Foreign Office find a Treaty's gone astray,
Or the Admiralty lose some plans and drawings by the way,
There may be a scrap of paper in the hall or on the stair—
30   But it's useless to investigate—*Macavity's not there!*
And when the loss has been disclosed, the Secret Service say:
'It *must* have been Macavity!'—but he's a mile away.
You'll be sure to find him resting, or a-licking of his thumbs,
Or engaged in doing complicated long division sums.

Macavity, Macavity, there's no-one like Macavity,
There never was a Cat of such deceitfulness and suavity.
He always has an alibi, and one or two to spare:
At whatever time the deed took place—MACAVITY WASN'T THERE!
And they say that all the Cats whose wicked deeds are widely known
40   (I might mention Mungojerrie, I might mention Griddlebone)
Are nothing more than agents for the Cat who all the time
Just controls their operations: the Napoleon of Crime!

The Love Song of J. Alfred Prufrock   *T. S. Eliot*

> *S'io credesse che mia risposta fosse*
> *A persona che mai tornasse al mondo,*
> *Questa fiamma staria senza piu scosse.*
> *Ma perciocche giammai di questo fondo*
> *Non torno vivo alcun, s'i'odo il vero,*
> *Senza tema d'infamia ti rispondo.*[1]

Let us go then, you and I,
When the evening is spread out against the sky
Like a patient etherised upon a table;
Let us go, through certain half-deserted streets,
The muttering retreats
Of restless nights in one-night cheap hotels

---

[1] This quotation is from Dante's *Inferno,* Canto XXVII. 11. 61–60. It is the reply of one of the damned who has been asked to identify himself. An approximate translation is "If I believed that my answer were to anyone who could ever return to the world, this flame would quiver no longer; but since as I hear, no one ever returns alive from this depth, I reply to you without fear of infamy."

And sawdust restaurants with oyster-shells:
Streets that follow like a tedious argument
Of insidious intent
10 To lead you to an overwhelming question . . .
Oh, do not ask, "What is it?"
Let us go and make our visit.

In the room the women come and go
Talking of Michelangelo.[2]

The yellow fog that rubs its back upon the window-panes,
The yellow smoke that rubs its muzzle on the window-panes
Licked its tongue into the corners of the evening,
Lingered upon the pools that stand in drains,
Let fall upon its back the soot that falls from chimneys,
20 Slipped by the terrace, made a sudden leap,
And seeing that it was a soft October night,
Curled once about the house, and fell asleep.

And indeed there will be time
For the yellow smoke that slides along the street,
Rubbing its back upon the window-panes;
There will be time, there will be time
To prepare a face to meet the faces that you meet;
There will be time to murder and create,
And time for all the works and days of hands
30 That lift and drop a question on your plate;
Time for you and time for me,
And time yet for a hundred indecisions,
And for a hundred visions and revisions,
Before the taking of a toast and tea.

In the room the women come and go
Talking of Michelangelo.

And indeed there will be time
To wonder, "Do I dare?" and, "Do I dare?"
Time to turn back and descend the stair,
40 With a bald spot in the middle of my hair—
(They will say: "How his hair is growing thin!")
My morning coat, my collar mounting firmly to the chin,

[2] Italian sculptor, painter, architect, and poet who lived from 1475–1564.

My necktie rich and modest, but asserted by a simple pin—
(They will say: "But how his arms and legs are thin!")
Do I dare
Disturb the universe?
In a minute there is time
For decisions and revisions which a minute will reverse.

For I have known them all already, known them all:
50 Have known the evenings, mornings, afternoons,
I have measured out my life with coffee spoons;
I know the voices dying with a dying fall
Beneath the music from a further room.
    So how should I presume?

And I have known the eyes already, known them all—
The eyes that fix you in a formulated phrase,
And when I am formulated, sprawling on a pin,
When I am pinned and wriggling on the wall,
Then how should I begin
60 To spit out all the butt-ends of my days and ways?
    And how should I presume?

And I have known the arms already, known them all—
Arms that are braceleted and white and bare
(But in the lamplight, downed with light brown hair!)
Is it perfume from a dress
That makes me so digress?
Arms that lie along a table, or wrap about a shawl.
    And should I then presume?
    And how should I begin?

              *   *   *

70 Shall I say, I have gone at dusk through narrow streets
And watched the smoke that rises from the pipes
Of lonely men in shirt-sleeves, leaning out of windows? . . .

I should have been a pair of ragged claws
Scuttling across the floors of silent seas.

              *   *   *

And the afternoon, the evening, sleeps so peacefully!
Smoothed by long fingers,

Asleep . . . tired . . . or it malingers,
Stretched on the floor, here beside you and me.
Should I, after tea and cakes and ices,
80   Have the strength to force the moment to its crisis?
But though I have wept and fasted, wept and prayed,
Though I have seen my head (grown slightly bald) brought in upon
   a platter,[3]
I am no prophet—and here's no great matter;
I have seen the moment of my greatness flicker,
And I have seen the eternal Footman hold my coat, and snicker,
And in short, I was afraid.

And would it have been worth it, after all,
After the cups, the marmalade, the tea,
Among the porcelain, among some talk of you and me,
90   Would it have been worth while,
To have bitten off the matter with a smile,
To have squeezed the universe into a ball
To roll it toward some overwhelming question,
To say: "I am Lazarus,[4] come from the dead,
Come back to tell you all, I shall tell you all"—
If one, settling a pillow by her head,
   Should say: "That is not what I meant at all;
   That is not it, at all."

And would it have been worth it, after all,
100   Would it have been worth while,
After the sunsets and the dooryards and the sprinkled streets,
After the novels, after the teacups, after the skirts that trail along
   the floor—
And this, and so much more?—
It is impossible to say just what I mean!
But as if a magic lantern threw the nerves in patterns on a screen:
Would it have been worth while
If one, settling a pillow or throwing off a shawl,
And turning toward the window, should say:

---

[3] When Salome, the wife of Herod Antipater, governor of Judea, so pleased her
husband by her dancing that he promised to grant whatever she desired, she demanded the head of John the Baptist on a platter. (Matthew 14:3–11; Mark
6:16–28).
[4] Jesus raised Lazarus from the dead after he had been four days in his grave.
(John 11:1–44).

"That is not it at all,
110 That is not what I meant, at all."

*   *   *

No! I am not Prince Hamlet, nor was meant to be;
Am an attendant lord, one that will do
To swell a progress, start a scene or two,
Advise the prince; no doubt, an easy tool,
Deferential, glad to be of use,
Politic, cautious, and meticulous;
Full of high sentence, but a bit obtuse;
At times, indeed, almost ridiculous—
Almost, at times, the Fool.

120 I grow old . . . I grow old . . .
I shall wear the bottoms of my trousers rolled.

Shall I part my hair behind? Do I dare to eat a peach?
I shall wear white flannel trousers, and walk upon the beach.
I have heard the mermaids singing, each to each.

I do not think that they will sing to me.

I have seen them riding seaward on the waves
Combing the white hair of the waves blown back
When the wind blows the water white and black.

We have lingered in the chambers of the sea
130 By sea-girls wreathed with seaweed red and brown
Till human voices wake us, and we drown.

Dulce et Decorum Est   *Wilfred Owen*

Bent double, like old beggars under sacks,
Knock-kneed, coughing like hags, we cursed through sludge,
Till on the haunting flares we turned our backs,
And towards our distant rest began to trudge.
Men marched asleep. Many had lost their boots,
But limped on, blood-shod. All went lame, all blind;

Drunk with fatigue; deaf even to the hoots
Of gas-shells dropping softly behind.

Gas! GAS! Quick, boys!—An ecstasy of fumbling,
10   Fitting the clumsy helmets just in time,
But someone still was yelling out and stumbling
And flound'ring like a man in fire or lime.—
Dim through the misty panes and thick green light,
As under a green sea, I saw him drowning.

In all my dreams before my helpless sight
He plunges at me, guttering, choking, drowning.

If in some smothering dreams, you too could pace
Behind the wagon that we flung him in,
And watch the white eyes writhing in his face,
20   His hanging face, like a devil's sick of sin,
If you could hear, at every jolt, the blood
Come gargling from the froth-corrupted lungs
Bitten as the cud
Of vile, incurable sores on innocent tongues,—
My friend, you would not tell with such high zest
To children ardent for some desperate glory,
The old Lie: *Dulce et decorum est
Pro patria mori.*[1]

The Parable of the Old Men and the Young[2]

Wilfred Owen

So Abram rose, and clave the wood, and went,
And took the fire with him, and a knife.
And as they sojourned both of them together,
Isaac the first-born spake and said, "My Father,
Behold the preparations, fire and iron,
But where the lamb for this burnt-offering?"

---

[1] A quotation from Horace: "It is sweet and proper to die for one's country."
[2] See Genesis 12–13 for the Biblical account of Abraham and Isaac.

Then Abram bound the youth with belts and straps,
And builded parapets and trenches there,
And stretched forth the knife to slay his son.
10 When lo! an angel called him out of heaven,
Saying, "Lay not thy hand upon the lad,
Neither do anything to him. Behold,
A ram, caught in a thicket by its horns;
Offer the Ram of Pride instead of him."
But the old man would not so, but slew his son,—
And half the seed of Europe, one by one.

Strange Meeting   *Wilfred Owen*

It seemed that out of battle I escaped
Down some profound dull tunnel, long since scooped
Through granites which titanic wars had groined.
Yet also there encumbered sleepers groaned,
Too fast in thought or death to be bestirred.
Then, as I probed them, one sprang up, and stared
With piteous recognition in fixed eyes,
Lifting distressful hands as if to bless.
And by his smile, I knew that sullen hall,
10 By his dead smile I knew we stood in Hell.
With a thousand pains that vision's face was grained,
Yet no blood reached there from the upper ground,
And no guns thumped, or down the flues made moan.
"Strange friend," I said, "here is no cause to mourn."
"None," said the other, "save the undone years,
The hopelessness. Whatever hope is yours,
Was my life also; I went hunting wild
After the wildest beauty in the world,
Which lies not calm in eyes, or braided hair,
20 But mocks the steady running of the hour,
And if it grieves, grieves richlier than here.
For by my glee might many men have laughed,
And of my weeping something had been left,
Which must die now. I mean the truth untold,

The pity of war, the pity war distilled.
Now men will go content with what we spoiled.
Or, discontent, boil bloody, and be spilled.
They will be swift with swiftness of the tigress,
None will break ranks, though nations trek from progress.
30 Courage was mine, and I had mystery,
Wisdom was mine, and I had mastery;
To miss the march of this retreating world
Into vain citadels that are not walled.
Then, when much blood had clogged their chariot-wheels
I would go up and wash them from sweet wells,
Even with truths that lie too deep for taint.
I would have poured my spirit without stint
But not through wounds; not on the cess of war.
Foreheads of men have bled where no wounds were.
40 I am the enemy you killed, my friend.
I knew you in this dark; for so you frowned
Yesterday through me as you jabbed and killed.
I parried; but my hands were loath and cold.
Let us sleep now. . . ."

Diogenes[1]   *Morris Bishop*

Diogenes lived in a tub,
Eating the plainest of grub;
And eminent people he'd snub.
He apparently did it for pub-
      licity.

Alexander the Great had the whim
To call; he looked over the rim
Of the tub. But the scholar was grim;
And "Kindly move out of my glim!"
Was all to be got out of him;

[1] A noted Greek cynic philosopher who lived from about 412 to 323 B.C., and, at least part of that time, according to legend, in a tub.

10   Which was thought at the time to be sim-
      plicity.

But what he was after, we know,
Was to get people talking, and so
To make his philosophy go,
And make the world conscious of sto-
      icity.

And what were the views of this cub?
Well, really, you know, there's the rub.
I cannot recall, like a dub.
But I know that he lived in a tub!
And there is the trouble with pub-
      licity!

Lines to a Daughter—Any Daughter   *Agnes Rogers Allen*

One of the things that you really should know
Is when to say "yes," and when to say "no."
It's terribly, terribly risky to guess
At when to say "no" and when to say "yes."
Girls who are slaving for Woolworth and Kress
Lament for the day when they might have said "yes,"
Others are crying at night apropos
Of moments when clearly they should have said "no."

There aren't any textbooks, there aren't many rules,
10   The subject's neglected in orthodox schools.
Experience helps, but you seldom remember
Your April mistakes by the first of November.
You can't be consistent; there's often a reason
For changing your mind with a change in the season.
You may be quite right in accepting at seven
Suggestions you'd better refuse at eleven.

Perhaps you'll consider these tentative hints:
"No" to a dirndl of highly glazed chintz,
"Yes" to the bashful young man at the dance,

20 "No" to the man who's been living in France,
   "Yes" to a walk in the park in the rain,
   "Yes" if he asks for a chance to explain,
   "No" to all slacks unless you're too thin,
   "No" to that impulse to telephone him,

   "Yes" to a baby, and "no" to a bore,
   "No" if you're asked if you've heard it before,
   "Yes" to the friend when she says, "Don't you think
   Rabbit is just as becoming as mink?"
   "Yes" to a Saturday, "no" to a Monday,
30 "Yes" to a salad and "no" to a sundae,
   "No" to a wastrel and "yes" to a ranger,
   "No" to a toady, and "yes" to a stranger

   (That is, providing you use some discretion),
   "No" to three cocktails in rapid succession,
   "No" to magenta and chocolate brown,
   "Yes" to a whisper and "no" to a frown,
   "No" if he's misunderstood by his wife,
   "Yes" if you want it the rest of your life.
   Remember, my darling, careers and caresses
40 Depend on our choices of "noes" and of "yesses."

---

nobody loses all the time   *e. e. cummings*

nobody loses all the time

i had an uncle named
Sol who was a born failure and
nearly everybody said he should have gone
into vaudeville perhaps because my Uncle Sol could
sing McCann He Was A Diver on Xmas Eve like Hell Itself
      which
may or may not account for the fact that my Uncle

Sol indulged in that possibly most inexcusable
of all to use a highfalootin phrase
10 luxuries that is or to

wit farming and be
it needlessly
added

my Uncle Sol's farm
failed because the chickens
ate the vegetables so
my Uncle Sol had a
chicken farm till the skunks
ate the chickens when

20 my Uncle Sol
had a skunk farm but
the skunks caught cold and
died and so
my Uncle Sol imitated the
skunks in a subtle manner

or by drowning himself in the watertank
but somebody who'd given my Uncle Sol a Victor
Victrola and records while he lived presented to
him upon the auspicious occasion of his decease a
30 scrumptious not to mention splendiferous funeral with
tall boys in black gloves and flowers and everything and

i remember we all cried like the Missouri
when my Uncle Sol's coffin lurched because
somebody pressed a button
(and down went
my Uncle
Sol

and started a worm farm)

The Persian Version   *Robert Graves*

Truth-loving Persians do not dwell upon
The trivial skirmish fought near Marathon.[1]

[1] Site of the decisive Greek victory over the Persians (490 B.C.)

As for the Greek theatrical tradition
Which represents that summer's expedition
Not as a mere reconnaissance in force
By three brigades of foot and one of horse
(Their left flank covered by some obsolete
Light craft detached from the main Persian fleet)
But as a grandiose, ill-starred attempt
10 To conquer Greece—they treat it with contempt;
And only incidentally refute
Major Greek claims, by stressing what repute
The Persian monarch and the Persian nation
Won by this salutary demonstration:
Despite a strong defence and adverse weather
All arms combined magnificently together.

Solitary Observation Brought Back from a Sojourn in Hell

Louise Bogan

At midnight tears
Run into your ears.

The Dream

Louise Bogan

O God, in the dream the terrible horse began
To paw at the air, and make for me with his blows.
Fear kept for thirty-five years poured through his mane,
And retribution equally old, or nearly, breathed through his
    nose.

Coward complete, I lay and wept on the ground
When some strong creature appeared, and leapt for the rein.
Another woman, as I lay half in a swound
Leapt in the air, and clutched at the leather and chain.

Give him, she said, something of yours as a charm.
¹⁰ Throw him, she said, some poor thing you alone claim.
No, no, I cried, he hates me; he's out for harm,
And whether I yield or not, it is all the same.

But, like a lion in a legend, when I flung the glove
Pulled from my sweating, my cold right hand,
The terrible beast, that no one may understand,
Came to my side, and put down his head in love.

Deferred   *Langston Hughes*

This year, maybe, do you think I can graduate?
I'm already two years late.
Dropped out six months when I was seven,
a year when I was eleven,
then got put back when we came North.
To get through high at twenty's kind of late—
But maybe this year I can graduate.

Maybe now I can have that white enamel stove
I dreamed about when we first fell in love
¹⁰ eighteen years ago.
But you know,
rooming and everything
then kids,
cold-water flat and all that.
But now my daughter's married
And my boy's most grown—
quit school to work—
and where we're moving
there ain't no stove—
²⁰ Maybe I can buy that white enamel stove!

Me, I always did want to study French.
It don't make sense—
I'll never go to France,
but night schools teach French.

Now at last I've got a job
where I get off at five,
in time to wash and dress,
so, si'l-vous plait, I'll study French!

Someday,
30 I'm gonna buy two new suits
at once!

All I want is
one more bottle of gin.

All I want is to see
my furniture paid for.

All I want is a wife who will
work with me and not against me. Say,
baby, could you see your way clear?

Heaven, heaven, is my home!
40 This world I'll leave behind
When I set my feet in glory
I'll have a throne for mine!

I want to pass the civil service.

I want a television set.

You know, as old as I am,
I ain't never
owned a decent radio yet?

I'd like to take up Bach.

Montage
50 *of a dream*
deferred.

Buddy, have you heard?

Harlem

Langston Hughes

What happens to a dream deferred?

Does it dry up
like a raisin in the sun?
Or fester like a sore—
And then run?
Does it stink like rotten meat?
Or crust and sugar over—
like a syrupy sweet?

Maybe it just sags
10 like a heavy load.

Or does it explode?

Any Man's Advice to His Son

Kenneth Fearing

If you have lost the radio beam, then guide yourself by the sun or the stars.
(By the North Star at night, and in daytime by the compass and the sun.)
Should the sky be overcast and there are neither stars nor a sun, then steer by dead reckoning.
If the wind and direction and speed are not known, then trust to your wits and your luck.

Do you follow me? Do you understand? Or is this too difficult to learn?
But you must and you will, it is important that you do.
Because there may be troubles even greater than these that I have said.

Because, remember this: Trust no man fully.
Remember: If you must shoot at another man squeeze, do not jerk

the trigger. Otherwise you may miss and die, yourself, at the hand
of some other man's son.

10 And remember: In all this world there is nothing so easily squan-
dered, or once gone, so completely lost as life.

I tell you this because I remember you when you were small,
And because I remember all your monstrous infant boasts and lies,
And the way you smiled, and how you ran and climbed, as no one
else quite did, and how you fell and were bruised,
And because there is no other person, anywhere on earth, who re-
members these things as clearly as I do now.

Very Like a Whale   *Ogden Nash*

One thing that literature would be greatly the better for
Would be a more restricted employment by authors of simile and
metaphor.
Authors of all races, be they Greeks, Romans, Teutons or Celts,
Can't seem just to say that anything is the thing it is but have to go
out of their way to say that it is like something else.
What does it mean when we are told
That the Assyrian came down like a wolf on the fold? [1]
In the first place, George Gordon Byron had had enough experience
To know that it probably wasn't just one Assyrian, it was a lot of
Assyrians.
However, as too many arguments are apt to induce apoplexy and thus
hinder longevity,

10 We'll let it pass as one Assyrian for the sake of brevity.
Now then, this particular Assyrian, the one whose cohorts were
gleaming in purple and gold,
Just what does the poet mean when he says he came down like a wolf
on the fold?
In heaven and earth more than is dreamed of in our philosophy there
are a great many things,
But I don't imagine that among them there is a wolf with purple
and gold cohorts or purple and gold anythings.

[1] See p. 508.

No, no, Lord Byron, before I'll believe that this Assyrian was actually like a wolf I must have some kind of proof;

Did he run on all fours and did he have a hairy tail and a big red mouth and big white teeth and did he say Woof woof woof?

Frankly I think it very unlikely, and all you were entitled to say, at the very most,

Was that the Assyrian cohorts came down like a lot of Assyrian cohorts about to destroy the Hebrew host.

But that wasn't fancy enough for Lord Byron, oh dear me no, he had to invent a lot of figures of speech and then interpolate them.

20 With the result that whenever you mention Old Testament soldiers to people they say Oh yes, they're the ones that a lot of wolves dressed up in gold and purple ate them.

That's the kind of thing that's being done all the time by poets, from Homer to Tennyson;

They're always comparing ladies to lilies and veal to venison,

And they always say things like that the snow is a white blanket after a winter storm.

Oh it is, is it, all right then, you sleep under a six-inch blanket of snow and I'll sleep under a half-inch blanket of unpoetical blanket material and we'll see which one keeps warm,

And after that maybe you'll begin to comprehend dimly

What I mean by too much metaphor and simile.

Polonius, Yes, Polonius, No[1]   *Ogden Nash*

I have always regretted that Hamlet slew Polonius,

With whom I think I would have got along very harmonious.

Polonius said, "Neither a borrower nor a lender be,"

And that applies to me,

Because, as he continued, "loan oft loseth both itself and friend,"

Which is grist for my mill, since I both have no credit to borrow on and no loans to lend.

However, Polonius also said, "Costly thy habit as thy purse can buy,"

[1] See p. 487.

Which is surely a personal matter between the little tailor around the
    corner and I.
If I want to dress parsimonious,
10 What's that to Polonius?
My own rule of thumb is, "Costly thy raiment
As the first payment,"
But even had I the gold of Ophir,[2]
I'd still feel entitled to go around wearing one wedgie and one loafer.
Obviously Polonius was a busybody whom no snub could embarrass,
So on second thought I don't regret that Hamlet stabbed him behind
    the arras.[3]

The Angry Man   *Phyllis McGinley*

The other day I chanced to meet
An angry man upon the street—
A man of wrath, a man of war,
A man who truculently bore
Over his shoulder, like a lance,
A banner labeled "Tolerance."

And when I asked him why he strode
Thus scowling down the human road,
Scowling, he answered, "I am he
10 Who champions total liberty—
Intolerance being, ma'am, a state
No tolerant man can tolerate."

"When I meet rogues," he cried, "who choose
To cherish oppositional views,
Lady, like this, and in this manner,
I lay about me with my banner
Till they cry mercy, ma'am." His blows
Rained proudly on prospective foes.

---

[2] A land rich in gold from which Solomon got his wealth (I Kings 12).
[3] A wall hanging, especially one made of tapestry.

²⁰ Fearful, I turned and left him there
Still muttering, as he thrashed the air,
"Let the Intolerant beware!"

The Unknown Citizen   *W. H. Auden*

(TO JS/07/M/378   THIS MARBLE MONUMENT IS ERECTED
BY THE STATE)

He was found by the Bureau of Statistics to be
One against whom there was no official complaint,
And all the reports on his conduct agree
That, in the modern sense of an old-fashioned word, he was a saint,
For in everything he did he served the Greater Community.
Except for the War till the day he retired
He worked in a factory and never got fired,
But satisfied his employers, Fudge Motors Inc.
Yet he wasn't a scab or odd in his views,
¹⁰ For his Union reports that he paid his dues,
(Our report on his Union shows it was sound)
And our Social Psychology workers found
That he was popular with his mates and liked a drink.
The Press are convinced that he bought a paper every day
And that his reactions to advertisements were normal in every way.
Policies taken out in his name prove that he was fully insured,
And his Health-card shows he was once in hospital but left it cured.
Both Producers Research and High-Grade Living declare
He was fully sensible to the advantages of the Installment Plan
²⁰ And had everything necessary to the Modern Man,
A phonograph, a radio, a car and a frigidaire.
Our researchers into Public Opinion are content
That he held the proper opinions for the time of year;
When there was peace, he was for peace; when there was war, he
went.
He was married and added five children to the population,
Which our Eugenist says was the right number for a parent of his
generation,

And our teachers report that he never interfered with their education.
Was he free? Was he happy? The question is absurd:
Had anything been wrong, we should certainly have heard.

Nothing Is Given: *W. H. Auden*
We Must Find Our Law

Nothing is given: we must find our law.
Great buildings jostle in the sun for domination;
Behind them stretch like sorry vegetation
The low recessive houses of the poor.

We have no destiny assigned us:
Nothing is certain but the body; we plan
To better ourselves; the hospitals alone remind us
Of the equality of man.

Children are really loved here, even by police:
10 They speak of years before the big were lonely,
And will be lost.

                    And only
The brass bands throbbing in the parks foretell
Some future reign of happiness and peace.

We learn to pity and rebel.

Dolor   *Theodore Roethke*

I have known the inexorable sadness of pencils,
Neat in their boxes, dolor of pad and paper-weight,
All the misery of manila folders and mucilage,
Desolation in immaculate public places,
Lonely reception room, lavatory, switchboard,
The unalterable pathos of basin and pitcher,

Ritual of multigraph, paper-clip, comma,
Endless duplication of lives and objects.
And I have seen dust from the walls of institutions,
10 Finer than flour, alive, more dangerous than silica,
Sift, almost invisible, through long afternoons of tedium,
Dripping a fine film on nails and delicate eyebrows,
Glazing the pale hair, the duplicate gray standard faces.

An Elementary School Classroom in a Slum
Stephen Spender

Far far from gusty waves, these children's faces.
Like rootless weeds the torn hair round their paleness.
The tall girl with her weighed-down head. The paper-
seeming boy with rat's eyes. The stunted unlucky heir
Of twisted bones, reciting a father's gnarled disease,
His lesson from his desk. At back of the dim class,
One unnoted, sweet and young: his eyes live in a dream
Of squirrels' game, in tree room, other than this.

On sour cream walls, donations. Shakespeare's head
10 Cloudless at dawn, civilized dome riding all cities.
Belled, flowery, Tyrolese valley. Open-handed map
Awarding the world its world. And yet, for these
Children, these windows, not this world, are world,
Where all their future's painted with a fog,
A narrow street sealed in with a lead sky,
Far far from rivers, capes, and stars of words.

Surely Shakespeare is wicked, the map a bad example
With ships and sun and love tempting them to steal—
For lives that slyly turn in their cramped holes
20 From fog to endless night? On their slag heap, these children
Wear skins peeped through by bones and spectacles of steel
With mended glass, like bottle bits on stones.
All of their time and space are foggy slum
So blot their maps with slums as big as doom.

Unless, governor, teacher, inspector, visitor,
This map becomes their window and these windows
That open on their lives like crouching tombs
Break, O break open, till they break the town
And show the children to the fields and all their world
30   Azure on their sands, to let their tongues
Run naked into books, the white and green leaves open
The history theirs whose language is the sun.

In Order To   *Kenneth Patchen*

Apply for the position (I've forgotten now for what) I
had to marry the Second Mayor's daughter by twelve noon.
The order arrived three minutes of.

I already had a wife; the Second Mayor was childless:
but I did it.

Next they told me to shave off my father's beard. All
right. No matter that he'd been a eunuch, and had succumbed
in early childhood: I did it, I shaved him.

Then they told me to burn a village; next, a fair-sized town;
then, a city; a bigger city; a small, down-at-heels country;
then one of 'the great powers'; then another (another, another)— In fact, they went right on until they'd told me
to burn up every man-made thing on the face of the earth!
And I did it, I burned away every last trace, I left nothing,
nothing of any kind whatever.

Then they told me to blow it all to hell and gone! And I
blew it all to hell and gone (oh, didn't I!) . . .

Now, they said, put it back together again; put it all back
the way it was when you started.

Well . . . it was my turn then to tell *them* something!
Shucks, I didn't want any job that bad.

In the Naked Bed, in Plato's Cave   *Delmore Schwartz*

In the naked bed, in Plato's cave,[1]
Reflected headlights slowly slid the wall,
Carpenters hammered under the shaded window,
Wind troubled the window curtains all night long,
A fleet of trucks strained uphill, grinding,
Their freights covered, as usual.
The ceiling lightened again, the slanting diagram
Slid slowly forth.
        Hearing the milkman's chop,
His striving up the stair, the bottle's chink,
I rose from bed, lit a cigarette,
10 And walked to the window. The stony street
Displayed the stillness in which buildings stand,
The street-lamp's vigil and the horse's patience.
The winter sky's pure capital
Turned me back to bed with exhausted eyes.

Strangeness grew in the motionless air. The loose
Film grayed. Shaking wagons, hooves' waterfalls,
Sounded far off, increasing, louder and nearer.
A car coughed, starting. Morning, softly
Melting the air, lifted the half-covered chair
20 From underseas, kindled the looking-glass,
Distinguished the dresser and the white wall.
The bird called tentatively, whistled, called,
Bubbled and whistled, so! Perplexed, still wet
With sleep, affectionate, hungry and cold. So, so,
O son of man, the ignorant night, the travail
Of early morning, the mystery of beginning
Again and again,
        while Time is unforgiven.

[1] Plato illustrated his belief that the material world is illusory by picturing men as bound in a cave with the shadows cast on the wall by a fire behind them as their only reality.

In My Craft or Sullen Art

Dylan Thomas

In my craft or sullen art
Exercised in the still night
When only the moon rages
And the lovers lie abed
With all their griefs in their arms,
I labour by singing light
Not for ambition or bread
Or the strut and trade of charms
On the ivory stages
10 But for the common wages
Of their most secret heart.
Not for the proud man apart
From the raging moon I write
On these spindrift pages
Not for the towering dead
With their nightingales and psalms
But for the lovers, their arms
Round the griefs of the ages,
Who pay no praise or wages
20 Nor heed my craft or art.

Do Not Go Gentle into That Good Night

Dylan Thomas

Do not go gentle into that good night,
Old age should burn and rave at close of day;
Rage, rage against the dying of the light.

Though wise men at their end know dark is right,
Because their words had forked no lightning they
Do not go gentle into that good night.

Good men, the last wave by, crying how bright
Their frail deeds might have danced in a green bay,
Rage, rage against the dying of the light.

¹⁰ Wild men who caught and sang the sun in flight,
And learn, too late, they grieved it on its way,
Do not go gentle into that good night.

Grave men, near death, who see with blinding sight
Blind eyes could blaze like meteors and be gay,
Rage, rage against the dying of the light.

And you, my father, there on the sad height,
Curse, bless, me now with your fierce tears, I pray.
Do not go gentle into that good night.
Rage, rage against the dying of the light.

The Death of the Ball Turret Gunner   *Randall Jarrell*

From my mother's sleep I fell into the State,
And I hunched in its belly till my wet fur froze.
Six miles from earth, loosed from its dream of life,
I woke to black flak[1] and the nightmare fighters.[2]
When I died they washed me out of the turret with a hose.

To David, About His Education   *Howard Nemerov*

The world is full of mostly invisible things,
And there is no way but putting the mind's eye,
Or its nose, in a book, to find them out,
Things like the square root of Everest
Or how many times Byron goes into Texas,
Or whether the law of the excluded middle
Applies west of the Rockies. For these
And the like reasons, you have to go to school
And study books and listen to what you are told,

[1] Anti-aircraft shell bursts.
[2] Fighter planes.

¹⁰ And sometimes try to remember. Though I don't know
   What you will do with the mean annual rainfall
   On Plato's Republic, or the calorie content
   Of the Diet of Worms,¹ such things are said to be
   Good for you, and you will have to learn them
   In order to become one of the grown-ups
   Who sees invisible things neither steadily nor whole,
   But keeps gravely the grand confusion of the world
   Under his hat, which is where it belongs,
   And teaches small children to do this in their turn.

The Triumph of Education   *Howard Nemerov*

   The children's eyes were like lakes of the sea
   And baffling with their false serenity
   When they were told, and given all the cause,
   "There is no Santa Claus."

   The children's eyes did not become more bright
   Or curious of sexual delight
   When someone said, "Man couples like the beast,
   The Stork does not exist."

   The children's eyes, like smoke or drifted snow,
¹⁰ White shifted over white, refused to show
   They suffered loss: "At first it may seem odd—
   There isn't any God."

   The children, not perturbed or comforted,
   Heard silently the news of their last bed:
   "For moral care you need not stint your breath,
   There's no Life after Death."

   The children's eyes grew hot, they glowed like stoves.
   Ambitious, and equipped with all our proofs,
   They ran forth little women, little men,
²⁰ And were not children then.

¹ At which Martin Luther was declared a heretic.

To be a giant and keep quiet about it,
To stay in one's own place;
To stand for the constant presence of process
And always to seem the same;
To be steady as a rock and always trembling,
Having the hard appearance of death
With the soft, fluent nature of growth,
One's Being deceptively armored,
One's Becoming deceptively vulnerable;
10 To be so tough, and take the light so well,
Freely providing forbidden knowledge
Of so many things about heaven and earth
For which we should otherwise have no word—
Poems or people are rarely so lovely,
And even when they have great qualities
They tend to tell you rather than exemplify
What they believe themselves to be about,
While from the moving silence of trees,
Whether in storm or calm, in leaf and naked,
20 Night or day, we draw conclusions of our own,
Sustaining and unnoticed as our breath,
And perilous also—though there has never been
A critical tree—about the nature of things.

Notes on Authors

AKUTAGAWA, RYONOSUKE (ä·kōō·tä·gä'·wä) (1892–1927), Japanese short story writer, was born in Tokyo, attended Tokyo Imperial University, and lived all his life in the capital. He produced a number of poems and essays and one brief novel, but most of his creative energies were devoted to some one hundred and fifty stories, which were published in seven collections. Many have been translated into English, French, German, and Spanish. His best known work, *Rashōmon*, was published in 1915. In 1927 he committed suicide by carefully administering an overdose of veronal.

ALLEN, AGNES ROGERS (b. 1893), American journalist and critic, was born in Hagerstown, Maryland, and is a Vassar graduate. In addition to a career in advertising, promotion, and editorial work, she has written several books including *Vassar Women* (1940), *From Man to Machine* (1941), and *Women Are Here to Stay* (1949). She collaborated with her husband, the late Frederick L. Allen, on several books of pictures and text depicting American life; among these are *The American Procession* (1933), *Metropolis* (1934), and *I Remember Distinctly* (1947).

ANDERSON, SHERWOOD (1876–1941), American novelist and short story writer, was born in Camden, Ohio, one of seven children. He left school frequently to work at odd jobs, and although he attended Wittenberg College briefly, his formal schooling seems to have ended when he was fourteen. He served in Cuba during the Spanish American War; later he became manager of a paint factory, a job he left abruptly one day to go to Chicago to become a writer. His first books were published through the efforts of the "Chicago group" of writers—Theodore

Dreiser, Floyd Dell, and others. In 1924 he became a newspaper editor, a job he kept for many years. Like D. H. Lawrence, Anderson was a rebel against modern industrial civilization. *Winesburg, Ohio* (1919) brought him his first recognition as a writer; these stories and those in *The Triumph of the Egg* (1921) are among his best. *A Story Teller's Story* (1924) is autobiographical.

ARNOLD, MATTHEW (1822–88), English poet and critic, was the son of Thomas Arnold, famous headmaster at Rugby. He was educated at Winchester, Rugby, and Balliol College, Oxford. From 1851–86 he served as an inspector of schools for the government, a position which entailed extensive travel both in England and on the continent. He was professor of poetry at Oxford from 1857–67. His works include *Poems* (1853–54), *Essays in Criticism, First Series* (1865), *Culture and Anarchy* (1869), and *Literature and Dogma* (1873).

ARRABAL, FERNANDO (är·rä·bäl′) (b. 1932), a young Spanish playwright, was born in Mellilla at the beginning of the Spanish Civil War, and grew up under the military dictatorship of Franco. In 1955 he went to Paris to live and now writes in French. His novel *Bael Babylone* (1961) evokes the conflicts in present-day Spain. This novel, and three plays of the absurd—*The Automobile Graveyard* (1960), *The Two Executioners* (1960), and *Picnic on the Battlefield* (1960)— have been published in English translations.

AUDEN, W. H. (b. 1907), Anglo-American poet and critic, was born in York, England, and educated at Gresham's School and Christ Church College, Oxford. He taught school for a short time, but soon became one of a group of young London poets. His rebellion against his conservative background led him to socialistic ideas; he drove an ambulance for the Loyalists in the Spanish Civil War, but later he lost faith in left-wing solutions for social problems. In 1939 he came to the United States and has become an American citizen. His poetry reflects the modern age; its themes are political, scientific, philosophic and religious. Among his publications are *Collected Poems* (1945), *Selected Poetry* (1960), and a collection of essays, *The Dyer's Hand* (1963). *The Age of Anxiety* poetry collection received the Pulitzer Prize in 1948.

BISHOP, MORRIS (b. 1893), American educator, humorist, and critic, was born in Willard, New York, and educated at Cornell University, where he has taught romance languages for many years. In 1964 he served as President of the Modern Language Association. He is the editor of *A Treasury of British Humor* (1942) and the author of many books. His chief interest has been in biography, and he has written two biographies of explorers and three of literary men. His light verse has appeared in the *Saturday Evening Post* and *The New Yorker*, and has been collected in *Spilt Milk* (1942) and *A Bowl of Bishop* (1954).

BLAKE, WILLIAM (1757–1827), English mystic, poet, and engraver, was the son of a London tradesman. After attending a drawing school, he was apprenticed at age fourteen to an engraver. Later he studied art at the Royal Academy. He began writing poems when he was twelve; his poems and the illustrations for them reflect his deep imagination and mysticism. He has been considered both a lunatic and a genius. His books include *Poetical Sketches* (1783), *Songs of Innocence* (1789), *Songs of Experience* (1794), and prophetic and mystical works, among them *The Book of Thel* (1787), *The Marriage of Heaven and Hell* (1790), *Milton* (1804), and *Jerusalem* (1804–18). His illustrations of such works as *The Divine Comedy, Paradise Lost,* and *The Book of Job* are considered by many to be great works of art.

BOGAN, LOUISE (b. 1897), American poet and critic, was born in Livermore Falls, Maine, and educated in New England country schools and at the Girls' Latin School in Boston. Since 1931 she has been poetry reviewer for *The New Yorker*. She has won numerous awards from *Poetry* magazine and in 1954 received the Bollingen Prize in Poetry for her *Collected Poems, 1923-53*. Her critical writing is collected in *Achievement in American Poetry, 1900–50* (1951) and in *Selected Criticism* (1955).

BROWNING, ROBERT (1812–89), English poet, was born in London. His father, a clerk in the Bank of England, had deep literary and artistic tastes, and much of Browning's education was received from his father's extensive library; his love of music and religious convictions came from his mother. He married the poet, Elizabeth Barrett, in 1846, and they lived in Italy until her death in 1861, when he returned to England. After publishing several books of poems, he wrote what is considered his most famous work, *The Ring and The Book* (1868–69), a long poem of twelve dramatic monologues about a Roman murder case. Browning's poetry shows deep insight into his characters. One of his best collections of shorter poems is *Men and Women* (1855).

BURNS, ROBERT (1759–96), the son of a poor farmer, was born near Ayr, Scotland. At home he learned many legends and songs of the Scottish peasants, although he had little formal education. He worked as a farm laborer, and published his first book, *Poems: Chiefly in the Scottish Dialect,* in 1786, in order to get passage money to emigrate to Jamaica. The book's success changed his plans and he became a social and literary sensation in Edinburgh where he stayed for about two years. He then married and settled on a farm at Ellisland, later giving up farming to become an exciseman. Burns' songs and tales are about peasant life in the Scottish lowlands, and are usually in his native Scottish dialect. They are famous for their vitality and human quality.

BYRON, GEORGE GORDON, sixth baron (1788–1824), was an English poet educated at Harrow and at Trinity College, Cambridge, where he published his first poems, *Hours of Idleness* (1807). The book was not well received by the critics, and Byron replied to their criticisms in a witty satirical poem, *English Bards and Scotch Reviewers* (1809). After taking his seat in the House of Lords, Byron and a friend toured Spain and the Mediterranean countries; the resulting poem, *Childe Harold's Pilgrimage,* a political narrative of travels through Southern Europe, brought him fame when its first two cantos were published in 1812. In much of his writing, the Byronic hero was a sad, embittered young man who brooded upon something evil and mysterious in his past. Personal difficulties caused Byron to leave England for the continent in 1816. In 1823 he joined the Greek rebels in their fight for independence, dying of fever the next year at Missolonghi. Among his important works are *Childe Harold* (1812–18), *Manfred* (1817), and *Don Juan* (1818).

CAMPION, THOMAS (1567–1620), English poet and musician, attended Cambridge and studied law at Gray's Inn, but later abandoned law for medicine and had a large medical practice in London. He published several volumes of lyrics for which he supplied both words and music; among these are several *Books of Aires* (1601–17), *Observations on the Arte of English Poesie* (1602), and four masques.

CHEKOV, ANTON (1860–1904), Russian novelist, dramatist, and short story writer, was the son of an ex-serf. He took a degree in medicine at the University of Moscow in 1884 and began practicing, although his own health was impaired. He completed around a thousand stories and a number of distinguished plays before dying of tuberculosis at the age of forty-four. Some of his plays are *The Sea Gull* (1898), *Uncle Vanya* (1899), *The Three Sisters* (1901), and *The Cherry Orchard* (1904); his fiction includes *The Chorus Girl* (1884), *Peasants* (1897), and *The Bishop* (1902).

CLARK, WALTER VAN TILBURG (b. 1909), American novelist and short story writer, was born in East Orland, Maine, but moved to Nevada at the age of eight. He later attended the University of Nevada, where his father was President, and the University of Vermont. He taught English and coached basketball for ten years in the East before returning to the West, where he has since lived and about which he has written. His novels include *The Ox-Bow Incident* (1940), *The City of Trembling Leaves* (1945), and *The Track of the Cat* (1949). His short stories are collected in *The Watchful Gods and Other Stories* (1950).

CLOUGH, ARTHUR HUGH (klŭf) (1819–61), English poet and educator, expressed his religious conflicts in his works. His books include *The Bothie of Tober-na-vvolich* (1848), *Amours de Voyage* (1858), *Mari Magno* (1862), and *Dipsychus* (1862). Matthew Arnold wrote the elegy *Thyrsis* in Clough's memory.

COLLINS, WILLIAM (1721–59), English poet, began writing poetry while an undergraduate at Oxford. Collins suffered from poverty and illness all his life, becoming insane becfore his death. His legacy of poems is small, consisting chiefly of odes, the best-known being "Ode to Evening" (1746), "How Sleep the Brave" (1746), and a dirge for Shakespeare's *Cymbeline* (1744). His collected *Odes* were published in 1747.

COWPER, WILLIAM (kō͞o′ pēr) (1731–1800), English poet, began late in life to write hymns, dialectic verse, nature lyrics, and introspective religious poetry. From his twenty-fourth year he suffered from a sense of overwhelming guilt and despair and intermittent attacks of insanity. His hymns are collected in *Olney Hymns* (1779), and "The Task" (1785) is his most famous poem.

CRANE, STEPHEN (1871–1900), American short story writer, poet, and novelist, was born in Newark, New Jersey, the son of a Methodist minister. He attended public schools in New Jersey and New York and studied one year at Lafayette College and another at Syracuse University, before becoming a reporter and free-lance writer. He was a war correspondent in Cuba and Greece, then went to England and Germany, where he died of tuberculosis before his twenty-ninth birthday. His first novel, *Maggie, a Girl of the Streets* (1893), was not a success with critics or readers; *The Red Badge of Courage* (1895), a realistic story of a civil war soldier in battle, brought him overnight fame. *The Black Riders* (1895) and *War Is Kind* (1899) are collections of his poems.

CUMMINGS, E(DWARD) E(STLIN) (1894–1962), American poet, whose father was a Congregational minister and a Harvard Professor of English, was born in Cambridge, Massachusetts. He was graduated from Harvard in 1915 and received his M.A. a year later. He served in an American ambulance corps in France in 1917, lived with American expatriates in France after World War I, and later in Greenwich Village. His works include *Tulips and Chimneys* (1923), *No Thanks* (1935), *1×1* (1944), and a collection called *Poems, 1923–54* which won him a special citation by the National Book Award Committee in 1955. *The Enormous Room* (1922), a prose account, is based upon his experiences in 1917 when he was confined to a detention camp for three months on an unfounded charge of treasonable correspondence.

DICKINSON, EMILY (1830–86), American poet, was the daughter of a successful lawyer and legislator. She was born and lived most of her life in Amherst, Massachusetts, becoming a recluse in her later life. Of the close to 1800 poems she wrote, only seven were published during her lifetime. The definitive edition of her poems was edited by Thomas H. Johnson and published by the Harvard University Press in 1955.

DONNE, JOHN (dŭn) (1573–1631), English metaphysical poet and churchman, was the son of a wealthy London merchant. He attended both Oxford and Cambridge, studied law at the Inns of Court, and participated in two naval expeditions. Brought up as a Roman Catholic, he was converted to Anglicanism and was made Dean of St. Paul's Cathedral in 1621. His works include love poems, religious verse including devotional poems, and the "holy" sonnets, and sermons. Among his works are *Divine Poems* (1607), *Cycle of Holy Sonnets* (1618), and the collection published posthumously in 1633 called *Songs and Sonnets*.

ELIOT, T(HOMAS) S(TERNS) (1888–1965), American poet, playwright, and critic, was born in St. Louis, Missouri, and educated at Harvard, the Sorbonne, and Oxford. He became a resident of London in 1914 and a British citizen in 1927. He was awarded the Nobel Prize for literature in 1948. Among his best-known poems are "The Love Song of J. Alfred Prufrock" (1917), "The Waste Land" (1922), "The Hollow Men" (1925), "Ash Wednesday" (1930), and "Four Quartets" (1943). His plays include *Murder in the Cathedral* (1935), *The Family Reunion* (1939), *The Cocktail Party* (1950), *The Confidential Clerk* (1954), and *The Elder Statesman* (1959). Most of his criticism is available in *Selected Essays* (1950). His *Collected Poems, 1909–62* was published in 1963.

FAULKNER, WILLIAM (1897–1962), American novelist and short story writer, was born in New Albany, Mississippi. After completing the tenth grade, he left high school for a job in his grandfather's bank. During World War I, he joined the Canadian Flying Corps and afterwards attended the University of Mississippi for one year, then worked in a book store, and as a carpenter, house painter, and postmaster before settling down in Oxford to a career of steady writing. Faulkner's novels and short stories are of the deep South; of more than a dozen novels, the following are probably the best known: *Sartoris* (1929), *The Sound and the Fury* (1929), *As I Lay Dying* (1930), *Sanctuary* (1931), *Light in August* (1932), *Absalom, Absalom* (1936), *The Hamlet* (1940), and *A Fable* (1954). He has also written short stories, many of which appear in the *Collected Stories of William Faulkner* (1950). Faulkner was awarded the Nobel Prize for literature in 1950. *A Fable* (1954) received both the National Book Award for fiction and the Pulitzer Prize for literature in 1955.

FEARING, KENNETH (1902–61), American poet and novelist, was born in Chicago and graduated from the University of Wisconsin. He worked as a salesman, mill hand, newspaper reporter, free-lance writer, teacher, novelist and poet. Among his books are *Angel Arms* (1929), *The Hospital* (1939), *Afternoon of a Pawnbroker* (1943), *The Big Clock* (1946), *Stranger at Coney Island* (1948), and *New and Selected Poems* (1956).

FORSTER, E(DWARD) M(ORGAN) (b. 1879), English short story writer, novelist, and critic, was born in London and educated at Tonbridge School and King's College, Cambridge, of which he is now an honorary Fellow. He has lived in Italy, India, and Egypt and has used all three countries as a background for his work. Among his novels are *Where Angels Fear to Tread* (1905), *The Longest Journey* (1907), *A Room with a View* (1908), *Howard's End* (1910), and *A Passage to India* (1927). The latter novel, probably his best known work, depicts the difficulties in human relationships experienced by an educated Indian and a Britisher in India. His short stories appear in *The Celestial Omnibus* (1911) and *The Eternal Moment* (1928) and were brought together in *Collected Tales* (1947). Further works include his study of fiction, *Aspects of the Novel* (1927), and two books of essays— *Abinger Harvest* (1936) and *Two Cheers for Democracy* (1951).

FROST, ROBERT LEE (1875–1963), American poet, was born in San Francisco but lived most of his life in New England. He attended high school in Massachusetts, then went to Dartmouth and Harvard. He farmed and taught school before moving to England in 1912 where his first two collections of poetry—*A Boy's Will* (1913) and *North of Boston* (1914)—were published. Upon his return he resumed farming but also taught at Amherst College and the Bread Loaf School of English in Vermont. He won the Pulitzer Prize for poetry four times. His *Complete Poems* appeared in 1949.

GALSWORTHY, JOHN (1867–1933), English novelist, short story writer, and playwright, was born in Surrey and educated at Harrow and Oxford. His father was a prominent attorney, and Galsworthy studied law; but at twenty-eight he turned to writing. He was awarded the Order of Merit in 1929 and the Nobel Prize in 1932. His most famous work, *The Forsyte Saga,* consists of two series of novels written over his entire career; his best known plays are *Strife* (1909), *Justice* (1910), and *Loyalties* (1922). Collections of short stories include *A Sheaf* (1916), *Five Tales* (1919), *The Burning Spear* (1923), *Captures* (1923), and *Caravan* (1925).

GIRAUDOUX, JEAN (zhē' rō' dōo') (1882–1934), French playwright, novelist, and diplomat, was born in Bellac, a small town in Limousin, which he always called the most beautiful town in the world. He attended the Ecole Normale Supérieure and the Lycée at Chateauraux. He spent a year at Harvard as a lecturer in French and served as a military instructor there during the First World War. When he was twenty-seven, he entered the French foreign service and later became Chief of Press and, eventually, Minister of Propaganda, a post he held until the German occupation. He has written novels, short stories, essays, and plays. Among the plays are *Amphitron 38* (1929), *The Tiger at the Gates* (1935), *Ondine* (1939), *The Madwoman of Chaillot* (1945), and *The Apollo of Bellac* (1942).

GRAVES, ROBERT (b. 1895), English poet and novelist, was born in London and educated at Oxford, where he has been a professor of poetry since 1961. Among his works are his autobiographies *Goodbye to All That* (1929), *But It Still Goes On* (1930), and *Occupation Writer* (1950); his historical novels *I, Claudius* (1934) and *Claudius the God* (1935); and his *Collected Poems* (1961) and *New Poems* (1963).

HARDY, THOMAS (1840–1928), English novelist, short story writer, and poet, was an architect's apprentice before he turned to novel writing. Hardy divided his prose work into three groups: novels of character and environment; romances and fantasies, and novels of ingenuity, stressing turns of plot. Among his novels are *The Return of the Native* (1878), *The Mayor of Casterbridge* (1886), *Tess of the D'Urbervilles* (1891), and *Jude The Obscure* (1896). His books of poetry include *Poems of the Past and Present* (1902), *Time's Laughing-stocks, and Other Verses* (1909), *Satires of Circumstance* (1911–14), and the poetic drama, *The Dynasts* (1903–08).

HEMINGWAY, ERNEST (1898–1962), American short story writer and novelist, was born in Oak Park, Illinois, where his father was a physician. After graduating from high school, he worked as a newspaper reporter on the Kansas City *Star* before joining an American ambulance unit in Italy during World War I. His first novel, *The Sun Also Rises,* brought him fame in 1926, and he received the Pulitzer Prize in fiction in 1953 and the Nobel Prize for literature in 1954. Other well-known novels are *A Farewell to Arms* (1929), *For Whom the Bell Tolls* (1940), and *The Old Man and the Sea* (1952). Some of his stories are collected in *The Fifth Column and the First Forty-Nine Stories* (1938).

HOPKINS, GERARD MANLEY (1844–89), English poet and Jesuit priest, was born in London and attended Oxford where he was converted to Roman Catholicism. After performing missionary work in the Liverpool slums, he taught classics at Stronghurst College and later became professor of Greek at the University of Dublin. Some of his poetry, unpublished during his lifetime, was collected in a single volume entitled *Poems* which appeared in 1918. A larger edition was published in 1930, to be followed by volumes of his correspondence in 1935 and 1938, and his *Notebooks and Papers* in 1937.

HOUSMAN, A(LFRED) E(DWARD) (1859–1936), English poet and classical scholar, was educated at Oxford. After working for ten years in a

British patent office, he became Professor of Latin at the University of London and, later, at Cambridge. His most famous work is his first collection of poems, *A Shropshire Lad* (1896). His *Collected Poems* appeared in 1940.

HUGHES, LANGSTON (b. 1902), American poet and translator, was born in Joplin, Missouri, and attended Columbia and Lincoln Universities. He has worked as a seaman on voyages to Europe and Africa and has lived in Mexico, France, and Italy. Author of a number of volumes of poetry and prose, including *Montage of a Dream Deferred* (1951), *Selected Poems* (1959), and his autobiography, *The Big Sea* (1940), he is also co-editor of an anthology, *The Poetry of the Negro* (1949).

JACKSON, SHIRLEY (1919–65), American short story writer, novelist, and essayist, was born in San Francisco. She graduated from Syracuse University in 1940 and married a fellow student, Stanley Edgar Hyman, who is now a well-known literary critic. Her collection of short stories, *The Lottery* or *The Adventures of James Harris,* appeared in 1949. Among her novels are *The Hangsman* (1951), *The Sundial* (1958), *The Haunting of Hill House* (1959), and *We Have Always Lived in the Castle* (1962). *Life Among the Savages* (1953) and *Raising Demons* (1957) are accounts of her life with her husband and children.

JARRELL, RANDALL (1914–65), American poet, novelist and critic, was born in Nashville, Tennessee, and educated at Vanderbilt University. He served in the Army Air Force during World War II and then taught at Kenyon College, the University of Texas, Sarah Lawrence, Princeton, and the Women's College of the University of North Carolina. He was awarded the National Book Award for poetry in 1960 and for fiction in 1962. His works include *Poetry and the Age* (1953), a book of criticism: *Pictures from an Institution* (1954), a satiric novel about campus life; *Selected Poems* (1955); *The Anchor Book of Stories* (1958); *The Woman at the Washington Zoo* (1960); and *A Sad Heart at the Supermarket* (1962).

JONSON, BEN (1572–1637), English poet and dramatist, worked briefly as a bricklayer and served as a soldier in Flanders. He later became leading author of masques at the court and was pensioned under both James I and Charles I as "King's Poet." His poetry includes odes, epigrams, songs, and letters in verse. Important plays are *Every Man in His Humour* (1598), *Volpone* (1606), *The Silent Woman* (1609), *The Alchemist* (1610), and *Bartholomew Fair* (1614). *Timber, Or Discoveries* (1640) is a book of short essays on literary topics.

JOYCE, JAMES (1882–1941), Irish novelist and short story writer, was born in Dublin, and educated for the priesthood at a Jesuit school, at Belvedere College, and at the Royal University in Dublin. He renounced both Catholicism and Ireland, leaving Ireland in 1902 to spend the rest of his life in Zurich, Paris, Trieste, and other European cities. Despite his self-imposed exile, Ireland is the subject of his works. He is famous for his experiments with the structure of the novel, for his use of the stream of consciousness technique, and for his language innovations. His best known works are *Dubliners* (1914), *A Portrait of the Artist as a Young Man* (1916), *Ulysses* (1922), and *Finnegan's Wake* (1939).

KEATS, JOHN (1795–1821), English poet, was born in London, where his father managed a livery stable. He was a medical student for two years but abandoned the study of medicine for literature. One of his first poems, "On First Looking into Chapman's Homer," was published in a London newspaper in 1815. His first small collection, *Poems,* was published in 1817. Other books include *Endymion* (1818) and *Lamia and Other Poems* (1820) which contained the now famous "Ode to a Nightingale," "Ode on a Grecian Urn," "Ode to Autumn," "Ode to Psyche," and "Ode on Melancholy." Keats died in Italy from tuberculosis in his twenty-seventh year.

LAWRENCE, D(AVID) H(ERBERT) (1885–1930), English novelist, short story writer, poet, and critic, was born in Eastwood, a small village near Nottingham, England, the son of a coal miner. He attended the University of Nottingham and taught school for a short time. In his constant search for a cure for his tuberculosis and for a place where he could put his ideas about primitive religions and his other controversial philosophies into practice, he traveled and lived in Italy, Australia, Ceylon, New Zealand, Tahiti, the French Riviera, Mexico, and the southwestern part of the United States. His best known novels are *Sons and Lovers* (1913), *The Rainbow* (1915), *Women in Love* (1920), and *Lady Chatterley's Lover* (1928). Among his short story collections are *The Prussian Officer* (1914) and *The Lovely Lady* (1933).

LOVELACE, RICHARD (1618–58), English poet, was a wealthy member of the Court of Charles I. In the royal army during the Civil War, he was imprisoned twice because of his connections with the Royalist group. While in prison he wrote some of his famous songs, including "To Althea, from Prison." Collections of his poems to Lucasta were published in 1649 and 1659. After King Charles was executed, Lovelace suffered additional ill fortune and died in poverty.

LUCIAN (c.120–c.180), Greek satirist and humorist was born in Samosta in Syria. An itinerant teacher of rhetoric and philosophy, he was the author of rhetorical, critical, and biographical works, romances, dialogues, and poems. He was often called "The Blasphemer" during his lifetime. Among his works are *Veracious History,* a mock narrative of travel, and *Dialogues of the Dead,* which are in reality satires of the living.

McGINLEY, PHYLLIS (b. 1905), American writer of light verse and prose, was born in Ontario, Oregon. After attending convent school and the Universities of Utah and California, she taught in public high schools before going to New York where she was a copy writer for an advertising agency and, later, assistant editor of *Town and Country.* She won the Pulitzer Prize for poetry in 1961; she has written essays and books for children, as well as poetry. The most recent collections of her work are *Times Three: Selected Verse from Three Decades* (1960) and *The Province of the Heart* (1960), a selection of essays.

MANSFIELD, KATHERINE (1888–1923), British short story writer, was born in Wellington, New Zealand, the daughter of a banker, and attended Queen's College in London. She was married to John Middleton Murray, with whom she edited a number of "little magazines" to which she also contributed. A victim of tuberculosis, she spent most of her later years in Italy, Switzerland, and France. Several collections of her stories appeared during her lifetime; a collected edition was published in 1937. Her husband has edited her *Journal* (1927), *Letters* (1930), *Scrapbook* (1939), and *Letters to John Middleton Murray* (1951).

MARQUIS, DON (1878–1937), American humorist, poet, and playwright, was born in Walnut, Illinois, and studied for a year and a half at the Corcoran School in Washington, D.C. He tried many occupations including teaching, clerking, working at the Census Bureau, and acting, before he started writing columns for the New York *Sun* and, later, for the New York *Herald Tribune*. His last six years were tragic as he became a penniless cripple before he died of a cerebral hemorrhage. Among his books are *Hermione* (1916), *Preface* (1919), *The Old Soal* (1921), *Archy and Mehitabel* (1927, 1930), *Master of the Revels* (1930), *Archy Does His Part* (1935), and *Sons of the Puritans* (1939).

MARVELL, ANDREW (1621–78), English poet, was born at Winestead, Yorkshire, England, the son of an Anglican clergyman. Educated at Cambridge, he later assisted Milton in the Latin secretaryship. Subsequently he was elected to Parliament, after which he held public office until his accidental death from an overdose of opiates. Among his best known poems are "To His Coy Mistress," "The Garden," and "Bermudas." Most of his poetry was not published until 1681, three years after his death.

MASTERS, EDGAR LEE (1869–1950), American poet, was born in Garnett, Kansas, but moved to Lewiston, Illinois, near the Spoon River, while still a boy. Although his education was sporadic, he studied law in his father's office and became a successful lawyer in Chicago. He published several volumes of poetry, plays, and essays, but his fame rests on one work, *Spoon River Anthology,* published in 1915.

MATUTE, ANA MARÍA (mä·tōō'tä) (b. 1926), Spanish novelist and short story writer, was born in Barcelona, Spain, and in 1966 holds a lectureship at Indiana University. Her one novel so far translated into English is *The Lost Children* (1965). "The Missing One," translated by Gloria Durán especially for this anthology, is from a Spanish collection called *Historias de la Artámila*.

MAUPASSANT, GUY DE (mō' pà' säN') (1850–93), French short story writer and novelist, held a number of official positions during his career. His first published story, "Boule de suif," in 1880 began a decade of successful literary production. But he became increasingly melancholy, and a disease contracted as a youth led to his insanity in 1892. Among his works are the story collections *La Maison Tellier* (1881), *Mademoiselle Fifi* (1883), *Contes de la Bécasse* (1883), and *Contes et Nouvelles* (1885), and the novels *Une Vie* (1883), *Bel-Ami* (1885), *Pierre et Jean* (1888), and *Notre Coeur* (1890).

MILTON, JOHN (1608–74), English poet and prose writer, was born in London, the son of a prosperous scrivener. After seven years at Cambridge, he spent several more at home and in travel, studying and writing poetry. Although trained in the Anglican faith, he became a puritan and served as Oliver Cromwell's Latin Secretary from 1649 until the Restoration, when he was arrested and fined but not imprisoned. He became totally blind in 1652, before he produced his greatest works—*Paradise Lost* (1667), *Paradise Regained* (1671) and *Samson Agonistes* (1671).

NASH, OGDEN (b. 1902), American writer of light verse, was born in Rye, New York, and attended St. George's School in Newport, Rhode Island, and Harvard. After spending several years in publishing work, he retired to devote his time to his own writing. His work has been published frequently in *The New Yorker*. Among his books are *Free Wheeling* (1931), *The Bad Parents' Garden of Verse* (1936), *I'm a Stranger Here Myself* (1938), *The Face Is Familiar* (1940), *Versus* (1949), *The Private Dining Room* (1953), *You Can't Get There from Here* (1957), *Verses from 1929 On* (1959), and *Everyone But Thee and Me* (1962).

NEMEROV, HOWARD (nĕm' ēr·ŏf) (b. 1920), American poet, novelist, and educator, was born in New York City and educated at Harvard. He was a fighter pilot with the Royal Canadian Air Force and later with the USAAF during World War II. He is now teaching at Bennington College. His collections of poetry are *The Image and the Law* (1947), *Guide to the Ruins* (1950), *The Salt Garden* (1955), *Mirrors and Windows* (1958), and *New and Selected Poems* (1960).

O'CONNOR, FRANK (1903), Irish short story writer, is the pen name of Michael O'Donovan, who was born and educated in Cork, Ireland. He worked as a librarian in County Cork and in Dublin and was once director of the Abbey Theatre. He was first recognized as a writer with the publication of *Guests of the Nation* (1931), a collection of stories which deal with the Irish civil war. Married to an American, he now lives in the United States and has taught writing courses at Harvard and at Northwestern University. A poet, dramatist, translator, and critic, as well as a short story writer, he has published extensively. Recent short story collections are *The Stories of Frank O'Connor* (1952) and *More Stories by Frank O'Connor* (1954). His autobiography, *An Only Child,* appeared in 1961.

O'NEILL EUGENE, (1888–1953) was born in New York City but spent his infancy and youth touring the country with his mother and father, the romantic actor James O'Neill. After a year at Princeton, he worked at miscellaneous jobs around the country and then went to sea. In 1914 he attended Professor Baker's famous English 47 class at Harvard. Afterwards he devoted himself to playwriting, publishing more than thirty plays. His works have been translated into many languages and performed in all civilized countries of the world. Three times winner of the Pulitzer Prize for drama, O'Neill was awarded the Nobel Prize for literature in 1936. Among his best known plays are *Desire Under the Elms* (1925), *Strange Interlude* (1928), *Mourning Becomes Electra* (1931), and the posthumously published *Long Day's Journey into Night* (1956). *A Touch of the Poet* (1957), the last of

Eugene O'Neill's full length plays, is complete in itself, but he intended it as part of a cycle which he did not live to complete.

OVID (PUBLIUS OVIDIUS NASO) (ŏv′ ĭd) (43 B.C.?–17 A.D.), Roman poet, was trained for a legal career but turned to literature instead. After years of popularity and fame in Rome, he was banished by the emperor Augustus and spent his last years in bitter exile. He is remembered for his elegies and for the Metamorphoses, poetic fables based on classic legends about miraculous transformations.

OWEN, WILFRED (1893–1918), English poet, was born in Oswestry, Shropshire, and attended the Birkenhead Institute in Liverpool. After working for two years as a private tutor, he served in France during World War I. He won the Military Cross for gallantry and became company commander in 1918, shortly before he was killed in action only a week prior to the Armistice. His poems were edited and published by his friend and fellow poet, Siegfried Sassoon, in 1920. An enlarged edition, *The Poems of Wilfred Owen,* appeared in 1931.

PATCHEN, KENNETH (1911), American poet and artist, was born in Niles, Ohio, and attended the University of Wisconsin. He has read his poems on radio and television, on the concert stage, and in nightclubs, usually accompaied by jazz groups. In addition he has made numerous recordings of them. Among his books are *The Selected Poems of Kenneth Patchen* (1947); *The Famous Boating Party* (1953), poems in prose; *Hurrah for Anything* (1957), poems and drawings; *Don't Look Now* (1959), drama; and *But Even So* (1963), poems and drawings.

PHOCYLIDES (fō·sĭl′ ĭ·dēz) (active about 540 B.C.), Greek poet, wrote hexameter and elegaic poems on moral subjects.

PIRANDELLO, LUIGI (pē′ rän·dĕl′ lō) (1867–1936), Italian short story writer, novelist, and playwright, was a professor of literature in an Italian girls' school during most of his early career. After he succeeded

as a playwright, he founded his own theater in Rome and took his acting company on tours performing his plays throughout Europe. His
most famous drama is *Six Characters in Search of an Author* (1918).
Collections of short stories include *A Character in Distre*ss (1938) and
The Medals, and Other Stories (1939).

POPE, ALEXANDER (1688–1744), English poet and satirist, was the
son of a London linen draper. He was a hunchback and cripple as a
result of a serious illness at the age of twelve. Although not permitted
to attend a public school or a university because of governmental re-
strictions against Roman Catholics after the Revolution of 1688, he
was educated by tutors. His best-known works are *Essay on Criticism*
(1711), which he claimed to have written at the age of twelve; *The
Rape of the Lock* (1712); *Essay on Man* (1733); and *Epistle to Dr.
Arbuthnot* (1735).

PORTER, KATHERINE ANNE (b. 1894), American short story writer and
novelist, was born in Indian Creek, Texas, and educated in convent
schools in Texas and Louisiana. She has lived in New York, Mexico,
and Europe, and has lectured at several colleges and universities across
the United States. Her works include *Flowering Judas and Other
Stories* (1930); *Pale Horse, Pale Rider* (1939), three novelettes; *The
Leaning Tower* (1944), a book of stories; *The Days Before* (1952),
a collection of personal recollections; and *Ship of Fools* (1962), a
long novel. *The Collected Stories of Katherine Anne Porter* was published in 1965.

POUND, EZRA LOOMIS (b. 1885), American poet, editor, and critic,
was born in Hailey, Idaho, and educated at the University of Pennsylvania and Hamilton College. He taught for a short time at Wabash
College before going to Europe in 1907 to live in various places, including Venice, London, Paris, Provence, and Rapollo, Italy, until
1945, when he was arrested and tried for high treason for supporting
Mussolini during World War II. He was adjudged insane and committed to a mental hospital near Washington, where he has continued
to work on his *Cantos,* his best known and mammoth work of which
several volumes have been published since 1930. Other collections of

poems are *Personae* (1926), including translations from the ancient Chinese and Japanese and other languages, *Selected Poems* (1928), and *Selected Poems* (1949).

PRIOR, MATTHEW (1664–1721), English poet and essayist, is remembered chiefly for his epigrams, satires, and "society" verse. He was a diplomat and took part in several important European treaty negotiations, including the Peace of Utrecht. His works include *Alma, Or the Progress of the Mind* (1718), a long poem on worldly vanity; *Solomon or the Vanity of the World* (1718); and *Four Dialogues on the Dead*.

RIHAKU (rē·hä' kōō) (701–62), Chinese lyric poet, was born in Chinese Turkestan. Rihaku is the Japanese translation of his Chinese name Li Po or Li Tai-Po. His aim in life was to free himself from the trammels of the world and, except for brief intervals, he led a wandering, Bohemian life. He was once called to the Court for a period of three years and in 757 was banished for complicity in a treasonable plot during a rebellion. His surviving poems number about eighteen hundred.

ROBINSON, EDWIN ARLINGTON (1869–1935), American poet, was born at Head Tide, Maine, and grew up in Gardiner, which became the "Tilbury Town" of his poems. He attended Harvard for two years, then went to New York to work as a subway laborer and advertising copy writer until President Theodore Roosevelt became interested in his poetry and found him a job in the New York Customs House. He received the Pulitzer Prize in 1921, 1925 and 1927. *The Collected Poems of Edwin Arlington Robinson* appeared in 1937.

ROETHKE, THEODORE (rŏth' kē) (1908–63), American poet, was born in Saginaw, Michigan, and educated at the University of Michigan and at Harvard. After serving as a public relations counsel and a tennis coach, he taught English at Lafayette College, Pennsylvania State College, Bennington College, and at the University of Washington, where he was a professor from 1947 until his death. Recipient of both the Pulitzer Prize and the National Book Award, he published several volumes of poetry including *Open House* (1941), *The Lost Son and Other Poems* (1948), *Praise to the End!* (1951), and *The Waking: Poems, 1933–53* (1953).

SCHORER, MARK (b. 1908), American short story writer, critic, and educator, was born in Sauk City, Wisconsin, and educated at the University of Wisconsin and Harvard. He has taught English at Dartmouth, Harvard, and the University of California. Among his books are *The State of Mind* (1947), a collection of thirty-two short stories; *William Blake: The Politics of Vision* (1946); and *Sinclair Lewis: An American Life* (1961).

SCHWARTZ, DELMORE (b. 1913), American author and critic, was born in Brooklyn and attended the University of Wisconsin, New York University, and Harvard, where he later taught English composition. He has served as editor of *The Partisan Review*, poetry editor of *The New Republic*, literary consultant for *New Directions*, and visiting lecturer at a number of schools and universities. Among his books are *In Dreams Begin Responsibilities* (1939), *The World Is a Wedding* (1947), and *Summer Knowledge: New and Selected Poems 1938–58* (1959).

SHAKESPEARE, WILLIAM (1564–1616), English poet and dramatist, was born at Stratford-on-Avon and attended the Stratford Grammar School. In 1585 he went to London, where he joined a theatrical company, and by 1592 became well-known as an actor and playwright. During the next twenty years he produced, in addition to the sonnets (published in 1609), the series of histories, comedies, and tragedies, universally acclaimed as the greatest in literature. They include *Romeo and Juliet, Julius Caesar, Hamlet, Othello, King Lear, Macbeth,* and *Antony and Cleopatra.* His works were first collected and published in folio in 1623.

SHAW, GEORGE BERNARD (1856–1950), Irish playwright, novelist, and critic, was born in Dublin. He left school at the age of fourteen and was thenceforth self-educated. Shaw was a London newspaper critic, reviewing music and drama, from 1885 to 1898. He wrote five novels and propaganda for the Fabian Society; but his fame rests chiefly on his plays, among the most famous of which are *Candida* (1898), *Mrs. Warren's Profession* (1898), *Caesar and Cleopatra* (1901), *Man and Superman* (1903), *Major Barbara* (1907), *Pygmalion* (1912), and *Saint Joan* (1924). He received the Nobel Prize for literature in 1925.

SHELLEY, PERCY BYSSHE (1792–1822), English poet, was the son of a county squire in Sussex. He attended Eton and Oxford, but was expelled from Oxford for circulating a pamphlet on atheism. During his brief life he lived in England, Ireland, Switzerland, and Italy. He was drowned while sailing on the Adriatic. His major works include *Queen Mab* (1813), *Prometheus Unbound* (1818–20), *The Cenci* (1819), and *Adonais* (1821).

SIMONIDES (sī·mŏn′ĭ–dēz) (c. 566–468 B.C.), Greek poet, is remembered for his odes, elegies, and epigrams, although only fragments of his work survive.

SOPHOCLES (sŏf′ ŏ·klēz) (c. 496–406 B.C.), Greek dramatist, was born at Colonus, near Athens. As a youth he was known for his excellence in singing, dancing, and gymnastics. He became first poet of Athens at the age of twenty-seven when he won first prize in tragedy at the Dionysian Festival. Only seven of the hundred or so plays he wrote survive. They are *Oedipus Rex, Oedipus at Colonus, Antigone, Electra, Philocetes, Ajax,* and *Maidens of Trachis.*

SPENDER, STEPHEN (b. 1909) English poet, short story writer, and critic, was born in London, the son of a prominent journalist. He was educated at Oxford. His works include *Collected Poems, 1928–53* (1954); *World Within World* (1951), his autobiography; *The Burning Cactus* (1936) and *The Backward Son* (1941), collections of short stories; and *The Destructive Element* (1935) and *The Creative Element* (1953), volumes of literary criticism.

STEVENS, WALLACE (1879–1955), American poet and essayist, was born in Reading, Pennsylvania, and attended Harvard and the New York Law School. He was admitted to the bar in 1904 and from 1916 until his death was associated with the Hartford Accident and Indemnity Company, becoming Vice-President in 1934. His *Collected Poems* appeared in 1954 and won the Pulitzer Prize for poetry in 1955.

SUCKLING, SIR JOHN (1609–42), English poet, was a member of an old Norfolk family from whom he inherited rich estates. He was a courtier, soldier, wit, and spendthrift, who was knighted by Charles I. At his own expense, he supplied a troop of horses and led it to the King's service at the outbreak of the Civil War. He spent his fortune lavishly and died in Paris a poor man, some accounts say a suicide, others, at the hand of a vengeful servant. The best known of his lyrics and songs is "Why So Pale and Wan, Fair Lover?" He published two collections of verse: *Fragmenta Aurea* (1646) and *The Last Remains* (1659).

TENNYSON, ALFRED, LORD (1809–92), English poet, was born at Somersky, where his father was a rector, and was educated at Cambridge. He was appointed poet laureate in 1850, a position he held until his death. He is buried in Westminister Abbey. Among his works are *Poems, by Two Brothers* (1827), *Poems, Chiefly Lyrical* (1830), *Poems* (1832), *Poems* (1842), *In Memoriam* (1850), and *Idylls of the King* (1859–85).

THOMAS, DYLAN (1914–53), British poet, was born in Swansea, South Wales, attended the Swansea Grammar School and worked as a newspaper reporter. During World War II he served as an anti-aircraft gunner and also read his poetry over the BBC. He gave lectures during his frequent visits to the United States and died in New York City while on a lecture tour. His works include *Collected Poems* (1953); *Portrait of the Artist as a Young Dog* (1940), a semi-autobiographical account; *Under Milk Wood* (1954), a poetic drama; and *Quite Early One Morning* (1954) and *A Prospect of the Sea* (1955), collections of stories, sketches, and essays.

THURBER, JAMES (1894–1961), American humorist and illustrator, was born in Columbus, Ohio, and attended Ohio State University. He worked as a newspaper reporter in the United States and abroad before joining the staff of *The New Yorker,* to which he contributed both articles and drawings for over thirty years. Among his books are *My Life and Hard Times* (1933), *Let Your Mind Alone* (1927), *Many Moons* (1943), *Fables for Our Times* (1940–56), and *The Thurber Album* (1952).

UPDIKE, JOHN (b. 1932), American poet, short story writer and novelist, was born in Shillington, Pennsylvania, and attended Harvard and Oxford's Ruskin School of Drawing and Fine Art. He was associated with *The New Yorker* from 1955–57. His works include a book of poems, *The Carpentered Hen* (1958); collections of short stories, *The Same Door* (1959) and *Pigeon Feathers* (1962); and the novels *The Poorhouse Fair* (1959), *Rabbit, Run* (1960), and *The Centaur* (1963).

WATTS, ISAAC (1674–1748), English clergyman and hymn writer, was pastor of the Independent Chapel in Mark Lane, London. He lived in semiretirement, however, because of ill health contracted in 1712. Among his several hundred hymns are "O God, Our Help in Ages Past," "Joy to the World," "When I Survey the Wondrous Cross," and "There Is a Land of Pure Delight." There are several editions of his collected works.

WELTY, EUDORA (b. 1909), American short story writer and novelist, was born in Jackson, Mississippi, and educated at Mississippi State College for Women, the University of Wisconsin, and Columbia. She has spent most of her life in her native state, which has been the setting for much of her work. Her books include *A Curtain of Green and Other Stories* (1941), *The Robber Bridegroom* (1942), *Delta Wedding* (1946), *The Golden Apples* (1949), *The Ponder Heart* (1954), and *The Bride of the Innisfallen* (1955).

WHITMAN, WALT (1819–92), American poet, was born in Huntington, Long Island, New York. His parents moved to Brooklyn when he was four and there he received his meager formal education, leaving school at eleven to work as office boy, printer's assistant, itinerant school teacher, reporter and editor before serving as editor of the Brooklyn *Eagle* from 1846 to 1848. He published his first edition of *Leaves of Grass* in 1855, then enlarged and revised it throughout his life until the eleventh and final edition appeared in 1892. He volunteered as a medical orderly in the Civil War and his books *Drum Taps* (1865) and *Sequel to Drum Taps* (1866), which contains "When Lilacs Last in the Dooryard Bloomed," reflect his experiences during the war. Among his prose works are *Democratic Vistas* (1871) and *Specimen Days* (1883).

WORDSWORTH, WILLIAM (1770–1850), English poet, was born in Cockermouth in the Lake District of Cumberland and educated at Cambridge. He was appointed poet laureate of England in 1843. In addition to his collaboration with Samuel Taylor Coleridge on *Lyrical Ballads* (1798), he wrote *The Prelude* (1805, published 1850) and the uncompleted *The Recluse,* long autobiographical poems, and several other volumes of poetry. His subjects are usually nature or ordinary people.

YEATS, WILLIAM BUTLER (yāts) (1865–1939), Irish poet and dramatist, was born near Dublin, the son of a painter, and educated in the Dublin schools and at the Royal Dublin Society of Art. He became, as a collector of Gaelic folklore and legends, many of which he translated, one of the leaders of the Irish literary revival. He was also one of the founders of the Irish Literary Theatre, forerunner of the Abbey Theatre, to which he contributed original plays. From 1922–28 he was a member of the Irish Senate and in 1923 he was awarded the Nobel Prize for literature. His plays are reprinted in *The Collected Plays of W. B. Yeats* (1953) and his poems, with his final revisions, in *Collected Poems* (1956).

A 6
B 7
C 8
D 9
E 0
F 1
G 2
H 3
I 4
J 5

Author-Title Index